ARBITRATION

THIRD EDITION

by

ALAN SCOTT RAU
Burg Family Professor of Law
The University of Texas at Austin School of Law

EDWARD F. SHERMAN
Moise F. Steeg, Jr. Professor of Law
Tulane University School of Law

SCOTT PEPPET
Associate Professor of Law
University of Colorado School of Law

FOUNDATION PRESS

2006

THOMSON
—*—
WEST
™

© 1996, 2002 FOUNDATION PRESS
© 2006 By FOUNDATION PRESS
        395 Hudson Street
        New York, NY 10014
        Phone Toll Free 1–877–888–1330
        Fax (212) 367–6799
        foundation–press.com

Printed in the United States of America
ISBN–13: 978–1–59941–071–5
ISBN–10: 1–59941–071–0

TEXT IS PRINTED ON 10% POST CONSUMER RECYCLED PAPER

PREFACE

Does anyone really read the preface to a casebook? We are reasonably confident that we could encrypt on this page the location of buried treasure and still, on retirement, manage to retain our wealth intact. But to honor custom—-and to reward the particularly conscientious student or instructor—-we will nevertheless include a few words here about what he have tried to do in this book.

This paperback dealing with arbitration was originally written as a chapter of our coursebook, *Processes of Dispute Resolution: The Role of Lawyers*, which is designed for a course on the full range of alternative dispute resolution procedures. With a growing interest in commercial arbitration, and a growing number of law school courses and seminars focusing specifically on that process, we thought it might be useful to reprint it separately, for use by instructors who wish to focus only on arbitration.

The teaching of arbitration must, of course, reflect at several points an awareness of the issues raised generally by resort to "alternative" processes. The Alternative Dispute Resolution field has certainly come of age since the first edition of this text was published seventeen years ago—-a time, incredibly, when most of our students were only entering primary school. We no longer need to defend the study of dispute resolution as a new and promising field; we no longer need to persuade lawyers, law school professors, and law students that ADR is a subject that practicing lawyers and judges will find important in their work. Alternative methods of dispute resolution have in fact become part and parcel of the processing of a wide range of disputes in our society. In a sizable number of state and federal courts, dispute resolution procedures are invoked in conjunction with the litigation process. Private companies and governmental agencies have adopted "system designs" incorporating ADR procedures to prevent, or to resolve, the inevitable disputes that arise in their operations. Delivery of mediation and arbitration services has moved to videoconferencing and cyberspace, as experimentation with different forms continues. And arbitration has expanded from such traditional fields as labor and construction to a wide range of contractual services such as investments, sales, banking, health care, and employment. It is obvious that lawyers today must have a grounding in all these various processes of dispute resolution in order to provide adequate advice and representation in many areas of the law.

Most law schools now offer courses in ADR. Still, stereotypes persist, and habits that developed over many decades change slowly. Within the first few months of law school, law students are often socialized to believe that the most prestigious role for a lawyer finds its principal outlet in the courtroom. Litigation is the standard; negotiation, mediation and arbitration are invisible processes. Our aim in this book is to bring litigation into perspective—to encourage students to see it as a system of dispute resolution, one with its own virtues and failings, but not an inevitable or the only process for resolving legal disputes. We want students to see that the many alternative processes of dispute resolution are not distinct from litigation, nor mutually exclusive, but usefully complementary processes. The contemporary lawyer needs to develop an ability to work effectively with all available processes, separately, in series, and even simultaneously.

The reasons for the explosion of interest in ADR over the last couple of decades are varied. They stem in part from the inadequacies of litigation as a dispute resolution mechanism. Parties have expressed dissatisfaction with a court system that imposes heavy costs in terms of time and money and that lacks flexibility in providing solutions. But there are other important dimensions of ADR than an anti-litigation bias that account for its new popularity, such as its potential for reducing the adversariness of the trial system and accomplishing a more satisfactory resolution of disputes. We will examine in this book both the philosophical well-springs of the ADR movement and the countervailing objections of its critics.

As the title to our book indicates, our focus is on process. At times, this is theoretical and policy-oriented. We think an understanding of the underlying philosophy, history, strengths, and weaknesses of each alternative dispute resolution process is necessary for a lawyer to appreciate how and when it can be used in helping clients resolve their disputes. But we place at least equal importance on practical application. Thus, we attempt to provide a comprehensive overview of the legal procedures and doctrines that a lawyer will need to know in order to use the processes effectively. These legal aspects are sometimes highly technical—with respect, for example, to the law governing arbitration practice—-and we believe these materials provide a solid introduction to their use. We have also, for this edition, added new sections that focus on two aspects of arbitration practice that can be expected to grow rapidly in importance—-the problems raised by complex and multiparty proceedings (including the use of class arbitrations), and problems posed by international commercial arbitration in an increasingly integrated and globalized economy.

As reflected in our subtitle, our focus is on "the role of lawyers." Our objective is to train lawyers to use ADR processes and not to train arbitrators, or other third-party neutrals. The student will certainly be exposed to these other roles and may be asked to perform in them in exercises and simulations. But learning how to be an arbitrator is secondary to our objective of exploring how lawyers can use ADR processes as adversaries on behalf of their clients. For this reason, there are many discussions of practice situations and techniques, professional ethical issues, and the law underlying

ADR processes. Throughout the book we have included extensive citations to cases and other sources so that these materials will also be a helpful reference book for students once they are in practice.

We place particular stress on the role of "the law" in alternative processes—-on the lawyer's role in choosing processes and implementing strategies, and on the lawyering skills needed to use the processes effectively. The skills component to the course can be substantial, depending on the specific objectives of the instructor. We believe that the more students practice ADR skills and become comfortable with ADR procedures, the better equipped they will be to serve their client's interests.

A note on form: We have substantially edited most cases and selections to delete unnecessary material. Deletions of text due to our editing are indicated by spaced asterisks. Citations in the text, and footnotes from the text, have usually been omitted without indication. Where footnotes to selections do appear, however, we have retained the number they have in the original material. A reader desiring to use the opinion as a research tool can, of course, go to the official case reporters.

We have benefited from the helpful comments and critiques of many colleagues and students who have used the prior editions of this book, and each of the institutions at which we teach has provided substantial financial support which helped make possible the completion of this project. We are also very grateful to Luemara Wagner, Sharon Stevenson, Melissa Bast, Rachel Ollar, and Michael Ross, for their able research and administrative assistance.

A.S.R.
E.F.S.
S.R.P.

July 2006

*

ACKNOWLEDGMENTS

The following authors and publishers gave us permission to reprint excerpts from copyrighted material; we gratefully acknowledge their assistance.

Drawing by Lorenz; copyright © 1991 The New Yorker Magazine, Inc.

Landes & Posner, Adjudication as a Private Good, 8 J. Legal Stud. 235, 235–40, 245–47 (1979). Copyright © 1979 by the University of Chicago. All rights reserved.

Fuller, Collective Bargaining and the Arbitrator, 1963 Wisc.L.Rev. 3, 11–12, 17.

Sperber, Overlooking Negotiating Tools, 20 Les Nouvelles 81 (June 1985).

Galanter, Justice in Many Rooms: Courts, Private Ordering, and Indigenous Law, 19 J. Pluralism & Unofficial L. 1, 17–18, 25 (1981).

Mentschikoff, The Significance of Arbitration-A Preliminary Inquiry, 17 Law & Contemporary Problems 698, 709 (1952). Copyright © 1952 Duke University School of Law.

Craver , The Judicial Enforcement of Public Sector Interest Arbitration, 21 B.C.L.Rev., 557, 558 n.8 (1980). Reprinted by permission of Boston College, Office of the Law Reviews.

Fuller, The Forms and Limits of Adjudication, 92 Harv. L. Rev. 353 (1978). Reprinted by permission of The Harvard Law Review.

Jones, Three Centuries of Commercial Arbitration on New York: A Brief Survey, 1956 Wash. U.L.Q. 193, 209–10, 218–19.

Mentschikoff, Commercial Arbitration, 61 Colum. L. Rev. 846, 848–54 (1961). Copyright © 1961 by the Directors of the Columbia Law Review Association Inc. All rights reserved. This article originally appeared at 61 Colum. L. Rev. 846 (1961). Reprinted by permission.

Craig, Park, & Paulsson, International Chamber of Commerce Arbitration 638, 29–30, 744 (3rd Ed. 2000).

Bühring-Uhle, Arbitration and Mediation in International Business 141–143 (1996). Reprinted by permission.

Tang, Arbitration—A Method Used in China to Settle Foreign Trade and Economic Disputes, 4 Pace L. Rev. 519, 533–34 (1984).

Hays, Labor Arbitration: A Dissenting View 112–3 (1966).

Getman, Labor Arbitration and Dispute Resolution, 88 Yale L.J. 916, 928–30 (1979). Reprinted by permission of The Yale Law Journal Company and William S. Hein Company from The Yale Law Journal, Vol. 88, pages 916–949.

Moller, Rolph, & Ebener, Private Dispute Resolution in the Banking Industry 12–13 (RAND 1993). RAND, MR–259–ICJ.

Terry, The Technical and Conceptual Flaws of Medical Malpractice Arbitration, 30 St. Louis U.L.J. 571, 572–73, 586 (1986). Reprinted with permission.

Henderson, Contractual Problems in the Enforcement of Agreements to Arbitrate Medical Malpractice, 58 Va.L.Rev. 947, 994 (1972). Reprinted by permission of Fred B. Rothman & Co.

St. Antoine, Judicial Review of Labor Arbitration Awards: *A Second Look at Enterprise Wheel* and its Progeny, 75 Mich. L. Rev. 1137, 1140, 1142 (1977).

Walters, Arbitration Decisions of the U.S. Supreme Court 2000–2001: Management Perspective, in Arbitration 2001: Arbitrating in an Evolving Legal Environment, Proceedings, 54th Annual Meeting, National Academy of Arbitrators 13, 28, 30–31 (2002). Reprinted by permission.

Hart & Sacks, The Legal Process 310 (1994).

Stein, The Selection of Arbitrators, N.Y.U Eighth Annual Conference on Labor 291, 293 (1955).

Giovannini, The Psychological Aspects of Dispute Resolution: Commentary, in International Council for Commercial Arbitration, Congress series no.11, International Commercial Arbitration: Important Contemporary Questions 348, 351.

Raffaele, Lawyers in Labor Arbitration, 37 Arb.J. No.3 (Sept. 1982).

Roth, When to Ignore the Rules of Evidence in Arbitration, 9 Litigation 20 (Winter 1983). Copyright © 1983 American Bar Association. Reprinted with permission from Vol. 9, No. 2, Litigation. All rights reserved.

Arnold & Hubert, Focus Points in Arbitration Practice 51-52 (1992) (unpublished).

Bond, "'Equality' Is Required When Naming Arbitrators, Cour de Cessation Rules," 3(3) World Arb. & Med. Rep. at p. 70 (Mar. 1992).

Allison, The Context, Properties, and Constitutionality of Nonconsensual Arbitration,1990 Journal of Dispute Resolution 1, 6, 15. Reprinted by permission from the *Journal of Dispute Resolution* and the Curators of the University of Missouri-Columbia.

Summers, Public Sector Bargaining: Problems of Governmental Decisionmaking, 44 U Cinn. L. Rev. 672 (1975). Reprinted with permission.

Raiffa, The Art and Science of Negotiation 118 (1982). Reprinted by permission of the publisher from THE ART AND SCIENCE OF NEGOTIATION: HOW TO RESOLVE CONFLICTS AND GET THE BEST OUT OF BARGAINING by Howard Raiffa, The Belknap Press of Harvard University Press, Copyright © 1982 by the President and Fellows of Harvard College.

Fuller, Collective Bargaining and the Arbitrator, Proceedings, Fifteenth Annual Meeting, National Academy of Arbitrators 8, 29–33, 37–48 (1962). Reprinted with permission. Chapter 2, pages 8, 29–33, and 37–48 and 34–41 from *Collective Bargaining and the Arbitrator's Role (Proceedings of the 15th Annual Meeting National Academy of Arbitrators)*, by Lon L. Fuller. Copyright © 1962, by The Bureau of National Affairs, Inc. Washington, D.C. 20037.

Folberg & Taylor, Mediation 277–78 (1984). Reprinted by permission of Jossey-Bass, Inc.

Telford, Med-Arb: A Viable Dispute Resolution Alternative 3 (Industrial Relations Centre 2000).

Christensen, Private Justice: California's General Reference Procedure, 1982 American Bar Foundation Research J. 79, 81–82, 103.

Note, The California Rent-A-Judge Experiment: Constitutional and Policy Considerations of Pay-As-You-Go Courts, 94 Harv. L. Rev. 1592, 1601–02, 1607–08 (1981). Copyright © 1981 by the Harvard law Review Association.

Bond, How to Draft an Arbitration Clause, 6(2) J. of Int'l Arb. 65, 66, 72, 74–75, 76, 78 (June, 1989).

Craig, Uses and Abuses of Appeals from Awards, 4 Arb. Int'l 174, 174-79, 182–85, 190–92 (1988).

Paulsson, The Case for Disregarding LSAs (local Standard Annulments) Under the New York Convention 7 Amer. Rev. of Int'l Arb. 99, 109 (1996).

Kaufmann-Kohler, Identifying and Applying the Law Governing the Arbitration Procedure: The Role of the Law of the Place of Arbitration, Int'l Council for Commercial Arb., Congress series no. 9 (Paris/1999) 336, 342–65.

Thomburg, Fast, Cheap, and Out of Control: Lessons from the ICANN Dispute Resolution Process, 6 J. Small & Emerging Bus. L. 191 (2002).

*

SUMMARY OF CONTENTS

*

TABLE OF CONTENTS

*

TABLE OF CASES

Principal cases are in bold type. Non-principal cases are in roman type. References are to Pages.

ARBITRATION

*

Snow White and the Wicked Queen submit the fairness question to binding arbitration.

•   •

ARBITRATION

A. THE PROCESS OF PRIVATE ADJUDICATION

1. INTRODUCTION

William M. Landes & Richard A. Posner, Adjudication As a Private Good

8 J. Legal Stud. 235, 235–40 (1979).

Adjudication is normally regarded as a governmental function and judges as public officials. Even economists who assign a highly limited role to government consider the provision of judicial services an indisputably apt function of government; this was, for example, Adam Smith's view. Few economists (and few lawyers) realize that the provision of judicial services precedes the formation of the state; that many formally public courts long had important characteristics of private institutions (for example, until 1825 English judges were paid out of litigants' fees as well as general tax revenues); and that even today much adjudication is private (commercial arbitration being an important example).

* * *

1. *Introduction.* A court system (public or private) produces two types of service. One is dispute resolution—determining whether a rule has been violated. The other is rule formulation—creating rules of law as a by-product of the dispute-settlement process. When a court resolves a dispute, its resolution, especially if embodied in a written opinion, provides information regarding the likely outcome of similar disputes in the future. This is the system of precedent, which is so important in the Anglo–American legal system.

* * *

The two judicial services are in principle severable and in practice often are severed. Jury verdicts resolve disputes but do not create precedents. Legislatures create rules of law but do not resolve disputes. In the Anglo–American legal system rule formation is a function shared by legislatures and (especially appellate) courts; elsewhere judicial law making tends to be less important.

2. *Dispute Resolution.* Imagine a purely private market in judicial services. People would offer their services as judges, and disputants would select the judge whom they mutually found most acceptable. The most popular judges would charge the highest fees, and competition among judges would yield the optimum amount and quality of judicial services at minimum social cost. This competitive process would produce judges who were not only competent but also impartial—would thus fulfill the ideals of procedural justice—because a judge who was not regarded as impartial could not get disputes submitted to him for resolution: one party would always refuse.

A voluntary system of dispute resolution does not presuppose that the dispute has arisen from a consensual relationship (landlord-tenant, employer-employee, seller-buyer, etc.) in which the method of dispute resolution is agreed on before the dispute arose. All that is necessary is that when a dispute does arise the parties to it choose a judge to resolve it. Even if they are complete strangers, as in the typical accident case, the parties can still choose a judge to determine liability.

Although dispute resolution could thus be provided (for criminal as well as civil cases) in a market that would operate free from any obvious elements of monopoly, externality, or other sources of "market failure," it may not be efficient to banish public intervention entirely. Public intervention may be required (1) to ensure compliance with the (private) judge's decision and (2) to compel submission of the dispute to adjudication in the first place. The first of these public functions is straightforward, and no more compromises the private nature of the adjudication system described above than the law of trespass compromises the private property rights system. The second function, compelling submission of the dispute to judge, is more complex. If A accuses B of breach of contract, the next step in a system of private adjudication is for the parties to select a judge. But suppose B, knowing that any impartial judge would convict him, drags his feet in agreeing to select a judge who will hear the case, rejecting name after name submitted by A for his consideration. Although a sanction for this kind of foot-dragging (a sanction analogous to the remedies that the National Labor Relations Board provides for refusals to bargain collectively in good faith) is conceivable, there may be serious difficulty in determining when the bargaining over the choice of the judge is in bad faith—it is not bad faith, for example, to reject a series of unreasonable suggestions by the other side.

Two ways of overcoming the submission problem come immediately to mind. The first is for the parties to agree on the judge (or on the method of selecting him) before the dispute arises, as is done in contracts with arbitration clauses. This solution is available, however, only where the dispute arises from a preexisting voluntary relationship between the parties; the typical tort or crime does not. * * *

Another type of private solution to the problem of enforcement and the selection of a private judge is available when both parties to the dispute are members of the same (private) group or association. The group can expel any member who unreasonably refuses to submit to an impartial adjudication (perhaps by a judge selected by the group) or to abide by the judge's decision. To the extent that membership in the group confers a value over and above alternative opportunities, members will have incentives to bargain in good faith over the selection of the judge and to abide by his decision. In these circumstances dispute resolution can operate effectively without public intervention.

* * *

3. *Rule Production.* Private production of rules or precedents involves two problems. First, because of the difficulty of establishing property rights in a precedent, private judges may have little incentive to produce precedents. They will strive for a fair result between the parties in order to preserve a reputation for impartiality, but why should they make any effort to explain the result in a way that would provide guidance for future parties? To do so would be to confer an external, an uncompensated, benefit not only on future parties but also on competing judges. If anything, judges might deliberately avoid explaining their results because the demand for their services would be reduced by rules that, by clarifying the meaning of the law, reduced the incidence of disputes. Yet, despite all this, private judges just might produce precedents. We said earlier that competitive private judges would strive for a reputation for competence and

impartiality. One method of obtaining such a reputation is to give reasons for a decision that convince the disputants and the public that the judge is competent and impartial. Competition could lead private judges to issue formal or informal "opinions" declaring their interpretation of the law, and these opinions—though intended simply as advertising—would function as precedents, as under a public judicial system. * * *

The second problem with a free market in precedent production is that of inconsistent precedents which could destroy the value of a precedent system in guiding behavior. If there are many judges, there is likely to be a bewildering profusion of precedents and no obvious method of harmonizing them. An individual contemplating some activity will have difficulty discovering its legal consequences because they will depend on who decides any dispute arising out of the activity.

* * *

[A] system of voluntary adjudication is strongly biased against the creation of precise rules of any sort. Any rule that clearly indicates how a judge is likely to decide a case will assure that no disputes subject to the rule are submitted to that judge since one party will know that it will lose. Judges will tend to promulgate vague standards which give each party to a dispute a fighting chance.

2.   ARBITRATION AND DISPUTE RESOLUTION

The traditional model of arbitration is precisely that of the "private tribunal"—private individuals, chosen voluntarily by the parties to a dispute in preference to the "official" courts, and given power to hear and "judge" their "case." The materials that follow explore the ramifications of this model, which is still the prevalent one. "Arbitration," however, cannot be so easily pigeon-holed, and in recent years the term has come to serve for a broad spectrum of dispute resolution processes. We will see later in this section how other models of arbitration have altered our conventional view of the process. Arbitration, for example, is sometimes imposed by law as a *mandatory,* non-consensual form of dispute resolution, and it has also been used to resolve kinds of disputes different from the traditional sort of "cases" which might otherwise have found their way into the judicial system.

There are many reasons why parties may choose arbitration as a more "efficient" means of dispute settlement than adjudication. To begin with, it seems likely that a dispute processed through arbitration will be disposed of more quickly than if the parties had made their way through the court system to a final judgment. In the commercial arbitration cases administered by the American Arbitration Association in 2001, an average of 3.7 months elapsed between the date the case was assigned to an arbitrator and the date the file was closed (by settlement, award or otherwise); the average time from assignment to *award* in all commercial arbitration cases was 9.2 months. Arbitration tends to be a speedier process in part because it allows the parties to bypass long queues at the courthouse door and to schedule hearings at their own convenience. In addition, as we will see, arbitration procedure is relatively "informal"; pre-trial procedures, pleading, motion practice, and discovery are substantially streamlined or in many cases completely eliminated. And the arbitrator's decision is likely to be final: There is no delay imposed by any appeal process, and court review is highly restricted. It is not surprising, therefore, that surveys of practicing attorneys indicate that arbitration is overwhelmingly considered a speedier means of dispute resolution than either jury trial or bench trial; see Stipanowich, Rethinking American Arbitration, 63 Ind.L.J. 425, 460 (1988). Any savings in time and in related pre-and post-trial work are also likely to be reflected in savings in expense—for example, in lawyers' fees—although there can be no assurance that this will always be the case.

There may be other benefits as well. Taking a dispute out of the courtroom and into the relative informality of arbitration may reduce the enmity and heightened contentiousness which so often accompany litigation, and which work against a future cooperative relationship. The privacy of the process may also contribute to a lessening of hostility and confrontation. An arbitration hearing (unlike a trial) is not open to the public, and unless the result later becomes the subject of a court proceeding it is not a matter of public record.

Most important of all, perhaps, the parties themselves are able to choose their "judges." They are free, therefore, to avail themselves of decision-makers with expert knowledge of the subject matter in dispute. The arbitrator may have a similar background to the parties, or be engaged in the same business; he is likely, then, to be familiar with the presuppositions and understandings of the trade. The usefulness of such expertise is particularly apparent when a contract dispute hinges on interpretation of the agreement—which in turn may depend on the content of trade custom and usage—or when the dispute is over whether goods sold meet the necessary technical standards. In such cases arbitration avoids the task (which may in some cases be insuperable) of educating judge or jury as to the content of these industry norms. In short, "the evidence from arbitration is that a single qualified lay judge is superior to six or twelve randomly selected laymen—on reflection, a not implausible suggestion."[1]

Lon Fuller, Collective Bargaining and the Arbitrator

1963 Wisc.L.Rev. 3, 11–12, 17.

Labor relations have today become a highly complicated and technical field. This field involves complex procedures that vary from industry to industry, from plant to plant, from department to department. It has developed its own vocabulary. Though the terms of this vocabulary often seem simple and familiar, their true meaning can be understood only when

---

1. William M. Landes & Richard A. Posner, Adjudication as a Private Good, 8 J.Legal Stud. 235, 252 (1979).

they are seen as parts of a larger system of practice, just as the umpire's "You're out!" can only be fully understood by one who knows the objectives, the rules and the practices of baseball. I might add that many questions of industrial relations are on a level at least equal to that of the infield fly rule. They are not suitable material for light dinner conversation.

In the nature of things few judges can have had any very extensive experience in the field of industrial relations. Arbitrators, on the other hand, are compelled to acquire a knowledge of industrial processes, modes of compensation, complex incentive plans, job classification, shift arrangements, and procedures for layoff and recall.

Naturally not all arbitrators stand on a parity with respect to this knowledge. But there are open to the arbitrator, even the novice, quick methods of education not available to courts. An arbitrator will frequently interrupt the examination of witnesses with a request that the parties educate him to the point where he can understand the testimony being received. This education can proceed informally, with frequent interruptions by the arbitrator, and by informed persons on either side, when a point needs clarification. Sometimes there will be arguments across the table, occasionally even within each of the separate camps. The end result will usually be a clarification that will enable everyone to proceed more intelligently with the case. There is in this informal procedure no infringement whatever of arbitrational due process. On the contrary, the party's chance to have his case understood by the arbitrator is seriously impaired if his representative has to talk into a vacuum, if he addresses his words to uncomprehending ears.

The education that an arbitrator can thus get, say, in a half an hour, might take days if it had to proceed by qualifying experts and subjecting them to direct and cross examination. The courts have themselves recognized the serious obstacle presented by traditional methods of proof in dealing with cases involving a complex technical background.

* * *

Courts have in fact had difficulty with complicated commercial litigation. The problems here are not unlike those encountered in dealing with labor agreements. There are really few outstanding commercial judges in the history of the common law. The greatest of these, Lord Mansfield, used to sit with special juries selected from among experienced merchants and traders. To further his education in commercial practice he used to arrange dinners with his jurors. In Greek mythology it is reported that Minos prepared himself for a posthumous career as judge of shades by first exposing himself to every possible experience of life. It is not only in labor relations that the impracticability of such a program manifests itself.

NOTES AND QUESTIONS

1. Consider the possible use of arbitration in the following circumstances, and weigh its advantages and disadvantages from the perspective of dispute settlement:

In 1986, the Hunt brothers of Dallas filed two lawsuits in federal court seeking a total of $13.8 billion against some of the country's biggest banks. The banks were accused of fraud, breach of contract, and banking and antitrust law violations after they refused to restructure about $1.5 billion in debts owed by certain Hunt companies, including Placid Oil Company. In December 1986 the Hunts hired a Houston attorney, Stephen Susman, to take charge of the two lawsuits. Placid Oil was then involved in Chapter 11 bankruptcy proceedings. In a court filing seeking the bankruptcy judge's approval to represent Placid, Susman proposed to charge $600 per hour for his time:

> If the Susman firm is terminated by the Hunts for any reason other than malpractice—or the Hunts drop their lawsuits—the firm can pocket the entire retainer [of $1 million]. A malpractice or fee dispute would be arbitrated by the dean of the University of Texas School of Law, Mr. Susman's alma mater. A decision by the dean is final, the fee agreement says.

The Wall Street Journal, December 30, 1986, p. 4.

2. In 1910, the King of England made Sir Adolf Tuck a baronet. He was anxious to ensure that his successors to the title should all be, like himself, of Jewish blood and Jewish faith: So in 1912 he made a settlement putting money in trust for "the Baronet for the time being if and when and so long as he shall be of the Jewish faith and shall be married to an approved wife"; an "approved wife" was defined as a woman of Jewish blood "who has been brought up in and has never departed from and .. continues to worship according to the Jewish faith." In case of "dispute or doubt," the decision of the Chief Rabbi in London "shall be conclusive."

Sir Adolf's grandson, after a divorce, married a woman who was not an "approved wife," and the question arose whether the settlement was valid. Attorneys for the estate argued that the definition of an "approved wife" was "so uncertain as to be void for uncertainty." The Court of Appeal disagreed; Lord Denning wrote:

> [T]he testator may even today think that the courts of law are not really the most suitable means of deciding the dispute or doubt. He would be quite right. As this very case shows, the courts may get bogged down in distinctions between conceptual uncertainty and evidential uncertainty, and between conditions subsequent and conditions precedent. The testator may want to cut out all that cackle, and let someone decide it who really will understand what the testator is talking about, and thus save an expensive journey to the lawyers and the courts. For my part, I would not blame him. I would give effect to his intentions. Take this very case: who better to decide these questions of "Jewish blood" and "Jewish faith" than a chief rabbi? ... I venture to suggest that his decision would be much more acceptable to all concerned that the decision of a court of law. I would let him decide it.

In re Tuck's Settlement Trusts, [1978] 1 All E.R. 1047 (C.A. 1977).

3. Later in this chapter we will consider in some detail the conduct of an arbitration proceeding, see Section D, infra. An arbitration, like a trial, entails the adversary presentation of evidence and argument before a neutral third party; as we will see, however, the rules of procedure and of evidence that constrain behavior at "trial" will be noticeably lacking. One federal court has observed that "[t]he present day penchant for arbitration may obscure for many parties who do not have the benefit of hindsight that the arbitration system is an inferior system of justice, structured without due process, rules of evidence, accountability of judgment and rules of law." Stroh Container Company v. Delphi Industries, Inc., 783 F.2d 743, 751 n. 12 (8th Cir.1986). As we proceed through this chapter, you should continue to ask if it is appropriate to consider arbitration as an "inferior system of justice." In what sense may this be true? Is the process merely another, somewhat streamlined, form of "trial"? Is there a danger that the pervasive influence of the judicial model may make it difficult for us to assess arbitration on its own terms? And in any event, isn't it clear that "whether to accept rougher justice in exchange for cost savings" is always "a question for contracting parties themselves"? Nagel v. ADM Investor Services, Inc., 65 F.Supp.2d 740, 745 (N.D. Ill. 1999).

4. Lawyers are quick to perceive the advantages that inhere in the expeditious, "businesslike," expert settlement of a controversy provided by arbitration. These are largely advantages of "efficiency." However, whether arbitration ultimately turns out to be a blessing or a curse may in fact depend upon the tactical position of the particular client. Rapid resolution of a dispute may in theory benefit everyone; nevertheless the party against whom a claim is being asserted will probably find that there are offsetting advantages in delaying the ultimate reckoning. The larger of the disputants may also prefer to exploit the fact that its smaller opponent does not have the financial resources for an extended struggle. In addition, a party for whom the stakes and risk of loss are high may for that reason become less interested in "informality"—and more reluctant to chance a decision without having taken every possible advantage of the full panoply of legal procedures, including the ability to play out his hand to the bitter end. Similarly, a party who is aware that his case is a weak one may not always find a knowledgeable arbiter to be desirable; he may prefer instead to take his chances with a decision maker who is somewhat less expert and considerably more malleable. The General Counsel of Refac Technology Development Corporation has in fact written this about his company's patent litigation strategy:

> [I]f patent validity or infringement is questionable, why take a chance with an arbitration expert who will know exactly how weak the patent is and how dubious infringement is? It makes sense to take one's chance with a judge inexperienced in the technical and legal aspects involved. If the infringer is much bigger than the patentee or an entire industry has copied the patent, a jury trial would be much more beneficial than arbitration because of the sympathy and deep-pocket doctrine that can be played to the hilt.

Sperber, Overlooked Negotiating Tools, 20 Les Nouvelles 81 (June 1985).

5.   The newly-appointed curator of drawings at the Getty Museum in Los Angeles came to believe that some of the Museum's expensive and highly-publicized acquisitions were in fact forgeries. "Some of the drawings were so patently bogus that they began to annoy me to look at them," he said. He was, however, instructed by the Museum director not to inform the Getty's trustees about the drawings' dubious authenticity. Over a number of years the relationship between the Museum and the curator worsened: The curator complained that the drawings department was being denied an adequate budget and gallery space—and in his opinion, the Museum "was punishing him and subverting his credibility in order to cast doubt on his forgery claims." He eventually sued the Museum for defamation, and the parties reached a settlement: The curator was to receive a large monetary payment and agreed to resign; the Getty promised to publish an exhaustive catalogue he had written of the Museum's drawings collection, part of which was devoted to the forgery allegations. The catalogue, however, was never published—and the curator was convinced that the Getty's intention was in fact to bury it in order to minimize embarrassment to the Museum. He later filed another suit, in which his allegations of fraud centered on the Getty's failure to publish his catalogue; the case was sent to arbitration.

In the course of the proceedings, the Getty's lawyers filed a motion with the arbitrator to keep the curator from discussing with the press anything discovered during the case: "The Getty argued that arbitration is an inherently confidential proceeding and so [the curator] should not be permitted to say anything to the media, especially about the forgeries." The motion, however, was denied—the arbitrator noting that after all, "*Erin Brockovich* was an arbitration." Peter Landesman, "A Crisis of Fakes," New York Times Magazine, March 18, 2001, at pp. 37, 38–40.

As we will see, arbitration has been used in a number of diverse contexts, to resolve many different types of disputes. However, it has flourished most in situations where parties to a contract have or aspire to have a continuing future relationship in which they will regularly deal with each other. The paradigm is the relationship between management and union in the administration of a collective bargaining agreement, or, perhaps, the relationship between a buyer and a seller of fabric in the textile industry. In both cases there is a history and a likelihood of continued mutual dependence by which both parties may profit; there also exist non-legal sanctions allowing either party to withdraw from (or seek to adjust) the relationship, or at least to withhold vital future cooperation. All this makes it easier to settle in advance on arbitration as a less disruptive method than litigation for resolving any future disputes. It also tends to induce the parties to comply with arbitration decisions once they are handed down (as does the feeling, in a long-term relation, that "awards are likely to be equalized over the long run and that erroneous awards can be dealt with through negotiation"[2]). In both cases there is an understandable reluctance to assert officially-defined legal "rights," or to rely on formal, technical arguments or on accusations of misconduct or impropriety—all of which may seem inappropriate in the context of a "family row" and which may hurt the prospects of future collaboration. And in both cases the parties may be more willing in advance to entrust to arbitrators the task of working out the details of their arrangement in accordance with the common values, the "shared norms," of the trade or of the "shop."

William M. Landes & Richard A. Posner, Adjudication As a Private Good

8 J.Legal Stud. 235, 245–47 (1979).

[I]f one party to a dispute expects that an impartial arbitrator would rule against him, he has an incentive to drag his feet in agreeing to the appointment of an arbitrator. Consistently with this point, writers on arbitration agree that the problem of selection makes arbitration a virtually unusable method of dispute resolution where there is no preexisting contractual or other relationship between the disputants. This suggests a clue to the superior ability of primitive compared to advanced societies to function without public institutions of adjudication. Primitive communities tend to be quite small and their members bound together by a variety of mutually advantageous relationships and interactions. Expulsion, outlawry, ostracism, and other forms of boycott or collective refusal to deal are highly effective sanctions in these circumstances. Another way of putting this point is that reputation, a factor recognized in the literature as deterring people from breaking contracts even in the absence of effective legal sanctions, is a more effective deterrent in a small community, where news travels rapidly throughout the entire circle of an individual's business and social acquaintances, than in large, modern, impersonal societies.

Yet even in modern society, certain trade, religious, and other associations correspond, to a degree, to the close-knit, primitive community. For example, securities or commodities exchanges whose members derive substantial benefits from membership can use the threat of expulsion as an effective sanction to induce members to submit to arbitration. So can a religious association in which excommunication is regarded by members as a substantial cost[30]; so can a university. Exchanges, religious associations, and (private) universities are in fact important examples of modern "communities" in which private adjudication (whether called arbitration or something else) is extensively utilized in preference to public adjudication.

2. Julius Getman, Labor Arbitration and Dispute Resolution, 88 Yale L.J. 916, 922–23 (1979).

30. The threat of excommunication was, for example, the ultimate sanction for refusal to submit to, or obey the decision of, the medieval English ecclesiastical courts, which had an immense jurisdiction covering matrimonial disputes, perjury, and a variety of other matters as well as strictly religious disputes.

In The Matter of the Arbitration Between Mikel and Scharf

Supreme Court, Special Term, Kings County New York, 1980.
105 Misc.2d 548, 432 N.Y.S.2d 602, aff'd, 85 A.D.2d 604, 444 N.Y.S.2d 690 (1981).

■ ARTHUR S. HIRSCH, J.

This is a motion to confirm an arbitration award rendered by a rabbinical court.

[Respondents are the shareholders of a corporation that operates a nursing home. In 1973, the corporation agreed to lease premises from a partnership. Negotiations on behalf of the partnership were conducted primarily by Barad, one of the partners, and the agreed monthly rental was $25,208.

In 1977 respondents contacted Barad and told him that because of business reverses, they would have to vacate the premises unless there were a substantial reduction in rent. After negotiations, an oral agreement was reached to reduce the monthly rental by $8000, and a writing to this effect was signed by respondents on behalf of the corporation and by Barad on behalf of the landlord.]

During the negotiations, respondents had met with other partners besides Barad, but at no time had they come in contact with petitioner or with his father, who acted as his son's surrogate in the arbitration proceedings and from whom petitioner had received the 6% interest in the partnership. * * *

In November, 1977, respondents received notice from the Union of Orthodox Rabbis to appear before a rabbinical court for a *"Din Torah"* or arbitration of a claim brought against them by petitioner. Respondents testified they refused to appear at first on grounds that they had no knowledge of petitioner, but did appear after receiving written notice that refusal would result in the court's invoking a "sirov."

The first meeting of the rabbinical court, presided over by the requisite three rabbis, took place on Sunday, May 14, 1978. The respondents appeared with their attorney, who was present as their legal representative and to testify as witness to all meetings between [landlord] and [tenant], at which the attorney was present.

Respondents are persistent in their claim that theirs was a special appearance before the rabbinical tribunal to establish that there was never a business nor contractual relationship between the claimant and themselves, and therefore, a *Din Torah,* or arbitration, would be improper and invalid. Their participation thereafter was to obtain a determination on this limited issue, i.e., whether a *Din Torah* should be convened and not for a determination as to the merits of the claim.

The respondents were required by the court to sign a Hebrew Document entitled a "Mediation Note" which, in effect, is an agreement to voluntarily arbitrate "the dispute existing" between the parties. Respondent Asher Scharf, who has a complete understanding of the Hebrew language, contends that much discussion ensued until it was unequivocally established that the "dispute" referred to in the "Mediation Note" was the question of the propriety of having a *Din Torah* and that he overcame his conceded reluctance to sign the document when he was assured by the court of the limited scope of the dispute. Respondents were summoned and attended two additional meetings. At the insistence of the rabbinical court, respondents' attorney did not attend any meeting after the first. On December 31, 1978, a written judgment of the rabbinical court was rendered, in which respondents were directed, among other things, to pay to petitioner a lump sum of $9,000 and to make monthly payments of 6% of $23,000, representing petitioner's share of the rental due and owing to the [landlord].

Petitioner has moved for an order confirming the award, with respondents opposing and moving to vacate the award on numerous grounds.

Rabbinical Court—Din Torah

As earlier indicated, the customary arbitration proceeding was not utilized by the parties. An accepted, but more unusual forum was selected, that of arbitration by a tribunal of rabbis conducting a *Din Torah*.

The beginnings of Jewish arbitral institutions are traceable to the middle of the second century. Throughout the centuries, thereafter, in every country in which Jews have been domiciled, Jewish judicial authority has existed, via the institute of arbitration conducted by special rabbinical courts. Orthodox Jews, prompted by their religious, national feelings, accepted Jewish judicial authority, by resorting to the arbitration procedure of their own free will. This method of arbitration has the imprimatur of our own judicial system, as a useful means of relieving the burdens of the inundated courts dealing with civil matters. Through Talmudic sages, it is learned that special rules or procedures have been provided under which the rabbinical courts function as a *Din Torah* (literally translated as torah judgment), with Judaic or torah law as its basis. * * *

In addition to the procedural rules established by Judaic Law, there are state, civil, procedural rules for arbitration (CPLR, Article 75) to which the rabbinical court, as an arbitration forum, must also adhere.

* * *

Respondents [challenge] the rabbinical court's award, claiming first, the arbitration agreement was entered involuntarily, under duress and is consequently void, [and] second, charging the arbitrators with misconduct * * *.

Involuntary Agreement—Duress

Both parties are members of the orthodox Jewish community. Respondent's denial of the existence of any disputable issue between themselves and petitioner convinced them to refuse to appear for a *Din Torah* and they would not have done so had they not received the threat of a "sirov." Rabbis testifying for respondents stated that a sirov, literally translated as contempt of court, is a prohibitionary decree that subjects the recipient to shame, scorn, ridicule and ostracism by his coreligionists, fellow members of his community. Ostensibly, he is ostracized and scorned. Other Jews refuse to eat or speak with him. He is discredited and dishonored. The respondents maintain that the draconian measures of a sirov are sufficiently threatening so as to compel their compliance with the demand to appear. They claim they would have become outcasts among their friends and coreligionists. However, from other testimony, it appears that the sirov, while most assuredly ominous in its potential power, is honored in its breach. The court cannot, of course, know the actual state of mind of respondents and it may be that their fear of a sirov decree was real. However, it seems more plausible that if respondents believed the consequences so fearful, they would not, at this point, be willing to defy the rabbinical court by refusing to accept the arbitrator's determination. Undoubtedly, pressure was brought to bear to have them participate in the *Din Torah,* but pressure is not duress. Their decision to acquiesce to the rabbinical court's urgings was made without the coercion that would be necessary for the agreement to be void.

Misconduct

CPLR 7511 (subd [b], par. 1, cl [i]) allows for the vacation of an award if the rights of a party are prejudiced by corruption, fraud or misconduct. Courts have used the term misconduct to denote actions of fundamental unfairness, whether intentional or unintentional.

Respondents charge misconduct by the rabbinical tribunal in their refusal to permit respondents to have legal representation and, further, to hear testimony or accept material documents offered by respondents' attorney, as witness to the lease negotiations. This, they contend, violated their due process rights. Respondents appeared at the first meeting with their attorney, Abraham Bernstein. From the beginning, it became apparent the tribunal would not tolerate the presence of an attorney at a *Din Torah.* Petitioner's father strenuously objected, claiming he had no attorney to represent petitioner. At first, attorney Bernstein was not permitted to speak, but later was allowed to make a short statement in which he attempted to establish the fact that a lease was executed between the corporation tenant and the landlord partnership without personal involvement of the parties and when he offered to submit the lease and other documents for the perusal of the court, the papers were returned to him. Thereafter, he interjected himself wherever possible to explain respondents' position regarding the lack of legal connection between the parties. For the most part, the court refused to acknowledge him, quelling his attempts to speak or take part in the proceedings. He was not permitted to ask questions of petitioner or his father, who at all times acted as representative and voice of petitioner.

* * *

Biblical law requires that parties appear before a magistrate in person and not by proxy (*Deuteronomy* 19:17). For many years, this supported a

Jewish judicial prejudice against proxies, including attorneys and even interpreters, it being determined essential that argument be heard directly from the mouths of litigants or witnesses. There was a tradition, however, that the high priest, when sued in court, could appoint an attorney to represent him (*Talmud Yerushalmi,* Sanhedrin 2:1, 19d). It may be this tradition that precipitated the admittance of defense attorneys into rabbinical courts. Where the parties were present to give testimony, thus permitting Judges to perceive their demeanor and evaluate their credibility, legal counsel was no longer considered to be anathema. The rabbinical court in the instant matter obviously did not abide by this accepted legal concept.

The tribunal's proclivity for conducting their court under outdated concepts resulted in inadvertent violations. Respondents were denied due process. The right of counsel, which is a constitutional right, is further enunciated in Article 75 of the CPLR, and is an unwaivable right. Consequently, respondent's participation without counsel, after receiving the court's warning to appear alone, did not have a negative effect on their inherent right to legal representation, the deprivation of which is sufficient to vitiate the award.

Respondent Asher Scharf's unrebutted testimony indicated that at a session he attended, one of the three rabbi arbitrators called him out to talk with him privately. The rabbi argued for a cash settlement, to be paid by respondent on the grounds that petitioner was a poor student. Scharf testified the rabbi asked, "Well, what does a few thousand dollars mean to you?"

Under Judaic law (*Deuteronomy* 1:17), a Judge must judge impartially in favoring the rich or the poor. In an interpretation of this portion of the Torah, the foremost authority, Rashi, in *Commentary Rashi,* states that the version should be understood as follows: A judge "should not say: 'This is a poor man and his fellow (opponent) is rich and he will consequently obtain some support in a respectable fashion.' "

To ensure fairness, it is axiomatic and imperative that an arbitrator's impartiality be above suspicion. The rabbinical court was obviously prejudiced against respondents because of their affluence and considered the financial status of the parties above the issues. Such conduct, forbidden by the Torah, the law under which the rabbinical court has jurisdiction, constitutes another instance in which the tribunal deviated from its own *Din Torah* precepts.

The procedural format of the sessions was haphazard; no prescribed order was followed. A rabbinical court normally operates in a set manner, with presentation of claims, counterclaims, testimony of witnesses and cross-examinations conducted in a fairly orderly manner. This is not to say that any formal hearings are required. However, it appears that no semblance of administrative court proceeding, formal or informal, was followed by this rabbinical court. Witnesses were not called, real evidence was not accepted and no recognizable and required *Din Torah* procedure was followed. Under these highly unusual and chaotic conditions, a fair award could not be given.

* * *

Despite the established and well-grounded precedent that courts rarely set aside an arbitration award, in this instance the court finds it obligatory to vacate the award of the rabbinical court for the reasons enunciated above. A new arbitration proceeding will not be scheduled, as the court is convinced that no legal dispute exists between these particular parties.

NOTES AND QUESTIONS

1.   Closely-knit Jewish communities throughout the Western world developed—out of necessity—a long-standing proscription against submitting intragroup disputes to hostile or uncomprehending secular courts. At the same time such communities developed their own systems of dispute resolution. See Lynn Cohen, "Inside the Beis Din," Canadian Lawyer, May 2000 at pp. 27, 30 (Toronto rabbi quoted as saying, "In this city, we actually push people a little to come because using the *Beis Din* is a *mitzvah*, a commandment from God, an obligation"). With assimilation into the wider society, the role of these autonomous tribunals has naturally declined—but even today a practice of rabbinical "arbitration" still persists in Jewish communities. The majority of cases heard in this country by Jewish courts seem to concern divorce matters. See, e.g., Avitzur v. Avitzur, 58 N.Y.2d 108, 459 N.Y.S.2d 572, 446 N.E.2d 136 (1983). But this is by no means always the case: In addition to *Mikel & Scharf*, see, e.g., Ghertner v. Solaimani, 254 Ga.App. 821, 563 S.E.2d 878 (2002)(financial dispute arising out of partnership agreement); Barak Richman, How Community Institutions Create Economic Advantage: Jewish Diamond Merchants in New York, 31:2 Law & Social Inquiry (Spring 2006)(brokers and cutters in New York's diamond industry, who handle 95% of the diamonds imported into the U.S., "are disproportionately comprised of ultra-Orthodox Jews, adherents to an insular and highly ritualistic version of Jewish practice"; the "Diamond Dealers Club" provides a mandatory arbitration system to resolve all disputes between merchants, and the DDC often in turn initiates proceedings before rabbinical courts—which can impose excommunication, or, less severely, compel an individual to make a charitable contribution to a community charity).

2.   In a business or employment dispute, it is usually understood by the parties that a Jewish rabbinical tribunal "may seek to compromise the parties' claims, and is not bound to decide strictly in accordance with the governing rules of Jewish law, but may more carefully weigh the equities of the situation." See Kingsbridge Center of Israel v. Turk, 98 A.D.2d 664, 469 N.Y.S.2d 732, 734 (1983). Is that what the tribunal attempted to do in the principal case?

3.   Examples of "faith-based" arbitrations are hardly limited to Jewish tribunals: See, e.g., Prescott v. Northlake Christian School, 244 F.Supp.2d

659 (E.D. La. 2002)(contract between school and principal required that all employment-related disputes be submitted to "biblically-based mediation and arbitration" under the Rules of Procedure for Christian Conciliation; the arbitrator concluded that the school had breached its contract "legally as well as Biblically" by wrongfully terminating the principal without following Matthew:18; held, "given the unique nature of this employment agreement," the award "was rationally related to the parties' agreement").

In Ontario, Canada, the Islamic Institute for Civil Justice was formed to appoint and train arbitrators—"imams and religious scholars"—to resolve civil disputes using *sharia*, or Islamic law; a report commissioned by the Government concluded that the "Arbitration Act should continue to allow disputes to be arbitrated using religious law." But after vigorous public protest, Ontario's Premier reversed course—and announced that henceforth "there will be no *sharia* law in Ontario": The Government introduced legislation that required any "family arbitration [to be] conducted exclusively in accordance with the law of Ontario or of another Canadian jurisdiction"; the arbitrators must apply "the substantive law of Ontario"—or of another Canadian province if the parties have expressly provided for it—and awards will be "enforceable only under the Family Law Act." In addition, family arbitration agreements could only be enforced if they were entered into after the dispute had arisen. For Ontario's Attorney–General, this means that "there is one family law for all Ontarians," and that resolutions based "on any other laws and principles * * * would have no legal effect. They would amount to advice only." See "Islamic law in civil disputes raises questions," Globe & Mail, Dec. 11, 2003; Bill 27, Family Statute Law Amendment, 2005, http://www.ontla.on.ca/library/bills/382/27382.htm; "McGuinty Government Declares One Law For All Ontarians," http://www.attorneygeneral.jus.gov.on.ca/ english/ news/ 2005/ 20051115- arbitration.asp; Legislative Assembly of Ontario, Hansard, Nov. 23, 2005, http://www.ontla.on.ca/ hansard/ house_debates/ 38_parl/ Session2/ L022.htm. See also "Decision on Sharia Sparks Jewish Protest," Globe & Mail, Sept. 13, 2005 ("Mubin Sheikh, with the Masjid-al-Noor mosque in Toronto, said he will still be guided by Islamic law when he mediates Muslims' disputes over child-support payments, custody and inheritance; '[a] ban will change nothing. And it hurts the women who were supposed to be protected by not affording them official state sanction of the arbitrated settlement' ").

4. Professor Marc Galanter has written that "[j]ust as health is not found primarily in hospitals or knowledge in schools, so justice is not primarily to be found in official justice-dispensing institutions. People experience justice (and injustice) not only (or usually) in forums sponsored by the state but at the primary institutional locations of their activity—home, neighborhood, workplace, business deal and so on * * *." This social ordering, found in a variety of institutional settings (such as universities, sports leagues, housing developments, and hospitals) he refers to as "indigenous law." He notes that although indigenous law may have the virtues of being familiar, understandable and independent of professionals, it is not always the expression of harmonious egalitarianism. It often reflects narrow and parochial concerns; it is often based on relations of domination; its coerciveness may be harsh and indiscriminate; protections that are available in public forums may be absent.

Galanter, Justice in Many Rooms: Courts, Private Ordering, and Indigenous Law, 19 J. Pluralism & Unofficial L. 1, 17–18, 25 (1981).

5. For further discussion of court review of "arbitration" awards, see Section C.4.a, infra.

3. ARBITRATION AND THE APPLICATION OF "RULES"

The Landes and Posner excerpt at the beginning of this chapter introduces another recurrent theme in these materials. Many writers suggest that arbitration, as a voluntary and private process, may not proceed by formulating, applying, and communicating general principles of decision, or "rules." A number of related points form an essential backdrop for this discussion.

- First of all—particularly outside the field of labor arbitration—arbitrators (unlike judges) commonly do not write reasoned opinions attempting to explain and justify their decisions. In fact the American Arbitration Association, which administers much commercial arbitration, actively discourages arbitrators from doing so.

- In addition, we do not in any event expect that an arbitrator will decide a case the way a judge does. We do not expect that he will necessarily "follow the law"—or indeed apply or develop any body of general rules as a guide to his decision. An arbitrator, it is said, "may do justice as he sees it, applying his own sense of law and equity to the facts as he finds them to be and making an award reflecting the spirit rather than the letter of the agreement."[1] Indeed, in the words of one older case, arbitrators "are a law unto themselves."[2]

- Furthermore, a decision by any particular arbitrator will not necessarily control the result of later cases involving other parties—or, indeed, have any precedential value at all for later arbitrators.

- And finally, an arbitrator's decision is not subject to later review and correction by a court to insure that general rules of law have been complied with. The highly restricted role courts play in passing on the decisions of arbitrators, and the implications of a system in which elaborate reasoned awards are rare, are discussed in some detail in Section C.4 infra.

1. In the Matter of the Arbitration between Silverman and Benmor Coats, Inc., 61 N.Y.2d 299, 308, 473 N.Y.S.2d 774, 779, 461 N.E.2d 1261, 1266 (1984).

2. Leach v. Harris, 69 N.C. 532 (N.C. 1873).

What are some of the implications of a system of private justice in which cases are "decided," but without the use or communication of consistent rules of decision? When cases are diverted into a private forum, operating without a formal system of precedent, any judicial function of shaping future activity may be neglected. In addition, it may be more difficult for private parties to predict the future results of cases heard in these private tribunals. Information disseminated by courts in the form of precedents is used every day by private actors in routine decisions concerning which claims they should assert, and under what circumstances they should settle those claims. With no certainty as to the rule a particular arbitrator would apply—and with no consistent application of rules across the entire community of "competing" arbitrators, purporting independently to decide particular cases without reference to each other or to generally accepted rules—any firm basis on which to build future conduct is undermined:

> You cannot say today that a check need not contain an unconditional promise or order to pay to be negotiable and tomorrow that it must. You cannot say today that F.O.B. means free on board and tomorrow that it means only that the seller must get the goods as far as his shipping room. And so on. Mankind needs an irreducible minimum of certainty in order to operate efficiently. That irreducible minimum would seem to be better handled by the courts than by arbitration even though in the particular case the result would have been better decided in arbitration.[3]

However, unless the parties to an arbitration are "repeat players"—with a stake in the rules applied that extends beyond the result in the particular case—creating and promulgating "rules" of decision could from their point of view serve only to confer a benefit on *other* people, at the cost of increasing the duration and the expense of their own proceedings.

Of course, much of the above discussion has to be qualified. Any dichotomy between an ad hoc, particularistic system of private arbitration and a rule-and precedent-bound judiciary can easily be overstated. All first-year law students know that such a characterization can grotesquely exaggerate the predictability of court decisions and the meaningfulness of rules of decision in predicting or explaining the results of litigation. Conversely, even in the absence of a formal system of precedent, criteria of decision can be agreed on, developed, and communicated in other ways: by private associations, through past practice and the evolution of trade custom, and particularly through the pre-existing contractual relations of the parties.[4] Lawyers who are experienced in arbitration tend to feel that

---

3. Soia Mentschikoff, The Significance of Arbitration—A Preliminary Inquiry, 17 Law & Contemporary Problems 698, 709 (1952).

4. See S.A. Wenger & Co., Inc. v. Propper Silk Hosiery Mills, Inc., 239 N.Y. 199, 146 N.E. 203 (1924)("It may be that under the rules of the Raw Silk Association matters of strict law are subordinated to a course of dealing or to the equities of the case," and "traders may prefer the decision of the arbitral tribunal to that of the courts" on questions of law as well as of fact).

they are able to predict the results of arbitration with some certainty, at least in part because these sources supply rules of decision likely to be consistently applied. It is, of course, a separate question whether the rules so applied will be consonant with officially-declared public values, or whether the arbitration process may implicate important public policy concerns which should be reserved to the official court system. This is a subject which is explored further in later sections.

In addition, the arbitration of disputes arising under collective bargaining agreements has come to evolve certain unique characteristics, distinguishing it from other forms of private dispute resolution. It does appear to be the general practice for *labor* arbitrators to write explanations and justifications—sometimes elaborate ones—for their decisions; these decisions are often publicly reported, cited to later arbitrators, and relied on in later cases. "An extensive survey of labor arbitration disclosed that 77 percent of the 238 responding arbitrators believed that precedents, even under *other* contracts, should be given 'some weight.' "[5] As we will see, there has developed a "common-law" of labor arbitration. In addition, the growth of labor arbitration over the last 50 years to a central place in the settlement of labor disputes has been accompanied by the development of the profession of "labor arbitrator." In the commercial area it may be unusual for an arbitrator to decide more than a handful of cases a year, but for many labor arbitrators arbitration constitutes a primary source of their livelihood. One may suspect that Landes and Posner's point concerning the advertising value of reasoned opinions may have particular relevance here.

4. "RIGHTS" ARBITRATION AND "INTEREST" ARBITRATION

"Interest" arbitration is distinguished from the more familiar grievance or "rights" arbitration by the fact that in the former situation the designated neutral is employed to determine the actual contract terms which will bind the parties during the life of their new agreement, while in the latter situation the arbitrator is only empowered to decide disputes concerning the interpretation and application of the terms of an already existing contract. The grievance arbiter is generally precluded from adding to or modifying the terms of the contract in dispute.[6]

The distinction between "rights" and "interest" arbitration is a familiar one. You will often see reference to it, particularly in relation to the arbitration of labor-management disputes. The paradigm of a "rights" arbitration is a hearing on the grievance of an employee alleging that he has been discharged "without just cause." The paradigm of an "interest" arbitration is a hearing held at the expiration of a collective bargaining agreement, after negotiations over a union's demand for higher wage rates in a "new" contract have failed. While "interest" arbitration remains an unusual and infrequent device in comparison to other forms of arbitration, it is quite commonly resorted to in resolving disputes over the terms of employment of public employees. Public employees, such as police or school teachers, are usually forbidden to engage in strikes; economic pressure, and the usual tests of economic strength used in the private sector to determine

---

5. Frank Elkouri & Edna A. Elkouri, How Arbitration Works 572 (Alan Miles Ruben et al. eds., 6th ed. 2003).

6. Charles B. Craver, The Judicial Enforcement of Public Sector Interest Arbitration, 21 B.C.L.Rev. 557, 558 n. 8 (1980).

contract terms after a bargaining impasse, are therefore limited in the public interest. "Interest" arbitration to determine the terms of a new contract when bargaining fails provides a common alternative mechanism. In many cases, in fact, state statutes impose this as a *mandatory* means of settlement. See Section E.1 infra. Such legislation in effect gives to public employee unions the "right" to resort to the arbitration mechanism to determine the future terms of employment.

Now compare the following three cases. Are these examples of "rights" or of "interest" arbitration? What precisely are the differences, if any, between them?

(a) A law firm entered into a lease of space in an office building. The term of the lease was ten years. At the firm's request, a clause was added to the lease by which it would have the option to renew the lease for an additional ten years; it provided that "rental for the renewal term shall be in such amount as shall be agreed upon by the parties based on the comparative rental values of similar properties as of the date of the renewal and on comparative business conditions of the two periods." The lease contained a general arbitration clause providing that "all disputes relating to" the lease shall be settled by arbitration. The parties fail to agree on a rental for the renewal term.

(b) A coal supply agreement provided that for a period of ten years a coal company would tender and a power company would purchase specified quantities of coal. There was a base price per ton, and a provision for the calculation of adjustments in base price upon changes in certain labor costs and in "governmental impositions." The agreement also provided:

> Any gross proven inequity that may result in unusual economic conditions not contemplated by the parties at the time of the execution of this Agreement may be corrected by mutual consent. Each party shall in the case of a claim of gross inequity furnish the other with whatever documentary evidence may be necessary to assist in effecting a settlement.

Another clause called for "any unresolved controversy between the parties arising under this Agreement" to be submitted to arbitration. Four years later, after a rapid escalation in the price of coal, the open market price of coal of the same quality was more than three times the current adjusted base price under the agreement. The coal company requested an adjustment in the contract price which the power company adamantly rejected.[7]

(c) An agreement between a newspaper and its employees was to last for three years, with a provision that "this contract shall remain in effect until all terms and conditions of employment for a succeeding contract term are resolved either through negotiation or through arbitration." After a bargaining deadlock, the union moved for arbitration. The employer presented to the arbitrator a number of items which it wanted included in the agreement for the new term, including the right to make layoffs on

---

7. See Georgia Power Co. v. Cimarron Coal Corp., 526 F.2d 101 (6th Cir.1975).

account of automation or the introduction of new processes. The Union also presented a number of issues to the arbitrator, including "wages; mailers brought up to mechanical department [wage] scale; proof room brought up to composing room scale; pension; sick leave; vacations; increased mileage; grievance procedure; jurisdiction of jobs—need for job descriptions; holidays; jury and witness duty; overtime after thirty hours during holiday weeks; night differential; life insurance; option under Blue Cross for eyeglasses; option under Dental Plan for payment for dentures; paid uniforms for pressmen; addition of grandparent and guardian to funeral leave."

As these examples illustrate, it may sometimes be difficult satisfactorily to distinguish an "interest" dispute from one concerning "rights." Moreover, from a broader perspective, even in what are assumed to be "rights" disputes (such as employee grievances) the process of interpretation must necessarily involve considerable flexibility. In complex and long-term relationships there will inevitably be some uncertainty concerning matters inadvertently (or purposely) left open when the contract was entered into, or where past solutions are no longer neatly adapted to changed needs. When the parties participate in this procedure, they are in a very real sense taking part in a process which "involves not only the settlement of the particular dispute but also interstitial rule-making"[8]—a process aimed at creating, refining, and elaborating for the future the rules which will govern their relationship.

The supposed distinction between "rights" and "interest" arbitration may then be—as are most distinctions in the law—a mere question of degree or emphasis. However, this is not to say that it is without analytic utility or practical importance. Parties to a contract who are considering arbitration as a device to handle future disputes must ask themselves a number of questions. The distinction between "rights" and "interest" arbitration forces them to ask some important ones. To what extent is arbitration suitable for establishing the basic structure, the essential parameters of the relationship? What important differences are there between doing this, and asking the arbitrator merely to spell out the implications of a bargain they have hammered out for themselves? Are there reasons to hesitate before confiding this task to arbitrators as a substitute for their own bargaining? A few of the relevant considerations are suggested in the paragraphs that follow.

Assume that the parties know from the outset—either because of a mandatory statutory procedure, or a contractual agreement—that they will later be able to turn to arbitration to determine their future rights. How might this affect the dynamics of the bargaining process? Is it likely that one or the other of them may assume more extreme positions at the bargaining stage, trusting that an arbitrator will later seek out a middle ground? Is there a danger that the parties may use the possibility of

---

8. See David E. Feller, A General Theory of the Collective Bargaining Agreement, 61 Calif.L.Rev. 663, 744–45 (1973).

arbitration as a crutch, and resort to it too readily rather than face the hard issues themselves? Is it likely that negotiators will resort to the arbitration mechanism to insulate themselves from the dissatisfaction of their own constituencies—union members, or taxpayers—who might personally hold them accountable for inevitable concessions made in negotiation?

If the contract confides to arbitrators the ultimate responsibility for determining the essential rights of the parties in the future, what standards are the arbitrators to use? The possible value choices are far more diverse, the possible criteria of decision far more nebulous, than in cases where an arbitrator acts more "judicially" in deciding whether particular goods are defective or whether certain employee conduct merited discharge.

In Twin City Rapid Transit Co., 7 Lab.Arb. 845 (1947), a collective bargaining agreement between a privately-owned company and an employee union provided that "if at the end of any contract year the parties are unable to agree upon the terms of a renewal contract, the matter shall be submitted to arbitration." In his decision, the arbitrator wrote:

> Arbitration of contract terms * * * calls for a determination, upon considerations of policy, fairness, and expediency, of what the contract rights ought to be. In submitting this case to arbitration, the parties have merely extended their negotiations—they have left it to this board to determine what they should, by negotiation, have agreed upon. We take it that the fundamental inquiry, as to each issue, is: what should the parties themselves, as reasonable men, have voluntarily agreed to?

> In answering that question, we think that prime consideration should be given to agreements voluntarily reached in comparable properties in the general area. For example, wages and conditions in Milwaukee, the city of comparable size nearest geographically to Minneapolis and St. Paul, whose transit company is neither bankrupt, municipally owned, nor municipally supported, might reasonably have had greater weight in the negotiations between the parties than Cleveland or Detroit, both municipally owned and farther distant, or Omaha and Council Bluffs, more distant in miles and smaller in population. Smaller and larger cities, however, and cities in other geographical areas should have secondary consideration, for they disclose trends and, by indicating what other negotiators, under different circumstances, have found reasonable, furnish a guide to what these parties, in view of the differing circumstances, might have found reasonable. * * * To repeat, our endeavor will be to decide the issues as, upon the evidence, we think reasonable negotiators, regardless of their social or economic theories might have decided them in the give and take process of bargaining. We agree with the company that the interests of stockholders and public must be considered, and consideration of their interests will enter into our considerations as to what the parties should reasonably have agreed on.

NOTES AND QUESTIONS

1. Does the inquiry in *Twin City Rapid Transit* ("what should the parties themselves, as reasonable men, have voluntarily agreed to?") seem meaningful to you in light of your understanding of the negotiation process? Should the arbitrator try to reconstruct the murky totality of the bargaining process, including the various dimensions of bargaining power, when the parties' own negotiations have failed? Can he do so? Or is he necessarily reduced to acting as a "legislator" and mandating what he thinks the "fair" result would be? Presented with all the outstanding bargaining issues with which the arbitrator was faced in case (c) above, how does he go about distinguishing between issues as to which the parties have reached a serious impasse and "throwaway" issues placed on the table for bargaining advantage? Is it feasible to impose criteria in advance on the arbitrator, by statute or contract? Or to structure the process so as to limit the scope of his discretion?

2. Of course, *courts* daily adjudicate grievances and disputes concerning "rights." Do they *also* handle types of disputes which might be characterized as "interest" disputes? In contracts cases, as you remember, the traditional wisdom is that courts "interpret" agreements, but they will not "make a contract for the parties" or enforce arrangements where the parties have merely "agreed to agree." The received learning has it that

> "[b]efore the power of law can be invoked to enforce a promise, it must be sufficiently certain and specific so that what was promised can be ascertained. Otherwise, a court, in intervening, would be imposing its own conception of what the parties should or might have undertaken, rather than confining itself to the implementation of a bargain to which they have mutually committed themselves. * * * [A] mere agreement to agree, in which a material term is left for future negotiations, is unenforceable."

Joseph Martin, Jr. Delicatessen, Inc. v. Schumacher, 52 N.Y.2d 105, 436 N.Y.S.2d 247, 417 N.E.2d 541 (1981).

Is that distinction in contract law the equivalent of the "rights"/"interest" dichotomy?

An economist would say that when courts insist on a certain level of clarity and completeness in the terms of a contract, they are attempting to insure that the deal is "allocatively efficient"—roughly, that it serves to reallocate resources to higher-valued uses—and that they do so by assuring that the deal has been bargained out by the parties themselves, in terms of their own assessments of their own interests. They may also be trying to prevent parties from taking a "free ride" on the public court system by shifting onto the courts the burden of determining contract terms. Do any of the same objections apply to "interest" arbitration?

The reluctance of courts to help in fashioning bargains left incomplete by the parties may be changing. Compare Sun Printing & Publishing Ass'n v. Remington Paper & Power Co., 235 N.Y. 338, 139 N.E. 470 (1923)—a wooden mainstay of the Contracts curriculum—with David Nassif Associates v. United States, 557 F.2d 249 (Ct.Cl.1977), 644 F.2d 4 (Ct.Cl.1981). See also Uniform Commercial Code §§ 2–204(3), 2–305; cf. Restatement, Second, Contracts § 204 & cmts. c, d ("where there is in fact no agreement, the court should supply a term which comports with community standards of fairness and policy rather than analyze a hypothetical model of the bargaining process"). Or is it fair to say that courts, like arbitrators, have been doing much the same thing all along, under the guise of "interpretation"—but without admitting it?

3. Lon Fuller has suggested that the adjudicative process may not be well-suited to resolve what he calls "polycentric" or "many-centered" disputes, in which the resolution of any one issue may have "complex repercussions" for other aspects of the dispute. See Lon Fuller, The Forms and Limits of Adjudication, 92 Harv. L. Rev. 353 (1978):

> Some months ago a wealthy lady by the name of Timken died in New York leaving a valuable, but somewhat miscellaneous, collection of paintings to the Metropolitan Museum and the National Gallery "in equal shares," her will indicating no particular apportionment. When the will was probated the judge remarked something to the effect that the parties seemed to be confronted with a real problem. The attorney for one of the museums spoke up and said, "We are good friends. We will work it out somehow or other." What makes this problem of effecting an equal division of the paintings a polycentric task? It lies in the fact that the disposition of any single painting has implications for the proper disposition of every other painting. If it gets the Renoir, the Gallery may be less eager for the Cezanne but all the more eager for the Bellows, etc. If the proper apportionment were set for argument, there would be no clear issue to which either side could direct its proofs and contentions. Any judge assigned to hear such an argument would be tempted to assume the role of mediator or to adopt the classical solution: Let the older brother (here the Metropolitan) divide the estate into what he regards as equal shares, let the younger brother (the National Gallery) take his pick.

Are any of the "interest" disputes we are looking at here "polycentric"? Do Fuller's objections apply to arbitration as well as to the judicial process? How might an "interest" arbitrator proceed so as to minimize the problems that Fuller raises?

4. In the case of a public employer, can the arbitrator weigh the claims of employees against other claims to public funds? Should the arbitrator take into account the employer's ability to pass on any increase in wages to others—to taxpayers or to the customers of a public utility? This may of course entail the exercise of some delicate judgment on matters of social and economic policy. In addition, the arbitrator is a creature of contract, hired and paid by employer and union: Is it appropriate for him in the course of making his decision to weigh the interests of those who are *not* parties to the agreement? See In re Nodak Rural Elect. Coop. and Int'l Bro. of Elect. Workers, 78 Lab.Arb. 1119 (1982) (rural North Dakota electrical cooperative; "This arbitrator grew up on an Iowa farm in the 1930's so he understands the meaning of a depressed farm economy and is sympathetic to the farmer's current conditions. * * * It is not likely that it would be wise for either the company or the union to ignore the condition of the farm economy. After all, the farmers and Nodak employees are dependent on each other. The farmers must be able to pay their bills in order for Nodak employees to retain their jobs and get paid.").

5. Can an existing "interest" arbitration clause be invoked in order to obtain inclusion of a similar clause in a *new* contract? Courts that have answered "no" have reasoned in this way:

> The contract arbitration system could be self-perpetuating; a party, having once agreed to the provision, may find itself locked into that procedure for as long as the bargaining relationship endures. Exertion of economic force to rid oneself of the clause is foreclosed, for the continued inclusion of the term is for resolution by an outsider. Parties may justly fear that the tendency of arbitrators would be to continue including the clause * * *.

> [T]he perpetuation of [interest] arbitration clauses in successive contracts may well serve to increase industrial unrest. Under [interest] arbitration, an outsider imposes contract terms, perhaps * * * unguided by any agreed-upon standards. In these circumstances, a disappointed party can readily believe that the arbitrator lacked appreciation of its needs or failed to apply appropriate standards, for example, "fair wages." * * * The result is that a party's dissatisfaction with an award may be aggravated by doubts about its legitimacy. The likelihood that one party will feel aggrieved by a contract arbitration award increases as parties move from contract to contract. The factors which determine the parties' relative strength for strikes and lockouts often changes with the passage of time. * * * Courts cannot bind the parties in perpetuity to forego use of economic weapons in support of bargaining positions.

NLRB v. Columbus Printing Pressmen & Assistants' Union No. 252, 543 F.2d 1161, 1169–70 (5th Cir.1976).

The *Columbus Printing* court also held that in negotiating the terms of a collective bargaining agreement, a union may not insist on the inclusion of an "interest" arbitration clause; to bargain to an "impasse" on this issue would constitute an "unfair labor practice."

6. One rarely comes across the term "interest arbitration" in the commercial arena. But as we have seen, contracting parties will frequently do something similar in cases where a close analogy to the world of collective bargaining exists—for example, in long-term supply contracts, where there may be a need to "adapt" the terms of an ongoing relationship to changing conditions—or in the internal affairs of close corporations. See, e.g., Vogel v. Lewis, 268 N.Y.S.2d 237 (App. Div. 1966), aff'd, 19 N.Y.2d 589, 278 N.Y.S.2d 236, 224 N.E.2d 738 (1967)(agreement between the two owners of a close corporation; held, a dispute over whether the company should exercise an option to purchase the warehouse where the business was carried on was arbitrable; "there seems to be no reason why arbitrators may not be useful in resolving issues which involve some business judgment so long as they are not required to assume a continuing burden of management"); cf. Ringling v. Ringling Bros.–Barnum & Bailey Combined Shows, Inc., 49 A.2d 603 (Del. Ch. 1946), modified, 53 A.2d 441 (Del. 1947)(shareholders agreed to "consult and confer" with each other and to "act jointly" in exercising their voting rights, and that if they failed to agree, the disagreement would be submitted to arbitration "to the end of assuring ... good management").

B.   Some Frequent Uses of Arbitration

1.   Commercial Arbitration

William C. Jones, Three Centuries of Commercial Arbitration in New York: A Brief Survey

1956 Wash.U.L.Q. 193, 209–10, 218–19.

[I]t is commonplace among those who write about arbitration that it has been in use for centuries.

* * *

[E]nough material on arbitration has been uncovered to show fairly conclusively that arbitration was in constant and widespread use throughout the colonial period in New York. * * * Seemingly, arbitration was used primarily in situations where the decision would not be entirely for one side or the other, but where there was, rather, considerable area for negotiation. The settlement of an account resulting from a long course of dealing between two merchants is an example. Land boundaries and the distribution of the proceeds from a privateering expedition are others. Evidently, from the way in which individuals felt it worthwhile to advertise in the newspapers their willingness to arbitrate, there was some social pressure to arbitrate a dispute before taking it to court, and even to submit it to arbitration after the suit was begun. This tends to substantiate a feeling that one function of arbitration was to supply a final stage in the negotiation process between two disputants and that a willingness to negotiate was highly esteemed in the community.

* * *

[T]he existence of the practice of extensive arbitration over so long a period of time in the mercantile community tends to show that, as used by merchants, arbitration is not really a substitute for court adjudication as something that is cheaper or faster or whatever,[112] but is rather a means of dispute settling quite as ancient—for all practical purposes anyway—as court adjudication, and that it has, traditionally, fulfilled quite a different function. The primary function of arbitration is to provide the merchants fora where mercantile disputes will be settled by merchants. This, in turn, suggests that merchants wish to form, and have for a long time succeeded in forming, a separate, and, to some extent, self-governing community, independent of the larger unit. For law this means that courts may perform, in the commercial field at least, a different function from that which we usually assign to them. In many cases, they may not be the primary fora for adjudication. If this is true, when they are called upon to

---

112. Though, interestingly enough, arbitration was presented as such an alternative in the eighteenth century in almost the same language as is used today.

decide a commercial case in one of these areas, it will be either after another adjudicatory agency has acted or because the other system cannot, or will not, cope with the case. In some areas, courts may almost never get a case. * * * Insofar as this area, in which arbitration is and—most importantly—has always been the primary dispute-settling agency, is an important one (and an area which includes stockbrokers, produce brokers, coffee merchants, etc., seems to be such an area), it cannot really be said that one has studied commercial law, in the sense of the rules that actually guide the settlement of disputes involving commercial matters, if he has studied only the reports of appellate courts and legislation. We cannot even understand the significance of the "law" contained in the reports and statutes until we have studied arbitration decisions. * * *

Having gone so far with hypothesis, one may be forgiven for going a little farther and suggesting that the existence of a sufficient sense of community identity or separateness on the part of merchants to cause them to have a separate adjudicatory system tends to show that there is a mercantile community which is, to a considerable degree, self-governing. This community has existed in this form for centuries. Its existence suggests that there may be others—religious and educational communities come to mind.

Soia Mentschikoff, Commercial Arbitration

61 Col.L.Rev. 846, 848–54 (1961).

The first thing to be noted is that although commonly thought of as a single type phenomenon, both the structure and the process of commercial arbitration are determined by the different institutional contexts in which it arises. There are three major institutional settings in which commercial arbitration appears as a mechanism for the settlement of disputes.

The simplest is when two persons in a contract delineating a business relationship agree to settle any disputes that may arise under the contract by resort to arbitration before named arbitrators or persons to be named at the time of the dispute. In this, which can be called individuated arbitration, the making of all arrangements, including the procedures for arbitration, rests entirely with the parties concerned. Although we do not know, we believe that the chief moving factors here are: (1) a desire for privacy as, for example, in certain crude oil situations where such arrangements exist; (2) the availability of expert deciders; (3) the avoidance of possible legal difficulties with the nature of the transaction itself; and (4) the random acceptance by many businessmen of the idea that arbitration is faster and less expensive than court action.

A second type of arbitration arises within the context of a particular trade association or exchange. The group establishes its own arbitration machinery for the settlement of disputes among its members, either on a voluntary or compulsory basis, and sometimes makes it available to non-members doing business in the particular trade. A particular association may also have specialist committees, which are investigatory in character, with the arbitration machinery handling only the private disputes involving nonspecialist categories of cases. * * *

The third setting for commercial arbitration is found in administrative groups, such as the American Arbitration Association, the International Chamber of Commerce, and various local chambers of commerce, which provide rules, facilities, and arbitrators for any persons desiring to settle disputes by arbitration. Many trade associations with insufficient business to warrant separate organizations make special arrangements with one of these groups to process disputes that arise among their members.

* * *

Factors Determining the Need for Arbitration

At this point it is useful to distinguish between those factors that can be said to produce a need for arbitration machinery in commercial groups and those factors that merely make it desirable. The reasons commonly given for arbitration—speed, lower expense, more expert decision, greater privacy—are appealing to all businessmen, and yet not all utilize arbitration. It seems reasonably clear, therefore, that for some trades these factors are of greater importance than for others, and that for some trades there must be countervailing values in not resorting to arbitration. We postulated three factors as being theoretically important in determining whether or not a particular trade needed institutionalized use of arbitration, and incorporated questions relating to these factors in our trade association questionnaire.

The first factor was the nature of the economic function being performed in relation to the movement of the goods by the members of the association. We postulated that persons primarily buying for resale, that is merchants in the original sense of the term, were much more likely to be interested in speed of adjudication, and that since price allowance would be a central remedy for defects in quality or, indeed, for nondelivery, the speed and low cost characteristics of arbitration would be particularly attractive to them, thus leading to the creation of institutionalized machinery. The trade associations in which such merchants constitute all or part of the membership reported as follows: 48 percent use institutionalized machinery, 34 percent make individual arrangements for arbitration, and only 18 percent never arbitrate. These figures are to be contrasted with the reports from those trade associations that stated that their memberships did not include any merchants. In those groups 23 percent reported the existence of institutionalized arbitration, 44 percent reported individual arrangements, and 33 percent reported no arbitration whatever.

The second major factor that we thought would be important in determining the need for arbitration was the participation of the members of the association in foreign trade. Apart from the enhanced possibility of delay inherent in transnational law suits, when the parties to a transaction are governed by different substantive rules of law, resort to the formal legal system poses uncertainty and relative unpredictability of result for at least one of the parties. This uncertainty and unpredictability is increased by the fact that the very rules governing the choice of the applicable law are themselves relatively uncertain and are not uniform among the nations of the world. Faced with such an uncertain formal legal situation, any affected trade group is apt to develop its own set of substantive rules or standards of behavior as the controlling rules for its members. Obviously, when a trade group develops its own rules of law, it requires as deciders of its disputes persons who are acquainted with the standards it has developed. Since this knowledgeability does not reside in the judges of any formal legal system, the drive toward institutionalized private machinery is reinforced.

* * *

The third factor that we thought would bear on the need for arbitration machinery relates to the kind of goods dealt with by the members of the association. One of the major areas of dispute among businessmen centers on the quality of the goods involved. If, therefore, the goods are such as not to be readily susceptible of quality determination by third persons, arbitration or, indeed, inspection, is an unlikely method of settling disputes. If goods are divided into raws, softs, and hards, the differences in their suitability for third party adjudication becomes relatively clear. On the whole, raws are a fungible commodity, one bushel of #1 wheat being very much like another bushel of #1 wheat. On the other hand, hards, which consist of items like refrigerators and automobiles, are not viewed by their producers as essentially fungible, however they may appear to the layman. We did not believe that Ford would like to have General Motors sitting on disputes involving the quality of Ford cars, or vice versa. Moreover, quality differentials in raws can normally be reflected by price differentials, but defects in hard goods frequently affect their usefulness and therefore price differential compensation is not feasible. Thus, the normal sales remedy for raws has come to be price allowance, whereas the normal sales remedy for hard goods has come to be repair or replacement. Raws, involving fungibility and ease of finding an appropriate remedy, are therefore highly susceptible to third party adjudication, whereas hard goods tend to move away from such adjudication. Soft goods, which are an intermediate category and range from textiles to small hardware, we thought would constitute a neutral category.

In our survey of exchanges dealing in grain and livestock, 100 percent of those responding reported the use of institutionalized arbitration. There are, of course, other reasons for such a unanimous response by the exchanges, but the nature of the goods involved is a very important one. The trade association survey showed that of all the reporting associations, dealings in raws, 46 percent had machinery, 29 percent made individual arrangements, and only 25 percent never arbitrated. On the other hand, only 4 percent of those reporting hards as their basic goods had machinery, 46 percent made individual arrangements, and 50 per cent never arbitrated. * * *

To the extent that the factors leading to institutionalized machinery reinforce each other, as, for example, in the case of an association reporting that its members have an import relationship to foreign trade, deal in raws, and consist of merchants, the existence of arbitration machinery rises to approximately 100 percent. When the contrary report is made, that is, that the membership consists of manufacturers of hard goods engaged only in domestic business, the percentage drops off to about 8 percent.

We can thus say that the presence of institutionalized arbitration is a strong index of the existence of a generally self-contained trade association having its own self-regulation machinery and that the forces leading to institutionalized arbitration also, therefore, tend to lead to the creation of self-contained, self-governing trade groups.

Note: The American Arbitration Association

The AAA is a private non-profit organization founded in 1926 "to foster the study of arbitration, to perfect its techniques and procedures under arbitration law, and to advance generally the science of arbitration." It works actively to publicize and promote arbitration. Of far greater importance, however, is its central role in the administration of much of the arbitration that takes place in this country. The parties to a contract will frequently stipulate that disputes which later arise are to be arbitrated under the auspices of the AAA. This means, for one thing, that the proceedings will automatically be governed by AAA rules. In a commercial case, the AAA's "Commercial Arbitration Rules" will resolve questions concerning the method of choosing arbitrators, their powers, time limits for various steps in the proceedings, and the conduct of the hearing. There are also alternative sets of rules available for adoption in particular trades. In the construction industry for example, use of the AAA's Construction Industry Arbitration Rules (recommended by such trade groups as the American Institute of Architects and the American Society of Civil Engineers) has become standard. The AAA also administers a large number of labor arbitrations under its Voluntary Labor Arbitration Rules, and uninsured motorist accident arbitrations under its Accident Claims Arbitration Rules. In all these cases, using contracts that incorporate pre-existing bodies of rules saves the parties the burden, costs, and delay of having to negotiate and spell out an entire code for the conduct of the arbitration.

Almost 158,000 arbitration cases were filed with the AAA in 2004. Of these, 12,679 were "commercial" cases [a figure that includes 3292 construction cases, 1633 individual employment cases, and 614 international cases]; there were, in addition, around 12,000 labor cases. (By far the largest part of the AAA's arbitration caseload was made up of uninsured-motorist and no-fault insurance cases).[1] The Association maintains a panel of approximately 6,700 arbitrators willing to serve on commercial cases, of whom 1,940 are also listed on a separate construction panel.[2] The parties

---

1. AAA, Corporate Communications Department; see also Thomas J. Stipanowich, ADR and the "Vanishing Trial": The Growth and Impact of "Alternative Dispute Resolu-tion," 1 J. Empirical Legal Studies 843 (2004).

2. In addition, the AAA in 2004 created a high-profile 90–member Construction Master Arbitration Panel. Members of the panel

select their arbitrators from a number of names suggested by AAA administrators, who furnish information concerning the background and experience of the candidates; if the parties cannot agree on a name, the AAA itself will appoint the arbitrator to hear the case. In addition, during the course of the proceeding the AAA staff will furnish a variety of administrative services, concerning, for example, notice to the parties, pre-hearing conferences, and the scheduling, location, and conduct of the hearing—all intended to insure that the process runs smoothly and that the chances of a successful later challenge to the award are minimized. Selection of arbitrators and arbitration procedure are discussed in some detail at Section D.1.a, infra.

While the AAA remains the dominant arbitral institution in the United States, it has in recent years been subject to increasing competition for business from a number of more entrepreneurial for-profit rivals—including the National Arbitration Forum (NAF), which administers around 50,000 cases per year, and Judicial Arbitration & Mediation Services, Inc., (JAMS), which administers around 10,000 cases per year. The overwhelming majority of the JAMS panel of neutrals is made up of retired judges.[3]

NOTES AND QUESTIONS

A survey of textile disputes arbitrated through the AAA found that much textile arbitration was handled by a relatively small group of lawyers: Only five lawyers were counsel to 43 of the 182 parties who submitted to arbitration in one of the years studied. "When asked to compare the predictability of an arbitrator's decision to that of a judge or the verdict of a jury, each of the five lawyers replied without hesitation that the decision of an arbitrator was by far the 'most predictable,' that a judge's decision was 'predictable at some but not all times,' and a jury's decision was 'virtually one of pure chance.'" Bonn, The Predictability of Nonlegalistic Adjudication, 6 Law & Soc'y Rev. 563 (1972). However, the author attributed this predictability largely to the fact that sellers would carefully "screen" or "preselect" cases they took to arbitration. Sellers would pursue arbitration primarily against "buyers who are marginal firms or who have weak or specious claims"; where a buyer had "a strong case, say one based on a legitimate quality claim," and was a good future business prospect, sellers would choose instead to settle the dispute informally.

In another survey of textile arbitration cases the same author found that out of 78 cases, "business relations were resumed" following the arbitration in only 14. Bonn, Arbitration: An Alternative System for Handling Contract Related Disputes, 17 Admin.Sci.Q. 254, 262 (1972). Is this clearly an indication that arbitration may be as "lethal to continuing relations" as litigation? Cf. Galanter, Reading the Landscape of Disputes:

are selected based on stringent criteria and work on large cases involving claims of $5 million or more.

3. See http://www.jamsadr.com/neutrals/ neutrals.asp; see also Pollock, "Arbitra-

tor Finds Role Dwindling as Rivals Grow," Wall St. J., April 28, 1993 at B1.

What We Know and Don't Know (And Think We Know) About Our Allegedly Contentious and Litigious Society, 31 U.C.L.A.L.Rev. 4, 25 n. 117 (1983). See also Baruch Bush, Dispute Resolution Alternatives and the Goals of Civil Justice: Jurisdictional Principles for Process Choice, 1984 Wisc.L.Rev. 893, 992–93. Bush suggests that the "informality" of arbitration may well contribute to reducing hostility between the parties—especially in comparison with litigation—in that it limits the amount and intensity of "direct party confrontation" in the form of evidentiary and procedural contentions. He argues, however, that this function is far more likely to be accomplished by a process like mediation that is aimed directly at facilitating mutual understanding and sympathy.

2. INTERNATIONAL COMMERCIAL ARBITRATION

Many of the same factors inducing parties to choose arbitration as a dispute settlement technique in domestic commercial transactions are likely to be present when the transaction expands across national boundaries. Indeed, as Professor Mentschikoff points out, the involvement of more than one body of law and more than one court system is likely to provide even further impetus to nonjudicial dispute resolution. The time, expense, and procedural complexities of litigating in another country's courts are likely to be considerable. There may not even be any effective protection against parallel litigation proceeding simultaneously in the courts of the United States and of a foreign country. There is likely to be far greater uncertainty with respect to the rules of decision that will govern the dispute in a foreign tribunal, and thus as to the outcome; the rules of "conflict of laws" will not always give a bankable answer even to the question of *which* nation's law will apply to the transaction. In addition, the "foreign" party to the litigation will not only feel disadvantaged by his relative unfamiliarity with the "rules of the game," but may also doubt how fairly and even-handedly he will be treated in comparison to his "local" opponent.

Another troubling cause of unpredictability in international litigation stems from uncertainty as to when and to what extent a judgment obtained in one country will be enforceable in another. A favorable decision against a French supplier in a New York court, for example, may be of little value if the courts of France will not recognize the New York judgment. However, compared with ordinary court decisions, arbitration is far ahead as far as enforcement in other countries is concerned: In many countries, enforcement of a foreign arbitral award is simpler and more assured than is enforcement of a foreign judgment—a difference in outcome perhaps explained by the common tendency to regard an arbitral award as "the outcome of contractual relationships, rather than of the exercise of state powers."[4] This favorable treatment of foreign arbitral awards has been reinforced by international treaty. See the United Nations Convention on

---

4. Gardner, Economic and Political Implications of International Commercial Arbi- tration, in Martin Domke (ed.), International Trade Arbitration 20–21 (1958).

the Recognition and Enforcement of Foreign Arbitral Awards, infra Appendix B.

It is therefore not surprising that in international commercial contracts, arbitration clauses "not only predominate but are nowadays almost universal" and are "virtually taken for granted."[5] The Supreme Court has on a number of occasions recognized the unique value of international arbitration in promoting "the orderliness and predictability essential to any international business transaction," and has drawn from it a strong policy favoring international commercial arbitration. See Scherk v. Alberto–Culver Co., 417 U.S. 506, 516 (1974); Mitsubishi v. Soler, infra p. 176. It has been suggested that international arbitrators have been moving towards a "common law of international arbitration"—that they have been developing a "customary law of international contracts"[6] that stresses general norms of conduct suited to international business practices independent of the rules of particular bodies of national law. This is particularly marked in arbitration decisions dealing with such thorny recurring problems in international trade as the effect on contracts of "impossibility" (*force majeure*) or currency fluctuations.

A large number of other organizations besides the AAA compete in the administration of international commercial arbitrations; by far the most important of these is the International Chamber of Commerce (ICC), based in Paris. However, parties to international transactions often prefer to proceed with arbitration outside of any institutional framework—and to administer the arbitration themselves on an "ad hoc" basis. However, dispensing with the administrative support of institutions like the AAA and the ICC is not likely to be successful in cases where the level of cooperation and trust between the parties is low, and where one of them may be dragging his feet in resolving the problem. "In non-administered arbitration, burdens such as objections to the continued service of the arbitrators, scheduling of hearings, and collection and disbursement of arbitration compensation will fall upon the parties [themselves] and can produce awkward results"; many of the administrative support functions performed by institutions will, in "ad hoc" arbitrations, have to be performed by the arbitrators themselves, which may become "excessively cost prohibitive."[7] And in addition, where a recognized institution has supervised the arbitration, the institution's reputation may lend credibility to the award should a national court ever come to review the arbitration.

Note: Investment Disputes

In many countries the government assumes a far more active role in economic transactions—particularly those involving capital investment and

5. Sir Michael Kerr, International Arbitration v. Litigation, [1980] J. Business Law 164, 165, 171.

6. W. Laurence Craig et al., International Chamber of Commerce Arbitration 638 (3rd ed. 2000). See also Rene David, Arbitration in International Trade §§ 16 ("Search for an autonomous commercial law"), 17 (1985).

7. William K. Slate II, International Arbitration: Do Institutions Make a Difference?, 31 Wake Forest L.Rev. 41, 53–55 (1996). [The author is the President and CEO of the AAA.].

the exploitation and development of national resources—than it does in the United States. The foreign state or one of its instrumentalities will often be a party to such contracts, which are likely to have political and economic implications and symbolic importance far greater than in the case of domestic transactions. This can be a factor which complicates the question of dispute resolution. A foreign state will understandably be reluctant to submit to the jurisdiction of the courts of another sovereign (as, of course, the foreign investor will be reluctant to submit to the courts of the host country.) However, capital-importing countries in particular have long been sensitive to the implications of submitting to *any* forum where the location or the decision-maker is foreign, and such reluctance has been extended to foreign arbitrations as well.

This unwillingness to submit to foreign arbitration is probably most marked in Latin American countries, where historical memory of one-sided international "arbitrations" dominated by European or North American partners is still vivid. A Brazilian writer has argued that:

> Functioning as an active element to denationalize (or internationalize) the contract, arbitration by removing a dispute from resolution by local courts applying local law, takes it to a plane where the rules are made by the great international commercial interests, a process from which Third World countries normally are excluded.[8]

(More pithily, it is said that developing countries during the late nineteenth and early twentieth centuries "often perceived investment arbitration as little more than an extension of gunboat diplomacy.").[9] For many years the "Calvo doctrine," incorporated in several Latin American constitutions or statutes, made impossible the litigation or arbitration abroad of state contracts and required foreign investors to consent to the dispute resolution processes of local courts.

Driven in large part by the desire to attract foreign investment, this traditional attitude has gradually been changing. One important development has been the creation of the International Center for Settlement of Investment Disputes (ICSID). ICSID was established by treaty in 1966 to reduce the fear of political risks that discourage the flow of private foreign capital to developing countries, by providing foreign investors with a neutral forum for the resolution of disputes. ICSID functions under the auspices of the World Bank and is a "public" body, administered by representatives of the various participating governments. 142 nations have ratified the treaty, including 15 Latin American states. Ratification involves

---

8. Quoted in Frank Nattier, International Commercial Arbitration in Latin America: Enforcement of Arbitral Agreements and Awards, 21 Tex.Int'l L.J. 397, 407 (1986). Extremely helpful, both as an historical survey and as an assessment of the current situation, is Horacio A. Grigera Naón, Arbitration and Latin America: Progress and Setbacks, 21 Arb. Int'l 127 (2005)("even to-day, in many Latin American countries two different schools of thought uneasily coexist: one adverse to commercial arbitration and the other favouring it").

9. Guillermo Aguilar Alvarez & William W. Park, The New Face of Investment Arbitration: NAFTA Chapter 11, 28 Yale J. Int'l L. 365, 367 (2003).

an unconditional commitment to enforce all ICSID awards—that is, there is no possibility of challenging an ICSID award in any national court.[10] Nevertheless ratification is not in itself equivalent to a consent to arbitrate—such consent must be given for each case, in the particular investment contract between the state agency and the private investor. As a result the rate of "contractual" ICSID arbitration has been low; most of the cases have involved disputes arising out of mining, construction, or joint venture agreements with developing states in sub-Saharan Africa and Latin America.

Most recently, however, there has been a dramatic increase in the use of investment arbitration, attributable to the proliferation of Bilateral Investment Treaties (BITs). Historically, the recourse available to an investor faced with adverse treatment by the host state—say, in the form of discrimination or even expropriation—was quite limited: In the absence of some supranational tribunal, neither litigation in the local courts, nor attempts to invoke the diplomatic protection of his home country, were likely to be entirely satisfactory. In a BIT, by contrast, each contracting state accords important substantive and remedial rights to investors who are nationals of the other state. Typical is the 1994 BIT between the United States and Argentina, in which each state agrees that it will:

- "observe any obligation it may have entered into" with respect to the foreign investment; and in addition, that it will:

- give "fair and equitable treatment" to the other state's investors;

- treat their investment no less favorably than it treats its own nationals or the nationals of any other country; and

- take no measures "tantamount to expropriation or nationalization" except "in a non-discriminatory manner" and "upon payment of prompt, adequate, and effective compensation."

And at the same time—and at the insistence of capital-exporting countries like the United States—the investor is given direct standing to enforce these provisions, by initiating arbitration proceedings against the state; arbitration may be either through ICSID or in an "ad hoc" arbitration. The largest number of ICSID cases now come to the organization through the arbitration provisions of BITs.[11]

---

10. Under arts. 53 and 54 of the ICSID Convention, awards "shall not be subject to any appeal or to any other remedy," and "each Contracting State shall recognize an award rendered pursuant to this Convention as binding." The treaty does, however, provide for the possibility of an internal appeal to an "*ad hoc* Committee" of ICSID, with the power to annul awards in limited circumstances—where:

    a) the Tribunal was not properly constituted;

    (b) the Tribunal has manifestly exceeded its powers;

    (c) there was corruption on the part of a member of the Tribunal;

    (d) there has been a serious departure from a fundamental rule of procedure; or

    (e) the award has failed to state the reasons on which it is based.

See art. 52; http://www.worldbank.org/icsid/basicdoc/partA-chap04.htm.

11. See the ICSID 2004 Annual Report, http://www.worldbank.org/icsid/pubs/1998ar/

The number of such treaties in force worldwide is in excess of 2200, and the United States is a party to 37 BITs. The BIT model has recently been generalized in Chapter 11 of the North American Free Trade Agreement [NAFTA], among Canada, Mexico, and the United States: Since the NAFTA entered into force in 1994 it appears, ironically, that more arbitration cases have been filed against the United States (13 as of 2005) than against either Mexico or Canada.[12]

NOTES AND QUESTIONS

1. It is inevitable that international arbitration will often turn out to be considerably more protracted and expensive than its domestic counterpart. A highly entertaining cautionary tale—which space constraints unfortunately prevent us from reproducing here—is Lord Justice Kerr's classic article, Arbitration v. Litigation: The Macao Sardine Case, 3 Arb. Int'l 79 (1987).

The ICC in particular is often criticized on this account. In ICC proceedings the administrative charges paid to the ICC for its services—as well as the fees paid to the arbitrators themselves—are calculated on the basis of the amount in dispute between the parties. In a $10 million case these may range from a bare—and unlikely—minimum of $71,550 to a maximum, if three arbitrators are used, of $479,000. The most articulate apologists for ICC arbitration respond to criticisms of excessive expense with a plea that:

> the cost must be evaluated in relation to the alternatives. Certainly, ICC arbitration seems cheaper than abandoning one's rights altogether. Litigation, even in one's own home courts, is not necessarily a less expensive alternative, given the possibility of one or more appeals. More importantly, it simply is not always reasonable to expect that one's home forum will be acceptable to a foreign contracting party. ICC arbitration is too often compared—unrealistically and unfairly—with a perfect world in which there are no administrative difficulties, no judicial prejudice against foreign parties, no language problems, no uncooperative parties, and where the just always prevail at no cost to themselves.

W. Laurence Craig, William Park, & Jan Paulsson, International Chamber of Commerce Arbitration 29–30 (3rd ed. 2000).

Moreover, a survey of "practitioners with extensive experience in international business disputes" suggests that the usual impetus behind the search for more "informal," "alternative" methods of dispute resolution—"the desire to achieve a process that is *faster, less expensive,* and *more amicable*"—seems to have "only marginal relevance for the choice of arbitration in international commerce":

2004_icsid_ar_en.pdf; see also Lucy Reed et al., Guide to ICSID Arbitration (2004).

12. See the U.S. Department of State website at http://www.state.gov/s/l/c3741.htm.

This may be due either to the perception that, in international arbitration, these advantages do not materialize, or that these qualities are not among the real priorities of the participants. Both reasons seem to be—at least in part—true: more than half of the respondents denied that arbitration is less expensive and more than one third disputed the notion that it was faster or more amicable. And only about one tenth of the respondents affirmed that speed, cost savings and amicability were "highly relevant" factors for the choice of arbitration as a method of dispute resolution. As one practitioner explained: "parties are often not that concerned with costs because their main preoccupation is with the outcome of the procedure; the advantage of arbitration is not to cut costs, it is a tailor-made procedure that emphasizes quality."

For such practitioners the most significant advantages of arbitration seem to be "the *neutrality* of the forum and the *international enforceability* of the results." Christian Bühring–Uhle, Arbitration and Mediation in International Business 141–143 (1996)(in the words of one participant, "if for judgments there existed a convention similar to the New York convention, 50% of the big international commercial arbitrations would be court litigation").

2. Athletes participating in the Olympic Games are required to sign entry forms in which they agree to settle all Games-related disputes through arbitration before the Court of Arbitration for Sport. The CAS was created in 1984 by the International Olympic Committee, but is now more or less independent, and operates under the general supervision of the International Council of Arbitration for Sport. (The ICAS is composed of twenty "high-level jurists," four of whom are appointed respectively by the IOC, by the Association of National Olympic Committees, and by the International Federations that govern individual sports such as swimming and gymnastics—with the remaining members chosen by those already appointed). The ICAS in turn selects a panel of arbitrators—there are currently around 300—who are supposed to have "legal training and who possess recognized competence with regard to sport": "From the professor of Sports Law, to the lawyer who once won an Olympic wrestling medal, the paths of 'specialization' are diverse." See Gabrielle Kaufmann–Kohler, "Art and Arbitration: What Lessons Can be Drawn from the Resolution of Sports Disputes," 11 Studies in Art Law 123, 128 (1999).

The CAS makes arbitrators available on-site at each Olympics—with a commitment to render awards within 24 hours after the demand for arbitration. (Under its rules, however, the "seat" of every arbitration panel is deemed to be in Lausanne, Switzerland, and the arbitration is to be governed by Swiss law). However, CAS jurisdiction is by no means limited to the Olympics: It is a permanent body that may decide any "matters of principle relating to sport or matters of pecuniary or other interests brought into play in the practice or the development of sport." Through 2004 the CAS had received 776 requests for arbitration and CAS arbitrators had issued 391 awards; most of the case load involved disciplinary matters such as substance abuse, but many cases were of a purely commercial nature—involving player transfers, endorsement contracts, or contracts between athletes and agents or managers.

Fairly typical of CAS case-law is a highly publicized award arising out of the 2000 Sydney games: A 16–year old Romanian gymnast was stripped of her gold medal by the IOC after testing positive for a banned substance—apparently she had been given two over-the-counter cold pills by the team's doctor. It was conceded that neither her intent, nor the effect of the drug, had been to enhance her performance. The CAS arbitration panel, made up of arbitrators from Australia, Switzerland, and the United States, nevertheless upheld the IOC's decision: The Anti–Doping Code must be "enforced without compromise," it said in a brief opinion; "the strict consequence of an automatic disqualification" is "a matter of fairness to all other athletes." Andreea Raducan v. IOC, award of 28 September 2000, II Digest of CAS Awards 665 (2002). A considerably more lenient approach, understandably, is taken in cases where the issue is not *the result of a particular contest* but *suspension from future competitions*: In such cases arbitrators may eliminate (or reduce) any period of future ineligibility where the athlete can show that she bears no (or no significant) fault or negligence. See A. v. FILA, award of 9 July 2001, III Digest of CAS Awards 159, 167 (2004)(with regard to suspension from future competition, "the so-called 'strict liability' rule ... does not, in the Panel's opinion, sufficiently respect the athlete's right of personality"); cf. the World Anti–Doping Code, art. 10.5 ("Elimination or Reduction of Period of Ineligibility Based on Exceptional Circumstances"), http://www.wada-ama.org/rtecontent/document/code_v3.pdf.

3. In December 1985, Walt Disney Productions and the French Government signed a letter of intent for the construction of a new Disneyland, to be located near Paris. France and Spain had both competed vigorously for this project, which French officials estimated would involve long-term American investment of as much as $6.7 billion and the creation of more than 30,000 jobs. The French Government had made commitments to build rail and highway networks linking the site to Paris and to develop an infrastructure, including roads and telephone trunk lines, for the area.

The contract negotiations, however, proved extremely difficult. Political opposition to the project—French Communists denounced it as "the encroachment of an alien civilization next to the city of enlightenment"—figured in the parliamentary elections held throughout France in March 1986. Another major snag was Disney's demand that any disputes which might later arise out of the French Government's undertakings be resolved by ICSID arbitration. Fear was expressed in France that acceding to Disney's demand would create a "precedent" by which all new foreign investments might have to go to arbitration. And one French official was said to have commented that "Disney's request for ICSID was shocking and a bit dumb. France is not a banana republic." International Herald Tribune, March 15, 1986, pp. 1, 15; see also Washington Post, August 21, 1986, p. C8; "The Real Estate Coup at Euro Disneyland," Fortune, April 28, 1986, p. 172.

The agreement between Disney and the French Government was finally signed in March 1987. It did contain a provision for dispute settlement by arbitration—but through the ICC, to take place in France.

4. In concluding commercial contracts with foreign businesses, negotiators from the People's Republic of China invariably try to obtain an agreement that any future disputes will be arbitrated in China by the China International Economic and Trade Arbitration Commission ("CIETAC"). CIETAC today has a caseload that makes it one of the world's busiest arbitration centers. For many years parties were required to select arbitrators from CIETAC's own list of panelists—a majority of whom are Chinese nationals (although about one-third of the names on the list are now from foreign countries, including Hong Kong); in addition, many Chinese members of the panel are either current or retired government officials. After much criticism, the rules have recently been amended, and now parties may choose arbitrators from outside the CIETAC list—although in such cases CIETAC confirmation is necessary. See Jerome A. Cohen, "Time to Fix China's Arbitration," Far Eastern Econ. Rev., Jan./Feb. 2005 ("unless the parties specify [otherwise] in their contract," the presiding arbitrator, chosen by CIETAC in the absence of agreement, "is most probably going to be Chinese"); Julius Melnitzer, "Reforms Make Arbitration in China a Safer Bet," Corporate Legal Times, July 2005 (nevertheless the new rules continue to allow CIETAC to use its own personnel as arbitrators, which creates "an obvious opportunity for the exercise of administrative influence"). See generally Michael J. Moser & Peter Yuen, The New CIETAC Rules, 21 Arb. Int'l 391 (2005).

Some insight into the nature of an arbitration conducted by CIETAC can be gleaned from this account by a leading official of the organization:

A foreign buyer ordered 500 cases of goods from a Chinese seller. According to the contract, the goods were to be shipped from a Chinese port to Hong Kong and then transshipped from Hong Kong to the port of destination. Upon arrival at the port of destination, part of the goods were found damaged. The buyer claimed against the seller for compensation of the losses incurred * * * on the grounds that the packing was defective. The seller argued that the packing was not defective because it was the normal packing he used for exporting the goods and no extra or special requirements for packing were specified in the contract. * * * The buyer then applied to [CIETAC] for arbitration. With the consent of both parties, the arbitration tribunal decided the case according to principles of conciliation. It was the opinion of the arbitration tribunal that although no extra or special requirements for packing were specified in the contract, the seller knew that the goods were to be transshipped at Hong Kong, which was different from shipment directly from a Chinese port to the port of destination. The packing should be suitable for that specific transportation. However, the nails and the wood used for the packing were not appropriate for the purpose. The arbitration tribunal proposed an appropriate compensation to the buyer for his losses. The seller accepted the arbitration tribunal's proposal but pointed out that the amount claimed by the buyer was too large and asked for a reduction. The arbitration tribunal consulted the buyer and eventually the buyer agreed to reduce his claim by seventy percent. Both parties came to a compromise agreement from which the arbitration tribunal delivered a Conciliatory Statement and closed the case.

Tang Houzhi, Arbitration—A Method Used by China to Settle Foreign Trade and Economic Disputes, 4 Pace L.Rev. 519, 533–34 (1984). See also Cheng Dejun, Michael J. Moser, & Wang Shengchang, International Arbitration in the People's Republic of China 12 (1995)("Arbitrators may act as judge, middleman and 'peace talker' at different times in the same proceedings").

CIETAC acts under the supervision of the China Chamber of International Commerce, which is nominally a non-governmental organization whose mission is to promote foreign investment and trade by promoting links between foreign companies and the Chinese government. Its arbitrators may understandably be reluctant to finally adjudicate the merits of a dispute between a Western trading company and a domestic state unit, since such a decision might well affect the future business relations between the parties. Cf. Chew, A Procedural and Substantive Analysis of the Fairness of Chinese and Soviet Foreign Trade Arbitrations, 21 Tex.Int'l L.J. 291, 330–34 (1986). In addition, a general aversion to formal third-party adjudication and a predilection for conciliation and compromise have long marked Chinese legal culture. See, e.g., Carlos de Vera, Arbitrating Harmony: "Med–Arb" and the Confluence of Culture and Rule of Law in the Resolution of International Commercial Disputes in China, 18 Colum. J. Asian L. 149 (2004)(the CIETAC regime is "a unique model that functions in the context of Confucian cultural predispositions"). In any event, as this excerpt illustrates, CIETAC will proceed to "decide" a dispute only in those cases where its efforts to induce a voluntary agreement through conciliation have failed. To what extent does this model correspond to the American understanding of the arbitration process? See also the discussion of "Med–Arb" at Section E.3 infra.

5. Fujitsu (Japan's largest computer company) developed and marketed IBM-compatible operating system software, which IBM claimed was in violation of its copyrights. The companies agreed to submit the dispute to two arbitrators (a law professor and a retired computer executive) under AAA auspices. The arbitrators were determined from the outset "to avoid becoming engulfed in an extensive adjudicatory fact-finding process with respect to hundreds of programs previously released by [Fujitsu]." "While this might determine in particular instances whether IBM's intellectual property rights had been violated, it would not directly address and resolve the parties' dispute with respect to [Fujitsu's] ongoing use of IBM programming material in its software development process."

Through their mediation efforts, the parties came instead to agree on the concept of a "coerced license" that was to be administered by these arbitrators into the future. The arbitrators' award allowed the Japanese company to examine IBM programs in a "secured facility" for a period of five to ten years and, "subject to strict and elaborate safeguards," to use such information in its software development; this would provide Fujitsu with a "reasonable opportunity to independently develop and maintain IBM–compatible operating system software." Fujitsu was to "fully and adequately compensate" IBM for such access in amounts to be determined by the arbitrators. In effect the arbitrators' award and subsequent decisions "will constitute the applicable intellectual property law until the end of the Contract Period, notwithstanding copyright decisions of U.S. or Japanese courts * * *." One of the arbitrators later commented that their decisions "will be considerably more detailed than existing copyright law, because there haven't been all that many cases and they haven't got into as many areas as we've gotten into." Wall. St. J., July 1, 1988, p. 4. See also Johnston, The IBM–Fujitsu Arbitration Revisited—A Case Study in Effective ADR, 7 Computer Law. 13 (May 1990).

6.   As we have seen, the practice in domestic commercial arbitration is to dispense with reasoned opinions. In contrast, parties in international cases *do* usually expect arbitrators to provide a written opinion that sets out the reasons for their award. The ICC requires its arbitrators to give reasoned awards; under the ICSID treaty, an award may be "annulled" by an ad hoc appellate committee if "the award has failed to state the reasons on which it is based." This expectation of a reasoned opinion in international arbitration reflects in part the pervasive influence of Continental legal systems, where unreasoned awards are often considered contrary to public policy and thus unenforceable. See W. Laurence Craig, William Park & Jan Paulsson, International Chamber of Commerce Arbitration § 19.04 (3rd ed. 2000); Domotique Secant Inc. v. Smart Systems Technologies Inc., 2005 CanLII 36874 (Quebec Sup. Ct.) (Quebec court refuses to recognize New Mexico award rendered "without giving reasons"; breach of the mandatory requirement "that reasons be provided" "violates * * * our notion of public order and natural justice as it applies to procedural fairness").

3.   LABOR ARBITRATION

A collective bargaining agreement between an employer and the union that represents the firm's employees is likely to be a complex document. It will deal with a large number of subjects, among many other things setting wages and other terms of employment, imposing limits on the employer's right to discharge or discipline employees, and providing for seniority for purposes of layoffs, promotion, and job assignments. It will constitute, in short, an overall framework for employer-employee relations.

Most agreements also spell out a process by which the inevitable questions of interpretation and application arising during the life of the contract will be settled. There are typically a number of steps in this process: At the beginning, for example, there may be informal attempts to adjust a grievance on the shop floor by consultations between the employee's immediate supervisor and the union shop steward; if the dispute is not settled at this stage it will move to successively higher levels. The agreement is likely to make it clear that at all stages work is not to be interrupted because of the dispute but is to continue pending a final settlement, and is likely also to impose strict time limits to insure that a grievance is heard and processed speedily. The final stage in the grievance process, to handle those cases that are not winnowed out by the process of day-to-day negotiation, is likely to be binding arbitration. In its survey of 4000 collective bargaining agreements, the Bureau of National Affairs reported that arbitration was called for in 99% of the contracts in its sample.[13]

Section 301 of the Labor Management Relations Act of 1947 (the Taft–Hartley Act) granted jurisdiction to federal district courts to hear suits for violation of collective bargaining agreements "in an industry affecting commerce." In Textile Workers Union v. Lincoln Mills, 353 U.S. 448 (1957), the Supreme Court held that § 301 was "more than jurisdictional," and that it "authorizes federal courts to fashion a body of federal law for the enforcement of these collective bargaining agreements." "Plainly the agreement to arbitrate grievance disputes is the *quid pro quo* for an agreement not to strike." Federal policy therefore was that promises to arbitrate grievances under collective bargaining agreements should be specifically enforced, and that "industrial peace can be best obtained only in that way."

Federal courts have for the past thirty years engaged in "fashioning" a federal common law dealing with the enforcement of arbitration agreements—to such an extent that it is not an exaggeration to say that the field of "labor law" is now to a large degree the law of labor arbitration. In 1960, in what is still the Supreme Court's most significant pronouncement on the subject, Justice Douglas undertook an evaluation of the purpose and function of labor arbitration and of the central place it occupies in our system of workplace bargaining. Some extracts from his discussion follow.

United Steelworkers of America v. Warrior & Gulf Navigation Co.

Supreme Court of the United States, 1960.
363 U.S. 574, 80 S.Ct. 1347, 4 L.Ed.2d 1409.

■ Opinion of the Court by Mr. Justice Douglas.

* * *

The present federal policy is to promote industrial stabilization through the collective bargaining agreement. A major factor in achieving industrial peace is the inclusion of a provision for arbitration of grievances in the collective bargaining agreement.

---

13. Bureau of National Affairs, Basic Patterns in Union Contracts v, 37 (14th ed. 1995).

Thus the run of arbitration cases * * * becomes irrelevant to our problem. There the choice is between the adjudication of cases or controversies in courts with established procedures or even special statutory safeguards on the one hand and the settlement of them in the more informal arbitration tribunal on the other. In the commercial case, arbitration is the substitute for litigation. Here arbitration is the substitute for industrial strife. Since arbitration of labor disputes has quite different functions from arbitration under an ordinary commercial agreement, the hostility evinced by courts toward arbitration of commercial agreements has no place here. For arbitration of labor disputes under collective bargaining agreements is part and parcel of the collective bargaining process itself.

* * *

A collective bargaining agreement is an effort to erect a system of industrial self-government. When most parties enter into [a] contractual relationship they do so voluntarily, in the sense that there is no real compulsion to deal with one another, as opposed to dealing with other parties. This is not true of the labor agreement. The choice is generally not between entering or refusing to enter into a relationship, for that in all probability preexists the negotiations. Rather it is between having that relationship governed by an agreed-upon rule of law or leaving each and every matter subject to a temporary resolution dependent solely upon the relative strength, at any given moment, of the contending forces. The mature labor agreement may attempt to regulate all aspects of the complicated relationship, from the most crucial to the most minute over an extended period of time. Because of the compulsion to reach agreement and the breadth of the matters covered, as well as the need for a fairly concise and readable instrument, the product of negotiations (the written document) is, in the words of the late Dean Shulman, "a compilation of diverse provisions: some provide objective criteria almost automatically applicable; some provide more or less specific standards which require reason and judgment in their application; and some do little more than leave problems to future consideration with an expression of hope and good faith." Gaps may be left to be filled in by reference to the practices of the particular industry and of the various shops covered by the agreement. Many of the specific practices which underlie the agreement may be unknown, except in hazy form, even to the negotiators. Courts and arbitration in the context of most commercial contracts are resorted to because there has been a breakdown in the working relationship of the parties; such resort is the unwanted exception. But the grievance machinery under a collective bargaining agreement is at the very heart of the system of industrial self-government. Arbitration is the means of solving the unforeseeable by molding a system of private law for all the problems which may arise and to provide for their solution in a way which will generally accord with the variant needs and desires of the parties. The processing of disputes through the grievance machinery is actually a vehicle by which meaning and content are given to the collective bargaining agreement.

Apart from matters that the parties specifically exclude, all of the questions on which the parties disagree must therefore come within the scope of the grievance and arbitration provisions of the collective agreement. The grievance procedure is, in other words, a part of the continuous collective bargaining process. It, rather than a strike, is the terminal point of a disagreement.

* * *

The labor arbitrator's source of law is not confined to the express provisions of the contract, as the industrial common law—the practices of the industry and the shop—is equally a part of the collective bargaining agreement although not expressed in it. The labor arbitrator is usually chosen because of the parties' confidence in his knowledge of the common law of the shop and their trust in his personal judgment to bring to bear considerations which are not expressed in the contract as criteria for judgment. The parties expect that his judgment of a particular grievance will reflect not only what the contract says but, insofar as the collective bargaining agreement permits, such factors as the effect upon productivity of a particular result, its consequence to the morale of the shop, his judgment whether tensions will be heightened or diminished. For the parties' objective in using the arbitration process is primarily to further their common goal of uninterrupted production under the agreement, to make the agreement serve their specialized needs. The ablest judge cannot be expected to bring the same experience and competence to bear upon the determination of a grievance, because he cannot be similarly informed.

Arbitration of labor disputes serves, then, to give "meaning and content" over time to the vague or ambiguous terms of the collective bargaining agreement. In addition, the very existence of this dispute resolution mechanism itself may affect the dynamic of the parties' relationship. Through the processing of a grievance dispute, for example, useful information may be communicated about the needs and attitudes of one party to the agreement, and about potential trouble spots in the relationship. Another function of labor arbitration was highlighted by Justice Douglas in a formulation which has now attained something of the status of a cliché: In a companion case to *Warrior & Gulf*, Justice Douglas noted that "[t]he processing of even frivolous claims may have therapeutic values of which those who are not a part of the plant environment may be quite unaware."[14]

Just what does it mean to claim that labor arbitration can have a "therapeutic" function? It has been suggested that the ability to participate in the selection of a neutral decisionmaker, and to present one's own story to him in an informal, "non-threatening" atmosphere, may be "empower-

14.   United Steelworkers of America v. American Mfg. Co., 363 U.S. 564, 568 (1960).

ing" for each of the parties to the dispute.[15] It is important also to bear in mind here that any particular grievance under a collective bargaining agreement is likely to be that of the individual *employee,* who may have been dismissed or whose job classification may have been changed. However, the parties to the bargaining agreement are the employer and the *union;* the union, as the exclusive representative of all the employees in the bargaining unit, is in exclusive control of the administration of the contract and controls access to the grievance procedure at every stage. In these circumstances, pursuing even a hopeless claim to arbitration has at least the virtue of giving the employee the assurance that his case has been heard and that he has been taken seriously. Grievance arbitration may thus serve as a "safety valve for troublesome complaints"; the employee's presence at the hearing watching management witnesses subjected to "searching and often embarrassing cross-examination" may result in "a kind of catharsis that helps to make even eventual defeat acceptable" to the grievant.[16]

Carrying a case through the arbitration process may have other advantages for the union. It is often more politic for union representatives to "pass the buck" to the arbitrator, who they know will reject the grievance, than to be obliged *themselves* to convince their constituent that he is wrong and that the claim should be dropped. In addition, a union that is found to have "arbitrarily" refused to pursue an employee's grievance to arbitration, or to have "process[ed] it in a perfunctory fashion," may well be open to a suit by the employee for "unfair representation."[17] Nevertheless, the fact remains that the overwhelming proportion of employee grievances are screened or settled without resort to arbitration, just as the overwhelming proportion of lawsuits are settled before trial. It has been estimated that a grievance rate of 10 to 20 per 100 employees per year is "typical" in this country.[18] If any substantial proportion of those cases were to go to arbitration the entire grievance system would collapse.

Awards handed down by labor arbitrators generally reveal considerable sensitivity to those considerations mentioned by Justice Douglas in his paean to labor arbitration in *Warrior & Gulf*—the need to reduce tensions and to foster a good working relationship within the plant setting, the need to pay attention to the "common law of the shop" and to the "customs and practices which the parties have come to consider as settled patterns of conduct."[19] Some selections from recent arbitral awards give a good flavor

---

15. See, e.g., Roger Abrams et al., Arbitral Therapy, 46 Rutgers L.Rev. 1751, 1765, 1767, 1769 (1994).

16. Archibald Cox, Current Problems in the Law of Grievance Arbitration, 30 Rocky Mt.L.Rev. 247, 261 (1958); Benjamin Aaron, The Role of the Arbitrator in Ensuring a Fair Hearing, 35 Proc.Nat'l Acad.Arb. 30, 32 (1983).

17. Vaca v. Sipes, 386 U.S. 171 (1967); see also Bowen v. U.S. Postal Service, 459 U.S. 212 (1983).

18. See David E. Feller, A General Theory of the Collective Bargaining Agreement, 61 Cal.L.Rev. 663, 755 (1973).

19. In re Standard Bag Corp. and Paper Bag, Novelty, Mounting, Finishing and Display Workers Union, 45 Lab.Arb. 1149 (1965).

of how labor arbitrators purport, at least, to see their role in the process. Would you expect to find opinions like these written by "judges"?

(a) The employee had worked for the employer for eight years and had never been disciplined. He was discharged for being disrespectful to the Company President ("If you don't like the way I'm doing the work, do it yourself") in the presence of a number of the company's other employees. The arbitrator held that the employer did not have "proper cause" to discharge the employee and that he should be reinstated, although without recovering back pay or accruing seniority or vacation benefits for the seven months he was off work:

> Since discharge is in essence "capital punishment" in the work place, it is necessary to examine with extreme care all of the evidence before determining whether it is appropriate or not. This would include the facts and circumstances leading to the discharge, the grievant's length of service, the degree of aggravation involved in the offense, whether the conduct was intended or rather an accidental outburst, the grievant's past record and finally whether the events are likely to recur were the grievant to be reinstated. * * *

> Management's main argument was that it would be difficult for [the President] to run his operation with employees knowing that they could talk back to the President of the Company and get away with it. However, with this employee having been off work for over seven months without pay, I doubt that any employee will seriously think that he "got away with" very much. Upholding the discharge would be the most severe form of industrial penalty, but giving the grievant his job back without the seven months of back pay is still a very significant penalty. In salary alone that amounts to approximately $6,000.00 of gross earnings. (The grievant did not collect unemployment compensation and has not worked.) * * *

> On the day he returns to work, but as a condition precedent to returning to work, the grievant will apologize to [the President] either privately or in front of the employees of Stylemaster. (The presence or lack thereof of other employees to be at the discretion of the Company.)

In re Stylemaster, Inc. and Production Workers Union of Chicago, 79 Lab.Arb. 76 (1982).

(b) A collective bargaining agreement provided that the employer, a grocery chain, would remain closed on January 1 "contingent upon similar limitations being contractually required of other organized food stores and/or being generally observed by major unorganized food competitors in the cities in which the Employer operated." The arbitrator found that the employer violated this agreement by opening on January 1. He then turned to the question of the proper remedy to be granted the Union. The arbitrator denied the Union's request for punitive damages, since he was "of the view that they are bad medicine when administered to a participant in an ongoing, union-management relationship." Although the employer's violation was "clear and unmistakable," "it is always hard to say that a beleaguered competitor, as Kroger undoubtedly considered itself, acted subjectively in bad faith. Moreover, it seems to me that a healing process is what is most needed in the relations between this Company and the Union, and I question whether punitive damages will contribute to that end." Nor, he held, was there any basis for awarding damages to the employees: "I do not mean that it would be impossible to attach a dollar value to a January 1 with family and friends, perhaps in front of the TV set watching a bowl game * * * but I do not find that such a showing was made here."

However, to prevent "unjust enrichment," the arbitrator did award to the union "restitution of any profits that may be attributable to the Company's operations on January 1." In re The Kroger Company and United Food and Commercial Workers, 85 Lab.Arb. 1198 (1985).

(c) The employee had worked for the employer for twenty-two years as a messenger; her job was to pick up and deliver advertising proofs and materials to customers. She was discharged for failing to report to work at the scheduled time: This was apparently "the fourth occurrence of this behavior in the past six months," and four months previously, she had been suspended for three days without pay in a similar incident. The arbitrator held that the discharge should be set aside, and that the employee should be returned to her former position without loss of seniority:

When [the grievant] was testifying at the Arbitration Hearing my personal observation of her demeanor and appearance indicated that she was emotionally distraught beyond the customary nervous reaction of a witness. I * * * believe that [the grievant] deserved compassionate understanding. * * *

If Grievant performed with reasonable competency essentially the same messenger duties for about twenty-two years and only during the past year * * * did she demonstrate incompetence there must be some reason. It could be possible that Grievant suddenly developed a contemptuous disregard for her supervisor's instructions, It is more likely that some other explanation accounts for her recent erratic work performance. * * *

It was not until the Arbitration Hearing that the [employer's] supervisor learned that [the grievant] lived with her mother who was suffering with Alzheimer's disease and Grievant had to assist her. Grievant, at 43 years of age, is within the age span of 40 to 54 years that physicians believe that the climacteric usually occurs. This aging process, commonly called the change of life, in women sometimes produces sudden emotional changes that usually are temporary but which disrupt normal activities. Such a condition could interfere with a woman's required work activities and responsibilities. * * *

The evidence proves that [the grievant's] work performance during the last year had declined to an unacceptable level. The time she has been suspended from work shall be considered a disciplinary penalty to impress upon her, and other employees, the necessity of conforming to proper standards of conduct. Perhaps this lengthy period [grievant] has been off duty provided an opportunity to regain her health and emotional stability.

It probably would be beneficial to both bargaining unit employees and Management if specific rules for reporting off and obtaining sick leave or vacation days would be set forth in writing and distributed to all employees in this department. In the past there seems to have been considerable laxity in enforcement of reporting off and attendance requirements and also some ambiguity as to what attendance standards employees were expected to observe.

In re Pittsburgh Post–Gazette and Pittsburgh Typographical Union, 113 Lab. Arb. 957 (1999).

Note: Compromise Decisions

POSNER: The arbitration literature says—something that is very difficult to find out independently—that arbitrators are not supposed to compromise. Arbitrators are supposed to decide a dispute as if they were judges.

LEFF: The literature says that for the same reason that signs in subways say, "Don't Smoke," because there is a very strong tendency to smoke and therefore you have to say it over and over again. That reflects the fact that arbitrators compromise a great deal * * *.[20]

Observers often note that arbitrators have a propensity to tailor their decisions so as to make them acceptable to both parties. Such a criticism is heard most vociferously perhaps with respect to labor arbitrators, although it is by no means confined to the labor area. It is often supposed that this is done to insure the future "acceptability" of the arbitrator *himself*. Labor arbitrators are paid, often quite handsomely, for their work; what would be more natural than for this to create an incentive to try to assure themselves of repeat business? This incentive may often result in compromise decisions, "splitting the difference" so as not to appear unduly to favor either of the two parties whose future goodwill must be retained. A similar dynamic might be reflected in a *course* of decisions by the same arbitrator which over time, taken together, appears to show a rough balance between awards favorable to labor and those favorable to management.

As might be expected, this tendency to engage in compromise decisions appears particularly marked in "interest" arbitrations. In such cases the arbitrator is likely to be aware that the stakes riding on his decision are high, that the impact of his decision may be great and felt in all sorts of ways that he cannot be sure of in advance, and that intense dissatisfaction with a "mistaken" award may adversely affect the working relationship of

---

20. Discussion by Seminar Participants, 8 J.Legal Stud. 323, 345 (1979)

the parties for some time to come. Do you expect that judges are often impelled to take such considerations into account in deciding cases?

Compare the following two excerpts, whose authors appear to take sharply differing views of the propriety of this behavior and of its function within the context of labor-management relations:

> A proportion of arbitration awards, no one knows how large a proportion, is decided not on the basis of the evidence or of the contract or other proper considerations, but in a way calculated to encourage the arbitrator's being hired for other arbitration cases. It makes no difference whether or not a large majority of cases is decided in this way. A system of adjudication in which the judge depends for his livelihood, or for a substantial part of his livelihood or even for substantial supplements to his regular income, on pleasing those who hire him to judge is per se a thoroughly undesirable system. In no proper system of justice should a judge be submitted to such pressures. On the contrary, a judge should be carefully insulated from any pressure of this type.

Paul R. Hays, Labor Arbitration: A Dissenting View 112–13 (1966).

Compare Julius Getman, Labor Arbitration and Dispute Resolution, 88 Yale L.J. 916, 928–930 (1979):

> In none of the literature is it suggested that an arbitrator's desire to promote acceptability might affect the process in a way that is basically desirable. However, if, as I contend, economic efficiency is promoted by arbitration partly because through it the parties conclude their negotiations, then it is likely that the desire to maintain acceptability plays a useful role in helping to achieve the resolution that the parties would have achieved had they had the opportunity to negotiate with respect to the issues in dispute. Such a resolution would by definition further the goal of efficiency.

> The negotiating process reflects both the relative economic strength and the differing priorities of the parties. * * * Economic strength is necessarily a factor in arbitration because it shapes the language of the collective-bargaining agreement, which is always the starting point, and sometimes the sole basis, for the arbitrator's decision. The parties' priorities are more difficult to ascertain. The arbitrator must pay careful attention to the clues that the parties give concerning how strongly they feel about a particular case. My judgment is that the need to maintain acceptability makes arbitrators more attentive to such clues than judges and more likely than judges would be to utilize them in their decision. Arbitrators whose decisions over time accurately reflect the priorities of the parties are likely to maintain and enhance their acceptability more than arbitrators who take either a more narrowly judicial role or a personally activist role. Thus, the process of selection will tend to produce arbitrators and a body of

arbitral precedent that facilitate and extend the process of negotiation.
* * *

The careful selection process also motivates arbitrators to try to please both sides, if possible, with their decision. Thus, the split award and the decision in which it is difficult to tell which side has won are frequent in labor relations. Although the parties constantly insist it is contrary to their wishes, this system of giving a little bit to each side permits the process to achieve the results of successful negotiation.

NOTES AND QUESTIONS

1. As Getman suggests, it is almost inevitable that in the course of a hearing an arbitrator will receive some intimation from the parties or their attorneys as to what an "acceptable" settlement will look like, and that he will be influenced by such hints or suggestions. In an extreme case this may even take the form of what is called a "rigged award." The union representative and the management may actually *agree* between themselves as to how a case should be resolved; this understanding is conveyed to the arbitrator, who incorporates it in the final award as "his" decision without openly revealing that it is in fact the result of the parties' compromise. The hearing itself then becomes a mere charade. The practice of the "rigged award" has been often and scathingly condemned as "the crassest infringement of adjudicative integrity," "the most severe criticism which could be made of arbitration," "vicious" and "a shocking distortion of the administration of justice." See Fuller, Collective Bargaining and the Arbitrator, 1963 Wisc.L.Rev. 3, 20 (1963); Eaton, Labor Arbitration in the San Francisco Bay Area, 48 Lab.Arb. 1381, 1389 (1967); Paul R. Hays, Labor Arbitration: A Dissenting View 113, 65 (1966).

Why might the parties want the arbitrator to proceed in this way, when they could simply "settle" the case and withdraw it from the purview of the arbitrator? And just *why* is the arbitrator not entitled to do this? What is wrong with the "rigged award"? Might there be a difference if this practice is used in "interest" arbitration rather than with respect to a "rights" dispute? Finally, if the arbitrator is unwilling merely to rubber-stamp the parties' understanding, how should he proceed? What as a practical matter is he able to do?

2. A labor arbitrator issued an award sustaining a grievance by the United Mine Workers against a coal company. The employer moved to vacate the award, alleging that the arbitrator had failed to disclose that his brother was employed by the UMW. The court, however, rebuffed this challenge: Neither the arbitrator nor his brother "had any discernible interest in the outcome of the proceeding." In addition, the court stressed that the coal industry decisions that this arbitrator had made in the past underlined the absence of any "partiality": He had served as a "coal industry arbitrator" for three years under procedures adopted by the UMW and the Bituminous Coal Operators Association; of his 66 awards, the Union had "won 30, lost 29, split 5, and settled 2 before a hearing."

Consolidated Coal Co. v. Local 1643, United Mine Workers of Amer., 48 F.3d 125 (4th Cir.1995).

3. One recent study has purported to refute the notion that arbitrators tend to "split the baby," by analyzing a sample of AAA awards in "international business disputes." The study found that 31% of the claimants received nothing, while 35% received 100% of the amounts they had claimed; 17% of the awards, however, were within 20% of the midpoint between the claimed amount and 0. The authors carefully distinguish the international business context from that of "interest" arbitration in labor cases, where "much of the collective bargaining process is a series of creative and skillful trade-offs, leaving the collective bargaining arbitrator with little to do but combine competing positions into a fair and balanced whole." Stephanie E. Keer & Richard W. Naimark, Arbitrators Do Not "Split the Baby," *in* Christopher R. Drahozal & Richard W. Naimark, Towards A Science of International Arbitration: Collected Empirical Research 311 (2005).

4. Some writers have suggested that the "procedures for arbitration that have been developed in the context of labor relations make the technique particularly adaptable to prison problems." To resolve disputes arising out of grievances by prison inmates, "third-party neutrals who have particular expertise in corrections may be chosen by both prisoners and the officials. Furthermore, the parties could stipulate in advance the rules to be followed and the issues to be settled." Goldfarb & Singer, Redressing Prisoners' Grievances, 39 Geo. Wash. L. Rev. 175, 316 (1970); see also Keating, Arbitration of Inmate Grievances, 30 Arb. J. 177 (1975). Do you agree?

4. ARBITRATION OF CONSUMER DISPUTES

The Bank of America, the nation's second-largest bank, announced in 1992 that all its contracts with depositors and credit-card holders would henceforth contain arbitration clauses. Under the Bank's new contract, any individual disputes would be decided by arbitration under the commercial rules of the AAA; any complaints brought as class actions would be "referred" to a neutral under California's "rent-a-judge" statute (See Section E.4. infra.) Notice of the arbitration clause was sent to the bank's customers as "stuffers" in their monthly statements; cardholders, for example, were told that if they continued to use their cards after receiving the notice, the arbitration provision would apply to all past and future transactions.

During the 1980's a number of California banks, including the Bank of America, had already begun to experiment with using arbitration in other product lines, particularly mid-range commercial loans. This was in reaction to a series of pro-borrower "lender liability" cases which seemed to broaden the scope of the duties owed to a borrower by a bank:

> [The banks] concluded that both their exposure and their transaction costs could be reduced by the adoption of arbitration provisions. First, they believed that their exposure would be both more predictable and

better contained with arbitration. In their view, arbitrators generally had a better grasp of underlying contractual issues than juries and were less likely to consider factors outside those presented in the case at issue; for example, the fact that the bank is a large institution able to spread out any losses relative to the individual, who may be forced into extreme hardship. Firms also believed that arbitrators were less likely to award punitive damages. Furthermore, firms anticipated that the fact that disputes would be heard before an arbitrator would, in turn, affect plaintiffs' and plaintiffs' attorneys' calculus in deciding whether to bring suit in the first place; as possible verdicts declined, plaintiffs would be less likely to bring suit.[21]

In 1998, the Bank's arbitration mechanism was held on narrow contract-law grounds to be unenforceable; the California Court of Appeals found that under the original terms of its customer agreements, the Bank had no right to unilaterally impose this modification on existing credit-card holders. (See p. 109 infra). But the Bank's example encouraged other companies to follow its lead: A few years later, a class action was brought in federal court on behalf of everyone holding a Visa or a Mastercard issued by the Bank of America, First USA, MBNA, Citibank, Chase, Diners Club, or Providian. One allegation was that these banks had "conspired" with American Express "to include compulsory arbitration clauses in their respective cardholder agreements"; plaintiffs alleged that the defendants, who "control more than 86% of the United States general purpose card market," had formed a group known as "the Arbitration Coalition" intended to "draw upon their collective market power * * * to develop, hone and implement their compulsory arbitration clauses." As the court described it, "the paradigm arbitration clause in cardholder agreements" imposed by all the defendants provided that

> Any claim, dispute or controversy. * * * arising from or relating in any way to this Agreement or your Account, including Claims regarding the applicability of this arbitration clause or the validity of the entire Agreement, shall be resolved by the National Arbitration Forum. * * * This arbitration agreement applies to all Claims now in existence or that may arise in the future * * * .

(The Bank of America agreement, sent to all cardholders in 2000 and titled "Important Notice Regarding Your Account," required arbitration under "the rules for arbitration of financial services disputes of JAMS"). See the various opinions in In re Currency Conversion Fee Antitrust Litigation, 361 F.Supp.2d 237, 243–44 (S.D.N.Y. 2005); 265 F.Supp.2d 385, 399 (S.D.N.Y. 2003); 2005 WL 2364969 (S.D.N.Y.) at 9. See also Ronald J. Mann, "Contracting" for Credit, 104 Mich. L. Rev. 899 (2006)("the major issuers have gravitated to a single provider (the National Arbitration Forum) that seems to be competing for business (at least in part) on a reputation for providing results that are satisfying to card issuers.").

---

21. Erik Moller et al., Private Dispute Resolution in the Banking Industry 12–13 (RAND 1993).

In the years following the earliest experiments, the possibilities for the use of arbitration in consumer contracts have expanded and now begin to seem endless:

- Securities brokers have long insisted that individual investors who wish to open a margin or an option account agree to arbitration; a substantial and increasing number of brokerage firms require arbitration even for investors wishing to open a cash account. Such a requirement is "never or almost never waived or negotiated."[22]

- After a customer orders a Gateway computer over the phone or online, the computer will eventually arrive in a box containing all the necessary equipment—along with a copy of Gateway's "Standard Terms and Conditions." The buyer who manages to go through this form will read that "You and Us agree that any Dispute between You and Us will be resolved exclusively and finally by arbitration administered by the National Arbitration Forum."[23]

- Home Buyers Warranty Corp. issues warranties that cover over 1,260,000 new and pre-owned homes. As "protection" against "rising consumer expectations and the epidemic of construction defect litigation against builders that is sweeping through our country,"[24] it now requires homeowners to agree to arbitration of any warranty claims through Construction Arbitration Services.[25]

In fact, as one newspaper article recently put it, arbitration clauses "are now migrating into the fine print of everyday consumer services, including cable TV, cellphones, online retailers, gyms, auto financing firms, travel agencies and summer camps."[26] A recent sampling of the businesses that "Joe ['our average U.S. consumer,' located in Los Angeles] was most likely to patronize," suggested that 35.4% included arbitration clauses in their consumer contracts—a figure that rose to 69.2% in the financial sector (that is, banks, credit cards, investment, and accounting/tax consulting).[27] And in 2005, McDonald's unveiled a number of customer promotions: In its

---

22. U.S. General Accounting Office, Securities Arbitration: How Investors Fare 28–30 (1992).

23. See http://content.gateway.com/www.gate-way.com/about/legal/warranties/ 8510306ConVAS88757B_306.pdf.

24. See http://www.2-10.com/warranty-holders/conciliation_arbitration.html.

25. CAS is itself to "appoint arbitrators from its panel of persons knowledgeable in residential construction," CAS Rules for the Arbitration of Home Warranty Disputes, R.3, http://www.cas-usa.org/rules/home_warranty/agreement_parties.php. Unless the case is "complex," the total cost for the arbitration, including one day of hearing, is between $500 and $700. R.26.

26. See Jane Spencer, "Signing Away Your Right to Sue," Wall St. J., Oct. 1, 2003 at p. D1. The article posits a "tough choice" for consumers: "Give up your legal rights—or forget about joining a gym, getting a cellphone, or even seeing your doctor." It does note, however, that a consumer can "avoid" arbitration if he obtains a credit card issued by an organization that has "negotiating power with credit-card issuers": Cards issued by the AARP, for example, do not contain arbitration clauses "since the organization refuses to accept them." Id. at p. D2.

27. Linda J. Demaine & Deborah R. Hensler, "Volunteering" to Arbitrate through Predispute Arbitration Clauses: The Average Consumer's Experience, 67 Law & Contemp. Probs. 55 (2004).

"Extreme Dream Sweepstakes," for example, a random drawing of entry forms (found on the Happy Meal Box) would determine winners of $5000 cash for a "dream room," a JVC Home Theater System, or Sharkboy or Lavagirl Pajamas: The contest rules, amidst much fine print—including a *force majeure* clause which exempted the sponsor from liability in the event of "terrorist threat" or "public health crisis"—contained an arbitration clause calling for any disputes over prizes to be resolved by the NAF.

Note: Medical Malpractice: Disputes Between Doctors and Patients

A dramatic increase in the number and size of medical malpractice claims and awards first entered the public consciousness during the 1970's, under the banner of the "malpractice crisis." The threatened effects of this "crisis" on the health and insurance industries spawned a large variety of legislative responses. These have ranged from tinkering with the formal legal standard of negligence or the statute of limitations in malpractice cases, to more dramatic reforms such as abolishing the collateral source rule or imposing ceilings on recoverable damages or on attorney's contingent fees. Among these legislative "reforms" there inevitably appeared changes in the *process* by which malpractice claims could be asserted, and attempts to divert such claims entirely from the time-honored system of tort litigation.

a. Medical Review Panels

Some states have imposed preliminary hurdles on malpractice litigation by *requiring* that claims first be submitted to a "medical review" or "professional liability review" panel. (These may sometimes be called "arbitration boards.") Under some statutes, this required panel must consist of three physicians.[28] Another common pattern is for the panel to consist of a physician, an attorney, and a member of the "general public"[29]; still other states simply provide for a "tripartite board" (with one member named by each party and a chairman selected by the other two members or by the court) without specifying the profession or background of the arbitrators. Under the various statutes the fees and expenses of the arbitrators may be shared equally by the parties, may be assessed by the arbitrators as an element of costs, or may in some cases come directly from state funds.

If either party is dissatisfied with the arbitration award, he has the right to demand a trial de novo to be held in the regular state courts. In consequence it is often said that the review panels serve not so much to "decide" disputes, as to provide "an expert opinion" based on evidence

---

28. See, e.g., Neb.Rev.St. § 44–2841 (each party selects one physician and the two thus chosen select a third; panel also includes attorney who acts in "advisory capacity" and has no vote).

29. See, e.g., Md.Code, Courts & Jud.Proceed. §§ 3–2A–03, 3–2A–04 (state "Health Claims Arbitration Office" circulates lists of arbitrators in each category to the parties, who may strike unacceptable names); Del.Code Tit. 18, §§ 6804, 6805 (each panel consists of two "health care providers," one attorney, and two "lay persons" chosen from a "list of 100 objective and judicious persons of appropriate education and experience" maintained by the Commissioner of Insurance).

submitted to them—that they act "in the nature of a pretrial settlement conference," or that, by giving the parties a preliminary, disinterested evaluation of the merits of a claim, they serve an "advisory" function and help to "promote an early disposition of many cases by a voluntary settlement."[30] See the discussion of such dispute-resolution processes at pp. 163–164 infra. In a number of states, however, decisions of review panels are given somewhat greater clout by being made admissible in any later trial of the malpractice claim.[31]

At some point 31 states provided by statute for medical review panels. However, the legislation was later repealed in at least seven states, and overturned by courts in another five—primarily on the ground that the panel requirement caused undue delay.[32] The practical effects of requiring these screening panels for malpractice litigation has been unclear: In some cases, it seems, the availability of a panel system may increase the number of claims asserted—because it "lowers the expected cost to plaintiffs of acquiring information about the outcome of their lawsuits." But in other cases, the panel requirement may instead *discourage* claiming—since the need to hold hearings and conduct discovery even before litigation may carry with it additional expense and the prospect for plaintiffs "of having to try their case twice"; panel proceedings may also "lower plaintiffs' expected returns by delaying the resolution of claims." For the same reasons, if the panel requirement does indeed promote pretrial resolution of claims, it may often do so not by facilitating settlement—but by leading the plaintiff to drop the claim entirely.[33]

b. Contractual agreements for binding arbitration

There has been some experimentation also with the use of *contractual* agreements to arbitrate malpractice claims between a patient and a medical defendant. As in the case of traditional arbitration, such agreements can be entered into either prior to treatment or as the submission of an existing dispute; where such an agreement is made, the arbitrator's decision will be binding on both parties.

In a number of states, statutes expressly authorize the arbitration of medical malpractice disputes:[34] These statutes are intended not only to encourage agreements to arbitrate but also to regulate the process; they commonly provide, for example, that notice that an agreement contains an

---

30. Prendergast v. Nelson, 199 Neb. 97, 256 N.W.2d 657, 666–67 (1977).

31. E.g., La.S.A.–Rev.Stat.40: 1299.47(H) (report of the "expert opinion" of the panel is "admissible," but not "conclusive").

32. The details appear in Catherine T. Struve, Expertise in Medical Malpractice Litigation: Special Courts, Screening Panels, and Other Options 56–57 (Pew Project on Medical Liability 2003), http://medliabilitypa.org/research/struve1003.

33. Id. at 61–64.

34. E.g., Alaska Stat. ch. 55 § 09.55.535; S.H.A.Ill.Comp.Stat. ch. 710 § 15/1; La.S.A.–Rev.Stat. § 9:4232; Ohio Rev. Code Tit. 27, § 2711.22; West's Ann.Cal.Code Civ.Proc. § 1295; see Pietrelli v. Peacock, 13 Cal.App.4th 943, 16 Cal.Rptr.2d 688, 689 (1993) ("The purpose of § 1295 was to encourage and facilitate arbitration of medical malpractice disputes"); cf. N.Y.–McKinney's C.P.L.R. 7550 et seq. (limited to HMO's).

arbitration clause must be printed in conspicuous "bold red type," and that an agreement to arbitrate "may not be made a prerequisite to receipt of care or treatment" by a doctor or hospital.[35] In other jurisdictions, voluntary arbitration agreements between patients and health care providers may also be enforceable under the state's general arbitration statute. A 2005 chart of all "state medical malpractice tort laws," including a column with information on "pre-trial screening and arbitration," has been prepared by the National Conference of State Legislatures and can be found at http://www.ncsl.org/standcomm/sclaw/sclaw.htm.

It appears that agreements for binding arbitration are not as yet widespread in the medical setting—although recent surveys do suggest "a dynamic innovation environment," since "organizations that are well positioned to stimulate use of agreements are aware of them, and alert to information that may demonstrate they have value." One California study reveals that while only 9% of physicians and hospitals in the state use arbitration agreements, 60% of the physicians using such agreements have adopted them since 1990—"suggesting that a reasonably persistent diffusion process is underway in the physician community."[36] About a third of the responding physicians and hospitals that did *not* use arbitration agreements attributed their reluctance to the fear that such agreements "set the wrong tone" for the patient,[37] creating "an uncomfortable situation."[38] Other possible reasons for the current lack of physician enthusiasm also might be suggested: For example, the supposed propensity of arbitrators to indulge in compromise decisions might not be attractive to physicians who in malpractice cases "possess a strong interest in vindicating their conduct."[39] And even where claims are subject to an arbitration agreement, defense attorneys will commonly fail to move to dismiss lawsuits filed by patients: Some defense attorneys in fact prefer to keep a case in court despite the existence of an arbitration agreement—apparently "for fear that a physician arbitrator would easily recognize that in that particular case, a deviation in the standard had occurred."[40]

In sharp contrast to the limited use by individual physicians and hospitals, the same California survey revealed that 71% of the state's HMO's do use binding arbitration agreements with their subscribers. Such arbitration agreements are usually designed by HMO's to apply to contract disputes only—and not to claims alleging medical malpractice. However, an important exception to this finding is the nation's largest HMO, Kaiser

35. West's Ann.Cal.Code Civ.Proc. § 1295(b); Alaska Stat. ch. 55, § 09.55.535(a).

36. Elizabeth Rolph et al., Arbitration Agreements in Health Care: Myths and Reality, 60 Law & Contemp. Probs. 153, 171–72, 180 (1997).

37. Id. at 175.

38. See U.S. General Accounting Office, Medical Malpractice: Few Claims Resolved Through Michigan's Voluntary Arbitration Program 6 (1990).

39. Thomas B. Metzloff, Alternative Dispute Resolution Strategies in Medical Malpractice, 9 Alaska L.Rev. 429, 440 (1992).

40. Brian W. Whitelaw, Health Care Arbitration in Michigan: An Effective Method of Alternative Dispute Resolution, 72 Mich. Bar J. 1158, 1162 (1993).

Permanente—which *does* require all of its subscribers in California and in three other states to agree to arbitrate any medical malpractice claims, as well as any other disputes arising out of their health care plans. (Over 6 million Kaiser subscribers are subject to mandatory arbitration agreements).

Kaiser's arbitration program was originally designed to be self-administered—with "administrative functions performed by outside counsel retained to defend Kaiser in an adversarial capacity."[41] In 1997, the California Supreme Court refused to compel arbitration against the estate of a deceased plan participant—finding that Kaiser had engaged in fraud both "in the inducement" and "in the application" of the arbitration agreement: An independent statistical analysis of Kaiser arbitrations found that in only 1% of all Kaiser cases was a neutral arbitrator appointed within the 60–day period mandated by the plan; on average it took 863 days to reach a hearing in a Kaiser arbitration. For the court, a fraud claim could be premised on Kaiser's conduct in setting up a self-administered arbitration system "in which delay for its own benefit and convenience was an inherent part"—and yet nevertheless "persist[ing] in its contractual promises of expeditiousness."[42] In response to such criticisms Kaiser promptly re-designed its arbitration mechanism to provide for independent administration. The Law Office of Sharon Oxborough—"a boutique law firm specializing in monitoring consent decrees and alternative dispute resolutions"—now serves as the "Office of the Independent Administrator," and has written new rules of procedure for Kaiser arbitrations, created a panel of qualified neutrals, and monitors the progress of the arbitrations "to assure that each case moves as expeditiously as possible." The latest annual report of the OIA can be found at www.oia-kaiserarb.com. The 2004 report indicates that the average time to select a neutral arbitrator is now 61 days; for those 16% of arbitration cases that closed with a final award, the average time from start to finish was 456 days.

Nevertheless a recent report by the California Research Bureau—the research arm of the California Legislature—has been highly critical of both the fairness and efficiency of patient-insurer arbitration. This 2000 report covered 50 health plans, although most of its data came from Kaiser. The Bureau noted that a substantial number of all Kaiser arbitrations under the OIA are dismissed on summary judgment (this figure was 8% in 2004; by contrast, the summary judgment rate in civil litigation was only 0.6%): This was attributed in part to the fact that it is "easier to file an arbitration claim" than to institute litigation (so that arbitrators see more plaintiffs who probably would never make it to court)—but also, in part, to the fact that many Kaiser arbitrations are conducted *pro se* (so that the

---

41. Engalla v. Permanente Medical Group, Inc., 15 Cal.4th 951, 64 Cal.Rptr.2d 843, 849, 938 P.2d 903 (1997).

42. Id. at 853, 858 (held, "there is evidence to support the [plaintiff's] claims that Kaiser fraudulently induced [plaintiff]

to enter the arbitration agreement in that it misrepresented the speed of its arbitration program, a misrepresentation on which [plaintiff's] employer relied by selecting Kaiser's health plan for its employees").

claimant may be unable to present necessary expert evidence, "or even understand what evidence needs to be presented."). Large malpractice awards are apparently less common in arbitration than in comparable jury trials: In 2004 patients were successful in only 34% of the cases leading to a final award; between 1999 and 2004, the average claimant award was $299,000 and the median award, $125,000; 45% of all the awards were under $100,000, and only 6% were more than $1 million.[43] The CRB report also pointed out that as a repeat player, Kaiser is likely to have far more information than the claimant with respect to the track record of potential arbitrators, and is therefore "in a good position to make informed decisions" in selecting them.[44] As a consequence—"[b]ecause the potential earnings, relative to the costs of preparing a case, are too limited"—lawyers are seldom willing to take such arbitration cases on a contingency basis.[45]

NOTES AND QUESTIONS

1. In this section you have been introduced to a use of arbitration quite different from the models presented in the labor and commercial areas. You can see that the term "arbitration" is commonly applied to describe any number of different processes, developing along different lines and responding to different needs. Indeed, the long-standing acceptability and respectability of "arbitration" make it a useful term to be co-opted by innovators in the dispute resolution field.

Some of the attributes traditionally claimed for arbitration may be present here as well. In consumer arbitration, an arbitrator is typically asked to apply fairly straightforward rules of decision to limited and tractable fact questions; in addition, the stakes are likely to be small and the procedure extremely informal. In such circumstances there are likely to be advantages, at least to the plaintiff, of reduced delay and costs—similar to the advantages often claimed for small claims courts. Studies indicate also that arbitration, at least where it is voluntary in inception and binding in result, may bring similar benefits to medical malpractice claimants in the form of increased speed and reduced expense. See, e.g., Note, Medical Malpractice Arbitration: A Patient's Perspective, 61 Wash.U.L.Q. 123, 153–155 (1983).

However, there are also some significant differences. The usefulness of arbitration may be diluted where the parties do not (as they may in labor and commercial disputes) "have an interest in the pie of continued collabo-

---

43. Between 1999 and 2004, 91% of the Kaiser arbitration cases were medical malpractice cases; only 2% involved disputes over benefits and coverage.

44. The CRB had strongly criticized the heavy use by Kaiser of a small number of repeat arbitrators—between 1999 and 2004 one neutral arbitrator had been selected 78 times—and noted also that none of the arbitrators in cases awarding more than $1 mil-

lion had ever been selected again. The 2004 OIA report attempts to answer this objection, stressing that 63% of the 309 neutral arbitrators on the Kaiser panel had been selected to serve on a case that year—none more than ten times.

45. Marcus Nieto & Margaret Hosel, Arbitration in California Managed Health Care Systems 2, 19 (CRB 2000).

ration." See Henry M. Hart & Albert M. Sacks, The Legal Process 315 (1994). Especially where the parties' autonomy in the choice of the process or in the selection of arbitrators is reduced, the decision-makers are no longer "their" arbitrators, spelling out the meaning of "their" agreement in terms of their probable preferences or past practice. It then becomes more appropriate to view arbitration not as part of the world of "private ordering" but simply as a form of economic regulation. Particularly in the field of medical malpractice such regulation is often responsive to a not-very-well-hidden agenda, as the following excerpt indicates:

> The push for the arbitration of malpractice claims * * * must not be seen as linked to the general interest in alternative dispute resolution mechanisms exhibited over the past two decades. This examination of alternative mechanisms has had as its primary goal the identification of fora and procedures suitable for the resolution of meritorious claims that, for essentially economic reasons, had been excluded from the litigation system. In direct contrast, malpractice claims have always been guaranteed judicial resolution because of the contingency fee system. * * *

> There are two primary goals set forth by those propounding the arbitration of malpractice claims: first, to chill attorney interest in what are labelled [as] frivolous or unmeritorious claims; and second, to reduce the size of damage awards in meritorious claims. Neither goal is related to providing a resolution for otherwise unresolvable claims. Both are intimately linked, however, to the widely held belief that the judiciary is unwilling or unable to exercise effective control over juries in civil trials. * * *

> Arbitration and pretrial review of medical malpractice claims serve different legislative goals. At the most general level, both are designed to freeze or slow the acceleration of the size of malpractice insurance premiums. The effect of pretrial review, however, is to chill plaintiff interest in pursuing marginal claims, both practically and psychologically, and to encourage settlement by forcing additional plaintiff expenditure without providing for concomitant recovery. Arbitration, on the other hand, is viewed primarily as a constitutionally safe method of avoiding jury determinations of liability and quantum of damages.

Terry, The Technical and Conceptual Flaws of Medical Malpractice Arbitration, 30 St. Louis U.L.J. 571, 572–73, 586 (1986).

2. A Florida statute provides that within 90 days after the plaintiff has given notice of his intent to initiate medical malpractice litigation, either party may request a "medical arbitration panel" to determine damages. An agreement by both parties to participate in arbitration binds both to the panel's decision. In such a case the plaintiff's noneconomic damages will be capped at $250,000 per incident and "calculated on a percentage basis with respect to capacity to enjoy life" (so, for example, a finding that the plaintiff had suffered a "50% reduction in his capacity to enjoy life" would warrant an award of not more than $125,000 in noneconomic damages). No punitive damages may be awarded, but the plaintiff is entitled to attorneys' fees of up to 15% of the award. If the defendant offers to arbitrate but *the plaintiff refuses,* the plaintiff may proceed to trial, although his noneconomic damages at trial will be limited to $350,000 per incident. If, however, it is the *defendant who refuses arbitration,* the plaintiff's noneconomic damages at trial are capped at $500,000 (or $1 million if because of "special circumstances" having caused "catastrophic injury," "manifest injustice" would otherwise occur)—and in addition the plaintiff may recover attorneys' fees up to 25% of the award.

What incentives are this statute intended to create? See West's Fla. Stat.Ann. §§ 766.118, 766.207, 766.209; St. Mary's Hospital, Inc. v. Phillipe, 769 So.2d 961, 970 (Fla. 2000)(the plaintiff "benefits from the requirement that a defendant quickly determine the merit of any defenses and the extent of its liability," and also "saves the costs of attorney and expert witness fees which would be required to prove liability"; in addition he benefits from "the relaxed evidentiary standard for arbitration proceedings" and "limited appellate review of the arbitration award"; on the other hand, "the most significant incentive for defendants to concede liability and submit the issue of damages to arbitration is the $250,000 cap on noneconomic damages," which "provides liability insurers with the ability to improve the predictability of the outcome of claims for the purpose of loss planning in risk assessment for premium purposes.").

3. In 2003 Utah enacted legislation under which physicians and hospitals could "require" patients to agree to arbitrate a claim instead of having the claim heard by a judge or jury; except in "the emergency department of a general acute hospital," care could be denied on the ground that the patient had refused to enter into such an agreement. The bill's sponsor pointed to the fact that malpractice insurance rates "for some specialists and for ob-gyns [were] 'rising substantially,' and 'we're going to do this as a trial and see if premiums can't come down.'" Michelle Andrews, "For Patients, Unpleasant Surprises in Arbitration," N.Y. Times, March 16, 2003. See also James Holbrook, Mandatory Binding Arbitration of Medical Malpractice Claims in Utah, Utah B.J., Oct. 2003 at pp. 8, 10 (counsel for state's Medical Insurance Association quoted as saying that "when arbitration is properly explained, over 95% of patients agree to sign an arbitration agreement"); "Doctors Don't Like Bill on Arbitration," Salt Lake Tribune, March 6, 2004, p. B1 (state MIA gave doctors who use arbitration agreements a 5% discount on malpractice insurance). After the state's largest HMO informed its patients that it would now require arbitration agreements, the public reaction from "trial lawyers and patients' advocacy groups" was vocal and hostile; the statute was promptly amended: It is now explicit that no patient may "be denied health care on the sole basis that [he or she] refused to enter into a binding arbitration agreement with a health care provider." Utah Code § 78–14–17(3); see "Suit Claims Care Tied to Mediation," Salt Lake Tribune, Oct. 12, 2004, p. C1.

4. Another area where there has been recent experimentation with use of the arbitration process has been in disputes between consumers and automobile manufacturers. General Motors and some other manufacturers, for example (including Honda, Nissan, and Volkswagen) have agreed to submit disputes over new-car warranties to the "Auto Line" program administered by the Better Business Bureau. In this program, the consumer's complaint is heard by volunteer arbitrators—"lawyers, professors, accountants, company executives, housewives, trade association personnel"—who have gone through a short training program but who have no necessary background in either the law or in automobile mechanics; they are told to "make common sense adjudications based on their own sense of fairness." General Motors Corp. v. Abrams, 897 F.2d 34, 37 (2d Cir.1990). "In the vast majority of cases both parties represent themselves, and do not find it necessary to involve an attorney." The arbitrators will hear any claims under an automobile warranty, although they will not consider claims for consequential damages such as for personal injury or lost wages. The program is funded by the manufacturer, operates at no cost to the consumer, and is designed to resolve any complaint within 40 days after filing. The manufacturer generally agrees in advance to be bound by the award. The consumer, however, is free either to reject any unfavorable award and pursue a warranty claim in court, or indeed, to bypass the arbitration process entirely. See generally the "Auto Line" website at http://www.dr.bbb.org/autoline/index.asp.

5. As part of the expansion of consumer protection legislation over the last two decades, most states have enacted so-called "lemon laws" aimed at insuring that automobile manufacturers conform the vehicle to any express warranty. These statutes grant additional rights to the consumer by requiring the manufacturer to refund the purchase price or provide the consumer a new replacement vehicle if it cannot correct any defect after a "reasonable number of attempts."

State "lemon laws" also commonly provide that where the manufacturer has set up or participates in a qualified "third party dispute resolution process" to hear warranty claims, then the consumer must first assert any "lemon law" claims through such a process before bringing suit. See Tanner Consumer Protection Act, Cal. Civ. Code § 1793.22 (c), (d). A number of states such as California have "certified" the BBB's AutoLine program as meeting the minimum standards of the state lemon law. According to a recent survey by California's Department of Consumer Affairs, consumers reported that in GM "Auto Line" cases, the arbitration decision was adverse to them 54% of the time—and that they were not "satisfied with the arbitration process" in 51% of the cases. Apparently, however, a post-arbitration lawsuit was filed by the consumer in only 6% of the cases. 2004 Annual Consumer Satisfaction Survey, available at http://www.dca.ca.gov/acp.

6. In New York, by contrast, a consumer has the option of selecting arbitration as an alternative to any process that the manufacturer sets up or sponsors (and is also free to initiate an arbitration under the state "lemon law" even if she has already resorted to the manufacturer's own non-binding process and been denied relief). The state "lemon law" arbitration is administered by a non-profit organization (the New York State Dispute Resolution Association) under state regulations, and is designed to be "accessible" "without the need for an attorney." Most notably, this arbitration mechanism is made *mandatory for the manufacturer* at the consumer's option. If the consumer elects arbitration and pays a filing fee she will, however, be bound by the result in the same way as the manufacturer.   See N.Y.Gen.Bus.Law § 198–a(k), (m). http://www.oag.state.ny.us/ consumer/cars/newcar_lemonlaw_brochure.pdf; http://www.nysra.org /about/about_index.html.

7.   Disputes between attorneys and clients over legal fees constitute the major share of all attorney-client conflict—it has even been said that such disputes constitute "the principal source of public dissatisfaction with the judicial system." Anderson v. Elliott, 555 A.2d 1042, 1049 (Me.1989). Litigation over fees is a highly unsatisfactory method of dispute resolution for the attorney; a suit over unpaid fees virtually guarantees a counterclaim for malpractice, so that "fee suits can be ugly affairs." Charles Wolfram, Modern Legal Ethics § 9.61 at 554 (1986). And litigation may be equally unattractive for the client. In addition to the cost, it may be difficult even to find a local lawyer willing to handle a fee case against another attorney; there is also the risk that in such litigation confidential information that had earlier been revealed to the attorney may become part of the public record. See Model Rules of Professional Conduct, Rule 1.6(b)(5), in Appendix D, infra.

As a consequence, a number of states have made binding arbitration of fee disputes mandatory for the attorney at the request of a client. See, e.g., Anderson v. Elliott, supra; In re LiVolsi, 85 N.J. 576, 428 A.2d 1268 (1981). In most other states, state or local bar associations offer programs by which attorney and client can voluntarily enter into binding arbitration after a fee dispute has arisen. These arbitration programs are usually administered by the bar association, and attorneys serve as the arbitrators (although in larger cases, where a panel of three arbitrators is used, it is common for one lay person to sit on the panel along with the attorneys.) See generally Alan Scott Rau, Resolving Disputes Over Attorneys' Fees: The Role of ADR, 46 S.M.U.L.Rev. 2005 (1993).

In addition, lawyers are increasingly experimenting with *pre-dispute* arbitration agreements, entered into with the client at the time the attorney is retained. Such agreements frequently purport to cover not only fee disputes but also later claims of malpractice. See, e.g., McGuire, Cornwell & Blakey v. Grider, 765 F.Supp. 1048 (D.Colo.1991) (agreement bound client to submit to arbitration "any fee disputes * * * and claims by you regarding [the firm's] handling of your matter," although it expressly permitted the firm to "[collect] amounts due to it in other ways, including litigation").

Might such pre-dispute agreements raise ethical problems for the attorney? Is any guidance to be found in Rule 1.8 of the Model Rules of Professional Conduct? In some ethics opinions Rule 1.8 has been thought to make such agreements impermissible unless the client has actually been "counseled by another attorney" before signing: See, e.g., Md. State Bar Comm. on Ethics Dock. 90–12 (1989) ("If the client refuses to seek independent counsel, then the lawyer is prohibited from entering into such a written agreement"). See also D.C. Bar Legal Ethics Comm., Op. 211 (1990)("the lawyer entering into a retainer agreement with a client for arbitration of all disputes, including malpractice, could not adequately explain the tactical considerations of arbitration versus litigation to the lay client—considerations such as lack of formal discovery, lack of a jury trial, and the closed nature of arbitration proceedings"); cf. Op. 218 (1991)(agreement calling for mandatory arbitration of *fee* disputes before the bar association's Attorney–Client Arbitration Board is ethically permissible given that the Board's procedures and rules are "relatively simple to understand" and that counseling is provided by the Board staff). An Ohio opinion concludes that since "it is impractical to expect most clients to 'hire a lawyer to hire a lawyer,'" the practice of requiring clients to prospectively agree to arbitrate legal malpractice disputes should be generally "discouraged"—and that such arbitration should in all cases "be a voluntary decision made by a client after opportunity to consider the facts and circumstances of the dispute." Ohio Bd. Comm. Griev. & Discip. Op. 96–9 (1996).

However, "commentators and most state bar ethics committees have concluded that mandatory arbitration provisions do not prospectively limit a lawyer's liability, but instead only prescribe a procedure for resolving such claims." ABA Formal Ethics Op. 02–425 (Feb. 20, 2002). Therefore, the ABA committee concluded that agreements for the binding arbitration of both fee and malpractice claims would be "ethically permissible" provided that (1) "the client has been fully apprised of the advantages and disadvantages of arbitration and has been given sufficient information to permit her to make an informed decision about whether to agree," and (2) "the arbitration provision does not insulate the lawyer from liability or limit the liability to which she would otherwise be exposed under common and/or statutory law." See also Maine Bd. of Bar Overseers Prof. Ethics Comm'n Op. 170 (1999)(the suggestion that someone is necessarily prejudiced by having to proceed to arbitration reflects a "jaundiced view of arbitration"). Is this rationale convincing?

8. Do you expect that resolution of consumer and malpractice claims that is "private"—that is, that uses non-"official" decision makers, does not establish precedent or communicate its decisions in reasoned opinions, and is otherwise withdrawn from public scrutiny—is likely to have the deterrent or accident-reduction effects of tort litigation?

9. Arbitration clauses found in consumer transactions are increasingly being challenged on the ground that they are not enforceable as contracts—because, for example, they are "unconscionable" contracts of adhesion. See the discussion at Section C.3.c. infra.

C. ARBITRATION AND THE COURTS

1. INTRODUCTION

The traditional attitude of judges towards arbitration has been one of considerable hostility, "explained," if at all, by ritual invocation of the phrase that agreements to submit disputes to arbitration "oust the jurisdiction of the courts." Perhaps this rhetorical flourish masked some concern over the diversion from the court system of cases implicating public values, or fear that private tribunals might ignore or undermine the enforcement of "legal" rules. Somewhat more cynically, one might also suppose that it originated in considerations of competition for business, at a time when judge's salaries still depended on fees paid by litigants.

At common law, if the parties did voluntarily submit a dispute to arbitration *and* the arbitrator proceeded to render an award, the award would be considered binding. Barring some exceptional defense such as arbitrator misconduct, the award could be enforced in a separate court action brought by the successful plaintiff. However, purely *executory* agreements to arbitrate had little force. A party could refuse to honor such an agreement and could revoke it at any time; a court would not specifically enforce an agreement to arbitrate existing or future disputes. While damages could in theory be awarded for breach of this contract, how could they possibly be calculated?[1] So a potential "defendant" could deprive the arbitration agreement of any effect simply by giving notice of his objection and refusing to participate in the process. A potential "plaintiff" could, after revocation, simply bring his own lawsuit, and the court would hear the case without regard to the agreement to arbitrate. A readable summary of the situation at common law can be found in Judge Frank's opinion in Kulukundis Shipping Co. S/A v. Amtorg Trading Corp., 126 F.2d 978 (2d Cir.1942).

Beginning with New York in 1920, almost all states have now passed statutes completely reversing the common law position on arbitration. The Uniform Arbitration Act, on which most of these modern statutes have been modeled, was adopted by the National Conference of the Commissioners on Uniform State Laws in 1955.[2] The Federal Arbitration Act (FAA) was enacted in 1925. All of these statutes are quite similar in their broad outlines, although there is considerable variation in detail. The Federal Act, because of its overwhelming importance, is set out in Appendix A, infra. Read the text of the Act carefully: It is deceptively simple for a statute which has grown to assume such pervasive importance. What does the Act do to change the common law attitude towards arbitration? How does it assure the enforceability of agreements to arbitrate?

The situation is further complicated by the fact that even in states with "modern" statutes modeled on the New York or Uniform Act, the statute is usually not interpreted to be exclusive. As a consequence,

---

1. See Munson v. Straits of Dover S.S. Co., 102 Fed. 926 (2d Cir.1900) (plaintiff sought damages, in the form of lawyer's fees and costs incurred in defending a lawsuit, for breach of agreement to arbitrate; held, plaintiff entitled to nominal damages only; judicial process is "theoretically at least, the safest and best devised by the wisdom and experience of mankind.").

2. A revised version of the Uniform Arbitration Act was approved by the NCCUSL at its Annual Meeting in August, 2000. The Revised Uniform Arbitration Act is available at http://www.law.upenn.edu/bll/ulc/ulc_frame.htm. Approved by the ABA and the AAA, it had been enacted in 12 states as of 2005.

"common law arbitration" still survives. Thus, even where the arbitration statute has not been complied with—for example, where there has been no written agreement to arbitrate or where the subject matter of the dispute has been specifically excluded from the coverage of the statute—the arbitrator's decision will have the same binding force it would have at common law, as long as consent to arbitrate has not been revoked and the parties have proceeded without objection to an award. See, e.g., L.H. Lacy Co. v. City of Lubbock, 559 S.W.2d 348 (Tex.1977) (arbitration statute did not apply to construction contracts); see generally Sturges and Reckson, Common–Law and Statutory Arbitration: Problems Arising From Their Coexistence, 46 Minn.L.Rev. 819 (1962).

Nor have state arbitration statutes frozen the independent *development* of the common law. On the contrary, in a number of places they seem to have aided in its growth. Increasingly, decisions can be found where courts will rely on the "pro-arbitration" policy of the state statute to enforce an arbitration agreement *outside* the statute's substantive scope, and *despite* one party's prior attempt to "revoke." See Olshan Demolishing Co. v. Angleton Independent School District, 684 S.W.2d 179 (Tex.App.— Houston [14th Dist.] 1984) (agreement to arbitrate lacked statutory notice; "[e]ncouraging arbitration will reduce some of the backlog in our trial courts"); Kodak Mining Co. v. Carrs Fork Corp., 669 S.W.2d 917 (Ky.1984) (statute then in force applied only to submission of existing disputes to arbitration).

2. THE FEDERAL ARBITRATION ACT AND STATE LAW

The FAA was enacted before *Erie v. Tompkins* (in 1938) called for a fundamental rethinking of the relationships between state and federal courts. Over the last 50 years, problems of federalism in the enforcement of arbitration agreements have surfaced on a number of occasions. Only recently have some fundamental issues been more or less settled.

Bernhardt v. Polygraphic Co. of America, Inc., 350 U.S. 198 (1956), was a diversity case in federal court. The contract provided that any future disputes would be settled by arbitration; the transaction was assumed *not* to "involve" interstate commerce. At that time, Vermont law made an agreement to arbitrate revocable at any time before an award was actually handed down. In such circumstances, could the federal court enforce the arbitration agreement? The Supreme Court said "no": In the absence of a "transaction involving commerce," *state* law on arbitration was to be applied in federal courts in diversity cases. Arbitration was therefore "substantive" for *Erie* purposes: "The change from a court of law to an arbitration panel may make a radical difference in ultimate result." Furthermore, the Court said, the "procedures" for enforcing arbitration agreements in section 3 of the Federal Act were limited by section 2; applying the FAA, therefore, even in a federal court, is dependent on the existence of "a transaction involving commerce."

It later became settled that the FAA had been enacted as an exercise of Congress' commerce and admiralty powers. The Act thus laid down substantive rules of decision, binding on federal courts even in diversity cases as long as interstate or foreign commerce or maritime matters were involved. In this respect, though, the FAA remains something of an anomaly among federal statutes: Although enacted under Congress' commerce power, of itself it confers no federal question *jurisdiction*. Therefore, an action to enforce an arbitration agreement under the Act does not "arise under" federal law but requires an *independent* source of federal jurisdiction, such as diversity or some other federal statute.

This line of cases raised still further questions: In cases that *do* involve foreign or interstate commerce, does the body of law fashioned by federal courts bind *state* courts as well? For example, would a Vermont court, in such a case, still be free to hold an arbitration agreement revocable, or is Vermont law to that effect preempted by the FAA?

Southland Corporation v. Keating

Supreme Court of the United States, 1984.
465 U.S. 1, 104 S.Ct. 852, 79 L.Ed.2d 1.

■ CHIEF JUSTICE BURGER delivered the opinion of the Court.

This case presents the questions (a) whether the California Franchise Investment Law, which invalidates certain arbitration agreements covered by the Federal Arbitration Act, violates the Supremacy Clause and (b) whether arbitration under the federal Act is impaired when a class-action structure is imposed on the process by the state courts.

Appellant Southland Corp. is the owner and franchisor of 7–Eleven convenience stores. Southland's standard franchise agreement provides each franchisee with a license to use certain registered trademarks, a lease or sublease of a convenience store owned or leased by Southland, inventory financing, and assistance in advertising and merchandising. The franchisees operate the stores, supply bookkeeping data, and pay Southland a fixed percentage of gross profits. The franchise agreement also contains the following provision requiring arbitration:

> Any controversy or claim arising out of or relating to this Agreement or the breach hereof shall be settled by arbitration in accordance with the Rules of the American Arbitration Association ... and judgment upon any award rendered by the arbitrator may be entered in any court having jurisdiction thereof.

Appellees are 7–Eleven franchisees. Between September 1975 and January 1977, several appellees filed individual actions against Southland in California Superior Court alleging, among other things, fraud, oral misrepresentation, breach of contract, breach of fiduciary duty, and violation of the disclosure requirements of the California Franchise Investment Law, Cal.Corp.Code § 31000 et seq. Southland's answer, in all but one of the individual actions, included the affirmative defense of failure to arbitrate.

In May 1977, appellee Keating filed a class action against Southland on behalf of a class that assertedly includes approximately 800 California franchisees. Keating's principal claims were substantially the same as those asserted by the other franchisees. After the various actions were consolidated, Southland petitioned to compel arbitration of the claims in all cases, and appellees moved for class certification.

The Superior Court granted Southland's motion to compel arbitration of all claims except those claims based on the Franchise Investment Law. The court did not pass on appellees' request for class certification. Southland appealed from the order insofar as it excluded from arbitration the claims based on the California statute. Appellees filed a petition for a writ of mandamus or prohibition in the California Court of Appeal arguing that the arbitration should proceed as a class action.

The California Court of Appeal reversed the trial court's refusal to compel arbitration of appellees' claims under the Franchise Investment Law. That court interpreted the arbitration clause to require arbitration of all claims asserted under the Franchise Investment Law, and construed the Franchise Investment Law not to invalidate such agreements to arbitrate. Alternatively, the court concluded that if the Franchise Investment Law rendered arbitration agreements involving commerce unenforceable, it would conflict with § 2 of the Federal Arbitration Act and therefore be invalid under the Supremacy Clause. The Court of Appeal also determined that there was no "insurmountable obstacle" to conducting an arbitration on a classwide basis, and issued a writ of mandate directing the trial court to conduct class-certification proceedings.

The California Supreme Court, by a vote of 4–2, reversed the ruling that claims asserted under the Franchise Investment Law are arbitrable. The California Supreme Court interpreted the Franchise Investment Law to require judicial consideration of claims brought under that statute and concluded that the California statute did not contravene the federal Act.

* * *

The California Franchise Investment Law provides:

Any condition, stipulation or provision purporting to bind any person acquiring any franchise to waive compliance with any provision of this law or any rule or order hereunder is void.

Cal.Corp.Code Ann. § 31512.

The California Supreme Court interpreted this statute to require judicial consideration of claims brought under the state statute and accordingly refused to enforce the parties' contract to arbitrate such claims. So interpreted the California Franchise Investment Law directly conflicts with § 2 of the Federal Arbitration Act and violates the Supremacy Clause.

In enacting § 2 of the federal Act, Congress declared a national policy favoring arbitration and withdrew the power of the states to require a judicial forum for the resolution of claims which the contracting parties agreed to resolve by arbitration. * * *

We discern only two limitations on the enforceability of arbitration provisions governed by the Federal Arbitration Act: they must be part of a written maritime contract or a contract "evidencing a transaction involving commerce" and such clauses may be revoked upon "grounds as exist at law or in equity for the revocation of any contract." We see nothing in the Act indicating that the broad principle of enforceability is subject to any additional limitations under state law.

The Federal Arbitration Act rests on the authority of Congress to enact substantive rules under the Commerce Clause. In Prima Paint Corp. v. Flood & Conklin Mfg. Co., 388 U.S. 395 (1967) [infra p. 87], the Court examined the legislative history of the Act and concluded that the statute "is based upon ... the incontestable federal foundations of 'control over interstate commerce and over admiralty.' " The contract in *Prima Paint,* as here, contained an arbitration clause. One party in that case alleged that the other had committed fraud in the inducement of the contract, although not of the arbitration clause in particular, and sought to have the claim of fraud adjudicated in federal court. The Court held that, notwithstanding a contrary state rule, consideration of a claim of fraud in the inducement of a contract "is for the arbitrators and not for the courts." The Court relied for this holding on Congress' broad power to fashion substantive rules under the Commerce Clause.

At least since 1824 Congress' authority under the Commerce Clause has been held plenary. Gibbons v. Ogden, 9 Wheat 1, 196 (1824). In the words of Chief Justice Marshall, the authority of Congress is "the power to regulate; that is, to prescribe the rule by which commerce is to be governed." The statements of the Court in *Prima Paint* that the Arbitration Act was an exercise of the Commerce Clause power clearly implied that the substantive rules of the Act were to apply in state as well as federal courts.

* * *

Although the legislative history is not without ambiguities, there are strong indications that Congress had in mind something more than making arbitration agreements enforceable only in the federal courts. The House Report plainly suggests the more comprehensive objectives:

The purpose of this bill is to make valid and enforceable agreements for arbitration contained *in contracts involving interstate commerce* or within the jurisdiction or admiralty, *or* which may be the subject of litigation in the Federal courts.

HR Rep No. 96, 68th Cong, 1st Sess, 1 (1924). (emphasis added).

This broader purpose can also be inferred from the reality that Congress would be less likely to address a problem whose impact was confined to federal courts than a problem of large significance in the field of commerce. The Arbitration Act sought to "overcome the rule of equity, that equity will not specifically enforce an[y] arbitration agreement." The House Report accompanying the bill stated:

The need for the law arises from.... the jealousy of the English courts for their own jurisdiction.... This jealousy survived for so lon[g] a period that the principle became firmly embedded in the English common law and was adopted with it by the American courts. The courts have felt that the precedent was too strongly fixed to be overturned without legislative enactment....

Surely this makes clear that the House Report contemplated a broad reach of the Act, unencumbered by state-law constraints.

* * *

Justice O'Connor argues that Congress viewed the Arbitration Act "as a procedural statute, applicable only in federal courts." If it is correct that Congress sought only to create a procedural remedy in the federal courts, there can be no explanation for the express limitation in the Arbitration Act to contracts "involving commerce." For example, when Congress has authorized this Court to prescribe the rules of procedure in the federal Courts of Appeals, District Courts, and bankruptcy courts, it has not limited the power of the Court to prescribe rules applicable only to causes of action involving commerce. We would expect that if Congress, in enacting the Arbitration Act, was creating what it thought to be a procedural rule applicable only in federal courts, it would not so limit the Act to transactions involving commerce. On the other hand, Congress would need to call on the Commerce Clause if it intended the Act to apply in state courts. Yet at the same time, its reach would be limited to transactions involving interstate commerce. We therefore view the "involving commerce" requirement in § 2, not as an inexplicable limitation on the power of the federal courts, but as a necessary qualification on a statute intended to apply in state and federal courts.

Under the interpretation of the Arbitration Act urged by Justice O'Connor, claims brought under the California Franchise Investment Law are not arbitrable when they are raised in state court. Yet it is clear beyond question that if this suit had been brought as a diversity action in a federal district court, the arbitration clause would have been enforceable. The interpretation given to the Arbitration Act by the California Supreme Court would therefore encourage and reward forum shopping. We are unwilling to attribute to Congress the intent, in drawing on the comprehensive powers of the Commerce Clause, to create a right to enforce an arbitration contract and yet make the right dependent for its enforcement on the particular forum in which it is asserted. And since the overwhelming proportion of all civil litigation in this country is in the state courts, we cannot believe Congress intended to limit the Arbitration Act to disputes subject only to *federal*-court jurisdiction.[9] Such an interpretation would

---

9. While the Federal Arbitration Act creates federal substantive law requiring the parties to honor arbitration agreements, it does not create any independent federal question jurisdiction under 28 USC § 1331 or otherwise. This seems implicit in the provisions in § 3 for a stay by a "court in which such suit is pending" and in § 4 that enforcement may be ordered by "any United States district court which, save for such agreement,

frustrate congressional intent to place "[a]n arbitration agreement ... upon the same footing as other contracts, where it belongs." HR Rep No. 96, 68th Cong, 1st Sess, 1 (1924).

In creating a substantive rule applicable in state as well as federal courts,[10] Congress intended to foreclose state legislative attempts to undercut the enforceability of arbitration agreements.[11] We hold that § 31512 of the California Franchise Investment Law violates the Supremacy Clause.

The judgment of the California Supreme Court denying enforcement of the arbitration agreement is reversed; as to the question whether the Federal Arbitration Act precludes a class-action arbitration and any other issues not raised in the California courts, no decision by this Court would be appropriate at this time. As to the latter issues, the case is remanded for further proceedings not inconsistent with this opinion.

■ JUSTICE STEVENS, concurring in part and dissenting in part.

The Court holds that an arbitration clause that is enforceable in an action in a federal court is equally enforceable if the action is brought in a state court. I agree with that conclusion. Although Justice O'Connor's review of the legislative history of the Federal Arbitration Act demonstrates that the 1925 Congress that enacted the statute viewed the statute as essentially procedural in nature, I am persuaded that the intervening developments in the law compel the conclusion that the Court has reached. I am nevertheless troubled by one aspect of the case that seems to trouble none of my colleagues.

For me it is not "clear beyond question that if this suit had been brought as a diversity action in a federal district court, the arbitration

---

would have jurisdiction under title 28, in a civil action or in admiralty of the subject matter of a suit arising out of the controversy between the parties."

10. The contention is made that the Court's interpretation of § 2 of the Act renders §§ 3 and 4 "largely superfluous." This misreads our holding and the Act. In holding that the Arbitration Act preempts a state law that withdraws the power to enforce arbitration agreements, we do not hold that §§ 3 and 4 of the Arbitration Act apply to proceedings in state courts. Section 4, for example, provides that the Federal Rules of Civil Procedure apply in proceedings to compel arbitration. The Federal Rules do not apply in such state-court proceedings.

11. * * * Justice Stevens dissents in part on the ground that § 2 of the Arbitration Act permits a party to nullify an agreement to arbitrate on "such grounds as exist at law or in equity for the revocation of any contract." We agree, of course, that a party may assert general contract defenses such as

fraud to avoid enforcement of an arbitration agreement. We conclude, however, that the defense to arbitration found in the California Franchise Investment Law is not a ground that exists at law or in equity "for the revocation of any contract" but merely a ground that exists for the revocation of arbitration provisions in contracts subject to the California Franchise Investment Law. Moreover, under this dissenting view, "a state policy of providing special protection for franchisees ... can be recognized without impairing the basic purposes of the federal statute." If we accepted this analysis, states could wholly eviscerate Congressional intent to place arbitration agreements "upon the same footing as other contracts" simply by passing statutes such as the Franchise Investment Law. We have rejected this analysis because it is in conflict with the Arbitration Act and would permit states to override the declared policy requiring enforcement of arbitration agreements.

clause would have been enforceable." The general rule prescribed by § 2 of the Federal Arbitration Act is that arbitration clauses in contracts involving interstate transactions are enforceable as a matter of federal law. That general rule, however, is subject to an exception based on "such grounds as exist at law or in equity for the revocation of any contract." I believe that exception leaves room for the implementation of certain substantive state policies that would be undermined by enforcing certain categories of arbitration clauses.

The exercise of state authority in a field traditionally occupied by state law will not be deemed preempted by a federal statute unless that was the clear and manifest purpose of Congress. Moreover, even where a federal statute does displace state authority, it "rarely occupies a legal field completely, totally excluding all participation by the legal systems of the states.... Federal legislation, on the whole, has been conceived and drafted on an ad hoc basis to accomplish limited objectives. It builds upon legal relationships established by the states, altering or supplanting them only so far as necessary for the special purpose." P. Bator, P. Mishkin, D. Shapiro, & H. Wechsler, Hart and Wechsler's The Federal Courts and the Federal System 470–471 (2d ed. 1973).

The limited objective of the Federal Arbitration Act was to abrogate the general common-law rule against specific enforcement of arbitration agreements, and a state statute which merely codified the general common-law rule—either directly by employing the prior doctrine of revocability or indirectly by declaring all such agreements void—would be pre-empted by the Act. However, beyond this conclusion, which seems compelled by the language of § 2 and case law concerning the Act, it is by no means clear that Congress intended entirely to displace state authority in this field. Indeed, while it is an understatement to say that "the legislative history of the ... Act ... reveals little awareness on the part of Congress that state law might be affected," it must surely be true that given the lack of a "clear mandate from Congress as to the extent to which state statutes and decisions are to be superseded, we must be cautious in construing the act lest we excessively encroach on the powers which Congressional policy, if not the Constitution, would reserve to the states."

The textual basis in the Act for avoiding such encroachment is the clause of § 2 which provides that arbitration agreements are subject to revocation on such grounds as exist at law or in equity for the revocation of any contract. The Act, however, does not define what grounds for revocation may be permissible, and hence it would appear that the judiciary must fashion the limitations as a matter of federal common law. In doing so, we must first recognize that as the " 'saving clause' in § 2 indicates, the purpose of Congress in 1925 was to make arbitration agreements as enforceable as other contracts, but not more so." The existence of a federal statute enunciating a substantive federal policy does not necessarily require the inexorable application of a uniform federal rule of decision notwithstanding the differing conditions which may exist in the several States and regardless of the decisions of the States to exert police powers as they deem best for the welfare of their citizens. Indeed the lower courts generally look to state law regarding questions of formation of the arbitration agreement under § 2, which is entirely appropriate so long as the state rule does not conflict with the policy of § 2.

A contract which is deemed void is surely revocable at law or in equity, and the California Legislature has declared all conditions purporting to waive compliance with the protections of the Franchise Investment Laws, including but not limited to arbitration provisions, void as a matter of public policy. Given the importance to the State of franchise relationships, the relative disparity in the bargaining positions between the franchisor and the franchisee, and the remedial purposes of the California Act, I believe this declaration of state policy is entitled to respect.

* * *

[A] state policy of providing special protection for franchisees, such as that expressed in California's Franchise Investment Law, can be recognized without impairing the basic purposes of the federal statute. Like the majority of the California Supreme Court, I am not persuaded that Congress intended the preemptive effect of this statute to be "so unyielding as to require enforcement of an agreement to arbitrate a dispute over the application of a regulatory statute which a state legislature, in conformity with analogous federal policy, has decided should be left to judicial enforcement."

Thus * * * I respectfully dissent from [the Court's] conclusion concerning the enforceability of the arbitration agreement. On that issue, I would affirm the judgment of the California Supreme Court.

■ JUSTICE O'CONNOR, with whom JUSTICE REHNQUIST joins, dissenting.

The majority opinion decides three issues. First, it holds that § 2 creates federal substantive rights that must be enforced by the state courts. Second, though the issue is not raised in this case, the Court states that § 2 substantive rights may not be the basis for invoking federal-court jurisdiction under 28 U.S.C. § 1331. Third, the Court reads § 2 to require state courts to enforce § 2 rights using procedures that mimic those specified for federal courts by FAA §§ 3 and 4. The first of these conclusions is unquestionably wrong as a matter of statutory construction; the second appears to be an attempt to limit the damage done by the first; the third is unnecessary and unwise.

One rarely finds a legislative history as unambiguous as the FAA's. That history establishes conclusively that the 1925 Congress viewed the FAA as a procedural statute, applicable only in federal courts, derived, Congress believed, largely from the federal power to control the jurisdiction of the federal courts.

In 1925 Congress emphatically believed arbitration to be a matter of "procedure." At hearings on the Act congressional Subcommittees were told: "The theory on which you do this is that you have the right to tell the Federal courts how to proceed."

* * *

Since *Bernhardt*, a right to arbitration has been characterized as "substantive," and that holding is not challenged here. But Congress in 1925 did not characterize the FAA as this Court did in 1956. Congress believed that the FAA established nothing more than a rule of procedure, a rule therefore applicable only in the federal courts.

* * *

Yet another indication that Congress did not intend the FAA to govern state-court proceedings is found in the powers Congress relied on in passing the Act. The FAA might have been grounded on Congress' powers to regulate interstate and maritime affairs, since the Act extends only to contracts in those areas. There are, indeed, references in the legislative history to the corresponding federal powers. More numerous, however, are the references to Congress' pre-Erie power to prescribe "general law" applicable in all federal courts. At the congressional hearings, for example: "Congress rests solely upon its power to prescribe the jurisdiction and duties of the Federal courts." * * * Plainly, a power derived from Congress' Art III control over federal-court jurisdiction would not by any flight of fancy permit Congress to control proceedings in state courts.

* * *

Section 2, like the rest of the FAA, should have no application whatsoever in state courts. Assuming, to the contrary, that § 2 *does* create a federal right that the state courts must enforce, state courts should nonetheless be allowed, at least in the first instance, to fashion their own procedures for enforcing the right. Unfortunately, the Court seems to direct that the arbitration clause at issue here must be *specifically* enforced; apparently no other means of enforcement is permissible.[20]

It is settled that a state court must honor federally created rights and that it may not unreasonably undermine them by invoking contrary local procedure. " '[T]he assertion of federal rights, when plainly and reasonably made, is not to be defeated under the name of local practice.' " Brown v. Western Ry. Co. of Alabama, 338 U.S. 294, 299 (1949). But absent specific direction from Congress the state courts have always been permitted to apply their own reasonable procedures when enforcing federal rights. Before we undertake to read a set of complex and mandatory procedures

---

20. If my understanding of the Court's opinion is correct, the Court has made § 3 of the FAA binding on the state courts. But * * * § 3 by its own terms governs only federal-court proceedings. Moreover, if § 2, standing alone, creates a federal right to specific enforcement of arbitration agreements §§ 3 and 4 are, of course, largely superfluous. And if § 2 implicitly incorporates §§ 3 and 4 procedures for making arbitration agreements enforceable before arbitration begins, why not also § 9 procedures concerning venue, personal jurisdiction, and notice for enforcing an arbitrator's award after arbitration ends? One set of procedures is of little use without the other.

into § 2's brief and general language, we should at a minimum allow state courts and legislatures a chance to develop their own methods for enforcing the new federal rights. Some might choose to award compensatory or punitive damages for the violation of an arbitration agreement; some might award litigation costs to the party who remained willing to arbitrate; some might affirm the "validity and enforceability" of arbitration agreements in other ways. Any of these approaches would vindicate § 2 rights in a manner fully consonant with the language and background of that provision.

The unelaborated terms of § 2 certainly invite flexible enforcement. At common law many jurisdictions were hostile to arbitration agreements. That hostility was reflected in two different doctrines: "revocability," which allowed parties to repudiate arbitration agreements at any time before the arbitrator's award was made, and "invalidity" or "unenforceability," equivalent rules that flatly denied any remedy for the failure to honor an arbitration agreement. In contrast, common-law jurisdictions that enforced arbitration agreements did so in at least three different ways— through actions for damages, actions for specific enforcement, or by enforcing sanctions imposed by trade and commercial associations on members who violated arbitration agreements. In 1925 a forum allowing any one of these remedies would have been thought to recognize the "validity" and "enforceability" of arbitration clauses.

* * *

The Court rejects the idea of requiring the FAA to be applied only in federal courts partly out of concern with the problem of forum shopping. The concern is unfounded. Because the FAA makes the federal courts equally accessible to both parties to a dispute, no forum shopping would be possible even if we gave the FAA a construction faithful to the congressional intent. In controversies involving incomplete diversity of citizenship there is simply no access to federal court and therefore no possibility of forum shopping. In controversies *with* complete diversity of citizenship the FAA grants federal-court access equally to both parties; no party can gain any advantage by forum shopping. Even when the party resisting arbitration initiates an action in state court, the opposing party can invoke FAA § 4 and promptly secure a federal court order to compel arbitration. See, e.g., Moses H. Cone Memorial Hospital v. Mercury Construction Corp., 460 U.S. 1 (1983).

* * *

Apparently confident that state courts are not competent to devise their own procedures for protecting the newly discovered federal right, the Court summarily prescribes a specific procedure, found nowhere in § 2 or its common-law origins, that the state courts are to follow.

Today's decision is unfaithful to congressional intent, unnecessary, and, in light of the FAA's antecedents and the intervening contraction of federal power, inexplicable. Although arbitration is a worthy alternative to litigation, today's exercise in judicial revisionism goes too far. I respectfully dissent.

NOTES AND QUESTIONS

1. Now that § 2 of the FAA makes arbitration agreements enforceable in state courts, does the enforcement mechanism provided by the rest of the Act accompany it? For example, to what extent are state courts required to supply remedies equivalent to those in § 3 (stay of court proceedings) and § 4 (order to compel arbitration)? Note that these sections appear to speak only in terms of proceedings *in federal district courts*. Compare footnote 10 of the majority opinion in *Southland* with footnote 20 of Justice O'Connor's dissent. What about Justice O'Connor's suggestion that specific performance of arbitration agreements is not necessary to vindicate the federal right because damages might be an acceptable alternative?

See Alan Scott Rau, "Does State Arbitration Law Matter At All? Part II: A Continuing Role for State Law," in ADR & The Law 208, 211 (15th ed. 1999):

> While the Supreme Court has been curiously and consistently coy on the question of whether state courts are bound by §§ 3 and 4, it seems obvious enough that these provisions exist to supply the remedial mechanisms necessary to make the core substantive mandate of § 2 effective. Once it is held that the states are bound by § 2 to treat arbitration agreements as enforceable, the suggestion that the remedy of specific performance is not necessary to vindicate the federal interest simply flies in the face of history, returning us to the era before modern arbitration statutes, when predispute arbitration clauses were enforceable only through the dubious means of actions for damages. In addition to the obligation to grant stays or compel arbitration, other provisions of §§ 3 and 4 may also call on states to align their procedures to some extent with the demands of federal arbitration policy. To say, for example, that courts "shall proceed summarily to the trial" of any issue concerning the making of the arbitration agreement may require applications to be heard under a state's local version of motion practice, or at least in some expeditious and summary hearing rather than in a plenary action.
>
> Other aspects of §§ 3 and 4 may not, however, "dig into" substantive rights in quite the same way. Section 4 provides for a jury determination of contested issues concerning the "making of the arbitration agreement." But a state might prefer that these issues be decided by the *court*. [*See* Rosenthal v. Great Western Fin. Securities Corp., 14 Cal.4th 394, 58 Cal.Rptr.2d 875, 926 P.2d 1061 (Cal. 1996)].
>
> To have a court rather than a jury pass on the existence of an arbitration agreement hardly appears to undermine or frustrate the arbitration process; moreover, a bench trial of the issue should not be expected to "frequently and predictably" lead to different outcomes. State rules denying a jury trial are certainly consistent both with the

summary nature of the proceeding, and with the traditional treatment of these specific performance actions as equitable—and they can only result in making arbitration a speedier and more efficient process. It is not particularly clear in any event what role the choice of a jury in § 4 was intended to play in the overall statutory scheme: For some reason it is only "the party alleged to be in default"—presumably the party who has "failed, neglected, or refused" to proceed with arbitration—who under § 4 is entitled to ask for a jury trial; the party "aggrieved" by such "failure, neglect, or refusal" has no equivalent right. After such an analysis it might be concluded that state law ought to govern on such matters, even where the parties themselves have not expressly chosen to adopt such law.

2. The same question might be raised in relation to other FAA provisions. Does § 12 (time limits for seeking to vacate or modify an award) override state law? See Jeereddi A. Prasad, M.D., Inc. v. Investors Associates, Inc., 82 F.Supp.2d 365 (D.N.J.2000)(state law permitted challenges to arbitration awards to be raised in opposition to a motion to confirm the award, even after 90 days; held, this contravenes federal policy favoring quick resolution of arbitrations and the enforcement of arbitration awards; "in the absence of contractual intent to the contrary, the FAA trumps the New York rule"). What about § 16 (appealability of trial-court orders dealing with arbitration)? See Bush v. Paragon Property, Inc., 165 Or.App. 700, 997 P.2d 882 (Or.App.2000)("Congress is without power under Article I to require a state to modify its normal judicial procedures, at least when those procedures do not absolutely defeat the congressional purpose").

The extent to which states, in deference to federal law, are required to abandon "state procedural law otherwise applicable in state court" is often referred to as the "reverse-*Erie*" problem. See generally Kevin M. Clermont, Reverse–*Erie* (Cornell Legal Studies Res. Paper 05–021, Aug. 2005)(the symmetry is not perfect, however, because in the "middle area between state and federal substantive law, state courts must apply federal procedural law to federally created claims more extensively than federal courts must apply state procedural law to state-created claims").

3. Virginia law requires automobile manufacturers to submit their standard franchise agreements to the Department of Motor Vehicles for approval. Saturn Corporation, a subsidiary of General Motors, includes binding arbitration clauses in all franchise agreements with its dealers. The Department refused to approve the Saturn agreement unless it contained "an opt out provision" for dealers; its position was that while arbitration clauses were permissible, they could not be made "nonnegotiable." Saturn's challenge to the Department's action was successful: State law that "singles out" arbitration clauses, or treats them "more harshly than other contracts," is preempted by the FAA; since Virginia "has no general contract law restricting nonnegotiable provisions in standardized contracts, Virginia may not bar automobile manufacturers from making arbitration provisions a nonnegotiable term of doing business. * * * If a dealer does not wish to agree to nonnegotiable arbitration provisions, the dealer need not do business with Saturn." Saturn Distribution Corp. v. Williams, 905 F.2d 719 (4th Cir.1990).

4.   Under Florida law, every arbitration agreement between a securities dealer and a customer must give the customer "the option" of arbitrating before the AAA "or other independent nonindustry arbitration forum" as well as before an "industry forum" such as a stock exchange. On what grounds could it be argued that such state law conflicts with the FAA? See Securities Industry Ass'n v. Lewis, 751 F.Supp. 205 (S.D.Fla.1990).

5.   Under the Michigan Franchise Investment Law, any "provision requiring *that arbitration or litigation* be conducted outside this state" is "void and unenforceable if contained in any document relating to a franchise." Is this part of the statute preempted by the FAA? See Flint Warm Air Supply Co., Inc. v. York Int'l Corp., 115 F.Supp.2d 820 (E.D.Mich.2000); see also Bradley v. Harris Research, Inc., 275 F.3d 884 (9th Cir. 2001)(California Franchise Relations Act provided that any "provision in a franchise agreement restricting venue to a forum outside this state is void"); OPE Int'l L.P. v. Chet Morrison Contractors, Inc., 258 F.3d 443 (5th Cir.2001)(with respect to construction projects to be carried on within Louisiana, Louisiana statute provided that any clause "requiring disputes * * * to be resolved in a forum outside of this state or requiring their interpretation to be governed by the laws of another jurisdiction [is] inequitable and against the public policy of this state").

6.   Individual investors opened an account with a discount brokerage firm registered in Delaware; the account agreement contained an arbitration clause. The firm advised the investors to buy certain stock that declined dramatically in value. The investors complained to the Division of Securities of the Delaware Department of Justice, and the state later instituted proceedings against the firm, alleging "fraudulent and unethical practices" in violation of state law in connection with the sale of stock. The state sought to impose fines and to revoke the firm's registration, and it also sought rescission of the stock transactions between the firm and the individual investors. The brokerage firm then brought suit to enjoin the state from pursuing this rescission action on behalf of the investors, alleging that the state could not properly pursue rescission since the firm "had a contractual right to arbitrate [the investors'] claims." The rescission remedy "circumvents [the firm's] rights under the FAA and thus violates the Supremacy Clause." What result? See Olde Discount Corp. v. Tupman, 1 F.3d 202 (3d Cir.1993).

7.   A state enacts a version of the Uniform Prudent Investor Act; the Uniform Act was adopted in 1994 to reverse the much-criticized historical rule prohibiting trustees from delegating investment and management functions. It permits a trustee to delegate such functions "that a prudent trustee of comparable skills could properly delegate under the circumstances." And if he exercises "reasonable care, skill and caution" in doing so, he is not liable to the trust, or to the beneficiaries, for any actions of the agent whom he selects. The state qualifies this, however, by adding one exception: The trustee remains liable if under the terms of the delegation, "the trustee or a beneficiary of the trust is required to arbitrate disputes with the agent." Tex. Prop. Code § 117.011. What can explain such a statute? Is it a permissible exercise of state power?

8. The FAA applies to any "maritime transaction" or "contract evidencing a transaction involving commerce." For many years it remained unclear just how broadly this language should be read as a Congressional exercise of control over "commerce." The FAA is the only federal statute that uses the word "involving" to describe a relation to interstate commerce, and different courts adopted different standards as to when transactions were considered to "involve" commerce for purposes of the Act. See, e.g., Metro Industrial Painting Corp. v. Terminal Construction Co., Inc., 287 F.2d 382, 388 (2d Cir.1961) (Lumbard, C.J., concurring) (FAA should apply only when the parties "contemplated substantial interstate activity," for only then would the Act advance their expectations at the time of contracting). Some state courts have naturally resisted a broad application of the FAA—warning that it "would tend to defeat the doctrine of federalism, making that doctrine a hollow shell," and that it would "stifle" the efforts of the states to develop "creative" solutions "other than those that catch the fancy of Congress," Sisters of the Visitation v. Cochran Plastering Co., Inc., 775 So.2d 759 (Ala. 2000).

However, the Supreme Court has recently made it clear that § 2 is to be given the broadest possible scope. The phrase "involving" commerce is the "functional equivalent" of "affecting" commerce, the Court has held, and both terms "signal an intent to exercise Congress's commerce power to the full." If a transaction "in fact" involves commerce, it is within the FAA even if the parties had never contemplated any connection to interstate commerce. The FAA therefore applied to a contract in which homeowners obtained a lifetime "Termite Protection Plan" from the local office of a Terminix franchisee—and state courts were therefore obligated to enforce the arbitration clause in such a contract, despite a state statute invalidating pre-dispute arbitration agreements. Allied–Bruce Terminix Cos., Inc. v. Dobson, 513 U.S. 265 (1995). Nor is it necessary that in any particular case the effect on interstate commerce be "substantial": It is clear that Congress' power to regulate economic activity extends to activity "that might, through repetition elsewhere," or "when viewed in the aggregate," come to substantially affect commerce—even though the effect in any individual case may be de minimis. See Citizens Bank v. Alafabco, Inc., 539 U.S. 52 (2003)(debt-restructuring agreements; "no elaborate explanation is needed to make evident the broad impact of commercial lending on the national economy or Congress' power to regulate that activity pursuant to the Commerce Clause"); see also Wickard v. Filburn, 317 U.S. 111 (1942)(upholding the application of the Agricultural Adjustment Act to the growing of wheat for home consumption).

9. The question whether the FAA applies to individual employment agreements also remained unsettled for many years. See the proviso to § 1 of the Act. A consensus gradually emerged in the lower courts, under which the § 1 exclusion should be narrowly limited to workers—like seamen and railroad employees—who are actually engaged "in the transportation industries or in the actual movement of goods in interstate commerce." E.g., Hampton v. ITT Corp., 829 F.Supp. 202 (S.D.Tex.1993) ("plaintiffs' employment in the loan servicing industry does not place them within [this] narrow category"). On this interpretation, except for workers literally engaged in interstate transportation, the FAA would apply to employment contracts to the same extent as to any other contract. The Supreme Court, narrowly divided 5–4, finally ratified this general understanding in Circuit City Stores, Inc. v. Adams, 532 U.S. 105 (2001). Justice Kennedy for the Court asserted that "the text of the FAA forecloses the construction" that all employment contracts are excluded from the scope of the Act: The "application of the maxim *ejusdem generis*" provides an "insurmountable textual obstacle" to that reading; in addition, "the plain meaning of the words 'engaged in commerce' [in § 1] is narrower than the more open-ended formulations 'affecting commerce' and 'involving commerce.' " And the Court should not, he added, "chip away at *Southland [v. Keating]* by indirection."

There has been little pressure to apply the Federal Arbitration Act to collective bargaining agreements, given the well-developed body of law enforcing arbitration clauses under § 301 of the Labor Management Relations Act—although, as the Supreme Court has noted, even in such cases "the federal courts have often looked to the [FAA] for guidance," United Paperworkers Int'l Union v. Misco, Inc., 484 U.S. 29, 40 n. 9 (1987). Cf. Coca–Cola Bottling Co. of New York v. Soft Drink & Brewery Workers, 242 F.3d 52 (2d Cir. 2001)("Given the difference in eras [between the respective dates of the two statutes] and the intervening revolution in labor policy, adherence to the FAA in Section 301 cases may led to anomalous or even bizarre results").

10.   The courts never tire of reminding us that arbitration is a "creature of contract"—and so "parties are generally free to structure their arbitration agreements as they see fit. Just as they may limit by contract the issues which they will arbitrate, so too may they specify by contract the rules under which that arbitration will be conducted." Volt Information Sciences, Inc. v. Board of Trustees of Leland Stanford Jr. Univ., 489 U.S. 468, 478–79 (1989). Should it not follow, then, that a particular state rule concerning arbitration—even one that would otherwise be preempted by the FAA—can still be "captured" by the parties, and validly incorporated as part of their agreement, if they choose to do so?

The answer appears to be "yes"—but since the FAA is now the "default rule," such an expression of contractual intent must be particularly explicit; a boilerplate choice-of-law clause will probably not suffice. See Stone & Webster, Inc. v. Baker Process, Inc., 210 F.Supp.2d 1177, 1183 (S.D. Cal. 2002)(joinder of parties; "if parties to an arbitration agreement subject to the FAA intend to be bound by state procedural rules, they must expressly incorporate those state procedural rules into their contract"; if they have not done so, "then the default presumption is that the FAA was intended to govern"); Sovak v. Chugai Pharmaceutical Co., 280 F.3d 1266,

1269 (9th Cir. 2002)(waiver; "the strong default presumption is that the FAA, not state law, supplies the rules for arbitration"); Puerto Rico Tel. Co., Inc. v. U.S. Phone Mfg. Corp., 427 F.3d 21 (1st Cir. 2005)(standard for vacatur; "the mere inclusion of a generic choice-of-law clause within the arbitration agreement is not sufficient to require the application of state law concerning the scope of review, since there is a strong federal policy requiring limited review," and "allowing more searching judicial review would inherently limit the authority of arbitrators"); Roadway Package System, Inc. v. Kayser, 257 F.3d 287, 289, 294 (3d Cir. 2001)(same; "because few (if any) federal statutes other than the FAA even *permit* parties to opt out of the standards contained in them, we are confident that this particular issue rarely occurs to contracting parties *ex ante*."). You can find a more detailed examination of this problem at pp. 238–40, and pp. 307–10, infra.

3. THE AGREEMENT TO ARBITRATE

a. ARBITRATION CLAUSES AND CONTRACT FORMATION

Under the modern federal and state statutes we have just been introduced to, the first requisite, of course, is an *enforceable agreement* providing for arbitration between the parties to the dispute. Where an arbitration clause calls for arbitration of any *future* dispute that may arise out of a contractual relationship, the clause may well be a small, little-noticed part of a much more complex document. Parties are likely to plan primarily for their performance, and only desultorily for what may happen should trouble arise from non-performance. And where firms exchange forms printed in advance, without separately agreeing (or even paying particularly careful attention) to everything that these forms contain, the challenge to the legal system to make some sense out of the transaction is at its most intense. The stage is then set for what lawyers and law students are trained to call "the battle of the forms."

Whether an arbitration clause has become part of a valid and enforceable contract is at least in the first instance a question of ordinary contract law. You may recall in fact the rather tortured attempt of the Uniform Commercial Code to provide some solution to the "battle of the forms" problem. UCC § 2–207 provides that

(1) A definite and seasonable expression of acceptance or a written confirmation which is sent within a reasonable time operates as an acceptance even though it states terms additional to or different from those offered or agreed upon, unless acceptance is expressly made conditional on assent to the additional or different terms.

(2) The additional terms are to be construed as proposals for addition to the contract. Between merchants such terms become part of the contract unless:

(a) the offer expressly limits acceptance to the terms of the offer;

(b) they materially alter it; or

(c) notification of objection to them has already been given or is given within a reasonable time after notice of them is received.

Assume that an exchange of forms creates a contract under UCC 2–207(1) but that only the *second* form contains a clause providing for the arbitration of future disputes. Does this clause become part of the contract?

The New York Court of Appeals considered this question in In the Matter of the Arbitration Between Marlene Industries Corp. v. Carnac Textiles, Inc., 45 N.Y.2d 327, 408 N.Y.S.2d 410, 380 N.E.2d 239 (1978). This case involved conflicting forms sent in confirmation of an *oral order* placed by the buyer; the seller's "acknowledgment" form, sent last, alone provided for arbitration but was not made "expressly conditional" on the buyer's assent to that or any other term. The Court of Appeals held that:

> the inclusion of an arbitration agreement materially alters a contract for the sale of goods, and thus, pursuant to section 2–207(2)(b) it will not become a part of such a contract unless both parties explicitly agree to it.

> It has long been the rule in this State that the parties to a commercial transaction "will not be held to have chosen arbitration as the forum for the resolution of their disputes in the absence of an express, unequivocal agreement to that effect; absent such an explicit commitment neither party may be compelled to arbitrate." The reason for this requirement, quite simply, is that by agreeing to arbitrate a party waives in large part many of his normal rights under the procedural and substantive law of the State, and it would be unfair to infer such a significant waiver on the basis of anything less than a clear indication of intent.

> Since an arbitration agreement in the context of a commercial transaction "must be clear and direct, and must not depend upon implication, inveiglement or subtlety ... [its] existence ... should not depend solely upon the conflicting fine print of commercial forms which cross one another but never meet." Thus, at least under this so-called "New York Rule", it is clear that an arbitration clause is a material addition which can become part of a contract only if it is expressly assented to by both parties. Applying these principles to this case, we conclude that the contract between Marlene and Carnac does not contain an arbitration clause; hence, the motion to permanently stay arbitration should have been granted.

In New York, therefore, an arbitration clause has been said to be a "per se material alteration" of any agreement.[1] Cf. Sibcoimtrex, Inc. v. American Foods Group, Inc., 241 F.Supp.2d 104 (D. Mass. 2003)(advocating a "fact specific, case-by-case analysis" to determine whether arbitration should become part of the contract; the court nevertheless found the arbitration clause to be "material" because as "an agreement to forego

---

1. Supak & Sons Mfg. Co., Inc. v. Pervel Industries, Inc., 593 F.2d 135, 136 (4th Cir.1979).

other available avenues of seeking relief"—"most notably including" trial by jury—the clause functioned as a "limitation of remedies," and noted that "a clause surrendering in advance any potential objection to personal jurisdiction in Minnesota [the site of the arbitration] 'is not a trivial or incidental concession' "); Jack Greenberg, Inc. v. Velleman Corp., 1985 WL 731677 n.1 (E.D.Pa.1985) (clause provided for arbitration under AAA rules "as supplemented or modified by the Meat Importers Council of America, Inc.'s Arbitration Rules"; held, "[e]ven assuming that it was not a per se material alteration, I would conclude that the clause here was material in that it would deprive Greenberg of its right to come into court to enforce the contract, without first bringing its claim before the Meat Importers Council of America").

NOTES AND QUESTIONS

1. The UCC does not define the term "materially alter." However Comment 4 to UCC § 2–207, in giving some examples, refers to clauses that would "result in surprise or hardship if incorporated without express awareness by the other party." The idea seems to be that a clause which is sufficiently important and unusual that a party would expect to have his attention specifically directed to it, should not come into the contract by way of a form that is by hypothesis commonly unread. Examples in Comment 5 of clauses which by contrast "involve no element of unreasonable surprise" are couched in terms of what is "within the range of trade practice" or "customary trade tolerances."

In many industries, of course, arbitration is a routinely-invoked, standard method of dispute resolution. Courts have even been willing to take "judicial notice" of the "common practice" of arbitration in the textile business. See Helen Whiting, Inc. v. Trojan Textile Corp., 307 N.Y. 360, 367, 121 N.E.2d 367, 370 (1954). Given the widespread acceptance of arbitration in these industries, could it be argued that an arbitration clause would not, in light of the policies behind UCC § 2–207, be a "material alteration"? See Aceros Prefabricados, S.A. v. TradeArbed, Inc., 282 F.3d 92 (2d Cir. 2002)(the seller "submitted unrebutted evidence that arbitration is standard practice within the steel industry, thereby precluding [the buyer] from establishing surprise or hardship"; therefore the arbitration provisions proposed in the seller's written confirmations "became part of the contract"); Schulze and Burch Biscuit Co. v. Tree Top, Inc., 831 F.2d 709 (7th Cir.1987) (given the prior course of dealing between the parties, the buyer "had ample notice" that the seller's confirmation might include an arbitration clause; the clause was therefore not a material alteration to the contract). Cf. Chelsea Square Textiles, Inc. v. Bombay Dyeing & Manufacturing Co., Ltd., 189 F.3d 289 (2d Cir. 1999), which held that an importer was obligated to arbitrate with a textile manufacturer even though the arbitration clause was "nearly illegible" and was "printed on very thin, tissue-style paper, which resulted in some of the text being obscured by typing on the reverse side": "We believe that a textile buyer is generally on notice that an agreement to purchase textiles is not only likely, but almost certain, to contain a provision mandating arbitration in the event of disputes."

2. Might the practice of dispute resolution through arbitration be so widespread in a given trade—or so well-established in the prior dealings of the parties—that under ordinary contract principles arbitration might be an implied term of the bargain *from the very beginning?* If so, then it would seem to follow that the arbitration term would not even be an "addition" to or an "alteration" of the contract *at all.* See UCC §§ 1–201(3)("agreement" means "the bargain of the parties in fact, as found in their language or inferred from other circumstances, including course of performance, course of dealing, or usage of trade"), 1–303m cmt. 3 (agreement "is to be sought for in the usages of trade, which furnish the background and give particular meaning to the language used, and are the framework of common understanding controlling any general rules of law which hold only when there is no such understanding"). In Schubtex, Inc. v. Allen Snyder, Inc., 49 N.Y.2d 1, 424 N.Y.S.2d 133, 399 N.E.2d 1154 (1979), a seller had confirmed a buyer's oral order by sending a form with an arbitration clause, and the buyer (as he had done several times in the past) retained the form without objection. The Court of Appeals suggested that "a determination that [the] oral agreement included a provision for arbitration could in a proper case be implied from a course of past conduct or the custom and practice in the industry," but concluded that such evidence was lacking in that case. See also International Tin Council v. Amalgamet Inc., 138 Misc.2d 383, 524 N.Y.S.2d 971 (1988) (retention of confirmation of sales form containing arbitration clause, without any objection to clause, constituted "tacit acceptance" of arbitration clause given "past contractual history" in which confirmation letters containing arbitration clauses were signed).

3. The United Nations Convention on Contracts for the International Sale of Goods, ratified by the United States in 1986, applies to all contracts for the sale of goods between parties "whose places of business are in different [Contracting] states." With respect to the formation of contracts, the Convention provides that a second printed form (e.g., a seller's "acknowledgement") that contains any additions to or modifications or the original offer may be treated as an acceptance, unless the additions or modifications "materially alter" the offer. If they *do* "materially alter" it, then the second form is presumed to be a counter-offer rather than an acceptance— with the result that *no contract is formed at all.* And additional or different terms "relating to the settlement of disputes" are *always* deemed to be "material" alterations, thereby preventing the formation of any contract by correspondence. Art. 19(3).

4. Sometimes the writings exchanged by the parties *will not create a contract* for the sale of goods under § 2–207(1): A second form, for example, may simply provide that it is not an "expression of acceptance" at all, and that any acceptance is "expressly conditional" on the other party's assent to its terms. Such a case is Commerce & Industry Ins. Co. v. Bayer Corp., 433 Mass. 388, 742 N.E.2d 567 (2001)(only the first form contained an arbitration clause; held, arbitration agreement is not enforceable because "a contract never came into being"). Nevertheless, the parties may still recognize the existence of a contract by their conduct—for example, by shipping, accepting, and paying for the goods before any dispute arises. In such a case, § 2–207(3) provides that the terms of the contract consist of "those terms on which the writings of the parties agree, together with any supplementary terms incorporated under any other provisions of this Act." May an agreement to arbitrate be brought back into the contract in such circumstances as a "supplementary term" implied from custom and usage?

Recall that the FAA provides for the enforceability of "*a written provision*" in a contract to submit future disputes to arbitration. Section 6 of the Revised Uniform Arbitration Act makes enforceable "*an agreement contained in a record*" to arbitrate future disputes. (A "record" is defined as "information that is inscribed on a tangible medium or that is stored in an electronic or other medium and is retrievable in perceivable form."). Does either of these statutes require the arbitration clause to be an *express* part of a valid written agreement—preventing an arbitration provision from being incorporated into a contract solely on the basis of custom, trade usage, or past dealing? See C. Itoh & Co. (America) Inc. v. Jordan Intern. Co., 552 F.2d 1228, 1238 (7th Cir.1977).

If the written contract between the parties provides for arbitration before the AAA, is an oral modification of this agreement—now providing for arbitration before JAMS—specifically enforceable? See Magness Petroleum Co. v. Warren Resources of Cal., Inc., 103 Cal.App.4th 901, 127 Cal.Rptr.2d 159 (2002).

5. A revision of Article 2 of the UCC was approved in 2003 by the National Conference of Commissioners on Uniform State Laws and by the American Law Institute. The new version of § 2–207 is radically simpler, and applies to all sales contracts even where there has been no "battle of the forms": Where a contract has been formed (either by the classic offer-and-acceptance mechanism—or by "conduct by both parties [that] recognizes the existence of a contract" although their writings do not otherwise establish one—or where an earlier informal contract is followed by a written confirmation with different or additional terms), then, in all cases, the terms of the contract are

- the terms "to which both parties agree" (whether in the writing or not), and

- "terms supplied or incorporated" under any other provision of the UCC.

The comments note also that "if the members of a trade, or if the contracting parties, expect to be bound by a term that appears in the record of only one of the contracting parties, that term is part of the agreement." Cmt. 4.

As of 2005, the revised Art. 2 has not yet been enacted in any state. Will it alter in any significant way the results reached under the current version of the statute?

6. A number of state statutes have traditionally imposed special requirements on the formation of arbitration agreements—presumably to guard against "surprise" and to insure that consent to arbitration has been knowing and informed. The Missouri arbitration statute, for example, requires a statement in ten point capital letters adjacent to or above the signature line, reading "THIS CONTRACT CONTAINS A BINDING ARBITRATION PROVISION WHICH MAY BE ENFORCED BY THE PARTIES." V.A.M.S. § 435.460. Another model singles out certain types of arbitration agreements and conditions their validity on the parties' having first received independent legal advice. The Texas statute requires that any agreement for arbitration in a contract where an individual acquires real or personal property, services, or money or credit, for an amount of $50,000 or less, must be signed by the attorneys of both parties. The same requirement applies to agreements to arbitrate any personal injury claim. Tex.Civ. Prac. & Rem.Code § 171.001.

All such statutes are now presumably dead letters in light of the Supreme Court's recent decision in Doctor's Associates, Inc. v. Casarotto, 517 U.S. 681 (1996). In *Casarotto,* the Court was faced with a Montana statute requiring notice that a contract is subject to arbitration to be "typed in underlined capital letters on the first page of the contract": The Court struck down the state statute on the predictable ground that by enacting the FAA, "Congress precluded States from singling out arbitration provisions for suspect status, requiring instead that such provisions be placed upon the same footing as other contracts." Courts may not "invalidate arbitration agreements under state laws applicable *only* to arbitration provisions."

7. The whole question of federal preemption may look quite different in cases involving the *business of insurance.* Given the tradition of intense state concern with this industry, Congress enacted the McCarran–Ferguson Act, which provides that:

> No Act of Congress shall be construed to invalidate, impair, or supersede any law enacted by any State for the purpose of regulating the business of insurance * * * unless such Act specifically relates to the business of insurance.

15 U.S.C. § 1012(b).

The FAA of course does not "specifically relate to the business of insurance." And so state statutes that focus on "protecting the relationship between the insurer and insured" will not be preempted by the FAA even if they purport to bar the submission of disputes to binding arbitration. See, e.g., Munich American Reinsurance Co. v. Crawford, 141 F.3d 585 (5th Cir. 1998)(Oklahoma has formulated a "complex and comprehensive scheme of insurance regulation" which vests state courts with "exclusive original jurisdiction" over all delinquency proceedings involving insolvent insurance companies; held, petition to compel arbitration was properly dismissed). In In re Kepka, 178 S.W.3d 279 (Tex. App.2005), a widow's suit against a nursing home for negligence in her husband's care was allowed to proceed, despite an arbitration clause that she and her husband had signed. By state statute every contract between a patient and a health care provider for the arbitration of a "health care liability claim" had to contain a written notice, in boldface type, "clearly and conspicuously stating" that "UNDER TEXAS LAW, THIS AGREEMENT IS INVALID AND OF NO LEGAL EFFECT UNLESS IT IS ALSO SIGNED BY AN ATTORNEY OF YOUR OWN CHOOSING." The court held that the McCarran–Ferguson Act saved the statute from preemption: The legislative provision was part of a broader enactment whose "overall scheme" was to "decrease the costs of health-care liability claims, through modifications of the insurance, tort, and medical-practice systems, in order to make insurance reasonably affordable"; the legislature could have determined that the section relating to arbitration "could reduce litigation over arbitration agreements' enforceability—thereby keeping down this aspect of litigation cost."

8. A bill introduced in the Texas legislature in 2005 made unenforceable any "provision waiving the right to demand a jury trial" in a consumer transaction, unless the waiver contained "the following statement in bold, underlined, capitalized, 16–point type: 'BY ENTERING INTO THIS AGREEMENT YOU ARE WAIVING YOUR RIGHT TO DEMAND A JURY TRIAL. THE LAW DOES NOT REQUIRE THAT YOU WAIVE THIS RIGHT.'" The bill never got out of committee. If it had been enacted, would it have survived a challenge based on the Supremacy Clause? Cf. note 6, supra.

A Massachusetts statute provides that any term in a residential lease "whereby the tenant agrees to waive his right to trial by jury in any subsequent litigation with the landlord * * * shall be deemed against public policy and void," Mass. Gen. Laws c. 186 § 15F. A court has recently held that this statute is preempted by federal law; "insofar as it voids arbitration agreements while leaving intact other aspects of rental agreements, the provision does not treat arbitration clauses equally with other contract terms," Patterson v. Piano Craft Guild Associates, L.P., 2002 WL 31931580 (Mass. Super.).

A recent California case has also held that any contractual predispute waiver of a jury trial in a civil action—even one "knowingly entered into between business entities armored with legal representation"—was unenforceable; a state statute that permits written waiver of a jury trial *"instead of a court trial"* necessarily envisages that the waiver occurs *"during the pendency of [a] civil action."* But the court carefully distinguished the case of predispute arbitration agreements: "The Legislature's authorization of agreements to resolve disputes in a *nonjudicial* forum, which leads to the loss of a package of procedural rights, does not necessarily imply approval of agreements to modify the *judicial* forum to eliminate one of these rights." Grafton Partners LP v. Superior Court, 9 Cal.Rptr.3d 511, 519–20 (Cal. App. 2004), aff'd, 36 Cal.4th 944, 32 Cal.Rptr.3d 5, 116 P.3d 479 (2005); see generally Stephen J. Ware, Arbitration Clauses, Jury–Waiver Clauses and other Contractual Waiver of Constitutional Rights, 67 Law & Contemp. Probs. 167 (2004).

9. An arbitration agreement might also run afoul of disclosure requirements applied generally to wide classes of contracts. New York, for example, imposes precise legibility requirements (not less than "eight points in depth or five and one-half points in depth for upper case") for printed contracts in all "consumer transactions." An arbitration clause in a customer's agreement with a stockbroker was invalidated for failure to meet this requirement in Hacker v. Smith Barney, Harris Upham & Co., Inc., 131 Misc.2d 757, 501 N.Y.S.2d 977 (Special Term 1986), aff'd, 136 Misc.2d 169, 519 N.Y.S.2d 92 (Sup.Ct.1987).

The court in *Hacker v. Smith Barney* perfunctorily dismissed a preemption argument based on *Southland v. Keating.* But *Hacker* is rather easily distinguishable from *Southland* and *Casarotto,* isn't it?

10. What about the "New York Rule" on contract formation exemplified by the *Marlene* case, supra? Is it likely that the FAA has any preemptive effect on this rule? The Tenth Circuit, rejecting this argument, noted that UCC § 2–207 is "a general principle of state law controlling issues of contract formation." "Presumptions against including terms, such as the New York rule, are routinely applied to any term considered significant to the contracting parties," such as disclaimers of warranty; "§ 2–207 does nothing under its general, or its specific New York application, to restrict enforcement of agreements to arbitrate to which the parties have expressly assented." Avedon Engineering, Inc. v. Seatex, 126 F.3d 1279 (10th Cir. 1997). The Second Circuit, on the other hand, has pointed out that the *general* New York law of contracts (unlike the rule in *Marlene*) requires that "nonarbitration agreements be proven only by a mere preponderance of the evidence"; it therefore followed that *Marlene*'s "discriminatory treatment of arbitration agreements * * * is preempted." Progressive Casualty Ins. Co. v. C.A. Reaseguradora Nacional De Venezuela, 991 F.2d 42 (2d Cir.1993).

b.   THE "SEPARABILITY" OF THE ARBITRATION CLAUSE

Prima Paint Corp. v. Flood & Conklin Mfg. Co.

Supreme Court of the United States, 1967.
388 U.S. 395, 87 S.Ct. 1801, 18 L.Ed.2d 1270.

■ MR. JUSTICE FORTAS delivered the opinion of the Court.

This case presents the question whether the federal court or an arbitrator is to resolve a claim of "fraud in the inducement," under a contract governed by the United States Arbitration Act of 1925, where there is no evidence that the contracting parties intended to withhold that issue from arbitration.

The question arises from the following set of facts. On October 7, 1964, respondent, Flood & Conklin Manufacturing Company, a New Jersey corporation, entered into what was styled a "Consulting Agreement," with petitioner, Prima Paint Corporation, a Maryland corporation. This agreement followed by less than three weeks the execution of a contract pursuant to which Prima Paint purchased F & C's paint business. The consulting agreement provided that for a six-year period F & C was to furnish advice and consultation "in connection with the formulae, manufacturing operations, sales and servicing of Prima Trade Sales account." These services were to be performed personally by F & C's chairman, Jerome K. Jelin, "except in the event of his death or disability." F & C bound itself for the duration of the contractual period to make no "Trade Sales" of paint or paint products in its existing sales territory or to current customers. To the consulting agreement were appended lists of F & C customers, whose patronage was to be taken over by Prima Paint. In return for these lists, the covenant not to compete, and the services of Mr. Jelin, Prima Paint agreed to pay F & C certain percentages of its receipts from the listed customers and from all others, such payments not to exceed $25,000 over the life of the agreement. The agreement took into account the possibility that Prima Paint might encounter financial difficulties, including bankruptcy, but no corresponding reference was made to possible financial problems which might be encountered by F & C. The agreement states that it "embodies the entire understanding of the parties on the subject matter." Finally, the parties agreed to a broad arbitration clause, which read in part:

> "Any controversy or claim arising out of or relating to this Agreement, or the breach thereof, shall be settled by arbitration in the City of New York, in accordance with the rules then obtaining of the American Arbitration Association...."

The first payment by Prima Paint to F & C under the consulting agreement was due on September 1, 1965. None was made on that date. Seventeen days later, Prima Paint did pay the appropriate amount, but into escrow. It notified attorneys for F & C that in various enumerated respects their client had broken both the consulting agreement and the earlier purchase agreement. Prima Paint's principal contention, so far as presently relevant, was that F & C had fraudulently represented that it was solvent and able to perform its contractual obligations, whereas it was in fact insolvent and intended to file a petition under Chapter XI of the Bankruptcy Act shortly after execution of the consulting agreement. Prima Paint noted that such a petition was filed by F & C on October 14, 1964, one week after the contract had been signed. F & C's response, on October 25, was to serve a "notice of intention to arbitrate." On November 12, three days before expiration of its time to answer this "notice," Prima Paint filed suit in the United States District Court for the Southern District of New York, seeking rescission of the consulting agreement on the basis of the alleged fraudulent inducement. The complaint asserted that the federal court had diversity jurisdiction.

Contemporaneously with the filing of its complaint, Prima Paint petitioned the District Court for an order enjoining F & C from proceeding with the arbitration. F & C cross-moved to stay the court action pending arbitration. F & C contended that the issue presented—whether there was fraud in the inducement of the consulting agreement—was a question for the arbitrators and not for the District Court. * * *

The District Court granted F & C's motion to stay the action pending arbitration, holding that a charge of fraud in the inducement of a contract containing an arbitration clause as broad as this one was a question for the arbitrators and not for the court. * * * The Court of Appeals for the Second Circuit dismissed Prima Paint's appeal.

* * *

[The Court first determined that "[t]here could not be a clearer case of a contract evidencing a transaction in interstate commerce."]

Having determined that the contract in question is within the coverage of the Arbitration Act, we turn to the central issue in this case: whether a claim of fraud in the inducement of the entire contract is to be resolved by the federal court, or whether the matter is to be referred to the arbitrators. The courts of appeals have differed in their approach to this question. The view of the Court of Appeals for the Second Circuit, as expressed in this case and in others, is that—except where the parties otherwise intend— arbitration clauses as a matter of federal law are "separable" from the contract in which they are embedded, and that where no claim is made that fraud was directed to the arbitration clause itself, a broad arbitration clause will be held to encompass arbitration of the claim that the contract itself was induced by fraud.[9] The Court of Appeals for the First Circuit, on the other hand, has taken the view that the question of "severability" is one of state law, and that where a State regards such a clause as inseparable a claim of fraud in inducement must be decided by the court.

With respect to cases brought in federal court involving maritime contracts or those evidencing transactions in "commerce," we think that Congress has provided an explicit answer. That answer is to be found in § 4 of the Act, which provides a remedy to a party seeking to compel compliance with an arbitration agreement. Under § 4, with respect to a matter within the jurisdiction of the federal courts save for the existence of an arbitration clause, the federal court is instructed to order arbitration to proceed once it is satisfied that "the making of the agreement for arbitration or the failure to comply [with the arbitration agreement] is not in issue." Accordingly, if the claim is fraud in the inducement of the arbitration clause itself—an issue which goes to the "making" of the agreement to arbitrate—the federal court may proceed to adjudicate it. But the statutory language does not permit the federal court to consider claims of fraud in the inducement of the contract generally. Section 4 does not expressly relate to situations like the present in which a stay is sought of a federal action in order that arbitration may proceed. But it is inconceivable that

9. The Court of Appeals has been careful to honor evidence that the parties intended to withhold such issues from the arbitrators and to reserve them for judicial resolution. We note that categories of contracts otherwise within the Arbitration Act but in which one of the parties characteristically has little bargaining power are expressly excluded from the reach of the Act. See § 1.

Congress intended the rule to differ depending upon which party to the arbitration agreement first invokes the assistance of a federal court. We hold, therefore, that in passing upon a § 3 application for a stay while the parties arbitrate, a federal court may consider only issues relating to the making and performance of the agreement to arbitrate. In so concluding, we not only honor the plain meaning of the statute but also the unmistakably clear congressional purpose that the arbitration procedure, when selected by the parties to a contract, be speedy and not subject to delay and obstruction in the courts.

* * *

In the present case no claim has been advanced by Prima Paint that F & C fraudulently induced it to enter into the agreement to arbitrate "[a]ny controversy or claim arising out of or relating to this Agreement, or the breach thereof." This contractual language is easily broad enough to encompass Prima Paint's claim that both execution and acceleration of the consulting agreement itself were procured by fraud. Indeed, no claim is made that Prima Paint ever intended that "legal" issues relating to the contract be excluded from arbitration, or that it was not entirely free so to contract. Federal courts are bound to apply rules enacted by Congress with respect to matters—here, a contract involving commerce—over which it has legislative power. The question which Prima Paint requested the District Court to adjudicate preliminarily to allowing arbitration to proceed is one not intended by Congress to delay the granting of a § 3 stay. Accordingly, the decision below dismissing Prima Paint's appeal is

Affirmed.

■ Mr. Justice Black, with whom Mr. Justice Douglas and Mr. Justice Stewart join, dissenting.

The Court here holds that the United States Arbitration Act, as a matter of federal substantive law, compels a party to a contract containing a written arbitration provision to carry out his "arbitration agreement" even though a court might, after a fair trial, hold the entire contract—including the arbitration agreement—void because of fraud in the inducement. The Court holds, what is to me fantastic, that the legal issue of a contract's voidness because of fraud is to be decided by persons designated to arbitrate factual controversies arising out of a valid contract between the parties. And the arbitrators who the Court holds are to adjudicate the legal validity of the contract need not even be lawyers, and in all probability will be nonlawyers, wholly unqualified to decide legal issues, and even if qualified to apply the law, not bound to do so. I am by no means sure that thus forcing a person to forgo his opportunity to try his legal issues in the courts where, unlike the situation in arbitration, he may have a jury trial and right to appeal, is not a denial of due process of law. I am satisfied, however, that Congress did not impose any such procedures in the Arbitration Act. And I am fully satisfied that a reasonable and fair reading of that Act's language and history shows that both Congress and the framers of the Act were at great pains to emphasize that nonlawyers designated to adjust and arbitrate factual controversies arising out of valid contracts would not trespass upon the courts' prerogative to decide the legal question of whether any legal contract exists upon which to base an arbitration.

* * *

Let us look briefly at the language of the Arbitration Act itself as Congress passed it. Section 2, the key provision of the Act, provides that "[a] written provision in . . . a contract . . . involving commerce to settle by arbitration a controversy thereafter arising out of such contract . . . shall be valid, irrevocable, and enforceable, *save upon such grounds as exist at law or in equity for the revocation of any contract.*" (Emphasis added.) Section 3 provides that "[i]f any suit . . . be brought . . . *upon any issue referable to arbitration* under an agreement in writing for such arbitration, the court . . . *upon being satisfied that the issue involved in such suit . . . is referable to arbitration under such an agreement,* shall . . . stay the trial of the action until such arbitration has been had . . ." (Emphasis added.) The language of these sections could not, I think, raise doubts about their meaning except to someone anxious to find doubts. They simply mean this: an arbitration agreement is to be enforced by a federal court unless the court, not the arbitrator, finds grounds "at law or in equity for the revocation of any contract." Fraud, of course, is one of the most common grounds for revoking a contract. If the contract was procured by fraud, then, unless the defrauded party elects to affirm it, there is absolutely no contract, nothing to be arbitrated. Sections 2 and 3 of the Act assume the existence of a valid contract. They merely provide for enforcement where such a valid contract exists. These provisions were plainly designed to protect a person against whom arbitration is sought to be enforced from having to submit his legal issues as to validity of the contract to the arbitrator. * * *

Finally, it is clear to me from the bill's sponsors' understanding of the function of arbitration that they never intended that the issue of fraud in the inducement be resolved by arbitration. They recognized two special values of arbitration: (1) the expertise of an arbitrator to decide factual questions in regard to the day-to-day performance of contractual obligations,[13] and (2) the speed with which arbitration, as contrasted to litigation, could resolve disputes over performance of contracts and thus mitigate the damages and allow the parties to continue performance under the contracts. Arbitration serves neither of these functions where a contract is sought to be rescinded on the ground of fraud. On the one hand,

---

13. "Not all questions arising out of contracts ought to be arbitrated. It is a remedy peculiarly suited to the disposition of the ordinary disputes between merchants as to questions of fact—quantity, quality, time of delivery, compliance with terms of payment, excuses for non-performance, and the like. It has a place also in the determination of the simpler questions of law—the questions of law which arise out of these daily relations between merchants as to the passage of title, the existence of warranties, or the questions of law which are complementary to the questions of fact which we have just mentioned." Cohen & Dayton, The New Federal Arbitration Law, 12 Va.L.Rev. 265, 281 (1926).

courts have far more expertise in resolving legal issues which go to the validity of a contract than do arbitrators.[14] On the other hand, where a party seeks to rescind a contract and his allegation of fraud in the inducement is true, an arbitrator's speedy remedy of this wrong should never result in resumption of performance under the contract. And if the contract were not procured by fraud, the court, under the summary trial procedures provided by the Act, may determine with little delay that arbitration must proceed. The only advantage of submitting the issue of fraud to arbitration is for the arbitrators. Their compensation corresponds to the volume of arbitration they perform. If they determine that a contract is void because of fraud, there is nothing further for them to arbitrate. I think it raises serious questions of due process to submit to an arbitrator an issue which will determine his compensation.

* * *

The avowed purpose of the Act was to place arbitration agreements "upon the same footing as other contracts." The separability rule which the Court applies to an arbitration clause does not result in equality between it and other clauses in the contract. I had always thought that a person who attacks a contract on the ground of fraud and seeks to rescind it has to seek rescission of the whole, not tidbits, and is not given the option of denying the existence of some clauses and affirming the existence of others. Here F & C agreed both to perform consulting services for Prima and not to compete with Prima. Would any court hold that those two agreements were separable, even though Prima in agreeing to pay F & C not to compete did not directly rely on F & C's representations of being solvent? The simple fact is that Prima would not have agreed to the covenant not to compete or to the arbitration clause but for F & C's fraudulent promise that it would be financially able to perform consulting services.

* * *

Prima here challenged in the courts the validity of its alleged contract with F & C as a whole, not in fragments. If there has never been any valid contract, then there is not now and never has been anything to arbitrate. If Prima's allegations are true, the sum total of what the Court does here is to force Prima to arbitrate a contract which is void and unenforceable before arbitrators who are given the power to make final legal determinations of their own jurisdiction, not even subject to effective review by the highest court in the land. That is not what Congress said Prima must do. It seems to be what the Court thinks would promote the policy of arbitration. I am completely unable to agree to this new version of the Arbitration Act * * *.

14. "It [arbitration] is not a proper remedy for ... questions with which the arbitrators have no particular experience and which are better left to the determination of skilled judges with a background of legal experience and established systems of law." Cohen & Dayton, supra, at 281.

NOTES AND QUESTIONS

1. There is a good review of authority in Ericksen, Arbuthnot, McCarthy, Kearney & Walsh, Inc. v. 100 Oak Street, 35 Cal.3d 312, 197 Cal.Rptr. 581, 673 P.2d 251 (1983). A law firm, complaining that the air conditioning in its offices was defective, brought suit against its landlord for breach of contract, of the covenant of quiet enjoyment, and of the warranty of habitability. The lease provided for arbitration "in the event of any dispute * * * with respect to the provisions of this Lease exclusive of those provisions relating to payment of rent." The lessor filed a motion to compel arbitration; the lessee responded that "[g]rounds exist for revocation of the agreement to arbitrate the alleged controversy in that [lessee] was falsely and fraudulently induced to enter into the lease agreement." The Supreme Court of California noted that "[t]he high courts of our sister states with cognate arbitration acts have followed the rule in *Prima Paint* with near unanimity" and held that the lessor's motion should have been granted:

> [T]he issue of fraud which is asserted here "seems inextricably enmeshed in the other factual issues of the case." Indeed, the claim of substantive breach—that the air conditioning did not perform properly—is totally embraced within the claim of fraud—that the lessor knew, at the time of the lease, that the air conditioning would not perform. Thus, if the trial court were to proceed to determine the fraud claim it would almost certainly have to decide the claim of substantive breach as well, and the original expectations of the parties—that such questions would be determined through arbitration—would be totally defeated. However the fraud claim were determined, there would be virtually nothing left for the arbitrator to decide.

Two dissenting judges found the majority's result "Incredible!" and commented that "[t]his is resupination: logic and procedure turned upside down."

2. The question of "separability" is posed also by challenges on a number of other contract-law grounds to the validity of the overall agreement. For example:

> **i.** *"Illegality."* See *Nuclear Electric Ins. Ltd. v. Central Power & Light Co.*, 926 F.Supp. 428 (S.D.N.Y.1996)(Texas Insurance Code rendered "unenforceable" any contract of insurance entered into by an unauthorized insurer; held, since "the claim of unenforceability does not specifically relate to the arbitration provision" but to "the entire policy," any claim that the policy is rendered unenforceable under Texas law "must be submitted to the arbitrator"); Wolitarsky v. Blue Cross of California, 53 Cal.App.4th 338, 61 Cal.Rptr.2d 629 (Cal.App. 1997)(policyholders argued that insurance dispute could not be arbitrated because the policy, by imposing an additional deductible for maternity care, discriminated against women in violation of the state Civil Rights Act,; held, when "the alleged illegality goes to only a portion of the contract (that does not include the arbitration agree-

ment), the entire controversy, including the issue of illegality, remains arbitrable").

See also Note (3) below.

ii. *"Unconscionability."* See Nagrampa v. Mailcoups Inc., 401 F.3d 1024 (9th Cir. 2005)(the arbitrator must decide whether an agreement containing an arbitration clause is a "contract of adhesion" because that issue "pertains to the making of the agreement as a whole and not to the arbitration clause specifically"); Bondy's Ford, Inc. v. Sterling Truck Corp., 147 F.Supp.2d 1283 (M.D.Ala.2001)(to the extent that one party claims that provisions of the agreement such as the waiver of punitive damages render the contract void because they are unconscionable, "the validity or invalidity of these provisions may be argued to the arbitral tribunal, and do not clearly implicate the arbitration clause itself").

iii. *Failure of a "meeting of the minds."* See Colfax Envelope Corp. v. Local No. 458–3M, Chicago Graphic Communications Int'l Union, 20 F.3d 750 (7th Cir. 1994)("even if" there was no "meeting of the minds" on the meaning of some critical term, at the least "there was a meeting of the minds on the mode of arbitrating disputes between the parties")(Posner, J.); Sphere Drake Ins. Ltd. v. All American Ins. Co., 256 F.3d 587, 590 (7th Cir. 2001)("if they have agreed on nothing else they have agreed to arbitrate")(Easterbrook, J.).

iv. *Duress and "coercion through bribery."* See Republic of the Philippines v. Westinghouse Electric Corp., 714 F.Supp. 1362 (D.N.J. 1989) ("if plaintiffs could demonstrate that the coercion or duress were directed specifically to the arbitration clause, this would satisfy *Prima Paint* and it would be appropriate to have a hearing on the issue").

v. *Frustration of purpose.* See Unionmutual Stock Life Ins. Co. of Amer. v. Beneficial Life Ins. Co., 774 F.2d 524 (1st Cir.1985) (defendant "never argued * * * that the arbitration clause itself was invalid because of either mutual mistake or frustration of purpose").

vi. *"Agreement to Agree."* See Toray Industries Inc. v. Aquafil S.p.a., 17(10) Int'l Arb. Rep., Oct. 2002 at p. D–1 (Sup. Ct. N.Y. 2002)(parties signed a document that one party contends "was no more than an agreement to agree and that the parties intended to negotiate further"; held, "the parties have agreed to arbitrate"—the parties "actively negotiated the choice of law and arbitration clause," which was not "inadvertently slipped in"—and so the arbitrators "will determine all questions including the meaning, effect, validity or enforceability of all other contract terms"); Republic of Nicaragua v. Standard Fruit Co., 937 F.2d 469 (9th Cir.1991) (in determining whether "Memorandum of Intent" was a "binding contract for the purchase and sale of bananas, or merely an 'agreement to agree' at some later date," the district court "improperly looked to the validity of the contract as a whole" and "ignored strong evidence in the record that both parties intended to be bound by the arbitration clause"; court should instead have "considered only the validity and scope of the arbitration clause itself").

vii. *Lack of "Consideration."* See Cline v. H.E. Butt Grocery Co., 79 F.Supp.2d 730 (S.D.Tex.1999)(an employee claimed that the employer's unilateral right to amend or terminate its occupational injury plan made its promises "illusory," but that "is an attack on the [plan] as a whole, and not the arbitration provision itself," and is therefore "properly referable to an arbitrator"); Matter of Exercycle Corp. v. Maratta, 9 N.Y.2d 329, 214 N.Y.S.2d 353, 174 N.E.2d 463 (N.Y. 1961)(although employment agreement contained an arbitration clause, the employer opposed arbitration, arguing that since the employee had the right to quit at any time, the employment contract was "lacking in mutuality" and therefore unenforceable; held, "the question whether the contract lacked mutuality of obligation" "is to be determined by the arbitrators, not the court").

viii. *Termination or Rescission.* See Rankin v. Allstate Ins. Co., 336 F.3d 8 (1st Cir. 2003)(policyholders claimed that Allstate's "undue delay" in payment constituted a "total breach" preventing Allstate from taking advantage of any other provision of the contract, including the arbitration clause; held, no; "[a]rbitration clauses are often invoked precisely because one side claims, and the other denies, that a contract has been violated"); Ambulance Billings Systems, Inc. v. Gemini Ambulance Services, Inc., 103 S.W.3d 507, 514 (Tex. App. 2003) (a claim that the parties had "mutually cancelled the contract" was contested; held, "a dispute regarding whether a settlement agreement was reached replacing or canceling" the original agreement is an issue "within the scope of the arbitration clause").

3. The plaintiff brought a class action alleging that the defendant had "made illegal usurious loans disguised as check cashing transactions" in violation of various Florida statutes. The defendant moved to stay proceedings and to compel arbitration pursuant to a clause in the contract. The lower appellate court ruled that the challenge to the validity of the underlying contract had to be resolved by an arbitrator, not a trial court, but the Supreme Court of Florida reversed:

> There is a key distinction between the claim in *Prima Paint* and the claim presently before us: in *Prima Paint,* the claim of fraud in the inducement, if true, would have rendered the underlying contract merely *voidable.* In the case before us today, however, the [contract] would be rendered void from the outset if it were determined that the contract indeed violated Florida's usury laws. Therefore, if the underlying contract is held entirely void as a matter of law, all of its provisions, including the arbitration clause, would be nullified as well. * * * We do not believe federal arbitration law was ever intended to be used as a means of overruling state substantive law on the legality of contracts.

Cardegna v. Buckeye Check Cashing, Inc., 894 So.2d 860 (Fla. 2005). The Supreme Court, relying on *Prima Paint,* reversed, 126 S.Ct. 1204 (2006).

For a particularly prescient account of what the Court would ultimately do, see Alan Scott Rau, " 'Separability,' 'Illegality,' and Federalism: The *Cardegna* Case in the Supreme Court," 20(10) Mealey's Int'l Arb. Rep. (Oct. 2005)("[t]his is simply about the contractual allocation of decision-making authority," and "if we can merely find * * * a willingness to arbitrate, we can draw the usual inferences about the agreed scope of arbitral power"; in addition, "I think we must fairly conclude that the presumption underlying *Prima Paint* has become part of the federal common law of arbitration [which] state courts, too, are now obliged to respect").

4. Compare Stevens/Leinweber/Sullens, Inc. v. Holm Development & Management, Inc., 165 Ariz. 25, 795 P.2d 1308 (1990). In this case a General Contractor entered into a standard-form construction contract with the Owner, providing that future disputes would be submitted to arbitration in accordance with the Construction Industry Arbitration Rules of the AAA. The contract also contained a non-standard clause drafted by the Owner, giving the Owner "the unilateral option of selecting either arbitration or litigation as the means of dispute resolution"; the Owner in fact had the right to reconsider its choice of dispute resolution "at any time, prior to a final judgment in the ongoing proceeding." The court noted that Arizona's arbitration statute contained language very similar to § 4 of the FAA and that it therefore "embod[ied] the concept of separability endorsed by the United States Supreme Court in *Prima Paint.*" "Because under the separability doctrine the arbitration provision is an independent and separate agreement, [the Owner] cannot 'borrow' consideration from the principal contract to support the arbitration provision. As a result, we conclude that the arbitration provision, which clearly lacks mutuality, is void for lack of consideration. * * * [Owner's] contention that the arbitration provision should be considered in isolation from the principal contract only when it is necessary to preserve the parties' agreement to arbitrate is without merit."

Note that the *overall* construction contract in *Holm* was not challenged on the ground of lack of "mutuality" or "consideration." See 1 A. Corbin, Contracts §§ 125 ("One Consideration Exchanged for Several Promises"), 164 (1963). This is truly "separability" with a vengeance, isn't it?

5. In some cases, courts seem to rebel at carrying the notion of "separability" to its logical extreme. Are the following cases consistent with *Prima Paint*?

i. Several local government authorities opened securities accounts with a brokerage firm, and later brought suit alleging that they had lost over $8 million as a result of the firm's unlawful conduct. The firm moved to stay the proceedings based on arbitration clauses in the customer agreements; the plaintiffs countered that the agreements were invalid because the individual purporting to sign on their behalf was not authorized to do so. The court held that this threshold issue whether the plaintiffs were bound by the customer agreements should be decided by the district court and not by the arbitrator: "A contrary rule would lead to untenable results. Party A could forge party B's name to a contract and compel party B to arbitrate the question of the genuineness of its signature." Three Valleys Municipal Water Dist. v. E.F. Hutton & Co., Inc., 925 F.2d 1136 (9th Cir.1991).

ii. A brokerage firm's customers (who could not read English) alleged that an employee of the firm had misrepresented to them that they were merely opening a money market account rather than a securities trading account. The court held that the customers were entitled to a trial on this issue, and that it was error to compel arbitration of the customers' claims before doing so: "Where misrepresentation of the character or essential terms of a proposed contract occurs, assent to the contract is impossible. In such a case there is no contract at all." Cancanon v. Smith Barney, Harris, Upham & Co., 805 F.2d 998 (11th Cir.1986). See also Strotz v. Dean Witter Reynolds, Inc., 223 Cal.App.3d 208, 272 Cal.Rptr. 680 (1990) (customer of brokerage firm alleged that she had not been told that the document entitled "Option Client Information" was actually a contract, the terms of which were set forth on the back of the form; "if a party is unaware he is signing any contract, obviously he also is unaware he is agreeing to arbitration").

6. That consent to an arbitration clause is a necessary condition of enforcement is made quite clear by the Court's opinion in *Prima Paint,*but in any event "is a truism reinforced by the language of both § 4 and of the savings clause of § 2 of the FAA." Courts that fail to perceive this simple point are likely to indulge in what has been called "bizarre and inexplicable misreadings" of the case. See generally Alan Scott Rau, Everything You Really Need to Know About "Separability" in Seventeen Simple Propositions, 14 Amer. Rev. of Int'l Arb. 1, 5, 14–18 (2003).

In one recent, astonishing, Fifth Circuit decision, a borrower brought suit against a lender for breach of contract, and the defendant moved to compel arbitration. The district court denied the motion after determining that the borrower "lacked the mental capacity to execute a contract under Mississippi law." The court of appeals, however, reversed—holding that this defense "is a defense to [the borrower's] entire agreement with [the lender] and not a specific challenge to the arbitration clause." So it seemed to follow that the defense of lack of capacity, as "part of the underlying dispute between the parties," must be submitted to the arbitrator. Primerica Life Ins. Co. v. Brown, 304 F.3d 469 (5th Cir. 2002); an equally bizarre holding on similar facts is In re Steger Energy Corp., 2002 WL 663645 (Tex. App.)(seller of mineral rights sued for rescission of the contract claiming that he "was incompetent at the time he signed the contracts—in the early stages of Alzheimer's"; held, motion to compel arbitration granted; "the defense asserted relates to the contract as a whole," and does not "specifically relate to the arbitration agreement itself"). Nor is this an isolated bit of lunacy. Consider, for example, the Alabama case in which the buyers of a mobile home claimed that the seller had "held all the documents * * * in one hand" and "pointed to where they needed to sign," without giving the agreement to them or allowing them to ask any questions about it. Since this allegation of fraud was that the seller had "concealed all portions of the agreement, not merely the arbitration clause" contained in it, the court pointed out that this was "in reality an attack on the entire" agreement. And since their challenge was "not only" to the enforceability of the arbitration clause, it was necessary under *Prima Paint* for the buyers, too, to make their arguments to the arbitrators. Green Tree Financial Corp. of Ala. v. Wampler, 749 So.2d 409 (Ala. 1999).

Is it necessary to point out the flaw in the reasoning here? *Prima Paint* does not merely preserve for the courts challenges that are "restricted" or "limited" to "just" the arbitration clause alone—which would be senseless—it preserves for the courts *any claim at all that necessarily calls an agreement to arbitrate into question*. To send a dispute to arbitration where "not only" the arbitration clause itself, but "also," in addition, the "entire" agreement is subject to challenge, is to lose sight of the only important question—which is the existence of a legally enforceable assent to submit to arbitration. It is reasonably safe to assume that someone lacking the requisite mental capacity to contract cannot assent to arbitrate anything at all. And isn't there something terminally silly about an analysis which permits arbitration just because the respondent has taken the pains to cover with his hand—not merely the arbitration clause—but *all the other provisions in the contract as well*? See Rau, supra at p. 18 ("Doctrine may certainly facilitate folly—but it rarely renders folly absolutely obligatory").

7. In an employee's suit against her employer, the employer moved for arbitration: The employee had signed a new employment contract, containing (in its article 15) an arbitration clause. (This new contract would replace, among other things, an arbitration agreement which had been entered into two years earlier.). The trial court found, however, that the employer had withheld her regularly scheduled pay—even for work already performed—unless she agreed to sign the new contract. At trial, the employee was asked by her attorney "whether she liked the arbitration clause." She replied:

> I did not. * * * The arbitration clause was going to allow me not to be able to be in a position that I needed to be in now, and that is, to have someone represent me to help me where I feel like the company did me wrong, and that is, not pay me correctly, not pay me at all, allow me to be in a position to have to quit so that I could not be making the kind of money that I had once made.

Of course, the employee had also "objected to other provisions in the contract."

The court refused to order arbitration, finding that "there was no valid, enforceable agreement to arbitrate because it was procured by economic duress." In re RLS Legal Solutions, L.L.C., 156 S.W.3d 160 (Tex. App. 2005). Are you convinced?

8. The Supreme Court in Scherk v. Alberto–Culver Co., 417 U.S. 506 (1974), characterized an agreement to arbitrate as "in effect, a specialized kind of forum-selection clause that posits not only the situs of suit but also the procedure to be used in resolving the dispute." Consider Marra v. Papandreou, 216 F.3d 1119 (D.C.Cir.2000). Here the plaintiff was an investor in a consortium that had won a license from the government of Greece to operate a casino near Athens. The license agreement contained no arbitration clause—it did, however, provide that any dispute concerning the license would be settled "by the Greek courts." After local political opposition to the casino developed, the Greek government revoked the license, citing legal defects. The plaintiff filed suit in the United States for breach of contract; it argued that—because the Greek government purported to have revoked the license "from the time it came into effect"—the government should be estopped from seeking refuge in the forum selection clause, which was a provision of a "nonexistent" license. The court nevertheless held that the forum selection clause was enforceable and that the plaintiff was required to file suit in Greece: The clause was properly understood as

> severable from the contract in which it is contained. Therefore while the Greek government's denial of its contractual obligations to Marra relieves her of her duty to perform her side of the contract's terms (for instance, she is no longer obligated to pay the annual license fee), that action does not work a repudiation of the forum-selection clause unless it is specifically directed at the clause itself. Were this not the case * * * the value of a forum-selection clause would be significantly diminished, since it will often be the case that a plaintiff can plausibly allege that the defendant's nonperformance constitutes a "repudiation" of its contractual obligations precluding it from recourse to the clause.

c. CONTRACTS OF ADHESION AND UNCONSCIONABILITY

Broemmer v. Abortion Services of Phoenix, Ltd.

Supreme Court of Arizona, En Banc, 1992.
173 Ariz. 148, 840 P.2d 1013.

■ MOELLER, VICE CHIEF JUSTICE. * * *

In December 1986, plaintiff, an Iowa resident, was 21 years old, unmarried, and 16 or 17 weeks pregnant. She was a high school graduate earning less than $100.00 a week and had no medical benefits. The father-to-be insisted that plaintiff have an abortion, but her parents advised against it. Plaintiff's uncontested affidavit describes the time as one of considerable confusion and emotional and physical turmoil for her.

Plaintiff's mother contacted Abortion Services of Phoenix and made an appointment for her daughter for December 29, 1986. During their visit to the clinic that day, plaintiff and her mother expected, but did not receive, information and counselling on alternatives to abortion and the nature of the operation. When plaintiff and her mother arrived at the clinic, plaintiff was escorted into an adjoining room and asked to complete three forms, one of which is the agreement to arbitrate at issue in this case. The agreement to arbitrate included language that "any dispute aris[ing] between the Parties as a result of the fees and/or services" would be settled by binding arbitration and that "any arbitrators appointed by the AAA shall be licensed medical doctors who specialize in obstetrics/gynecology." The two other documents plaintiff completed at the same time were a 2–page consent-to-operate form and a questionnaire asking for a detailed medical history. Plaintiff completed all three forms in less than 5 minutes and returned them to the front desk. Clinic staff made no attempt to explain the agreement to plaintiff before or after she signed, and did not provide plaintiff with copies of the forms.

After plaintiff returned the forms to the front desk, she was taken into an examination room where pre-operation procedures were performed. She was then instructed to return at 7:00 a.m. the next morning for the termination procedure. Plaintiff returned the following day and Doctor Otto performed the abortion. As a result of the procedure, plaintiff suffered a punctured uterus that required medical treatment.

Plaintiff filed a malpractice complaint in June 1988, approximately 1 1/2 years after the medical procedure. By the time litigation commenced, plaintiff could recall completing and signing the medical history and consent-to-operate forms, but could not recall signing the agreement to arbitrate. Defendants moved to dismiss, contending that the trial court lacked subject matter jurisdiction because arbitration was required. In opposition, plaintiff submitted affidavits that remain uncontroverted. The trial court considered the affidavits, apparently treated the motion to dismiss as one for summary judgment, and granted summary judgment to the defendants. Plaintiff's motion to vacate, quash or set aside the order, or to stay the claim pending arbitration, was denied.

On appeal, the court of appeals held that although the contract was one of adhesion, it was nevertheless enforceable because it did not fall outside plaintiff's reasonable expectations and was not unconscionable. * * * We granted plaintiff's petition for review. * * *

Some of the parties and amici have urged us to announce a "bright-line" rule of broad applicability concerning the enforceability of arbitration agreements. Arbitration proceedings are statutorily authorized in Arizona, A.R.S. §§ 12–1501 to–1518, and arbitration plays an important role in dispute resolution, as do other salutary methods of alternative dispute resolution. Important principles of contract law and of freedom of contract are intertwined with questions relating to agreements to utilize alternative methods of dispute resolution. We conclude it would be unwise to accept the invitation to attempt to establish some "bright-line" rule of broad applicability in this case. We will instead resolve the one issue which is dispositive: Under the undisputed facts in this case, is the agreement to arbitrate enforceable against plaintiff? We hold that it is not.

I.   The Contract is One of Adhesion

* * * [T]he enforceability of the agreement to arbitrate is determined by principles of general contract law. The court of appeals concluded, and we agree, that, under those principles, the contract in this case was one of adhesion.

An adhesion contract is typically a standardized form "offered to consumers of goods and services on essentially a 'take it or leave it' basis without affording the consumer a realistic opportunity to bargain and under such conditions that the consumer cannot obtain the desired product or services except by acquiescing in the form contract." Wheeler v. St. Joseph Hosp., 63 Cal.App.3d 345, 356, 133 Cal.Rptr. 775, 783 (1976). The *Wheeler* court further stated that "[t]he distinctive feature of a contract of adhesion is that the weaker party has no realistic choice as to its terms." Likewise, in Contractual Problems in the Enforcement of Agreements to Arbitrate Medical Malpractice, 58 Va.L.Rev. 947, 988 (1972), Professor Stanley Henderson recognized "the essence of an adhesion contract is that bargaining position and leverage enable one party 'to select and control risks assumed under the contract.'" (quoting Friedrich Kessler, Contracts of Adhesion—Some Thoughts About Freedom of Contract, 43 Colum.L.Rev. 629 (1943)).

The printed form agreement signed by plaintiff in this case possesses all the characteristics of a contract of adhesion. The form is a standardized contract offered to plaintiff on a "take it or leave it" basis. In addition to removing from the courts any potential dispute concerning fees or services, the drafter inserted additional terms potentially advantageous to itself requiring that any arbitrator appointed by the American Arbitration Association be a licensed medical doctor specializing in obstetrics/gynecology. The contract was not negotiated but was, instead, prepared by defendant and presented to plaintiff as a condition of treatment. Staff at the clinic neither explained its terms to plaintiff nor indicated that she was free to refuse to sign the form; they merely represented to plaintiff that she had to complete the three forms. The conditions under which the clinic offered plaintiff the services were on a "take it or leave it" basis, and the terms of service were not negotiable. Applying general contract law to the undisputed facts, the court of appeals correctly held that the contract was one of adhesion.

II.   Reasonable Expectations

Our conclusion that the contract was one of adhesion is not, of itself, determinative of its enforceability. "[A] contract of adhesion is fully enforceable according to its terms unless certain other factors are present which, under established legal rules—legislative or judicial—operate to render it otherwise." Graham v. Scissor–Tail, Inc., 28 Cal.3d 807, 171 Cal.Rptr. 604, 611, 623 P.2d 165, 172 (1981) To determine whether this contract of adhesion is enforceable, we look to two factors: the reasonable expectations of the adhering party and whether the contract is unconscionable. As the court stated in *Graham:*

Generally speaking, there are two judicially imposed limitations on the enforcement of adhesion contracts or provisions thereof. The first is that such a contract or provision which does not fall within the reasonable expectations of the weaker or "adhering" party will not be enforced against him. The second—a principle of equity applicable to all contracts generally—is that a contract or provision, even if consistent with the reasonable expectations of the parties, will be denied enforcement if, considered in its context, it is unduly oppressive or "unconscionable."

* * *

The comment to [Restatement (Second) of Contracts § 211] states in part: "Although customers typically adhere to standardized agreements and are bound by them without even appearing to know the standard terms in detail, they are not bound to unknown terms which are beyond the range of reasonable expectation." The Restatement focuses our attention on whether it was beyond plaintiff's reasonable expectations to expect to arbitrate her medical malpractice claims, which includes waiving her right to a jury trial, as part of the filling out of the three forms under the facts and circumstances of this case. Clearly, there was no conspicuous or explicit waiver of the fundamental right to a jury trial or any evidence that such rights were knowingly, voluntarily and intelligently waived. The only evidence presented compels a finding that waiver of such fundamental rights was beyond the reasonable expectations of plaintiff. Moreover, as Professor Henderson writes, "[i]n attempting to effectuate reasonable expectations consistent with a standardized medical contract, a court will find less reason to regard the bargaining process as suspect if there are no terms unreasonably favorable to the stronger party." In this case failure to explain to plaintiff that the agreement required all potential disputes, including malpractice disputes, to be heard only by an arbitrator who was a licensed obstetrician/gynecologist requires us to view the "bargaining" process with suspicion. It would be unreasonable to enforce such a critical term against plaintiff when it is not a negotiated term and defendant failed to explain it to her or call her attention to it.

Plaintiff was under a great deal of emotional stress, had only a high school education, was not experienced in commercial matters, and is still not sure "what arbitration is." Given the circumstances under which the agreement was signed and the nature of the terms included therein, [we are compelled] to conclude that the contract fell outside plaintiff's reasonable expectations and is, therefore, unenforceable. Because of this holding, it is unnecessary for us to determine whether the contract is also unconscionable.

III. A Comment on the Dissent

In view of the concern expressed by the dissent, we restate our firm conviction that arbitration and other methods of alternative dispute resolution play important and desirable roles in our system of dispute resolution. We encourage their use. When agreements to arbitrate are freely and fairly entered, they will be welcomed and enforced. They will not, however, be exempted from the usual rules of contract law * * *. * * *

The dissent is concerned that our decision today sends a "mixed message." It is, however, our intent to send a clear message. That message is: Contracts of adhesion will not be enforced unless they are conscionable and within the reasonable expectations of the parties. This is a well-established principle of contract law; today we merely apply it to the undisputed facts of the case before us.

Those portions of the opinion of the court of appeals inconsistent with this opinion are vacated. The judgment of the trial court is reversed and this case is remanded for further proceedings consistent with this opinion. * * *

■ MARTONE, JUSTICE, dissenting.

The court's conclusion that the agreement to arbitrate was outside the plaintiff's reasonable expectations is without basis in law or fact. I fear today's decision reflects a preference for litigation over alternative dispute resolution that I had thought was behind us. I would affirm the court of appeals.

We begin with the undisputed facts that the court ignores. At the top [of the agreement to arbitrate] it states in bold capital letters "PLEASE READ THIS CONTRACT CAREFULLY AS IT EFFECTS [sic] YOUR LEGAL RIGHTS." Directly under that in all capital letters are the words "AGREEMENT TO ARBITRATE." The recitals indicate that "the Parties deem it to be in their respective best interest to settle any such dispute as expeditiously and economically as possible." The parties agreed that disputes over services provided would be settled by arbitration in accordance with the rules of the American Arbitration Association. They further agreed that the arbitrators appointed by the American Arbitration Association would be licensed medical doctors who specialize in obstetrics/gynecology. Plaintiff, an adult, signed the document. * * *

The court seizes upon the doctrine of reasonable expectations to revoke this contract. But there is nothing in this record that would warrant a finding that an agreement to arbitrate a malpractice claim was not within the reasonable expectations of the parties. On this record, the exact opposite is likely to be true. For all we know, both sides in this case might wish to avoid litigation like the plague and seek the more harmonious waters of alternative dispute resolution. Nor is there anything in this record that would suggest that arbitration is bad. Where is the harm? In the end, today's decision reflects a preference in favor of litigation that is not shared by the courts of other states and the courts of the United States. * * *

NOTES AND QUESTIONS

1. Is it critical to the court's decision in *Broemmer* that under the contract the arbitrators were required to be "medical doctors who specialize in obstetrics/gynecology"?

Cf. Graham v. Scissor–Tail, Inc., 28 Cal.3d 807, 171 Cal.Rptr. 604, 623 P.2d 165 (1981), relied on by the court in *Broemmer. Graham* involved a contract for a series of concerts entered into between a promoter and Leon Russell, a recording artist and leader of a musical group. The contract was on a standard form prepared by Russell's union, the American Federation of Musicians, and provided that any disputes would be submitted to the International Executive Board of the Federation for final determination. After a dispute arose over the amount due to Russell out of the proceeds of the concerts, the Board issued an award in favor of Russell on the basis of a recommendation by a "referee"—a former executive officer of the union— named by the union president. The California Supreme Court refused to confirm this award. The court first found the agreement to be a "contract of adhesion"—"a standardized contract, which, imposed and drafted by the party of superior bargaining strength, relegates to the subscribing party only the opportunity to adhere to the contract or reject it." "All concert artists and groups of any significance or prominence" are members of the A.F. of M., and the promoter "was required by the realities of his business" to sign A.F. of M. form contracts with any concert artist with whom he wished to deal. Given that adhesion contracts are widely used and are "an inevitable fact of life for all citizens," that fact alone could not render the contract invalid. However, the court went on to find the agreement "unconscionable and unenforceable" because "it designates an arbitrator who, by reason of its status and identity, is presumptively biased in favor of one party":

> [W]hen as here the contract designating [the] arbitrator is the product of circumstances suggestive of adhesion, the possibility of overreaching by the dominant party looms large; contracts concluded in such circumstances, then, must be scrutinized with particular care to insure that the party of lesser bargaining power, in agreeing thereto, is not left in a position depriving him of any realistic and fair opportunity to prevail in a dispute under its terms. * * * [W]e * * * must insist— most especially in circumstances smacking of adhesion—that certain "minimum levels of integrity" be achieved if the arrangement in question is to pass judicial muster.

Further discussion of the selection of arbitrators and of arbitrator impartiality appears in Section D.1 infra.

2. As we saw in Section B.4 supra, legislation in certain states imposes in medical malpractice cases the requirement of a prior "screening" or "review panel," which will commonly include at least one physician. A recent study questions whether "the presence of doctors on the review panels improves the panels' accuracy," and also questions whether practicing physicians are reliably able "to judge other doctors objectively": Surveys have in fact found "a marked variation among physicians in their willingness to label certain kinds of medical outcomes as iatrogenic, and an even more pronounced reluctance to label as negligent those treatment decisions that, *ex post* at least, were clearly erroneous." See Catherine T. Struve, Expertise in Medical Malpractice Litigation: Special Courts, Screening

Panels, and Other Options 66–67 (Pew Project on Medical Liability 2003), http://medliabilitypa.org/research/struve1003.

3. Absent such elements of potential bias on the part of the arbitrators that the court found in *Graham,* supra note (1), under what circumstances is an arbitration clause in an adhesion contract likely to be found unenforceable?

Many state courts are inclined to strike down such clauses as "unconscionable" when they suspect that one party was not aware of it or that adequate efforts were not made to bring it to his attention. One such case is Wheeler v. St. Joseph Hospital, 63 Cal.App.3d 345, 133 Cal.Rptr. 775 (1976), also relied on in *Broemmer.* Wheeler was admitted to the hospital one evening "for an angiogram and catheterization studies in connection with a coronary insufficiency." On admission he signed a form entitled "CONDITIONS OF ADMISSION" which included a paragraph entitled "ARBITRATION OPTION." There was a blank space which the patient could initial to indicate his refusal of arbitration, but Wheeler did not do so. After the tests were performed, Wheeler suffered a brainstem infarction rendering him a total quadriplegic. The court held that he was not required to submit his malpractice claim to arbitration. According to his wife he had signed the admission form without reading it, and neither of them was aware that it contained an arbitration clause; "it was hurriedly signed under the stressful atmosphere of a hospital admitting room without any procedures calculated to alert the patient to the existence of the 'ARBITRATION OPTION.' Nor was the patient given a copy of the agreement to permit him to study its terms under less anxious circumstances":

> Although an express waiver of jury trial is not required, by agreeing to arbitration, the patient does forfeit a valuable right. The law ought not to decree a forfeiture of such a valuable right where the patient has not been made aware of the existence of an arbitration provision or its implications. Absent notification and at least some explanation, the patient cannot be said to have exercised a "real choice" in selecting arbitration over litigation. We conclude that in order to be binding, an arbitration clause incorporated in a hospital's "CONDITIONS OF ADMISSION" form should be called to the patient's attention and he should be given a reasonable explanation of its meaning and effect, including an explanation of any options available to the patient. These procedural requirements will not impose an unreasonable burden on the hospital. The hospital's admission clerks need only direct the patient's attention to the arbitration provision, request him to read it, and give him a simple explanation of its purpose and effect, including the available options. Compliance will not require the presence of the hospital's house counsel in the admission office.

4. If the patient in *Wheeler* had had the opportunity to consult you in advance of treatment, would you have advised him that it was in his best interests to sign the arbitration agreement? Is it likely that the "disclosures" required in cases like this will have the same effect?

5. Professor Budnitz argues that "[w]ithout a brochure explaining the consequences of signing the [arbitration] agreement, a consumer cannot intelligently and knowingly waive his or her right to access to the judicial process." He proposes therefore that banks in their contracts with customers be made to include "a copy of the AAA rules," Mark E. Budnitz, Arbitration of Disputes Between Consumers and Financial Institutions: A Serious Threat to Consumer Protection, 10 Ohio St. J. on Disp. Resol. 267, 304, 334 (1995); see also id. at 276–77 (criticizing a bank contract because it "does not discuss the circumstances under which a court may review an arbitrator's order").

Do you agree? Cf. William Whitford, The Functions of Disclosure Regulation in Consumer Transactions, 1973 Wisc. L. Rev. 400, 423–27 (1973)("[s]ellers have long known that it is precisely in the contract, and only in the contract, that information consumers are *not* supposed to notice is to be put"); Robert A. Hillman & Jeffrey J. Rachlinski, Standard–Form Contracting in the Electronic Age, 77 N.Y.U. L. Rev. 429, 436 (2002)("the consumer, engaging in a rough but reasonable cost-benefit analysis ... understands that the costs of reading, interpreting, and comparing standard terms outweigh any benefits of doing so and therefore chooses not to read the form carefully or even at all"); Melvin Aron Eisenberg, The Limits of Cognition and the Limits of Contract, 47 Stan. L. Rev. 211, 247 (1995)("most form takers will be rationally ignorant of most preprinted terms. Accordingly, it should not matter whether a preprinted term is clearly written and conspicuous"); Hylton, Agreements to Waive or to Arbitrate Legal Claims: An Economic Analysis, 8 Sup. Ct. Econ. Rev. 209, 252 (2000)("rational apathy" may justify enforcement of arbitration clauses in "shrink wrap" and other cases where consumers purchase goods before reading or understanding the contract terms; "it is costly to discover information about the probability of loss, and the expected rewards for discovering such information are too low to justify the research costs"— because "either the probability or the severity of harm, even after the [possibility of filing a lawsuit] is removed, is extremely low").

More fundamentally, perhaps, the results of the National Adult Literacy Survey suggest that few American adults could "understand and use contract documents and disclosures" even "if they actually chose to read them": "While design and readability experts could improve contracts and disclosure forms, the terms of modern consumer contracts are so complex that legal mandates to make contract forms readable may be futile." Alan M. White & Cathy Lesser Mansfield, Literacy and Contract, 13 Stan. L. & Policy Rev. 233, 234, 242 (2002).

6. Investors entered into a margin account agreement with a stock brokerage firm. The firm later sold securities worth $3 million that were held in the account as collateral for the repayment of loans it had made to the investors. The investors brought suit claiming that this sale violated the agreement; the firm moved to compel arbitration in accordance with an arbitration clause. The investors asserted that they had been "fraudulently induced" to enter into the arbitration agreement by the firm's "failure to disclose the effect of the arbitration clause.'' The court held that the investors were not entitled to a jury trial of this issue:

> We know of no case holding that parties dealing at arm's length have a duty to explain to each other the terms of a written contract. We decline to impose such an obligation where the language of the contract clearly and explicitly provides for arbitration of disputes arising out of the contractual relationship. This is not a criminal case; the [plaintiffs'] argument that there was no ''showing of intelligent and knowing waiver of the substantive rights at issue'' is simply beside the point. * * * We see no unfairness in expecting parties to read contracts before they sign them.

Cohen v. Wedbush, Noble, Cooke, Inc., 841 F.2d 282 (9th Cir.1988). Is this consistent with cases like *Wheeler,* note (2) above?

7. After *Southland v. Keating,* (Section C.2 above), the focus of resistance to arbitration seems to have shifted from state legislatures to state courts, called upon to apply their own law of contract in a neutral fashion. In East Ford, Inc. v. Taylor, 826 So.2d 709 (Miss. 2002), for example, the buyer of a pickup truck brought suit against the seller alleging that the truck had been represented to him ''as new'' whereas in reality it was used. The contract contained an arbitration clause that the buyer alleged was ''unconscionable because although he signed the provision, he did not read it because the salesman did not tell him that he should.'' The court agreed that the arbitration clause was unconscionable: For it was ''not in boldface''; appeared along with other provisions ''in very fine print and regular typing font,'' did ''not have any underlining nor any other effect which would alert the reader of the importance of its terms,'' and was ''preprinted on the document.'' See also Raiteri v. NHC Healthcare/Knoxville, Inc., 2003 WL 23094413 (Tenn. App.)(arbitration clause in nursing home contract held to be unenforceable because ''the dispute resolution procedures do not contain any type of short explanation encouraging patients to ask questions,'' and the terms, ''including the provision waiving a jury trial, are printed in the same font size, type, and color as the rest of the agreement'').

Can these cases possibly be consistent with *Doctor's Associates v. Casarotto,* (Section 3.a, Note (6) above?). See also Kloss v. Edward D. Jones & Co., 310 Mont. 123, 54 P.3d 1 (2002), which involved a 95–year old widow who had opened several accounts with a brokerage firm. She did not read the contract, and the broker ''explained significant features of the account'' but did not explain the arbitration provision. Reversing the district court, the Supreme Court of Montana, in an opinion by Justice Trieweiler, found that ''the arbitration provision by which [she] waived her right of access to this State's courts, her right to a jury trial, her right to reasonable discovery, her right to findings of fact based on the evidence, and her right to enforce the law applicable to her case by way of appeal were clearly not within [her] reasonable expectations'' and was therefore unenforceable. Professor Knapp has termed Justice Trieweiler's ''forthrightness'' in arbitration cases ''a remarkable example of principled courage or pigheadedness, depending on your point of view." Charles L. Knapp, Taking Contracts Private: The Quiet Revolution in Contact Law, 71 Ford. L. Rev. 761, 777 n. 61 (2002). Which of these alternatives would you choose?

8. In addition to one party's lack of awareness of the arbitration clause, what other defects might there be in an arbitration agreement which could give rise to an argument of unconscionability? See Stanley D. Henderson, Contractual Problems in the Enforcement of Agreements to Arbitrate Medical Malpractice, 58 Va.L.Rev. 947, 994 (1972):

> Assuming the conventional expectations test is applied widely to medical arbitration clauses, it is essential to underscore the point that the primary reason for application of such a test is that the disadvantaged bargaining party is harmed or unfairly overreached. The factor of harm or prejudice measures the range of reasonable expectation induced by a standardized contract. * * * So unless it can be said that a medical arbitration term operates in a coercive or oppressive manner, it is difficult to see that the courts will regard it as exceeding the expectations of the average patient who accepts it.

One possible illustration of an arbitration clause that "operates in a coercive or oppressive manner" might be Patterson v. ITT Consumer Financial Corp., 14 Cal.App.4th 1659, 18 Cal.Rptr.2d 563 (1993). Plaintiffs, "individuals of modest means, some self-employed or temporarily jobless," borrowed "relatively small amounts of money." The loan agreements provided that any disputes "shall be resolved by binding arbitration by the National Arbitration Forum, Minneapolis, Minnesota." The court found this arbitration provision "unconscionable and thus unenforceable." The NAF's rules were unclear as to just where the arbitration would be held, but "the provision on its face suggests that Minnesota would be the locus for the arbitration"—and "[w]hile arbitration per se may be within the reasonable expectation of most consumers, it is much more difficult to believe that arbitration in Minnesota would be within the reasonable expectation of California consumers." Cf. Bank v. WorldCom, Inc., 2002 WL 171629 (N.Y. Sup. Ct.)(resident of New York City claimed that his refund payment of $51.25 from WorldCom "was untimely and should have included interest"; the court "upholds Washington, D.C. as a venue for the arbitration" even though it "believes that there may be something inherently wrong and unfair in setting the venue for an arbitration in a distant city, when the amount in issue is a relatively small amount.").

The arbitration "distant forum" cases seem curiously uninformed by the Supreme Court's celebrated decision in Carnival Cruise Lines, Inc. v. Shute, 499 U.S. 585 (1991). See also Effron v. Sun Line Cruises, Inc., 67 F.3d 7 (2d Cir. 1995), in which a resident of Palm Beach, Florida purchased a "17–day South American vacation package" including a cruise on a ship of Greek registry; the passenger contract required any action to be brought in Athens. After being injured as a result of a shipboard fall, she unsuccessfully tried to bring suit in New York: "We are concerned here with a forum of contract," said the court, "not of convenience." "Unsupported statements concerning financial difficulties are less than persuasive when made by someone who owns homes in Palm Beach and New York and who has just returned from an expensive foreign vacation." And after all, "a plaintiff may have his 'day in court' without ever setting foot in a courtroom."

9. The use of arbitration clauses by Gateway in the direct sales of its computers (see p. 53 supra) has also been the subject of a flurry of recent litigation. The terms of Gateway's standard arbitration clause were found to be "substantively unconscionable" in Brower v. Gateway 2000, Inc., 246 A.D.2d 246, 676 N.Y.S.2d 569 (1998). The clause, as originally drafted, provided for arbitration to take place in Chicago under ICC rules. The court held that the "possible inconvenience of the chosen site" did not "alone" rise to the level of unconscionability. However, "the excessive cost factor that is necessarily entailed in arbitrating before the ICC is unreasonable and surely serves to deter the individual consumer from invoking the process." (For the smallest of cases ICC rules required an advance payment of $4000—greater than the cost of most Gateway products—of which the $2000 registration fee was nonrefundable even if the consumer prevailed at the arbitration.). Nevertheless, the court did not strike down the arbitration clause in its entirety—instead, it remanded the case to the trial court "so that the parties have the opportunity to seek appropriate substitution of an arbitrator" pursuant to § 5 of the FAA. More recently, the standard Gateway arbitration clause has been amended so that it now requires an arbitration to be administered by the NAF, and to be held "at any reasonable location near [the customer's] residence."

The possible burden of substantial filing fees has in recent years become an increasingly important focus of litigation, especially where the claimant is attempting to vindicate a right granted by civil rights or other regulatory legislation. For further discussion, see the *Armendariz* case and the notes following in Section C.4, infra.

10. The Bank of America's arbitration program for all its depositors and credit-card holders (see pp. 51–52 supra) was quickly challenged in court. The plaintiffs argued that "the Bank's unprecedented ADR provision does not fall within the reasonable expectations of the Bank's consumer account-holders," and that "the Bank's unilateral imposition of ADR deprives consumers without their consent of rights that are constitutionally guaranteed." (Plaintiffs' Trial Brief, pp. 23, 25). Outside of court, the plaintiffs' attorney put the matter somewhat more luridly: "[A]rbitration, like sex, must be based on consent, not on coercion." 1 ABA Disp.Res.Mag., p. 5 (Summer 1994).

The plaintiffs were successful in having the Bank's arbitration clause held unenforceable in Badie v. Bank of America, 67 Cal.App.4th 779, 79 Cal.Rptr.2d 273 (Cal.App.1998). The credit-card agreements had provided that the Bank "may change any term, condition, service or feature of your Account at any time"—such change-of-terms provisions had in fact been standard industry practice since bank credit cards first became available in the 1960's. Nevertheless the court held that it was a violation of the covenant of good faith and fair dealing for the Bank to "attempt to 'recapture' a foregone opportunity by adding an entirely new term, which has no bearing on any subject * * * addressed in the original contract and which was not within the reasonable contemplation of the parties when the contract was entered into"; the absence of any such limitation "would open the door to a claim that the agreements are illusory." There was nothing that would have alerted a customer to the possibility that the Bank might one day in the future invoke this provision to add clauses that were not "integral to the Bank/creditor relationship". Nor was the customer's failure to close an account after receiving the "bill stuffers" sufficient to constitute a waiver of his right to a jury trial—because the Bank's notice was not "direct, clear and unambiguous" and was not "designed to achieve knowing consent" to arbitration. Federal policy favoring arbitration, added the court, "does not even come into play unless it is first determined that the Bank's customers agreed to use some form of ADR to resolve disputes regarding their deposit and credit card accounts"—a determination that in turn "requires analysis of the account agreements in light of ordinary state law principles" governing contracts.

11. The following year, Delaware enacted a statute that permitted a bank to amend any revolving credit plan "in any respect, whether or not the amendment * * * was originally contemplated or addressed by the parties or is integral to the relationship between the parties." Such amendment "may change terms by the addition of new terms" "of any kind whatsoever," expressly including "arbitration or other alternative dispute resolution mechanisms," and notice of any such amendment may be sent by the bank "in the same envelope with a periodic statement." 5 Del. Code § 952 (1999).

The Delaware statute has been applied to bind credit card customers in later suits against issuers, e.g., Marsh v. First USA Bank, N.A., 103 F.Supp.2d 909 (N.D.Tex.2000)(it was enough for the Bank to show that notice of the arbitration clause was designed to be routinely included in monthly credit-card statements, and that there were in place "multi-level quality assurance controls" to "detect errors"); Kurz v. Chase Manhattan Bank USA, N.A., 319 F.Supp.2d 457 (S.D.N.Y.2004)("the continued charges by authorized users, coupled with plaintiff's failure to submit to defendant the required written objection, evinces plaintiff's consent to the arbitration amendment").

12. The problem of "assent to unknown terms" has also arisen where retailers like Gateway ship computers—and contracts—only in response to an order placed by phone or on line. An arbitration clause sent under these circumstances was enforced by the Seventh Circuit in Hill v. Gateway 2000, Inc., 105 F.3d 1147 (7th Cir.1997). Under Gateway's standard terms, the "form in the box" would govern unless the customer returned the computer within 30 days. Therefore, the court held, the contract had not been formed when the telephone order was placed—nor when the goods were delivered—but only *after* the customer had retained the computer beyond that time limit. "By keeping the computer beyond 30 days, the Hills accepted Gateway's offer, including the arbitration clause." Judge Easterbrook pointed out that "cash now-terms later" transactions were quite common in our economy, for example, in air travel and insurance transactions; "cashiers cannot be expected to read legal documents to customers before ringing up sales." And of course, "a contract need not be read to be effective; people who accept take the risk that the unread terms may in retrospect prove unwelcome."

A number of courts have declined to follow *Hill*, and have insisted that the proper analysis should instead be under § 2–207 of the UCC. The court in Klocek v. Gateway, Inc., 104 F.Supp.2d 1332 (D.Kan.2000) denied Gateway's motion to dismiss a consumer's breach of warranty suit. For purposes of the motion, it assumed that an offer to purchase the computer had originally been made by *the consumer*, and that Gateway had accepted the offer, "either by completing the sales transaction in person or by agreeing to ship and/or shipping the computer to plaintiff." Because the plaintiff was not a "merchant," it followed that Gateway's "additional" arbitration term could only become part of the agreement under § 2–207(2) if the plaintiff had "expressly agreed" to it—and merely retaining the computer was insufficient to show such express agreement. Cf. Lively v. IJAM, Inc., 114 P.3d 487 (Okla. Civ. App.2005)(forum selection clause; the consumer "had already paid for the computer before it was shipped and a contract existed before [he] opened the box and found the invoice").

13. "When introduced as a method to control soil erosion, kudzu was hailed as an asset to agriculture, but it has become a creeping monster. Arbitration was innocuous when limited to negotiated commercial contracts, but it developed sinister characteristics when it became ubiquitous." In re Knepp, 229 B.R. 821 (Bankr.N.D.Ala.1999).

The *Knepp* court held that an arbitration clause in a contract for the sale of a used car was "void under the doctrine of unconscionability": The buyer lacked "meaningful choice," since "in today's market it is virtually impossible to purchase an automobile without the sales contract containing an arbitration clause." The court noted that since "automobiles are a necessity in our society, consumers can ill afford to forsake this necessity even at the price of their constitutional rights." Under such reasoning, what *other* clauses in a standard sales, employment, or insurance contract could one justify invalidating?

See also Jean Sternlight, Creeping Mandatory Arbitration: Is It Just?, 57 Stan. L. Rev. 1631, 1653–54 (2005):

> [While it is true that] "adhesive contracts" are rampant and typically enforced by courts, these facts do not justify the use of adhesive mandatory arbitration agreements. * * * [I]t can at least be argued that it is more inappropriate to deprive a person of access to court on a nonconsensual basis than it is to increase their interest rate without actual subjective consent. After all, the right to a jury trial is guaranteed by the federal Constitution, and more general access to court is assured by many state constitutions. Surely we would not allow police to use adhesive contracts to deprive alleged criminals of their rights to an attorney?

d. "ARBITRABILITY"

Even if a valid agreement to arbitrate exists, that does not end the matter. The question may still arise whether the particular dispute falls within the ambit of the agreement—that is, whether the parties have agreed to submit *this* matter in controversy to decision by arbitration. In the United States this is often referred to as an inquiry into whether the dispute is "arbitrable"—in effect, an inquiry into the "subject matter jurisdiction" of the arbitrator to hear the case.

AT & T Technologies, Inc. v. Communications Workers of America

Supreme Court of the United States, 1986.
475 U.S. 643, 106 S.Ct. 1415, 89 L.Ed.2d 648.

■ Justice White delivered the opinion of the Court.

The issue presented in this case is whether a court asked to order arbitration of a grievance filed under a collective-bargaining agreement must first determine that the parties intended to arbitrate the dispute, or whether that determination is properly left to the arbitrator.

I

AT & T Technologies, Inc. (AT & T or the Company) and the Communications Workers of America (the Union) are parties to a collective-bargaining agreement which covers telephone equipment installation workers. Article 8 of this agreement establishes that "differences arising with respect to the interpretation of this contract or the performance of any obligation hereunder" must be referred to a mutually agreeable arbitrator upon the written demand of either party. This Article expressly does not cover disputes "excluded from arbitration by other provisions of this contract."[1] Article 9 provides that, "subject to the limitations contained in the provisions of this contract, but otherwise not subject to the provisions of the arbitration clause," AT & T is free to exercise certain management functions, including the hiring and placement of employees and the termination of employment.[2] "When lack of work necessitates Layoff," Article 20

---

1. Article 8 provides, in pertinent part, as follows:

If the National and the Company fail to settle by negotiation any differences arising with respect to the interpretation of this contract or the performance of any obligation hereunder, such differences shall (provided that such dispute is not excluded from arbitration by other provisions of this contract, and provided that the grievance procedures as to such dispute have been exhausted) be referred upon written demand of either party to an impartial arbitrator mutually agreeable to both parties.

2. Article 9 states:

The Union recognizes the right of the Company (subject to the limitations contained in the provisions of this contract, but otherwise not subject to the provisions of the arbitration clause) to exercise the functions of managing the business which involve, among other things, the hiring and placement of Employees, the termination of employment, the assignment of work, the determination of

prescribes the order in which employees are to be laid off.[3]

On September 17, 1981, the Union filed a grievance challenging AT & T's decision to lay off 79 installers from its Chicago base location. The Union claimed that, because there was no lack of work at the Chicago location, the planned layoffs would violate Article 20 of the agreement. Eight days later, however, AT & T laid off all 79 workers, and soon thereafter, the Company transferred approximately the same number of installers from base locations in Indiana and Wisconsin to the Chicago base. AT & T refused to submit the grievance to arbitration on the ground that under Article 9, the Company's decision to lay off workers when it determines that a lack of work exists in a facility is not arbitrable.

The Union then sought to compel arbitration by filing suit in federal court pursuant to § 301(a) of the Labor Management Relations Act, 29 U.S.C. § 185(a). Ruling on cross-motions for summary judgment, the District Court reviewed the provisions of Articles 8, 9, and 20 and set forth the parties' arguments as follows:

> "Plaintiffs interpret Article 20 to require that there be an actual lack of work prior to employee layoffs and argue that there was no such lack of work in this case. Under plaintiffs' interpretation, Article 20 would allow the union to take to arbitration the threshold issue of whether the layoffs were justified by a lack of work. Defendant interprets Article 20 as merely providing a sequence for any layoffs which management, in its exclusive judgment, determines are necessary. Under defendant's interpretation, Article 20 would not allow for an arbitrator to decide whether the layoffs were warranted by a lack of work but only whether the company followed the proper order in laying off the employees."

Finding that "the union's interpretation of Article 20 was at least 'arguable,'" the court held that it was "for the arbitrator, not the court to decide whether the union's interpretation has merit," and accordingly, ordered the Company to arbitrate.

The Court of Appeals for the Seventh Circuit affirmed. The Court of Appeals understood the District Court to have ordered arbitration of the threshold issue of arbitrability. The court acknowledged the "general rule" that the issue of arbitrability is for the courts to decide unless the parties stipulate otherwise, but noted that this Court's decisions in *Steelworkers v. Warrior & Gulf Navigation Co.,* 363 U.S. 574 (1960), and *Steelworkers v. American Mfg. Co.,* 363 U.S. 564 (1960), caution courts to avoid becoming entangled in the merits of a labor dispute under the guise of deciding arbitrability. From this observation, the court announced an "exception" to

---

methods and equipment to be used, and the control of the conduct of work.

3. Article 20 provides, in pertinent part, "[w]hen lack of work necessitates Layoff, Employees shall be Laid-Off in accordance with Term of Employment and by

Layoff groups as set forth in the following [subparagraphs stating the order of layoff]." Article 1.11 defines the term "Layoff" to mean "a termination of employment arising out of a reduction in the force due to lack of work."

the general rule, under which "a court should compel arbitration of the arbitrability issue where the collective bargaining agreement contains a standard arbitration clause, the parties have not clearly excluded the arbitrability issue from arbitration, and deciding the issue would entangle the court in interpretation of substantive provisions of the collective bargaining agreement and thereby involve consideration of the merits of the dispute."

All of these factors were present in this case. Article 8 was a "standard arbitration clause," and there was "no clear, unambiguous exclusion from arbitration of terminations predicated by a lack of work determination." Moreover, although there were "colorable arguments" on both sides of the exclusion issue, if the court were to decide this question it would have to interpret not only Article 8, but Articles 9 and 20 as well, both of which are "substantive provisions of the Agreement." The court thus "decline[d] the invitation to decide arbitrability," and ordered AT & T "to arbitrate the arbitrability issue."

* * *

We granted certiorari and now vacate the Seventh Circuit's decision and remand for a determination of whether the Company is required to arbitrate the Union's grievance.

II

The principles necessary to decide this case are not new. They were set out by this Court over 25 years ago in a series of cases known as the *Steelworkers Trilogy: Steelworkers v. American Mfg. Co.; Steelworkers v. Warrior & Gulf Navigation Co.;* and *Steelworkers v. Enterprise Wheel & Car Corp.,* 363 U.S. 593 (1960). These precepts have served the industrial relations community well, and have led to continued reliance on arbitration, rather than strikes or lockouts, as the preferred method of resolving disputes arising during the term of a collective-bargaining agreement. We see no reason either to question their continuing validity, or to eviscerate their meaning by creating an exception to their general applicability.

The first principle gleaned from the *Trilogy* is that "arbitration is a matter of contract and a party cannot be required to submit to arbitration any dispute which he has not agreed so to submit." This axiom recognizes the fact that arbitrators derive their authority to resolve disputes only because the parties have agreed in advance to submit such grievances to arbitration.

The second rule, which follows inexorably from the first, is that the question of arbitrability—whether a collective-bargaining agreement creates a duty for the parties to arbitrate the particular grievance—is undeniably an issue for judicial determination. Unless the parties clearly and unmistakably provide otherwise, the question of whether the parties agreed to arbitrate is to be decided by the court, not the arbitrator.

The Court expressly reaffirmed this principle in *John Wiley & Sons, Inc. v. Livingston,* 376 U.S. 543 (1964). The "threshold question" there was whether the court or an arbitrator should decide if arbitration provisions in a collective-bargaining contract survived a corporate merger so as to bind the surviving corporation. The Court answered that there was "no doubt" that this question was for the courts. " 'Under our decisions, whether or not the company was bound to arbitrate, as well as what issues it must arbitrate, is a matter to be determined by the Court on the basis of the contract entered into by the parties.' ... The duty to arbitrate being of contractual origin, a compulsory submission to arbitration cannot precede judicial determination that the collective bargaining agreement does in fact create such a duty."

The third principle derived from our prior cases is that, in deciding whether the parties have agreed to submit a particular grievance to arbitration, a court is not to rule on the potential merits of the underlying claims. Whether "arguable" or not, indeed even if it appears to the court to be frivolous, the union's claim that the employer has violated the collective-bargaining agreement is to be decided, not by the court asked to order arbitration, but as the parties have agreed, by the arbitrator. "The courts, therefore, have no business weighing the merits of the grievance, considering whether there is equity in a particular claim, or determining whether there is particular language in the written instrument which will support the claim. The agreement is to submit all grievances to arbitration, not merely those which the court will deem meritorious."

Finally, it has been established that where the contract contains an arbitration clause, there is a presumption of arbitrability in the sense that "[a]n order to arbitrate the particular grievance should not be denied unless it may be said with positive assurance that the arbitration clause is not susceptible of an interpretation that covers the asserted dispute. Doubts should be resolved in favor of coverage." *Warrior & Gulf,* 363 U.S. at 582–583. Such a presumption is particularly applicable where the clause is as broad as the one employed in this case, which provides for arbitration of "any differences arising with respect to the interpretation of this contract or the performance of any obligation hereunder...." In such cases, "[i]n the absence of any express provision excluding a particular grievance from arbitration, we think only the most forceful evidence of a purpose to exclude the claim from arbitration can prevail." *Warrior & Gulf,* 363 U.S., at 584–585.

This presumption of arbitrability for labor disputes recognizes the greater institutional competence of arbitrators in interpreting collective bargaining agreements, "furthers the national labor policy of peaceful resolution of labor disputes and thus best accords with the parties' presumed objectives in pursuing collective bargaining." The willingness of parties to enter into agreements that provide for arbitration of specified disputes would be "drastically reduced," however, if a labor arbitrator had the "power to determine his own jurisdiction...." Cox, Reflections Upon Labor Arbitration, 72 Harv.L.Rev. 1482, 1509 (1959). Were this the applicable rule, an arbitrator would not be constrained to resolve only those disputes that the parties have agreed in advance to settle by arbitration, but instead, would be empowered "to impose obligations outside the contract limited only by his understanding and conscience." This result undercuts the longstanding federal policy of promoting industrial harmony through the use of collective-bargaining agreements, and is antithetical to the function of a collective-bargaining agreement as setting out the rights and duties of the parties.

With these principles in mind, it is evident that the Seventh Circuit erred in ordering the parties to arbitrate the arbitrability question. It is the court's duty to interpret the agreement and to determine whether the parties intended to arbitrate grievances concerning layoffs predicated on a "lack of work" determination by the Company. If the court determines that the agreement so provides, then it is for the arbitrator to determine the relative merits of the parties' substantive interpretations of the agreement. It was for the court, not the arbitrator, to decide in the first instance whether the dispute was to be resolved through arbitration.

The Union does not contest the application of these principles to the present case. Instead, it urges the Court to examine the specific provisions of the agreement for itself and to affirm the Court of Appeals on the ground that the parties had agreed to arbitrate the dispute over the layoffs at issue here. But it is usually not our function in the first instance to construe collective-bargaining contracts and arbitration clauses, or to consider any other evidence that might unmistakably demonstrate that a particular grievance was not to be subject to arbitration. The issue in the case is whether, because of express exclusion or other forceful evidence, the dispute over the interpretation of Article 20 of the contract, the layoff provision, is not subject to the arbitration clause. That issue should have been decided by the District Court and reviewed by the Court of Appeals; it should not have been referred to the arbitrator.

The judgment of the Court of Appeals is vacated, and the case is remanded for proceedings in conformity with this opinion.

■ JUSTICE BRENNAN, with whom THE CHIEF JUSTICE and JUSTICE MARSHALL join, concurring.

I join the Court's opinion and write separately only to supplement what has been said in order to avoid any misunderstanding on remand and in future cases.

The Seventh Circuit's erroneous conclusion that the arbitrator should decide whether this dispute is arbitrable resulted from that court's confusion respecting the "arbitrability" determination that we have held must be judicially made. Despite recognizing that Article 8 of the collective-bargaining agreement "is a standard arbitration clause, providing for arbitration of 'any differences arising with respect to the interpretation of this contract or the performance of any obligation hereunder,' " and that "there is no clear, unambiguous exclusion [of this dispute] from arbitration," the Court of Appeals thought that "there [were] colorable arguments both for and against exclusion." The "colorable arguments" referred to by the Court of Appeals were the parties' claims concerning the meaning of

Articles 9 and 20 of the collective-bargaining agreement: the Court of Appeals thought that if the Union's interpretation of Article 20 was correct and management could not order lay-offs for reasons other than lack of work, the dispute was arbitrable; but if AT & T's interpretation of Article 20 was correct and management was free to order lay-offs for other reasons, the dispute was not arbitrable under Article 9. Because these were the very issues that would be presented to the arbitrator if the dispute was held to be arbitrable, the court reasoned that "determining arbitrability would enmesh a court in the merits of th[e] dispute," and concluded that the arbitrability issue should be submitted to the arbitrator.

The Court of Appeals was mistaken insofar as it thought that determining arbitrability required resolution of the parties' dispute with respect to the meaning of Articles 9 and 20 of the collective-bargaining agreement. This is clear from our opinion in *Steelworkers v. Warrior & Gulf Navigation Co.* In *Warrior & Gulf,* the Union challenged management's contracting out of labor that had previously been performed by Company employees. The parties failed to resolve the dispute through grievance procedures, and the Union requested arbitration; the Company refused, and the Union sued to compel arbitration under § 301 of the Labor Management Relations Act, 29 U.S.C. § 185. The collective-bargaining agreement contained a standard arbitration clause similar to Article 8 of the AT & T/CSA contract, i.e., providing for arbitration of all differences with respect to the meaning or application of the contract. We held that, in light of the congressional policy making arbitration the favored method of dispute resolution, such a provision requires arbitration "unless it may be said with positive assurance that the arbitration clause is not susceptible of an interpretation that covers the asserted dispute. Doubts should be resolved in favor of coverage."

The Company in *Warrior & Gulf* relied for its argument that the dispute was not arbitrable on a "Management Functions" clause which, like Article 9 of the AT & T/CWA agreement, excluded "matters which are strictly a function of management" from the arbitration provision. We recognized that such a clause "might be thought to refer to any practice of management in which, under particular circumstances prescribed by the agreement, it is permitted to indulge." However, we also recognized that to read the clause this way would make arbitrability in every case depend upon whether management could take the action challenged by the Union; the arbitrability of every dispute would turn upon a resolution of the merits, and "the arbitration clause would be swallowed up by the exception." Therefore, we held that, where a collective-bargaining agreement contains a standard arbitration clause and the "exception" found in the Management Functions clause is general, "judicial inquiry . . . should be limited to the search for an explicit provision which brings the grievance under the cover of the [Management Functions] clause. . . ." "In the absence of any express provision excluding a particular grievance from arbitration, . . . only the most forceful evidence of a purpose to exclude the claim from arbitration can prevail. . . ."

The Seventh Circuit misunderstood these rules of contract construction and did precisely what we disapproved of in *Warrior & Gulf*—it read Article 9, a general Management Functions clause, to make arbitrability depend upon the merits of the parties' dispute. As *Warrior & Gulf* makes clear, the judicial inquiry required to determine arbitrability is much simpler. The parties' dispute concerns whether Article 20 of the collective-bargaining agreement limits management's authority to order lay-offs for reasons other than lack of work. The question for the court is "strictly confined" to whether the parties agreed to submit disputes over the meaning of Article 20 to arbitration. Because the collective-bargaining agreement contains a standard arbitration clause, the answer must be affirmative unless the contract contains explicit language stating that disputes respecting Article 20 are not subject to arbitration, or unless the party opposing arbitration—here AT & T—adduces "the most forceful evidence" to this effect from the bargaining history. Under *Warrior & Gulf,* determining arbitrability does not require the court even to consider which party is correct with respect to the meaning of Article 20.

NOTES AND QUESTIONS

1. The presumption of arbitrability established by the *Steelworkers* "Trilogy" rested in large part on the unique value that arbitration was thought to have, as a "substitute for industrial strife," in the context of the administration of a collective bargaining agreement. See the excerpts from Justice Douglas' opinion in the *Warrior and Gulf* case, supra p. 42. Is there any reason to apply a similar presumption in other areas? See Schneider Moving & Storage Co. v. Robbins, 466 U.S. 364, 104 S.Ct. 1844, 80 L.Ed.2d 366 (1984) (*Steelworkers* presumption of arbitrability "is not a proper rule of construction" in a case brought against employers by the trustees of certain multi-employer trust funds; since the trustees "have no recourse" to the "economic weapons of strikes and lock-outs," "requiring them to arbitrate disputes with the employer would promote labor peace only indirectly, if at all").

However, in cases within the coverage of the FAA, the statute's "liberal federal policy favoring arbitration agreements" has led to a similar presumption—that "any doubts concerning the scope of arbitrable issues should be resolved in favor of arbitration." Moses H. Cone Memorial Hospital v. Mercury Construction Corp., 460 U.S. 1, 24–25, 103 S.Ct. 927, 941, 74 L.Ed.2d 765 (1983); see also Mitsubishi Motors Corp. v. Soler Chrysler–Plymouth, infra p. 176. After all, said one district court judge, "the more the arbitrators do, the less I have to do." Block 175 Corp. v. Fairmont Hotel Management Co., 648 F.Supp. 450, 454 (D. Colo. 1986).

Courts applying the FAA will tend even in commercial arbitration cases to cite routinely and to rely indiscriminately on the labor precedents. See, e.g., In the Matter of the Arbitration Between the Singer Co. and Tappan Co., 403 F.Supp. 322, 330 (D.N.J.1975), aff'd, 544 F.2d 513 (3d Cir.1976) (if the policy of judicial noninterference in labor cases is grounded on the belief that "a labor arbitrator is better able to decide complex labor issues than a judge, then it can likewise be said here that the accounting complexities which led to disagreement between well known and highly regarded accounting firms should likewise be best left for arbitration").

2. The *Steelworkers* "Trilogy" is also thought to stand for the principle that questions of "arbitrability" are not affected by the fact that the claim asserted may clearly be without any substantive merit. "Issues do not lose their quality of arbitrability because they can be correctly decided only one way." New Bedford Defense Prods. Div. v. Local No. 1113, 258 F.2d 522, 526 (1st Cir.1958). Is the same proposition true, as a general matter, of the "subject matter jurisdiction" of a court?

In an influential article relied on by Justice Douglas in the "Trilogy," Professor Cox argued that a dispute can rarely be confidently labeled as "frivolous" until "its industrial context," "the parties' way of life and general industrial practice," have all been brought to light: "Since the true nature of a grievance often cannot be determined until there is a full hearing upon the facts, the reasonable course is to send all doubtful cases to arbitration * * *." Cox, Reflections Upon Labor Arbitration, 72 Harv. L.Rev. 1482, 1515, 1517 (1959). Recall also the frequently-made claim that in collective bargaining cases the airing even of claims that *are* clearly "frivolous" might have a "therapeutic" or "cathartic" value. Is this likely to be true of disputes outside of the collective bargaining area?

3. A collective bargaining agreement provided that any layoffs would be in order of seniority, provided that "aptitude and ability [were] equal." One year after the agreement had expired, the employer laid off a number of senior employees, and the Union brought a grievance. The Supreme Court (in a 5–4 decision) held that this dispute did not "arise under" the expired agreement and was therefore not arbitrable. The grievances "would be arbitrable only if they involve rights which accrued or vested under the Agreement, or rights which carried over after expiration of the Agreement * * * as continuing obligations under the contract," and this was not the case: Since aptitude and ability "do not remain constant, but change over time," they "cannot be said to vest or accrue." The Court rejected the Union's argument that this was an issue of contract interpretation that should be submitted in the first instance to the arbitrator: The presumption of arbitrability cannot be applied "wholesale in the context of an expired bargaining agreement, for to do so would make limitless the contractual obligation to arbitrate. * * * [W]e must determine whether the parties agreed to arbitrate this dispute, and we cannot avoid that duty because it requires us to interpret a provision of a bargaining agreement." A footnote in the opinion conceded that the Court's determination that the dispute was not arbitrable "does, of necessity, determine that * * * the employees lacked any vested contractual right to a particular order of layoff." Litton Financial Printing Div. v. NLRB, 501 U.S. 190, 111 S.Ct. 2215, 115 L.Ed.2d 177 (1991).

Is *Litton* consistent with *AT & T?* See also Independent Lift Truck Builders Union v. Hyster Co., 2 F.3d 233 (7th Cir.1993) (after *Litton,* "the rule that courts must decide arbitrators' jurisdiction takes precedence over the rule that courts are not to decide the merits of the underlying dispute'').

4. The AAA recommends the following standard arbitration clause for use in all commercial contracts:

Any controversy or claim arising out of or relating to this contract, or the breach thereof, shall be settled by arbitration in accordance with the Commercial Arbitration Rules of the American Arbitration Association, and judgment upon the award rendered by the Arbitrator(s) may be entered in any Court having jurisdiction thereof.

"This is precisely the kind of broad arbitration clause that justifies a presumption of arbitrability," Oldroyd v. Elmira Sav. Bank, 134 F.3d 72, 76 (2d Cir. 1998).

One of the advantages of arbitration is that this grant of jurisdiction can be limited or tailored to meet the particular needs and circumstances of the parties. However, more detailed clauses are likely to invite litigation over arbitrability, and may invite courts to speculate as to just what the parties were aiming at. And the departure from hallowed formulas may leave the door open to idiosyncratic judicial rulings.

For example, in Beckham v. William Bayley Co., 655 F.Supp. 288 (N.D.Tex.1987) the parties had provided for arbitration of "any disagreement * * * as to the intent of this contract." The plaintiff, a general contractor, complained that the casements and doors delivered by the defendant were warped and otherwise defective. The court held that this complaint concerning the defendant's *performance* under the contract was not covered by the arbitration clause. The court did not suggest *why* the parties might have wanted to distinguish between disputes over "intent" and disputes over "performance." (Aren't issues of the quality of "performance" precisely the kind of factual questions for which arbitration may be most suited?) See also United Offshore Co. v. Southern Deepwater Pipeline Co., 899 F.2d 405 (5th Cir.1990) (clause provided for arbitration of "any controversy or claim * * * arising out of the interpretation of the provisions of the agreement"; held, arbitrator was "powerless to decide matters on which the agreement was silent; '[i]t is clear that the parties intended that only the contract be interpreted by the arbitrator and not general principles of justice or industry custom or course of dealing between the parties' ").

5. Should the attitude of a court be different if the case to be decided by an arbitrator falls towards the "interest" side of the dispute spectrum? In such cases should a court begin with a different presumption as to arbitrability?

Consider Bowmer v. Bowmer, 50 N.Y.2d 288, 428 N.Y.S.2d 902, 406 N.E.2d 760 (N.Y. 1980). Husband and wife entered into a 37–page separation agreement providing for payment of alimony and child support according to a complex formula. Certain matters such as adjustments to the formula in the event of changes in the tax laws or in the Government's cost of living index were expressly made arbitrable. The agreement also provided for arbitration in the event of "any claim, dispute or misunderstanding arising out of or in connection with this Agreement."

Five years later the husband gave notice that because of changed circumstances he would be reducing his support payments, and sought to compel arbitration of this issue. The court held that the husband's claim was not arbitrable since the arbitration clause "was not intended to encompass the dispute here":

> [What the husband] seeks, in essence, is to have the arbitrator rewrite the terms of the agreement because he now views them as onerous. This cannot be considered merely a claim arising from the contract. Instead, it requires the making of a new contract, not by the parties, but by the arbitrator. Obviously, the parties never agreed to such a procedure for it would mean that, once the agreement made provision for arbitration, the arbitrator would be completely unfettered by the terms of the contract in resolving disputes.

Compare Egol v. Egol, 118 A.D.2d 76, 503 N.Y.S.2d 726 (App. Div.), aff'd, 68 N.Y.2d 893, 508 N.Y.S.2d 935, 501 N.E.2d 584 (1986), where a husband and wife in a pre-divorce agreement expressly provided for arbitration of any claims for reduction in the husband's maintenance and support obligations should he "suffer a substantial, adverse and involuntary change in his financial circumstances, making his support obligations under this Agreement inequitable or a substantial hardship for him." The court granted a motion to compel arbitration: "This is not a case where the arbitrator is asked to reform the instrument. The arbitrator is called upon only to interpret it."

6. Agreements between brokerage firms and their employees commonly provide for arbitration of disputes "arising out of employment or the termination of employment." A former account executive brought suit against his employer for prima facie tort and slander, alleging that his superiors had (1) made defamatory statements to former customers and falsely informed others that his broker's license had been suspended, (2) attempted to "scrounge up" complaints from former customers concerning the handling of their investments, and (3) told fellow office workers that the plaintiff had stolen things from their desks at night. The court held that the first two claims were arbitrable, because they "involved significant aspects of the employment relationship," but that the third was not: "No customers or securities agencies are implicated, and no significant issue of [plaintiff's] job performance *qua* broker is implicated." Morgan v. Smith Barney, Harris Upham & Co., 729 F.2d 1163 (8th Cir.1984). See also Dean Witter Reynolds, Inc. v. Ness, 677 F.Supp. 866 (D.S.C.1988) (brokerage firm caused former employee to be arrested for trespass when he repeatedly visited the office; employee's suit for false arrest, imprisonment, and intentional infliction of emotional distress held not arbitrable).

7. Mr. and Mrs. Seifert contracted with U.S. Home for the construction of a house; the contract provided for arbitration of "any controversy or claim arising out of or related to this Agreement." After they moved into their home, their car was left running in the garage, and the air conditioning system located in the garage picked up the carbon monoxide emissions and distributed them through the house, killing Mr. Seifert. U.S. Home moved that Mrs. Seifert's claim for negligence be referred to arbitration. Mrs. Seifert "concedes that an action for breach of contract or any of the warranties or other rights and obligations arising out of the contract would be subject to arbitration": However, the court held, "because the wrongful death action here is predicated upon a tort theory of common law negligence unrelated to the rights and obligations of the contract," the action "was not contemplated by the parties when the contract was made and should not be subject to arbitration." According to the court, this result was also "supported" by "public policy"—since referral to arbitration would "deprive [the plaintiff] of her rights to a trial by jury, due process and access to the courts." A concurring judge concluded that "the authors of these arbitration provisions need to go back to the drafting board." Seifert v. U.S. Home Corp., 750 So.2d 633 (Fla.1999).

Cf. Scrosati v. McRoy–Wilbur Communities, Inc., 2005 WL 590626 (Cal. App.)(appellate court ordered arbitration of homeowner's claim against developer for personal injuries arising from "toxic mold," although the trial court had denied the developer's motion to compel arbitration because "I'm just not comfortable with the idea of a construction arbitration service determining issues of personal injury claims"); Snyder v. Belmont Homes, Inc., 899 So.2d 57 (La. App. 2005)(same; " 'but for' the defects in the product resulting in the mold, [plaintiff] would have no tort claim against defendants for toxic mold").

Note: Determining the "Jurisdiction" of the Arbitrator

Any "presumption" in favor of arbitration remains, at least in theory, only a rule of construction: "Thus, as with any other contract, the parties' intentions control, but those intentions are generously construed as to issues of arbitrability."[1] The ultimate goal is to effectuate the parties' intent, and the presumption that a dispute is "arbitrable" can be overcome by language or other evidence indicating an intent to *exclude* certain items or claims from the arbitrator's consideration. See, e.g., Instructional Television Corp. v. National Broadcasting Co., 45 A.D.2d 1004, 357 N.Y.S.2d 915 (1974) (clause provided that "[a]ny unresolved questions of fact, as distinguished from questions of law, shall at the behest of either party be submitted to arbitration").

Now, who is to make this determination? It is at least conceivable that the parties could go so far as to entrust to *the arbitrator alone* the authority to determine the scope *of his own jurisdiction.* After all, is not a dispute about "arbitrability" a dispute (in the language of the arbitration clause involved in *Warrior & Gulf*) "as to the meaning and application of [one of] the provisions of [the] Agreement"? Nevertheless, is it likely that the parties will have wanted to do this? Are arbitrators likely to be entirely objective in deciding whether or not they have the authority to hear the merits of a case? "Once they have bitten into the enticing fruit of contro-

---

1. *Mitsubishi Motors Corp. v. Soler Chrysler–Plymouth, Inc.,* infra p. 176.

versy, they are not apt to stay the satisfying of their appetite after one bite."[2]

The Supreme Court has repeated several times that as to this question, we should start with a presumption that is different from the usual one: After all the question, "who should decide arbitrability?" is "rather arcane," and "a party often might not focus upon the question or upon the significance of having arbitrators decide the scope of their own powers." The leading case here is First Options of Chicago v. Kaplan, 514 U.S. 938, 944 (1995). An options trader ("MKI") had incurred a substantial trading deficit leaving it in debt to a clearinghouse firm ("First Options"), and the parties had entered into a series of agreements aimed at "working out" the debt. Kaplan, the President and sole shareholder of MKI, signed several of these, containing an arbitration clause, on behalf of MKI; in addition, he signed one such agreement in his individual capacity that did *not* contain an arbitration clause. First Options later initiated arbitration proceedings against both MKI and Kaplan individually; the arbitrators took jurisdiction and issued an award against both. The Supreme Court ultimately held that the award should be vacated: Where a proper objection has been raised, a court must make a *de novo* determination of consent to arbitration without any deference to the arbitrators' findings: Echoing the opinion in *AT & T,* it warned that lower courts "should not assume" that contracting parties have empowered the arbitrator to decide questions of arbitrability, in the absence of "clear and unmistakable evidence that they did so."

But just what constitutes such "clear and unmistakable" evidence? The *First Options* case, it will be noticed, involved the question of whether Kaplan himself, in his personal capacity, had ever agreed *to arbitrate anything at all.* But what of the case where, by contrast, the parties *do* have a contract that at least "provides for *arbitration of some issues*"?[3] Here the tendency in lower courts has been to find even in the most banal, "broad" arbitration clause, a contractual intention to submit the coverage of the clause—the scope of arbitrable issues—to the arbitrators themselves. It has sufficed to say that "all controversies and disputes" concerning the "meaning [and] construction" of the agreement are to be arbitrated[4]—or that "any dispute, controversy or claim arising out of, or relating to, this agreement" shall be arbitrated.[5] In such cases, it is hard to see how the parties could have done much less.

---

2. Trafalgar Shipping Co. v. International Milling Co., 401 F.2d 568, 573–74 (2d Cir.1968) (Lumbard, C.J., dissenting).

3. *First Options of Chicago, Inc. v. Kaplan,* supra, 514 U.S. at 945.

4. Fraternity Fund Ltd. v. Beacon Hill Asset Management LLC, 371 F.Supp.2d 571 (S.D.N.Y. 2005)("disputes with respect to the 'meaning' and 'construction' of the agreement ... cover a dispute over whether a claim falls within the scope of the arbitration clause"). See also Ryan, Beck & Co., LLC v. Fakih, 268 F.Supp.2d 210 (E.D.N.Y. 2003)("all disputes ... arising out of or relating to [the investor's] Accounts ... or any construction, performance, or breach of this or any other agreement between [the parties]"; language "is sufficiently plain and sweeping to encompass disputes over the scope of the arbitration clause, and to manifest the parties' intent to have the arbitrators decide that issue").

5. Gruner v. Blumen, 1999 WL 669844 (Conn. Super)("the language is broad enough to empower the arbitrator to rule on the

Such results may in fact be quite sensible. See Alan Scott Rau, "The Arbitrability Question Itself," 10 Amer. Rev. of Int'l Arb. 287, 362–69 (1999):

> While there is obviously no one "right" way to conceptualize disputes over the scope of an undoubted arbitration agreement, in many cases these too can be treated as discrete controversies, dependent on the interpretative skills of the arbitrators themselves and thus entrusted to them by the parties. * * * So, for example, whether an agreement grants arbitrators the power to award punitive damages will usually be a question as to which an arbitrator's judgment should be expected to command considerable deference. * * *
>
> [W]here the parties are found to have entered into some sort of arbitration agreement, it seems unfair and tendentious to treat such decisionmakers wholly as intermeddling, officious strangers: Parties who agree to arbitration cannot rationally claim to be wholly astonished when they find that "their" arbitrators have been tempted to expand their own jurisdiction through self-interest—nor is it unfair to charge them with the risk that this might sometimes occur. As one member of the Court in fact suggested at the time of oral argument in *Kaplan*, "[w]henever you submit issues to arbitration, in effect you're consenting to a kind of rough-and-ready disposition of whatever your claims or disputes may be, and therefore there's no reason to sort of draw fine lines as to what you were rough and ready about."[6] There is more reason, then, to think that the parties—merely by settling upon the language of the conventional, expansive arbitration clause—were willing to submit such questions of "arbitrability" to the arbitrators. * * *
>
> I think it clear also that the model put forward here brings strong advantages of administrative efficiency. It is not merely that what has been termed "one-stop adjudication"[7] is inevitably more economical,

question of arbitrability"); see also The Shaw Group Inc. v. Triplefine Int'l Corp., 322 F.3d 115 (2d Cir. 2003)("all disputes . . . concerning or arising out of this Agreement"; language "reflects such a broad grant of power to the arbitrators as to evidence the parties' clear intent to arbitrate issues of arbitrability").

6. *See* Oral Argument in First Options of Chicago, Inc. v. Kaplan, 1995 WL 242250 at *43–*44. This suggestion took the form of one Justice's insistent attempt to be helpful to counsel for the Kaplans: "[W]hy don't you say that there is, in fact, a superior value to be served by making this distinction between subject and person, and the person agreement at least must be clear and unmistakable, regardless of what the subject agreement is?"

The fact that the parties have chosen an arbitrator to do *something*—and that they therefore have incentives both to find out what they can about him in advance, and to monitor his behavior—may also minimize the likelihood of a runaway tribunal and of "outlier" awards, including an unjustified assumption of jurisdiction. * * *

7. *Cf.* Harbour Assurance Co. (UK) Ltd. v. Kansa Gen. Int'l Assurance Co. Ltd., [1993] Q.B. 701, 724, 726 (C.A.)(Hoffmann, L.J.)(discussing whether "illegality also strikes down the arbitration clause," and referring to "the practical advantages of one-stop adjudication, or in other words, the inconvenience of having one issue resolved by the court and then, contingently on the outcome of that decision, further issues decided by the arbitrator"; "I would be very slow to

and thus likely to have been desired by both parties *ex ante*—that questions of "arbitrability" and questions "going to the merits" are often so intertwined that we can expect similar arbitral competence to be relevant, and similar factual considerations to come into play. It is also true that arbitrators will be in a far better position than courts to appreciate the submissions made by the parties in the course of the proceedings—submissions which if properly understood can define, alter or expand the scope of actual consent. * * *

Nothing that I have written, finally, need disqualify the courts in any way from continuing their supervisory role, both before and after the award, as benign if occasionally distracted gatekeepers to the arbitration process. To be sure, limited or idiosyncratic arbitration clauses might perhaps present a court with "sufficient ambiguity"—so that it requires the reassurance of "clear and unmistakable" evidence to the effect that scope or timeliness issues were to be for the arbitrators. But in the run-of-the-mill case, where the conventional "broad" form has not been distorted, this should be quite unnecessary. As institutional draftsmen naturally respond to the invitation that *Kaplan* seems to extend, even this individualized examination will progressively become superfluous.

Indeed, in 1999 the AAA revised its Commercial Arbitration Rules precisely in order to address the holding in *First Options*: The Rules now expressly empower the arbitrator "to rule on his or her own jurisdiction, including any objections with respect to the existence, scope or validity of the arbitration agreement."[8] See Sleeper Farms v. Agway, Inc., 211 F.Supp.2d 197 (D. Me. 2002)(since the AAA rules constitute "a clear and unmistakable delegation of scope-determining authority to an arbitrator," the court "refers this dispute" to the arbitrator "to determine * * * what issues * * * are covered by the arbitration clause").

One further indication that the courts are moving in the same direction can be found in the Supreme Court's recent opinion in Pacificare Health Systems, Inc. v. Book, 538 U.S. 401 (2003). In this case, agreements between physicians and HMO's called for arbitration of any dispute that "arises out of or relates to this agreement or its terms"—but also specified that "punitive damages shall not be awarded." The physicians brought an action alleging, among other things, violations of the Racketeer Influenced and Corrupt Organizations Act ["RICO"] based on the defendants' failure to reimburse them for health-care services provided to patients under their health plans.[9] The lower courts refused to compel arbitration, on the ground that the contractual restriction on punitive damages served to bar the recovery of treble damages as provided for by the RICO statute—and that such limitations were unenforceable as a matter of public policy

---

attribute to reasonable parties an intention that there should in any foreseeable eventuality be two sets of proceedings").

8. AAA Commercial Arbitration Rules, R.7(a).

9. The RICO statute is at 18 U.S.C.A. § 1961; see further at p. 195 infra.

because they prevented the plaintiffs "from obtaining any meaningful relief for [their] statutory claims."

The Supreme Court, however, reversed: Writing for a unanimous court, Justice Scalia thought that to address the public-policy related question was simply "premature": The terms of the agreement were "ambiguous," and the intent of the parties "uncertain"—in particular, whether the contractual limitation was even applicable to RICO claims for treble damages "is, to say the least, in doubt." So the arbitration clause was "at least initially, enforceable": Courts should not take upon themselves "the authority to decide the antecedent question of how the ambiguity is to be resolved," and the arbitrators must first be called on to tell us just what the agreement meant. Is it fair to say that the result of compelling arbitration in *Pacificare* was that the *coverage of the arbitration clause* ("Did the parties intend to bar, or rather to retain, a claimant's right to treble damages under RICO?") *was made a matter for final determination by the arbitrators* themselves?[10]

NOTES AND QUESTIONS

1. In some state courts, the list of possible reasons to find an arbitration clause "unconscionable" continues to expand rapidly. For the Alabama Supreme Court, for example, the fact that a consumer loan agreement contains an "unusually broad" arbitration clause may itself be an "indicium of unconscionability." Another such "indicium" apparently is a provision that "all issues and disputes as to the arbitrability of claims must also be resolved by the arbitrator" himself. American Gen. Finance, Inc. v. Branch, 793 So.2d 738, 748–49 (Ala. 2000).

2. A respondent refuses to participate in arbitration, asserting that he never agreed to arbitrate the dispute. May the claimant simply proceed without him? The AAA Commercial Arbitration Rules permit arbitrators to proceed despite the absence of one party, although the award may not be made solely by default and the party who is present must submit evidence supporting his claim. (Rule 29).

Or, alternatively, should the claimant first seek an order under § 4 of the FAA to compel arbitration? The court in Waterspring, S.A. v. Trans Marketing Houston Inc., 717 F.Supp. 181 (S.D.N.Y. 1989), held that since the parties' arbitration clause allowed the claimant to proceed *ex parte*, and since "the very purpose of such a self-executing mechanism in an arbitration clause is to avoid the time and expense of Federal Court motion practice," then the claimant was simply not a party "aggrieved" within the meaning of § 4 by the respondent's refusal to arbitrate. In Raytheon Co. v. Ashborn Agencies, Ltd., 372 F.3d 451 (D.C. Cir. 2004), the court reached

---

10. See Pacificare Health Systems, Inc. v. Book, 538 U.S. at 407 fn. 2 ("If the contractual ambiguity could itself be characterized as raising a 'gateway' question of arbitrability, then it would be appropriate for a court to answer it in the first instance . . . [But] we think the preliminary question whether the remedial limitations at issue here prohibit an award of RICO treble damages is not a question of arbitrability").

the same result, this time on constitutional grounds: Here too, the parties' agreement—as well as the rules of the ICC—allowed the claimant to proceed *ex parte*. As a consequence, it was held that the claimant had not "demonstrated it suffered any injury-in-fact" as a result of the respondent's refusal—and thus that it lacked "standing to sue" under Art. III of the Constitution. The respondent's absence "should, if anything, make it easier for [the claimant] to obtain a favorable award." Are these sensible results? Does it matter that if the respondent should later successfully challenge the existence of a binding arbitration agreement, the claimant would then find that the arbitration had turned out to be nothing more than an expensive and useless gesture?

3. If the respondent fails to appear, and the arbitration does proceed without him, may he later resist judicial enforcement of the resulting award? It is clear at the very least—as in the case of default in litigation—that the respondent has lost the ability to defend the claim on the merits. May he also be found to have waived the right to assert any defense of lack of agreement? It is usually assumed that a respondent who remains out of the proceeding may still at a later time challenge the existence of an agreement to arbitrate. See MCI Telecommunications Corp. v. Exalon Industries, Inc., 138 F.3d 426 (1st Cir.1998)(if there is no written agreement to arbitrate, "the actions of the arbitrator have no legal validity"; "in both the FAA and personal jurisdiction contexts, albeit for different reasons, the non-appearing party can subsequently challenge the authority of the decision-maker, but not the merits of the decision"). This seems also to be the sense of the Revised Uniform Arbitration Act, which allows a court to vacate an arbitration award where "[t]here was no agreement to arbitrate, unless the person participated in the arbitration proceeding without raising the objection . . . not later than the commencement of the arbitration hearing." § 23(a)(5).

However, cf. Comprehensive Accounting Corp. v. Rudell, 760 F.2d 138 (7th Cir.1985). The respondents in this case refused to participate in an arbitration, and later opposed confirmation of the award on the ground that they did not actually know about the arbitration clause when they signed the agreement. The court commented that this was "irrelevant," even if the respondents could make out a claim of fraud in the inducement. "[A]fter an award has been entered, § 4 [of the FAA] is no longer in play." It was "too late" for the respondents to "sit back and allow the arbitration to go forward, and only after it was all done * * * say: oh by the way, we never agreed to the arbitration clause. That is a tactic that the law of arbitration, with its commitment to speed, will not tolerate." See also Ramonas v. Kerelis, 102 Ill.App.2d 262, 243 N.E.2d 711 (Ill.App.1968) ("in refusing to appear," respondent "acted at [his] own peril," and his "defense that he did not sign the contract nor was a party to the contract was lost due to a situation of his own creation").

If, on the other hand, the respondent *does* appear before the arbitrators to argue that he had never agreed to arbitrate the dispute, he may also incur certain risks: Might his conduct be taken as a consent to allow *the arbitrators themselves* to determine the threshold question of their own jurisdiction? See, e.g., Yorkaire, Inc. v. Sheet Metal Workers Int'l Ass'n, 758 F.Supp. 248 (E.D.Pa.1990), aff'd mem., 931 F.2d 53 (3d Cir.1991) ("Although [the employer] vigorously argued from the start that the panel did not have jurisdiction to resolve the substance of the Union's grievances, it did not contest the arbitration panel's authority to determine whether the grievances fell within its jurisdiction"); Mytech Corp. v. Ausman, 1999 WL 230942 (Tex. App.)("because [respondent had] raised the question of the existence of an [arbitration] agreement before the arbitrator, it may not reurge the same argument before the trial court"). And if the arbitrators go on to conclude that the dispute is in fact arbitrable, will that decision benefit from the same degree of deference that is enjoyed by arbitral awards generally?

Such a risk for the respondent should be considerably attenuated in light of the Supreme Court's decision in *First Options of Chicago, Inc. v. Kaplan*, supra. The Court here seems to have concluded, as Justice Scalia noted in oral argument, that to confront a respondent with such a cruel dilemma was "just not fair, it really isn't." In such a case, the Court declared,

> merely arguing the arbitrability issue to an arbitrator does not indicate a clear willingness to arbitrate that issue, *i.e.,* a willingness to be effectively bound by the arbitrator's decision on that point. To the contrary, insofar as the [respondents] were forcefully objecting to the arbitrators deciding their dispute with [the claimant], one naturally would think that they did *not* want the arbitrators to have binding authority over them. * * * [B]ecause the [respondents] did not clearly agree to submit the question of arbitrability to arbitration, the Court of Appeals was correct in finding that the arbitrability of the * * * dispute was subject to independent review by the courts.

Cf. Mays v. Lanier Worldwide, Inc., 115 F.Supp.2d 1330 (M.D. Ala. 2000)("at the very least, a specific objection is necessary in order to entitle the objector to raise the issue in court" after the conclusion of the arbitration).

What other steps are open to a defendant who does not believe that he is subject to a valid agreement to arbitrate?

4. When a party's obligation to arbitrate is challenged, every legal system has to make some difficult procedural choices. In France, for example, the so-called doctrine of *"compétence/compétence"* gives first crack at the question to the arbitrators themselves: Unless the arbitration clause is "manifestly null or non-existent," the courts are not to intervene. See generally William W. Park, The Arbitrability Dicta in First Options v. Kaplan: What Sort of Kompetenz–Kompetenz Has Crossed the Atlantic?, 12 Arb. Int'l 137, 150–152 (1996); John J. Barceló III, Who Decides the Arbitrator's Jurisdiction? Separability and Competence–Competence in Transnational Perspective, 36 Vand. J. Transnat'l L. 1115 (2003). However, *after* the award is rendered, judicial review of the arbitrator's authority is possible on a de novo basis; the arbitrator's "decision" is provisional only. In sharp contrast, American procedural law has been exceptionally generous in providing an abundance of devices through which legal challenges to arbitral authority can be made—for legislation "allows an objecting party to seek judicial determination of the scope of consent *either before, during, or after an arbitration.*" Grad v. Wetherholt Galleries, 660 A.2d 903, 908 (D.C. App. 1995)(state law). As Justice (then Judge) Breyer has remarked, to enjoin a party from arbitrating where an agreement to arbitrate is absent is nothing more than "the concomitant of the power to compel arbitration where it is present," Société Générale de Surveillance S.A. v. Raytheon European Management & Systems Co., 643 F.2d 863, 868 (1st Cir. 1981). In this country, then, the doctrine of *compétence/compétence* takes on the air of a local solution with little or no relevance to American procedure.

Now the choice between these polar mechanisms is at bottom a matter of cost/benefit analysis: Is it best, as we have tended to assume, that the question of "arbitrability" be resolved with finality as soon as possible— thereby obviating an extended procedure that might turn out in the end to have been pointless? Or is it best, instead, to allow the arbitration to proceed—preventing delay and obstructive tactics by recalcitrant parties— bearing in mind that quite often

- a preliminary arbitral award on jurisdictional matters alone may expedite matters by making the question ripe for immediate review, and that in any event,

- an arbitral award in favor of the respondent will render the "arbitrability" question completely moot?

5. The "separability" principle of *Prima Paint* is also nominally a rule of construction. See fn. 9 of the Supreme Court's opinion, p. 89 supra. A court will frequently compel arbitration only after indulging in mock deference to the parties' presumed "intention" to entrust to the arbitrator the question whether the overall agreement had been induced by fraud. See, e.g., Weinrott v. Carp, 32 N.Y.2d 190, 344 N.Y.S.2d 848, 298 N.E.2d 42 (1973) (proceeding to confirm arbitration award; "technical argument about separability or nonseparability has often obscured the main goal of the court's inquiry which is to discern the parties' intent"). It need hardly be pointed out that this is usually little more than a fiction: It will be rare indeed that parties resisting arbitration will be able to present sufficient evidence to satisfy "their heavy burden of proving an intent not to arbitrate" the issue of fraudulent inducement. See Stateside Machinery Co., Ltd. v. Alperin, 591 F.2d 234 (3d Cir.1979).

Nevertheless, judicial reliance on rules of construction may occasionally entail some curious consequences in terms of party planning and drafting. Some courts continue to hold, for example, that a clause merely requiring arbitration of "any disputes arising hereunder" must be considered a "narrow" clause—and thus, may not encompass an allegation of fraudulent inducement. See Bristol–Myers Squibb Co. v. SR Int'l Bus. Ins. Co. Ltd., 354 F.Supp.2d 499 (S.D.N.Y. 2005)(grumbling, however, that its holding, dictated by circuit precedent, "is out of step with the overwhelming body of law favoring arbitration in circumstances like these"); see also Tracer Research Corp. v. National Environmental Services Co., 42 F.3d 1292 (9th Cir. 1994)(clause calling for arbitration of claims "arising under" an agreement—but omitting reference to claims "relating to" it—does not cover a tort claim for misappropriation of trade secrets, even though the defendant obtained the secrets during the term of a license; the clause covers only those disputes "relating to the interpretation and performance of the contract itself." Cf. S.A. Mineracao Da Trindade–Samitri v. Utah Int'l, Inc., 745 F.2d 190 (2d Cir. 1984)(clause calling for arbitration of *any question or dispute [that] shall arise or occur under* this [agreement]" is, however, broad enough to include a claim of fraudulent inducement); Genesco, Inc. v. T. Kakiuchi & Co., 815 F.2d 840 (2d Cir. 1987)(so is a clause calling for arbitration of *"all claims and disputes of whatever nature arising under* this contract").

Note: Loss of the Right to Arbitrate through Delay or "Waiver"

A particular dispute may be conceded to be within the scope of a valid arbitration clause. However, one of the parties may resist on the ground that the other has *lost* the right to arbitrate—perhaps through delay in asserting the right, or by engaging in some action supposedly "inconsistent" with arbitration. This defense may be phrased indiscriminately in terms of "waiver," or "laches," or may be based on the other party's failure to comply with time limits or procedures specified in the contract for seeking arbitration. Is this a matter for the court or the arbitrator to decide? And why does this matter?

The cases have traditionally distinguished between "substantive" and "procedural arbitrability," and hold that the latter is always a question for the arbitrator: "Once it is determined * * * that the parties are obligated to submit the subject matter of a dispute to arbitration, 'procedural' questions which grow out of the dispute and bear on its final disposition should be left to the arbitrator." John Wiley & Sons, Inc. v. Livingston, 376 U.S. 543, 557 (1964). In *Wiley* the employer argued that the union had failed to follow the various grievance steps required in the collective bargaining agreement as prerequisites to arbitration; the Supreme Court held that this question was itself arbitrable. The Court noted that "procedural" questions will often be intertwined with the merits of the dispute, and that reserving "procedural" issues for the court "would thus not only create the difficult task of separating related issues, but would also produce frequent duplication of effort" and delay in a final decision. See also Trafalgar Shipping Co. v. International Milling Co., 401 F.2d 568 (2d Cir.1968) (laches) ("in the often esoteric field of commercial dealings," severity of prejudice suffered through delay should be submitted to "expertise of the arbitrators").

One much-litigated example can be found in securities arbitration, where the rules of administering institutions like the NYSE and NASD impose a limit of six years after which no customer claim "shall be eligible for submission to arbitration." Brokerage firms will usually prefer that the *courts* decide whether this time limit has passed, while on the other hand customers will argue that this should be an issue for the *arbitrators*. (Why?) Now it would be perfectly plausible to say that this rule of "eligibility" calls into question the very power of the arbitrator to act: After all, it is not clear that there was *any "agreement" at all* to arbitrate claims not brought within the contractual time limit—and if there is no consent to arbitration in those circumstances, how in the world can the arbitrator come by his authority to determine whether the claim is properly brought? See, e.g., Smith Barney Shearson Inc. v. Sacharow, 91 N.Y.2d 39, 666 N.Y.S.2d 990, 992–93, 689 N.E.2d 884 (1997)(contractual proviso "limits the subject of, entitlement to, and range of arbitrable matters" and thus "creates a substantive feature that may affect the right and obligation to arbitrate"). But the Supreme Court has recently held—relying heavily on the *Wiley* case—that such " 'procedural' questions which grow out of the dispute and bear on its final disposition are presumptively *not* for the judge, but for an arbitrator, to decide." The parties to this contract "would normally expect a forum-based decisionmaker" to decide such "forum-specific procedural gateway matters." Howsam v. Dean Witter Reynolds, Inc., 537 U.S. 79 (2002).

Another common scenario goes something like this: One party who now wishes to arbitrate will have earlier taken an active part in litigation concerning the very same dispute—for example, he may have earlier filed a counterclaim, or engaged in discovery. He may then be met with the assertion that he has "waived" his right to arbitration. In such cases, courts will often pass directly on the "waiver" issue, sometimes without expressly addressing the appropriateness of their doing so. It has in fact been suggested that a claim of waiver "predicated solely upon participation in the lawsuit by the party seeking arbitration" should be decided by a court, while the issue of waiver "by other conduct" should be for the arbitrator. See The Brothers Jurewicz, Inc. v. Atari, Inc., 296 N.W.2d 422 (Minn.1980). Why should this be true? See also Marie v. Allied Home Mortgage Corp., 402 F.3d 1 (1st Cir. 2005)(allowing courts to decide waiver issues arising out of litigation-related activity "furthers a key purpose of the FAA: to permit speedy resolution of disputes"; "comparative expertise" also argues for judges to decide this issue as they are "well-trained to recognize abusive forum shopping"). Does the final proviso of § 3 of the FAA have any bearing at all on this question?

Some state courts seem to approach this question of waiver in a fairly rigid and mechanical way, asking whether the party now seeking arbitration had earlier acted in a way that is "inconsistent" with an assertion of the right to arbitrate or had made "an election" between a judicial and an arbitral forum. E.g., Sanford Construction Co., Inc. v. Rosenblatt, 25 Ohio Misc. 99, 266 N.E.2d 267 (Ohio Mun.Ct.1970) (defendant's statement, "If you want to collect, sue us!" constituted an "express waiver" of arbitration); Lapidus v. Arlen Beach Condominium Ass'n, Inc., 394 So.2d 1102 (Fla.App.1981) ("filing an answer without asserting the right for arbitration acts as waiver"). Such cases seem to counsel that a decision whether or not to pursue arbitration under an arbitration clause should be made at the earliest possible moment. See also Texas International Commercial Arbitration and Conciliation Act, V.T.C.A., Civ.Prac. & Rem.Code § 172.174(b)(a party "may not make a request for a stay [of litigation] after the time the requesting party submits the party's first statement on the substance of the dispute").

In contrast, many *federal* cases seem to be considerably slower in finding "waiver" where a party has vacillated and participated in litigation before moving to compel arbitration. Given the "strong federal policy favoring enforcement of arbitration agreements between knowledgeable business people," a finding of waiver is not favored in federal court; the party asserting waiver is said to bear a heavy burden of proof. Knorr Brake Corp. v. Harbil, Inc., 556 F.Supp. 489 (N.D.Ill.1983). But cf. Cabinetree of Wisconsin, Inc. v. Kraftmaid Cabinetry, Inc., 50 F.3d 388 (7th Cir.1995) (Posner, J.) ("[i]n determining whether a waiver has occurred, the court is not to place its thumbs on the scales").

The majority of federal courts therefore tend to ask whether one of the parties will have been "prejudiced" if his adversary is permitted to take part in litigation and then later demand arbitration. Without such a finding of "prejudice," the mere fact that a party has delayed in calling for arbitration will not be enough to cause a waiver of his right to arbitrate. (In many cases, of course, delay in demanding arbitration will simply reflect the fact that negotiations over settlement of the dispute are being carried on.) Nor will the fact that he has filed pleadings in the lawsuit. So, for example, a party has been allowed to seek arbitration thirteen months after a suit was filed, even though he had answered the complaint, served several interrogatories and requests for the production of documents, and participated in a pretrial conference. Walker v. J.C. Bradford & Co., 938 F.2d 575 (5th Cir.1991). See also Blumenthal–Kahn Electric Ltd. v. American Home Assurance Co., 236 F.Supp.2d 575 (E.D. Va. 2002)(more than five months after the complaint was filed, and more than four months after filing an answer, the defendant moved to compel arbitration; "[a]lthough the matter has been pending in litigation for only six months, ... discovery is largely completed, with the parties having exchanged documents and taken depositions of the various party representatives"; held, defendant's motion granted).

Whether a party has suffered enough "prejudice" to warrant a finding of waiver is obviously an inquiry heavily dependent on the facts of the particular case. Courts will often rely on the fact that the party resisting arbitration has incurred substantial costs in preparing for trial and in defending against the litigation moves of his opponent. See, e.g., Fraser v. Merrill Lynch Pierce, Fenner & Smith, Inc., 817 F.2d 250 (4th Cir.1987) (the parties "participated in four status conferences, five hearings on pending motions, and two pretrial conferences"; waiver was found in light of "the extent of the moving party's trial-oriented activity" and the "substantial time and effort" expended by the plaintiff); Ritzel Communications, Inc. v. Mid–American Cellular Telephone Co., 989 F.2d 966 (8th Cir. 1993)(defendant moved to stay litigation and compel arbitration, but its motion was denied; it appealed this ruling, but continued nevertheless to litigate in district court, where after a six-day trial judgment was entered against it; held, "by failing to make the simple effort of requesting a stay in [the court of appeals] and by proceeding to trial on the merits in the district court, [defendant] defeated the whole purpose of the arbitration clause on which it claims to rely").

In addition, courts often find it important that the party now demanding arbitration had earlier benefited from using judicial discovery mechanisms to which he might not have been entitled in arbitration. See, e.g., Zwitserse Maatschappij Van Levensverzekering En Lijfrente v. ABN Int'l Capital Markets Corp., 996 F.2d 1478 (2d Cir.1993) (defendant "suffered prejudice because the deposition-type discovery obtained [by plaintiff] in the Netherlands would not have been available" in securities arbitration in the United States). In other cases, however, the benefits of pre-trial discovery obtained by the party now seeking arbitration seem to play a smaller role: See Microstrategy, Inc. v. Lauricia, 268 F.3d 244 (4th Cir. 2001). Here an employer engaged in a "remarkably aggressive" spate of preemptive lawsuits against an employee who had filed discrimination claims with the EEOC; the employer only requested arbitration after the employee herself had filed a discrimination lawsuit. Reversing the district court, the Fourth Circuit found that there had been no waiver because "the bulk of the activity" [sic] in the employer's three lawsuits sought to prevent the employee from disclosing trade secrets or other confidential information—thus raising different legal and factual issues from the employee's discrimination claim. In addition, the court held, the fact that the employer had engaged in discovery in its own lawsuits did not satisfy "the heavy burden of proving waiver"—because the employee had offered "no evidence generally showing how often discovery is permitted by arbitrators conducting proceedings under the rules to which she agreed or the extent of discovery that typically is permitted by such arbitrators." On the availability of discovery in arbitration, see generally Section D.2.d. infra.

NOTES AND QUESTIONS

1.   Are the state cases and statutes referred to in the text consistent with federal policy? Is a separate state standard of waiver permissible in cases falling within the ambit of the FAA? See Alan Scott Rau, The UNCITRAL Model Law in State and Federal Courts: The Problem of "Waiver," 6 Am.Rev.Int'l Arb. 223 (1995).

2.   A finding of waiver is more readily made where it is the *plaintiff* in a lawsuit who later seeks to compel arbitration of the dispute. See, e.g., Christensen v. Dewor Developments, 33 Cal.3d 778, 191 Cal.Rptr. 8, 661 P.2d 1088 (Cal. 1983) (plaintiff filed complaint in order to "have some feel for what the Defendants' position would be at arbitration"). See also Note, Contractual Agreements to Arbitrate Disputes: Waiver of the Right to Compel Arbitration, 52 So.Cal.L.Rev. 1513 (1979), which advocates that a plaintiff who files suit over an arbitrable issue should be "deemed" to have waived any right to arbitration. Are there any virtues in such a mechanical rule? What of the case where a plaintiff files a complaint and then, the same day, changes his mind and makes a formal demand for arbitration? See Cavac Compania Anonima Venezolana de Administracion y Comercio v. Board for Validation of German Bonds in the U.S., 189 F.Supp. 205 (S.D.N.Y.1960).

3. A plaintiff brings a lawsuit, and the defendant successfully moves for a stay on the ground that the parties had agreed to arbitrate. So the plaintiff acquiesces, and makes a demand for arbitration. Then the defendant tries to claim that the plaintiff—by originally instituting the suit—has waived his right to arbitration. Can the defendant thereby accomplish the "stunning tour de force" of denying the plaintiff any forum at all? See 795 Fifth Ave. Corp. v. Trusthouse Forte (Pierre) Management, Inc., 131 Misc.2d 291, 499 N.Y.S.2d 857 (1986) (no).

4. A finding that the right to arbitration has been "waived" is often a value-laden judgment, comprehensible only as a response to other, unarticulated policies. An extreme example of this point is Davis v. Blue Cross of Northern California, 25 Cal.3d 418, 158 Cal.Rptr. 828, 600 P.2d 1060 (1979). A number of insureds alleged in a class action that Blue Cross had refused to pay for hospital expenses to which they were entitled. Shortly after the filing of the complaint Blue Cross moved to submit the disputes to a "medical arbitration panel" as required by the policies. The trial court found that the arbitration clause had been "buried in an obscure provision" of the agreements and that Blue Cross, in rejecting claims, had failed to bring the arbitration procedure to its insureds' attention. The Supreme Court of California agreed with the trial court that Blue Cross had "breached its duty of good faith and fair dealing" to its insureds "by failing timely or adequately to apprise them of the availability" of arbitration and that "as a consequence, Blue Cross waived any right subsequently to compel its insureds to resort to arbitration."

Is this a case of "waiver"? How have the plaintiffs been prejudiced by Blue Cross's failure to inform them of the availability of arbitration? In the course of its opinion, the Supreme Court also noted that:

> Under hospitalization policies, in which disputes over benefits may frequently involve a simple disagreement between the insured's physician and the insurer's medical consultant as to the reasonableness of fees or the necessity for certain medical procedures, the existence of an arbitral process will often enable the insured to obtain an impartial review of the insurer's decision without the need to incur the significant expense of legal counsel; as a consequence, the reduced cost of the process may make it practicable for the insured to secure a binding resolution of disputes over smaller claims than would otherwise be financially feasible.

How does the court's finding of "waiver" respond to this rhetoric about the advantages of the arbitration process?

5. The respondent in an arbitration asserts that if the dispute had been litigated, the state's statute of limitations would have barred the underlying claim. The arbitrator finds that questions relating to the statute of limitations are within the scope of the arbitration clause, and rules in favor of the claimant. On a motion to vacate the award, what result? See NCR Corp. v. CBS Liquor Control, Inc., 874 F.Supp. 168 (S.D.Ohio 1993), aff'd, 43 F.3d 1076 (6th Cir.1995) ("the effect of a statute of limitations is to bar an action at law, not arbitration"); Hanes Corp. v. Millard, 531 F.2d 585 (D.C.Cir.1976) ("the arbitrator may be forced to decide at what point any breach might have occurred and when the [plaintiffs] did or should have acquired knowledge of the alleged breach. Such an inquiry will require considerable factual probing"). A New York statute permits a party, by application to the court, to assert the statute of limitations "as a bar to arbitration"; "the failure to assert such bar by such application shall not preclude its assertion before the arbitrators, who may, in their sole discretion, apply or not apply the bar." N.Y.C.P.L.R. § 7502(b).

6. A contract involving a natural gas project in Australia was entered into between the operator ("Tri–Star") and the non-operating owners ("Tipperary"). After a few years of operations, a dispute arose as to the propriety of certain charges made by the operator to the joint account (a proportionate share of which was the contractual responsibility of the non-operating owners). So the parties entered into an agreement providing that "a 'Big Six' accounting firm familiar with international petroleum operations" would make a final and binding determination as to which expenses should properly be chargeable to the joint account. Ernst & Young was engaged and eventually issued a report; Tri–Star moved both to confirm the report as an arbitration award and to compel arbitration of further disputes that had arisen between the parties.

The court held that both motions should be denied: The trial court had found that Tri–Star had "hired Ernst & Young not as a neutral arbitrator but in the capacity of its own accounting firm," and had exercised "undue influence" over it; that Tri–Star had "engaged in a conscious effort to exclude Tipperary from access" to the accountant; that the arbitration process had been "extremely long, costly, and inefficient" as a result of Tri–Star's "misconduct"; that "valuable productive time in the drilling program was lost because of the flawed arbitration process, the 'efficacy' of which had been 'irretrievably compromised,' so that it was now 'impossible for Tipperary to obtain the benefit it reasonably anticipated from the arbitration agreement—a speedy and inexpensive resolution of the controversy.'" As a consequence Tri–Star was found to have "materially breached" the arbitration agreement—which had been "rendered no longer enforceable." Because material breach is "a ground for revoking [any] contract" under the arbitration statute, then it should be a ground for revoking an "arbitration agreement," and so the agreement "effectively no longer exists." Tri–Star Petroleum Co. v. Tipperary Corp., 107 S.W.3d 607 (Tex. App. 2003). The word "waiver" appears nowhere in the court's opinion.

7. A contract for the sale of the "Nancy Lea" provided that if after accepting the vessel the buyer failed by March 17, 2005 to pay the balance of the purchase price and execute all necessary papers, then "the parties shall be relieved of all obligations under this agreement." On March 17, the buyer requested a one-week extension—he later claimed that the seller "would not provide payoff information in a sufficient time for the contract to close"—but on March 22, the seller responded that he had changed his mind about the whole deal. The court held that "the expiration of the agreement" on March 17 precluded arbitration of the dispute: "Under any reasonable interpretation," the termination of "all obligations" "must necessarily include the obligation to arbitrate," and "as a matter of straightforward contract interpretation" the agreement "excluded from arbitration" any disputes arising after March 17 where the buyer had failed to make payment in full by that date, "irrespective of the reason for that failure." In the view of the court, "no other reading * * * makes sense," and the buyer had not suggested "any viable reconciliation" of the arbitration clause and the expiration clause that would enable the former to survive—"it is not incumbent on this Court to develop or articulate his arguments for him." Clements v. Preston, 2005 WL 1840239 (S.D. Ala.)

Can you do a better job?

4. JUDICIAL SUPERVISION AND REVIEW

For arbitration to function as an efficient process of private dispute resolution—to realize the benefits of expert decision-making with reduced cost and delay—litigation challenging the process, or aimed at upsetting the resulting award, must be minimized. One danger is exemplified by a tongue-in-cheek comment of a lawyer from Latin America, a region where arbitration was for many decades neither familiar nor generally accepted:

> "We lawyers like arbitration. It assures us three litigations: one before, one during and one after the arbitration."[1]

In addition, arbitrators faced with heightened judicial scrutiny might ultimately come to focus less on the merits of the particular dispute, or the relationship between the parties, and more on the task of producing opinions or building a record that would enable their awards to survive later challenge.

There is thus a need to prevent a "judicialization" of the arbitral process. But at the same time, some sort of "public" supervision and control may be necessary to protect wider social interests that may be ignored or jeopardized by "private" arbitrators. The inevitable tension between these two values is a theme that figures in much of these materials.

The occasion for judicial supervision and control of the arbitral process may arise at a number of different stages. Such supervision may be exercised at the time an award made by arbitrators comes before a court for review and enforcement. Or it may be exercised at a still earlier stage—

---

1. Quoted in Nattier, International Commercial Arbitration in Latin America: Enforcement of Arbitral Agreements and Awards, 21 Tex.Int'l L.J. 397, 408 (1986).

when the question is posed whether a particular dispute is at all suitable for arbitration in the first place: This is the question whether "public policy" demands that the full panoply of judicial procedure remain available to an aggrieved party, despite his earlier agreement to submit to arbitration. Even at that threshold stage, however, an inquiry into whether "public policy" forbids arbitration of the dispute must take into account the fact that any ultimate award is likely to be treated with considerable deference by a reviewing court, even with respect to matters of "law." We begin, therefore, with an overview of the critical subject of the judicial review of arbitral awards.

a. JUDICIAL REVIEW OF ARBITRAL AWARDS

By far the greatest number of the many awards rendered by arbitrators are voluntarily complied with. This seems especially true in collective bargaining cases: It has been suggested in fact that fewer than 1% of labor arbitration awards in the private sector are ever challenged in court.[2] However, where one party is recalcitrant, official sanctions to enforce the award may be needed. Modern arbitration statutes make available the assistance of courts in enforcing arbitration awards: See, for example, §§ 9 and 13 of the FAA. How closely will a court scrutinize an arbitration award? Under what circumstances will it decline to give the award legal effect?

The conventional wisdom is that successful challenges to arbitration awards are rare. Four decades ago one commentator could write that in "the overwhelming majority of that miniscule portion which are appealed, only an infinitesimal few have ever been vacated."[3] In more recent years, the amount of "litigious wrangling" over the enforcement of awards—and thus the number of successful challenges—has unquestionably increased, so as to make that something of an overstatement.[4] Nonetheless the essential point about judicial deference to arbitral awards still appears to be valid.[5]

---

2. Peter Feuille & Michael LeRoy, Grievance Arbitration Appeals in the Federal Courts: Facts and Figures, 45 Arb.J. 35 (Mar. 1990).

3. Jones, Evidentiary Concepts in Labor Arbitration: Some Modern Variations on Ancient Legal Themes, 13 U.C.L.A.L.Rev. 1241, 1296 (1966).

4. See Gould, Judicial Review of Labor Arbitration Awards—Thirty Years of the Steelworkers Trilogy : The Aftermath of AT & T and Misco, 64 Notre Dame L.Rev. 464, 467, 474 (1989). Gould attributes this phenomenon at least in part to the decline in the number of employees represented by unions, which has "simultaneously encouraged and emboldened employers to challenge arbitration awards and unions as well."

5. While "the odds of a successful appeal have improved somewhat" in recent years, federal courts are still enforcing arbitration awards over 70% of the time in collective bargaining cases, and over 80% of the time in individual employment disputes. See Michael LeRoy & Peter Feuille, The Steelworkers Trilogy and Grievance Arbitration Appeals: How the Federal Courts Respond, 13 Ind.Rel.L.J. 78, 103, 117 (1991); Michael LeRoy & Peter Feuille, Final and Binding, but Appealable to Courts: Empirical Evidence of Judicial Review of Labor and Employment Arbitration Awards, in Arbitration 2001: Arbitrating in an Evolving Legal Environment, Proceedings, 54th Annual Meeting, National Academy of Arbitrators (2002).

Modern arbitration statutes provide only limited grounds on the basis of which a court may refuse to enforce an award. See §§ 10 and 11 of the FAA. What does it mean to say (as in § 10(d)) that an award can be overturned if the arbitrators have "exceeded their powers"? Among other things, this can often be a peg on which to hang a challenge—even after an award is rendered—to the "arbitrability" of the dispute, at least if the point has been preserved by a proper objection before the arbitrator. The question then becomes whether the arbitrator has in fact determined an issue which the parties in their agreement have empowered him to decide. See also § 11(b).

Does § 10 of the FAA have a bearing on *other* challenges to arbitration awards besides assertions that under the agreement the underlying dispute was not "arbitrable"? And are the grounds specified in the federal statute *exclusive*? Or are there other grounds on which a court can rely in refusing to enforce an award? In the materials that follow you will come across a number of variant formulations, sometimes in terms borrowed from labor arbitration cases. Do these constitute alternative grounds to vacate an award? Or do they instead amount to nothing more than dressing up the same idea in different semantic garb?

United Paperworkers International Union v. Misco, Inc.

Supreme Court of the United States, 1987.
484 U.S. 29, 108 S.Ct. 364, 98 L.Ed.2d 286.

■ JUSTICE WHITE delivered the opinion of the Court.

The issue for decision involves several aspects of when a federal court may refuse to enforce an arbitration award rendered under a collective-bargaining agreement.

I

Misco, Inc. operates a paper converting plant in Monroe, Louisiana. The Company is a party to a collective-bargaining agreement with the United Paperworkers International Union, AFL–CIO, and its union local; the agreement covers the production and maintenance employees at the plant. Under the agreement, the Company or the Union may submit to arbitration any grievance that arises from the interpretation or application of its terms, and the arbitrator's decision is final and binding upon the parties. The arbitrator's authority is limited to interpretation and application of the terms contained in the agreement itself. The agreement reserves to management the right to establish, amend, and enforce "rules and regulations regulating the discipline or discharge of employees" and the procedures for imposing discipline. Such rules were to be posted and were to be in effect "until ruled on by grievance and arbitration procedures as to fairness and necessity." For about a decade, the Company's rules had listed as causes for discharge the bringing of intoxicants, narcotics, or controlled substances on to plant property or consuming any of them there, as well as reporting for work under the influence of such substances.[2] At the time of the events involved in this case, the Company was very concerned about the use of drugs at the plant, especially among employees on the night shift.

Isiah Cooper, who worked on the night shift for Misco, was one of the employees covered by the collective-bargaining agreement. He operated a slitter-rewinder machine, which uses sharp blades to cut rolling coils of paper. The arbitrator found that this machine is hazardous and had caused numerous injuries in recent years. Cooper had been reprimanded twice in a few months for deficient performance. On January 21, 1983, one day after the second reprimand, the police searched Cooper's house pursuant to a warrant, and a substantial amount of marijuana was found. Contemporaneously, a police officer was detailed to keep Cooper's car under observation at the Company's parking lot. At about 6:30 p.m., Cooper was seen walking in the parking lot during work hours with two other men. The three men entered Cooper's car momentarily, then walked to another car, a white Cutlass, and entered it. After the other two men later returned to the plant, Cooper was apprehended by police in the backseat of this car with marijuana smoke in the air and a lighted marijuana cigarette in the front-seat ashtray. The police also searched Cooper's car and found a plastic scales case and marijuana gleanings. Cooper was arrested and charged with marijuana possession.[3]

On January 24, Cooper told the Company that he had been arrested for possession of marijuana at his home; the Company did not learn of the marijuana cigarette in the white Cutlass until January 27. It then investigated and on February 7 discharged Cooper, asserting that in the circumstances, his presence in the Cutlass violated the rule against having drugs on the plant premises.[4] Cooper filed a grievance protesting his discharge the same day, and the matter proceeded to arbitration. The Company was not aware until September 21, five days before the hearing before the arbitrator was scheduled, that marijuana had been found in Cooper's car. That fact did not become known to the Union until the hearing began. At the hearing it was stipulated that the issue was whether the Company had "just cause to discharge the Grievant under Rule II.1" and, "[i]f not, what if any should be the remedy."

The arbitrator upheld the grievance and ordered the Company to reinstate Cooper with backpay and full seniority. The arbitrator based his finding that there was not just cause for the discharge on his consideration

---

2. Rule II.1 lists the following as causes for discharge:

"Bringing intoxicants, narcotics, or controlled substances into, or consuming intoxicants, narcotics or controlled substances in the plant, or on plant premises. Reporting for duty under the influence of intoxicants, narcotics, or controlled substances."

3. Cooper later pleaded guilty to that charge, which was not related to his being in a car with a lighted marijuana cigarette in it. The authorities chose not to prosecute for the latter incident.

4. The Company asserted that being in a car with a lit marijuana cigarette was a direct violation of the company rule against having an illegal substance on company property.

of seven criteria.[5] In particular, the arbitrator found that the Company failed to prove that the employee had possessed or used marijuana on company property: finding Cooper in the backseat of a car and a burning cigarette in the front-seat ashtray was insufficient proof that Cooper was using or possessed marijuana on company property. The arbitrator refused to accept into evidence the fact that marijuana had been found in Cooper's car on company premises because the Company did not know of this fact when Cooper was discharged and therefore did not rely on it as a basis for the discharge.[6]

The Company filed suit in District Court, seeking to vacate the arbitration award on several grounds, one of which was that ordering reinstatement of Cooper, who had allegedly possessed marijuana on the plant premises, was contrary to public policy. The District Court agreed that the award must be set aside as contrary to public policy because it ran counter to general safety concerns that arise from the operation of dangerous machinery while under the influence of drugs, as well as to state criminal laws against drug possession. The Court of Appeals affirmed, with one judge dissenting. The court ruled that reinstatement would violate the public policy "against the operation of dangerous machinery by persons under the influence of drugs or alcohol." The arbitrator had found that Cooper was apprehended on company premises in an atmosphere of marijuana smoke in another's car and that marijuana was found in his own car on the company lot. These facts established that Cooper had violated the Company's rules and gave the company just cause to discharge him. The arbitrator did not reach this conclusion because of a "narrow focus on Cooper's procedural rights" that led him to ignore what he "knew was in fact true: that Cooper *did* bring marijuana onto his employer's premises." [The Court of Appeals also suggested that the arbitrator's "baffling view of evidence that would with ease have sustained a civil verdict and probably a criminal conviction" might in part be explained by his formal training "as an engineer and not as a lawyer." 768 F.2d 739, 741 n. 2.] * * *

Because the Courts of Appeals are divided on the question of when courts may set aside arbitration awards as contravening public policy, we granted the Union's petition for a writ of certiorari, and now reverse the judgment of the Court of Appeals.

II

The Union asserts that an arbitral award may not be set aside on public policy grounds unless the award orders conduct that violates the

---

5. These considerations were the reasonableness of the employer's position, the notice given to the employee, the timing of the investigation undertaken, the fairness of the investigation, the evidence against the employee, the possibility of discrimination, and the relation of the degree of discipline to the nature of the offense and the employee's past record.

6. The arbitrator stated: "One of the rules in arbitration is that the Company must have its proof in hand before it takes disciplinary action against an employee. The Company does not take the disciplinary action and then spend eight months digging up supporting evidence to justify its actions. * * *"

positive law, which is not the case here. But in the alternative, it submits that even if it is wrong in this regard, the Court of Appeals otherwise exceeded the limited authority that it had to review an arbitrator's award entered pursuant to a collective-bargaining agreement. Respondent, on the other hand, defends the public policy decision of the Court of Appeals but alternatively argues that the judgment below should be affirmed because of erroneous findings by the arbitrator. We deal first with the opposing alternative arguments.

A

Collective-bargaining agreements commonly provide grievance procedures to settle disputes between union and employer with respect to the interpretation and application of the agreement and require binding arbitration for unsettled grievances. In such cases, and this is such a case, the Court made clear almost 30 years ago that the courts play only a limited role when asked to review the decision of an arbitrator. The courts are not authorized to reconsider the merits of an award even though the parties may allege that the award rests on errors of fact or on misinterpretation of the contract. "The refusal of courts to review the merits of an arbitration award is the proper approach to arbitration under collective bargaining agreements. The federal policy of settling labor disputes by arbitration would be undermined if courts had the final say on the merits of the awards." *Steelworkers v. Enterprise Wheel & Car Corp.,* 363 U.S. 593, 596 (1960). As long as the arbitrator's award "draws its essence from the collective bargaining agreement," and is not merely "his own brand of industrial justice," the award is legitimate.

> "The function of the court is very limited when the parties have agreed to submit all questions of contract interpretation to the arbitrator. It is confined to ascertaining whether the party seeking arbitration is making a claim which on its face is governed by the contract. Whether the moving party is right or wrong is a question of contract interpretation for the arbitrator. In these circumstances the moving party should not be deprived of the arbitrator's judgment, when it was his judgment and all that it connotes that was bargained for." * * * *Steelworkers v. American Mfg. Co.,* 363 U.S. 564, 567–568 (1960).

The reasons for insulating arbitral decisions from judicial review are grounded in the federal statutes regulating labor-management relations. These statutes reflect a decided preference for private settlement of labor disputes without the intervention of government. * * * Because the parties have contracted to have disputes settled by an arbitrator chosen by them rather than by a judge, it is the arbitrator's view of the facts and of the meaning of the contract that they have agreed to accept. Courts thus do not sit to hear claims of factual or legal error by an arbitrator as an appellate court does in reviewing decisions of lower courts. To resolve disputes about the application of a collective-bargaining agreement, an arbitrator must find facts and a court may not reject those findings simply because it disagrees with them. The same is true of the arbitrator's interpretation of the contract. The arbitrator may not ignore the plain language of the contract; but the parties having authorized the arbitrator to give meaning to the language of the agreement, a court should not reject an award on the ground that the arbitrator misread the contract. So, too, where it is contemplated that the arbitrator will determine remedies for contract violations that he finds, courts have no authority to disagree with his honest judgment in that respect. If the courts were free to intervene on these grounds, the speedy resolution of grievances by private mechanisms would be greatly undermined. Furthermore, it must be remembered that grievance and arbitration procedures are part and parcel of the ongoing process of collective bargaining. It is through these processes that the supplementary rules of the plant are established. * * * [A]s long as the arbitrator is even arguably construing or applying the contract and acting within the scope of his authority, that a court is convinced he committed serious error does not suffice to overturn his decision. Of course, decisions procured by the parties through fraud or through the arbitrator's dishonesty need not be enforced. But there is nothing of that sort involved in this case.

B

The Company's position, simply put, is that the arbitrator committed grievous error in finding that the evidence was insufficient to prove that Cooper had possessed or used marijuana on company property. But the Court of Appeals, although it took a distinctly jaundiced view of the arbitrator's decision in this regard, was not free to refuse enforcement because it considered Cooper's presence in the white Cutlass, in the circumstances, to be ample proof that Rule II.1 was violated. No dishonesty is alleged; only improvident, even silly, factfinding is claimed. This is hardly sufficient basis for disregarding what the agent appointed by the parties determined to be the historical facts.

Nor was it open to the Court of Appeals to refuse to enforce the award because the arbitrator, in deciding whether there was just cause to discharge, refused to consider evidence unknown to the Company at the time Cooper was fired. The parties bargained for arbitration to settle disputes and were free to set the procedural rules for arbitrators to follow if they chose. Section VI of the agreement, entitled "Arbitration Procedure," did set some ground rules for the arbitration process. It forbade the arbitrator to consider hearsay evidence, for example, but evidentiary matters were otherwise left to the arbitrator. Here the arbitrator ruled that in determining whether Cooper had violated Rule II.1, he should not consider evidence not relied on by the employer in ordering the discharge, particularly in a case like this where there was no notice to the employee or the Union prior to the hearing that the Company would attempt to rely on after-discovered evidence. This, in effect, was a construction of what the contract required when deciding discharge cases: an arbitrator was to look only at the evidence before the employer at the time of discharge. As the arbitrator noted, this approach was consistent with the practice followed by other arbitrators.[8] And it was consistent with our observation in *John Wiley & Sons, Inc. v. Livingston,* 376 U.S. 543, 557 (1964), that when the subject matter of a dispute is arbitrable, "procedural" questions which grow out of the dispute and bear on its final disposition are to be left to the arbitrator.

Under the Arbitration Act, the federal courts are empowered to set aside arbitration awards on such grounds only when "the arbitrators were guilty of misconduct ... in refusing to hear evidence pertinent and material to the controversy." If we apply that same standard here and assume that the arbitrator erred in refusing to consider the disputed evidence, his error was not in bad faith or so gross as to amount to affirmative misconduct.[10] Finally, it is worth noting that putting aside the evidence about the marijuana found in Cooper's car during this arbitration did not forever foreclose the Company from using that evidence as the basis for a discharge.

Even if it were open to the Court of Appeals to have found a violation of Rule II.1 because of the marijuana found in Cooper's car, the question remains whether the court could properly set aside the award because in its view discharge was the correct remedy. Normally, an arbitrator is authorized to disagree with the sanction imposed for employee misconduct. In *Enterprise Wheel,* for example, the arbitrator reduced the discipline from discharge to a 10–day suspension. The Court of Appeals refused to enforce the award, but we reversed, explaining that though the arbitrator's decision must draw its essence from the agreement, he "is to bring his informed judgment to bear in order to reach a fair solution of a problem. *This is especially true when it comes to formulating remedies.*" The parties, of course, may limit the discretion of the arbitrator in this respect; and it may be, as the Company argues, that under the contract involved here, it was within the unreviewable discretion of management to discharge an employee once a violation of Rule II.1 was found. But the parties stipulated that the issue before the arbitrator was whether there was "just" cause for the discharge, and the arbitrator, in the course of his opinion, cryptically observed that Rule II.1 merely listed causes for discharge and did not expressly provide for immediate discharge. Before disposing of the case on the ground that Rule II.1 had been violated and discharge was therefore proper, the proper course would have been remand to the arbitrator for a definitive construction of the contract in this respect.

8. Labor arbitrators have stated that the correctness of a discharge "must stand or fall upon the reason given at the time of discharge," see, e.g., West Va. Pulp & Paper Co., 10 Lab.Arb. 117, 118 (1947), and arbitrators often, but not always, confine their considerations to the facts known to the employer at the time of the discharge.

10. Even in the very rare instances when an arbitrator's procedural aberrations rise to the level of affirmative misconduct, as a rule the court must not foreclose further proceedings by settling the merits according to its own judgment of the appropriate result, since this step would improperly substitute a judicial determination for the arbitrator's decision that the parties bargained for in the collective-bargaining agreement. Instead, the court should simply vacate the award, thus leaving open the possibility of further proceedings if they are permitted under the terms of the agreement. The court also has the authority to remand for further proceedings when this step seems appropriate. See [FAA] § 10(e).

C

The Court of Appeals did not purport to take this course in any event. Rather, it held that the evidence of marijuana in Cooper's car required that the award be set aside because to reinstate a person who had brought drugs onto the property was contrary to the public policy "against the operation of dangerous machinery by persons under the influence of drugs or alcohol." We cannot affirm that judgment.

A court's refusal to enforce an arbitrator's award under a collective-bargaining agreement because it is contrary to public policy is a specific application of the more general doctrine, rooted in the common law, that a court may refuse to enforce contracts that violate law or public policy. *W.R. Grace & Co. v. Rubber Workers,* 461 U.S. 757, 766 (1983). That doctrine derives from the basic notion that no court will lend its aid to one who founds a cause of action upon an immoral or illegal act, and is further justified by the observation that the public's interests in confining the scope of private agreements to which it is not a party will go unrepresented unless the judiciary takes account of those interests when it considers whether to enforce such agreements. In the common law of contracts, this doctrine has served as the foundation for occasional exercises of judicial power to abrogate private agreements.

In *W.R. Grace,* we recognized that "a court may not enforce a collective-bargaining agreement that is contrary to public policy," and stated that "the question of public policy is ultimately one for resolution by the courts." We cautioned, however, that a court's refusal to enforce an arbitrator's interpretation of such contracts is limited to situations where the contract as interpreted would violate "some explicit public policy" that is "well defined and dominant, and is to be ascertained 'by reference to the laws and legal precedents and not from general considerations of supposed public interests.' " In *W.R. Grace,* we identified two important public policies that were potentially jeopardized by the arbitrator's interpretation of the contract: obedience to judicial orders and voluntary compliance with Title VII. We went on to hold that enforcement of the arbitration award in that case did not compromise either of the two public policies allegedly threatened by the award. Two points follow from our decision in *W.R. Grace.* First, a court may refuse to enforce a collective-bargaining agreement when the specific terms contained in that agreement violate public policy. Second, it is apparent that our decision in that case does not otherwise sanction a broad judicial power to set aside arbitration awards as against public policy. Although we discussed the effect of that award on two broad areas of public policy, our decision turned on our examination of whether the award created any explicit conflict with other "laws and legal precedents" rather than an assessment of "general considerations of supposed public interests." At the very least, an alleged public policy must be properly framed under the approach set out in *W.R. Grace,* and the violation of such a policy must be clearly shown if an award is not to be enforced.

As we see it, the formulation of public policy set out by the Court of Appeals did not comply with the statement that such a policy must be "ascertained 'by reference to the laws and legal precedents and not from general considerations of supposed public interests.' " The Court of Appeals made no attempt to review existing laws and legal precedents in order to demonstrate that they establish a "well defined and dominant" policy against the operation of dangerous machinery while under the influence of drugs. Although certainly such a judgment is firmly rooted in common sense, we explicitly held in *W.R. Grace* that a formulation of public policy based only on "general considerations of supposed public interests" is not the sort that permits a court to set aside an arbitration award that was entered in accordance with a valid collective-bargaining agreement.

Even if the Court of Appeals' formulation of public policy is to be accepted, no violation of that policy was clearly shown in this case. In pursuing its public policy inquiry, the Court of Appeals quite properly considered the established fact that traces of marijuana had been found in Cooper's car. Yet the assumed connection between the marijuana gleanings found in Cooper's car and Cooper's actual use of drugs in the workplace is tenuous at best and provides an insufficient basis for holding that his reinstatement would actually violate the public policy identified by the Court of Appeals "against the operation of dangerous machinery by persons under the influence of drugs or alcohol." A refusal to enforce an award must rest on more than speculation or assumption.

In any event, it was inappropriate for the Court of Appeals itself to draw the necessary inference. To conclude from the fact that marijuana had been found in Cooper's car that Cooper had ever been or would be under the influence of marijuana while he was on the job and operating dangerous machinery is an exercise in factfinding about Cooper's use of drugs and his amenability to discipline, a task that exceeds the authority of a court asked to overturn an arbitration award. The parties did not bargain for the facts to be found by a court, but by an arbitrator chosen by them who had more opportunity to observe Cooper and to be familiar with the plant and its problems. Nor does the fact that it is inquiring into a possible violation of public policy excuse a court for doing the arbitrator's task. If additional facts were to be found, the arbitrator should find them in the course of any further effort the Company might have made to discharge Cooper for having had marijuana in his car on company premises. Had the arbitrator found that Cooper had possessed drugs on the property, yet imposed discipline short of discharge because he found as a factual matter that Cooper could be trusted not to use them on the job, the Court of Appeals could not upset the award because of its own view that public policy about plant safety was threatened. In this connection it should also be noted that the award ordered Cooper to be reinstated in his old job or in an equivalent one for which he was qualified. It is by no means clear from the record that Cooper would pose a serious threat to the asserted public policy in every job for which he was qualified.[12]

12. We need not address the Union's position that a court may refuse to enforce an award on public policy grounds only when the award itself violates a statute, regulation,

The judgment of the Court of Appeals is reversed.

So ordered.

■ JUSTICE BLACKMUN, with whom JUSTICE BRENNAN joins, concurring.

* * *

I agree with the Court that the judgment of the Court of Appeals must be reversed and I summarize what I understand to be the three alternative rationales for the Court's decision:

1. The Court of Appeals exceeded its authority in concluding that the company's discharge of Cooper was proper under the collective-bargaining agreement. The Court of Appeals erred in considering evidence that the arbitrator legitimately had excluded from the grievance process, in second-guessing the arbitrator's factual finding that Cooper had not violated Rule II.1, and in assessing the appropriate sanction under the agreement. Absent its overreaching, the Court of Appeals lacked any basis for disagreeing with the arbitrator's conclusion that there was not "just cause" for discharging Cooper.

2. Even if the Court of Appeals properly considered evidence of marijuana found in Cooper's car and legitimately found a Rule II.1 violation, the public policy advanced by the Court of Appeals does not support its decision to set aside the award. The reinstatement of Cooper would not contravene the alleged public policy "against the operation of dangerous machinery by persons under the influence of drugs or alcohol." The fact that an employee's car contains marijuana gleanings does not indicate that the employee uses marijuana on the job or that he operates his machine while under the influence of drugs, let alone that he will report to work in an impaired state in the future. Moreover, nothing in the record suggests that the arbitrator's award, which gives the company the option of placing Cooper in a job equivalent to his old one, would require Cooper to operate hazardous machinery.

3. The public policy formulated by the Court of Appeals may not properly support a court's refusal to enforce an otherwise valid arbitration award. In *W.R. Grace & Co. v. Rubber Workers,* 461 U.S. 757 (1983), we stated that the public policy must be founded on "laws and legal precedents." The Court of Appeals identified no law or legal precedent that demonstrated an "explicit public policy" against the operation of dangerous machinery by persons under the influence of drugs. Far from being "well defined and dominant," as *W.R. Grace* prescribed, the Court of Appeals' public policy was ascertained merely "from general considerations of supposed public interests." I do not understand the Court, by criticizing the company's public policy formulation, to suggest that proper framing of an alleged public policy under the approach set out in *W.R. Grace* would be sufficient to justify a court's refusal to enforce an arbitration award on

or other manifestation of positive law, or compels conduct by the employer that would violate such a law.

public policy grounds. Rather, I understand the Court to hold that such compliance is merely a necessary step if an award is not to be enforced.

It is on this understanding that I join the opinion of the Court.

NOTES AND QUESTIONS

1. In Hill v. Norfolk and Western Ry. Co., 814 F.2d 1192, 1194–95 (7th Cir.1987), Judge Posner wrote that

> As we have said too many times to want to repeat again, the question for decision by a federal court asked to set aside an arbitration award—whether the award is made under the Railway Labor Act, the Taft–Hartley Act, or the United States Arbitration Act—is not whether the arbitrator or arbitrators erred in interpreting the contract; it is not whether they clearly erred in interpreting the contract; it is not whether they grossly erred in interpreting the contract; it is whether they interpreted the contract. * * * A party can complain if the arbitrators don't interpret the contract—that is, if they disregard the contract and implement their own notions of what is reasonable and fair. * * * But a party will not be heard to complain merely because the arbitrators' interpretation is a misinterpretation. Granted, the grosser the apparent misinterpretation, the likelier it is that the arbitrators weren't interpreting the contract at all. But once the court is satisfied that they were interpreting the contract, judicial review is at an end, provided there is no fraud or corruption and the arbitrators haven't ordered anyone to do an illegal act.

In *Hill,* the district court had refused to disturb an award against a discharged employee. Finding that the employee's appeal was "based largely on frivolous grounds," the Seventh Circuit on its own initiative imposed sanctions on his attorney. Judge Posner remarked that "[t]his court has been plagued by groundless lawsuits seeking to overturn arbitration awards * * *. [W]e have said repeatedly that we would punish such tactics, and we mean it." Cf. B.L. Harbert Int'l LLC v. Hercules Steel Co., 441 F.3d 905 (11th Cir.2006)("this Court is exasperated by those who attempt to salvage arbitration losses through litigation that has no sound basis in the law applicable to arbitration awards"; "we are ready, willing and able to consider imposing sanctions in appropriate cases," although the court declined to do so in this case since the "poor loser" "did not have the benefit of this notice and warning").

2. Different arbitrators may on different occasions come to hear cases arising under the same collective bargaining agreement, and they may, on identical facts, give opposite or conflicting interpretations of the same contractual provision. In such circumstances a court may well conclude that *neither* award should be vacated, since *each* "draws its essence" from the agreement. E.g., Graphic Arts Int'l Union Local 97–B v. Haddon Craftsmen, Inc., 489 F.Supp. 1088 (M.D.Pa.1979); Consolidation Coal Co. v. United Mine Workers of America, 213 F.3d 404 (7th Cir.2000). Cf. Connecticut Light & Power Co. v. Local 420, Int'l Brotherhood of Elec. Workers,

718 F.2d 14 (2d Cir.1983) (first arbitrator had issued cease and desist order for the future; where both awards could not be implemented, the court must "select that interpretation which most nearly conforms to the intent of the parties").

3.   Assume that after the Supreme Court's decision in *Misco,* the employer wishes to discharge Cooper on the ground that it *now* knows marijuana was found in his car on company premises on January 21: Would this be consistent with the arbitral award ordering that the employee be reinstated? See part "II.B." of the Supreme Court's opinion. In a similar case, an employee was discharged for sexual harassment, and the arbitrator ordered reinstatement. The employer acquiesced in the confirmed award and reinstated the employee, but then discharged him *the same day* on the basis of earlier incidents which had come to light after the original termination, but which the arbitrator had refused to consider. The union requested that the employer be held in contempt for attempting to evade the court's order enforcing the award but the district court denied the motion "because it concluded that [the employer] had complied with its order by reinstating [the employee]". The court of appeals affirmed in Chrysler Motors Corp. v. International Union, Allied Industrial Workers of America, 2 F.3d 760 (7th Cir.1993).

Compare United States Postal Service v. National Ass'n of Letter Carriers, 64 F.Supp.2d 633 (S.D.Tex.1999), in which an employee was discharged for committing workers' compensation fraud; the arbitrator, finding a "procedural defect" in the process by which the worker was terminated, ordered reinstatement. The employer then sent a second notice of termination predicated on the same misconduct and began a disciplinary process in an attempt to "cure the procedural defect." The arbitrator determined that the collective bargaining agreement precluded a "collateral attack" on the original award through a second discipline, and the court confirmed this award: The remedy sought by the employer "is analogous to a police department's illegally executing a search warrant, seizing evidence, and on seeing it suppressed, returning the evidence to the apartment, correctly executing the warrant, and attempting to reintroduce it at trial." The worker should not become "a pinata that the government strikes until it gets a 'good' result." Is this case distinguishable from *Chrysler Motors?*

Note: Arbitral Decision–Making and Legal "Rules"

"Some years ago a survey of commercial arbitrators found that 80 per cent of the studied arbitrators 'thought that they ought to reach their decisions within the context of the principles of substantive rules of law, but almost 90 per cent believed that they were free to ignore these rules whenever they thought that more just decisions would be reached by so doing.' "[1] A later poll of AAA construction arbitrators asked whether respondents "always follow the law" in formulating their awards; 72% answered "yes," and 20% "no." "Of the 33 who explained their 'no' answer, 11 stated they did not know the law and therefore could not follow

---

1.   Soia Mentschikoff, Commercial Arbitration, 61 Col.L.Rev. 846, 861 (1961).

it." (On this last point, it is suggestive that 73% of the respondents also thought that a three-person arbitration panel should ideally be composed of a single attorney, plus one design professional and one contractor—a fairly typical arrangement in the construction field.).[2]

The readiness of arbitrators to depart from legal "rules" varies, of course. It will depend in part on the presumed willingness of the parties to allow them to do so, as well as on the presence or absence of attorneys and the arbitrator's own profession and degree of expertness. For example, in the highly informal "Autoline" program administered by the Better Business Bureau, volunteer arbitrators are expressly enjoined not to try to interpret state law or even the language of the automobile manufacturer's warranty: Rather than basing an award on the fact that a car may be "out of warranty," for example, they are told instead to "make a decision that [they believe] is fair based on the facts of your case."[3]

At the other end of the spectrum, international commercial contracts regularly contain provisions that stipulate which substantive law the arbitrator is to apply. In international transactions the choice of law is likely to affect any number of questions, from warranty obligations to prejudgment interest, as to which the various national legal systems involved may give radically different answers. Where the parties are of different nationalities they may think it fairer to insure that the transaction is governed by the law of a *third* country, unrelated to either. Another possibility is exemplified by a contract between a German and an English company, where the arbitrators were instructed to apply German law if the English company was the claimant, and English law if the German company was the claimant![4] Nevertheless there does exist a familiar alternative in international arbitration. The parties may sometimes expressly provide that the arbitrators shall decide "according to natural justice and equity" or "ex aequo et bono." (The comparable French phrase, rooted in civil law tradition, is that the arbitrators shall act as "*amiables compositeurs.*") The rules of international arbitral institutions such as the ICC make this device available to parties who expressly choose to give the arbitrator such authority, as do the Arbitration Rules promulgated by the United Nations Commission on International Trade Law ("UNCITRAL") for non-administered arbitrations. In what sorts of cases might the parties prefer that their arbitrators proceed on the basis of general "equitable" standards of fairness? In what sorts of cases might they prefer instead that their arbitrators apply a particular body of national law?

---

2. Dean B. Thomson, Arbitration Theory & Practice: A Survey of AAA Construction Arbitrators, 23 Hofstra L.Rev. 137, 151, 154–55 (1994).

3. See "How BBB Autoline Works," http://www.dr.bbb.org/autoline/alprocess.asp. Only in California are consumers assured that the arbitrator will take into account "legal and equitable factors" including the manufacturer's warranty, the state "lemon law," the UCC, and state-mandated emissions controls. California BBB Autoline Process, http://www.dr.bbb.org/autoline/caprocess.asp.

4. See Kerr, International Arbitration v. Litigation, [1980] J.Bus.Law 164, 172.

The extent to which arbitrators are expected to follow external legal "rules" has given rise to considerable controversy in labor relations cases. The classic statement of the dilemma usually goes like this: Assume that an industrial plant begins Sunday operations; when work crews cannot be filled with volunteers, the employer selects workers for Sunday work on a rotating basis. An employee refuses to work on Sunday for religious reasons; he is discharged and a grievance is filed which proceeds to arbitration. The collective bargaining agreement forbids discharge without "just cause." Title VII of the 1964 Civil Rights Act makes it unlawful for an employer to discriminate on the basis of religion unless he can demonstrate "that he is unable to reasonably accommodate" the employee's religious practices "without undue hardship" on the conduct of his business. How should the arbitrator proceed?

The "orthodox" position among labor arbitrators has been that the arbitrators should adhere to the agreement and "ignore the law." The arbitrator, on this view, is merely:

> the parties' officially designated "reader" of the contract. He (or she) is their joint *alter ego* for the purpose of striking whatever supplementary bargain is necessary to handle the anticipated unanticipated omissions of the initial agreement. * * * [T]he arbitrator's mandate is plain: tell the parties (and the courts) what the contract means and let them worry about the legal consequences.[5]

Finding "the law" and interpreting statutes and cases are tasks likely to be beyond the special competence of most arbitrators, whether legally trained or not—beyond, that is, the reasons for which they were chosen by the parties, and beyond the reasons supporting the presumption of arbitrability and the practice of deference to arbitral awards. So the conventional view is that whether an agreement is in accord with the external "law" is "irrelevant";[6] it is a question best "postponed" for later determination by the courts.[7] The fear is frequently expressed that by presuming to decide such questions themselves, arbitrators might actually be inviting closer judicial scrutiny and thus more active judicial intervention in the arbitral process— for professional arbitrators, one of the most menacing of nightmares.

There exist in the literature all sorts of nuanced variations on this "orthodox" view. An exception is usually made for situations where the parties themselves seem to "invite" the arbitrator to decide according to the law: It is, for example, increasingly common to find cases where the parties have expressly tracked the language of a statute in their agreement, or have stipulated that the award must be "consistent with applicable laws" and in such cases it is likely that they will be found to have

---

5. St. Antoine, Judicial Review of Labor Arbitration Awards: A Second Look at Enterprise Wheel and its Progeny, 75 Mich.L.Rev. 1137, 1140, 1142 (1977).

6. Feller, Arbitration and the External Law Revisited, 37 St. Louis U.L.J. 973, 975 (1993).

7. Meltzer, Ruminations about Ideology, Law and Labor Arbitration, Proceedings, 20th Annual Meeting, Nat'l Academy of Arbitrators 1, 17 n. 40 (1967).

"necessarily bargained for the arbitrator's interpretation of the law."[8] In a recent survey of the members of the National Academy of Arbitrators, four out of five respondents reported that they had in fact arbitrated a dispute within the prior three years that required them to interpret or apply a statute.[9] It may well be, after all, that this entire subject is of more academic than practical interest. The paradigm case—where both law and agreement are clear and irreconcilably in conflict—will not often arise. There is usually plenty of room to reinterpret the agreement in light of the arbitrator's understanding of the requirements of the external law, and most arbitrators can be expected to deploy adequate resourcefulness to avoid any contradiction.[10]

———

After an arbitral award has been handed down, the *Misco* case clearly teaches that the arbitrator should not be treated as a sort of "lower court": For over a century the cases have been full of reminders to the effect that "if an arbitrator makes a mistake either as to law or fact, it is the misfortune of the party, and there is no help for it. There is no right of appeal, and the court has no power to revise the decisions of 'judges who are of the parties' own choosing.' "[11]

Alan Scott Rau, The Culture of American Arbitration and the Lessons of ADR

40 Tex. Int'l L.J. 449, 518–521 (2005).

After an award is rendered, we may become convinced that a court would have acted somewhat differently—but after all, "the court's interpretation is the 'correct' one only in some positivist sense, and only, perhaps,

8. American Postal Workers Union v. United States Postal Serv., 789 F.2d 1, 6 (D.C.Cir.1986) (Edwards, J.).

See, e.g., Butler Mfg. Co. v. United Steelworkers of Amer., 336 F.3d 629 (7th Cir. 2003)(district court held that the arbitrator had "strayed too far beyond his powers when he applied the Family and Medical Leave Act" to help resolve a grievance involving the termination of an employee and "possible excuses" for her absences; held, reversed; the collective bargaining agreement stated that the employer "offers ... continuation of employment to all qualified individuals in accordance with the provisions of law," and this clause "conferred on the arbitrator the authority to consider the FMLA"); In re Los Angeles Community College District, 112 Lab. Arb. 733, 738 (1999)(employer agreed "to comply with all federal * * * laws regarding non-discrimination"; "[I]t becomes, then, the Arbitrator's unenviable task to decide the matter, even if it presents a novel issue under the ADA not previously settled by the courts").

9. Michel Picher et al., The Arbitration Profession in Transition: A Survey of the National Academy of Arbitrators 26 (Cornell/PERC Institute on Conflict Resolution 2000).

10. For a recent review of the controversy—and a demonstration that "the debate may be more limited than it first appears"—see Laura Cooper et al., ADR in the Workplace 170–198 (2nd ed. 2005).

11. Patton v. Garrett, 116 N.C. 847, 21 S.E. 679, 682–83 (1895).

for the moment."[281] As the late Leon Green wrote, memorably, a decision of a court is no more "the law" "than the light from last night's lamp is electricity."[282]

Granted, the elaborate and costly apparatus of common-law litigation—the extensive discovery, the reasoned awards subject to appellate review—are all in a sense designed to ensure close and accurate compliance with legal rules. (For the parties, the trade-off of arbitration consists precisely in allowing them to escape all this—in exchange for their willingness to receive a somewhat less than perfect replication of what would happen in the public forum.) But can we really take for granted the continuing ability of judges and juries to produce, over time, reliable results that remain responsive to the needs of participants in the market? If not, it may be the peculiar contribution of arbitrators to test—"in terms of their inherent soundness"—these rules of law, questioning, qualifying, and reshaping them, constructing brick by brick the *lex mercatoria* by realigning arbitral decisions with changing commercial practices.[285]

I find an excellent illustration of this point in a highly obscure, but immensely suggestive, Texas case of the beginning of the last century. In *Panhandle Grain & Elevator Co. v. Dorsey*,[286] the seller was to deliver 10,000 pounds of cane seed in "sound, strong bags." The buyer rejected the shipment on the ground that it had not been properly sacked—and the court assumed that it had been "conclusively shown" that he was indeed justified in doing so. Now as soon as the buyer objected, the seller had immediately offered to resack the seed and protect the buyer against any loss—but the buyer declined the offer, "thus throwing the seed back on [the seller, who was] forced to resell on a declining market." An arbitration panel of the Grain Dealers' Association gave an award in favor of the seller, and the award was enforced: Although the buyer "may have been warranted, in a strictly legal, technical sense, in arbitrarily terminating the whole contract," the sellers had "sought to, and could, fully repair the damage" and tried to place the buyer "just where it would have been had there been no breach." The arbitrators had the power to "disregard any strict legal

---

281. [Cf. Luca G. Radicati di Brozolo, L'Illicéité "qui crève les yeux": critère de contrôle des sentences au regard de l'ordre public international, [2005] Rev. de l'Arb. 529, 548, 553 ("national judges hardly have a monopoly on the 'correct' application of the law," and "errors and oversights in applying competition law are hardly the exclusive domain of arbitral tribunals")].

282. Leon Green, The Duty Problem in Negligence Cases, 28 Col. L. Rev. 1014, 1015 (1928).

285. The role of arbitrators in helping to work out more functional solutions—in being the harbingers of legal change, in serving (even unwittingly) in the vanguard of reform—can go much further than the rather banal truism that they are likely to be sensitive to custom and usage. Cf. Ole Lando, The *Lex Mercatoria* in International Commercial Arbitration, 34 Int'l & Comp. L.Q. 747, 752–53 (1985), to the effect that an arbitrator applying the *lex mercatoria* will often act "as an inventor," taking "advantage of [his] freedom to select the better rule of law which courts sometimes miss." This seems particularly plausible in the case of an arbitrator who may be inclined to subordinate a local—the appropriate pejorative term is apparently "parochial"—rule to one that seems better adapted for use in international sales.

286. Panhandle Grain & Elevator Co. v. Dorsey, 242 S.W. 255 (Tex.Civ.App. 1922).

right or objection" and adjust the matters in dispute on the basis of the "equities growing out of the transaction as evidenced by the circumstances surrounding it"—and here, they found that "equity and good conscience required [the buyer] to accept [the seller's] offer to make it whole."

Now we cannot know for sure whether the buyer in *Panhandle,* in rejecting the seller's offer to resack, was simply looking for a means of escape from what had turned out to be a bad bargain: Under the state of sales law at the time, that would not in any event have been particularly relevant. But it is clear that the law of sales has continued to evolve—and along precisely that path laid out by the Texas arbitrators. The principle that sellers should be able to "cure" defects in their tender—now embodied in the UCC—may be a "novel legal doctrine," but as Professors White and Summers note, "it does no more than give legal recognition to a practical right that sellers have long exercised"—and, perhaps, that arbitrators have long honored.[289] There must be an endless number of similar cases in which departure by arbitrators from "the law" equally signals a greater sensitivity to business norms—and equally places them ahead of their time.[290]

Finally, in thinking about judicial review on matters of "law" we must of course distinguish between mere rules of construction—which come into

---

289. James J. White & Robert S. Summers, Uniform Commercial Code 332 (5th ed. 2000)(UCC § 2–508 "simply recognizes a general pattern of business behavior and adds a legal sanction to those economic and nonlegal sanctions which the parties had and have"). Even after the time for performance has expired, the seller has a right to cure—and thereby cut off the buyer's right to reject or revoke acceptance of a non-conforming delivery—if he "has performed in good faith," and "if the cure is appropriate and timely under the circumstances." UCC § 2–508(2). Whether a cure is "appropriate and timely" will be tested "based upon the circumstances and needs of the buyer"; an "offered cure would be untimely if the buyer has reasonably changed its position in good faith reliance on the nonconforming tender." Preliminary Comments, cmt. 4. * * *

290. Here is another one: Courts in a given jurisdiction may take the position that a builder who has "substantially failed to perform"—in circumstances "where performance is to precede payment and becomes a condition thereof"—"can recover nothing for his labor and materials, notwithstanding the owner has chosen to occupy and enjoy the erection." Smith v. Brady, 17 N.Y. 173, 182 (1858). "[N]o encouragement has ever been given to that loose and dangerous doctrine which allows a person to violate his most solemn engagements and then to draw the injured party into a controversy concerning

the amount and value of the benefits received." Id. at 186. Dobbs refers to this "older doctrine" as a "grim guillotine," Dan B. Dobbs, Handbook on the Law of Remedies 918 (1973). See also id. at 883 (contracts of sale), 928–29 (contracts of employment).

Yet in such a case an arbitrator may think it fairer to grant some recovery to the builder—say, in an amount by which the benefit that he has conferred upon the owner by part performance exceeds the damages that the owner has suffered from the breach; his award to that effect will be enforced. See Fudickar v. Guardian Mut. Life Ins. Co., 62 N.Y. 392, 400–01 (1875)(dictum). What this arbitrator has done amounts to nothing more than a forward-looking application of the principle of Britton v. Turner, 6 N.H. 481 (1834)—a principle that only gradually and belatedly won general acceptance in public fora. See, e.g., Maxton Builders, Inc. v. Lo Galbo, 502 N.E.2d 184, 187 (N.Y. 1986)(the "modern rule" "permits the party in default to recover for part performance in excess of actual damages, but places the burden on him to prove the net benefit conferred"); Dobbs, supra at 921 (a "reason for rejecting the old rule [denying] restitutionary recovery or conditioning such a recovery on the contractor's 'good faith' is that such a rule is not only punitive but whimsical") * * *.

play in the absence of an agreement to the contrary—and mandatory rules. After all, most "rules" of contract or commercial law are nothing more than "gap-fillers," supplying a term where the parties have not expressly supplied one themselves. These "general rules of law" hold only when there is no "common understanding" that is directly furnished by the parties themselves—or which can be found in the background, of usage and prior conduct, against which they have dealt with each other.

Where, however, the parties have bargained for dispute resolution through arbitration, the particular method *they* have chosen to fill any gaps—to define their "common understanding"—is the arbitrator's reading of both the agreement and the surrounding landscape: His construction "*is* their bargain.*" Those "legal rules" that arbitrators are occasionally willing to temper with considerations of common business practice, and notions of honorable behavior, are likely to be precisely the "gap fillers" that could in any event have been varied directly by the parties themselves. Doctrine would not be doing its job properly should it fail to give effect to such exercises of private autonomy—here, the parties' commitment to the choice of a common agent to work out the implications of an inchoate deal. And commentary that does not even glance in this direction is without any value whatever.

Alan Rau, On Integrity in Private Judging

14 Arbitration International 115, 146–150 (1998).

It is a familiar enough proposition that an arbitrator's freedom from the need to explain or justify his award is closely linked to his lack of accountability in terms of judicial review: The naked award that is the norm in domestic commercial arbitrations can be explained as much by a desire to insulate decisions from judicial scrutiny as to any desire to avoid the delay or added expense that written opinions would entail. And this tactic of ensuring the finality of arbitration by harnessing Delphic decisions to a hard-to-rebut presumption of validity has been extremely effective. Conversely, one can expect that any attempt to impose reasoned awards on arbitrators will be motivated at least in part by the desire to expand judicial supervision of the process.

For arbitrators as for jurors, our present lack of accountability can be both liberating and intoxicating. And for arbitrators and jurors equally, decisionmaking that is so safe and easy can just as readily lead to lazy and uninformed judgment—where minds have not been concentrated nor strenuous efforts made to question initial impulses.[149] From this point of view,

---

149. See Christine Cooper, *Where Are We Going with Gilmer?—Some Ruminations on the Arbitration of Discrimination Claims,* 11 St Louis U. Pub. Law. Rev. 203, 219 (1992)(an arbitrator "who is not a professional arbitrator and who knows the scope of judicial review cannot be expected to view the case as seriously as a federal judge who is developing public law"); Margaret Jacobs, "Men's Club: Riding Crop and Slurs: How Wall Street Dealt With a Sex–Bias Case," Wall St J, June 9, 1994, at A1, A8 (arbitrator in employment discrimination case explained that "[u]sually you see and hear things and

reasoned opinions can be seen as one means of imposing transparency on the decisionmaking process and in particular, of imposing a certain self-discipline on the decisionmakers themselves. This is the phenomenon in which the judge or arbitrator supposedly finds—at the point where it becomes necessary to turn inclination into reasoned judgment—that it simply "will not write":[150] Forced to think through the implications of his decision, he may in the course of explanation be surprised to find that it is not internally consistent, that it does not take account of all relevant interests, that it overlooks authority or ignores factual complexities. "[W]hen institutional designers have grounds for believing that decisions will systematically be the product of bias, self-interest, insufficient reflection, or simply excess haste, requiring decisionmakers to give reasons may counteract some of these tendencies."[151]

However, one need not be inordinately cynical to suspect that in arbitration, a requirement of reasoned awards would be somewhat less likely to affect outcomes in this way than it would be to serve merely as a challenge to an arbitrator's craftsmanship. It is hard to take issue with the proposition that a mandate to give reasons will "drive out illegitimate reasons when they are the only plausible explanation for particular outcomes"[152]—but surely in most cases we can expect the qualifying phrase to swallow up whatever possible interest inheres in the original claim. Surely an arbitrator obligated to make a reasoned award may be expected to deploy his rhetorical ability, ingenuity, creativity and imagination in articulating the narrowest, the most plausible, or the most conventional rationale for his decision—all in the interest of commanding the acquiescence of the disputing parties or a reviewing court.[153] The claim here is not that

you get a feeling, and the decision is based on that").

I think it would be a serious error, though, to underestimate the sobering and disciplining effects on decisionmaking that one sees simply as a result of deliberation on a panel of three arbitrators—especially when the members of the panel are experienced attorneys and businesspeople, willing to invest some care in taking apart the elements of a dispute, and anxious to demonstrate to their colleagues that they have done so.

150. See * * * Frederick Schauer, Giving Reasons, 47 Stan. L. Rev. 633, 652 (1995); see also Rt. Hon. Lord Justice Bingham, Reasons and Reasons for Reasons: Differences Between a Court Judgment and an Arbitration Award, 4 Arb. Int'l 141, 143 (1988) ("I cannot, I hope, be the only person who has sat down to write a judgment, having formed the view that A must win, only to find in the course of composition that there are no sustainable grounds for that conclusion and that on any rational analysis B must succeed").

151. Schauer, supra n. 150 at 657. The CPR's "Non–Administered Arbitration Rules" provide that awards "shall state the reasoning on which the award rests unless the parties agree otherwise," Rule 13.2. In its Commentary, the drafting Committee suggested that it would be "good discipline for arbitrators to require them to spell out their reasoning. Sometimes this process gives rise to second thoughts as to the soundness of the result."

152. Schauer, supra n.150 at 657–58.

153. This of course has been a commonplace of Realist insight for some time. See, e.g., Letter from O.W. Holmes, Jr. to Harold Laski, 19 February 1920, in 1 Holmes–Laski Letters 243 (1953) ("I always say in conference that no case can be settled by general propositions, that I will admit any general proposition you like and decide the case either way") * * * .

reasoned opinions must always and necessarily be products of a conscious "Houdini-like manipulation"—when they are not indeed the result of self-deception or rationalization[154]—although this will very often be the case. The point is just that even under the very best of circumstances, the process of crafting reasoned awards will not be congruent with the decision-making process; the award must be an imperfect "reconstruction" after the fact of actual decision, the product of a struggle to marshal arguments in support of the result in such a way that it will "pass without objection in the trade."

European academics and arbitrators, accustomed to reasoned awards as a matter of course, often find it paradoxical that it is only in this country—where a common law, case-based jurisprudence has become so highly developed—that we are so willing to dispense with such opinions from arbitrators. But as with most paradoxes, this observation makes possible a further leap of insight. I should think that it is precisely our common law background that enables us to do this: More particularly, it is precisely because our legal education has so carefully honed the skills of deconstructing judicial opinions, and so laboriously trained us to debunk their explanatory power, that we can no longer believe in the presence of such opinions as an indispensable element of a just decision.

* * *

While reasoned opinions often do not constrain choice as much as we would like to believe, there is also a counter-proposition that may seem somewhat paradoxical—that at the same time they often constrain more than we would think desirable. The case for "naked" awards thus has an important positive as well as a defensive aspect. Here the continual dialectic between "rule-based decisionmaking" on the one hand, and "particularistic decisionmaking" or "case by case optimization" on the other—which lies at the heart of the judicial enterprise—has a particular resonance. When we talk about the arbitrator's freedom from reasoned awards, it will frequently be the case that we are really talking about his freedom from over-broad rules or time-honored categories that might otherwise appear to dictate a result he would prefer to avoid. This is, then, a freedom that makes possible an arbitrator's flexibility in decisionmaking and a maximum attention to context.

Some concrete examples may illustrate the point. Where a buyer has refused to perform under an installment sales contract, an arbitrator's decision may award damages to the seller for breach but at the same time relieve the buyer of any further performance. As a teacher of Contracts, I would find it rather difficult to rationalize this result in doctrinal terms—but it may nevertheless make some rough sense in terms of the business situation and the equities of the parties. Or again, a strong claim may be made based on fraud for the rescission of a joint venture agreement; the

---

154. See Scott Altman, Beyond Candor, 89 Mich. L. Rev. 296, 311 (1990) ("Houdini is willing to manipulate. By manipulation, I mean intentionally ignoring what one believes to be the most convincing argument and instead offering legal arguments that one believes to be less strong, while failing to disclose one's reasons for doing so").

arbitrators may be sympathetic to the claim but feel that the plaintiff is at least in part responsible for its own dilemma and at least in part to blame for its reliance—and so they may resort to the analogy of "comparative negligence" to reduce its recovery. Here too, lawyer-arbitrators obligated to justify this result in the form of a reasoned opinion might well feel the need to do so in terms of existing contract doctrine: Should they find that they are not in fact up to the task, they would inexorably be led to apply "that most ubiquitous of principles, winner-take-all, which is more typical of a judicial forum."

It has been suggested that a major source of the common law's commitment to an "all-or-nothing bias" has been the "combative aspects of the search for reality in our courts": It is a "reflection of the egocentric dialectic of the adversary system," and of our "fighting instinct." But the prevalence of hard-fought arbitrations suggests that this may give us at best an incomplete account. Perhaps a more satisfactory explanation might be found in the mandate to our courts to rationalize results in written opinions. It is striking that by contrast to the judicial forum, arbitration shares with other processes of private settlement two major characteristics: both a tendency to look for intermediate solutions—responsive to the uniqueness of each dispute—and the absence of any need to justify the outcome.

So a naked award in the cases I mentioned above might appear at first glance to be nothing more than further examples of unprincipled arbitral "compromise". Yet such awards do not readily fit our usual understanding of "compromise" as a response to factual or legal indeterminacy, or as the reflection of an arbitrator's insecurity of tenure, or of his inadequate energy or care. Still less do they strike us as a kind of "formless and unpredictable qadi justice." Lack of a reasoned opinion here may make possible an arbitral decisionmaking which, while departing from the judicial model, is nevertheless infused with attention to such things as commercial understanding, good business practice and notions of honorable behavior, and with practical reasoning from familiar legal norms.[164] And we should remember that private dispute settlement—which lacks any adjudicative dimension whatever—may often work in the same way. In a sense, then, we are returning here to where we began—with the premise that the process of arbitration can only be understood in terms of bargain and contract, as part of a private exercise in the planning of transactions.

Alan Rau, Contracting Out of the Arbitration Act

8 American Review of International Arbitration 225 (1997).

The parties to an international joint venture agreed to arbitration to be held under ICC Rules in San Francisco. Under the terms of their

---

164. Cf. Lisa Bernstein, Opting Out of the Legal System: Extralegal Contractual Relations in the Diamond Industry, 21 J. Leg. Stud. 115, 127 (1992)(arbitrators in the diamond industry's arbitration mechanism "explain that they decide complex cases on the basis of trade custom and usage, a little common sense, some Jewish law, and, last, common-law legal principles").

arbitration clause, the arbitration panel was instructed to issue a written award that was to include "detailed findings of fact and conclusions of law"; the federal district court for the Northern District of California could then:

> vacate, modify or correct any award (i) based upon any of the grounds referred to in the Federal Arbitration Act, (ii) where the arbitrators' findings of fact are not supported by substantial evidence, or (iii) where the arbitrators' conclusions of law are erroneous.

An award was ultimately rendered, but the district court resolutely refused to look into the arbitrators' findings of fact or conclusions of law: It found that its "options" were "limited" by the provisions of the FAA "and may not be extended by agreement of the parties." "The role of the federal courts cannot be subverted to serve private interests at the whim of contracting parties." So the court restricted its inquiry to the "permissible statutory grounds" found in § 10 of the Act, and summarily confirmed the award. The arbitrators had not "exceeded their powers." * * * [T]hey were hardly required to apply California law "without error."

* * *

[On appeal, a three-judge panel of the Ninth Circuit reversed, and instructed the district court "to apply the parties' contractually expanded standard of review of unsupported factual findings or errors of law." The district court then again confirmed the award—this time, after duly examining it under the contractual standard. A second appeal followed—and this time the Ninth Circuit en banc overturned the decision of the earlier panel: The law of the Circuit was "corrected" to hold that "a federal court may only review an arbitral decision on the grounds set forth in the [FAA]. Private parties have no power to alter or expand those grounds, and any contractual provision purporting to do so is, accordingly, legally unenforceable":

> Congress had good reason to preclude more expansive federal court review. Arbitration is a dispute resolution process designed, at least in theory, to respond to the wishes of the parties more flexibly and expeditiously than the federal courts' uniform rules of procedure allow.]

This [is] the celebrated case of *Lapine Technology Corp. v. Kyocera Corp.*[4] I must say that I have been astonished at the extent to which this issue seems to have excited the attention of the arbitration community. It might, then, not be out of place for me to say just why I think the [position ultimately taken by the Ninth Circuit en banc is so clearly wrong.].

* * *

II. WHAT IS THE POINT OF § 10?

It seems symptomatic of a particularly rigid cast of mind to assume that where the arbitration statute allocates certain powers to a court,

---

4. 130 F.3d 884, 891 (9th Cir.1997) [overruled, 341 F.3d 987 (9th Cir. 2003)].

then—by that very fact—any *contractual re-allocation* by the parties themselves must necessarily be forbidden. Section 3 of the FAA, for example, tells us that before staying litigation, the court must be "satisfied that the issue involved in such suit or proceeding is referable to arbitration." Are we really and truly required to conclude from this that the courts have "exclusive jurisdiction" to determine whether an arbitration clause covers a particular dispute—even *though the parties themselves* may have agreed to entrust this question of "arbitrability" to the arbitrator? The Supreme Court has sensibly indicated that the answer to this question is "no"[25]— that is, that the statute's default allocation of authority *between courts and arbitrators* need not implicate in any way the power of the *parties themselves* to structure the arbitration mechanism so as to advance their own interests.

Similarly, §§ 9 and 10 of the Act direct courts to confirm awards unless certain specified grounds for vacatur are present; the "merits"— that is, arbitral determinations of fact and interpretations of law—are not reviewable, being presumably left to the arbitrators. Are we really and truly required to conclude from this that *the parties themselves* may not entrust to courts—rather than to the arbitrators—the final authority to decide legal and factual questions? Must we conclude [as some commentators have argued] that giving effect to such an agreement would constitute a "patent violation" of the Act? Presented with such an assertion—and with no attempt at a functional or purposive reading of the statute—the diagnosis seems justified that we are in the presence of that most common of legal ailments, "hardening of the categories."

By contrast, I have always thought that the principal purpose of § 10 of the FAA—and for that matter, of equivalent provisions found in all modern arbitration laws—is rather to insulate from parochial or intrusive judicial review awards *that the parties intended in the usual sense to be binding.* That is, § 10 serves to assure the parties to an arbitral proceeding that they need not fear an officious or meddlesome inquiry into the merits which would impair the efficacy of the arbitral process for them. But such a purpose has nothing at all, as far as I can see, to do with the situation where the parties are eager to depart from the protective rule of § 10. It is one thing to say that their awards must have legal currency in accordance with the parties' presumed wishes; it is something totally different to say that their awards *will* have this currency, by God, over the parties' expressed wishes to the contrary. I should think that such interference with private autonomy would have to be justified—and on other than paternalistic grounds.

---

25. See First Options of Chicago, Inc. v. Kaplan, 514 U.S. 938, 943 (1995)(the question "who has the primary power to decide arbitrability" "turns upon what the parties agreed about that matter"; if the parties agreed to submit the arbitrability question to arbitration, "then the court's standard for reviewing the arbitrator's decision about that matter should not differ from the standard courts apply when they review any other matter that parties have agreed to arbitrate").

It is in this sense then that I see the provisions of § 10, not as an imperative command of public policy, but as no more than a set of "default rules" intended to reflect the traditional historical understanding concerning the binding effect of arbitral awards. Like any default rules, these supply a ready-made stock of implied terms, allocating the burden of being explicit and chosen at least in part to mirror the "hypothetical bargain" that the parties are assumed to have intended. And so whatever we can characterize as a "default rule" may naturally be varied by an express agreement of the parties, who may stray in the direction of expanding the statutory grounds of review—or even, perhaps, in the direction of restricting them still further.

Since a default rule is no more than a rebuttable presumption—the mere beginning of the inquiry—it by definition grants the ultimate power of decisionmaking to the parties rather than to the State. * * * Now it is of course entirely a separate question whether § 10 represents the *most desirable background* rule to govern arbitral determinations of "legal" issues. The arbitration law of England, for example, adopts more or less the opposite presumption: Judicial review for errors of law is possible, at least with leave of the court, unless the parties expressly exclude it.[33] But the English legislation at least demonstrates that it is plausible to treat this issue as I am suggesting it should be treated—as the search for the appropriate presumption—and for the moment, the default rule of § 10 is the only default rule we have.

III. ARBITRABILITY AND COMPARATIVE ADVANTAGE

It is at least plausible to say—it is, after all, a proposition of some antiquity—that arbitration has its greatest utility in providing expert determinations of contested matters of fact (such as the "determination of the quality of a commodity or the amount of money due under a contract").[34] By contrast, the legitimacy of the arbitration process—and any

---

33. See Arbitration Act 1996 (1996 c.23) § 69.

In the absence of an exclusion agreement, the right to appeal on questions of law is generally discretionary with the court. But note that under the English Arbitration Act no leave of court is necessary *if all the parties agree to such an appeal.* And such an "agreement" for appeal may be contained in a predispute arbitration clause, or even in "rules incorporated into that clause;" see David St. John Sutton et al., Russell on Arbitration 428 & n.14 (21st ed. 1997). In that respect at least the English regime is not too different from what was [attempted by the parties] in *Kyocera.*

34. Wilko v. Swan, 346 U.S. 427, 435 (1953). See also Philip G. Phillips, Rules of Law or Laissez–Faire in Commercial Arbitra-

tion, 47 Harv. L. Rev. 590, 599–600, 626 (1934)("the attention of business has been on arbitration as an escape from the jury method of fact determination and not as an escape from substantive law"); Paul L. Sayre, Development of Commercial Arbitration Law, 37 Yale L. J. 595, 615 (1928)(the "full usefulness of arbitration lies" in making it serve "as a substitute for the preliminary stages of a court trial"; "arbitration works much more cheaply and quickly when the arbitrators confine themselves to their specialty, that of passing on technical questions of fact in modem business"); Julius Henry Cohen & Kenneth Dayton, The New Federal Arbitration Law, 12 Va. L. Rev. 265, 281 (1926)("[n]ot all questions arising out of contracts ought to be arbitrated;" arbitration "is a remedy peculiarly suited to the disposition of the ordinary disputes between merchants as to questions

comparative advantage that it may possess over litigation—may be weakest when arbitrators attempt to follow national courts in laying down disputed legal norms. In fact such a judgment once reflected our dominant view of arbitration, and presumably explains the traditional reluctance of courts in decisions like *Wilko v. Swan*,[35] or *Alexander v. Gardner–Denver*,[36] to defer to arbitrators—or even to find arbitration permissible—in cases where the decisionmaker was called upon to interpret and apply regulatory legislation.

Now of course, the law has progressed far beyond the stage where the competence of arbitrators to decide difficult "legal" questions was systematically doubted—and cases like *Wilko*, as restrictions on the arbitral process in the name of "public policy," are long dead. But might not *the parties themselves*—who are, after all, the ultimate consumers of the process—still reasonably adopt the same attitude in individual cases?

I am at a loss to understand why parties to commercial transactions should ever be compelled to adopt one unitary model of arbitration—making judicial oversight of awards, for example, into a Procrustean bed to which the parties must adapt themselves even at the cost of amputated limbs. But that is precisely what it means to assert that once parties choose arbitration, they must necessarily accept arbitral determinations on all "legal issues." * * *

I had always assumed it to be a commonplace that parties to a contract are able—and indeed, should be encouraged—to tailor the scope of "arbitrable issues" to fit their own particular needs, circumstances, or desires. The ability to do this is in fact one of the principal selling points of the arbitration process: As the prophets of private ordering suggested long ago, arbitration is in this respect "the parties' dream."[39] The parties are free, as the Supreme Court wrote in *Volt*, "to structure their arbitration agreements as they see fit. Just as they may limit by contract the issues which they will arbitrate, so too may they specify by contract the rules under which that arbitration will be conducted." So, for example, they are free, if they think it advisable, to:

- draw a distinction between disputes over fees "due and owing" under a distributorship agreement, and disputes over alleged copy-

---

of fact—quantity, quality, time of delivery, compliance with terms of payment, excuses for non-performance, and the like") * * *.

35. Wilko v. Swan, 346 U.S. 427, 437 (1953)("the protective provisions of the Securities Act require the exercise of judicial direction to fairly assure their effectiveness").

36. Alexander v. Gardner–Denver Co., 415 U.S. 36, 56–57 (1974)(employee's statutory right to trial under Title VII of the Civil Rights Act of 1964 is not foreclosed by prior submission of his claim to arbitration under arbitration clause in collective bargaining agreement; "[a]rbitral procedures, while well suited to the resolution of contractual disputes, make arbitration a comparatively inappropriate forum for the final resolution of rights created by Title VII"; "the specialized competence of arbitrators pertains primarily to the law of the shop, not the law of the land"). [See pp. 198–203 infra].

39. Henry M. Hart, Jr. & Albert M. Sacks, The Legal Process: Basic Problems in the Making and Application of Law 310 (1994 ed.).

right and trademark infringement—and choose to arbitrate only the former;[41] * * *

- draw a distinction between disputes over past breaches of contract, and disputes relating to future adjustments of the contract—and choose to arbitrate only the former.

Certain well-established "rules" of arbitration law are also in essence little more than background presumptions, which the parties may vary by redefining in their contract the scope of arbitrable issues. So, for example, the parties may:

- draw a distinction between disputes over breach of contract and disputes alleging fraudulent inducement of the contract—and choose to arbitrate only the former, thereby reversing the default rule of *Prima Paint*[44] * * *.

- Now, given this familiar background, is it not understandable that the parties—relying here on hoary considerations of comparative advantage—might choose to draw a distinction between "any unresolved questions of fact" and "questions of law"? If they do so, they may prefer to draft an arbitration clause by which they agree to submit only the former to arbitration—thereby entrusting factual determinations to arbitrators chosen specifically for that purpose, while *withholding* from their arbitrators the power to make ultimate determinations of "legal" issues.

Would this not, in fact, be just one more example of the unremarkable, everyday practice by which parties "agree to submit to arbitration only some of the disputes that may arise between them"? The contract in *Kyocera* might then be understood simply as an attempt to limit the scope of authority of the arbitrators and to carve out a particular class of disputes as "arbitrable": And from this point of view, [a court's decision enforcing the contract] becomes nothing more than a natural corollary of a half-dozen or more cases in which the Supreme Court's "presumption of arbitrability" left abundant room for an inquiry into whether the parties had agreed on anything to the contrary.

* * *

41. Zenger–Miller, Inc. v. Training Team, GmbH, 757 F.Supp. 1062 (N.D.Cal. 1991); see also Coady v. Ashcraft & Gerel, 996 F.Supp. 95, 98, 109 (D.Mass. 1998)(employment agreement provided for arbitration of "any ambiguities or questions of interpretation of this contract"; held, claim of breach of fiduciary duty is not subject to arbitration since "fiduciary duties arise out of agency law and do not depend on any interpretation of the Employment Agreement"); Tracer Research Corp. v. National Environmental Services Co., 42 F.3d 1292, 1295 (9th Cir.1994)(arbitration clause covering "any controversy or claim arising out of this Agreement" refers only to disputes "re-

lating to the interpretation and performance of the contract itself"; tort claim for misappropriation of trade secrets is not arbitrable). * * *

44. See Carro v. Parade of Toys, Inc., 950 F.Supp. 449, 452 (D.P.R.1996) (agreement to arbitrate any dispute arising under this "Purchase Order" reflected "an intent to arbitrate only a limited range of disputes," those "relating to the interpretation and performance of a contract," and did not cover allegations of fraud in the inducement of the entire contract, nor claims for negligent misrepresentation or conversion). * * *

IV. CONTRACTING FOR NON–BINDING ARBITRATION

[The same conclusion—that a court should review the arbitration award in *Kyocera* by following the standards laid down by the parties in their contract—can also be reached by taking a somewhat different route.]. While it would be unusual to do so, the parties to an agreement might wish to alter in some respects the binding effect of an arbitral award. * * * [There are cases, for example,] where commercial parties dealing at arm's length have stipulated that their arbitral award shall be completely non-binding. These are the cases where the parties may see the virtues of what is in effect an "advisory opinion" as an aid to evaluating a case for settlement purposes—although they may be unwilling to give up all notion of recourse to litigation. In particular the parties may think that a "trial run" of the case, ending in a prediction by a neutral expert, may cause the more recalcitrant among them to reassess their own partisan estimates of the likely outcome of adjudication. Another object may be for attorneys or management representatives to be able to use the opinion of a third party to "sell" a compromise settlement to reluctant clients or constituents, allowing them to withdraw without loss of face from hardened positions. In this respect "non-binding arbitration" has much in common with other formal "reality testing" devices such as "court-annexed arbitration," the "summary jury trial," the "mini-trial," and fact finding in public-sector employment disputes. The utility of such non-binding evaluative processes has long been recognized, to the point that they have become commonplace and unremarkable remedies in the ADR armamentarium.

Such agreements for non-binding arbitration have been held to be within the Federal Arbitration Act for the purposes of stays or orders to compel under §§ 3 and 4. (The leading case probably remains *AMF Inc. v. Brunswick*,[71] but there are a number of more recent holdings to the same effect.)[72] However, the applicability of the FAA seems to be a question of largely theoretical interest—given the undoubted power of a court to enforce such agreements as a matter of ordinary contract law. A federal court with the requisite jurisdiction over the case would be expected routinely to apply this general corpus of state law—under which compliance with the prescribed arbitration process becomes merely a precondition to litigation in accordance with the intention of the parties.[74] Should the

71. AMF Inc. v. Brunswick Corp., 621 F.Supp. 456, 458 (E.D.N.Y.1985)(settlement agreement between competitors provided that any future dispute involving an advertised claim of "data based comparative superiority" would be submitted to the National Advertising Division of the Council of Better Business Bureaus "for the rendition of an advisory opinion"). * * *

72. See Wolsey, Ltd. v. Foodmaker, Inc., 144 F.3d 1205 (9th Cir. 1998)(agreement between franchiser of Jack in the Box restaurants and Hong Kong corporation established a three-step dispute resolution process, in which non-binding arbitration under AAA rules could be followed by litigation in federal court); Kelley v. Benchmark Homes, Inc., 250 Neb. 367, 550 N.W.2d 640, 642–43 (Neb. 1996)(warranty contract entered into by home buyers provided for arbitration which "shall not be legally binding, but shall be a condition precedent to the commencement of any litigation"). * * *

74. * * * Similar results are reached without difficulty in other cases that do not even consider it necessary to use the word

process fail in its goal of inducing settlement, the court would then of course proceed to hear the case in the usual manner.

From this point of view, then, aren't *Kyocera* and similar cases—where parties merely wish courts to honor their preference that arbitral determinations of "legal" issues not be binding—merely natural corollaries *of AMF Inc. v. Brunswick?* The thesis that the parties may preserve the right to reject an arbitrator's "conclusions of law" should be fairly unobjectionable, should it not, once one concedes an even broader proposition—that they may preserve the right to a trial *de novo* on *all issues* in the case?

In stark contrast to this analysis, [some distinguished commentators have argued that]:

> Obtaining a resolution of a dispute ... in a speedy and efficient manner provides a compelling reason for limiting the scope of judicial review to the bare essentials needed to afford due process and to protect the state's own interests.... [I]f arbitral awards could be reviewed for errors of law or fact, arbitration would easily degenerate into a device for adding still another instance to the usual three instances of litigation in the ordinary courts.... [P]ermitting contractual modification of the scope of judicial review would undermine the public policy of encouraging arbitration. For it would inexorably cause arbitral awards to be final dispositions to a far lesser extent and thus lessen the social desirability of arbitration.[76]

But I find the argument that parties should not be permitted to alter the binding character of their awards, "because it would impair the efficacy of arbitration," to be extremely troubling. More than anything, it reminds me of the stereotypical librarian resentful of the whole practice of borrowing books—because the annoying tendency of patrons to do so disrupts the

---

"arbitration." See, e.g., Haertl Wolff Parker, Inc. v. Howard S. Wright Construction Co., 1989 WL 151765 (D.Or.)(parties agreed to submit future disputes to a neutral third party "for a recommendation;" held, claim dismissed "with leave to refile without prejudice if the disputes are not resolved after referral" to the neutral; "the court cannot say that it would be futile to refer the deadlocked issues to him"); DeValk Lincoln Mercury, Inc. v. Ford Motor Co., 811 F.2d 326, 334–38 (7th Cir.1987)(agreement between automobile dealership and manufacturer provided that any claim by the dealer arising out of termination or nonrenewal "shall be appealed" to the company's Dealer Policy Board as "a condition precedent to the Dealer's right to pursue any other remedy;" the company, but not the dealer, "shall be bound by the decision of the Policy Board;" held, because "the mediation (sic) clause demands strict compliance with its requirement of appeal," summary judgment ordered for manufacturer).

76. Hans Smit, Contractual Modification of the Scope of Judicial Review of Arbitral Awards, 8 Am. Rev. Int'l Arb. 147, 149, 150 (1997). See also Andreas Lowenfeld, Can Arbitration Coexist with Judicial Review? A Critique of LaPine v. Kyocera, ADR Currents, Sept. 1998 at pp. 1, 15 ("judicial review of the merits would inevitably prolong the process, negating the expeditiousness that is one of the important advantages of arbitration") * * *.

This has long been a familiar point. Cf. Fudickar v. Guardian Mut. Life Ins. Co., 62 N.Y. 392, 400 (1875)("If courts should assume to judge the decision of arbitrators upon the merits, the value of this method of settling controversies would be destroyed, and an award instead of being a final determination of a controversy would become but one of the steps in its progress").

symmetry and orderly appearance of the shelves, and the comforting assurance that everything can always be found in its rightful place.

However, the arbitration process—just like the public library—exists and is designed above all to serve the interests of its users, not those of the guardians of the temple. The Supreme Court has reminded us often enough that "efficiency" is not an ultimate value in arbitration: The overriding goal of the FAA, in the eyes of the Court, is not "to promote the expeditious resolution of claims" but rather to "rigorously enforce agreements to arbitrate"—even though this may admittedly "thwart" our interest in "speedy and efficient decisionmaking." But in any event there is a more fundamental point: It is to the practice of contracting parties—and to that exclusively—that we must look to determine what under the circumstances is efficient *for them*. The quoted argument strikes me as excellent drafting advice—a sage warning to transactional attorneys that inserting into their arbitration agreements a clause of the sort involved in *Kyocera* may be folly.[78] But would it not be just a tad dogmatic to assert that there exist no cases where the parties might ever rationally choose to make a different choice?

So in high-stakes cases I can imagine that a desire to ensure predictability in the application of legal standards, a desire to guard against a "rogue tribunal," or against the distortions of judgment that can often result from the dynamics of tripartite arbitration—may all weigh heavily in the decision to limit by contract the binding effect of an arbitral award. Parties who, through risk aversion or inadequate confidence, have *ex ante* the perspective of a "potential loser" may particularly be impelled in this direction. * * * Similarly, I find it quite plausible to assert that review of awards for "errors of law"—with all the formality and need for reasoned opinions that are likely to come in its wake—is quite likely to impair the ability of arbitrators to "fashion creative solutions"; arbitrators might shun reasonable solutions if they had to worry that courts might not be willing or able to endorse the legal bases on which they rest. Indeed I have argued elsewhere that it is precisely an arbitrator's "freedom from overbroad rules or time-honored categories" that makes possible arbitration's "flexibility in decisionmaking and a maximum attention to context." But in the absence of externalities, here too surely the proper tradeoff is for the parties themselves—who may be less enamored of clever and creative solutions than those of us who do not have to live with the practical consequences.

* * *

78. It is interesting to note, though, that among all the reasons why parties prefer to submit their disputes to arbitration rather than litigation, savings in time and in cost appear—at least in international cases—to be factors of "slight" or even "non-existent" importance, see Christian Bühring–Uhle, Arbitration and Mediation in International Business 137–39 (1996). This survey of practitioner attitudes also suggests that the "ab-sence of appeals" is a somewhat "ambivalent" attribute of the arbitration process: For a large number of respondents, this was "crucial for the aim of obtaining a final decision within a reasonable time span"—although "according to some of the practitioners interviewed [the absence of appeals was] seen as a disadvantage since the possibility to correct even grave errors of the arbitral tribunal is very restricted." Id. at 137.

During oral argument before the Ninth Circuit in *Kyocera,* Judge Kozinski asked pointedly what could account for the sudden popularity of clauses in which the binding effect of awards was restricted: What, he wondered, "was happening in the middle of the 1980's that caused the parties to start drafting arbitration agreements that departed from the standard clause. . . . [T]here's no case law there, there's no legislation. Suddenly it starts popping up." He didn't receive much of an answer, but the question was certainly a good one.

Reasons for drafting clauses of the sort involved in *Kyocera* have always existed, of course, but in light of a number of developments the moment does indeed seem "right" for lawyers increasingly to resort to them. The blanket assumption of arbitral competence that has in recent years swept whole areas of statutory and regulatory law into arbitration has certainly contributed to a countervailing impulse—the desire to ensure that awards in such cases are not too discordant with "public" jurisprudence. The growing use of custom-tailored arbitration clauses—whether intended to diminish the finality of awards or to increase formality in arbitral procedure—is surely but one manifestation of what is often described and decried as the "judicialization" or "legalization" of arbitration; it is in a sense the natural consequence of the capture of the ADR movement by lawyers intent on remaking all dispute resolution in the image of the courtroom. In international cases, this process has been attributed to an increased involvement on the part of American litigators in transnational arbitration;[142] the habits—and perceived duties—of such litigators, may, it is said, lead them "to push to enlarge the limited means of appeal and therefore expand the control of the courts over private justice."

The increasingly altered appearance of arbitration may also suggest that one of the principal messages of the ADR movement—that parties can experiment with dispute resolution, shaping and adapting different processes to meet their own particular needs—is at last beginning to percolate through the profession. On a more mundane level, the diffusion of information about particular innovations in dispute resolution will inevitably encourage, if not coerce, imitation. * * *

One can expect that it is attorneys least familiar and comfortable with the peculiar nature of arbitration who will be most tempted to tinker with the default rules that govern arbitral finality. Long-term, repeat users will by contrast have the greatest stake in the proper functioning of the system—and will be most likely to understand that combining private justice with judicial oversight of the merits represents some considerable conceptual confusion, certain over time to lessen the potential utility of

142. See Yves Dezalay & Bryant G. Garth, Dealing in Virtue: International Commercial Arbitration and the Construction of a Transnational Legal Order 33–58 (1996)("Arbitration as Litigation"; electing arbitration, says an American practitioner, "doesn't mean that I necessarily want to give up all the trappings of full-scale litigation and what might come with it"; "[o]ne understands the irritation of the founding fathers confronted by these newcomers who permit themselves to transform the nature of arbitration by multiplying the incidents of procedure and technical appeals").

arbitration to contracting parties. In this sense I am tempted to join Professor Lowenfeld in the hope that what he calls "arbitration plus" "does not catch on" generally.[148] But clearly there will be occasions when limits on the binding effect of an award may be critical to acceptance of the process: For some litigators, I imagine, arbitration will only be tolerated at all with what appears to be the added safeguard of a controlled outcome firmly grounded in "the law." In such cases, the persistent feeling that people will unfailingly make the wrong decisions if allowed to choose for themselves is a poor basis for lawmaking.

NOTES AND QUESTIONS

1. The standard of judicial review of arbitration awards "has taken on various hues and colorations in its formulations," some courts suggesting that awards may be set aside if they are "arbitrary and capricious" or "completely irrational." "Although the differences in phraseology have caused a modicum of confusion, we deem them insignificant. We regard the standard of review undergirding these various formulations as identical, no matter how pleochroic their shadings and what terms of art have been employed to ensure that the arbitrator's decision relies on his interpretation of the contract as contrasted with his own beliefs of fairness and justice. However nattily wrapped, the packages are fungible." Advest, Inc. v. McCarthy, 914 F.2d 6, 9 (1st Cir.1990).

2. A casino hired a construction manager to supervise major renovations. In an arbitration initiated by the casino, "after four years and sixty-four days, the arbitrators simply awarded $14 million to [the claimant for lost profits] without any explanation whatsoever other than a finding that [the respondent] had 'failed to properly perform its obligations * * * pursuant to the contract * * *.' There are no reasons, no findings of fact, no conclusions of law, nothing other than the foregoing. For all we know, the arbitrators concluded that the sun rises in the west, the earth is flat, and damages have nothing to do with the intentions of the parties or the foreseeability of the consequences of a breach." Perini Corp. v. Greate Bay Hotel & Casino, Inc., 129 N.J. 479, 534–35, 610 A.2d 364, 392 (1992) (Wilentz, C.J., concurring). The award was confirmed.

3. One California judge has advised commercial arbitrators that in the event "they feel impelled by some uncontrollable urge, literary fluency, good conscience, or mere garrulousness to express themselves about a case they have tried, the opinion should be a separate document and not part of the award itself." Loew's, Inc. v. Krug (Cal.Super.1953); *quoted in* Sherman, Analysis of Pennsylvania's Arbitration Act of 1980, 43 U.Pitts.L.Rev. 363, 397 n. 94 (1982). Or, as the AAA's Guide for Commercial Arbitrators (1985) puts it, "The obligations to the parties are better fulfilled when the award leaves no room for attack."

---

148. Lowenfeld, supra n.76 at 17.

4. Section 20(d) of the Revised Uniform Arbitration Act permits a reviewing court to resubmit a case to the arbitrators "to clarify the award," and courts proceeding under the FAA have asserted a similar power to demand "clarification." Such power is occasionally used to determine the effect or scope of an award—to determine just what it was that the arbitrator had in fact decided. See, e.g., Tri–State Business Machines, Inc. v. Lanier Worldwide, Inc., 221 F.3d 1015 (7th Cir. 2000)(arbitrators decided that the termination of a dealership agreement triggered an obligation on the part of the manufacturer to repurchase "any inventory that [the dealer] currently owns"; held, because the term "inventory" in the award was "ambiguous," the district court engaged in "impermissible interpretation" of the award when it included sales literature within the repurchase requirement; the district court therefore "erred in not remanding the issue of the sales literature to the arbitration panel for clarification"). But such power is rarely if ever used to compel the arbitrator to explain his reasoning process.

See Sargent v. Paine Webber Jackson & Curtis, Inc., 882 F.2d 529 (D.C.Cir.1989). In this case the arbitrators, without any explanation, had awarded the plaintiffs a fraction of the amount they were claiming. The district court vacated the award and remanded to the arbitrators "for a full explanation of the manner in which damages were computed," reasoning that in order for the court to be able to engage in "meaningful judicial review" the "basis for the calculations underlying the award must be made known." However, the court of appeals reversed. It noted that "the absence of a duty to explain is presumably one of the reasons why arbitration should be faster and cheaper than an ordinary lawsuit"; the interest "in assuring that judgment be swift and economical * * * must generally prevail" over any interest "in rooting out possible error." See also Robbins v. Day, 954 F.2d 679 (11th Cir.1992) ("an arbitration award that only contains a lump sum award is presumed to be correct"; the burden is on the party seeking to overturn the award to refute "every rational basis upon which the arbitrator could have relied"); Container Technology Corp. v. J. Gadsden Pty., Ltd., 781 P.2d 119 (Colo.App.1989) (taking deposition of arbitrators is not permitted if the purpose is to inquire into their "thought processes").

But compare Hardy v. Walsh Manning Securities, L.L.C., 341 F.3d 126 (2d Cir. 2003). Here an investor brought proceedings against a (1) an account executive, (2) the brokerage firm he worked for, and (3) the firm's CEO. The account executive settled with the claimant; the arbitrators issued an award against the remaining two respondents, holding them "jointly and severally liable * * * in the amount of [$2 million] based upon the principles of respondeat superior." The district court confirmed the award: Although he noted that the CEO was himself "technically only an employee," he held that "it would not be proper to remand the Award to the Panel for clarification as to its intent regarding [his] liability," since the arbitrators were "crystal clear" in directing both respondents to pay a "sum certain." The Second Circuit disagreed—holding that a remand for clarification as to the underlying legal basis of the CEO's liability was indeed called for: The award itself "states no other ground of liability but respondeat superior," but "no reading of the facts" could possibly support the legal conclusion of liability under that theory—after all the principle that respondeat superior "cannot be imposed upon the fellow employee of a wrongdoer is certainly well-defined and explicit in New York." The court noted that it was "reluctant to announce that the Award is void outright"—but the arbitrators *did* after all choose "to make an explicit legal conclusion in the award, a conclusion that may very well be wrong. [They] should be given the opportunity to explain themselves."

5. Except in the most complex or technical cases, it is not common practice to make a record or transcript of the proceedings in commercial arbitration. See Martin Domke, Commercial Arbitration § 24:07 (rev. ed.). This of course reinforces the absence of a reasoned opinion in making the work of a reviewing court that much more problematical. See House Grain Co. v. Obst, 659 S.W.2d 903 (Tex.App.1983) (in absence of transcript, there was insufficient evidence to support trial court's finding that arbitration award was the result of "such gross mistake as would imply bad faith and failure to exercise honest judgment").

6. The Internet Corporation for Assigned Names and Numbers [ICANN] is a private nonprofit corporation to which the United States Government has delegated control of the Internet's system of domain names. Anyone seeking to register a domain name (for example, a ".com" name) must contract with an ICANN-approved registrar; all such contracts incorporate by reference the Uniform Domain Name Dispute Resolution Policy [UDRP]. See http://www.icann.org/dndr/udrp/policy.htm. The UDRP in turn requires the registrant to submit to a "mandatory administrative proceeding" whenever the owner of a trademark makes an allegation against him of "cybersquatting"—that is, contends that his domain name is infringing on the trademark. The proceedings are conducted before one of four approved dispute-resolution services at the choice of the plaintiff: the NAF; the CPR Institute for Dispute Resolution; the World Intellectual Property Organization [WIPO]; and the Asian Domain Name Dispute Resolution Center. If the proceeding leads to a finding of infringement, the panel may order that the domain name be cancelled or transferred to the complainant. However, the proceedings are completely non-binding: The registrant may suspend any cancellation or transfer by beginning a lawsuit against the complainant within ten days. See Sallen v. Corinthians Licenciamentos LTDA, 273 F.3d 14 (1st Cir. 2001)(in the Anticybersquatting Consumer Protection Act, Congress provided registrants with "an affirmative cause of action to recover domain names lost in UDRP proceedings"; a favorable ACPA ruling in an independent proceeding in national court will thus "trump the panel's finding of noncompliance with the UDRP").

Is this "arbitration"? In Dluhos v. Strasberg, 321 F.3d 365 (3d Cir. 2003), the court held that UDRP proceedings obviously "do not fall under" the FAA for the purposes of applying the "extremely deferential" standards of judicial review in § 10. The more fundamental problem, however, is not so much that the UDRP proceedings are not intended to be "final"—it is rather that they are not even intended to be *exclusive*: The court in *Dluhos* stressed that the UDRP in no way "prevents a party *from filing suit before, after or during the administrative proceedings*"; since the trademark holder "is not required to avail itself of the dispute resolution policy before moving ahead in the district court," party participation cannot be compelled and the proceedings are therefore "remov[ed] .. from the warmth of the FAA blanket." To the same effect see Richard E. Speidel, ICANN Domain Name Dispute Resolution, the Revised Uniform Arbitration Act, and the Limitations of Modern Arbitration Law, 6 J. Small & Emerging Bus. L. 167, 174 (2002); in French law, see Le Parmentier v. La Société Miss France (Cour d'Appel de Paris, 1ère ch., June 17, 2004) ("Miss France" v. "Miss Francophonie"; "in contrast with the mandatory effect of an arbitration clause, [the UDRP] preserves recourse to state courts before the administrative procedure is begun, during the course of the proceedings ... or after it is concluded, so that it can be adjudicated again").

7. An insured was injured in an automobile accident and made a claim under the uninsured motorist provision of his policy. The policy contained an arbitration clause, which provided that if the damages awarded by the arbitrators exceeded the statutory minimum coverage for uninsured motorists ($25,000), then either party might demand a trial de novo. The arbitrators awarded the insured $45,000. The court held that the insurer had no right to a new trial; the trial de novo provision was unenforceable since it "would result in complete frustration of the very essence of the public policy favoring arbitration" and would operate "to defeat goals designed to promote judicial economy and respect for the judicial system." Schmidt v. Midwest Family Mutual Ins. Co., 426 N.W.2d 870 (Minn.1988).

What precisely is the nature of the "public policy" argument here? Are you convinced? Cf. Little v. Auto Stiegler, Inc., 29 Cal.4th 1064, 63 P.3d 979, 130 Cal.Rptr.2d 892 (2003)(provision in employment agreement that permits either party to "appeal" an award of more than $50,000 to a second arbitrator, is "unconscionable").

8. Is even greater judicial deference due to an award in an "interest" arbitration? Why might this be true? See Local 58, Int'l Brotherhood of Elec. Workers v. Southeastern Mich. Chapter, Nat'l Elec. Contractors Ass'n, Inc., 43 F.3d 1026 (6th Cir.1995) (because the arbitrator is "acting as a legislator, fashioning new contractual obligations" rather than "as a judicial officer, construing the terms of an existing agreement and applying them to a particular set of facts").

9. A number of states have enacted statutes that purport to govern international commercial arbitrations (that is, arbitrations arising out of contracts between parties of different nationalities or that envisage performance abroad). Such statutes are patterned after the "Model Law" adopted in 1985 by a United Nations Commission, and provide—in accordance with the general understanding in international arbitration—that the arbitral tribunal may "decide ex aequo and bono * * * if the parties have expressly authorized it to do so." See, e.g., Cal.Code Civ.Pro. § 1297.284; Tex. Int'l Commercial Arbitration and Conciliation Act, Tex.

Civ.Prac. & Rem.Code § 172.251(d). What is the effect of such provisions? Are these statutes not in fact more restrictive than the general practice in American commercial arbitration? After all, isn't it true that when American arbitrators decide *ex aequo et bono,* they "do not think of themselves as doing anything special"? See W. Laurence Craig, William Park, & Jan Paulsson, International Chamber of Commerce Arbitration 110 (3rd ed. 2000); see also Rene David, Arbitration in International Trade 119, 332 (1985).

Note: Judicial Review of Awards and "Public Policy"

At the end of his shift a worker suffered a nervous breakdown; he "flew into a rage," attacked other employees, and damaged company property. He was discharged and later spent 30 days in a hospital psychiatric ward. The arbitrator found that the likelihood of a recurrence was "remote" and that he was "not at fault for his outburst"; the company was ordered to reinstate him. The district court vacated the award, noting "public policy concerns regarding the safety of the workplace." The Court of Appeals reversed, E.I. DuPont de Nemours & Co. v. Grasselli Employees Ind. Ass. of East Chicago, Inc., 790 F.2d 611 (7th Cir.1986). In his concurring opinion, Judge Easterbrook wrote:

> Suppose DuPont's contract expressly excused a single psychotic tantrum, provided the problem was unlikely to recur, or suppose a contract excused a single episode of larceny from the employer. If the firm, honestly implementing its contract with the employees, reinstated the berserker or the thief (or never discharged him), no public policy would stand in the way. If the person's immediate supervisor fired him, and someone higher in the line of command reversed that decision as a result of a grievance, there would be no greater reason for review. A contract of arbitration transfers the power of this manager to the arbitrator. If the arbitrator carries out the contract, the decision should be treated the same as the management's own. Firms may place decisionmaking authority where they please, and the Arbitration Act restricts the court to ascertaining that the arbitrator was a faithful agent of the contracting parties. * * *

> [I]f because of potential liability to its workers for having an unsafe working environment no firm would adopt a clause giving a psychotic worker a second chance, an arbitrator who provides a second chance is expressing sympathy, administering home-brewed justice rather than the contract. Public policy may be a useful guide to the sorts of provisions that will not appear in contracts, and when no one will write the provisions expressly arbitrators may not infer them. If a court concludes, however, that the implication of a rule by the arbitrator is not a frolic, that a rational firm could have such a rule and apply it prospectively, then the only further role for public policy is to determine whether the rule violates positive law.

The Supreme Court seems to have adopted Judge Easterbrook's position. In Eastern Associated Coal Corp. v. United Mine Workers of America, 531 U.S. 57, 121 S.Ct. 462 (2000), a truck driver twice tested positive for marijuana, was twice discharged, and was twice reinstated by arbitrators who found that there was no "just cause" for termination. (The second arbitrator made reinstatement conditional on suspension without pay, participation in a substance abuse program, and continued random drug testing). The employer claimed that "considerations of public policy" made the second award unenforceable, but both the lower courts and the Supreme Court disagreed. Six Justices joined Justice Breyer's opinion:

> In considering this claim, we must assume that the collective-bargaining agreement itself calls for [the employee's] reinstatement. That is because both employer and union have granted to the arbitrator the authority to interpret the meaning of their contract's language, including such words as "just cause." They have "bargained for" the "arbitrator's construction" of their agreement. * * * Hence we must treat the arbitrator's award as if it represented an agreement between [the employer] and the union as to the proper meaning of the contract's words "just cause." For present purposes, the award is not distinguishable form the contractual agreement. * * * And, of course, the question to be answered is not whether [the employee's] drug use itself violates public policy, but whether the agreement to reinstate him does so. To put the question more specifically, does a contractual agreement to reinstate [the employee] with specified conditions run contrary to an explicit, well-defined, and dominant public policy, as ascertained by reference to positive law and not from general considerations of supposed public interests?

> In this case, "neither Congress [in the Omnibus Transportation Employee Testing Act of 1991, 49 U.S.C. § 31306(b)(1)(A)] nor the Secretary [of Transportation] has seen fit to mandate the discharge of a worker who twice tests positive for drugs."

NOTES AND QUESTIONS

1. During an overnight layover the "Pilot in Command" of a Delta flight consumed large quantities of alcohol, and when he arrived at the airport the next morning shortly before departure, "[h]is face was very red; his eyes were glassed over; and he appeared to be very disoriented." He nevertheless flew the aircraft between Bangor, Maine and Boston. A later blood test indicated that at the time of the flight his blood alcohol level was .13. The pilot's license was suspended by the FAA, and Delta discharged him. An arbitrator, however, found that the discharge was "without just cause," since Delta had not enforced its alcohol policy "uniformly or fairly" and the pilot, after being discharged, "had pursued a rehabilitation program with effective results." Delta was ordered to reinstate him and to cooperate with him and with the FAA so that he could be relicensed. The court set aside the award: "We emphasize that we have found no state that approves of operation of an aircraft while drunk." Delta Air Lines, Inc. v. Air Line Pilots Ass'n Int'l, 861 F.2d 665 (11th Cir.1988).

Four nurses' aides, employees of a nursing home, were discovered sleeping on the job; as a result of their neglect several patients had been left unattended—incontinent patients were soaked with urine and fecal matter; one patient had her hands tied to the bedside without any authorization from a doctor, and a number of firedoors had been tied shut. The aides were fired, and their union filed a grievance on their behalf; an arbitrator found that their conduct constituted "gross negligence" and "a complete disregard for patient care" which "cannot be tolerated in a health care institution where the needs of patients, including their dignity, are paramount." Nevertheless he ruled that they should be reinstated—although without back pay—since discharge was "an excessive penalty." But "under circumstances such as this," the court held, it "would be remiss in its duties if it were to uphold the award." Edgewood Convalescent Center v. District 1199, New England Health Care Employees, 1985 WL 5779 (D. Mass.).

Is it likely that in these cases the process of labor arbitration—so oriented towards "industrial due process" and the maintenance of good working relations between employer and union—will adequately protect the interests of society generally? How would Judge Easterbrook or Justice Breyer have voted to decide these cases?

2. An attorney specializing in labor law from the "management perspective" wrote the following comment on *Eastern Associated Coal:*

> The employer had an employee who was randomly tested for drugs twice and was discharged both times. Someone in the company's management was thinking to himself or herself, What happens if the employee gets busted a third time and it is not a random test but a post-accident test after he's run his bulldozer into a school bus carrying third-grade children? I think that is the sort of thought that goes through management's mind. * * * And if parents and relatives of injured schoolchildren sue, those lawsuits are going to have claims for negligent retention and so forth. The best affirmative defense I think a company like Eastern Associated Coal could have in that sorry circumstance would be to say that it wanted to get rid of the employee, but a majority of U.S. Supreme Court justices told it that they had to take him back.

James Walters, Arbitration Decisions of the U.S. Supreme Court 2000–2001: Management Prospective, in Arbitration 2001: Arbitrating in an Evolving Legal Environment, Proceedings, 54th Annual Meeting, National Academy of Arbitrators 13, 28, 30–31 (2002).

Would that indeed be an effective defense for the employer? Compare EEOC v. Indiana Bell Tel. Co., 256 F.3d 516, 523, 527–28 (7th Cir. 2001)((Easterbrook, J.):

> [Take the case of] a truck driver who ran down a pedestrian while on company business. In the ensuing tort litigation, * * * it would not be a defense to liability even if [the employer] had fired the driver, and an arbitrator had reinstated him over the company's vigorous opposition.

It would remain vicariously liable for its employee's misdeeds. [However, while an] arbitrator's award reinstating a poor driver, who later injured a pedestrian, would not eliminate the employer's tort liability for the pedestrian's actual loss, [it might nevertheless] persuade a jury not to award punitive damages or to reduce the size of any punitive award.

3. Stroehmann Bakeries discharged one of its drivers for "immoral conduct while on duty" after a store clerk complained that he had sexually assaulted her when he was making a delivery. The arbitrator found that the driver had been dismissed without just cause, and the employer was ordered to reinstate him with full back pay and benefits. "Considerations referred to by the arbitrator in conjecturing on the matter" included the observation that the victim lacked a social life, had a female roommate, was "unattractive and frustrated," and that she might have fabricated the entire incident in order to "titillate herself and attract her mother's caring attention." The court vacated the award and remanded the matter for a *de novo* hearing before another arbitrator: The arbitrator's "reasoning process, language, tone, considerations, and award violate public policy." "The manner in which the award was reached could easily deter other victims," and the award also "sends a message" to the company's other employees and to the public "that complaints of sexual assault are not treated seriously [or] sensitively." Stroehmann Bakeries, Inc. v. Local 776 Int'l Brotherhood of Teamsters, 762 F.Supp. 1187 (M.D.Pa.1991), aff'd, 969 F.2d 1436 (3d Cir.1992). Cf. Note, Arbitral Decision–Making and Legal "Rules," supra.

4. In an effort to promote the sale of its fighter aircraft to Saudi Arabia, Northrop entered into a "marketing agreement" with Triad. In exchange for commissions on sales, Triad was to act as Northrop's exclusive agent in soliciting contracts for aircraft for the Saudi Air Force. Some of the sales were to be made through the United States Government as a result of contracts between Northrop and the Defense Department. The agreement was to be governed by California law and contained an arbitration clause.

Several years later the Saudi Arabian government issued a decree prohibiting the payment of commissions in connection with armaments contracts, and requiring that existing obligations for the payment of commissions be suspended. Northrop ceased paying commissions and the dispute was submitted to arbitrators, who awarded Triad over $31 million. The district court held that the arbitrator's award was "contrary to law and public policy." California's Civil Code provides that "performance of an obligation" is "excused" when it is "prevented * * * by the operation of law." The court interpreted the Saudi decree as applying to and indeed "formulated specifically with the Northrop–Triad agency relationship in mind." And it noted that the Defense Department "wished to conform its policy precisely to that announced by Saudi Arabia" and was now requiring that arms suppliers under contract to the Department certify that their price included no costs for agent's commissions not approved by the purchasing country.

On appeal, what result? See Northrop Corp. v. Triad Int'l Marketing S.A., 811 F.2d 1265 (9th Cir.1987).

5. A "weighmaster" at a town landfill was terminated after pleading nolo contendere to the charge of larceny by embezzlement for pocketing daily landfill fees. He purportedly made the decision to enter the plea because he could not afford the legal fees he would incur by contesting the charges at trial. Because the city relied exclusively on the plea, and did not seek to independently prove the charge, an arbitrator found that the city lacked "just cause" for the termination and ordered reinstatement. The court vacated the award on the ground that it "violated the clear public policy against embezzlement," which "encompasses the policy that an employer should not be compelled to reinstate an employee who has been convicted of embezzling the employer's funds, irrespective of whether the conviction followed a trial, a guilty plea or a nolo contendere plea." The employer "is entitled to expect that he be able to trust an employee who is in a position of financial responsibility." Town of Groton v. United Steelworkers of America, 254 Conn. 35, 757 A.2d 501 (2000).

What exactly is the "public policy" implicated here? Is the term being used in the same sense as in the foregoing cases?

6. The United Nations Convention on the Recognition and Enforcement of Foreign Arbitral Awards (the "New York Convention") has been ratified by most important commercial nations, including the United States. See Appendix B. Adherence to the Convention obligates the United States to recognize commercial arbitration awards rendered in another contracting state, and to enforce them with only the most limited exceptions.

American cases have narrowly confined the "public policy" defense of Art. V(2)(b) to the exceptional situation "where enforcement would violate the forum country's most basic notions of morality and justice." Parsons & Whittemore Overseas Co., Inc. v. Société Générale De L'Industrie Du Papier (RAKTA), 508 F.2d 969 (2d Cir.1974). In *Parsons & Whittemore* an American business had refused to perform a contract in Egypt after the severance of diplomatic relations between the United States and Egypt following the 1967 "Six Day War"; it then argued that an arbitration award against it should not be enforced on the grounds of "public policy." The court disagreed: "To read the public policy defense as a parochial device protective of national political interests would seriously undermine the Convention's utility. This provision was not meant to enshrine the vagaries of international politics under the rubric of 'public policy.' " In addition, "considerations of reciprocity" counsel courts to invoke the public policy defense "with caution lest foreign courts frequently accept it as a defense to enforcement of arbitral awards rendered in the United States." For another case making it equally clear that "public policy" should not be equated with "American foreign policy," see National Oil Corp. v. Libyan Sun Oil Co., 733 F.Supp. 800 (D.Del.1990) (award of $20 million to entity wholly owned by Libyan Government was not against "public policy" despite defendant's claim that enforcement would "undermine the internationally-supported antiterrorism policy" and make possible the transfer to

Libya of funds "which could be employed to finance its continuing terrorist activities").

b. "PUBLIC POLICY" AND ARBITRABILITY

Mitsubishi Motors Corp. v. Soler Chrysler–Plymouth, Inc.

Supreme Court of the United States, 1985.
473 U.S. 614, 105 S.Ct. 3346, 87 L.Ed.2d 444.

■ JUSTICE BLACKMUN delivered the opinion of the Court.

The principal question presented by these cases is the arbitrability, pursuant to the federal Arbitration Act and the Convention on the Recognition and Enforcement of Foreign Arbitral Awards (Convention), of claims arising under the Sherman Act, 15 U.S.C. § 1 et seq., and encompassed within a valid arbitration clause in an agreement embodying an international commercial transaction.

I

Petitioner-cross-respondent Mitsubishi Motors Corporation (Mitsubishi) is a Japanese corporation which manufactures automobiles and has its principal place of business in Tokyo, Japan. Mitsubishi is the product of a joint venture between, on the one hand, Chrysler International, S.A. ("CISA"), a Swiss corporation registered in Geneva and wholly owned by Chrysler Corporation, and, on the other, Mitsubishi Heavy Industries, Inc., a Japanese corporation. The aim of the joint venture was the distribution through Chrysler dealers outside the continental United States of vehicles manufactured by Mitsubishi and bearing Chrysler and Mitsubishi trademarks. Respondent-cross-respondent Soler Chrysler–Plymouth, Inc. (Soler), is a Puerto Rico corporation with its principal place of business in Pueblo Viejo, Guaynabo, Puerto Rico.

On October 31, 1979, Soler entered into a Distributor Agreement with CISA which provided for the sale by Soler of Mitsubishi-manufactured vehicles within a designated area, including metropolitan San Juan. On the same date, CISA, Soler, and Mitsubishi entered into a Sales Procedure Agreement (Sales Agreement) which, referring to the Distributor Agreement, provided for the direct sale of Mitsubishi products to Soler and governed the terms and conditions of such sales. Paragraph VI of the Sales Agreement, labeled "Arbitration of Certain Matters," provides:

> "All disputes, controversies or differences which may arise between [Mitsubishi] and [Soler] out of or in relation to Articles I–B through V of this Agreement or for the breach thereof, shall be finally settled by arbitration in Japan in accordance with the rules and regulations of the Japan Commercial Arbitration Association."

Initially, Soler did a brisk business in Mitsubishi-manufactured vehicles. As a result of its strong performance, its minimum sales volume, specified by Mitsubishi and CISA, and agreed to by Soler, for the 1981 model year was substantially increased. In early 1981, however, the new-car market slackened. Soler ran into serious difficulties in meeting the expected sales volume, and by the spring of 1981 it felt itself compelled to request that Mitsubishi delay or cancel shipment of several orders. About the same time, Soler attempted to arrange for the transshipment of a quantity of its vehicles for sale in the continental United States and Latin America. Mitsubishi and CISA, however, refused permission for any such diversion, citing a variety of reasons, and no vehicles were transshipped. Attempts to work out these difficulties failed. Mitsubishi eventually withheld shipment of 966 vehicles, apparently representing orders placed for May, June, and July 1981 production, responsibility for which Soler disclaimed in February 1982.

The following month, Mitsubishi brought an action against Soler in the United States District Court for the District of Puerto Rico under the federal Arbitration Act and the Convention.[2] Mitsubishi sought an order to compel arbitration in accord with ¶ VI of the Sales Agreement. Shortly after filing the complaint, Mitsubishi filed a request for arbitration before the Japan Commercial Arbitration Association.

Soler denied the allegations and counterclaimed against both Mitsubishi and CISA. It alleged numerous breaches by Mitsubishi of the Sales Agreement, raised a pair of defamation claims, and asserted causes of action under the Sherman Act; the federal Automobile Dealers' Day in Court Act; the Puerto Rico competition statute; and the Puerto Rico Dealers' Contracts Act. In the counterclaim premised on the Sherman Act, Soler alleged that Mitsubishi and CISA had conspired to divide markets in restraint of trade. To effectuate the plan, according to Soler, Mitsubishi had refused to permit Soler to resell to buyers in North, Central, or South America vehicles it had obligated itself to purchase from Mitsubishi; had refused to ship ordered vehicles or the parts, such as heaters and defoggers, that would be necessary to permit Soler to make its vehicles suitable for resale outside Puerto Rico; and had coercively attempted to replace Soler and its other Puerto Rico distributors with a wholly owned subsidiary which would serve as the exclusive Mitsubishi distributor in Puerto Rico.

After a hearing, the District Court ordered Mitsubishi and Soler to arbitrate each of the issues raised in the complaint and in all the counterclaims save two and a portion of a third. [The Court of Appeals agreed that the arbitration clause "encompass[ed] virtually all the claims arising under the various statutes, including all those arising under the Sherman Act."[9]

---

2. The complaint alleged that Soler had failed to pay for 966 ordered vehicles; that it had failed to pay contractual "distress unit penalties," intended to reimburse Mitsubishi for storage costs and interest charges incurred because of Soler's failure to take shipment of ordered vehicles; that Soler's failure to fulfill warranty obligations threatened Mit-

subishi's reputation and good will; * * * and that the Distributor and Sales Agreements had expired by their terms or, alternatively, that Soler had surrendered its rights under the Sales Agreement.

9. As the Court of Appeals saw it, "[t]he question ... is not whether the arbitration clause mentions antitrust or any oth-

It held, however, that arbitration of Soler's antitrust claims could not be compelled.]

* * *

II

At the outset, we address the contention raised in Soler's cross-petition that the arbitration clause at issue may not be read to encompass the statutory counterclaims stated in its answer to the complaint. In making this argument, Soler does not question the Court of Appeals' application of ¶ VI of the Sales Agreement to the disputes involved here as a matter of standard contract interpretation. Instead, it argues that as a matter of law a court may not construe an arbitration agreement to encompass claims arising out of statutes designed to protect a class to which the party resisting arbitration belongs "unless [that party] has expressly agreed" to arbitrate those claims, by which Soler presumably means that the arbitration clause must specifically mention the statute giving rise to the claims that a party to the clause seeks to arbitrate. Soler reasons that, because it falls within the class for whose benefit the federal and local antitrust laws and dealers' acts were passed, but the arbitration clause at issue does not mention these statutes or statutes in general, the clause cannot be read to contemplate arbitration of these statutory claims.

We do not agree, for we find no warrant in the Arbitration Act for implying in every contract within its ken a presumption against arbitration of statutory claims. * * *

[T]he first task of a court asked to compel arbitration of a dispute is to determine whether the parties agreed to arbitrate that dispute. The court is to make this determination by applying the "federal substantive law of arbitrability, applicable to any arbitration agreement within the coverage of the Act." And that body of law counsels "that * * * any doubts concerning the scope of arbitrable issues should be resolved in favor of arbitration * * *." Thus, as with any other contract, the parties' intentions control, but those intentions are generously construed as to issues of arbitrability.

There is no reason to depart from these guidelines where a party bound by an arbitration agreement raises claims founded on statutory

---

er particular cause of action, but whether the factual allegations underlying Soler's counterclaims—and Mitsubishi's bona fide defenses to those counterclaims—are within the scope of the arbitration clause, whatever the legal labels attached to those allegations." * * *

The court read the Sherman Act counterclaim to raise issues of wrongful termination of Soler's distributorship, wrongful failure to ship ordered parts and vehicles, and wrongful refusal to permit transshipment of stock to the United States and Latin America. Be-cause the existence of just cause for termination turned on Mitsubishi's allegations that Soler had breached the Sales Agreement by, for example, failing to pay for ordered vehicles, the wrongful termination claim implicated [several] provisions within the arbitration clause [including]: Article I–D(1), which rendered a dealer's orders "firm" * * * and Article I–F, specifying payment obligations and procedures. The court therefore held the arbitration clause to cover this dispute. * * *

rights. * * * Of course, courts should remain attuned to well-supported claims that the agreement to arbitrate resulted from the sort of fraud or overwhelming economic power that would provide grounds "for the revocation of any contract." [FAA, § 2]. But, absent such compelling considerations, the Act itself provides no basis for disfavoring agreements to arbitrate statutory claims by skewing the otherwise hospitable inquiry into arbitrability.

That is not to say that all controversies implicating statutory rights are suitable for arbitration. There is no reason to distort the process of contract interpretation, however, in order to ferret out the inappropriate. Just as it is the congressional policy manifested in the federal Arbitration Act that requires courts liberally to construe the scope of arbitration agreements covered by that Act, it is the congressional intention expressed in some other statute on which the courts must rely to identify any category of claims as to which agreements to arbitrate will be held unenforceable. For that reason, Soler's concern for statutorily protected classes provides no reason to color the lens through which the arbitration clause is read. By agreeing to arbitrate a statutory claim, a party does not forego the substantive rights afforded by the statute; it only submits to their resolution in an arbitral, rather than a judicial, forum. It trades the procedures and opportunity for review of the courtroom for the simplicity, informality, and expedition of arbitration. We must assume that if Congress intended the substantive protection afforded by a given statute to include protection against waiver of the right to a judicial forum, that intention will be deducible from text or legislative history. Having made the bargain to arbitrate, the party should be held to it unless Congress itself has evinced an intention to preclude a waiver of judicial remedies for the statutory rights at issue. Nothing, in the meantime, prevents a party from excluding statutory claims from the scope of an agreement to arbitrate.

In sum, the Court of Appeals correctly conducted a two-step inquiry, first determining whether the parties' agreement to arbitrate reached the statutory issues, and then, upon finding it did, considering whether legal constraints external to the parties' agreement foreclosed the arbitration of those claims. We endorse its rejection of Soler's proposed rule of arbitration-clause construction.

III

We now turn to consider whether Soler's antitrust claims are nonarbitrable even though it has agreed to arbitrate them. In holding that they are not, the Court of Appeals followed the decision of the Second Circuit in *American Safety Equipment Corp. v. J.P. Maguire & Co.*, 391 F.2d 821 (1968). Notwithstanding the absence of any explicit support for such an exception in either the Sherman Act or the federal Arbitration Act, the Second Circuit there reasoned that "the pervasive public interest in enforcement of the antitrust laws, and the nature of the claims that arise in such cases, combine to make ... antitrust claims ... inappropriate for arbitration." We find it unnecessary to assess the legitimacy of the *Ameri-*

can Safety doctrine as applied to agreements to arbitrate arising from domestic transactions. As in *Scherk v. Alberto–Culver Co.,* 417 U.S. 506 (1974), we conclude that concerns of international comity, respect for the capacities of foreign and transnational tribunals, and sensitivity to the need of the international commercial system for predictability in the resolution of disputes require that we enforce the parties' agreement, even assuming that a contrary result would be forthcoming in a domestic context.

* * *

[The Court in *Scherk*] Court emphasized:

"A contractual provision specifying in advance the forum in which disputes shall be litigated and the law to be applied is . . . an almost indispensable precondition to achievement of the orderliness and predictability essential to any international business transaction. . . .

"A parochial refusal by the courts of one country to enforce an international arbitration agreement would not only frustrate these purposes, but would invite unseemly and mutually destructive jockeying by the parties to secure tactical litigation advantages. . . . [It would] damage the fabric of international commerce and trade, and imperil the willingness and ability of businessmen to enter into international commercial agreements."

* * *

Thus, we must weigh the concerns of *American Safety* against a strong belief in the efficacy of arbitral procedures for the resolution of international commercial disputes and an equal commitment to the enforcement of freely negotiated choice-of-forum clauses.

At the outset, we confess to some skepticism of certain aspects of the *American Safety* doctrine. As distilled by the First Circuit, the doctrine comprises four ingredients. First, private parties play a pivotal role in aiding governmental enforcement of the antitrust laws by means of the private action for treble damages. Second, "the strong possibility that contracts which generate antitrust disputes may be contracts of adhesion militates against automatic forum determination by contract." Third, antitrust issues, prone to complication, require sophisticated legal and economic analysis, and thus are "ill-adapted to strengths of the arbitral process, i.e., expedition, minimal requirements of written rationale, simplicity, resort to basic concepts of common sense and simple equity." Finally, just as "issues of war and peace are too important to be vested in the generals, . . . decisions as to antitrust regulation of business are too important to be lodged in arbitrators chosen from the business community—particularly those from a foreign community that has had no experience with or exposure to our law and values."

Initially, we find the second concern unjustified. The mere appearance of an antitrust dispute does not alone warrant invalidation of the selected forum on the undemonstrated assumption that the arbitration clause is tainted. A party resisting arbitration of course may attack directly the validity of the agreement to arbitrate. See *Prima Paint Corp.* Moreover, the party may attempt to make a showing that would warrant setting aside the forum-selection clause—that the agreement was "[a]ffected by fraud, undue influence, or overweening bargaining power"; that "enforcement would be unreasonable and unjust"; or that proceedings "in the contractual forum will be so gravely difficult and inconvenient that [the resisting party] will for all practical purposes be deprived of his day in court." But absent such a showing—and none was attempted here—there is no basis for assuming the forum inadequate or its selection unfair.

Next, potential complexity should not suffice to ward off arbitration. We might well have some doubt that even the courts following *American Safety* subscribe fully to the view that antitrust matters are inherently insusceptible to resolution by arbitration, as these same courts have agreed that an undertaking to arbitrate antitrust claims entered into after the dispute arises is acceptable. And the vertical restraints which most frequently give birth to antitrust claims covered by an arbitration agreement will not often occasion the monstrous proceedings that have given antitrust litigation an image of intractability. In any event, adaptability and access to expertise are hallmarks of arbitration. The anticipated subject matter of the dispute may be taken into account when the arbitrators are appointed, and arbitral rules typically provide for the participation of experts either employed by the parties or appointed by the tribunal. Moreover, it is often a judgment that streamlined proceedings and expeditious results will best serve their needs that cause parties to agree to arbitrate their disputes; it is typically a desire to keep the effort and expense required to resolve a dispute within manageable bounds that prompts them mutually to forgo access to judicial remedies. In sum, the factor of potential complexity alone does not persuade us that an arbitral tribunal could not properly handle an antitrust matter.

For similar reasons, we also reject the proposition that an arbitration panel will pose too great a danger of innate hostility to the constraints on business conduct that antitrust law imposes. International arbitrators frequently are drawn from the legal as well as the business community; where the dispute has an important legal component, the parties and the arbitral body with whose assistance they have agreed to settle their dispute can be expected to select arbitrators accordingly.[18] We decline to indulge the presumption that the parties and arbitral body conducting a proceeding

---

18. * * * [T]he arbitration panel selected to hear the parties' claims here is composed of three Japanese lawyers, one a former law school dean, another a former judge, and the third a practicing attorney with American legal training who has written on Japanese antitrust law.

The Court of Appeals was concerned that international arbitrators would lack "experience with or exposure to our law and values."

The obstacles confronted by the arbitration panel in this case, however, should be no greater than those confronted by any judicial or arbitral tribunal required to determine foreign law. See, e.g., Fed.Rule Civ.Proc. 44.1. Moreover, while our attachment to the antitrust laws may be stronger than most, many other countries, including Japan, have similar bodies of competition law.

will be unable or unwilling to retain competent, conscientious, and impartial arbitrators.

We are left, then, with the core of the *American Safety* doctrine—the fundamental importance to American democratic capitalism of the regime of the antitrust laws. Without doubt, the private cause of action plays a central role in enforcing this regime. As the Court of Appeals pointed out:

> "A claim under the antitrust laws is not merely a private matter. The Sherman Act is designed to promote the national interest in a competitive economy; thus, the plaintiff asserting his rights under the Act has been likened to a private attorney-general who protects the public's interest."

The treble-damages provision wielded by the private litigant is a chief tool in the antitrust enforcement scheme, posing a crucial deterrent to potential violators.

The importance of the private damages remedy, however, does not compel the conclusion that it may not be sought outside an American court. Notwithstanding its important incidental policing function, the treble-damages cause of action conferred on private parties by § 4 of the Clayton Act, and pursued by Soler here by way of its third counterclaim, seeks primarily to enable an injured competitor to gain compensation for that injury.

> "Section 4 ... is in essence a remedial provision. It provides treble damages to '[a]ny person who shall be injured in his business or property by reason of anything forbidden in the antitrust laws....' Of course, treble damages also play an important role in penalizing wrongdoers and deterring wrongdoing, as we also have frequently observed.... It nevertheless is true that the treble-damages provision, which makes awards available only to injured parties, and measures the awards by a multiple of the injury actually proved, is designed primarily as a remedy." *Brunswick Corp. v. Pueblo Bowl–O–Mat, Inc.,* 429 U.S. 477, 485–486 (1977).

* * *

There is no reason to assume at the outset of the dispute that international arbitration will not provide an adequate mechanism. To be sure, the international arbitral tribunal owes no prior allegiance to the legal norms of particular states; hence, it has no direct obligation to vindicate their statutory dictates. The tribunal, however, is bound to effectuate the intentions of the parties. Where the parties have agreed that the arbitral body is to decide a defined set of claims which includes, as in these cases, those arising from the application of American antitrust law, the tribunal therefore should be bound to decide that dispute in accord with the national law giving rise to the claim.[19] And so long as the

---

19. In addition to the clause providing for arbitration before the Japan Commercial Arbitration Association, the Sales Agreement includes a choice-of-law clause which reads: "This Agreement is made in, and will be governed by and construed in all respects

prospective litigant effectively may vindicate its statutory cause of action in the arbitral forum, the statute will continue to serve both its remedial and deterrent function.

Having permitted the arbitration to go forward, the national courts of the United States will have the opportunity at the award enforcement stage to ensure that the legitimate interest in the enforcement of the antitrust laws has been addressed. The Convention reserves to each signatory country the right to refuse enforcement of an award where the "recognition or enforcement of the award would be contrary to the public policy of that country." Art. V(2)(b). While the efficacy of the arbitral process requires that substantive review at the award-enforcement stage remains minimal, it would not require intrusive inquiry to ascertain that the tribunal took cognizance of the antitrust claims and actually decided them.[20]

As international trade has expanded in recent decades, so too has the use of international arbitration to resolve disputes arising in the course of that trade. The controversies that international arbitral institutions are called upon to resolve have increased in diversity as well as in complexity. Yet the potential of these tribunals for efficient disposition of legal disagreements arising from commercial relations has not yet been tested. If they are to take a central place in the international legal order, national courts will need to "shake off the old judicial hostility to arbitration," and also their customary and understandable unwillingness to cede jurisdiction of a claim arising under domestic law to a foreign or transnational tribunal. To this extent, at least, it will be necessary for national courts to subor-

---

according to the laws of the Swiss Confederation as if entirely performed therein." The United States raises the possibility that the arbitral panel will read this provision not simply to govern interpretation of the contract terms, but wholly to displace American law even where it otherwise would apply. Brief for United States as Amicus Curiae 20. The International Chamber of Commerce opines that it is "[c]onceivabl[e], although we believe it unlikely, [that] the arbitrators could consider Soler's affirmative claim of anti-competitive conduct by CISA and Mitsubishi to fall within the purview of this choice-of-law provision, with the result that it would be decided under Swiss law rather than U.S. Sherman Act." Brief for International Chamber of Commerce as Amicus Curiae 25. At oral argument, however, counsel for Mitsubishi conceded that American law applied to the antitrust claims and represented that the claims had been submitted to the arbitration panel in Japan on that basis. The record confirms that before the decision of the Court of Appeals the arbitral panel had taken these claims under submission.

We therefore have no occasion to speculate on this matter at this stage in the proceedings, when Mitsubishi seeks to enforce the agreement to arbitrate, not to enforce an award. Nor need we consider now the effect of an arbitral tribunal's failure to take cognizance of the statutory cause of action on the claimant's capacity to reinitiate suit in federal court. We merely note that in the event the choice-of-forum and choice-of-law clauses operated in tandem as a prospective waiver of a party's right to pursue statutory remedies for antitrust violations, we would have little hesitation in condemning the agreement as against public policy.

20. See n. 19, supra. We note, for example, that the rules of the Japan Commercial Arbitration Association provide for the taking of a "summary record" of each hearing, for the stenographic recording of the proceedings where the tribunal so orders or a party requests one, and for a statement of reasons for the award unless the parties agree otherwise.
* * *

dinate domestic notions of arbitrability to the international policy favoring commercial arbitration.

Accordingly, we "require this representative of the American business community to honor its bargain," by holding this agreement to arbitrate "enforce[able] . . . in accord with the explicit provisions of the Arbitration Act."

The judgment of the Court of Appeals is affirmed in part and reversed in part, and the cases are remanded for further proceedings consistent with this opinion.

■ Justice Stevens, with whom Justice Brennan joins, and with whom Justice Marshall joins except as to Part II, dissenting.

One element of this rather complex litigation is a claim asserted by an American dealer in Plymouth automobiles that two major automobile companies are parties to an international cartel that has restrained competition in the American market. Pursuant to an agreement that is alleged to have violated § 1 of the Sherman Act, those companies allegedly prevented the dealer from transshipping some 966 surplus vehicles from Puerto Rico to other dealers in the American market.

The petitioner denies the truth of the dealer's allegations and takes the position that the validity of the antitrust claim must be resolved by an arbitration tribunal in Tokyo, Japan. Largely because the auto manufacturers' defense to the antitrust allegation is based on provisions in the dealer's franchise agreement, the Court of Appeals concluded that the arbitration clause in that agreement encompassed the antitrust claim. * * *

* * * Because I am convinced that the Court of Appeals' construction of the arbitration clause is erroneous, and because I strongly disagree with this Court's interpretation of the relevant federal statutes, I respectfully dissent. In my opinion, (1) a fair construction of the language in the arbitration clause in the parties' contract does not encompass a claim that auto manufacturers entered into a conspiracy in violation of the antitrust laws; (2) an arbitration clause should not normally be construed to cover a statutory remedy that it does not expressly identify; (3) Congress did not intend § 2 of the Federal Arbitration Act to apply to antitrust claims; and (4) Congress did not intend the Convention on the Recognition and Enforcement of Foreign Arbitral Awards to apply to disputes that are not covered by the Federal Arbitration Act.

* * *

Until today all of our cases enforcing agreements to arbitrate under the Arbitration Act have involved contract claims. * * * [T]his is the first time the Court has considered the question whether a standard arbitration clause referring to claims arising out of or relating to a contract should be construed to cover statutory claims that have only an indirect relationship to the contract. In my opinion, neither the Congress that enacted the Arbitration Act in 1925, nor the many parties who have agreed to such standard clauses, could have anticipated the Court's answer to that question.

* * *

In view of the Court's repeated recognition of the distinction between federal statutory rights and contractual rights, together with the undisputed historical fact that arbitration has functioned almost entirely in either the area of labor disputes or in "ordinary disputes between merchants as to questions of fact," it is reasonable to assume that most lawyers and executives would not expect the language in the standard arbitration clause to cover federal statutory claims. Thus, in my opinion, both a fair respect for the importance of the interests that Congress has identified as worthy of federal statutory protection, and a fair appraisal of the most likely understanding of the parties who sign agreements containing standard arbitration clauses, support a presumption that such clauses do not apply to federal statutory claims.

* * *

It was Chief Justice Hughes who characterized the Sherman Anti–Trust Act as "a charter of freedom" that may fairly be compared to a constitutional provision. * * * More recently, the Court described the weighty public interests underlying the basic philosophy of the statute:

> "Antitrust laws in general, and the Sherman Act in particular, are the Magna Carta of free enterprise. They are important to the preservation of economic freedom and our free-enterprise system as the Bill of Rights is to the protection of our fundamental personal freedoms. And the freedoms guaranteed each and every business, no matter how small, is the freedom to compete—to assert with vigor, imagination, devotion, and ingenuity whatever economic muscle it can muster."
> * * * *United States v. Topco Associates, Inc.,* 405 U.S. 596, 610 (1972).

The Sherman and Clayton Acts reflect Congress' appraisal of the value of economic freedom; they guarantee the vitality of the entrepreneurial spirit. Questions arising under these Acts are among the most important in public law.

The unique public interest in the enforcement of the antitrust laws is repeatedly reflected in the special remedial scheme enacted by Congress. Since its enactment in 1890, the Sherman Act has provided for public enforcement through criminal as well as civil sanctions.

* * *

The provision for mandatory treble damages—unique in federal law when the statute was enacted—provides a special incentive to the private enforcement of the statute, as well as an especially powerful deterrent to violators. What we have described as "the public interest in vigilant enforcement of antitrust laws through the instrumentality of the private treble damage action" is buttressed by the statutory mandate that the injured party also recover costs, "including a reasonable attorney's fee."

The interest in wide and effective enforcement has thus, for almost a century, been vindicated by enlisting the assistance of "private Attorneys General"; we have always attached special importance to their role because "[e]very violation of the antitrust laws is a blow to the free-enterprise system envisaged by Congress."

There are, in addition, several unusual features of the antitrust enforcement scheme that unequivocally require rejection of any thought that Congress would tolerate private arbitration of antitrust claims in lieu of the statutory remedies that it fashioned. * * * [A]n antitrust treble damage case "can only be brought in a District Court of the United States." The determination that these cases are "too important to be decided otherwise than by competent tribunals" surely cannot allow private arbitrators to assume a jurisdiction that is denied to courts of the sovereign States.

* * *

Arbitration awards are only reviewable for manifest disregard of the law, and the rudimentary procedures which make arbitration so desirable in the context of a private dispute often mean that the record is so inadequate that the arbitrator's decision is virtually unreviewable.[31] Despotic decision making of this kind is fine for parties who are willing to agree in advance to settle for a best approximation of the correct result in order to resolve quickly and inexpensively any contractual dispute that may arise in an ongoing commercial relationship. Such informality, however, is simply unacceptable when every error may have devastating consequences for important businesses in our national economy and may undermine their ability to compete in world markets.[32] Instead of "muffling a grievance in the cloakroom of arbitration," the public interest in free competitive markets would be better served by having the issues resolved "in the light of impartial public court adjudication."

* * *

In my opinion, the elected representatives of the American people would not have us dispatch an American citizen to a foreign land in search of an uncertain remedy for the violation of a public right that is protected by the Sherman Act. This is especially so when there has been no genuine bargaining over the terms of the submission, and the arbitration remedy provided has not even the most elementary guarantees of fair process. Consideration of a fully developed record by a jury, instructed in the law by

---

31. The arbitration procedure in this case does not provide any right to evidentiary discovery or a written decision, and requires that all proceedings be closed to the public. Moreover, Japanese arbitrators do not have the power of compulsory process to secure witnesses and documents, nor do witnesses who are available testify under oath. Cf. [FAA] § 7 (arbitrators may summon witnesses to attend proceedings and seek enforcement in a district court).

32. The greatest risk, of course, is that the arbitrator will condemn business practices under the antitrust laws that are efficient in a free competitive market. In the absence of a reviewable record, a reviewing district court would not be able to undo the damage wrought. Even a Government suit or an action by a private party might not be available to set aside the award.

a federal judge, and subject to appellate review, is a surer guide to the competitive character of a commercial practice than the practically unreviewable judgment of a private arbitrator.

Unlike the Congress that enacted the Sherman Act in 1890, the Court today does not seem to appreciate the value of economic freedom. I respectfully dissent.

NOTES AND QUESTIONS

1. Consider carefully footnote 19 to the Court's opinion in *Mitsubishi*. The ICC's concession that it was "unlikely" the arbitrators would apply Swiss law in deciding Soler's antitrust claims "came as a bad surprise to many long time users of ICC arbitration," according to one commentator: One of "the very basics" of arbitration is that it functions within the limits fixed by the agreement of the parties, and "what is indeed very unlikely, to say the least, is that arbitrators would accept to apply U.S. antitrust law to claims to be ruled, according to [the] parties' clear will, by Swiss law!" Jacques Werner, A Swiss Comment on *Mitsubishi*, 3 J. of Int'l Arb. 81, 83 (1986).

Cf. Andreas Lowenfeld, The *Mitsubishi* Case: Another View, 2 Arb.Int'l 178, 186 (1986) ("antitrust law is 'mandatory law,' on the same level as export controls, criminal law, or tax law, i.e., law that cannot ordinarily be avoided by party choice of law in the same way that, for instance, otherwise applicable statutes of limitations, or law governing the extent of implied warranties, or the measure of damages for breach of contract, can be avoided by the parties through a choice of law clause."). The opposing views are canvassed thoroughly in Pierre Mayer, Mandatory Rules of Law in International Arbitration, 2 Arb.Int'l 274 (1986)("One might find the Supreme Court's confidence in the conduct of arbitrators somewhat naïve"; "in at least some quarters of the arbitration milieu, there is a manifest hostility to the application of mandatory rules of law that do not belong to the law governing the contract").

2. In PPG Industries, Inc. v. Pilkington Plc, 825 F.Supp. 1465 (D.Ariz. 1993), the contract between the parties contained a clause by which "the Agreement shall be governed by the laws of England." The court compelled arbitration, but warned that:

> the Court may, and certainly will, withdraw the reference to arbitration if U.S. antitrust law does not govern the substantive resolution of [the plaintiff's] claims. In addition, the Court directs that any damages determination, or arbitral award, made by the arbitrators shall be determined according to U.S. antitrust law irrespective of any conflict that may exist between those laws and the laws of England.

Similar questions have arisen in a number of recent securities fraud cases brought against Lloyd's of London, in which underwriters have suffered massive losses arising out of liability for asbestos and toxic-waste damage. Standardized contracts in such cases did not mandate arbitration, but they commonly joined an English choice-of-law clause with a choice-of-forum clause giving jurisdiction to English courts. See, e.g., Haynsworth v. The Corporation, 121 F.3d 956 (5th Cir.1997)("The view that every foreign forum's remedies must duplicate those available under American law would render all forum selection clauses worthless and would severely hinder Americans' ability to participate in international commerce"; "[t]he plaintiffs' remedies in England are adequate to protect their interests and the policies behind the statutes at issue"); Lipcon v. Underwriters at Lloyd's, London, 148 F.3d 1285 (11th Cir.1998)("the Court in *Mitsubishi* recognized and affirmed *Scherk's* policy of treating international commercial agreements as *sui generis*"; "[w]e will not invalidate choice clauses * * * simply because the remedies available in the contractually chosen forum are less favorable than those available in the courts of the United States"). Cf. Simula, Inc. v. Autoliv, Inc., 175 F.3d 716 (9th Cir. 1999)("even if Swiss law is applied to the dispute, there has been no showing that it will not provide [the plaintiff] with sufficient protection [in its Sherman Act claim]"; "we do not consider [footnote 19 in *Mitsubishi]* to be binding").

3. How convincing is the Supreme Court's assurance that the arbitral award, once rendered, can be effectively reviewed at the enforcement stage to "ensure that the legitimate interest in the enforcement of the antitrust laws has been addressed"? In light of the highly restricted scope of judicial review of the merits of awards, is this a realistic prospect?

See Baxter Int'l, Inc. v. Abbott Laboratories, 315 F.3d 829 (7th Cir. 2003). Here the arbitrators had prohibited Baxter, the inventor and patent-holder of sevoflurane, from competing with its licensee, finding that this would "violate the exclusivity term of the license." The arbitrators rejected the argument that if the license were so construed, it would amount to a "territorial allocation unlawful per se under § 1 of the Sherman Act." The court held that the award should be enforced: It is true, wrote Judge Easterbrook, that arbitrators are not allowed to command the parties to violate rules of positive law, "but *whether* the tribunal's construction of [the license] has that effect was a question put to, and resolved by, the arbitrators," and as between the parties "their answer is conclusive." The arbitral tribunal did, as commanded by *Mitsubishi,* take "cognizance of the antitrust claims and actually decided them," and "ensuring this is as far as our review legitimately goes." If the arrangement "really does offend the Sherman Act, then the United States, the FTC, or any purchaser of sevoflurane is free to sue and obtain relief," since none of them would be bound by the award. Dissenting, Judge Cudahy wrote that "this cannot be correct":

> While *Mitsubishi* and its progeny make clear that the choice of the arbitral forum is to be respected, they do not confer on the arbitrators a prerogative to preemptively review their own decisions and receive deference on that review in subsequent judicial evaluations.

Cf. pp. 93–96 supra ("Illegality").

4. Professor Eric Posner notes that the *Mitsubishi* case has been much criticized on the ground that the holding and the dicta in footnote 19 "contradict each other": "If the Court meant to hold that all arbitration clauses must be enforced, then international arbitration will flourish but arbitrators will not respect mandatory rules in the hope of attracting clients." If, on the other hand, the Court included footnote 19 "in order to signal that courts will review arbitration clauses in de novo trials, then courts can ensure that mandatory rules are enforced but international arbitration will lose its value." Posner argues, however, that these polar solutions are not the only ones possible: The "optimal strategy" of courts may instead be to engage in *random* de novo review of awards—a strategy that would result "in arbitrators frequently respecting mandatory rules" (since they would "fear the possibility of de novo review"), and courts refraining from *always* reviewing arbitration awards ("creating savings in congestion"). And he goes on to argue that the Court in *Mitsubishi* implemented precisely this strategy ("though perhaps not intentionally")— by creating conditions of "ambiguous threat": If parties are "not sure whether American courts will review arbitration awards or not—and if American courts occasionally do review arbitration awards—that would be a good thing." Eric A. Posner, Arbitration and the Harmonization of International Commercial Law: A Defense of *Mitsubishi,* 39 Va. J. Int'l L. 647, 651–52, 667–68 (1999).

5. Yves Dezalay and Bryant Garth have written that "the key" to the *Mitsubishi* opinion "is that it could invoke the elite image of international commercial arbitration": The amicus brief submitted by the ICC "gave the unmistakable impression that the academics, judges and practitioners who served as ICC arbitrators were comparable in status to U.S. Supreme Court judges. The list of recent arbitrators contained in the brief pointedly included the name of Justice Potter Stewart, who had retired recently from the Supreme Court."

> No doubt the increased caseload mattered, as did perhaps a relative decline in the prestige of federal rights, but the international dimension and prestige overcame formidable arguments and a strong alliance of a conservative government and judicial liberals * * * [T]he international dimension revalorized the image of arbitration from "sloppy litigation" to a potential elite private justice.

Yves Dezalay and Bryant Garth, Dealing in Virtue: International Commercial Arbitration and the Construction of a Transnational Legal Order 158–159 (1996).

6. Despite Justice Blackmun's careful disclaimer that it was "unnecessary [in *Mitsubishi]* to assess the legitimacy of the *American Safety* doctrine as applied to agreements to arbitrate arising from domestic transactions," can the rationale of *Mitsubishi* possibly be limited to international arbitration? Or is an antitrust claim now arbitrable even in a purely domestic case? See Nghiem v. NEC Electronic, Inc., 25 F.3d 1437 (9th Cir.1994)(referring to *Mitsubshi*'s "meticulous step-by-step disembowelment of the *American Safety* doctrine"); Seacoast Motors of Salisbury, Inc. v. DaimlerChrysler Motors Corp., 271 F.3d 6, 10 (1st Cir. 2001)("It is time to lay [*American Safety]* to rest").

7. ILC Peripherals Leasing Corp. v. International Business Machines Corp., 458 F.Supp. 423 (N.D.Cal.1978) was a suit against IBM for monopolizing or attempting to monopolize various markets in the computer industry. The trial lasted for five months and consumed 96 trial days; the parties called 87 witnesses whose testimony filled more than 19,000 pages of transcript. After deliberating for 19 days, the jury reported itself hopelessly deadlocked, and the court declared a mistrial. "Throughout the trial, the court felt that the jury was having trouble grasping the concepts that were being discussed by the expert witnesses." Only one of the jurors had even "limited technical education." "While the court was appreciative of the effort they put into deciding the case, it is understandable that people with such backgrounds would have trouble applying concepts like cross-elasticity of supply and demand, market share and market power, reverse engineering, product interface manipulation, discriminatory pricing, barriers to entry, exclusionary leasing, entrepreneurial subsidiaries, subordinated debentures, stock options, modeling, and etc." Cf. John R. Allison, Arbitration Agreements and Antitrust Claims: The Need for Enhanced Accommodation of Conflicting Public Policies, 64 N. Car. L. Rev. 219., 246 (1986)("One is led to wonder whether the rule prohibiting arbitration of antitrust claims actually contributes to the interest that a party with a weak claim has in generating confusion.").

8. Each nation has a list of disputes that are not deemed capable of resolution by arbitration—"because of their perceived public importance or a felt need for formal judicial procedures and protections." See Gary B. Born, International Commercial Arbitration 245–57 (2nd ed. 2001). A state may, for example, prohibit arbitration of disputes involving labor or employment, intellectual property, antitrust claims, real estate, domestic relations, bankruptcy, consumer transactions, or franchise agreements. In the United States, by contrast, the category of "inarbitrable" disputes is now virtually a null set. See, e.g., Borowiec v. Gateway 2000, Inc., 209 Ill.2d 376, 283 Ill.Dec. 669, 808 N.E.2d 957 (2004)("the text, legislative history, and purposes of the [Magnuson–Moss Act, 15 U.S.C. § 2301], do not evince a congressional intent to bar arbitration of written warranty claims"); In re Cooker Restaurant Corp., 292 B.R. 308 (S.D. Ohio 2003)("in non-core proceedings [that is, as to claims not created by the Bankruptcy Code itself], the policies expressed in favor of arbitration in the [FAA] are not overridden, either expressly or implicitly, by provisions of the Bankruptcy Code," and a bankruptcy court "has no discretion to deny a stay and compel arbitration").

One rare, isolated exception is Alexander v. U.S. Credit Management, Inc., 384 F.Supp.2d 1003 (N.D.Tex.2005)(under the "Credit Repair Organization Act," 15 U.S.C § 1679c(a), any "credit repair organization" is required to inform a consumer in writing that "you have a right to sue a credit repair organization that violates" the Act; the Act's "non-waiver of rights provisions, combined with its proclamation of a consumer's right to sue, represent precisely the expression of congressional intent required by *Mitsubishi* and its progeny"). In Garrett v. Circuit City Stores, Inc., 338 F.Supp.2d 717 (N.D. Tex. 2004), the same court held that a claim for discrimination based on the employee's military status—in alleged violation of the Uniformed Services Employment and Reemployment Rights Act [38 U.S.C. § 4301]—was not arbitrable because the Act's guarantee of a federal jury trial superseded any arbitration clause. This time, however, the Fifth Circuit reversed: The Act may grant unwaivable "substantive rights" to soldiers and reservists with respect to "reemployment, to leaves of absence, to protection against discrimination and to health and pension plan benefits"—but, the court held, these rights "relate to compensation and working conditions, not to affording a particular forum for dispute resolution." 449 F.3d 672 (5th Cir. 2006).

9. A federal statute enacted in 2002 has ironically reversed the precise result of *Mitsubishi* itself: The "Motor Vehicle Franchise Contract Arbitration Act" now makes unenforceable any arbitration clause in a contract between an automobile manufacturer (or importer) and a dealer, unless the parties "consent in writing to use arbitration" *"after [the] controversy arises."* 15 U.S.C. § 1226 (a)(2). This piece of special-interest legislation was necessary, according to the Senate Committee report, on the ground of "the imbalance in bargaining power" by which "manufacturers possess unparalleled leverage over dealers and potential franchisees," making the dealers their "virtual economic captives." 107 S. Rpt. 266, 107th Cong., 2nd Sess., Sept. 10, 2002. But "readers of John O'Hara will hardly confuse the local GM dealer, often the leading businessman in town, with the proverbial widow or orphan or the purchaser of a Gateway computer," Richard W. Hulbert, Should the FAA Be Amended?, 18 (12) Mealey's Int'l Arb. Rep., Dec. 2003, at pp. 35, 38.

10. Separation agreements usually contain detailed provisions relating to the children of the marriage. Where children are involved, the unraveling of the family can never be complete, and so there will be a need to lay down ground rules for all sorts of matters: custody and visitation rights, child support, and various other continuing incidents of the family relationship (such as the choice of a school or summer camp, religious training, medical treatment, or trips and vacations). With increasing frequency, agreements provide that the inevitable disputes over such matters will be settled by arbitration. Nevertheless some courts deny on grounds of "public policy" that such disputes can ever be arbitrable. See, e.g., Glauber v. Glauber, 192 A.D.2d 94, 600 N.Y.S.2d 740 (App. Div. 1993) ("when circumstances require determining which living arrangements are in the best interests of children, the courts alone must undertake the task"); Kelm v. Kelm, 92 Ohio St.3d 223, 749 N.E.2d 299 (2001)(while an arbitration clause is enforceable as to matters "relating to spousal and child support," such a rule should not be extended to allow "matters of custody and visitation" to be resolved by arbitration).

Other courts enforce arbitration agreements, but with the caveat that "a special review" of the resulting award is necessary: "The courts should conduct a de novo review unless it is clear on the face of the award that the award could not adversely affect the substantial best interests of the child." Faherty v. Faherty, 97 N.J. 99, 477 A.2d 1257 (1984); see also Miller v.

Miller, 423 Pa.Super. 162, 620 A.2d 1161 (1993) ("an award rendered by an arbitration panel would be subject to the supervisory power of the court in its parens patriae capacity in a proceeding to determine the best interests of the child"; the trial court is not "bound by the narrow scope of review" set out in the local arbitration act). What is the justification for compelling arbitration of a domestic dispute—but at the same time treating the process as something of a rehearsal for a separate judicial inquiry, with an inevitable duplication of time and expense? Are there aspects of arbitration that make it particularly attractive as a device for resolving domestic disputes over child support and custody? Cf. Agur v. Agur, 32 A.D.2d 16, 298 N.Y.S.2d 772 (App. Div. 1969) (separation agreement provided that custody disputes would be decided by three arbitrators, including an Orthodox rabbi, versed in "Jewish religious law"; court refused to order arbitration). One court has observed that "the process of arbitration, useful when the mundane matter of the amount of support is in issue, is less so when the delicate balancing of the factors comprising the best interests of a child is the issue. The judicial process is more broadly gauged and better suited in protecting these interests." Nestel v. Nestel, 38 A.D.2d 942, 331 N.Y.S.2d 241 (App. Div. 1972). What precisely do you think this means? Do you agree?

Still another solution is suggested by a Texas statute which permits a court, "on written agreement of the parties," to "refer a suit affecting the parent-child relationship to arbitration." If the parties have agreed that the arbitration is to be binding the court is to enforce the award, unless it determines independently that the award is "not in the best interest of the child": But the burden of proof on this issue is on the party seeking to *avoid* enforcement of the award. Tex. Fam. Code § 153.0071(a),(b).

11. An important tenet of American patent law is that the validity of patents must be freely challengeable, so as not to impede free competition in the exploitation of the "public domain." Invalid patents are "vicious Zombis." Aero Spark Plug Co. v. B.G. Corp., 130 F.2d 290, 299 (2d Cir.1942) (Frank, J., concurring). Patent licensees, therefore, are free to attack the patents of their licensors. Lear, Inc. v. Adkins, 395 U.S. 653 (1969). And once a patent has been successfully challenged in court, its invalidity is established not only between the litigants but as to the world generally; the owner of the patent will be estopped from claiming infringement in a later suit against a third party. Blonder–Tongue Labs., Inc. v. University of Illinois Found., 402 U.S. 313 (1971).

Given this public interest in challenging invalid patents, it was traditionally assumed that patent disputes were not arbitrable. See, e.g., Diematic Mfg. Corp. v. Packaging Industries, Inc., 381 F.Supp. 1057 (S.D.N.Y. 1974), appeal dismissed, 516 F.2d 975 (2d Cir.1975) ("Questions of patent law are not mere private matters"). In 1982, however, Congress expressly authorized the arbitration of "any dispute relating to patent validity or infringement." 35 U.S.C.A. § 294. The statute provides that the arbitration award is to be "final and binding between the parties to the arbitration," but that it "shall have no force or effect on any other person." What does this language mean? See Goldstein, Arbitration of Disputes Relating to Patent Validity or Infringement, 72 Ill.Bar.J. 350, 351 (1984) ("phrase is intended to remove the defense of collateral estoppel and permit the patentee to enforce a patent against others").

The AAA has issued a set of "Patent Arbitration Rules" and maintains a "National Panel of Patent Arbitrators, [made up of] individuals having experience in patent law and/or special technical expertise." It appears, however, that the potential for arbitration in patent cases has not as yet been widely exploited. One survey of practice in patent disputes suggested that corporations "overwhelmingly favor arbitration for disputes involving smaller stakes," but "only a very small percentage prefer arbitration where the risks exceed six figures." Wesley & Peterson, "Patent Arbitration," BNA ADR Rep., vol. 4 no. 2 (1990), at 30. Similar results were found in Field & Rose, Prospects for ADR in Patent Disputes: An Empirical Assessment of Attorneys' Attitudes, 32 Idea 309, 317–18 (1992). Why might this be true?

12.   Plaintiff, a minor, brought suit against Cigna Healthplans for medical malpractice, and also for violation of the California Consumer Legal Remedies Act [CLRA]—claiming that Cigna had deceptively advertised the quality of medical services which would be provided under its health care plan. Alleging that the plaintiff's mother had received "substandard prenatal medical services" that caused the plaintiff to suffer severe injuries at birth, the suit asked for actual and punitive damages and for "an order enjoining [Cigna's] deceptive practices." The trial court granted the motion to compel arbitration of the medical malpractice action, but denied the motion as to the CLRA claim, and Cigna appealed. The Supreme Court of California held that the plaintiff's *damage* claim under CLRA was indeed "fully arbitrable," but that his claim for an *injunction* was not. Distinguishing *Mitsubishi,* the court held that there was an "inherent conflict" between arbitration and the injunctive relief provisions of the CLRA: The "evident purpose" of the latter was not to "resolve a private dispute" or to "compensate for an individual wrong," but instead to "prohibit and enjoin conduct injurious to the general public"; in seeking an injunction, the plaintiff was in effect here "playing the role of a private attorney general." Furthermore, arbitration would not be a "suitable forum" because of "evident institutional shortcomings": A court, unlike an arbitrator, could "retain its jurisdiction over a public injunction until it is dissolved," providing "a necessary continuity and consistency for which a series of arbitrators is an inadequate substitute"; also unlike arbitrators, courts are "publicly accountable" and thus "the most appropriate overseers of injunctive remedies explicitly designed for public protection." Broughton v. Cigna Healthplans of California, 21 Cal.4th 1066, 90 Cal.Rptr.2d 334, 988 P.2d 67 (1999).

Note: Investor/Broker Disputes Under the Securities Acts

The Securities Act of 1933 imposes liability for making misleading statements in the sale of a security "by means of a prospectus or oral communication."[1] The SEC's Rule 10b–5, promulgated under the Securities Exchange Act of 1934, prohibits the making of false statements or the failure to disclose material facts in connection with the sale of securities, and also makes it unlawful to engage "in any act, practice, or course of business which operates or would operate as a fraud or deceit upon any person, in connection with the purchase or sale of any security."[2] Provisions of this Rule have been used to attack a wide variety of securities practices such as "insider trading" and the "churning" of customer accounts by brokers (making numerous trades in order to increase commissions); a private cause of action for those injured by violations of the Rule has long been implied.

For many years, disputes arising under both of these statutes were thought to be not arbitrable as a matter of "public policy." The Supreme Court held in Wilko v. Swan, 346 U.S. 427 (1953), that an investor could litigate a misrepresentation claim against a brokerage firm under the Securities Act of 1933, despite the fact that the investor's agreement with the firm contained an arbitration clause. The Court noted that arbitrators must make determinations "without judicial instruction on the law" and that an award "may be made without explanation of their reasons and without a complete record of their proceedings"; it concluded that "the protective provisions of the Securities Act require the exercise of judicial direction to fairly assure their effectiveness." The statute should therefore be read as preventing a "waiver of judicial trial and review," and any agreement to arbitrate future disputes was invalid.

However, the Supreme Court—in line with its increasing tendency to presume arbitral competence even as to statutory or "public policy" matters—has reversed course. In Shearson/American Express, Inc. v. McMahon, 482 U.S. 220 (1987), the Court held that arbitration of claims against a broker under the Securities Exchange Act and Rule 10b–5 could be compelled where the customer had earlier signed an arbitration agreement. The Court reached this conclusion by relying heavily on *Mitsubishi,* noting that "the mistrust of arbitration that formed the basis for the *Wilko* opinion in 1953 is difficult to square with the assessment of arbitration that has prevailed since that time." The Court pointed to the fact that the SEC had specifically approved the arbitration procedures of the various stock exchanges, and has exercised its "oversight authority" to ensure that the procedures of the exchanges "adequately protect statutory rights." Nor were arbitration agreements made unenforceable by § 29(a) of the Securities Exchange Act, which prohibits any agreement by which a party undertakes "to waive compliance with any provision of [the Act]". The Court—in what has now become a familiar rhetorical move—concluded that by "agreeing to arbitrate a statutory claim, a party does not forego the substantive rights afforded by the statute; it only submits to their resolution in an arbitral, rather than a judicial, forum."

1. 15 U.S.C.A. §§ 77a, 77l.

2. 15 U.S.C.A. §§ 78a, 78j; 17 C.F.R. § 240.10b–5.

At the same time the Supreme Court held in *McMahon* that claims under the Racketeer Influenced and Corrupt Organizations Act ("RICO") were also subject to arbitration under a pre-dispute arbitration clause. "RICO" makes it unlawful to use any money derived "from a pattern of racketeering activity" in the operation of an interstate enterprise.[3] As Justice O'Connor noted in *McMahon,* the scope of RICO has in recent years been dramatically extended far beyond the activities of "the archetypal, intimidating mobster," to reach ordinary business disputes involving "respected and legitimate" enterprises.[4] The RICO statute follows the model of the antitrust laws in giving a private cause of action, including the right to attorney's fees and treble damages, to persons injured by such conduct. "Although the holding in *Mitsubishi* was limited to the international context, much of its reasoning is equally applicable here." 482 U.S. at 239.

While the *McMahon* case did not expressly overrule *Wilko v. Swan,* it did not take long for the Supreme Court to give *Wilko* a formal burial: In Rodriguez de Quijas v. Shearson/American Express, Inc., 490 U.S. 477 (1989), the Court held that claims under the Securities Act of 1933 were also arbitrable where the parties had entered into a pre-dispute arbitration agreement.

At the present time, virtually all brokerage firms require customers to sign a pre-dispute arbitration agreement as a condition for opening an account, particularly in the case of margin or option accounts. Broker-customer contracts commonly provide for arbitration under the auspices of an industry organization such as the New York Stock Exchange (NYSE) or the National Association of Securities Dealers (NASD). In 2004, 8201 cases were filed with NASD, which handles approximately 90% of all securities arbitrations; in cases where a hearing was held, the average "turnaround time" from filing to final award was 17 months.[5] Under current NASD rules, cases involving more than $50,000 are presumptively to be heard by a panel of three arbitrators, two of whom must be "public" arbitrators, that is, not from the securities industry.

These exchange-administered arbitrations have been the subject of frequent and vocal criticism for many years. See, e.g., "When Investors Bring Claims Against Brokers," New York Times, March 29, 1987, Sec. 3, pp. 1, 8 (lawyer who represents investors says, "I would rather defend a capitalist before the comrades' court than a client before an arbitration panel of the New York Stock Exchange"); "Wall Street's Dispute Process Is Under Fire," Wall St. J., July 20, 2004, p. C1. The suspicion has persisted (in the words of Justice Blackmun's dissent in *McMahon*) that "[t]he uniform opposition of investors to compelled arbitration and the overwhelming support of the securities industry for the process suggest that

---

3. 18 U.S.C.A. § 1961.

4. "Racketeering activity" under the statute is defined as the violation of certain predicate statutes—for example, those dealing with bribery and narcotics sales, but also including "mail fraud" and "fraud in the sale of securities"; a "pattern" of such activity is found when at least two such violations occur within a period of ten years.

5. These and other securities arbitration statistics are available at the NASD web site at www.nasd.com.

there must be *some* truth to the investors' belief that the securities industry has an advantage in a forum under its own control."[6]

Arbitration of disputes between members of a trade and "outsiders" often brings to the surface a tension between two widely-accepted values underlying the arbitration process. On the one hand, there are the often-cited advantages of expert knowledge and experience on the part of decision-makers familiar with industry practice. The task, for example, of educating a jury or even the average judge in the conventions of securities or commodities trading may be a daunting one. On the other hand, there is a need to preserve the fairness of the process by avoiding onesidedness. Even decision-makers who think of themselves as scrupulously neutral are often hard put to avoid the predispositions and preconceptions that seem to accompany technical "expertise." This is particularly true where one of the parties claims to have observed "trade standards," and the dispute seems likely to call into question long-standing practices and patterns of behavior widespread throughout an entire industry. "Expertise provides a powerful basis to determine what behavior is reasonable, economically efficient, or even economically necessary." And "[p]ressures to decide cases quickly without an intrusive investigation into motives and the like * * * may enforce the failure to challenge" long-standing practices.[7] The arbitration of broker-customer disputes illustrates the inevitable tension; how to draw the balance between these values is a persistent theme in discussions of arbitration.

Following the Supreme Court's decision in *McMahon,* the industry's arbitration rules were amended in an attempt to address some of these concerns. The definition of just who can serve as a "public" arbitrator has several times been clarified and tightened "to reduce a perception of bias by NASD arbitration panel members":[8] Under current NASD rules individuals cannot serve as "public" arbitrators if they have been associated with a broker or dealer within the past 5 years, or if they worked in the industry for 20 years or more (regardless of how long ago the association ended); if they are attorneys or accountants who in the past two years devoted 20% of their work to securities industry clients, or if their firm derived 10% or more of its annual revenue from such clients; or if they are spouses or immediate family members of anybody in any of these categories.[9]

---

6. See also Cheryl Nichols, Arbitrator Selection at the NASD: Investor Perception of a Pro–Securities Industry Bias, 15 Ohio St. J. Disp. Res. 63, 129 (1999) (amended NASD rules illustrate "the difficulty, maybe the impossibility, of eliminating the perception of pro-securities industry bias in the NASD arbitrator pool when an economically dependent relationship exists between one of the parties (securities industry respondents) and the arbitrators deciding the dispute").

7. Bryan Garth, Privatization and the New Market for Disputes: A Framework for Analysis and a Preliminary Assessment, 12 Studies in Law, Politics and Society 367, 382 (1992).

8. SEC, Order Granting Approval to a Proposed Rule Change Relating to Arbitrator Classification and Disclosure in NASD Arbitrations, April 16, 2004, 69 Fed. Reg. 21871, 21873 (2004).

9. NASD, Code of Arbitration Procedure § 10308(a)(4), (a)(5). Under NYSE rules, by contrast, attorneys and accountants "whose firms have close securities industry ties will still be classified as public arbitrators

One frequently-expressed concern has been that in disputes between customers and "repeat players" like brokers, the decisions of arbitrators who hope to decide a large number of cases may be affected by the desire to obtain future assignments—and that an appearance of partiality toward the industry may be exacerbated by a tendency of some exchanges to call frequently on particular arbitrators.[10] Under the NYSE rules the exchange itself—rather than the parties—names the members of the arbitration panel in most cases. This was formerly the NASD's practice as well, but in 1998 the NASD moved to a system of arbitration selection similar to that of the AAA—in which the parties are provided lists of potential arbitrators, strike the names of those found to be unacceptable, and rank the remaining names in order of preference.[11] A software program will now generate names for forwarding to the parties "on a random basis." In addition, arbitral awards are now made publicly available; the NASD has also recently proposed a rule change to require that awards contain a "written explanation" of the result if the customer requests one prior to the hearing.[12]

A 1992 study conducted by the United States General Accounting Office could find "no indication of pro-industry bias in arbitration decisions at industry-sponsored forums";[13] in fact a later report prepared for the SEC by Professor Michael Perino asserts that both "regulatory oversight and economic self-interest" would appear, "at least in theory, to provide a significant check" on any systematic tendency to "yield pro-industry out-

provided [they do] not routinely represent industry firms or individuals," NYSE Arbitration Rules, "Guidelines for Classification of Arbitrators." See also "Wall Street Panels For Settling Fights Draw Renewed Fire," Wall St. J., March 17, 2005, p. A1 (lawyer who worked for 30 years for Wall Street law firm, and who since represented Morgan Stanley and Prudential Securities, was "slightly taken aback" when he was "reclassified as a public arbitrator" under NASD rules).

In July 2005 the NASD filed with the SEC a proposal for a further amendment to its rules: This would bar from serving as a "public" arbitrator any director, officer, or employee of a company that is affiliated with ["directly or indirectly controls, is controlled by, or is under common control with"] a securities broker-dealer.

10. See Robbins, Securities Arbitration from the Arbitrators' Perspective, 23 Rev. Sec. & Commodities Reg. 171, 175 (1990) ("arbitration should not be a supplement to social security. * * * [W]hen they sit on cases day after day, arbitrators build up an immunity to outrageous conduct").

Arbitrators in securities cases are compensated for their services—although not handsomely. At the NASD, they receive an "honorarium" of $200 for a four-hour "hearing session."

11. NASD Code of Arbitration Procedure, R. 10308(b),(c); cf. NYSE Arbitration Rules R. 607(b), R. 608, R. 609 (each party has right to one peremptory challenge, and unlimited challenges for cause). See generally pp. 246–47 infra.

12. SEC, Notice of Filing of Proposed Rule Change (July 11, 2005), 70 Fed. Reg. 41065 (2005)("The lack of reasoning or explanations in awards is one of the most common complaints of non-prevailing participants in NASD's arbitration forum"; however, "requiring the inclusion of legal authorities and damage calculations would significantly increase the processing time of awards because it would result in the drafting of complex and lengthy judicial-type decisions").

13. GAO, Securities Arbitration : How Investors Fare 35 (1992), GGD–92–74. [This and other GAO reports are available at http://www.gao.gov.].

comes."[14] The 1992 report indicated that investors were successful in about 59% of the cases in which they initiated claims against broker-dealers, and that those receiving awards got an overall average of 61% of the amount they claimed. (More recent figures show a somewhat less favorable pattern.).[15] Since investors with small monetary claims against broker-dealers often have difficulty obtaining legal representation in arbitration, around 40% of investors represent themselves in securities arbitration—and as might be expected, investors represented by counsel achieve a significantly higher recovery rate than pro se claimants.[16]

Note: Employment Disputes and the Statutory Rights of Employees

A large number of federal statutes have been enacted in recent years that extend protection to employees against various forms of discrimination in the workplace. Perhaps the most important of these is Title VII of the Civil Rights Act of 1964, which makes it an "unlawful employment practice" to "fail or refuse to hire or to discharge any individual, or otherwise to discriminate against any individual with respect to his compensation, terms, conditions, or privileges of employment, because of such individual's race, color, religion, sex, or national origin." 42 U.S.C. § 2000e–2(a)(1). When—if at all—may claims brought under such statutes be subject to mandatory and binding arbitration? This is a question that has been the focus of much litigation—and the cause of considerable and continuing confusion.

14. Michael A. Perino, Report to the Securities and Exchange Commission Regarding Arbitrator Conflict Disclosure Requirements in NASD and NYSE Securities Arbitrations 8–9 (2002)("Systemic procedural inequities would likely increase the costs of the arbitration system as more dissatisfied parties attempted to overturn arbitration awards. The presence of systemic conflicts or other procedural inequities might invite closer judicial scrutiny of arbitration awards, yielding more successful challenges and therefore less finality"). See http://www.sec.gov/pdf/arbconflict.pdf.

15. A later GAO study published in June 2000 found that the percentage of cases favoring investors averaged around 51% in the years 1992–1996, then rose to 57% in 1998. The amount of awards made to investors as a percentage of what they had claimed also declined to about 51% during those years, although an increase in the percentage of cases settled—generally 50–60% of the total cases concluded—"may have changed the mix of cases going to a final arbitration award." [Why might this be true?] GAO, Securities Arbitration: Actions Needed to Ad-

dress Problem of Unpaid Awards (2000), GAO/GGD–00–115.

According to the NASD, investors as claimants received monetary damages, or non-monetary relief, in 48% of arbitration cases decided in 2003, and in 46% of cases decided in 2004.

The 2000 GAO report also found that in 1998, 49% of the awards rendered in favor of customers remained totally unpaid, and that an additional 12% were only partially paid—although when investors complained, suspensions or the threat of suspensions by the NASD against noncomplying broker-dealers resulted in many of these awards being satisfied. Most of the unpaid awards had been rendered against broker-dealers who were no longer in business. For recent rule changes adopted to address this problem, see GAO, "Evaluation of Steps Taken to Address the Problem of Unpaid Arbitration Awards," (2001), GAO–01–654R; GAO, "Follow–Up Report on Matters Relating to Securities Arbitration" (2003), GAO–03–162R.

16. See U.S. Securities and Exchange Commission, Office of Inspector General, "Oversight of Self–Regulatory Organization Arbitration" (1999).

In Alexander v. Gardner–Denver Co., 415 U.S. 36 (1974), the Supreme Court was presented with a collective bargaining agreement protecting employees from discharge without "just cause," and also prohibiting "discrimination against any employee on account of race." After being fired, an employee claimed at an arbitration hearing that his discharge was the result of racial discrimination. The arbitrator made no explicit reference to the racial discrimination claim but found that the employee had been fired for "just cause," and denied the grievance. The employee then sued the employer, alleging that his discharge was in violation of Title VII. The district court granted the employer's motion for summary judgment, finding "that the claim of racial discrimination had been submitted to the arbitrator and resolved adversely" to the employee: Having "voluntarily elected to pursue his grievance to final arbitration under the nondiscrimination clause of the collective bargaining agreement," the employee "was bound by the arbitral decision and thereby precluded from suing his employer under Title VII." Before the Supreme Court, the employer argued that federal courts should defer to arbitral decisions on discrimination claims, at least "where (i) the claim was before the arbitrator; (ii) the collective-bargaining agreement prohibited the form of discrimination charged in the suit under Title VII; and (iii) the arbitrator has authority to rule on the claim and to fashion a remedy."

The Supreme Court, however, rejected this argument and reversed:

> The purpose and procedures of Title VII indicate that Congress intended federal courts to exercise final responsibility for enforcement of Title VII; deferral to arbitral decisions would be inconsistent with that goal. * * * [The employer's] deferral rule is necessarily premised on the assumption that arbitral processes are commensurate with judicial processes and that Congress impliedly intended federal courts to defer to arbitral decisions on Title VII issues. We deem this supposition unlikely.

Gardner–Denver was followed by two other important cases, also dealing with the effects of an arbitral award under a collective bargaining agreement on the statutory rights of employees. In Barrentine v. Arkansas–Best Freight System, Inc., 450 U.S. 728 (1981), an employee had unsuccessfully submitted wage claims to arbitration; the Court held that this did not preclude a later suit, based on the same underlying facts, alleging a violation of the minimum wage provisions of the Fair Labor Standards Act.

In McDonald v. City of West Branch, 466 U.S. 284 (1984), a police officer was discharged by a city and filed a grievance pursuant to the collective bargaining agreement. Here too the arbitrator ruled against him, finding that there was "just cause" for the discharge. McDonald did not challenge the award, but later filed an action against the city under 42 U.S.C. § 1983 (imposing liability on any person who "under color of" state law deprives another "of any rights, privileges, or immunities secured by the Constitution and laws" of the United States; McDonald alleged that he had been discharged for exercising his First Amendment rights.) The court of appeals concluded that McDonald's First Amendment claims were barred by res judicata and collateral estoppel, but the Supreme Court, relying heavily on *Gardner–Denver,* reversed: While "arbitration is well suited to resolving contractual disputes," it said, it cannot in a § 1983 action "provide an adequate substitute for a judicial trial. Consequently, according preclusive effect to arbitration awards in § 1983 actions would severely undermine the protection of federal rights that the statute is designed to provide."

The Court buttressed this conclusion by pointing to a number of characteristics of arbitration. Noting first that "many arbitrators are not lawyers," the Court suggested that:

> [A]n arbitrator's expertise "pertains primarily to the law of the shop, not the law of the land." An arbitrator may not, therefore, have the expertise required to resolve the complex legal questions that arise in § 1983 actions.

> Second, because an arbitrator's authority derives solely from the contract, an arbitrator may not have the authority to enforce § 1983. As we explained in *Gardner–Denver:* "The arbitrator ... has no general authority to invoke public laws that conflict with the bargain between the parties.... If an arbitral decision is based 'solely upon the arbitrator's view of the requirements of enacted legislation,' rather than on an interpretation of the collective-bargaining agreement, the arbitrator has 'exceeded the scope of the submission,' and the award will not be enforced." * * *

> Third, when, as is usually the case, the union has exclusive control over the "manner and extent to which an individual grievance is presented," there is an additional reason why arbitration is an inadequate substitute for judicial proceedings. The union's interests and those of the individual employee are not always identical or even compatible. As a result, the union may present the employee's grievance less vigorously, or make different strategic choices, than would the employee. Thus, were an arbitration award accorded preclusive effect, an employee's opportunity to be compensated for a constitutional deprivation might be lost merely because it was not in the union's interest to press his claim vigorously.

> Finally, arbitral factfinding is generally not equivalent to judicial factfinding. * * * The record of the arbitration proceedings is not as complete; the usual rules of evidence do not apply; and rights and procedures common to civil trials, such as discovery, compulsory process, cross-examination, and testimony under oath, are often severely limited or unavailable.

Even though an arbitral award would not preclude a later action by the employee, the Court nevertheless suggested that the award might still be admitted as evidence in the lawsuit. The weight to be given the award "must be determined in the court's discretion with regard to the facts and circumstances of each case":

Relevant factors include the existence of provisions in the collective-bargaining agreement that conform substantially with [the statute or Constitution], the degree of procedural fairness in the arbitral forum, adequacy of the record with respect to the issue [in the judicial proceeding], and the special competence of particular arbitrators. Where an arbitral determination gives full consideration to an employee's [statutory or constitutional] rights, a court may properly accord it great weight. This is especially true where the issue is solely one of fact, specifically addressed by the parties and decided by the arbitrator on the basis of an adequate record.

See, e.g., Wilmington v. J.I. Case Co., 793 F.2d 909 (8th Cir.1986) ("the arbitrator's decision [that the employee was fired for "just cause"] was simply another piece of evidence presented to the jury, and it was for the jury to decide what weight to give it"; however, the trial court properly refused to admit into evidence the text of the award, since the arbitrator's comments and findings "would either usurp the jury's role in assessing credibility [of witnesses who also testified at trial] or would be unfairly prejudicial").

However, the relentless federal policy favoring arbitration has in recent years caused the pendulum to swing in the opposite direction. Gilmer v. Interstate/Johnson Lane Corporation, 500 U.S. 20 (1991), involved an individual employee who was hired as a "Manager of Financial Services" by a brokerage house, and required to register as a securities representative with the New York Stock Exchange; NYSE rules at the time required the arbitration of any dispute "arising out of the employment or termination of employment" of registered representatives. Gilmer later brought suit against his employer alleging that he had been discharged in violation of the Age Discrimination in Employment Act of 1967 (ADEA), 290 U.S.C. § 621. The Supreme Court—relying again on *Mitsubishi* as well as on *Shearson/American Express, Inc. v. McMahon* and *Rodriguez de Quijas v. Shearson/American Express*—held that arbitration of the claim should be compelled. Again the Court repeated that "[b]y agreeing to arbitrate a statutory claim, a party does not forgo the substantive rights afforded by the statute; it only submits to their resolution in an arbitral, rather than a judicial, forum." Again the Court stressed that "generalized attacks" on arbitration—to the effect that the arbitration process may not adequately permit vindication of the claimant's statutory rights—rested on an unwarranted "suspicion of arbitration," and were "far out of step with our current strong endorsement of the federal statutes favoring this method of resolving disputes."

For example, while it is true that discovery permitted in arbitration is more limited than in the federal courts, the Court found it "unlikely"

that age discrimination claims require more extensive discovery than other claims that we have found to be arbitrable, such as RICO and antitrust claims. Moreover, there has been no showing in this case that the NYSE discovery provisions, which allow for document production, information requests, depositions, and subpoenas, will prove insufficient to allow ADEA claimants such as Gilmer a fair opportunity to present their claims. Although those procedures might not be as extensive as in the federal courts, by agreeing to arbitrate, a party "trades the procedures and opportunity for review of the courtroom for the simplicity, informality, and expedition of arbitration." Indeed, an important counterweight to the reduced discovery in NYSE arbitration is that arbitrators are not bound by the rules of evidence.

Nor was the Court persuaded by the contention that "there often will be unequal bargaining power between employers and employees.":

> Mere inequality in bargaining power * * * is not a sufficient reason to hold that arbitration agreements are never enforceable in the employment context. Relationships between securities dealers and investors, for example, may involve unequal bargaining power, but we nevertheless held in *Rodriguez de Quijas* and *McMahon* that agreements to arbitrate in that context are enforceable. * * * There is no indication in this case * * * that Gilmer, an experienced businessman, was coerced or defrauded into agreeing to the arbitration clause in his registration application. As with the claimed procedural inadequacies discussed above, this claim of unequal bargaining power is best left for resolution in specific cases.

But how could *Gilmer* be distinguished from earlier cases like *Alexander v. Gardner–Denver* and its progeny? Most notably, the Court pointed out, in that the arbitration in those cases occurred in the context of a collective-bargaining agreement—where the claimants were represented by their unions in the arbitration proceedings. So "an important concern [was] the tension between collective representation and individual statutory rights, a concern not applicable to the present case." This seems critical, and other purported distinctions seem considerably less persuasive—and more like mere makeweights.[17]

The relationship between *Gilmer* and *Gardner-Denver* was revisited—although inconclusively—by the Supreme Court in Wright v. Universal Maritime Service Corp., 525 U.S. 70 (1998). Here, an employee subject to a collective bargaining agreement filed suit alleging an employer's violation of the Americans with Disability Act of 1990, 42 U.S.C. § 12101. The Supreme Court acknowledged that there was "obviously some tension between these two lines of cases." The employee's contention—that "federal forum rights" could not be waived at all in union-negotiated collective bargaining agreements, even if they could be waived in individually executed contracts—"assuredly finds support in the text of *Gilmer.*" The employer, on the other hand, argued that *Gilmer* "has sufficiently undermined

---

17. The Court also pointed out, for example, that the *Gardner–Denver* line of cases, unlike *Gilmer*, were not decided under the FAA—which (alone?) "reflects a liberal federal policy favoring arbitration agreements." And it also stressed that those cases did not—unlike *Gilmer*—"involve the issue of the [initial] enforceability of an agreement to arbitrate statutory claims. Rather, they involved the quite different issue whether arbitration of contract-based claims precluded subsequent judicial resolution of statutory claims." 500 U.S. at 35. Why are you not persuaded by these distinctions?

Gardner–Denver" that henceforth a union too should be able to surrender an employee's right to litigate a statutory claim. The Court found it "unnecessary to resolve" this question: For *"Gardner-Denver* at least stands for the proposition that the right to a federal judicial forum is of sufficient importance to be protected against less-than-explicit union waiver in a [collective bargaining agreement]." Matters which "go beyond the interpretation and application of contract terms"—like the meaning of a federal statute—will not be *presumed* to be arbitrable, but any such requirement in a collective bargaining agreement must instead be *"particularly clear."* And since the agreement in *Wright* could not meet such a standard, the employer's attempt to compel arbitration was denied. In *Gilmer*, by contrast—since it involved "an individual's waiver of his own rights, rather than a union's waiver of the rights of represented employees"—such a "clear and unmistakable" standard did not apply.

NOTES AND QUESTIONS

1. In 1990, Congress enacted the Older Workers Benefit Protection Act, 29 U.S.C. § 626(f), which amended the ADEA to prohibit waiver of "any right or claim" under the Act that is not "knowing and voluntary." Any such waiver must be "written in a manner calculated to be understood" by the employee; the employee must be "advised in writing to consult with an attorney" prior to signing it, and in any event there could be no waiver of "rights or claims that may arise after the date the waiver is executed." Should this amendment affect the validity of agreements providing for the arbitration of ADEA claims?

See Rosenberg v. Merrill Lynch, Pierce, Fenner & Smith, Inc., 170 F.3d 1 (1st Cir.1999)(to interpret the OWBPA to include "the right to a judicial forum" "would be to ignore the Supreme Court's repeated statements that arbitral and judicial fora are both able to give effect to the policies that underlie legislation"). But cf. Hammaker v. Brown & Brown, Inc., 214 F.Supp.2d 575 (E.D. Va. 2002), in which the employment agreement provided that both parties "waive any right either may have to a trial by jury." The court held that "the plain meaning of the statute requires that waivers of any statutory right, including the right to a jury trial, must conform to the OWBPA to be enforceable." Cases like *Rosenberg* were distinguishable because in such cases, "employees waived their rights to a judicial forum altogether"—whereas in *Hammaker* the employee's claim "will be heard in a judicial forum, whether by a bench trial or jury trial."

2. The holding in *Gilmer* has been routinely applied by lower courts to other federal legislation extending rights to individual employees against job discrimination. See, e.g., EEOC v. Luce, Forward, Hamilton & Scripps, 345 F.3d 742 (9th Cir. 2003)(district court enjoined law firm from requiring job applicants to agree to arbitrate Title VII claims and from enforcing existing agreements to arbitrate those claims; held, reversed; "the view that compulsory arbitration weakens Title VII conflicts with the Supreme Court's stated position that arbitration affects only the choice of forum, not substantive rights"); Bercovitch v. Baldwin School, Inc., 133 F.3d 141 (1st Cir.1998)(Americans with Disabilities Act [ADA]). But see Campbell v. General Dynamics Government Systems Corp., 407 F.3d 546 (1st Cir. 2005)(mass e-mail sent to employer's entire work force regarding implementation of new dispute resolution policy "would not have apprised a reasonable employee" that his right to a judicial forum for resolution of statutory employment discrimination claims was being "extinguished," and so it "would not be appropriate" to enforce a waiver of the right to litigate ADA claims).

See also McNulty v. Prudential–Bache Securities, Inc., 871 F.Supp. 567 (E.D.N.Y.1994) (claim under Jurors' Act, making it unlawful to discharge an employee "by reason of such employee's jury service"); Saari v. Smith Barney, Harris Upham & Co., Inc., 968 F.2d 877 (9th Cir.1992) (claim under Employee Polygraph Protection Act); Jones v. Fujitsu Network Communications, Inc., 81 F.Supp.2d 688 (N.D.Tex.1999)(claim under Family Medical Leave Act); Orcutt v. Kettering Radiologists, Inc., 199 F.Supp.2d 746 (S.D. Ohio 2002)(claim under whistleblower protection provision of the False Claims Act). In Williams v. Katten, Muchin & Zavis, 837 F.Supp. 1430 (N.D.Ill.1993), a claim under the Civil Rights Act of 1870 [42 U.S.C.A. § 1981, equal rights "to make and enforce contracts"] was held arbitrable; the court rejected arguments that racial discrimination is a more serious offense "morally distinguishable" from gender and age claims, and that § 1981 is more "constitutional in nature" than statutes enacted pursuant to the commerce clause such as Title VII.

3. The district court in *Alexander v. Gardner–Denver* had granted summary judgment to the employer; it feared that "[t]o hold that an employee has a right to an arbitration of a grievance which is binding on an employer but is not binding on the employee—a trial balloon for the employee, but a moon shot for the employer—would sound the death knell for arbitration clauses in labor contracts." 346 F.Supp. 1012, 1019 (D.Colo.1971). This prediction has not of course been borne out. Many collective bargaining agreements now include non-discrimination clauses and often incorporate Title VII or similar state statutes; labor arbitrators regularly decide such cases and engage in interpreting this language. See the discussion at pp. 150–51 supra ("Arbitral Decision–Making and Legal 'Rules' "). But given the holdings in *Gardner–Denver* and *McDonald,* what incentive is there for employers to agree to submit such disputes to arbitration if employees are able to get "a second bite of the apple"?

4. Strictly speaking, *Gardner–Denver* and *McDonald* were only concerned with the preclusive effect of *a prior arbitration award* on a *later* judicial claim. However, it seems clear that an employee subject to a collective bargaining agreement may always proceed *directly* to pursue litigation under Title VII or other civil rights statutes, without first exhausting his rights under the agreement. See 2 Larson, Employment Discrimination §§ 49.14, 49.15 (1990) (since courts in Title VII actions are not bound by the results of grievance and arbitration procedures in collective bargaining agreements, requiring exhaustion would "needlessly prolong the deprivation of rights"). This option of course no longer remains open to an employee in the position of Robert Gilmer. Is it not something of a paradox that statutory rights against discrimination are apparently subject to binding arbitration only in individual employment agreements—which are so often contracts of adhesion—and not in the hard-fought and actually "dickered" collective bargaining agreements between employers and unions?

5. In the securities industry, employees like Gilmer were for many years required by NASD and NYSE rules to submit employment disputes to arbitration before industry fora, under the same procedures as customers. A 1994 study found that arbitrators in such fora were not selected on the basis of any particular "expertise" in employment or discrimination law, and that most of them were "white men, averaging 60 years of age." U.S. General Accounting Office, Employment Discrimination: How Registered Representatives Fare in Discrimination Disputes 2, 8, 12 (1994)(of the 726 arbitrators in NYSE's New York arbitrator pool, 89% were men; of the 349 arbitrators whose race could be identified, 97% were white).

Commentators predictably seized on this fact to conclude that the awards of such arbitrators must tend to disfavor minority or female complainants—indeed, the presence of at least "unconscious bias" is usually taken to be self-evident without the need for any further discussion. (How, though, would you characterize the typical federal judge? See Alan Rau, On Integrity in Private Judging, 14 Arb. Int'l 115, 135–40 (1998)).

Similarly, a number of anecdotal accounts of the security industry's arbitration procedures in employment discrimination cases have been highly critical and widely-publicized. One NYSE panel apparently decided against the claimant in a sexual harassment case because her supervisor's behavior "was common within the industry"; the arbitrators were unfamiliar with the current state of antidiscrimination law and, in the words of one law professor, were "10 years behind where the courts are." One article concluded that "So grim are the prospects for most women who go through the securities-industry arbitration process that lawyers say they now advise their clients not to bother with arbitration at all. Instead, they urge women to take modest settlements and walk away." See Jacobs, "Men's Club: Riding Crop and Slurs: How Wall Street Dealt With a Sex–Bias Case," Wall St.J., June 9, 1994 at p. A1.

Studies and stories like these have naturally prompted calls for legislation to restrict the use of arbitration in resolving discrimination claims. See, e.g., the "Preservation of Civil Rights Protections Act of 2005," H.R. 2969, 109th Cong., 1st Sess. (which would make unenforceable any employment agreement that "requires arbitration of a claim arising under the Constitution or laws of the United States"). After being introduced, these bills invariably go nowhere. However, recent amendments to the rules of both the NASD and the NYSE have eliminated any *industry-wide* requirement of mandatory arbitration with respect to statutory discrimination claims. (Nevertheless industry employees are still required under these rules to arbitrate any common-law claims, such as wrongful termination or infliction of emotional distress. In addition, under NASD rules individual brokerage firms remain free to insert pre-dispute arbitration clauses in their employment agreements should they wish to do so, thereby making mandatory the arbitration of even discrimination claims. See SEC, Release No. 34–40109, 1998 WL 339422 (F.R.); SEC, Release No. 34–40858, 1999 WL 3315 (F.R.)). The NASD has also amended its rules to provide that all arbitrators in employment discrimination cases must be "public" arbitrators; the chairman must be an attorney with ten or more years of legal experience and "substantial familiarity with employment law," and must not have "represented primarily the views of employers or of employees" within the past five years. See NASD Code of Arbitration Procedure, § 10211.

6. Outside the (now much diminished) sphere of cases like *Gardner–Denver* and *McDonald,* arbitration awards can be expected to have res judicata and collateral estoppel effects on later proceedings. The Restatement of Judgments, for example, generally provides that "a valid and final award by arbitration" will have the same preclusive effects as a judgment of a court. "If the arbitration award were not treated as the equivalent of a judicial adjudication for purposes of claim preclusion, the obligation to arbitrate would be practically illusory." Restatement (Second) of Judgments, § 84 and comment b. In addition, the arbitrators' determination of a particular *issue* will prevent later relitigation of the same issue (i.e., will have "collateral estoppel" effect), at least where the proceedings possess "the elements of adjudicatory procedure"—including notice to the parties, the right to present and rebut evidence and legal argument, and "such other procedural elements as may be necessary to constitute the proceeding a sufficient means of conclusively determining the matter in question." Id. at §§ 84(3), 83(2). Under modern arbitration statutes, once an award is confirmed by a court it is given "the same force and effect" as a judgment rendered in a suit, FAA § 13. But judicial confirmation is not necessary in order for an award to have a preclusive effect barring later relitigation. See generally 4 Ian Macneil, Richard Speidel, & Thomas Stipanowich, Federal Arbitration Law § 39.6 (1994).

In some cases, however, the collateral estoppel effects of an arbitration award may be limited by the "informality" of the arbitration proceeding. For example, where there is no transcript and where the arbitrators do not write a reasoned opinion, it may often be difficult to tell just what it is that they have actually decided. See, e.g., Tamari v. Bache & Co. (Lebanon) S.A.L., 637 F.Supp. 1333 (N.D.Ill.1986). In this case a customer initiated arbitration proceedings against a brokerage firm, seeking to hold it accountable for the acts of its subsidiary, and the arbitrators denied the claim without an opinion. This was held not to preclude a later suit against the subsidiary itself, since "it is impossible to tell" the basis for the arbitrators' award. After all, the court reasoned, the arbitrators could have found *either* that the subsidiary had done nothing wrongful, *or* that the subsidiary had simply not been acting as an agent of the parent. See also Clark v. Bear Stearns & Co., Inc., 966 F.2d 1318 (9th Cir.1992) (dismissal by arbitrators of state-law claims against broker did not preclude a later suit on federal-law claims; the award did not mention the applicable law selected by the arbitrators and if they chose California law "the defendants' alleged negligence need not have been addressed by the arbitrators at all," since the common-law claim would be barred by the state's statute of limitations); Shell, Res Judicata and Collateral Estoppel Effects of Commercial Arbitration, 35 U.C.L.A. L.Rev. 623 (1988).

In addition, in the absence of some express agreement between the parties, even a confirmed arbitration award may not be given a *nonmutual* collateral estoppel effect. This is the situation in which A & B arbitrate a particular dispute, and A loses. In later litigation between A & C involving some of the same issues, C argues that A should be bound by adverse findings made by the arbitrator in the earlier proceeding. The Supreme Court of California rejected that argument in Vandenberg v. Superior Court, 21 Cal.4th 815, 88 Cal.Rptr.2d 366, 982 P.2d 229 (1999). The earlier arbitration had been between a landowner and its lessee for contamination of soil and groundwater; the court held that findings adverse to the lessee did not prevent him, in a later indemnification action against his insurers, from arguing that the discharge was "sudden and accidental" and thus not excluded from pollution coverage under the policy. The court noted that while in arbitration the parties have voluntarily traded "the safeguards and formalities of court litigation for an expeditious, sometimes roughshod means of resolving their dispute," "these same features can be serious, unexpected disadvantages if issues decided by the arbitrators are given leveraged effect in favor of strangers to the arbitration." But cf. Riverdale Development Co. v. Ruffin Building Systems, Inc., 356 Ark. 90, 146 S.W.3d 852 (2004). Here a development company (Riverdale) had hired a contractor (May) to erect a commercial office building, and May was to use a pre-engineered metal building manufactured by Ruffin. In an arbitration between Riverdale and May, the arbitrator ruled against Riverdale—finding that there was "no credible evidence of [damages] for repairs or for the cost of correcting defects." In a later suit brought by Riverdale against Ruffin for breach of implied warranties and negligence, the court held that Ruffin was entitled to summary judgment: "It is apparent that Riverdale had a full and fair opportunity to litigate the issues it raised, and those issues were actually decided by the arbitrator and were necessary to the decision."

7. After an employee was discharged in 1989, her union filed a grievance alleging unjust termination under the collective bargaining agreement; she also filed discrimination charges with the state Commission on Human Rights and with the EEOC. Two years later, the employer and the employee agreed to be bound by an arbitration decision. A "Stipulated Arbitration Award" was later confirmed by a state court: Under it, the employee was to be reinstated and compensated for lost wages, and she was to withdraw the discrimination charges filed with state and federal agencies. The employee later filed a lawsuit alleging a series of unlawful acts—up to and including her 1989 termination—which allegedly constituted discrimination and retaliation under Title VII and a deprivation of her civil rights under 42 U.S.C. § 1983. The employer moved to dismiss. The court noted that

- "if the prior resolution was an arbitration award, the plaintiff may proceed with the case, even if the only act of discrimination she can prove is the 1989 termination"—for, as in *Gardner–Denver,* "the arbitration was limited to determining the plaintiff's rights under a collective bargaining agreement." On the other hand,

- "if the prior resolution was a settlement," the plaintiff can only recover if she can prove "discriminatory acts which occurred *after* the settlement"—for an employee "who freely settles her demand with the employer may not sue on the same cause of action later merely because she grows dissatisfied with the payment for which she settled."

For purposes of the motion to dismiss, the court accepted the plaintiff's characterization of the earlier resolution as "an arbitration award," and denied the motion to dismiss. Tang v. State of Rhode Island Department of Elderly Affairs, 904 F.Supp. 69 (D.R.I.1995).

Armendariz v. Foundation Health Psychcare Services, Inc.

Supreme Court of California, 2000.
24 Cal.4th 83, 99 Cal.Rptr.2d 745, 6 P.3d 669.

■ MOSK, J.

* * *

I. STATEMENT OF FACTS AND PROCEDURAL ISSUES

Marybeth Armendariz and Dolores Olague–Rodgers (hereafter the employees) filed a complaint for wrongful termination against their former employer, Foundation Health Psychcare Services, Inc. (hereafter the employer). * * * In July and August of 1995, the employer hired the employees in the "Provider Relations Group" and they were later given supervisory positions with annual salaries of $38,000. On June 20, 1996, they were informed that their positions were "being eliminated" and that they were "being terminated." During their year of employment, they claim that their supervisors and coworkers engaged in sexually based harassment and discrimination. The employees alleged that they were "terminated ... because of their perceived and/or actual sexual orientation (heterosexual)."

Both employees had filled out and signed employment application forms, which included an arbitration clause pertaining to any future claim of wrongful termination. Later, they executed a separate employment arbitration agreement, containing the same arbitration clause. The clause states in full: "I agree as a condition of my employment, that in the event my employment is terminated, and I contend that such termination was wrongful or otherwise in violation of the conditions of employment or was in violation of any express or implied condition, term or covenant of employment, whether founded in fact or in law, including but not limited to the covenant of good faith and fair dealing, or otherwise in violation of any of my rights, I and Employer agree to submit any such matter to binding arbitration * * * . I and Employer further expressly agree that in any such arbitration, my exclusive remedies for violation of the terms, conditions or covenants of employment shall be limited to a sum equal to the wages I would have earned from the date of any discharge until the date of the arbitration award. I understand that I shall not be entitled to any other remedy, at law or in equity, including but not limited to reinstatement and/or injunctive relief."

The employees' complaint against the employer alleges a cause of action for violation of the [California Fair Employment and Housing Act, Gov. Code § 12900 (FEHA)] and three additional causes of action for wrongful termination based on tort and contract theories of recovery. The complaint sought general damages, punitive damages, injunctive relief, and the recovery of attorney fees and costs of suit.

The employer countered by filing a motion for an order to compel arbitration * * *. [T]he trial court denied the motion on the ground that the arbitration provision in question was an unconscionable contract, * * * [finding] that several of the provisions of the contract are "so one-sided as to shock the conscience." * * *

After the employer filed a timely appeal, the Court of Appeal reversed. * * * We granted review.

II. DISCUSSION

* * *

C. Arbitration of FEHA Claims

The United States Supreme Court's dictum that a party in agreeing to arbitrate a statutory claim, "does not forgo the substantive rights afforded by the statute but only submits to their resolution in an arbitral ... forum" (*Mitsubishi Motors Corp.*, 473 U.S. at p. 628) is as much prescriptive as it is descriptive. That is, it sets a standard by which arbitration agreements and practices are to be measured, and disallows forms of arbitration that in fact compel claimants to forfeit certain substantive statutory rights.

Of course, certain statutory rights can be waived. But arbitration agreements that encompass unwaivable statutory rights must be subject to particular scrutiny. This unwaivability derives from two statutes that are themselves derived from public policy. First, Civil Code section 1668 states: "All contracts which have for their object, directly or indirectly, to exempt anyone from responsibility for his own fraud, or willful injury to the person or property of another, or violation of law, whether willful or negligent, are against the policy of the law." "Agreements whose object, directly or indirectly, is to exempt [their] parties from violation of the law are against public policy and may not be enforced." Second, Civil Code section 3513 states, "Anyone may waive the advantage of a law intended solely for his benefit. But a law established for a public reason cannot be contravened by a private agreement."

There is no question that the statutory rights established by the FEHA are "for a public reason." * * * As we stated in [Rojo v. Kliger, 276 Cal. Rptr. 130 (1990)]: "The public policy against sex discrimination and sexual harassment in employment, moreover, is plainly one that inures to the benefit of the public at large rather than to a particular employer or employee. No extensive discussion is needed to establish the fundamental public interest in a workplace free from the pernicious influence of sexism. So long as it exists, we are all demeaned." It is indisputable that an employment contract that required employees to waive their rights under the FEHA to redress sexual harassment or discrimination would be contrary to public policy and unlawful.

In light of these principles, it is evident that an arbitration agreement cannot be made to serve as a vehicle for the waiver of statutory rights created by the FEHA. * * *

The employees argue that arbitration contains a number of shortcomings that will prevent the vindication of their rights under the FEHA. In determining whether arbitration is considered an adequate forum for securing an employee's rights under FEHA, we begin with the extensive discussion of this question in Cole v. Burns Intern. Security Services, 105 F.3d 1465 (*Cole*), in the context of Title VII claims. In that case, the employee, a security guard, filed Title VII claims against his former employer alleging racial discrimination and harassment. He had signed an arbitration form committing himself to arbitrate such claims.

The court began its analysis by acknowledging the difficulties inherent in arbitrating employees' statutory rights, difficulties not present in arbitrating disputes arising from employee rights under collective bargaining agreements. "The reasons for this hesitation to extend arbitral jurisprudence from the collective bargaining context are well-founded. The fundamental distinction between contractual rights, which are created, defined, and subject to modification by the same private parties participating in arbitration, and statutory rights, which are created, defined, and subject to modification only by Congress and the courts, suggests the need for a public, rather than private, mechanism of enforcement for statutory rights." Although *Gilmer* had held that statutory employment rights outside of the collective bargaining context are arbitrable, the *Cole* court recognized that *Gilmer*, both explicitly and implicitly, placed limits on the arbitration of such rights. "Obviously, *Gilmer* cannot be read as holding that an arbitration agreement is enforceable no matter what rights it waives or what burdens it imposes. Such a holding would be fundamentally at odds with our understanding of the rights accorded to persons protected by public statutes like the ADEA and Title VII. The beneficiaries of public statutes are entitled to the rights and protections provided by the law."

* * *

Based on *Gilmer*, and on the basic principle of nonwaivability of statutory civil rights in the workplace, the *Cole* court formulated five minimum requirements for the lawful arbitration of such rights pursuant to a mandatory employment arbitration agreement. Such an arbitration agreement is lawful if it "(1) provides for neutral arbitrators, (2) provides for more than minimal discovery, (3) requires a written award, (4) provides for all of the types of relief that would otherwise be available in court, and (5) does not require employees to pay either unreasonable costs or any arbitrators' fees or expenses as a condition of access to the arbitration forum. Thus, an employee who is made to use arbitration as a condition of employment effectively may vindicate [his or her] statutory cause of action in the arbitral forum."

Except for the neutral-arbitrator requirement, which we have held is essential to ensuring the integrity of the arbitration process and is not at issue in this case, the employees claim that the present arbitration agreement fails to measure up to the Cole requirements enumerated above. We consider below the validity of those requirements and whether they are met by the employer's arbitration agreement.[8]

1. Limitation of Remedies

The principle that an arbitration agreement may not limit statutorily imposed remedies such as punitive damages and attorney fees appears to be undisputed.

* * *

The employer does not contest that the damages limitation would be unlawful if applied to statutory claims, but instead contends that the limitation applies only to contract claims, pointing to the language in the penultimate sentence that refers to "my exclusive remedy for violation of the terms, conditions or covenants of employment.... " Both the trial court and the Court of Appeal correctly rejected this interpretation. While the above quoted language is susceptible to the employer's interpretation, the final sentence—"I understand that I shall not be entitled to any other remedy.... "—makes clear that the damages limitation was all-encompassing. We conclude this damages limitation is contrary to public policy and unlawful.

2. Adequate Discovery

The employees argue that employers typically have in their possession many of the documents relevant for bringing an employment discrimina-

---

8. We emphasize at the outset that our general endorsement of the Cole requirements occurs in the particular context of mandatory employment arbitration agreements, in order to ensure that such agreements are not used as a means of effectively curtailing an employee's FEHA rights. These requirements would generally not apply in situations in which an employer and an employee knowingly and voluntarily enter into an arbitration agreement after a dispute has arisen. In those cases, employees are free to determine what trade-offs between arbitral efficiency and formal procedural protections best safeguard their statutory rights. Absent such freely negotiated agreements, it is for the courts to ensure that the arbitration forum imposed on an employee is sufficient to vindicate his or her rights under the FEHA.

tion case, as well as having in their employ many of the relevant witnesses. The denial of adequate discovery in arbitration proceedings leads to the de facto frustration of the employee's statutory rights. They cite a report by the Department of Labor's Commission on the Future of Worker–Management Relations, chaired by former Secretary of Labor John Dunlop and including employee and employer representatives, which concludes that "if private arbitration is to serve as a legitimate form of private enforcement of public employment law," it must among other things provide "a fair and simple method by which the employee can secure the necessary information to present his or her claim." (Com. on the Future of Worker–Management Relations, Reported Recommendations (1994) p. 31 (hereafter Dunlop Commission Report).)

We agree that adequate discovery is indispensable for the vindication of FEHA claims. The employer does not dispute the point, but contends that the arbitration agreement at issue in this case does provide for adequate discovery by incorporating by reference all the rules set forth in the CAA. Adequate provisions for discovery are set forth in the CAA at Code of Civil Procedure section 1283.05, subdivision (a).[10]

The employees point out that the provisions of Code of Civil Procedure section 1283.05 are only "conclusively deemed to be incorporated into" an agreement to arbitrate under section 1283.1 if the dispute arises "out of ... any injury to, or death of, a person caused by the wrongful act or neglect of another", and argue that this language does not apply to FEHA claims. They further argue that because adequate discovery is not guaranteed under the arbitration agreement, FEHA claims should not be deemed arbitrable.

We note that one Court of Appeal case has held that a FEHA sexual harassment claim is considered an "injury to ... a person" within the meaning of Code of Civil Procedure section 1283.1, subdivision (a). * * * The scope of this provision is not before us. But even assuming that the claim in this case is not the sort of injury encompassed by section 1283.1, subdivision (a), subdivision (b) of that section permits parties to agree to incorporate section 1283.05. We infer from subdivision (b), and from the fundamentally contractual nature of arbitration itself, that parties incorporating the CAA into their arbitration agreement are also permitted to agree to something less than the full panoply of discovery provided in section

---

10. Code of Civil Procedure section 1283.05, subdivision (a), states: "To the extent provided in Section 1283.1 depositions may be taken and discovery obtained in arbitration proceedings as follows:

(a) After the appointment of the arbitrator or arbitrators, the parties to the arbitration shall have the right to take depositions and to obtain discovery regarding the subject matter of the arbitration, and, to that end, to use and exercise all of the same rights, remedies, and procedures, and be subject to all of the same duties, liabilities, and obligations in the arbitration with respect to the subject matter thereof, * * * as if the subject matter of the arbitration were pending before a superior court of this state in a civil action other than a limited civil case, subject to the limitations as to depositions set forth in subdivision (e) of this section." Subdivision (e) states that depositions may only be taken with the approval of the arbitrator.

1283.05. We further infer that when parties agree to arbitrate statutory claims, they also implicitly agree, absent express language to the contrary, to such procedures as are necessary to vindicate that claim. As discussed above, it is undisputed that some discovery is often necessary for vindicating a FEHA claim. Accordingly, whether or not the employees in this case are entitled to the full range of discovery provided in Code of Civil Procedure section 1283.05, they are at least entitled to discovery sufficient to adequately arbitrate their statutory claim, including access to essential documents and witnesses, as determined by the arbitrator(s) * * *.[11]

Therefore, although the employees are correct that they are entitled to sufficient discovery as a means of vindicating their sexual discrimination claims, we hold that the employer, by agreeing to arbitrate the FEHA claim, has already impliedly consented to such discovery. Therefore, lack of discovery is not grounds for holding a FEHA claim inarbitrable.

3. Written Arbitration Award and Judicial Review

The employees argue that lack of judicial review of arbitration awards makes the vindication of FEHA rights in arbitration illusory. * * * Arbitration, they argue, cannot be an adequate means of resolving a FEHA claim if the arbitrator is essentially free to disregard the law.

* * *

We are not faced in this case with a petition to confirm an arbitration award, and therefore have no occasion to articulate precisely what standard of judicial review is "sufficient to ensure that arbitrators comply with the requirements of [a] statute." (*McMahon*, 482 U.S. at p. 232.) All we hold today is that in order for such judicial review to be successfully accomplished, an arbitrator in a FEHA case must issue a written arbitration decision that will reveal, however briefly, the essential findings and conclusions on which the award is based. While such written findings and conclusions are not required under the CAA, nothing in the present arbitration agreement precludes such written findings, and to the extent it applies to FEHA claims the agreement must be interpreted to provide for such findings. In all other respects, the employees' claim that they are unable to vindicate their FEHA rights because of inadequate judicial review of an arbitration award is premature.

4. Employee Not to Pay Unreasonable Costs and Arbitration Fees

The employees point to the fact that the agreement is governed by Code of Civil Procedure section 1284.2, which provides that "each party to the arbitration shall pay his pro rata share of the expenses and fees of the neutral arbitrator, together with other expenses of the arbitration incurred

---

11. We recognize, of course, that a limitation on discovery is one important component of the "simplicity, informality and expedition of arbitration." (Gilmer, 500 U.S. at p. 31.) The arbitrator and reviewing court must balance this desirable simplicity with the requirements of the FEHA in determining the appropriate discovery, absent more specific statutory or contractual provisions.

or imposed by the neutral arbitrator.'' They argue that requiring them to share the often substantial costs of arbitrators and arbitration effectively prevents them from vindicating their FEHA rights.

In considering the employees' claim, we start with the extensive discussion of this issue in *Cole*. The *Cole* court held that it was unlawful to require an employee who is the subject of a mandatory employment arbitration agreement to have to pay the costs of arbitration. The issue in that case was an arbitration agreement that was to be governed by the rules of the American Arbitration Association (AAA). Under these rules, the court noted that the employee may well be obliged to pay arbitrators' fees ranging from $500 to $1,000 per day or more, a $500 filing fee, and administrative fees of $150 per day, in addition to room rental and court reporter fees. The court's reasons for requiring employer-financed arbitration are worth quoting at length:

> In *Gilmer* the Supreme Court endorsed a system of arbitration in which employees are not required to pay for the arbitrator assigned to hear their statutory claims. There is no reason to think that the Court would have approved arbitration in the absence of this arrangement. Indeed, we are unaware of any situation in American jurisprudence in which a beneficiary of a federal statute has been required to pay for the services of the judge assigned to hear her or his case. Under *Gilmer*, arbitration is supposed to be a reasonable substitute for a judicial forum. Therefore, it would undermine Congress's intent to prevent employees who are seeking to vindicate statutory rights from gaining access to a judicial forum and then require them to pay for the services of an arbitrator when they would never be required to pay for a judge in court.

> There is no doubt that parties appearing in federal court may be required to assume the cost of filing fees and other administrative expenses, so any reasonable costs of this sort that accompany arbitration are not problematic. However, if an employee like Cole is required to pay arbitrators' fees ranging from $500 to $1,000 per day or more, . . . in addition to administrative and attorney's fees, is it likely that he will be able to pursue his statutory claims? We think not. * * * [I]t is unacceptable to require Cole to pay arbitrators' fees, because such fees are unlike anything that he would have to pay to pursue his statutory claims in court.

> Arbitration will occur in this case only because it has been mandated by the employer as a condition of employment. Absent this requirement, the employee would be free to pursue his claims in court without having to pay for the services of a judge. In such a circumstance— where arbitration has been imposed by the employer and occurs only at the option of the employer—arbitrators' fees should be borne solely by the employer.

The Tenth and Eleventh Circuit Courts of Appeal have adopted a position on arbitration fees for statutory employment claims essentially in accord with *Cole*. In Shankle [v. B–G Maintenance Management of Colorado, Inc., 163 F.3d 1230, (10th Cir.1999)], the court estimated that the employee would have to pay between $1,875 and $5,000 in forum costs to resolve his claim. As the court stated: "Mr. Shankle could not afford such a fee, and it is unlikely other similarly situated employees could either. The Agreement thus placed Mr. Shankle between the proverbial rock and a hard place—it prohibited use of the judicial forum, where a litigant is not required to pay for a judge's services, and the prohibitive cost substantially limited use of the arbitral forum. Essentially, B–G Maintenance required Mr. Shankle to agree to mandatory arbitration as a term of continued employment, yet failed to provide an accessible forum in which he could resolve his statutory rights. Such a result clearly undermines the remedial and deterrent functions of the federal anti-discrimination laws."

* * *

[I]f it is possible that the employee will be charged substantial forum costs, it is an insufficient judicial response to hold that he or she may be able to cancel these costs at the end of the process through judicial review. Such a system still poses a significant risk that employees will have to bear large costs to vindicate their statutory right against workplace discrimination, and therefore chills the exercise of that right. Because we conclude the imposition of substantial forum fees is contrary to public policy, and is therefore grounds for invalidating or "revoking" an arbitration agreement and denying a petition to compel arbitration, * * * we hold that the cost issues should be resolved not at the judicial review stage but when a court is petitioned to compel arbitration.

Accordingly, consistent with the majority of jurisdictions to consider this issue, we conclude that when an employer imposes mandatory arbitration as a condition of employment, the arbitration agreement or arbitration process cannot generally require the employee to bear any type of expense that the employee would not be required to bear if he or she were free to bring the action in court. This rule will ensure that employees bringing FEHA claims will not be deterred by costs greater than the usual costs incurred during litigation, costs that are essentially imposed on an employee by the employer.

[Several] objections have been raised to imposing the forum costs of arbitration on the employer. The first is that such a system will compromise the neutrality of the arbitrator. As the *Cole* court recognized, however, it is not the fact that the employer may pay an arbitrator that is most likely to induce bias, but rather the fact that the employer is a "repeat player" in the arbitration system who is more likely to be a source of business for the arbitrator. Furthermore, as the *Cole* court recognized, there are sufficient institutional safeguards, such as scrutiny by the plaintiff's bar and appointing agencies like the AAA, to protect against corrupt arbitrators.

The second objection is that although employees may have large forum costs, the cost of arbitration is generally smaller than litigation, so that the employee will realize a net benefit from arbitration. Although it is true that the costs of arbitration is on average smaller than that of litigation, it is also true that amount awarded is on average smaller as well. The payment of large, fixed, forum costs, especially in the face of expected meager awards, serves as a significant deterrent to the pursuit of FEHA claims.

To be sure, it would be ideal to devise a method by which the employee is put in exactly the same position in arbitration, costwise, as he or she would be in litigation. But the factors going into that calculus refuse to admit ready quantification. Turning a motion to compel arbitration into a mini-trial on the comparative costs and benefits of arbitration and litigation for a particular employee would not only be burdensome on the trial court and the parties, but would likely yield speculative answers. Nor would there be an advantage to apportioning arbitration costs at the conclusion of the arbitration rather than at the outset. Without clearly articulated guidelines, such a post arbitration apportionment would create a sense of risk and uncertainty among employees that could discourage the arbitration of meritorious claims.

Moreover, the above rule is fair, inasmuch as it places the cost of arbitration on the party that imposes it. Unlike the employee, the employer is in a position to perform a cost/benefit calculus and decide whether arbitration is, overall, the most economical forum. Nor would this rule necessarily present an employer with a choice between paying all the forum costs of arbitration or forgoing arbitration altogether and defending itself in court. There is a third alternative. Because this proposed rule would only apply to mandatory, predispute employment arbitration agreements, and because in many instances arbitration will be considered an efficient means of resolving a dispute both for the employer and the employee, the employer seeking to avoid both payment of all forum costs and litigation can attempt to negotiate postdispute arbitration agreements with its aggrieved employees.

* * *

We therefore hold that a mandatory employment arbitration agreement that contains within its scope the arbitration of FEHA claims impliedly obliges the employer to pay all types of costs that are unique to arbitration. Accordingly, we interpret the arbitration agreement in the present case as providing, consistent with the above, that the employer must bear the arbitration forum costs. The absence of specific provisions on arbitration costs would therefore not be grounds for denying the enforcement of an arbitration agreement.

D. Unconscionability of the Arbitration Agreement

1. General Principles of Unconscionability

In the previous section of this opinion, we focused on the minimum requirements for the arbitration of unwaivable statutory claims. In this section, we will consider objections to arbitration that apply more generally to any type of arbitration imposed on the employee by the employer as a condition of employment, regardless of the type of claim being arbitrated. These objections fall under the rubric of "unconscionability."

We explained the judicially created doctrine of unconscionability in [*Graham v. Scissor–Tail,* see p. 104 supra]. Unconscionability analysis begins with an inquiry into whether the contract is one of adhesion. "The term [contract of adhesion] signifies a standardized contract, which, imposed and drafted by the party of superior bargaining strength, relegates to the subscribing party only the opportunity to adhere to the contract or reject it." If the contract is adhesive, the court must then determine whether "other factors are present which, under established legal rules—legislative or judicial—operate to render it [unenforceable]." "Generally speaking, there are two judicially imposed limitations on the enforcement of adhesion contracts or provisions thereof. The first is that such a contract or provision which does not fall within the reasonable expectations of the weaker or 'adhering' party will not be enforced against him. The second—a principle of equity applicable to all contracts generally—is that a contract or provision, even if consistent with the reasonable expectations of the parties, will be denied enforcement if, considered in its context, it is unduly oppressive or 'unconscionable.' " * * *

Because unconscionability is a reason for refusing to enforce contracts generally, it is also a valid reason for refusing to enforce an arbitration agreement under Code of Civil Procedure section 1281, which, as noted, provides that arbitration agreements are "valid, irrevocable, and enforceable, save upon such grounds as exist at law or in equity for the revocation of any contract." The United States Supreme Court, in interpreting the same language found in section 2 of the FAA, recognized that "generally applicable contract defenses, such as fraud, duress, or unconscionability, may be applied to invalidate arbitration agreements...."

"[U]nconscionability has both a 'procedural' and a 'substantive' element," the former focusing on "oppression" or "surprise" due to unequal bargaining power, the latter on "overly harsh" or "one-sided" results. "The prevailing view is that [procedural and substantive unconscionability] must both be present in order for a court to exercise its discretion to refuse to enforce a contract or clause under the doctrine of unconscionability." But they need not be present in the same degree. "Essentially a sliding scale is invoked which disregards the regularity of the procedural process of the contract formation, that creates the terms, in proportion to the greater harshness or unreasonableness of the substantive terms themselves." In other words, the more substantively oppressive the contract term, the less evidence of procedural unconscionability is required to come to the conclusion that the term is unenforceable, and vice versa.

2. Unconscionability and Mandatory Employment Arbitration

Applying the above principles to this case, we first determine whether the arbitration agreement is adhesive. There is little dispute that it is. It was imposed on employees as a condition of employment and there was no opportunity to negotiate.

* * *

Aside from FEHA issues discussed in the previous part of this opinion, the employees contend that the agreement is substantively unconscionable because it requires only employees to arbitrate their wrongful termination claims against the employer, but does not require the employer to arbitrate claims it may have against the employees. In asserting that this lack of mutuality is unconscionable, they rely primarily on the opinion of the Court of Appeal Stirlen v. Supercuts, Inc., 60 Cal. Rptr.2d 138 (Cal.App. 1997). The employee in that case was hired as a vice president and chief financial officer; his employment contract provided for arbitration "in the event there is any dispute arising out of [the employee's] employment with the Company," including "the termination of that employment." The agreement specifically excluded certain types of disputes from the scope of arbitration, including those relating to the protection of the employer's intellectual and other property and the enforcement of a post-employment covenant not to compete, which were to be litigated in state or federal court. The employee was to waive the right to challenge the jurisdiction of such a court. The arbitration agreement further provided that the damages available would be limited to "the amount of actual damages for breach of contract, less any proper offset for mitigation of such damages." When an arbitration claim was filed, payments of any salary or benefits were to cease "without penalty to the Company," pending the outcome of the arbitration.

The *Stirlen* court concluded that the agreement was one of adhesion, even though the employee in question was a high-level executive, because of the lack of opportunity to negotiate. The court then concluded that the arbitration agreement was substantively unconscionable. * * * The employee pursuing claims against the employer had to bear not only with the inherent shortcomings of arbitration—limited discovery, limited judicial review, limited procedural protections—but also significant damage limitations imposed by the arbitration agreement. The employer, on the other hand, in pursuing its claims, was not subject to these disadvantageous limitations and had written into the agreement special advantages, such as a waiver of jurisdictional objections by the employee if sued by the employer.

The *Stirlen* court did not hold that all lack of mutuality in a contract of adhesion was invalid. "We agree a contract can provide a 'margin of safety' that provides the party with superior bargaining strength a type of extra protection for which it has a legitimate commercial need without being unconscionable. However, unless the 'business realities' that create the special need for such an advantage are explained in the contract itself, which is not the case here, it must be factually established." The *Stirlen* court found no "business reality" to justify the lack of mutuality, concluding that the terms of the arbitration clause were " 'so extreme as to appear unconscionable according to the mores and business practices of the time and place.' "

* * *

We conclude that *Stirlen* [is] correct in requiring this "modicum of bilaterality" in an arbitration agreement. Given the disadvantages that may exist for plaintiffs arbitrating disputes, it is unfairly one-sided for an employer with superior bargaining power to impose arbitration on the employee as plaintiff but not to accept such limitations when it seeks to prosecute a claim against the employee, without at least some reasonable justification for such one-sidedness based on "business realities." As has been recognized unconscionability turns not only on a "one-sided" result, but also on an absence of "justification" for it. If the arbitration system established by the employer is indeed fair, then the employer as well as the employee should be willing to submit claims to arbitration. Without reasonable justification for this lack of mutuality, arbitration appears less as a forum for neutral dispute resolution and more as a means of maximizing employer advantage. Arbitration was not intended for this purpose.

The employer cites a number of cases that have held that a lack of mutuality in an arbitration agreement does not render the contract illusory as long as the employer agrees to be bound by the arbitration of employment disputes. We agree that such lack of mutuality does not render the contract illusory, i.e., lacking in mutual consideration. We conclude, rather, that in the context of an arbitration agreement imposed by the employer on the employee, such a one-sided term is unconscionable. Although parties are free to contract for asymmetrical remedies and arbitration clauses of varying scope, *Stirlen* [is] correct that the doctrine of unconscionability limits the extent to which a stronger party may, through a contract of adhesion, impose the arbitration forum on the weaker party without accepting that forum for itself.

* * *

Applying these principles to the present case, we note the arbitration agreement was limited in scope to employee claims regarding wrongful termination. Although it did not expressly authorize litigation of the employer's claims against the employee, as was the case in *Stirlen*, such was the clear implication of the agreement. Obviously, the lack of mutuality can be manifested as much by what the agreement does not provide as by what it does.

This is not to say that an arbitration clause must mandate the arbitration of all claims between employer and employee in order to avoid invalidation on grounds of unconscionability. Indeed, as the employer points out, the present arbitration agreement does not require arbitration of all conceivable claims that an employee might have against an employer, only wrongful termination claims. But an arbitration agreement imposed in an adhesive context lacks basic fairness and mutuality if it requires one contracting party, but not the other, to arbitrate all claims arising out of the same transaction or occurrence or series of transactions or occurrences.

The arbitration agreement in this case lacks mutuality in this sense because it requires the arbitration of employee—but not employer—claims arising out of a wrongful termination. An employee terminated for stealing trade secrets, for example, must arbitrate his or her wrongful termination claim under the agreement while the employer has no corresponding obligation to arbitrate its trade secrets claim against the employee.

The unconscionable one-sidedness of the arbitration agreement is compounded in this case by the fact that it does not permit the full recovery of damages for employees, while placing no such restriction on the employer. Even if the limitation on FEHA damages is severed as contrary to public policy, the arbitration clause in the present case still does not permit full recovery of ordinary contract damages. The arbitration agreement specifies that damages are to be limited to the amount of back pay lost up until the time of arbitration. This provision excludes damages for prospective future earnings, so-called "front pay," a common and often substantial component of contractual damages in a wrongful termination case. The employer, on the other hand, is bound by no comparable limitation should it pursue a claim against its employees.

The employer in this case, as well as the Court of Appeal, claim the lack of mutuality was based on the realities of the employees' place in the organizational hierarchy. As the Court of Appeal stated: "We . . . observe that the wording of the agreement most likely resulted from the employees' position within the organization and may reflect the fact that the parties did not foresee the possibility of any dispute arising from employment that was not initiated by the employee. Plaintiffs were lower-level supervisory employees, without the sort of access to proprietary information or control over corporate finances that might lead to an employer suit against them."

The fact that it is unlikely an employer will bring claims against a particular type of employee is not, ultimately, a justification for a unilateral arbitration agreement. It provides no reason for categorically exempting employer claims, however rare, from mandatory arbitration. Although an employer may be able, in a future case, to justify a unilateral arbitration agreement, the employer in the present case has not done so.

E. Severability of Unconscionable Provisions

The employees contend that the presence of various unconscionable provisions or provisions contrary to public policy leads to the conclusion that the arbitration agreement as a whole cannot be enforced. The employer contends that, insofar as there are unconscionable provisions, they should be severed and the rest of the agreement enforced.

Civil Code section 1670.5, subdivision (a) provides that "if the court as a matter of law finds the contract or any clause of the contract to have been unconscionable at the time it was made the court may refuse to enforce the contract, or it may enforce the remainder of the contract without the unconscionable clause, or it may so limit the application of any unconscionable clause as to avoid any unconscionable result." Comment 2 of the Legislative Committee Comment on section 1670.5, incorporating the comments from the Uniform Commercial Code, states: "Under this section the court, in its discretion, may refuse to enforce the contract as a whole if it is permeated by the unconscionability, or it may strike any single clause or group of clauses which are so tainted or which are contrary to the essential purpose of the agreement, or it may simply limit unconscionable clauses so as to avoid unconscionable results."

Thus, the statute appears to give a trial court some discretion as to whether to sever or restrict the unconscionable provision or whether to refuse to enforce the entire agreement. But it also appears to contemplate the latter course only when an agreement is "permeated" by unconscionability.

* * *

Two reasons for severing or restricting illegal terms rather than voiding the entire contract appear implicit in case law. The first is to prevent parties from gaining undeserved benefit or suffering undeserved detriment as a result of voiding the entire agreement—particularly when there has been full or partial performance of the contract. Second, more generally, the doctrine of severance attempts to conserve a contractual relationship if to do so would not be condoning an illegal scheme. The overarching inquiry is whether "the interests of justice ... would be furthered" by severance. Moreover, courts must have the capacity to cure the unlawful contract through severance or restriction of the offending clause, which, as discussed below, is not invariably the case.

* * *

In this case, two factors weigh against severance of the unlawful provisions. First, the arbitration agreement contains more than one unlawful provision; it has both an unlawful damages provision and an unconscionably unilateral arbitration clause. Such multiple defects indicate a systematic effort to impose arbitration on an employee not simply as an alternative to litigation, but as an inferior forum that works to the employer's advantage. In other words, given the multiple unlawful provisions, the trial court did not abuse its discretion in concluding that the arbitration agreement is permeated by an unlawful purpose.[13]

13. We need not decide whether the unlawful damages provision in this arbitration agreement, by itself, would be sufficient to warrant a court's refusal to enforce that agreement. We note, however, that in the analogous case of overly broad covenants not to compete, courts have tended to invalidate rather than restrict such covenants when it appears they were drafted in bad faith, i.e., with a knowledge of their illegality. The reason for this rule is that if such bad faith restrictive covenants are enforced, then "employers are encouraged to overreach; if the covenant is overbroad then the court will redraft it for them." This reasoning applies with equal force to arbitration agreements that limit damages to be obtained from challenging the violation of unwaivable statutory rights. An employer will not be deterred from routinely inserting such a deliberately illegal clause into the arbitration agreements it mandates for its employees if it knows that the worst penalty for such illegality is the severance of the clause after the employee has litigated the matter. In that sense, the enforcement of a form arbitration agreement containing such a clause drafted in bad faith would be condoning, or at least not discour-

Second, in the case of the agreement's lack of mutuality, such permeation is indicated by the fact that there is no single provision a court can strike or restrict in order to remove the unconscionable taint from the agreement. Rather, the court would have to, in effect, reform the contract, not through severance or restriction, but by augmenting it with additional terms. * * * Code of Civil Procedure section 1281.2 authorizes the court to refuse arbitration if grounds for revocation exist, not to reform the agreement to make it lawful. Nor do courts have any such power under their inherent, limited authority to reform contracts. (See Kolani v. Gluska, 64 Cal. App. 4th 402, 407–408 (1998)) [power to reform limited to instances in which parties make mistakes, not to correct illegal provisions]. Because a court is unable to cure this unconscionability through severance or restriction, and is not permitted to cure it through reformation and augmentation, it must void the entire agreement.

* * *

The approach described above is consistent with our holding in *Scissor–Tail*. In that case, we found an arbitration agreement to be unconscionable because the agreement provided for an arbitrator likely to be biased in favor of the party imposing the agreement. We nonetheless recognized that "the parties have indeed agreed to arbitrate" and that there is a "strong public policy of this state in favor of resolving disputes by arbitration." The court found a way out of this dilemma through the [California Arbitration Act,] which provides in part: "In the absence of an agreed method [for appointing an arbitrator], or if the agreed method fails or for any reason cannot be followed, or when an arbitrator appointed fails to act and his or her successor has not been appointed, the court, on petition of a party to the arbitration agreement, shall appoint the arbitrator." Citing this provision, the court stated: "We therefore conclude that upon remand the trial court should afford the parties a reasonable opportunity to agree on a suitable arbitrator and, failing such agreement, the court should on petition of either party appoint the arbitrator." Other cases, both before and after *Scissor-Tail,* have also held that the part of an arbitration clause providing for a less-than-neutral arbitration forum is severable from the rest of the clause.

Thus, in *Scissor–Tail* and the other cases cited above, the arbitration statute itself gave the court the power to reform an arbitration agreement with respect to the method of selecting arbitrators. There is no comparable provision in the arbitration statute that permits courts to reform an unconscionably one-sided agreement.

* * *

aging, an illegal scheme, and severance would be disfavored unless it were for some other reason in the interests of justice. The refusal to enforce such a clause is also consistent with the rule that a party may waive its right to arbitration through bad faith or willful misconduct. Because we resolve this case on other grounds, we need not decide whether the state of the law with respect to damages limitations was sufficiently clear at the time the arbitration agreement was signed to lead to the conclusion that this damages clause was drafted in bad faith.

The employer also points to two cases in which unconscionably one-sided provisions in arbitration agreements were severed and the agreement enforced. [Saika v. Gold, 56 Cal. Rptr.2d 922 (Cal.App.1996)] involved an arbitration agreement with a provision that would make the arbitration nonbinding if the arbitration award were $25,000 or greater. In Beynon v. Garden Grove Medical Group [161 Cal. Rptr. 146 (Cal.App.1980)], a provision of the arbitration agreement gave one party, but not the other, the option of rejecting the arbitrator's decision. The courts in both instances concluded, in *Saika* implicitly, in *Beynon* explicitly, that the offending clause was severable from the rest of the arbitration agreement.

The provisions in these two cases are different from the one-sided arbitration provision at issue in this case in at least two important respects. First, the one-sidedness in the above two cases were confined to single provisions regarding the rights of the parties after an arbitration award was made, not a provision affecting the scope of the arbitration. As such, the unconscionability could be cured by severing the unlawful provisions. Second, in both cases, the arguments against severance were made by the party that had imposed the unconscionable provision in order to prevent enforcement of an arbitration award against them, and the failure to sever would have had the effect of accomplishing the precise unlawful purpose of that provision the invalidation of the arbitration award. As discussed, courts will generally sever illegal provisions and enforce a contract when nonenforcement will lead to an undeserved benefit or detriment to one of the parties that would not further the interests of justice. In *Beynon* and *Saika*, the interests of justice would obviously not have been furthered by nonenforcement. The same considerations are not found in the present case.

The judgment of the Court of Appeal upholding the employer's petition to compel arbitration is reversed, and the cause is remanded to the Court of Appeal with directions to affirm the judgment of the trial court.

■ BROWN, J., CONCURRING. Although I agree with most of the majority's reasoning, I write separately on the issue of apportioning arbitral costs. The majority takes the simple approach: where the employer imposes mandatory arbitration and the employee asserts a statutory claim, the employer must bear all costs "unique to arbitration." Simplicity, however, is not a proxy for correctness. * * *

In adopting the bright-line approach advocated by *Cole,* supra, the majority argues that the mere risk that an employee may have to bear certain arbitral costs necessarily "chills the exercise" of her statutory rights. Thus, arbitration is not a reasonable substitute for a court if arbitral costs, such as the arbitrator's fees, may be imposed on the employee. The majority, however, assumes too much. "Arbitration is often far more affordable to plaintiffs and defendants alike than is pursuing a claim in court." Because employees may incur fewer costs and attorney fees in arbitration than in court, the potential imposition of arbitration forum costs does not automatically render the arbitral forum more expensive than—and therefore inferior to—the judicial forum.

The majority's approach also ignores the unique circumstances of each case. Not all arbitrations are costly, and not all employees are unable to afford the unique costs of arbitration. Thus, the imposition of some arbitral costs does not deter or discourage employees from pursuing their statutory claims in every case. (See, e.g., Williams v. Cigna Financial Advisors Inc.,197 F.3d 752, 764–765 (5th Cir.1999) [compelling arbitration because the employee did not show that he was unable to pay the arbitral costs or that these costs would deter him from pursuing his claims]; McCaskill v. SCI Management Corp., 2000 WL 875396 (N.D.Ill.) [compelling arbitration because there was no evidence that the costs of arbitration would be prohibitively expensive for the employee]). Indeed, the uniqueness of each case makes it impossible for any court to "conclude that the payment of fees will constitute a barrier to the vindication of . . . statutory rights" without knowing the exact amount the employee must pay.

Accordingly, I would reject the majority's approach and follow the approach suggested by courts in several other jurisdictions. As long as the mandatory arbitration agreement does not require the employee to front the arbitration forum costs or to pay a certain share of these costs, apportionment should be left to the arbitrator. When apportioning costs, the arbitrator should consider the magnitude of the costs unique to arbitration, the ability of the employee to pay a share of these costs, and the overall expense of the arbitration as compared to a court proceeding. Ultimately, any apportionment should ensure that the costs imposed on the employee, if known at the onset of litigation, would not have deterred her from enforcing her statutory rights or stopped her from effectively vindicating these rights.

If the employee feels that the arbitrator's apportionment of costs is unreasonable, then she can raise the issue during judicial review of the arbitration award. I believe such an approach is preferable because it accounts for the particular circumstances of each case without sacrificing the employee's statutory rights.

NOTES AND QUESTIONS

1. As the *Armendariz* case indicates, arbitration agreements are increasingly common in nonunion employment agreements outside of the securities industry. Companies like Rockwell International, Brown and Root, Borg–Warner, and Hughes Electronics are now requiring such clauses, which usually call for arbitration under the auspices of an organization like the AAA: The AAA estimates that six million employees are now covered by agreements that call for it to administer the arbitration of employment disputes. See Elizabeth Hill, Due Process at Low Cost: An Empirical Study of Employment Arbitration Under the Auspices of the American Arbitration Association, 18 Ohio St. J. on Disp. Res. 777, 780 (2003).

2. Does Justice Brown have the better of the argument when he urges that the issue of costs should be postponed, until such time as a court is asked to confirm or vacate the award? This was in fact the approach of the

United States Supreme Court in a recent non-employment case, Green Tree Financial Corp.-Alabama v. Randolph, 531 U.S. 79 (2000). Here a buyer of a mobile home had financed the purchase, and later brought suit against the lender alleging violations of the Truth in Lending Act, 15 U.S.C. § 1601. The Eleventh Circuit held that the arbitration clause in the agreement was unenforceable: Since the agreement was silent with respect to the payment of filing fees and arbitrator compensation, there was a risk that the plaintiff's ability to assert her statutory rights under the TILA would be undone by "steep" arbitration costs. The Supreme Court reversed.

The Court acknowledged the possibility that "the existence of large arbitration costs could preclude a litigant such as [the plaintiff] from effectively vindicating her federal statutory rights in the arbitral forum." However, if a party seeks to invalidate an arbitration agreement on the ground that arbitration "would be prohibitively expensive," she must "bear the burden of showing the likelihood of incurring such costs." Here, the "risk" that the plaintiff "will be saddled with prohibitive costs is too speculative to justify the invalidation of an arbitration agreement," and the agreement's silence on the subject of costs "alone is plainly insufficient to render it unenforceable." Four dissenting justices would have preferred to remand for "clarification" and "further consideration of the accessibility of the arbitral forum" to the plaintiff, rather than "leaving the issue unsettled until the end of the line," that is, until after the arbitration. They noted that under the AAA's Consumer Arbitration Rules, consumers in small-claims arbitration incur no filing fee and are required to pay only $125 of the total fees charged by the arbitrator—but stressed that "there is no reliable indication in this record that [the plaintiff's] claim will be arbitrated under any consumer-protective fee arrangement."

3. In scores of cases following *Green Tree,* claimants have attempted to carry the burden imposed by the Supreme Court and show that the arbitration would be "prohibitively expensive" for them.

Obviously, substantial filing fees may affect the claimant's very access to the arbitral forum—at least to the extent that such fees are not advanced by the attorney-entrepreneur. Administrative fees and the compensation of the arbitrators may have precisely the same deterrent effect where the panel or the institution is prudent enough to require an advance deposit, see AAA, Commercial Arbitration Rules, R. 52 (AAA may require the parties to deposit "in advance of any hearings" such amounts as it deems necessary to cover the expenses of the arbitration, including the arbitrator's fee); Ting v. AT & T, 182 F.Supp.2d 902, 934 (N.D. Cal. 2002), aff'd, 319 F.3d 1126 (9th Cir.2003)(claimant's "potential cost before arbitration begins would be $5800"; "[t]he arbitrator's authority to alter the allocation of the costs of arbitration at the conclusion of he case does little to mitigate the cost of 'buying into' arbitration"). Does this call for an individualized inquiry into the claimant's particular financial condition? See Cooper v. MRM Investment Co., 367 F.3d 493, 512 (6th Cir. 2004)(courts will "regularly find arbitration costs too high to permit enforcement of a lower-or middle-income employee's duty to arbitrate," while finding that "high-level managerial employees and others with substantial means can afford the costs of arbitration"); Scovill v. WSYX/ABC, 425 F.3d 1012, 1021 (6th Cir. 2005)(although the plaintiff/employee had made nearly $100,000 a year, he had "recently lost his job, his future income is uncertain as he just began a business, he has children to support, and it does not appear as though he amassed a great savings to use in arbitration proceedings"); cf. Michael H. Leroy & Peter Feuille, When Is Cost An Unlawful Barrier to Alternative Dispute Resolution? The Ever Green Tree of Mandatory Employment Arbitration, 50 U.C.L.A. L.Rev. 143, 193 (2002)("the two leading appellate decisions that rejected cost arguments involved professional employees," whereas "in the three leading appellate decisions that responded favorably to employee cost arguments, the plaintiffs were a train station security guard, an airport security agent, and a janitorial supervisor").

But compare the court's warning in *Armendariz* that arbitration agreements may not "require the employee to bear *any type of expense* that the employee would not be required to bear if he or she were free to bring the action in court." Can we possibly be expected to take this literally? See, e.g., Ingle v. Circuit City Stores, Inc., 328 F.3d 1165, 1177 (9th Cir. 2003)(California law). Here a filing fee of $75 was held to be "substantively unconscionable" because it is "not the type of expense that the employee [would] be required to bear" in court: Since the fee was to be paid "directly to [the employer] rather than to the arbitration service," this meant that in effect "the employee is required to pay [the employer] for the privilege of bringing a complaint," which may well "deter employees from initiating complaints."

On the other hand, what of the case where an assessment of costs will abide the result, and be part of the ultimate award? In such cases, shouldn't we compare the relative burdens of arbitration and litigation on a "total cost" basis—thus taking into account all the legal costs of pre-trial and appellate practice that will be minimized by an alternative process that requires less "lawyering"? And mightn't we take account also of the possible impact that greater time and expense in litigation may have on the very availability of contingent-fee legal services? How can it be sensible to instead compare the *total costs of arbitration* merely with the *institutional costs of invoking the judicial system*? But for precisely such an approach, see Phillips v. Associates Home Equity Services, Inc., 179 F.Supp.2d 840, 846 (N.D. Ill. 2001)("the cost of pursuing arbitration" "is likely to be at least twelve times *what it currently costs to file a case in federal court*"). Cf. Morrison v. Circuit City Stores, Inc., 317 F.3d 646, 654–55 (6th Cir. 2003) (clause required employer to advance all arbitration costs, but—following issuance of the award—each party was to pay one-half of the costs of arbitration, unless the arbitrator used her discretionary power to impose all costs on the losing party; held, court should look to the possible "chilling effect" of this cost-splitting provision on "similarly situated potential litigants, as opposed to its effect merely on the actual plaintiff"; it should refuse to enforce the cost-splitting provision if it finds that the provision "would deter a substantial number" of such litigants).

4. The California Supreme Court has recently broadened the analysis in *Armendariz* to extend beyond the context of statutory rights, to include claims of wrongful discharge allegedly in violation of "public policy"—and thus "almost by definition unwaivable." But it has refused to extend the *Armendariz* holding to clauses that require an insured to share "the costs of arbitration and the arbitrators' fees" when the claim is against an insurance company for "breach of contract, pure and simple." Boghos v. Certain Underwriters at Lloyd's of London, 36 Cal.4th 495, 30 Cal.Rptr.3d 787, 115 P.3d 68 (2005)(noting, however, that the lower courts had not yet addressed the question whether the clause was "unenforceable under the general law of unconscionability," and suggesting that "considerations of judicial economy make it appropriate" to leave this question to them in the first instance).

5. An employee resists a motion to stay litigation on the ground that arbitration would be "prohibitively expensive" for her—and in response, the employer immediately offers to cover the cost of the process. Is the objection of expense therefore "obviated," "mooted," or "foreclosed"? Jung v. Association of American Medical Colleges, 300 F.Supp.2d 119, 149 (D.D.C. 2004); Large v. Conseco Finance Servicing Corp., 292 F.3d 49, 56–57 (1st Cir. 2002). Or does this come too late? Popovich v. McDonald's Corp., 189 F.Supp.2d 772, 779 (N.D. Ill. 2002)(this "amounts to an offer for a new contract," and "as a matter of elementary contract law," one party cannot "unilaterally modify the existing agreement").

6. Plaintiffs had bought a home that allegedly contained undisclosed structural defects, and brought suit against Affordable Inspection Service for negligence and breach of contract. Their contract with the inspection service provided that "the inspector's liability for mistakes or omissions in this inspection report is limited to a refund of the fee paid"; it also mandated arbitration through Construction Arbitration Services. The trial court denied a motion to compel arbitration, and the appellate court affirmed: The plaintiffs had paid only $169 for the inspection services, and CAS required a filing fee of $650: Therefore "the arbitration provision operates to deter a claimant from pursuing any claim under the contract and, therefore, we find that it is unenforceable." McDonough v. Thompson, 2004 WL 2847818 (Ohio App.). Is *McDonough* distinguishable from the cases in Note (3) above? Is the result justifiable?

7. On the subject of "non-mutual" arbitration clauses—where only one of the parties to the agreement is obligated to arbitrate—compare *Stevens/Leinweber/Sullens, Inc. v. Holm Development and Management, Inc.*, supra p. 96. Cf. Oblix, Inc. v. Winiecki, 374 F.3d 488, 491 (7th Cir. 2004)(Easterbrook, J.):

> That [the employer] did not promise to arbitrate all of its potential claims is neither here nor there. [The employee] does not deny that the arbitration clause is supported by consideration—her salary. [The employer] paid her to do a number of things; one of the things it paid

her to do was agree to non-judicial dispute resolution. It is hard to see how the arbitration clause is any more suspect, or any less enforceable, than the others—or for that matter, than her salary.

8. Note that in *Armendariz* the Supreme Court of California apparently assumed that it was *for a court—rather than for an arbitrator*—to determine whether the terms of the agreement were "unlawful" or "unconscionable." Cf. p. 94 supra; see also Margaret M. Harding, The Redefinition of Arbitration By Those With Superior Bargaining Power, 1999 Utah L. Rev. 857, 922–23 ("The claim that an arbitration clause is invalid because it improperly restricts statutory remedies should be distinguished from the situation where the parties in the container contract exclude certain types of damages"; "a defense to arbitration based on public policy stemming * * * from the unsuitability of the particular arbitral scheme crafted for determining the claim does indeed challenge the validity of the arbitration agreement and the arbitrability of the dispute"). Do you see the argument here? Do you agree? Cf. Rollins, Inc. v. Lighthouse Bay Holdings, Ltd., 898 So.2d 86 (Fla. App. 2005)("the adequacy of arbitration remedies has nothing to do with whether the parties agreed to arbitrate or if the claims are in the scope of the arbitration agreement," and so "whether an arbitration provision is unenforceable because it limits statutory remedies is for the arbitrator, not the trial court").

9. Assume, though, that this is indeed a question for the court: Does it follow that a judicial finding of "unconscionability" necessarily means that *the arbitration agreement as a whole* "is tainted and cannot be enforced"? See Harding, supra at 944 (courts should "penalize parties who attempt to use the arbitral process for improper means"; "[w]hen a party attempts to abuse the arbitral process and gets caught, that party should completely lose the privilege—gained only by its superior economic position—of requiring the weaker party to arbitrate"). Do you agree? See Graham Oil Co. v. ARCO Prods. Co., 43 F.3d 1244 (9th Cir. 1994). A distribution agreement between ARCO and a franchisee contained an arbitration clause barring the arbitrators from awarding punitive damages or attorneys' fees. After ARCO terminated the franchise, the distributor brought suit under the Petroleum Marketing Practices Act, 15 U.S.C. § 2801. The court held that the dealer was not required to submit to arbitration: The arbitration clause "contravenes the Act," which was enacted to protect franchisees of oil companies against arbitrary termination, and grants successful plaintiffs the right to punitive damages and attorneys' fees. Nor could the offending provisions be severed; instead, "the entire clause must be eliminated": "[T]he offensive provisions clearly represent an attempt by ARCO to achieve through arbitration what Congress has expressly forbidden," and such a "blatant misuse of the arbitration procedure serves to taint the entire clause." Dissenting, Judge Fernandez suggested that "the only reason [for the decision], subliminal as it is, may be that arbitration is [a] bad thing for companies" like the distributor.

Cf. Booker v. Robert Half Int'l, Inc., 413 F.3d 77 (D.C. Cir. 2005)(Roberts, J.), in which an employment agreement also barred the arbitrator from awarding punitive damages, but at the same time made the various provisions of the agreement "severable." The employee brought suit for racial discrimination under the D.C. Human Rights Act, and the employer moved to compel arbitration, although it conceded that the bar on punitive damages made the clause "unenforceable as written." In granting the motion, the court relied on the severability clause—and it also noted that to compel the employee to arbitrate with the offending clause severed would be "entirely consistent with the intent to arbitrate he manifested" in signing the agreement in the first place; he was after all allowed to arbitrate "under more favorable terms than those to which [he had originally] agreed." It is only when the "illegality pervades the arbitration agreement such that only a disintegrated fragment would remain after hacking away the unenforceable parts" that a court would be unlikely to sever the offending clauses.

10. On the "adequacy of discovery," compare Fitz v. NCR Corp., 118 Cal.App.4th 702, 13 Cal.Rptr.3d 88 (2004). Here an employer's dispute resolution policy for employees—known as "Addressing Concerns Together"—set forth a three-stage process ending in binding arbitration. The agreement provided that the employer and employee each had the right "to take the sworn deposition statements of two individuals" as well as of any expert witnesses; all documents to be used as exhibits were to be exchanged two weeks before the hearing; but "no other discovery (i.e., depositions or demands for documents/information) will be permitted unless the arbitrator finds a compelling need to allow it"; the arbitrator was to override the goal of "a prompt and inexpensive resolution to the dispute" only "if a fair hearing is impossible without additional discovery." The court held this provision to be unconscionable: "Given the complexity of employment disputes * * * it will be the unusual instance where the deposition of two witnesses will be sufficient to present a case." *Armendariz* was distinguishable in that the express language in the ACT policy was "contrary to [the Supreme Court's assumption in *Armendariz*] that where there is an agreement to arbitrate statutory claims, there is at the same time an 'implicit agreement' to procedures necessary to vindicate that claim."

Generally on discovery in arbitration, see Section D.2.d. below.

11. Once it is clear that asserted violations of statutory rights may now be sent to arbitration, is it inevitable that a more intensive judicial scrutiny of arbitral awards will follow? One distinguished labor arbitrator has warned that "[w]hen arbitrators start interpreting statutes * * * there is no reason why their interpretations of the proper application of statutes should be given greater weight than that of the district courts. District courts' interpretations of statutes are constantly being reviewed by appellate courts." Feller, Arbitration and the External Law Revisited, 37 St. Louis U.L.J. 973, 980 (1993).

See, e.g., Halligan v. Piper Jaffray, Inc., 148 F.3d 197 (2d Cir. 1998). Although a discharged employee had presented the arbitrators with "overwhelming evidence" of age-based discrimination, an NASD arbitration panel denied any relief in an award that contained no explanation or rationale. The Second Circuit held that the award should be vacated: An arbitration award may be vacated if it is in " 'manifest disregard' of the law," which requires findings both that the arbitrators "knew of a governing legal principle yet refused to apply it or ignored it altogether," and that the law was "well defined, explicit, and clearly applicable." "In view of the strong evidence that Halligan was fired because of his age and the agreement of the parties that the arbitrators were correctly advised of the applicable legal principles, we are inclined to hold that they ignored the law or the evidence or both." The court stressed that in making this decision, the arbitrators' failure to explain their award "can be taken into account." If the arbitrators had given as their rationale that they had simply believed the employer's witnesses rather than the employee's, "on this record it would have been extremely hard to accept—but they did not do even that." The court disclaimed any holding that arbitrators must write reasoned awards in every case or "even in most cases"—but it observed that "where a reviewing court is inclined to find that arbitrators manifestly disregarded the law or the evidence and that an explanation, if given, would have strained credulity, the absence of explanation may reinforce the reviewing court's confidence that the arbitrators engaged in manifest disregard."

Is it possible that too great an enthusiasm for arbitration in cases that touch on individual rights may create the danger of a "backlash" of hostility to the process generally?

12. The theoretical notion that an arbitration award could be overturned for "manifestly disregarding the law"—suggested by the court in *Halligan* and by many others—has always been in considerable tension with a view of arbitration as a "nonlegal" process—a model in which arbitrators are "free to ignore" substantive rules of law in order to "do justice as they see it." See pp. 17–19, 148–51 supra. As disputes over statutory rights are increasingly swept into arbitration, courts naturally come under increasing pressure to ensure that these rights are being adequately addressed. But cf. Alan Scott Rau, The Culture of American Arbitration and the Lessons of ADR, 40 Tex. Int'l L.J. 449, 509, 524–27 (2005)("the red herring of manifest disregard"):

> [F]or the moment the notion of "manifest disregard," as it has reemerged in cases like *Cole* and *Halligan,* has had a legacy quite as impoverished as that of the *Mitsubishi* Court's quixotic footnote 19. The echo has been faint indeed. * * * "Manifest disregard of the law" has been safely confined to those exceedingly rare instances where some egregious impropriety on the part of the arbitrators is apparent— but where none of the other provisions of the FAA can readily be made to fit. * * * [It may be] unacceptable hyperbole to say that [vacatur on this ground] "will never happen in our lifetimes," but * * * I will stand by Captain Corcoran's formulation in *Pinafore:* "Hardly ever."

More recently, the Seventh Circuit has attempted to put the doctrine of "manifest disregard" squarely in its place—by essentially equating it with the review of awards on grounds of "public policy," and suggesting that it is subject to the same limitations as "public policy" review. In George

Watts & Son, Inc. v. Tiffany & Co., 248 F.3d 577 (7th Cir.2001), an arbitrator granted relief to a distributor under the state's "Fair Dealership Law," but failed, allegedly in violation of the statute, to award attorneys' fees and costs. The court nevertheless upheld confirmation of the award: "Manifest disregard of the law," according to Judge Easterbrook, means simply that "an arbitrator may not direct the parties to violate the law." "The judiciary may step in when the arbitrator has commanded the parties to violate legal norms," but "judges may not deprive arbitrators of authority to reach compromise outcomes that legal norms leave within the discretion of the parties to the arbitration agreement." Here, the parties themselves could certainly have negotiated a settlement under which each side would bear its own fees and costs. And if the parties "may resolve their differences without fees changing hands, why can't an arbitrator, as their agent, prescribe the same outcome?" "People who want their arbitrators to have fewer powers need only provide this by contract." For a similar rationale in "public policy" cases, see *Eastern Associated Coal Corp. v. United Mine Workers*, supra pp. 171–72.

13.   Another response to growing criticism of employment arbitration may be found in rules that have recently been approved by the AAA for the arbitration of employment disputes. The AAA's National Rules for the Resolution of Employment Disputes now provide that in the case of "employer-promulgated plans"—as opposed to "individually-negotiated employment agreements"—the employee is to pay only a filing fee capped at $125; all other administrative fees, as well as the arbitrator's compensation, are to be paid by the employer. At the same time these rules provide that the arbitrators must be "experienced in the field of employment law," and that "[t]he parties shall bear the same burdens of proof and * * of producing evidence as would apply if their claims * * * had been brought in court." The arbitrator has "the authority to order such discovery, by way of deposition, interrogatory, document production, or otherwise," as he considers necessary; he may grant any relief that he deems "just and equitable, including any remedy or relief that would have been available to the parties had the matter been heard in court." The arbitrator must also "provide the written reasons for the award unless the parties agree otherwise," and the resulting award (with the exception of the names of the parties and witnesses) "shall be publicly available, on a cost basis."

According to one attorney who helped draft them, by arbitrating under the new rules "you are getting something close to the type of hearing that you would have had, [in] a bench trial in state or federal court." Aquino, "Revamping Employment Arbitration," The Recorder, Aug. 4, 1994 at p. 1. Are these changes desirable?

14.   Attorneys who represent management in employment matters have cautioned that there might be some dangers in using arbitration agreements: For example, arbitrators might "borrow from the experience of labor arbitrators" under collective bargaining agreements that require "just cause" for discharge, and thereby expand the rights of "at-will" employees. Piskorski & Ross, Private Arbitration as the Exclusive Means of

Resolving Employment–Related Disputes, 19 Employee Relations L.J. 205, 210 (1993); see also Guidry & Huffman, Legal and Practical Aspects of Alternative Dispute Resolution in Non–Union Companies, 6 Lab.Law. 1, 25 (1990) (employer may be "hoist on its own petard"). Is this a serious risk? In PaineWebber, Inc. v. Agron, 49 F.3d 347 (8th Cir.1995), arbitrators found that a brokerage firm had "improperly fired" one of its vice-presidents. The employer objected that this award "manifestly disregard-ed" the state's employment-at-will doctrine, but the court disagreed. Even if a "manifest disregard of the law" standard applied, "the use of the arbitration procedure as a means of settling employment-related disputes * * * necessarily alters the employment relationship from at-will to some-thing else—some standard of discernable cause is inherently required in this context where an arbitration panel is called on to interpret the employment relationship." If the plaintiff's employment was purely at-will, "the arbitration procedure designed to interpret that employment relation-ship would serve no identifiable purpose."

15. The Supreme Court in *Gilmer* was "unpersuaded" by the employee's argument that compelling arbitration would "undermine" the role of the EEOC in enforcing statutes like the Age Discrimination in Employment Act: After all, it noted, a claimant subject to an arbitration agreement "will still be able to file a charge with the EEOC, even though [he] is not able to institute a private judicial action." And in any event, the EEOC's role in combating age discrimination is not dependent on the filing of a charge by a claimant—since the agency may receive information concerning alleged violations of the Act "from any source" and has independent authority to investigate discrimination. 500 U.S. at 28.

What possibilities then are open to the EEOC if it is convinced that Gilmer's employer had been violating the ADEA? It seems generally accept-ed (as the Supreme Court made clear in *Gilmer* itself) that arbitration agreements will not preclude the EEOC from bringing actions seeking class-wide and injunctive relief. The EEOC, however, is also empowered to seek remedies, such as back pay, reinstatement, and damages, to "make whole" aggrieved employees: May it do so on behalf of employees like Gilmer who are bound to arbitrate their own claims?

The Supreme Court finally addressed this issue in EEOC v. Waffle House, Inc., 534 U.S. 279 (2002). The Fourth Circuit had held that the EEOC was barred from pursuing "victim-specific judicial relief" in an ADA action where the employee was subject to a mandatory arbitration agree-ment: "When the EEOC seeks 'make-whole' relief for [an employee], the federal policy favoring enforcement of private arbitration agreements out-weighs the EEOC's right to proceed in federal court because in that circumstance, the EEOC's public interest is minimal, as the EEOC seeks primarily to vindicate private, rather than public, interests." 193 F.3d 805, 812 (4th Cir. 1999). The Supreme Court, however, reversed: "No one asserts that the EEOC is a party to the contract, or that it agreed to arbitrate its claims." Whenever, pursuant to Title VII and the ADA, "the EEOC chooses from among the many charges filed each year to bring an enforcement action in a particular case, the agency may be seeking to vindicate a public interest, not simply provide make-whole relief for the employee, even when it pursues entirely victim-specific relief." The Court noted, however, that the employee in this case had not sought arbitration, nor had he entered into settlement negotiations with the employer: "It is an open question whether a settlement or arbitration judgment would affect the validity of the EEOC's claim or the character of relief the EEOC may seek." See also Olde Discount Corp. v. Tupman, supra p. 77.

16. The obstacles faced by an employee in pursuing an employment discrimination claim—whether through the EEOC's enforcement mechanism, or through a private suit—may be considerable. To seek relief on a federal statutory claim—under Title VII, the ADEA, or the ADA—an individual must first file a charge of discrimination with the EEOC. If its investigation suggests the existence of a valid claim the EEOC must attempt conciliation, and may ultimately bring suit on behalf of the individual claimant. If for any reason the agency determines *not* to pursue the case, it must issue a "right to sue" notice informing the individual that she is free to initiate her own court action. In *each* of the years 2002 through 2004, between 79,000 and 84,000 charges of discrimination were filed by employees, former employees, or rejected job applicants; in these years the EEOC filed 332, 361, and 379 lawsuits respectively. The average processing time for a charge is "upwards of 300 days," and in some district offices is considerably higher.

As for discrimination lawsuits brought by individual employees, "plaintiffs have a rough row to hoe. * * * They win a lower proportion of cases during pre-trial and at trial. [The overall success rate at trial for employment discrimination plaintiffs is approximately 33%]. Then, more of their successful cases are appealed. On appeal, they have a harder time upholding their successes and reversing adverse outcomes." [Plaintiffs' wins at trial are reversed approximately 42% of the time; defendants' wins, by contrast, only 8%; for the victorious plaintiff, "the appellate process offers a chance of retaining victory that cannot meaningfully be distinguished from a coin flip."]. Kevin M. Clermont & Stewart J. Schwab, How Employment Discrimination Plaintiffs Fare in Federal Court, 1 J. of Empirical Leg. Studies 429 (2004). See also Kevin M. Clermont & Theodore Eisenberg, Plaintiphobia in the Appellate Courts: Civil Rights Really Do Differ from Negotiable Instruments, 2002 U. of Ill. L. Rev. 947; cf. Ruth Colker, The Americans with Disabilities Act: A Windfall for Defendants, 34 Harv. C.R.-C.L. L. Rev. 99, 108–109 (1999)(study of ADA cases shows that defendant-employer prevailed in 93% of cases, 39% through summary judgment and 54% through a decision on the merits).

In these circumstances, it is hardly surprising that employees may have some difficulty enlisting an attorney willing to pursue discrimination litigation on a contingent-fee basis: "Experienced litigators across the country tell me that the good plaintiffs' attorneys will accept on the average only about one in a hundred of the discrimination claimants who seek their help. One of the Detroit area's top employment specialists was more precise. His secretary kept an actual count; he took on one out of eighty-seven persons who contacted him for possible representation." Theodore J. St. Antoine, Mandatory Arbitration of Employment Discrimination Claims: Unmitigated Evil or Blessing in Disguise?, 15 T.M. Cooley L. Rev. 1 (1998)(arbitration "may well be the most realistic hope of the ordinary claimant"); see also Samuel Estreicher, Saturns for Rickshaws: The Stakes in the Debate over Predispute Employment Arbitration Agreements, *in* Alternative Dispute Resolution in the Employment Arena: Proceedings, N.Y.U. 53rd Annual Conference on Labor 639, 644 (2004)("in a world without employment arbitration as an available option, we would essentially have a 'Cadillac' system for the few and a 'rickshaw' system for the many"; "the people who benefit under a litigation-based system are those whose salaries are high enough to warrant the costs and risks of a law suit undertaken by competent counsel"; "the system works well for high-end claimants and most plaintiff lawyers, and not very well for average claimants").

17. Professor Jerome Cohen once remarked, in a very different context, that the worst kind of Comparative Law thinking is that which compares *"our* theory" with *"their* reality"—and, inevitably, finds the latter deficient. Might the same thing be said about some of the literature critical of employment arbitration—redolent as it is with what has been termed "litigation romanticism"? See Carrie Menkel–Meadow, Mothers and Fathers of Invention: The Intellectual Founders of ADR, 16 Ohio St. J. on Disp. Resol. 1, 20 (2000).

18. One recent empirical study compared data from employment arbitrations administered by the AAA with litigated employment cases: The results were "consistent with arbitrators acting like in-court adjudicators in cases *in which higher-pay employees bring non-civil rights claims."* That is, there was "no statistically significant difference" between the arbitration and litigation outcomes [in fact employees won 65% of the time, compared with 57% in state trials]; nor was there any statistically significant difference in the amounts awarded successful plaintiffs [although the trial mean was substantially higher than the mean for arbitrations, the median for arbitration cases was higher than the trial median]. Arbitration was also considerably more rapid. [The mean and median times in arbitration from filing to final disposition was about 8 to 9 months; in both federal and state courts, they exceeded 20 months]. By contrast, the number of *discrimination* cases was too small to support firm inferences, and comparison was also difficult for lower-paid employees who were compelled to arbitrate pursuant to an employer-promulgated arbitration policy: The absence of litigation data for such employees "is likely explained by the fact that [they] seem to lack ready access to court." Theodore Eisenberg & Elizabeth Hill, Arbitration and Litigation of Employment Claims: An Empirical Comparison, Disp. Res. J., Nov. 2003/Jan. 2004, at p. 44. See also Elizabeth Hill, supra n. 1, 18 Ohio St. J. on Disp. Res. at 818 (in study of sample of AAA employment arbitrations, one third of employees bound by employer-promulgated plans proceeded *pro se,* but succeeded at the same rate as such employees with counsel).

Similar results appear in another study comparing discrimination claims asserted in NASD/NYSE arbitration and in federal litigation: It found employees won 19% of bench trials, 38% of jury trials, and 48% of arbitrations. The author did note that the average recovery in cases actually litigated through trial was "significantly greater than in arbitration." However, plaintiffs' lawyers typically required minimum provable damages of $60,000–$65,000, and a retainer of $3,000 to $3,600, before they would even accept a case—suggesting that "only the larger cases are litigated," William Howard, Arbitrating Claims of Employment Discrimination, Disp. Resol. J., Oct./Dec. 1995, at pp. 40, 45. And to the same effect, Michael Delikat & Morris M. Kleiner, Comparing Litigation and Arbitration of Employment Disputes: Do Plaintiffs Better Vindicate Their Rights in Litigation?, 6 (3) Conflict Management (ABA Committee on ADR 2003).

It is hard to know what to make of studies like these as long as we lack any reliable information about the relative *merits* of the cases involved. Cf. David Sherwyn et al., Assessing the Case for Employment Arbitration: A New Path for Empirical Research, 57 Stan. L. Rev. 1557, 1565–66 (2005)(where arbitration is mandated by employer policy, there is invariably a procedure by which employees must first go through a number of internal steps before formally initiating arbitration, and this "form of internal review" performs "critical filtering functions"; if the company's internal review has any value at all, "there may well be a systematic difference in the 'quality' of the cases that make it to arbitration as opposed to those cases that make it to the final stages of litigation"); Scott Baker, A Risk–Based Approach to Mandatory Arbitration, 83 Ore. L. Rev. 861, 885–87 (2004)(a large number of discrimination claims that are litigated end in summary judgment for the employer; this may "reflect the fact that the employers most likely to lose on summary judgment—the repeat discriminators—have opted out of litigation and are now using arbitration," and *"for this same reason*, a higher percentage of arbitration cases should be resolved in favor of employees").

19. Assume nevertheless—as is often casually asserted—that employees can indeed be expected regularly to do better before a jury than before a panel of arbitrators: What do you think of the argument that the lower arbitration awards would be "really the more fair assessments of redress"—since "the preconceived anti-employer sentiment of juries results in inflated court awards for plaintiffs"? David Sherwyn et al., In Defense of Mandatory Arbitration of Employment Disputes, 2 U. Pa. J. Lab. & Employment L. 73, 142–143 (1999). Aren't we still committed to the proposition that a jury verdict is necessarily the baseline for any notion of a "correct" result? Cf. Marc Galanter, The Vanishing Trial: An Examination of Trials and Related Matters in Federal and State Courts, 1 J. of Empirical Leg. Stud. 459, 462–653 (2004)(only 1.2% of federal civil cases are resolved by juries, down from 5.5% in 1962); William Glaberson, "Juries, Their Powers Under Siege, Find Their Role Is Being Eroded," N.Y. Times, March 2, 2001 at pp. A1, A15 (in a survey of federal trial judges, 27.4% said "juries should decide fewer types of cases"); Kent Syverud, ADR and the Decline of the American Civil Jury, 44 U.C.L.A. L. Rev. 1935 (1997)("Other than the trial bar and an occasional exhilarated juror, is there anyone left in America whose impression of a civil jury trial is so positive that he or she is willing to pay for one?'').

20. A job applicant signed an agreement to arbitrate. The agreement was included by the employer, Ryan's Family Steak House, in its application packet and was made a condition of employment. (Curiously, the agreement did not run directly between Ryan's and the potential employee; it was instead between the employee and ''Employment Dispute Services, Inc.,'' with Ryan's purportedly being a third-party beneficiary of the employee's agreement). Arbitrators were to be chosen by the parties from three separate pools selected by EDSI: One of them was made up of supervisors or managers of other employers that had signed an agreement with EDSI (there were only six others, including Golden Corral Steak Houses, K & W Cafeterias, and Sticky Fingers Restaurants); another pool was made up of employees from another signatory. The employee later filed suit against Ryan's for failure to pay the minimum wage in violation of the Fair Labor Standards Act; Ryan's filed a motion to compel arbitration. The court held that the motion should be denied on the ground that ''EDSI's arbitral forum is not neutral'':

> EDSI is clearly a for-profit business, and Ryan's annual fee accounted for over 42% of EDSI's gross income. * ** * Given the symbiotic relationship between Ryan's and EDSI, Ryan's effectively determines the three pools of arbitrators.

Walker v. Ryan's Family Steak Houses, Inc., 400 F.3d 370 (6th Cir. 2005). See also Penn v. Ryan's Family Steakhouses, Inc., 95 F.Supp.2d 940 (N.D.Ind.2000)(since the employer is a ''repeat'' customer of EDSI, EDSI has an incentive to ''load'' its lists of arbitrators ''with names that have sided with * * * any EDSI customers/employers in the past'') aff'd 269 F.3d 753 (7th Cir. 2001) (but criticizing trial court for ''plac[ing] too much weight on certain specifics of this system that * * * do not distinguish it from many others that have passed muster'').

21. Another study of AAA employment arbitrations suggests that the process may give an advantage to employers who are ''institutional repeat players'': Employees who arbitrated with ''repeat player employers''—that is, those who were in the case sample more than once—prevailed around 16% of the time, while employees arbitrating with ''one-time player'' employers prevailed over 70% of the time. In cases involving non-repeat player employers, employees recovered an average of 48% of their demands, while against repeat player employers they recovered only 11%. Lisa Bingham, On Repeat Players, Adhesive Contracts, and the Use of Statistics in Judicial Review of Employment Arbitration Awards, 29 McGeorge L. Rev. 223 (1998).

Where, as in AAA arbitrations, arbitrators are chosen from a panel list submitted to the parties, only the institutional repeat player is likely to develop an ''institutional memory'': That is, it is only the employer, and not the employee, who is likely to have the ability and incentive to invest in information about the arbitrator's background—and to monitor his past awards. Such asymmetry may suggest the need for some incremental reform of the arbitral process—perhaps in the form of tinkering with the institutional rules that are presented to the parties for adoption. The AAA's new National Rules for the Resolution of Employment Disputes— not yet in effect at the time of the Bingham study—now require that prospective arbitrators disclose their "service as a neutral in any past or pending case involving any of the parties and/or their representatives," Rule 11(b). (Is this an adequate response?) A further response is the AAA's 1995 "Due Process Protocol" for the arbitration of statutory claims in employment cases, which calls for the administering institution to provide each side with the names, addresses and phone numbers of the attorneys for the parties in that arbitrator's six most recent cases, in order "to aid them in selection"; see Lisa Bingham & Shimon Sarraf, Employment Arbitration Before and After the Due Process Protocol: Preliminary Evidence that Self–Regulation Makes a Difference, *in* Alternative Dispute Resolution in the Employment Arena: Proceedings, N.Y.U. 53rd Annual Conference on Labor 303, 326 (2004)(Protocol thereby "provided employees with a substitute for institutional memory"). Cf. Estreicher, supra n.16 at 648 ("the real repeat players in arbitration are not the parties themselves but the lawyers involved"; "the emergency of an organized plaintiff's bar * * * should drive down considerably any claimed systematic advantage for employers").

Note: Punitive Damages and Other Remedies

For many years federal courts have routinely asserted that arbitrators had the power under the FAA to award punitive damages: They would readily presume that the parties had been willing to grant such power, especially where the arbitration clause was broadly phrased so as to make "all disputes" arbitrable, or to give the arbitrators power (in the language of the AAA rules) to grant "any remedy or relief [that they deem] just and equitable." See Raytheon Co. v. Automated Business Systems, Inc., 882 F.2d 6 (1st Cir.1989) ("inasmuch as agreements to arbitrate are generously construed, it would seem sensible to interpret [such] phrases to indicate, at a minimum, an intention * * * to allow the chosen dispute resolvers to award the same varieties and forms of damages or relief as a court would be empowered to award"); Kelley v. Michaels, 830 F.Supp. 577 (N.D.Okl. 1993) (NASD Code of Arbitration; agreement to arbitrate "any dispute, claim or controversy" includes a claim for punitive damages). In such cases it would take a "clear and express exclusion" in the agreement to deprive the arbitrator of the power to award punitive damages.

And if authorized by the parties' agreement, an award of punitive damages by arbitrators was not considered by these courts to be against any "public policy." "[A]n arbitrator steeped in the practice of a given trade is often better equipped than a judge not only to decide what behavior so transgresses the limits of acceptable commercial practice in that trade as to warrant a punitive award, but also to determine the amount of punitive damages needed to (1) adequately deter others in the trade from engaging in similar misconduct, and (2) punish the particular defendant in accordance with the magnitude of his misdeed." Willoughby Roofing & Supply Co., Inc. v. Kajima Int'l, Inc., 598 F.Supp. 353 (N.D.Ala. 1984), aff'd, 776 F.2d 269 (11th Cir.1985).

However, difficult issues arose when state law was otherwise: A number of states (notably New York) have taken the position that arbitrators may *not* award punitive damages. In these states, an arbitral award of punitive damages is against "public policy" *even though the parties had granted the arbitrators the power to award such damages—and even though on a similar cause of action a court or jury could impose them.* The leading case is Garrity v. Lyle Stuart, Inc., 40 N.Y.2d 354, 386 N.Y.S.2d 831, 353 N.E.2d 793 (1976), in which the court vacated an award of punitive damages to an author for his publisher's "malicious withholding of royalties":

> If arbitrators were allowed to impose punitive damages, [arbitration] would become a trap for the unwary given the eminently desirable freedom from judicial overview of law and facts. It would mean that the scope of determination by arbitrators, by the license to award punitive damages, would be both unpredictable and uncontrollable. * * *
>
> In imposing penal sanctions in private arrangements, a tradition of the rule of law in organized society is violated. One purpose of the rule of law is to require that the use of coercion be controlled by the State. * * * For centuries the power to punish has been a monopoly of the State, and not that of any private individual. The day is long past since barbaric man achieved redress by private punitive measures.

What would be the practical result of a rule such as New York's? Either the parties must be deemed to have completely "waived" any right to punitive damages merely by entering into an arbitration agreement—thus surrendering (as they would not in litigation) this important right—or there would have to be an additional trial, on essentially the same facts, on a separate claim for punitives—a wasteful exercise that would undermine many of the advantages of arbitration. *Compare* Surman v. Merrill, Lynch, Pierce, Fenner & Smith, 733 F.2d 59, 63 (8th Cir. 1984)(plaintiffs argued that if their fraud claims were referred to arbitration, they would not be able to recover punitive damages; "this, however, is what the parties contracted for"), *with* DiCrisci v. Lyndon Guaranty Bank of New York, 807 F.Supp. 947, 953 (W.D.N.Y.1992)("arbitrable claims" are severed and ordered to arbitration; further proceedings on claim for punitive damages are stayed "pending the completion of arbitration").

The Supreme Court finally addressed this problem in Mastrobuono v. Shearson Lehman Hutton, Inc. 514 U.S. 52, 115 S.Ct. 1212, 131 L.Ed.2d 76 (1995). An agreement between a brokerage house and its customer provided that it "shall be governed by the laws of the State of New York"; a panel of arbitrators, sitting in Illinois, awarded punitive damages. The Supreme Court was then presented with the question "whether a contractual choice-of-law provision may preclude an arbitral award of punitive damages that otherwise would be proper." The answer it gave was "no":

- It was axiomatic that state law could have no regulatory force in this area at all *where the intention of the parties was otherwise*:
  - If, for example, "contracting parties agreed to include claims for punitive damages within the issues to be arbitrated, the FAA ensures that their agreement will be enforced according to its terms even if a rule of state law would otherwise exclude such claims from arbitration." That much was already made abundantly "clear" by *Southland v. Keating.*
  - Now of course, even if the contract contained no choice-of-law clause at all, New York law might still govern under normal conflict-of-laws analysis—because, say, it was signed and was to be performed within the state. But in such a case, also, arbitrators would be able to award punitive damages—because "there would be nothing in the contract that could possibly constitute evidence of an *intent to exclude* punitive damages claims." That is, punitive damages would be allowed "because, *in the absence of contractual intent to the contrary,* the FAA would preempt the *Garrity* rule."
- Thus, the Court said, what the case came down to was what the contract actually had to say about the arbitrability of the claim for punitive damages. And the Court suggested that the "best way" to read the New York choice-of-law clause was as a reference only to the *"substantive rights and obligations" that New York courts* would apply, and not to "'any' special rules limiting the authority of arbitrators": "The choice-of-law provision covers the rights and duties of the parties, while the arbitration clause covers arbitration . . ."

  > At the worst, though, the choice-of-law clause would have introduced "an *ambiguity* into an arbitration agreement that would otherwise allow punitive damages awards." "*It is not, in itself, an unequivocal exclusion of punitive damages claims.*" And "when a court interprets such provisions in an agreement covered by the FAA, due regard must be given to the federal policy favoring arbitration, and ambiguities as to the scope of the arbitration clause itself resolved in favor of arbitration."

The result in *Mastrobuono* thus "derived both from an explicit interpretative strategy and a conscious choice of a default rule. Choosing to construe the choice-of-law clause as inapplicable to state restrictions on arbitral power was a means of furthering the time-honored 'federal policy favoring arbitration' and its 'presumption of arbitrability'; it was also a response to those consumer protection concerns behind the 'common-law rule of contract interpretation' that ambiguous language should be construed against the drafter."[1] See also Section C.2, supra, note 10 ("The FAA and State Law"); Section C.3.d., supra, note 1 ("Arbitrability"). And

---

1. See Alan Scott Rau, The UNCITRAL Model Law in State and Federal Courts: The Case of "Waiver," 6 Amer. Rev. of Int'l Arb. 223, 256 (1995).

finally, the Court noted in *Mastrobuono* that its own interpretation of the parties contract "accords with that of the only decision-maker arguably entitled to deference—the arbitrator."[2] See Section C.3.d., supra (Note, "Determining the 'Jurisdiction' of the Arbitrator").

For a while, New York courts were ready to indulge in the grossest forms of wishful thinking—believing that they still remained free independently to construe choice-of-law clauses differently from the way the Supreme Court did it in *Mastrobuono,* and that, should they do so, federal courts would have to defer to their reading even where the result would be to exclude punitive damage awards. See Dean Witter Reynolds, Inc. v. Trimble, 166 Misc.2d 40, 631 N.Y.S.2d 215, 217 n. 4 (Sup. Ct. 1995)("the interpretation of contracts is a matter of state law"). This, however, failed to take very seriously that "liberal federal policy favoring arbitration agreements" that has been the subject of a relentless Supreme Court jurisprudence. In more recent cases the New York courts seem, at last, to have sensibly capitulated—and they now appear to consider themselves bound by *Mastrobuono*'s reading of choice-of-law clauses to permit arbitral awards of punitive damages. See Olde Discount Corp. v. Dartley, N.Y.L.J., Dec. 12, 1997, at pp. 26–27 (Sup. Ct.)(under the FAA, "a reference to the substantive law of a particular State, without more, is simply insufficient to bar arbitrators from considering the question of punitive damages"); cf. Smith Barney Shearson Inc. v. Sacharow, 91 N.Y.2d 39, 689 N.E.2d 884, 666 N.Y.S.2d 990 ("While a choice of law clause incorporates substantive New York principles, it does not also pull in conflicting restrictions on the scope of the authority of the arbitrators and the competence of parties to contract for plenary alternative dispute resolution").

NOTES AND QUESTIONS

1. The Oregon Constitution prohibited judicial review of jury awards of punitive damages "unless the court can affirmatively say there is no evidence to support the verdict." In Honda Motor Co., Ltd. v. Oberg, 512 U.S. 415 (1994), the Supreme Court held that this violated the due process clause of the 14th Amendment:

> Punitive damages pose an acute danger of arbitrary deprivation of property. Jury instructions typically leave the jury with wide discretion in choosing amounts, and the presentation of evidence of a defendant's net worth creates the potential that juries will use their verdicts to express biases against big businesses, particularly those without strong local presences. Judicial review of the amount awarded was one of the few procedural safeguards which the common law provided against that danger.

Oregon apparently did permit judicial review to ensure only "that there is evidence to support *some* punitive damages, not that there is evidence to support the amount actually awarded." But "evidence of guilt

---

2. 514 U.S. at 60 n.4.

warranting some punishment is not a substitute for evidence providing at least a rational basis for the particular deprivation of property imposed by the State to deter future wrongdoing.''

Is the reasoning in *Honda Motor Co.* at all relevant to the problems in this note?

2. Compare BMW of North America, Inc. v. Gore, 517 U.S. 559 (1996). After Dr. Ira Gore bought a new black BMW sports sedan for $40,750, he learned that it been repainted (at a cost of $600) before delivery—presumably because of exposure to acid rain during transit. He brought suit against BMW of North America, alleging that the failure to disclose this fact constituted fraud; a jury awarded compensatory damages of $4000 and punitive damages of $4 million (later reduced by the state courts to $2 million). The Supreme Court (5–4) held that the award of punitive damages was ''grossly excessive'' in relation to ''the state's legitimate interests in punishing unlawful conduct and deterring its repetition,'' and thus amounted to a denial of due process. See also State Farm Mutual Auto. Ins. Co. v. Campbell, 538 U.S. 408 (2003)(action against insurance company for ''bad faith'' refusal to settle; held, a punitive damages award of $145 million, where compensatory damages were $1 million, is ''excessive''; ''in practice, few awards exceeding a single-digit ratio between punitive and compensatory damages * * * will satisfy due process'').

Is the analysis in *Gore* and *State Farm* applicable to judicial review of arbitration awards? Courts have regularly held that ''because an arbitration award does not constitute state action and is not converted into state action by [judicial confirmation], an arbitration panel's award of punitive damages does not implicate the due process clause, regardless of how excessive the award may be.'' MedValUSA Health Programs, Inc. v. Memberworks, Inc., 273 Conn. 634, 872 A.2d 423 (2005). In *MedValUSA* a punitive damage award of $5 million—in the absence of any compensatory damages at all—was also held not to violate public policy, because the state had no ''well-defined public policy against the award of excessive punitive damages'': We should be wary, the court warned, of ''constitutionalizing a wide variety of private conduct through public policy analysis,'' thereby countenancing an ''indirect imposition of constitutional norms on private actors.''

But cf. Sawtelle v. Waddell & Reed, Inc., 304 A.D.2d 103, 754 N.Y.S.2d 264 (2003). After multiple hearing sessions over a period of several years, an NASD panel awarded a broker $1 million in compensatory damages, $747,000 in attorneys' fees, and $25 million in punitive damages for his former employer's ''campaign of deception'' against him. Relying on *Gore*, the court found this award to be ''in manifest disregard of the law'' (''A grossly excessive award that is arbitrary and irrational under *Gore* should be equally arbitrary and irrational under the FAA''), although it rejected the argument that it violated ''public policy.'' The case was remanded to the original panel of arbitrators for reconsideration. After a one-day hearing, the arbitrators changed their characterization of the employer's conduct—they now found the employer had carried on a ''horrible campaign of deception, defamation and persecution" against the claimant—but returned with an identical amount. This second award was vacated once again—and this time, the trial court directed that the issue of punitive damages be submitted to a different panel. The claimant asked the court to order a conditional remittitur—modifying the award "in the same way that the court would modify a legally excessive jury verdict"—but the court found that it had no power to do so: This would "require legislative action." 6 Misc.3d 487, 789 N.Y.S.2d 857 (N.Y. Sup. 2004), aff'd, 21 A.D.3d 820, 801 N.Y.S.2d 286 (2005).

3. Strictures against arbitral "punishment" (such as those in the earlier New York cases) may as a practical matter turn out to be meaningless unless the arbitrator is ingenuous enough to label his award as punitive. As all first-year law students quickly learn, calculating "compensatory" damages in contract cases is hardly an exact science. In addition, arbitrators may find in particular cases that remedies other than the traditional award of damages are warranted; for example they may think it appropriate, on a theory of unjust enrichment, to require the defendant to "disgorge" the benefits he has made from breach. Cf. International Union of Operating Engineers v. Mid–Valley, Inc., 347 F.Supp. 1104 (S.D.Tex.1972). In the absence of a reasoned opinion or a transcript, it will be difficult to say that the arbitrator has in fashioning appropriate remedies gone beyond permitted "flexibility" to forbidden "punishment."

4. Staklinski was hired as an executive. His contract provided that should he become "permanently disabled" he would receive reduced compensation for the next three years, and then the contract would end. Several years later the company's Board determined that Staklinski had become permanently disabled; he disagreed with this finding and the dispute was submitted to arbitration. The arbitrator found in favor of Staklinski and ordered the corporation to reinstate him. The court confirmed the award: "The power of an arbitrator to order specific performance in an appropriate case has been recognized from early times. * * * Whether a court of equity could issue a specific performance decree in a case like this is beside the point." In the Matter of the Arbitration Between Staklinski and Pyramid Electric Co., 6 N.Y.2d 159, 188 N.Y.S.2d 541, 160 N.E.2d 78 (1959). See also Coopertex, Inc. v. Rue De Reves, Inc., 1990 WL 6548 (S.D.N.Y.) (specific performance of a contract for the sale of goods; "[w]hether or not a court would have awarded specific performance in this case is not the issue").

5. As the preceding note suggests, arbitrators are usually assumed to have broad discretion in fashioning a remedy for the particular circumstances of the case. An important recent decision is Advanced Micro Devices, Inc. v. Intel Corp., 9 Cal.4th 362, 885 P.2d 994, 36 Cal.Rptr.2d 581 (1994). AMD and Intel had entered into a contract under which each company could acquire the right to manufacture under license semiconductor products initially developed by the other. After an arbitration that lasted almost five years, an arbitrator found that Intel had "breached the implied covenant of good faith and fair dealing" under this contract. The arbitrator found that Intel's breach had prevented AMD from acquiring the right to manufacture Intel's highly successful "386" computer chip, and had also delayed AMD's efforts to independently develop its own competitive product by "reverse engineering" Intel's chip. AMD's actual damages were found to be "immeasurable." So the arbitrator gave AMD a permanent, royalty-free license to any of Intel's intellectual property that was embodied in AMD's competing chip—thereby providing AMD with "a complete and dispositive defense" against "legal harassment by Intel over AMD's alleged use of Intel intellectual property," notably in patent and copyright infringement claims that were being pressed by Intel in separate litigation. In confirming the award, the California Supreme Court rejected the proposition that arbitrators could not award a party "benefits different from those the party could have acquired through performance of the contract." The court also rejected any rule by which the remedial power of arbitrators would be limited to remedies "that a court could award on the same claim." "The choice of remedy * * * may at times call on any decision maker's flexibility, creativity and sense of fairness."

The dissenting judges protested that "the majority has greatly increased the risks and uncertainty of arbitration," and that the decision "will make businesses think twice about whether they should agree to resolve disputes by arbitration." They acknowledged that a number of reasons might contribute to granting wide remedial powers to *labor* arbitrators—such as the impossibility of reducing all aspects of a labor-management relationship to writing, and the need for "an ongoing process during the life of a collective bargaining agreement that adjusts and modifies the agreement to meet the changing conditions of the workplace." By contrast, in *commercial* arbitration the "possibility of unlimited and unpredictable forms of relief is not one of the advantages that a party normally expects to receive from choosing to arbitrate." Under the majority test, the dissent wrote, "it is theoretically possible for an arbitrator to order the losing party to be placed in the stocks or the pillory, or to direct that the contractual relationship be repaired by ordering the marriage of the parties' first-born children."

See also Alan Rau, Resolving Disputes Over Attorneys' Fees: The Role of ADR, 46 S.M.U.L.Rev. 2005, 2071 (1993) (in fee dispute between attorney and client, an arbitrator awarded the attorney $356 "to be paid with no more than 12 hairstylings"; "[i]f the client was in fact a hairstylist, this is surely an efficient settlement, reducing the cost of settlement 'with the same net gain to plaintiff at a lower cost to the defendant' "); David Co. v. Jim W. Miller Construction, Inc., 444 N.W.2d 836 (Minn.1989) (developer sought monetary damages against contractor who had built defective townhouses; the arbitrators (a contractor and two engineers) fashioned an "innovative and unique remedy" that ordered the builder—who was himself a real estate developer—to purchase from the plaintiff the townhouses and the land on which they were built).

D. THE ARBITRATION PROCEEDING

Within broad limits * * * private parties who submit an existing dispute to arbitration may write their own ticket about the terms of submission, if they can agree to a ticket. [The authors refer to an old story about a person who, in a dream, was threatened by an ominous character and who asked, tremulously, "Wh-what are you going to do now?"—only to receive the answer, "How do I know? This is *your* dream."] The arbitration of an existing dispute is the parties' dream, and they can make it what they want it to be.

The trouble is that it takes time and money to draft elaborate private laws * * *. Only in the most exceptional circumstances can a private disputant stop to negotiate and draft a complete constitution, together with a substantive and procedural code, for the governance of his private court.[1]

It is quite common to find leading members of the ADR community willing to question whether arbitration is "really" an "ADR process" at all—who may suggest, for example, that it is somehow inappropriate to include a discussion of the arbitration process in a conference or law school course devoted primarily to "the gentler arts of reconciliation and accommodation."[2] We gather that this is true because, paradoxically, arbitration "matters"—that is, that it is merely "adjudication." "Where is the empowerment"?[3] Nevertheless it should be obvious enough that what the arbitration process is in fact all about is private ordering and self-determination. "In the run-of-the-mill case, the task of planning for dispute resolution necessarily requires a high level of party participation. Choosing a dispute resolution process, designing its structure, and selecting the decisionmaker, all proceed through negotiation and agreement—and giving thought to such matters may thus make the same calls on the parties' creativity and imagination as do more openly 'empowering' ADR processes."[4]

Rather than draft their own "procedural code," however, parties to arbitration agreements commonly prefer to incorporate by reference the standard rules for the conduct of arbitration proceedings prepared by institutions like the AAA. This allows them to avoid having to reinvent the wheel through lengthy negotiation and drafting—especially at a time when there may not be much incentive for cooperation—and instead to build upon the experience of others. In the materials that follow, frequent reference will be made to the practice of the AAA and particularly to its Commercial Arbitration Rules. But it must be remembered that arbitration remains ultimately "the parties' dream." It is always necessary to consider

---

1. Henry Hart & Albert Sacks, The Legal Process 310 (1994).

2. Derek Bok, A Flawed System of Law Practice and Training, 33 J. Legal Educ. 570, 582–83 (1983).

3. Jean Sternlight, Is Binding Arbitration A Form of ADR?: An Argument That the Term "ADR" Has Begun to Outlive its Usefulness, 2000 J. of Disp. Resol. 97, 103–04; see id. at 106 ("It makes no more sense to group all these techniques together than it would to group together contracts, torts,

property, UCC, etc. in a single three credit course called 'private law' "); see also William Howard, Arbitrating Employment Discrimination Claims: Do You Really Have To? Do You Really Want To?, 43 Drake L. Rev. 255, 279–80 (1994)(since arbitration is "nonconsensual," it "has nothing in common with the other ADR techniques beyond not being a state institution").

4. See Alan Rau, Integrity in Private Judging, 38 So. Tex. L. Rev. 485, 486 (1997).

carefully the special features of each individual transaction, with a view to adding to the pre-existing structure or adapting it in light of the parties' particular circumstances.

1.   THE DECISION-MAKERS

a.   SELECTION OF ARBITRATORS

Selecting the arbitrators is obviously a critical aspect of the arbitration process. After all, the ability to have a dispute decided by "judges" of one's own choosing is perhaps the most distinctive characteristic of this dispute resolution mechanism. How to provide for arbitrator selection is therefore an essential question for the parties in their planning.

The parties may, of course, simply try to agree by name on the individuals who will arbitrate their dispute. The arbitrator might, for example, be named in the original agreement. Or selection of the arbitrator might be left for later agreement on an ad hoc basis after a dispute arises. The choice of the most appropriate arbitrator may in fact often be a function of the nature of the dispute which has arisen, or of the issues which happen to be in contention. In labor arbitration, for example, the parties may prefer lawyers as arbitrators when the issue is one of arbitrability, but may well prefer economists for wage disputes in "interest" arbitration, and industrial engineers for disputes over job evaluation.[5]

However, reliance on this method of arbitrator selection carries obvious dangers. When the arbitrator is named in advance, he may have become unwilling or unable to serve by the time a dispute later arises. This may then open up a challenge to the whole process; one party may argue that his agreement to arbitration was not unconditional but dependent on the personal choice of this "known and trusted expert," and that therefore arbitration should not proceed in his absence.[6] Such an argument will

---

5. See Retzer and Petersen, Strategies of Arbitrator Selection, 70 Lab.Arb. 1307, 1319 (1978).

6. See Uniform Commercial Code § 2–305, cmt. 4 ("there may be cases in which a particular person's judgment is not chosen merely as a barometer or index of a fair price but is an essential condition to the parties' intent to make a contract at all"; in such a case it would be plausible to find that "the parties did not intend to make a binding agreement if that expert were unavailable"); cf. Madison Teachers, Inc. v. Wisconsin Educational Ass'n Council, 285 Wis.2d 737, 703 N.W.2d 711 (App. 2005)(trial court found that the arbitrator specifically named in the agreement was "central to the agreement" and was a "condition precedent to arbitrating disputes," so that "there [could] be no arbitration" if he was unavailable due to age or

infirmity; held, rev'd; "the history between these parties demonstrates that arbitration was the overriding consideration, rather than the existence of a specifically named arbitrator").

Similar questions arise when the arbitration forum agreed on by the parties declines jurisdiction over the case, see In re Salomon Inc. Shareholders' Derivative Litigation, 68 F.3d 554, 559 (2d Cir.1995) ("[b]ecause the parties had contractually agreed that only the NYSE could arbitrate any disputes between them, [the lower court] properly declined to appoint substitute arbitrators and compel arbitration in another forum"), or is simply nonexistent, see Stinson v. America's Home Place, Inc., 108 F.Supp.2d 1278 (M.D.Ala. 2000)(the "National Academy of Conciliators, the arbitrator designated in the contract for resolution of disputes, was not in existence at

rarely be found persuasive, but in any event a means must be found to select a replacement.

On the other hand, where the agreement contemplates only that the parties will select their arbitrator *after* a dispute arises, there is an obvious potential for a recalcitrant party to drag his feet. The larger the stakes in the transaction, the more likely it is that the parties will wish to retain at least a veto over the identity of the decision-maker. Consider for example the agonizingly prolonged contract dispute between the Hunt brothers of Texas and the major oil-producing companies, a complex case arising out of various interests in Libyan oil concessions and involving sixteen parties and a welter of legal issues. The arbitration extended over a period of seven years; more than *two years* were consumed by the process of screening arbitrators, "as arbitrators proposed by one party were rejected by one or more of the other parties." The complexity of the issues in the case made the search for the requisite "arbitrators of unusual legal qualifications and broad experience in complicated transactions" particularly difficult. The court, however, made it clear that much of the delay was due to the tactics of the Hunts and their "campaign of obstruction to impede and defeat the arbitration."[7]

Under AAA rules, as soon as a demand for arbitration is made the AAA distributes to the parties a short list of potential arbitrators. It chooses these from its extensive panel of arbitrators, trying to match the names to the nature of the dispute and the industry involved. It may, for example, suggest arbitrators who have had experience in solar heating or landscape architecture if the dispute centers on practice in those trades. The parties may in their agreement have already specified the background or qualification of their arbitrators. In maritime arbitration, for example, it is the usual practice to stipulate that the arbitrators "shall be commercial men"—a phrase not meant to exclude women, but definitely meant to exclude lawyers.[8] Unless the parties have ruled out the possibility, however, it is customary to have at least one attorney on the list. Lawyers in fact play a dominant part in many AAA arbitrations: As of January 2006, for example, 51% of the names on the AAA's construction arbitration panel were attorneys—far outnumbering the next largest professional category, engineers. And a recent survey of the members of the National Academy of Arbitrators [NAA] reported that 61.4% had a law degree.[9]

---

the time the contract was formed or at any time thereafter").

7. See Hunt v. Mobil Oil Corp., 654 F.Supp. 1487 (S.D.N.Y.1987).

8. In W.K. Webster & Co. v. American President Lines, Ltd., 32 F.3d 665 (2d Cir. 1994), the Society of Maritime Arbitrators took the position (as *amicus curiae*) that a person cannot be a "commercial man" and a practicing attorney at one and the same time. The court disagreed, however, and upheld the appointment of an attorney who "had substantial practical experience on the commercial side of the maritime industry"—it noted that the attorney had not obtained his experience "*solely* as [a] practicing" attorney.

9. Michel Picher et al., The Arbitration Profession in Transition: A Survey of the National Academy of Arbitrators 12 (Cornell/PERC Institute on Conflict Resolution 2000).

The information that the parties are given about a potential arbitrator is not extensive; it usually contains summary biographical information indicating the arbitrator's profession, present and past employment, education, areas in which he claims expertise, and of course his stated rate of compensation. There is no mechanism analogous to voir dire in which the parties have the opportunity to examine potential arbitrators prior to selection—although in large cases they have an obvious incentive to do some research on their own. Under AAA procedure, each party is allowed to cross off the list any names he finds unacceptable. Each then ranks the remaining names in order of preference, and from these the AAA is supposed to appoint an arbitrator "in accordance with the designated order of mutual preference." (The British refer to this method as "knocking the brains out of the panel.")[10] In the (unusual) event that every name turns out to be objectionable to one or both of the parties, the AAA may at that point simply choose another name from its panel without submitting any further lists; barring disqualification for cause, this selection is final.

Arbitration can proceed before any number of arbitrators—it is, again, "the parties' dream." But the most common pattern is to use either a single individual or three arbitrators. Under AAA rules, a single arbitrator is to be used unless the parties specify otherwise or unless the AAA "in its discretion" selects a larger number. In 2005, 42% of the AAA's commercial and construction cases involved claims of $75,000 or less and were administered under its "Expedited Procedures," where a single arbitrator is always used. However, in complex cases, or cases where the stakes are large, it is common to use three neutral arbitrators: The current rule of thumb for both the AAA and the ICC is to appoint three arbitrators wherever the amount in controversy exceeds $1 million. With three arbitrators, of course, far more time is consumed in selection, in scheduling the hearings, and, probably, in hearing time; the fees paid to the arbitrators are also likely to be higher.

What do parties look for in selecting arbitrators? In labor cases, where a large cadre of professional arbitrators has developed, it is often observed that parties have a strong preference for only the most experienced and active arbitrators. One survey submitted a sample case to a selected number of union and management representatives and asked for their preferences as to whom they wanted to hear the case: 47.6% of the management representatives and 61.5% of the union representatives chose a decision-maker whose primary occupation was as a "full-time arbitrator."[11] The fact that many labor arbitration opinions are published not only helps the parties in doing "research" on potential arbitrators; it also serves to focus even greater attention on the well-known "name" arbitrators whose cases appear regularly in the reports.

10. Bernstein, Nudging and Shoving All Parties to a Jurisdictional Dispute Into Arbitration: The Dubious Procedure of *National Steel*, 78 Harv.L.Rev. 784, 790–91 (1965).

11. See Nelson, The Selection of Arbitrators, Lab.L.J., October 1986, at 703, 711.

This leads to a classic "Catch–22." Without experience, it is difficult for an arbitrator to be chosen to hear a labor case—and difficult therefore to develop the experience and reputation that will enable her to be chosen to hear *future* cases. One survey's estimate of the number of labor arbitrators "willing and able to practice" in 1986 was 3,669. Only 16% of these practiced full-time as arbitrators. At the other extreme, approximately 22% of the entire group did not work at all as arbitrators during the year, largely because no assignments were offered to them.[12] So "a small percentage of arbitrators do most of the business."[13] Experienced observers can suggest, with only mild rhetorical excess, that "ten percent of labor arbitrators do ninety percent of the arbitrations."[14]

The National Academy of Arbitrators is an elite group of highly-experienced arbitrators who primarily work in labor-management cases: The average Academy member is 63 years old—88% of the members are male, and 94% are white—and over 66% of them work as "full-time neutrals." The average yearly caseload for Academy members is around 55—but approximately one-quarter of the membership reported that they had rendered awards in at least 200 labor-management arbitrations over the three year period between 1996 and 1998. Direct appointment by the parties was "the most significant means" by which most Academy members obtained cases, "perhaps reflecting the members' vast experience and the parties' knowledge of their reputations."[15] In commercial cases, also, parties "will necessarily want someone who is well known," particularly when the stakes are high: "It helps to come from a strong corporate law firm, to produce strong writings on corporate law issues, to have friends or colleagues who will refer 'starter' cases to a trusted novice, or to have served as a judge with a reputation as safe for business."[16]

The natural result of this selective demand is that there are often lengthy delays before the chosen arbitrator will have the time to hear and dispose of a given case; the most experienced arbitrators may not be available for a hearing within several months after being asked to serve. While this is not perhaps a long time in comparison with some crowded judicial dockets, it is still troubling for a supposedly "expeditious" dispute

---

12. Bognanno & Smith, The Demographic and Professional Characteristics of Arbitrators in North America, Proceedings, 41st Annual Meeting, Nat'l Academy of Arbitrators 266, 269, 277–79 (1988).

13. Mario Bognanno & Charles Coleman, Labor Arbitration in America: The Profession and Practice 89 (1992).

14. See Bryant Garth, Tilting the Justice System: From ADR as Idealistic Movement to a Segmented Market in Dispute Resolution, 18 Ga. St. U. L. Rev. 927, 939 fn.34 (2002)(remarks by Phil LaPorte, Director of Labor Studies at the Usery Center of Georgia State University). See also The Chronicle (Journal of the Nat'l Academy of Arbitrators), May 1988 at p. 3 (11.9% of all active arbitrators handled 60 or more cases in 1986, representing 50.5% of the total grievance arbitration case load).

15. Picher et al., supra n.9 at 11–12, 14, 18.

16. Garth, supra n. 14 at 941–42 (in international commercial arbitration, "third world" arbitrators had to work twice as hard as those from countries such as Switzerland or the Netherlands to prove that they could be "neutral").

resolution process—particularly in cases where an employee has been discharged, and the employer is facing potential liability for back pay.

The profession of "labor arbitrator" is made possible by the often substantial fees that arbitrators are regularly paid for their services in labor cases. The average "lowest daily fee" that NAA members with law degrees report charging, is $688; the average "highest daily fee" is $949.[17] In the commercial arena the supply of acceptable arbitrators is relatively more elastic, and the "full-time" arbitrator is extremely uncommon. For many years, the AAA's Commercial Arbitration Rules provided that commercial arbitrators were expected to serve without compensation for the first day of hearing—presumably as a form of public service. Under the current rules, however, arbitrators are paid beginning with the first day of hearing; they may also be paid for "study time" prior to the hearing, and, more exceptionally, a "cancellation" fee should there be changes after the arbitrator has reserved time for the case.[18] Arbitrators are free to state their own rate of compensation, and rates do tend to be considerably higher than in labor cases—a $2000 per diem fee has been termed not "excessively high" or "far beyond the applicable standard for such services."[19] This is in addition to the administrative fee, based on the amount of the claim, which is paid to institutions like the AAA and the ICC for their services in supervising the arbitration.

NOTES AND QUESTIONS

1.   It is possible of course for the parties to vary the usual "list" procedure in any number of ways: See, e.g., Brook v. Peak Int'l, Ltd., 294 F.3d 668 (5th Cir. 2002)(under the agreement the AAA was to submit a list of nine potential arbitrators; the employer and employee were then to "alternately remove names from this list (beginning with the party which wins a flip of the coin) until one person remains and this person shall serve as the impartial arbitrator").

2.   Another traditional pattern in arbitration is a "tripartite" panel, in which each party is allowed to select one arbitrator and a third, "neutral" chairman is chosen by the other two (or in the absence of agreement, by an institution like the AAA).

17.   Picher et al., supra n.9 at 22–25.

18.   See generally John Gotanda, Setting Arbitrators' Fees: An International Survey, 33 Vand. J. Transnat'l L. 779 (2000).

19.   Polin   v.   Kellwood   Co.,   103 F.Supp.2d 238, 257 n. 27 (S.D.N.Y.2000), aff'd, 34 Fed. Appx. 406 (2d Cir. 2002).

In California arbitrators who handle disputes between Kaiser and its HMO patients charge fees ranging from $100/hour to $600/hour, with the average hourly fee being $314.

Sixth Annual Report of the Office of the Independent Administrator (2004), http://www.oia-kaiserarb.com/oia/6th% 20report.htm; see Section B.4. supra. A random sampling of arbitrators on the AAA's Commercial Panel in Northern California indicated that their rate of compensation ranged from $600 to $3850 per day, with the average daily rate of arbitrator compensation being $1899. Ting v. AT & T, 182 F.Supp.2d 902, 917 (N.D. Cal. 2002).

What effects might this kind of panel have on the decision-making process? The AAA's Commercial Arbitration Rules provide that where there is a panel of more than one arbitrator, decision is to be by *majority vote* unless the agreement provides otherwise. To the same effect is § 4 of the Uniform Arbitration Act, which has been enacted by most states. Where the party-appointed arbitrators agree on a particular result, may the neutral be led to acquiesce in what is in reality a negotiated settlement being given the prestige of an arbitral award? And where the other two arbitrators *disagree,* may the neutral be forced to trim or compromise his own views in order to obtain a majority? Consider In re Publishers' Ass'n of N.Y. and N.Y. Typographical Union, 36 Lab.Arb. 706 (1961). The neutral arbitrator here voted with the employer to discharge a worker but wrote, in an unusually candid opinion, that this penalty had been "forced upon" him. While he would have preferred a lesser penalty such as a disciplinary suspension, his most "patient and painstaking efforts" had convinced him that "there was no possibility whatever of an award issuing which would reflect a view intermediate to the polar position of my colleagues." He therefore saw no choice other than to join in the position which was *closest* to the one he preferred!

Would it have been possible or appropriate for the neutral in *Publishers' Association* to have acted differently? To avoid placing such a burden on the neutral, would it not be better simply to stipulate that in the absence of a majority decision the final decision is to be made by the neutral alone—or even that the function of the party-appointed arbitrators is always to be merely advisory? This is in fact commonly provided in collective bargaining agreements. And in that case, is any purpose ever served by having a tripartite board at all? Can you think of any countervailing advantages to using a tripartite board with party-named representatives? See Zack, Tripartite Panels: Asset or Hindrance in Dispute Settlement?, Proceedings, 34th Annual Meeting, Nat'l Academy of Arbitrators 273, 279 (1982) (deliberations between neutral and party-appointed arbitrators can help clarify technical issues, provide assurance that the neutral fully understands the issues and background of the case, and allow discussion and review of the possible implications of the neutral's written opinion); Lowenfeld, The Party–Appointed Arbitrator in International Controversies: Some Reflections, 30 Tex.Int'l L.J. 59, 65–67 (1995) (in international disputes a party-appointed arbitrator can help in the "translation of legal culture * * * when matters that are self-evident to lawyers from one country are puzzling to lawyers from another"; such an arbitrator also gives some "confidence that at least one member of the tribunal is listening, and listening sympathetically, to the submission of counsel").

3. Where the parties are unable to agree on an arbitrator and the proceeding is not being administered by an institution like the AAA, modern statutes empower a court to make the choice. See FAA, § 5.

A contract for the delivery of rice provided that any disputes "shall be resolved by means of the judgment of arbitrators *appointed by mutual agreement.* This could be in Nicaragua or the Rice Millers' Association

[RMA] in the United States." When a dispute arose over the condition of the rice, the buyer made a demand for arbitration with the RMA. Under RMA rules, the RMA arbitration committee appoints the arbitrators; the panel appointed by this committee proceeded to arbitrate the dispute and awarded the buyer $1.3 million. The court vacated the award, holding that the seller was instead "entitled" to an arbitration before arbitrators chosen by mutual agreement of the parties. "The arbitration clause does not set forth how this choice of arbitrators by the parties should be conducted." The district court was therefore instructed to require that arbitration "be conducted under the standard method, where both parties choose an arbitrator and these arbitrators select a third arbitrator"; if the two party-appointed arbitrators cannot agree, then the third arbitrator would be appointed by the court under § 5 of the FAA. Cargill Rice, Inc. v. Empresa Nicaraguense Dealimentos Basicos, 25 F.3d 223 (4th Cir.1994). Does this make any sense at all?

4. Three members of a family were parties to a partnership agreement: Charles, Albert (Charles' son), and Isidore (Charles' brother). The agreement provided for arbitration in which Charles and Albert would jointly name one arbitrator, Isidore would name another, and the two arbitrators would select a third.

However, the drafting of this clause proved to be inept. There was a change of alignment in the partnership not originally contemplated; Isidore and Charles, complaining about Albert's lack of concern for the partnership, sought arbitration. Charles and Albert could not jointly agree on an arbitrator; Albert insisted that he be permitted to select an arbitrator independently since the interests of the other two parties were identical and adverse to his. On application to the court to name an arbitrator, what result? See Lipschutz v. Gutwirth, 304 N.Y. 58, 106 N.E.2d 8 (1952).

5. One study of party preferences in labor arbitration suggests that employers tend to prefer economists over lawyers as arbitrators, while unions on the other hand "prefer arbitrators with legal training and dislike economists." Why might this be true? The authors speculate that this result may be explained by "the fact that economists are likely to be heavily influenced by efficiency considerations, whereas lawyers are more likely to place greater emphasis on equity." David E. Bloom & Christopher L. Cavanagh, An Analysis of the Selection of Arbitrators, 76 Am.Econ.Rev. 408, 418, 421 (1986). Cf. W. Daniel Boone, How Union Advocates Select Arbitrators, *in* Arbitration 2003: Arbitral Decision–Making: Confronting Current and Recurrent Issues, Proceedings, 56th Annual Meeting, National Academy of Arbitrators 266, 269 (2004): "I want a discipline case tried before an arbitrator who has life experiences more than going to law school, working as an attorney or academician, and then becoming an arbitrator. * * * [I]n almost all workplaces, nothing works the way it is supposed to. * * * [A]n arbitrator should understand that most rules and procedures are not followed 100 percent."

6. A "routine contract suit" was assigned to a magistrate judge. "Protracted efforts at settlement ensued but were unsuccessful. Then the lawyers had a brainstorm: appoint [the magistrate judge] the arbitrator of their dispute." An order, drafted by the lawyers and signed by the judge, provided that an independent auditor selected by the parties would determine the actual losses sustained, and "the Court will retain jurisdiction to act as the arbitrator * * * and shall make a decision binding upon the parties." The auditor submitted a report; the magistrate judge then held two hearings to consider the parties' objections and issued a document, captioned "judgment," calling for the defendant to pay $125,000.

The Seventh Circuit (in an opinion by Judge Posner) affirmed this "judgment"—"if that is what it is"—but seemed puzzled by just what it was that the parties and the magistrate judge had done. Had the judge issued an award as arbitrator, and then judicially confirmed his own award? If so, his order would clearly be void: "[A]rbitration is not in the job description of a federal judge"; "since 'alternative dispute resolution' is all the rage these days * * * the day may not be distant when federal judges will be recommissioned (or issued supplementary commissions) as arbitrators. But it has not arrived." However, there was an alternative characterization of what the parties had done that was "slightly more plausible": Perhaps they had simply "stipulated to an abbreviated, informal procedure for [the magistrate judge's] deciding the case in his judicial capacity. * * * [T]hey agreed that the judge would make a decision on a record consisting of the auditor's report plus the parties' objections, * * * and that they would not appeal the decision. So viewed, the procedure was not improper." By "talking the language of arbitration" the parties had essentially intended to limit judicial review of the magistrate judge's decision. DDI Seamless Cylinder Int'l, Inc. v. General Fire Extinguisher Corp., 14 F.3d 1163 (7th Cir.1994).

b. ARBITRAL IMPARTIALITY

Commonwealth Coatings Corp. v. Continental Casualty Co.

Supreme Court of the United States, 1968.
393 U.S. 145, 89 S.Ct. 337, 21 L.Ed.2d 301.

■ Mr. Justice Black delivered the opinion of the Court.

At issue in this case is the question whether elementary requirements of impartiality taken for granted in every judicial proceeding are suspended when the parties agree to resolve a dispute through arbitration.

[Having read this far, what do you think the answer is going to be?—Eds.]

The petitioner, Commonwealth Coatings Corp., a subcontractor, sued the sureties on the prime contractor's bond to recover money alleged to be due for a painting job. The contract for painting contained an agreement to arbitrate such controversies. Pursuant to this agreement petitioner appointed one arbitrator, the prime contractor appointed a second, and these two together selected the third arbitrator. This third arbitrator, the supposedly neutral member of the panel, conducted a large business in Puerto Rico, in which he served as an engineering consultant for various people in connection with building construction projects. One of his regular customers in this business was the prime contractor that petitioner sued in this case. This relationship with the prime contractor was in a sense sporadic in that the arbitrator's services were used only from time to time at irregular intervals, and there had been no dealings between them for about a year immediately preceding the arbitration. Nevertheless, the prime contractor's patronage was repeated and significant, involving fees of about $12,000 over a period of four or five years, and the relationship even went so far as to include the rendering of services on the very projects involved in this lawsuit. An arbitration was held, but the facts concerning the close business connections between the third arbitrator and the prime contractor were unknown to petitioner and were never revealed to it by this arbitrator, by the prime contractor, or by anyone else until after an award had been made. Petitioner challenged the award on this ground, among others, but the District Court refused to set aside the award. The Court of Appeals affirmed.

    * * * [B]oth sides here assume that [the FAA] governs this case. Section 10 sets out the conditions upon which awards can be vacated. The two courts below held, however, that § 10 could not be construed in such a way as to justify vacating the award in this case. We disagree and reverse. Section 10 does authorize vacation of an award where it was "procured by corruption, fraud, or undue means" or "[w]here there was evident partiality * * * in the arbitrators." These provisions show a desire of Congress to provide not merely for *any* arbitration but for an impartial one. It is true that petitioner does not charge before us that the third arbitrator was actually guilty of fraud or bias in deciding this case, and we have no reason, apart from the undisclosed business relationship, to suspect him of any improper motives. But neither this arbitrator nor the prime contractor gave to petitioner even an intimation of the close financial relations that had existed between them for a period of years. We have no doubt that if a litigant could show that a foreman of a jury or a judge in a court of justice had, unknown to the litigant, any such relationship, the judgment would be subject to challenge. This is shown beyond doubt by Tumey v. State of Ohio, 273 U.S. 510 (1927), where this Court held that a conviction could not stand because a small part of the judge's income consisted of court fees collected from convicted defendants. Although in *Tumey* it appeared the amount of the judge's compensation actually depended on whether he decided for one side or the other, that is too small a distinction to allow this manifest violation of the strict morality and fairness Congress would have expected on the part of the arbitrator and the other party in this case. Nor should it be at all relevant, as the Court of Appeals apparently thought it was here, that "[t]he payments received were a very small part of [the arbitrator's] income * * *." For in *Tumey* the Court held that a decision should be set aside where there is "the slightest pecuniary interest" on the part of the judge, and specifically rejected the State's contention that the compensation involved there was "so small that it is not to be regarded as

likely to influence improperly a judicial officer in the discharge of his duty
* * *.'' Since in the case of courts this is a *constitutional* principle, we can
see no basis for refusing to find the same concept in the broad statutory
language that governs arbitration proceedings and provides that an award
can be set aside on the basis of "evident partiality" or the use of "undue
means." It is true that arbitrators cannot sever all their ties with the
business world, since they are not expected to get all their income from
their work deciding cases, but we should, if anything, be even more
scrupulous to safeguard the impartiality of arbitrators than judges, since
the former have completely free rein to decide the law as well as the facts
and are not subject to appellate review. We can perceive no way in which
the effectiveness of the arbitration process will be hampered by the simple
requirement that arbitrators disclose to the parties any dealings that might
create an impression of possible bias.

[Justice Black then referred to the AAA rules of procedure which,
"while not controlling in this case," called on an arbitrator "to disclose any
circumstances likely to create a presumption of bias or which he believes
might disqualify him as an impartial Arbitrator."]

[B]ased on the same principle as this Arbitration Association rule is
that part of the 33d Canon of Judicial Ethics which provides:

33.   Social Relations

* * * [A judge] should, however, in pending or prospective litigation
before him be particularly careful to avoid such action as may reasonably
tend to awaken the suspicion that his social or business relations or
friendships, constitute an element in influencing his judicial conduct.

This rule of arbitration and this canon of judicial ethics rest on the
premise that any tribunal permitted by law to try cases and controversies
not only must be unbiased but also must avoid even the appearance of bias.
We cannot believe that it was the purpose of Congress to authorize litigants
to submit their cases and controversies to arbitration boards that might
reasonably be thought biased against one litigant and favorable to another.

Reversed.

■ MR. JUSTICE WHITE, with whom MR. JUSTICE MARSHALL joins, concurring.

While I am glad to join my Brother Black's opinion in this case, I desire
to make these additional remarks. The Court does not decide today that
arbitrators are to be held to the standards of judicial decorum of Article III
judges, or indeed of any judges. It is often because they are men of affairs,
not apart from but of the marketplace, that they are effective in their
adjudicatory function. This does not mean the judiciary must overlook
outright chicanery in giving effect to their awards; that would be an
abdication of our responsibility. But it does mean that arbitrators are not
automatically disqualified by a business relationship with the parties before
them if both parties are informed of the relationship in advance, or if they
are unaware of the facts but the relationship is trivial. I see no reason
automatically to disqualify the best informed and most capable potential
arbitrators.

The arbitration process functions best when an amicable and trusting atmosphere is preserved and there is voluntary compliance with the decree, without need for judicial enforcement. This end is best served by establishing an atmosphere of frankness at the outset, through disclosure by the arbitrator of any financial transactions which he has had or is negotiating with either of the parties. In many cases the arbitrator might believe the business relationship to be so insubstantial that to make a point of revealing it would suggest he is indeed easily swayed, and perhaps a partisan of that party.* But if the law requires the disclosure, no such imputation can arise. And it is far better that the relationship be disclosed at the outset, when the parties are free to reject the arbitrator or accept him with knowledge of the relationship and continuing faith in his objectivity, than to have the relationship come to light after the arbitration, when a suspicious or disgruntled party can seize on it as a pretext for invalidating the award. The judiciary should minimize its role in arbitration as judge of the arbitrator's impartiality. That role is best consigned to the parties, who are the architects of their own arbitration process, and are far better informed of the prevailing ethical standards and reputations within their business.

Of course, an arbitrator's business relationships may be diverse indeed, involving more or less remote commercial connections with great numbers of people. He cannot be expected to provide the parties with his complete and unexpurgated business biography. But it is enough for present purposes to hold, as the Court does, that where the arbitrator has a substantial interest in a firm which has done more than trivial business with a party, that fact must be disclosed. If arbitrators err on the side of disclosure, as they should, it will not be difficult for courts to identify those undisclosed relationships which are too insubstantial to warrant vacating an award.

■ Mr. Justice Fortas, with whom Mr. Justice Harlan and Mr. Justice Stewart join, dissenting.

I dissent and would affirm the judgment.

* * *

Both courts below held, and petitioner concedes, that the third arbitrator was innocent of any actual partiality, or bias, or improper motive. There is no suggestion of concealment as distinguished from the innocent failure to volunteer information.

The third arbitrator is a leading and respected consulting engineer who has performed services for "most of the contractors in Puerto Rico." He was well known to petitioner's counsel and they were personal friends. Petitioner's counsel candidly admitted that if he had been told about the arbitrator's prior relationship "I don't think I would have objected because I know Mr. Capacete [the arbitrator]."

---

* In fact, the District Court found—on the basis of the record and petitioner's admissions—that the arbitrator in this case was entirely fair and impartial. I do not read the majority opinion as questioning this finding in any way.

Clearly, the District Judge's conclusion, affirmed by the Court of Appeals for the First Circuit, was correct, that "the arbitrators conducted fair, impartial hearings; that they reached a proper determination of the issues before them, and that plaintiff's objections represent a 'situation where the losing party to an arbitration is now clutching at straws in an attempt to avoid the results of the arbitration to which it became a party.'"

* * *

Arbitration is essentially consensual and practical. The United States Arbitration Act is obviously designed to protect the integrity of the process with a minimum of insistence upon set formulae and rules. The Court applies to this process rules applicable to judges and not to a system characterized by dealing on faith and reputation for reliability. Such formalism is not contemplated by the Act nor is it warranted in a case where no claim is made of partiality, of unfairness, or of misconduct in any degree.

NOTES AND QUESTIONS

1. Did Justice White really "join" in Justice Black's opinion? Note that the votes of Justices White and Marshall were essential to a majority in *Commonwealth Coatings*.

2. The current version of the AAA's Commercial Arbitration Rules requires any person named as an arbitrator to "disclose to the AAA any circumstance likely to give rise to justifiable doubt as to the arbitrator's impartiality or independence, including any bias or any financial or personal interest in the result of the arbitration or any past or present relationship with the parties or their representatives." The AAA communicates this information to the parties and if any of them objects, "the AAA shall determine whether the arbitrator should be disqualified * * * and shall inform the parties of its decision, which decision shall be conclusive." (Rules 16, 17).

A "Code of Ethics for Arbitrators in Commercial Disputes" has also been adopted by the AAA and by the American Bar Association. Canon II of this Code provides that "an arbitrator shall disclose any interest or relationship likely to affect impartiality or which might create an appearance of partiality":

A. Persons who are requested to serve as arbitrators should, before accepting, disclose:

(1) any known direct or indirect financial or personal interest in the outcome of the arbitration;

(2) any known existing or past financial, business, professional or personal relationships which might reasonably affect impartiality or lack of independence in the eyes of any of the parties. For example, prospective arbitrators should disclose any such relationships which

they personally have with any party or its lawyer, with any co-arbitrator, or with any individual whom they have been told will be a witness. They should also disclose any such relationships involving their families or household members or their current employers, partners, or professional or business associates that can be ascertained by reasonable efforts;

(3) the nature and extent of any prior knowledge they may have of the dispute. * * *

B. Persons who are requested to accept appointment as arbitrators should make a reasonable effort to inform themselves of any interests or relationships described in paragraph A. * * *

G. If an arbitrator is requested by all parties to withdraw, the arbitrator must do so. If an arbitrator is requested to withdraw by less than all of the parties because of alleged partiality, the arbitrator should withdraw unless either of the following circumstances exists:

(1) An agreement of the parties, or arbitration rules agreed to by the parties, or applicable law establishes procedures for determining challenges to arbitrators, in which case those procedures should be followed; or

(2) In the absence of applicable procedures, if the arbitrator, after carefully considering the matter, determines that the reason for the challenge is not substantial, and that he or she can nevertheless act and decide the case impartially and fairly.

Notes to the Code also warn that

A prospective arbitrator is not necessarily partial or prejudiced by having acquired knowledge of the parties, the applicable law or the customs and practices of the business involved. Arbitrators may also have special experience or expertise in the areas of business, commerce, or technology which are involved in the arbitration. Arbitrators do not contravene this Canon if, by virtue of such experience or expertise, they have views on certain general issues likely to arise in the arbitration, but an arbitrator may not have prejudged any of the specific factual or legal determinations to be addressed during the arbitration.

3. What use can be made of the AAA Rules and Canons in a judicial proceeding to vacate an arbitral award? Judge Posner has written that:

[E]ven if the failure to disclose was a material violation of the ethical standards applicable to arbitration proceedings, it does not follow that the arbitration award may be nullified judicially. * * * The arbitration rules and code do not have the force of law. If [a party] is to get the arbitration award set aside it must bring itself within the statute * * *.

The American Arbitration Association is in competition not only with other private arbitration services but with the courts in providing—in the case of the private services, selling—an attractive form of dispute settlement. It may set its standards as high or as low as it thinks its customers want. The [FAA] has a different purpose—to make arbitration effective by putting the coercive force of the federal courts behind arbitration decrees that affect interstate commerce or are otherwise of federal concern. * * * The standards for judicial intervention are therefore narrowly drawn to assure the basic integrity of the arbitration process without meddling in it. Section 10 is full of words like corruption and misbehavior and fraud. The standards it sets are minimum ones. * * * The fact that the AAA went beyond the statutory standards in drafting its own code of ethics does not lower the threshold for judicial intervention.

Merit Ins. Co. v. Leatherby Ins. Co., 714 F.2d 673 (7th Cir.1983).

Do you agree? Cf. Art. V(1)(d) of the New York Convention, in Appendix B.

4. The arbitration statutes of some states impose more explicit and stringent obligations of disclosure on potential arbitrators. For example, recent California legislation requires any potential arbitrator to disclose the existence of any facts that would warrant the disqualification of a *judge*. It further provides that any potential arbitrator must disclose the "names of any prior or pending cases involving any party to the arbitration agreement or the lawyer for a party" for whom she served or is serving as an arbitrator, as well as "the results of each case arbitrated to conclusion * * * and the amount of monetary damages awarded, if any." The proposed arbitrator "shall be disqualified on the basis of the disclosure statement" if any party "serves a notice of disqualification"; failure to make the requisite disclosures would give rise to vacatur. Cal.Code Civ.Pro. §§ 1281.85, 1281.9, 1281.91,1286.2.

At the same time the legislature delegated to the state Judicial Council the task of promulgating additional minimum ethical standards, which could "expand but may not limit" those in the statute. The resulting "Ethics Standards for Neutral Arbitrators in Contractual Arbitration" came into effect in 2002 and are highly complex and detailed: They would apparently require disqualification because an arbitrator's "spouse used to serve on a bar committee with an associate of a party's lawyer, even if the associate is uninvolved in the case." They would also require disclosure of an arbitrator's membership in any organization that practices "invidious discrimination on the basis of race, sex, religion, national origin, or sexual orientation." Most burdensome are the requirements for consumer and employment arbitrations administered by an organization like the AAA or the NASD: In such cases the arbitrator would have to disclose any financial or professional relationship between the *institution* and a party or lawyer to the arbitration, as well as whether the institution had ever administered any other arbitrations in which a present party or lawyer was involved— and in such cases, the result and the amount of damages awarded. "The sheer collective volume of disclosure requirements is enough to make a conscientious arbitrator nervous, and provide a disappointed lawyer potential ammunition with which to pursue another try or an improved negotiated outcome." Jay Folberg, Arbitration Ethics: Is California the Future?, 18 Ohio St. J. on Disp. Res. 343, 352 (2003)(the author chaired the California Judicial Council Blue Ribbon Panel of Experts on Arbitrator Ethics); see also Michael A. Perino, Report to the Securities and Exchange Commission Regarding Arbitrator Conflict Disclosure Requirements in NASD and NYSE Securities Arbitrations 45, 47 (2002)("These provisions could effectively eliminate [securities] arbitration in California," since such conflicts "will exist in all [NASD-and NYSE-] sponsored arbitrations and could serve as a basis for disqualifying all arbitrators"); see generally http://www.sec.gov/pdf/arbconflict.pdf.

The NASD immediately suspended the conduct of all arbitrations in California. (It later announced that it would resume only if the customer/claimant were willing to waive the application of the state Ethics Standards). It also brought suit against the Judicial Council and its individual members, seeking a declaratory judgment that the Standards were an impermissible attempt to "usurp federal law," NASD Dispute Resolution, Inc. v. Judicial Council of California, 232 F.Supp.2d 1055 (N.D. Cal. 2002)(held, defendants are immune from suit under Eleventh Amendment). In another case, the Ninth Circuit found that the federal Securities Exchange Act preempted application of the California Ethics Standards to NASD-appointed arbitrators, so that the Standards were "without effect" as to these arbitrations: The SEC's approval of NASD arbitration procedures "included a thorough review and eventual approval of the NASD Code's disclosure and disqualification rules," and if each state could institute its own regulation, this would create "a patchwork of laws that would interfere with Congress's chosen approach" of delegating nationwide regulatory authority to the SEC and the NASD. The added disclosure requirements were "unnecessary because empirical evidence reveals little evidence of bias in [securities] arbitration outcomes"; nevertheless they would "increase the complexity, cost and uncertainty of the arbitration process," deter "well-qualified individuals" from being willing to serve on NASD panels, and in general "create an obstacle to the accomplishment and execution of the full purposes and objectives of Congress." Credit Suisse First Boston Corp. v. Grunwald, 400 F.3d 1119 (9th Cir. 2005).

The court in *Grunwald* found "no need to consider" whether the FAA also preempted the state Ethics Standards, 400 F.3d at 1136 fn. 26. This question was directly addressed in Ovitz v. Schulman, 133 Cal.App.4th 830, 35 Cal.Rptr.3d 117 (2005): While an arbitration was pending, an arbitrator accepted an appointment as arbitrator in another proceeding involving different parties but one of the same law firms; however, he did not disclose that fact. The court held that the state statute "leaves no room for discretion" and required vacatur: The court rejected the argument that the FAA preempted the state legislation: The California statute "does not undermine the enforceability of arbitration agreements," since it "neither limits the rights of contracting parties to submit disputes to arbitration, nor discourages persons from using arbitration"; the California scheme merely "seeks to enhance both the appearance and reality of fairness in arbitration proceedings, thereby instilling public confidence."

5. If courts held arbitrators to the same standards of isolation and purity to which they hold Article III judges, an adverse decision might invariably become the occasion for frantic research by the losing party into possible links between his adversary and the arbitrator. The obvious dangers to the arbitral process have led courts to be unreceptive to such attempts.

In their reluctance to set aside awards on these grounds courts have also been sensitive to the need for decision-makers with extensive professional experience and knowledge, and to what Judge Posner has called the necessary "tradeoff between impartiality and expertise." *Merit Ins. Co.*, supra note (3), 714 F.2d at 679; see also Sphere Drake Ins. Ltd. v. All American Life Ins. Co., 307 F.3d 617, 620 (7th Cir. 2002)(Easterbrook, J.):

> Industry arbitration, the modern law merchant, often uses panels composed of industry insiders, the better to understand the trade's norms of doing business and the consequences of proposed lines of decision. The more experience the panel has, and the smaller the number of repeat players, the more likely it is that the panel will contain some actual or potential friends, counselors or business rivals of the parties. Yet all participants may think the expertise-impartiality tradeoff worthwhile; the Arbitration Act does not fasten on every industry the model of the disinterested generalist judge.

See also Lefkovitz v. Wagner, 395 F.3d 773, 780 (7th Cir. 2005)(Posner, J.)("[s]tricter rules cabin the generalist because he is more apt to be led astray by the lawyers and witnesses in a matter in which his only knowledge comes from them. When disputants repose their trust in a specific individual rather than having to take the luck of the draw, it is right that they should have to take the bad with the good unless the individual runs completely off the rails").

A good example is presented by International Produce, Inc. v. A/S Rosshavet, 638 F.2d 548 (2d Cir.1981). This was a maritime arbitration in which the neutral arbitrator was the Vice–President of a management firm retained by owners of various commercial vessels. After the hearings had begun, this arbitrator's firm became involved in an unrelated arbitration involving another vessel. It happened that the law firms representing the parties in the second arbitration were the same firms that were handling the *International Produce* arbitration; in this second proceeding the arbitrator appeared as a non-party witness, prepared in his testimony by one of the law firms and cross-examined by the other. Although requested to withdraw, the arbitrator refused to do so, and his award was successfully challenged in district court. The Second Circuit held that the award should not have been vacated:

> It is not unusual that those who are selected as arbitrators in maritime arbitrations have had numerous prior dealings with one or more of the parties or their counsel. * * * Arbitrator Klosty aptly analogized New York's maritime-arbitration community to a busy harbor, where the wakes of the members often cross.

The most sought-after arbitrators are those who are prominent and experienced members of the specific business community in which the dispute to be arbitrated arose. Since they are chosen precisely because of their involvement in that community, some degree of overlapping representation and interest inevitably results. Those chosen as arbitrators in important shipping arbitrations have typically participated in a great number of prior maritime disputes, not only as arbitrators but also as parties and witnesses. They have therefore almost inevitably come into contact with a significant proportion of the relatively few lawyers who make up the New York admiralty bar. Under these circumstances, a decision on our part to vacate arbitration awards whenever a mere appearance of bias can be made out would seriously disrupt the salutary process of settling maritime disputes through arbitration.

6. Of course, the alleged conflict of interest in *International Produce* was immediately known to both of the parties in the case as soon as it arose. Would the matter be different—should a higher standard be imposed—if one party is claiming that the arbitrator failed before the hearing to disclose facts about his relationship with the other? See Schmitz v. Zilveti, 20 F.3d 1043 (9th Cir. 1994)(in a nondisclosure case, "the integrity of the process by which arbitrators are chosen is at issue," and showing a "reasonable impression of partiality" is sufficient because of the policy that "parties should choose their arbitrators intelligently"; by contrast, "in an actual bias determination, the integrity of the arbitrators' decision is directly at issue"; that a "reasonable impression of partiality" is present does not mean that the arbitration award itself was necessarily "the product of impropriety"). But cf. *Sphere Drake Ins. Ltd.*, supra note (5). In *Sphere Drake*, an arbitrator had—four years previously—worked on an unrelated matter as counsel to the Bermuda subsidiary of the party who had appointed him. It was held that his failure to make a full disclosure of these facts "may sully his reputation for candor but does not demonstrate 'evident partiality' and thus does not spoil the award." On those same facts, after all, the arbitrator could even "have served as a federal judge * * * without challenge on grounds of partiality"—and if "the full truth would not have disclosed even a risk of partiality," his failure to make a complete disclosure should not be treated differently: *Commonwealth Coatings* "did not hold * * * that disclosure is compulsory for its own sake, and its absence fatal even if the arbitrator meets judicial standards of impartiality."

7. A wealthy Colorado businessman alleged that "the star telecommunications analyst" at Salomon Smith Barney, a unit of Citigroup, had persuaded him to hold onto his WorldCom stock "even as the company spiraled into bankruptcy": He sought $900 million in an NASD arbitration, but the arbitrators ruled against him. He later learned that one of the arbitrators was the general counsel of a firm that—the previous year—had won underwriting business to take public a company represented by a law firm that had represented Citigroup and other WorldCom-related defendants. Eight years previously, the arbitrator had also been a defendant in a securities fraud case in which he had asked to be dismissed on the same legal basis that Citigroup used in its defense in the current arbitration with the claimant. Does the failure to disclose these facts warrant vacatur of the award? See Gretchen Morgenson, "Arbitrator in Citigroup Case Accused of Conflicts of Interest," N.Y. Times, Feb. 23, 2006 at p. C1.

8. Since the concept of "evident partiality" rests so heavily on a failure to disclose, it is been held that an arbitrator cannot be guilty of "evident partiality" absent *"actual knowledge* of a real or potential conflict," see Gianelli Money Purchase Plan & Trust v. ADM Investor Services, Inc., 146 F.3d 1309 (11th Cir. 1998); Mariner Financial Group, Inc. v. Bossley, 79 S.W.3d 30 (Tex. 2002)(Owen, J., concurring)("an impression of partiality cannot be created simply by the existence of facts, unknown to the arbitrator, that the arbitrator's 'reasonable effort to inform himself' would have revealed"). But cf. *Schmitz v. Zilveti,* note (6) above (lawyer ran a conflict check for a party but not for its parent company, which his law firm had represented many times over a period of 35 years; held, award vacated; "though lack of knowledge may prohibit actual bias, it does not always prohibit a reasonable impression of partiality"; that a lawyer "forgot to run a conflict check or had forgotten that he had previously represented the party is not an excuse").

9. There are at least some cases in which one can recognize "evident partiality" without a great deal of trouble. In one major insurance arbitration, the claimant was awarded $92 million by a "tripartite" panel. After the award was rendered—but before confirmation by a court—the losing attorneys surreptitiously made videotapes indicating that the claimant's lawyer and the panel's "neutral" arbitrator had spent several nights together in the lawyer's hotel room. "She says he spent the two nights in question in a separate room in her suite, one night because she was sick and another night because he didn't have a room of his own." (A full account appears in Schmitt, "Suite Sharing: Arbitrator's Friendship With Winning Lawyer Imperils Huge Victory," Wall St. J., Feb. 14, 1990, p. 1.) We understand that the award was later vacated by stipulation of the parties.

10. A sole arbitrator in a case in which Federal Vending was the claimant issued a written opinion upholding the validity of the company's form-contract liquidated damages provision. When he was selected to serve as an arbitrator in another Federal Vending case, he failed to disclose his prior arbitration experience; at the hearing, the defendant argued that the liquidated damages clause was an unenforceable penalty, and Federal Vending, in support of the clause, merely attached a copy of the arbitrator's decision in its favor in the prior case. "It is reasonable to assume that the validity of Federal Vending's form-contract liquidated damages provision is a recurring issue in every one of its contractual disputes." Should the award in favor of Federal Vending be vacated? Federal Vending, Inc. v. Steak & Ale of Fla., Inc., 71 F.Supp.2d 1245 (S.D. Fla. 1999)(held, motion to vacate denied since the respondent has failed to demonstrate any "actual prejudice" from the failure to disclose; any prejudice is "too speculative" in light of the fact that when the prior case did come to light, the AAA rejected the respondent's request to have the arbitrator removed; that the arbitrator "might likely decide the same issue the same way in a later arbitration does not mean that he has a bias for or against either party").

11.   Where an arbitration takes place under the AAA rules and a challenge is made to an arbitrator *before the hearing has begun*, the AAA "recognizes that it is preferable and more economical in the long run * * * to arrange for the prompt substitution of an arbitrator so that the arbitration can proceed without the threat of subsequent litigation." When a challenge is made *after the hearings have begun*, however, the AAA will be much less likely to disqualify the arbitrator—and will naturally require much more stringent proof of bias. See remarks by Michael Hoellering, then General Counsel of the AAA, reproduced in BNA ADR Rep., Jan. 5, 1989 at pp. 13, 15.

Where the AAA has rejected a challenge to an arbitrator, concerns for arbitral finality may be reinforced by deference to the institution's judgment and to its interpretation of its own rules. See Portland General Elec. Co. v. U.S. Bank Trust Nat'l Ass'n, 38 F.Supp.2d 1202, 1212 (D. Ore. 1999), rev'd on other grounds, 218 F.3d 1085 (9th Cir. 2000)("as the contract appoints the AAA as the entity charged with choosing who the appraiser would be, it was, in effect, the arbitrator of that portion of the dispute"; "the AAA's resolution was in itself an arbitral decision"); Reeves Bros., Inc. v. Capital–Mercury Shirt Corp., 962 F.Supp. 408 (S.D.N.Y.1997) (where the parties have adopted AAA rules, they "are also obligated to abide by the [AAA's] determinations under those rules"; the court also noted that after challenges to the arbitrator's qualifications were rejected in accordance with AAA rules, the losing party "fully participated in the arbitration without seeking a stay"). But, predictably, compare Azteca Construction, Inc. v. ADR Consulting, Inc., 121 Cal.App.4th 1156, 18 Cal.Rptr.3d 142 (2004)(party challenged a proposed arbitrator based on his required disclosure, but the AAA reaffirmed the appointment under its rules and the arbitration proceeded to an award; held, award vacated, "the provisions for arbitrator disqualification established by the California Legislature may not be waived or superseded by a private contract").

12.   Are party-appointed representatives on "tripartite" boards held to the same standards as other arbitrators? Section 23(a)(2) of the Revised Uniform Arbitration Act permits a court to vacate an award where there was "corruption by an arbitrator," "misconduct by an arbitrator prejudicing the rights of a party," or "evident partiality by an arbitrator *appointed as a neutral.*" What do the italicized words add?

American courts have long recognized that in domestic practice, "party-appointed arbitrators are *supposed* to be advocates." *Sphere Drake Ins. Ltd.*, supra note (5). After all, "the right to appoint one's own arbitrator * * * would be of little moment were it to comprehend solely the choice of a 'neutral' "; a party will only bargain for this valued right "if it involves a choice of one believed to be sympathetic to his position or favorably disposed to him." *Astoria Med. Group v. Health Ins. Plan of Greater N.Y.*,

11 N.Y.2d 128, 227 N.Y.S.2d 401, 182 N.E.2d 85, 88 (1962). One might see this as simply an advance "waiver" by each party of the right to an entirely neutral panel. And the clear lesson of the cases is that parties to an arbitration agreement are taken to have contracted with reference to established practice and usage in the field of arbitration—and that courts are bound to respect these choices. In any event, the right to an effectively neutral tribunal can be safeguarded merely by "building in presumably offsetting biases." Tate v. Saratoga Savings & Loan Ass'n, 216 Cal.App.3d 843, 265 Cal.Rptr. 440, 445 (1989).

In one case an arbitrator, after being appointed, assisted the party that had named him "in preparing its case by attending and participating in meetings with [its] witnesses [and suggesting] lines or areas of testimony." The court found this conduct "not only unobjectionable, but common-place," Sunkist Soft Drinks, Inc. v. Sunkist Growers, Inc., 10 F.3d 753 (11th Cir.1993). See also Delta Mine Holding Co. v. AFC Coal Properties, Inc., 280 F.3d 815 (8th Cir. 2001)(one of the party-appointed arbitrators was present at his party's witness preparation and strategy sessions, acted as that party's "expert in preparing witnesses," disclosed to that party "the substance of the panel's deliberations and the neutral arbitrator's draft decisions, and obtained input from [his party] before responding to [the neutral's] proposed offset;" held, vacatur is not warranted).

Assuming then that proper disclosure is made, can a party appoint a member of its Board of Directors as "its" arbitrator on a tripartite board? See *Astoria Medical Group*, supra (yes). Does it follow, then, that an individual party can *himself* sit as his own arbitrator? See Edmund E. Garrison, Inc. v. International Union of Operating Engineers, 283 F.Supp. 771 (S.D.N.Y.1968)(no). What about the arbitrator appointed by a claimant in a personal injury case who agreed to be compensated on the basis of a percentage of the award? See Aetna Casualty & Surety Co. v. Grabbert, 590 A.2d 88 (R.I.1991).

At the urging of the international arbitration bar—for whom American domestic practice was an embarrassing aberration—the "Code of Ethics for Arbitrators" has recently been revised so that there will henceforth be "a presumption of neutrality for *all* arbitrators, including party-appointed arbitrators." Revisions to the Code have necessarily been accompanied by parallel changes in the Rules themselves: See R.12(b)(effective July 1, 2003)(party-appointed arbitrators "must meet the [usual] standards with respect to impartiality and independence unless the parties have specifical-ly agreed ... that [they] are to be non-neutral and need not meet those standards"); R. 18 (b) (bar on ex parte communications "does not apply to arbitrators directly appointed by the parties who [the parties] have agreed in writing are non-neutral"). As the text indicates, these new rules operate only by default: But is it likely that contracting parties in AAA arbitrations will often exercise their power to reverse this presumption? Already at the drafting stage, little enough thought is given to the contours of any possible future arbitration; the "stickiness" of default rules—and their normative power—further suggest that authoritative statements of what constitutes "normal" practice are unlikely to be re-examined. Nor can we underestimate the effects of simple sheepishness: After all, after an arbitration has been initiated—and even more clearly ex ante—might it not seem rather delicate to suggest that "all our" arbitrators should be biased? Cf. Code of Ethics, Canon IX(c)(1) (it may be appropriate for party-appointed arbitrators, as part of their duty to determine their status, to inquire into "agreements that have not been expressly set forth, but which may be implied from an established course of dealings of the parties or well-recognized custom and usage in their trade or profession").

13. In international commercial arbitrations, the "tripartite" model is in fact a norm which will be surrendered only with difficulty—to many, indeed, the right to choose one member of the panel is the very essence of arbitration. And in such arbitrations the general understanding calls for a rule that is nominally different from what has traditionally been our domestic practice: Arbitrators on international panels are expected to be both independent of the party appointing them and impartial. Apparently there is no room for debate that a party-appointed arbitrator may be partisan, and ICC practice, for example, is to refuse confirmation to an arbitrator where there exists a professional or financial relationship with any of the parties.

Cf. Alan Scott Rau, On Integrity in Private Judging, 14 Arb. Int'l 115, 230–31 (1998):

> Nevertheless it is usually conceded that without violating in any way this theoretical obligation of independence, the arbitrator may quite acceptably share the nationality, or political or economic philosophy, or "legal culture" of the party who has nominated him—and may therefore be supposed from the very beginning to be "sympathetic" to that party's contentions, or "favorably disposed" to its position. * * *

> I would think it very doubtful that this could possibly be considered an improvement over the practice in our domestic commercial arbitrations. Even in the best of circumstances an official rhetoric of "independence" and a tolerated latent "sympathy" must exist in an uneasy tension. * * * .

> When the Continental jurist writes that a party-appointed arbitrator must be impartial—but can be impartial "in his own fashion"—the echo of Cole Porter is undoubtedly inadvertent. But in such circumstances the potential for ambiguity, uncertainty and confusion seems obvious. Even the arbitrator himself may be unaware of the extent to which his identification with the party who has appointed him may be affecting his view of a given procedural or substantive issue—and what is more important, this may be appreciated still less by his two colleagues, particularly the chairman. A mythology that promotes the belief that international arbitrators can be relied on not to allow their sympathy "to override their conscience and professional judgment"—regardless of whether this is taken as empirical description or as a mere aspiration—seems calculated only to increase these dangers of self-deception and sandbagging.

It is true of course that too visible an advocacy is likely to be simply counterproductive. Once he is perceived as little more than an agent for the party appointing him, an arbitrator may well lose all his clout with the rest of the panel and all his ability to influence the course of the proceedings. But these are counsels of prudence and discreet self-presentation, not of impartiality. In the course of discussions aimed at selecting party-appointed arbitrators in international cases, the highest praise one can give, apparently—one actually hears this said—is that the potential arbitrator "knows just how far he can go in advocacy" without losing all credibility with his colleagues. By contrast, to recognize quite openly the inevitability of partisanship once party-appointed arbitrators are used might instead * * * be "the only intellectually honest approach to the situation".

Another engaging note to the same effect is David J. Branson, American Party–Appointed Arbitrators: Not the Three Monkeys, 30 U. Dayton L. Rev. 1 (2004)(in an arbitration proceeding, "sympathy must be equivalent to partiality").

14. Westinghouse entered into a contract with the New York City Transit Authority (NYCTA) for the delivery of equipment for the New York subway system. Numerous disputes arose between the parties; NYCTA declared Westinghouse in default, and Westinghouse submitted a claim for additional compensation. Under the contract, disputes were to be submitted to the Superintendent of the NYCTA—who was an NYCTA employee and its Chief Electrical Officer; judicial review was to be limited to the question whether the Superintendent's decision was "arbitrary, capricious, or grossly erroneous to evidence bad faith." Westinghouse later challenged an adverse determination by the Superintendent, arguing that the contract "imposes a procedure for dispute resolution by a functionary inseparable from one of the parties to the dispute and, thus, fosters a predisposed adjudication process" contrary to public policy. The court, however, rejected this argument: "Westinghouse chose, with its business eyes open, to accept the terms, specifications and risk" of the contract; this was "part of the calculated business risk it undertook." Private contractors are "often economic giants in their own right," and the fact that municipalities may enjoy a "virtual monopolistic-kind of power" on their public works jobs "does not make these contracts adhesion agreements. * * * [W]here, as here, the parties are dealing at arm's length with relative equality of bargaining power, they ought to be left to themselves." The court found its conclusion buttressed by the fact that the contract "allows broader review than the usual and stricter standards" of judicial review of arbitration awards. Westinghouse Electric Corp. v. New York City Transit Authority, 82 N.Y.2d 47, 603 N.Y.S.2d 404, 623 N.E.2d 531 (1993). See also Parke Construction Co. v. Construction Management Co., 37 N.C.App. 549, 246 S.E.2d 564 (1978)(agreement named as sole arbitrator, "for absolute and final decision," the Chairman of the Board of the parent company of the respondent).

The leading treatise on federal arbitration law peremptorily asserts that cases like these have "no proper role to play in the interpretation of the FAA." Ian Macneil et al., Federal Arbitration Law 28:36 n.106 (1994). Why should this be true? How different, after all, is the agreement in *Westinghouse* from the common contractual device in which one party's payment is made subject to the "condition" that he be "satisfied" with performance by the other? See, e.g., Thompson–Starrett Co. v. La Belle Iron Works, 17 F.2d 536 (2d Cir. 1927)("the work included under this contract is to be done under the direction and to the satisfaction of the general superintendent of mines"; held, contractor's complaint dismissed; "the promisee of a conditional promise always runs the chance of losing what he has done, if he fails to fulfill the condition"; the superintendent "was not in any sense, as the plaintiff appears to suppose, an arbiter chosen by both sides because of his presumptive impartiality"; as he was "the representative of a party to the contract ... impartiality could not be expected of him, though honesty could")(L.Hand, J.). Cf. Morin Building Prods. Co. v. Baystone Construction, Inc., 717 F.2d 413, 417 (7th Cir.1983)(contract required all work to be done "subject to the final approval of the Architect or Owner's authorized agent, and his decision in matters relating to artistic effect shall be final"; "if it appeared from the language or circumstances of the contract that the parties really intended [the Owner] to have the right to reject [the Contractor's] work for failure to satisfy the private aesthetic taste of [the Owner's] representative, the rejection would have been proper even if unreasonable")(Posner, J.). Compare Graham v. Scissor–Tail, Inc., supra p. 104. ("Contracts of Adhesion and Unconscionability").

If it is thought desirable that the dispute resolution mechanism in *Westinghouse* be invalidated, should courts then go on to engage in a readjustment of the contract price—forcing Westinghouse to surrender the premium it undoubtedly was able to extract in return for subjecting itself to this risk—a premium which would now be unearned?

15. The CPR Institute for Dispute Resolution has published a set of rules for "non-administered arbitration"—rules "that could be used by sophisticated users who didn't need a babysitter," see 18 Alternatives to the High Cost of Litigation 149, 151–52 (Sept. 2000). A recent revision of these rules provides for an optional "screened" selection of party-appointed arbitrators—designed "in such a manner so that the arbitrators wouldn't know who picked them." Under the new rules, parties wishing to follow this procedure are given a copy of the CPR "Panel of Distinguished Neutrals," and each party is to designate three candidates, in order of preference, "as candidates for its party-designated arbitrator." A party may object to any appointment "on independent and impartial grounds by written and reasoned notice to CPR," which is to make a final decision with respect to any objection. "Neither CPR nor the parties shall advise or otherwise provide any information or indication to any arbitrator candidate or arbitrator as to which party selected either of the party-designated arbitrators." Rule 5.4(d); see http://www.cpradr.org/pdfs/arb-rules2005.pdf.

What do you think of this solution?

16.   On occasion a losing party, claiming that the arbitrator did not decide fairly or that he proceeded in violation of the rules, will bring a suit directly against the arbitrator or the administering institution. Such claims are usually rebuffed with an invocation of "arbitral immunity." Just as with judges, it is thought that "the independence necessary for principled and fearless decision-making can best be preserved by protecting these persons from bias or intimidation caused by the fear of a lawsuit arising out of the exercise of official functions within their jurisdiction." Corey v. New York Stock Exchange, 691 F.2d 1205 (6th Cir.1982). This "federal policy" dictates that the only remedy for a disgruntled party is under § 10 and § 11 of FAA and not by means of collateral attacks on the award. A similar interest in protecting arbitrators also means that when a court *does* hear a motion under § 10 or § 11, it is unlikely to permit examination of the arbitrators themselves aimed at developing a factual basis for impeaching the award. See, e.g., Woods v. Saturn Distribution Corp., 78 F.3d 424 (9th Cir. 1996)(although "it may be difficult to prove actual bias without deposing the arbitrators, deposition of arbitrators are repeatedly condemned by courts" and they must be "limited to situations where clear evidence of impropriety has been presented"; in arbitration between franchisee and automobile manufacturer, the franchisee "could have compiled evidence showing, e.g., the percentage of arbitration decisions that have been in favor of Saturn * * * to provide some indicia of improper motive").

The Revised Uniform Arbitration Act also provides that "an arbitrator or an arbitration organization acting in such capacity is immune from civil liability to the same extent as a judge of a court of this State acting in a judicial capacity"; where a suit against an arbitrator or an arbitral institution is dismissed on the ground of immunity, the defendants are entitled to recover "reasonable attorney's fees and other reasonable expenses of litigation." § 14(a),(e).

Now it is at least conceivable that arbitrators might *by contract choose to accept* potential liability for negligence—thereby giving rise to a market for insurance. However, the Revised Act makes the rule of arbitrator immunity mandatory and unwaivable; see § 4(c) (a party "may not waive," and the parties "may not vary the effect of," § 14). Why should this be the case? The only suggested rationale for such a position is that waiver would affect "the inherent rights of an arbitrator," § 4, cmt. 5: Does this advance the ball very far? Obviously, the mandatory nature of the immunity rule makes it unnecessary for arbitrators to "buy" immunity from users—and also makes it impossible for them to compete in terms of their relative willingness to bear the risk of liability, or, stated more positively, to signal their greater "confidence in their ability to reach a legally defensible decision," see Scott Hughes, Mediator Immunity: The Misguided and Inequitable Shifting of Risk, 83 Or. L. Rev. 107, 158, 191–93 (2004). Is it possible that permitting a waiver of immunity would be likely to skew the playing field in favor of the drafting party in contracts of adhesion?

17.   Who is acting as an "arbitrator" for purposes of "arbitral immunity"? Can former New York City mayor Edward Koch, who presided over a televised episode of "The People's Court," be liable for allegedly defamatory statements made in the course of the hearing? See Kabia v. Koch, 186 Misc.2d 363, 713 N.Y.S.2d 250 (City Ct.2000)(no; this is "arbitration" under state law even though any award is to be paid by the producers of the television program and not by the losing party; "arbitrators in contractually agreed upon arbitration proceedings are absolutely immune from liability for all acts within the scope of the arbitral process").

Should immunity be extended to an architect, employed and paid by the owner of a construction project and charged with interpreting the contract documents and deciding whether the contractor has substantially performed? See Lundgren v. Freeman, 307 F.2d 104, 116–19 (9th Cir.1962) (granting immunity when architect was acting as "quasi-arbitrator"). What about an accountant who is hired by both parties to a contract for the sale of stock to determine the earnings of the company? See Wasyl, Inc. v. First Boston Corp., 813 F.2d 1579 (9th Cir.1987) (claim of breach of contract and gross negligence by defendant in appraisal of value of partnership interest; immunity granted, relying on state arbitration statute that expressly "includes * * * valuations [and] appraisals"); contra, Comins v. Sharkansky, 38 Mass.App.Ct. 37, 644 N.E.2d 646 (1995)(defendant-accountant "is neither an arbitrator exercising 'quasi-judicial' functions nor an expert rendering expert services to the court"; "[w]hile an arbitration may be less formal than court proceedings, the parties contemplate that an arbitrator will hold hearings and will take evidence in the presence of the parties"). Cf. Arenson v. Casson Beckman Rutley & Co., [1975] 3 All E.R. 901 (H.L.) (Lord Kilbrandon) ("It would be absurd if the situation were that, when an expert is asked by one customer to value a picture, he is liable in damages if he is shown to have done so negligently, but that if two customers had jointly asked him to value the same picture he would have been immune from suit").

Do the reasons justifying arbitral immunity extend to protecting an arbitrator from a lawsuit that alleges he is liable for "breach of contract" for simply failing to render any award at all? See Baar v. Tigerman, 140 Cal.App.3d 979, 189 Cal.Rptr. 834 (1983) (arbitrator did not meet deadline imposed for decision under AAA rules; cases granting immunity were distinguished because here the arbitrators were not "acting in a quasi-judicial capacity" and plaintiffs had not alleged "misconduct in arriving at a decision").

2.   CONDUCT OF THE PROCEEDING

a.   INTRODUCTION

In any discussion of arbitration it is almost mandatory to mention the supposed "informality" of the process: "Submission of disputes to arbitration always risks an accumulation of procedural and evidentiary shortcuts that would properly frustrate counsel in a formal trial."[1] However, there is not merely one form of procedure for arbitration in the United States, but an almost infinite variety:

> At one extreme, we have what is practically courtroom procedure, with carefully drawn submissions, formal procedures, emphasis upon technicalities, formal opening and closing statements, arguments as to the admissibility and relevance of evidence, qualifications of witnesses, and the burden of proof, and briefs, rebuttal briefs, and sur-rebuttal briefs. At the other extreme, we have an atmosphere which is barely distinguishable from a mediation proceeding; the issue is vague and ill-defined, everybody talks at the same time, says irrelevant things, no standards of evidence appear, and the arbitrator seems to be working chiefly at the task of securing agreement between the disputants. Between the extremes are innumerable shadings and variations.[2]

The personality and the professional background of the arbitrator, the attitudes and the relationship of the parties, the issues in contention—all will influence the way the arbitration proceeds.

We should not be surprised to find a considerable amount of procedural innovation in the practice of arbitration—stemming, first, from the unbounded ability of the parties to "write their own ticket," and, second, from the traditionally broad discretion of arbitrators in structuring the proceedings. "Indeed, short of authorizing trial by battle or ordeal or, more doubtfully, by a panel of three monkeys, parties can stipulate to whatever procedures they want to govern the arbitration of their disputes."[3] In one large and complex antitrust dispute, for example, the parties had selected as their arbitrator a noted antitrust scholar and law professor:

> Based on his reading of briefs and affidavits, [the arbitrator] advised counsel which witnesses he wanted to have at the hearing. Rather than putting on the plaintiff's case in full, followed by defendant's case in full, [the arbitrator] proceeded by topic or category of witness; and in several instances, he put corresponding witnesses for the two sides on the stand at the same time. In so doing, he was able to let both parties' witnesses respond in succession to the same question and then engage in dialogue to explore differences of opinion. Throughout the proceeding, [he] peppered counsel with questions to explore the bases for and merits of various legal theories.

This technique avoided both the rigidity of traditional direct and cross-examination, and the usual "ships-passing-in-the-night" quality of most competing expert testimony. In fact most of the questioning at the hearing was done by the arbitrator, and only "limited follow-up questioning" was conducted by counsel. In addition, the parties agreed that the arbitrator

---

1. Forsythe Int'l, S.A. v. Gibbs Oil Co. of Texas, 915 F.2d 1017, 1022 (5th Cir.1990).

2. Stein, The Selection of Arbitrators, N.Y.U. Eighth Annual Conference on Labor 291, 293 (1955).

3. Baravati v. Josephthal, Lyon & Ross, Inc., 28 F.3d 704, 709 (7th Cir.1994)(Posner, C.J.).

would write a reasoned opinion that "could be published because of its potential value to other parties who might be faced with similar issues."[4]

One more illustration of the enormous flexibility permitted by the arbitration process is provided by a recent international arbitration, involving the dissolution of a joint venture. After the closing of the hearings, the arbitral tribunal

> Issued an Order by which it gave its tentative "inclination" regarding the outcome of the dispute and—simultaneously—put some additional questions to the parties, * * * reserving any modifications of its final judgment depending upon the parties' answers to the questions put. This Order actually gave the parties the possibility to see—before the final award was issued—that any and all issues raised were duly taken into consideration by the tribunal and also to realize that the tribunal had actually understood the core of the dispute. Indeed, the losing party tried—through the answers required by the tribunal—to redress the situation through what it considered its strongest arguments. In that case, it was in vain. But clearly, the losing party had been given a "voice" in a very efficient process.[5]

b.   THE ROLE OF LAWYERS

"[E]ven in the most informal of proceedings certain minimum requirements of 'due process' must be met if the award is to be legally binding."[6] State and federal statutes governing arbitration mandate certain elements supposed to be essential to a fair hearing. Under the Revised Uniform Arbitration Act, "the parties to the arbitration proceeding are entitled to be heard, to present evidence material to the controversy and to cross-examine witnesses appearing at the hearing." § 15(d). The parties also have the right to be represented by an attorney, and any waiver of that right "before a controversy arises" subject to the arbitration agreement is ineffective. §§ 4(b)(4), 16.

Attorneys can play a useful role in arbitration. In framing and focusing the issues, and in eliciting and marshalling the evidence, the attorney can help create a more coherent and rational process. However, the use of attorneys—along with the adversarial proceedings that seem to be envisaged by the arbitration statutes—may be responsible for some of the vociferous complaints about the growing "legalization" of the arbitration process. These complaints seem to be heard most loudly in the self-

4. Baker, Alexander, Cohan & Heike, "The First Texas–Pulse Arbitration: A Case Study," reprinted in John Murray, Alan Rau, and Edward Sherman, Dispute Resolution: Materials for Continuing Legal Education IV–136, IV–141 (NIDR 1991).

5. Teresa Giovannini, "The Psychological Aspects of Dispute Resolution: Commentary," *in* International Council for Commercial Arbitration, Congress series no. 11, International Commercial Arbitration: Important Contemporary Questions 348, 351 (2003).

6. Smith, Merrifield & Rothschild, Collective Bargaining and Labor Arbitration 212 (1970).

contained enclave of labor arbitration. One observer, for example, has written:

> In the past two decades, a change in orientation of labor arbitrators and a rise in the use of attorneys as advocates have accelerated the introduction into labor arbitration of procedures that approximate those of the courts. * * *

[The former president of the NAA has written that]

* * * The ratio of hard fought, legalistic arbitration presentations to problem-solving presentations is increasing. I now have more long, drawn-out cases in which employers and unions present prehearing briefs, spend endless hours haggling over the language of the submitted issue, have stenographic records made of the hearings and insist upon briefs, reply briefs, and sometimes, reply briefs to the reply briefs. * * *

Legalism adds to the complexity of arbitration, and correspondingly to the confusion of an employee. The impersonality that legalism brings to the process undermines its credibility. Employees who have been assisted in their grievances by union representatives who may have known them for years may be represented at the arbitration by attorneys whom they have seen for the first time on the day of the arbitration. When these attorneys, competent though they may be, neglect to raise questions that the grievants feel are important, which they feel would have been asked by union representatives, the grievants feel cheated.[7]

In this debate, however, as in most others, where one ends up may well depend upon one's starting point. The author of the preceding excerpt is a "Professor of Human Resource Development" in a College of Business. A lawyer, by contrast, is far more likely to be using a judicial yardstick when he evaluates arbitration. He may be struck most forcibly by the way in which the process *falls short* of the ritual trappings and judicial solemnity of the model with which he is most comfortable.

Commercial arbitrations are considerably more likely even than labor cases to involve lawyers (acting either as arbitrators or as advocates), and to look like "loose approximations of judicial proceedings."[8] This is a tendency that may be accelerating. More than half a century ago, Lon Fuller could advise advocates that the commercial arbitrator, "who will usually be a layman, * * * will be unimpressed by arguments resting upon the abstract 'rights' of the parties. The arbitrator will chiefly want to know whether the parties conducted themselves honorably and fairly and made a

---

7. Raffaele, Lawyers in Labor Arbitration, 37 Arb.J. No. 3 (Sept. 1982). See also Alleyne, Delawyerizing Labor Arbitration, 50 Ohio St. L.J. 93 (1989)("creeping formalism took sway with the commonly held notion that representation by a lawyer in an adversary proceeding, even a labor arbitration hearing, enhances the possibility of a successful outcome").

8. Shell, ERISA and Other Federal Employment Statutes: When Is Commercial Arbitration an "Adequate Substitute" for the Courts?, 68 Tex.L.Rev. 509, 534 (1990).

genuine effort to settle their differences by negotiation."[9] Given the remedial flexibility and freedom from the constraint of legal rules that typify arbitration, there remains much truth in this counsel. On the other hand, pressures by lawyers "always to guarantee as much due process as possible" may be creating subtle changes in the appearance of arbitration—and might well cause it "over time by accretion" to become almost "indistinguishable from the system you were trying to get away from."[10] When important questions of external law are routinely entrusted to arbitrators—and when the paradigm arbitration case increasingly becomes, not a dispute over the quality of goods delivered but over alleged violations of the Sherman Act or Title VII—then the attention to legal rules, and the accompanying level of procedural formality, may be expected to be much higher.

The attorney can still however expect in all forms of arbitration to encounter an environment that is noticeably different from that of litigation. Lawyers who are unfamiliar with the process may at first find it difficult to adapt themselves to the different quality of advocacy expected in arbitration, and must struggle to adjust their behavior to the different style and atmosphere of an arbitration proceeding. Such a mainstay of a litigator's life as pre-"trial" motion practice is for all practical purposes absent from arbitration. And a forensic style carefully honed for courtroom use may be totally out of place in an arbitration proceeding, where the parties and the arbitrators are all seated together around a conference-room table. In this more relaxed setting a non-theatrical, even conversational style is likely to be much more effective. A less confrontational and less argumentative approach may be hardest to pull off in the cross-examination of the opponent's witnesses—although this may be all the more important if the arbitrators are prone to identify closely with witnesses from the industry involved in the dispute.

c. EVIDENCE

The classic illustration of the relative "informality" of the arbitration process is the usual absence of the rules of evidence, which play such a dominant role in any courtroom. Under the AAA's Commercial Arbitration Rules, "[c]onformity to legal rules of evidence shall not be necessary"; "[t]he arbitrator shall determine the admissibility, relevance, and materiality of the evidence offered and may exclude evidence deemed by the arbitrator to be cumulative or irrelevant." (Rule 31). It is not unusual for evidence to be presented in the form of affidavits rather than live testimony, despite the absence of any possibility for cross-examination. See Commercial Arbitration Rules, Rule 32 (but it shall be given "only such weight as the arbitrator deems it entitled to after consideration of any objection made to its admission"); Pierre v. General Accident Ins., 100 A.D.2d 705,

---

9. Lon Fuller, Basic Contract Law 713 (1947).

10. McKeen, "Med–Mal Arbitration in California: Murky Results," Legal Times, Sept. 13, 1993, at pp. 10, 13 (quoting the general counsel for the Association for California Tort Reform).

474 N.Y.S.2d 622 (1984) (widow's claim for death benefit under automobile insurance policy was denied; arbitrator accepted "an unsworn report, in the form of a letter, from respondent's expert cardiologist, who did not testify or make himself available for cross-examination").

An arbitrator is in fact more likely to get into trouble by following the rules of evidence than by ignoring them—and far more likely to get into trouble by excluding evidence than by admitting it. Section 10(a)(3) of the FAA allows a court to vacate an award where the arbitrator was "guilty of misconduct" "in refusing to hear evidence pertinent and material to the controversy." There is a serious risk, then, that an arbitrator's disregard of testimony in reliance on rules of evidence may cause his award to be vacated, on the ground that a party has been denied a "fair hearing." See, e.g., Harvey Alum. v. United Steelworkers of America, 263 F.Supp. 488 (C.D.Cal.1967)(arbitrator refused to permit a witness to testify in full, and refused to consider his testimony, on the ground that he should have "appeared as a part of petitioner's 'principal case' and that his appearance as a rebuttal witness was not timely"; held, award vacated; "this does not mean that the Arbitrator may not insist on orderly proceeding but it does not appear that legalistic technicalities are to prevail or control particularly where no statement of ground rules for the hearing is made by the Arbitrator in the initial stages"). Perhaps as a consequence, the common tendency of arbitrators seems to be to admit most proffered evidence and to consider it "for whatever it may be worth." "I am prepared to listen to just about anything a party wants me to hear."[11]

A good example of how this can work in practice is provided by one lawyer's account of his service on an arbitration panel. In this construction case a contractor who had built a building for a private school submitted a substantial claim for "extras," work done but supposedly not covered by the contract price:

> In his opening statement to the panel, the lawyer for the school asserted that even without the extras, the contractor had made a profit. He then gave the arbitrators an affidavit from the school's controller. It stated that the school, which enjoyed an excellent reputation in the community, would have to raise each student's tuition at least $1,300 a year just to pay the interest on the amount sought by the contractor. The affidavit also stated that the school had granted scholarships to at least 28 students, who might have to withdraw if the contractor obtained the award he was seeking.

> [Over an objection by the contractor's lawyer that the affidavit was "incompetent, irrelevant, hearsay, prejudicial, and not probative on any issue in dispute," the panel (which also included an architect and an engineer) received it in evidence. The arbitration lasted for weeks, with copious, and confusing, evidence offered on each of the contractor's claims:]

11. McDermott, An Exercise in Dialectic: Should Arbitration Behave As Does Litigation?, Proceedings, 33rd Annual Meeting, Nat'l Academy of Arbitrators 1, 14 (1981).

Among the few facts which retained their persuasive power throughout the arbitration were the points the school lawyer had made at the outset. Almost every day, in private conversations over lunch or over an early evening drink, or during any one of the several recesses taken during the day, one or more of the arbitrators mentioned that the contractor had already made a profit and that granting the claim would injure the school and hurt innocent scholarship students.

The ultimate decision was in favor of the school. [12]

NOTES AND QUESTIONS

1.   The lowering of barriers to the admission of evidence in arbitration is often the subject of serious criticism, particularly on the part of lawyers, who are likely to find it chaotic, sloppy—and worse. For example, one prominent attorney and arbitrator has written:

> [T]he common arbitration practice often admits costly immaterial and/or prejudicial evidence. * * * The arbitrators do that out of [a desire] to appear to be fair and * * * [t]hereby they become unfair by receiving prejudicial evidence or making parties spend effort and money responding to immaterial evidence. * * * It is fairly common knowledge that uncross-examined affidavit evidence is *extremely* unreliable. Lawyers hear a narrative, draft a preliminary affidavit proposal with many voids filled in out of their own imagination, send it to the affiant perhaps "to check and execute if it is OK." * * * The wildest hearsay upon hearsay is often pretended to be "personal knowledge." A party ought not [to] have to fight such irresponsible evidence presented by the adversary.

Arnold & Hubert, Focus Points in Arbitration Practice 51–52 (1992, unpublished), quoted in Alan Scott Rau & Edward Sherman, Tradition and Innovation in International Arbitration Procedure, 30 Tex.Int'l L.J. 89, 95, 101 (1995).

In many cases such criticism is undoubtedly well-founded. In some kinds of cases, however, may criticisms of this sort overlook some of the premises of arbitration? The opportunity to present evidence that is not particularly relevant or even particularly reliable by the usual standards of the courtroom may nevertheless provide arbitrators with an insight into the "total situation" of the parties not afforded by a narrower scope of inquiry. (This may be true of the school construction arbitration discussed above.) And when the parties are engaged in a continuing relationship, such an opportunity can permit a useful "ventilation" of a grievance; as in mediation, when the parties are given a sense that they have had a full opportunity to "have their say" on points that are personally important to them, the process is legitimated and their confidence in it increased: "This

---

12.   Roth, When to Ignore the Rules of Evidence in Arbitration, 9 Litigation 20 (Winter 1983).

is therapy evidence." Edgar A. Jones, Evidentiary Concepts in Labor Arbitration: Some Modern Variations on Ancient Legal Themes, 13 U.C.L.A.L.Rev. 1241, 1254 (1966). In addition, it is far from clear that generosity in admitting evidence will necessarily prolong the hearings: Laying a proper "foundation" for evidence and qualifying witnesses, making a series of witnesses personally available for the purposes of cross-examination—and resolving the inevitable attorney wranglings over admissibility—all may consume at least as much if not more time than does the present practice.

Although it is well known that arbitrators are not bound by "rules of evidence," it is nevertheless quite common to find lawyers objecting in arbitration to the introduction of what, in litigation, would be "inadmissible" evidence. The goal here, obviously, is not so much to keep the evidence out—as it is to emphasize its unreliability, and to reduce the weight it might have for the arbitrator.

2.   On the tendency of labor arbitrators to admit evidence "for what it is worth," see W. Daniel Boone, A Debate: Should Labor Arbitrators Receive Evidence "For What It's Worth"?: The Union Perspective, Proceedings, 51st Annual Meeting, Nat'l Academy of Arbitrators 89, 92 (1999):

> Within the arbitrator community in Northern California, I take this to mean, "this evidence is not worth anything, but I'll let it in anyway." I understand the arbitrator to be saying (1) the evidence is neither relevant nor probative, (2) it has no persuasive impact, (3) it will not assist in making a decision, (4) the opposing party need not respond with evidence or argument, and (5) the proponent may proceed only if a truly short amount of time is taken.

3.   In none of the statutes governing arbitration is there any mention of improperly *admitting* evidence as a form of arbitral "misconduct." Can an award ever be vacated on such grounds? It is quite common for arbitrators to hear testimony in the form of what would be "hearsay" in a court of law, and this clearly is not a ground for overturning an award. E.g., Farkas v. Receivable Financing Corp., 806 F.Supp. 84 (E.D.Va.1992). See also In the Matter of the Arbitration between Norma Brill and Muller Brothers, Inc., 40 Misc.2d 683, 243 N.Y.S.2d 905 (Sup. Ct. 1962), in which the arbitrator received in evidence a detective agency report consisting of a "dime-novel series of stories about the petitioner and her behavior, said to be gathered from her former neighbors" and "detailing specific acts of alleged avarice, malice and chicanery." The trial court, calling this "hearsay on hearsay" and "thoroughly unfair evidence," "inflammatory and prejudicial to the highest degree," vacated the award. Higher courts, however, reversed, 17 A.D.2d 804, 232 N.Y.S.2d 806 (1962), aff'd, 13 N.Y.2d 776, 242 N.Y.S.2d 69, 192 N.E.2d 34 (N.Y. 1963*)*. See also Hayne, Miller & Farni v. Flume, 888 F.Supp. 949 (E.D.Wis.1995) (claimant introduced evidence of an FBI investigation of the respondent; held, "the improper admission of evidence does not warrant vacation of the arbitration award"; respondent's "reliance on cases involving the introduction of unfairly prejudicial evidence at a court trial is misplaced").

4. In a Better Business Bureau arbitration between General Motors and a car owner, the owner requested that GM be made to buy back the car; he had bought it second-hand, and had replaced the engine after driving it for an additional 23,000 miles. "The arbitrator awarded the owner half the cost of the second engine, or $875. The rationale was that, during mediation, the manufacturer had indicated a willingness to assume half the cost of the engine * * *." This anecdote is reported—without any comment—in Note, Virginia's Lemon Law: The Best Treatment for Car Owner's Canker?, 19 U.Rich.L.Rev. 405, 421 (1985).

See Bowles Financial Group, Inc. v. Stifel, Nicolaus & Co., Inc., 22 F.3d 1010 (10th Cir.1994). In this case the attorney for the claimant had "deliberately, intentionally, affirmatively and repeatedly communicated to the arbitrators an offer of settlement" from the respondent, arguing that the settlement offer "evidenced [the respondent's] admission of liability." "Counsel also indicated he routinely submitted settlement offers to the arbitrators in the cases where he represented clients in arbitration." The arbitrators, "after receiving the settlement offer, commented they would not consider it," but they subsequently made an award to the claimant that exceeded the offer. The court held that the respondent "has not proven it was subjected to a fundamentally unfair hearing":

> Had [the claimant's] counsel done before a court of law what he did before the arbitrators, significant sanctions would have been imposed and a mistrial ordered. But however well-established may be the judicial rules of evidence, they legitimately did not apply to this arbitration.

See also Mantle v. Upper Deck Co., 956 F.Supp. 719 (N.D.Tex.1997) (arbitrator reviewed allegedly privileged material, including the "mental impressions" of respondent's general counsel concerning "his assessment of the settlement value" of the case; "it is not widely held that arbitrators are so impressionable that exposure to prejudicial documents inexorably leads to partiality"); United States ex rel. National Roofing Services, Inc. v. Lovering–Johnson, Inc., 53 Supp.2d 1142 (D. Kan. 1999)("if [the parties] wished to arbitrate under rules which prohibit the introduction or consideration of settlement offer evidence, they should contract for such rules"). Cf. Rule 408, Federal Rules of Evidence.

5. "Skepticism about the ability of jurors to ignore inadmissible information is widespread," and "empirical research confirms that this skepticism is well-founded." Can judges—or arbitrators—accomplish what jurors cannot? A recent experimental study concludes that "like jurors, judges are not reliably able to avoid being influenced by relevant but inadmissible information of which they are aware." Judges in this study "had difficulty disregarding" such things as demands disclosed during settlement talks or conversations protected by attorney-client privilege; this information influenced the judges' decisions even when they had ruled the evidence inadmissible. Indeed, the problem may even be exacerbated in bench trials—because "judges presiding in a jury trial can protect juries from encountering inadmissible evidence in a way that they cannot protect themselves":

Jurors, for example, "will never be exposed to the inadmissible evidence that judges encounter during the pre-trial phase of litigation" or through *in camera* review. Andrew J. Wistrich et al., Can Judges Ignore Inadmissible Information? The Difficulty of Deliberately Disregarding, 153 U. Pa. L. Rev. 1251 (2005).

6. Should the arbitrator be expected to make a decision based solely on the evidence received at the hearing? After all, one of the premises of arbitration is that the arbitrator may himself be an "expert," chosen to bring to the process his own knowledge and familiarity with the subject matter. It seems clear that an arbitrator, unlike a judge, is free to draw on this background. In one commercial dispute, for example, the arbitrators awarded the buyer money damages for non-delivery even though no evidence as to the market price of the goods had been introduced. Judge Learned Hand dismissed the seller's argument that this constituted arbitral "misconduct," remarking that if the arbitrators "were of the trade, they were justified in resorting to their personal acquaintance with its prices." When the parties have chosen arbitration, he added, "they must be content with its informalities; they may not hedge it about with those procedural limitations which it is precisely its purpose to avoid." American Almond Prods. Co. v. Consolidated Pecan Sales Co., 144 F.2d 448, 450–51 (2d Cir.1944). See also In the Matter of the Arbitration between Oinoussian Steamship Corp. of Panama and Sabre Shipping Corp., 224 F.Supp. 807 (S.D.N.Y.1963) (arbitrators allegedly relied on trade custom not mentioned at hearing; "it would be carrying coals to Newcastle to require presentation of evidence to experts in the field").

However, the arbitrator's relative freedom in supplementing the evidence introduced by the parties is hardly a license to make his own independent investigation into the facts of the dispute. Where the quality of goods is in dispute, an arbitrator who gives samples of the goods to his own salesmen for the purpose of obtaining an opinion as to "merchantability" is inviting a court to vacate his award for "misconduct.". See Stefano Berizzi Co. v. Krausz, 239 N.Y. 315, 146 N.E. 436 (1925) (Cardozo, J.) ("The plaintiff, knowing nothing of the evidence, had no opportunity to rebut or even to explain it."). So is the arbitrator who, in attempting to fix the rental value of commercial real estate, asks his assistant to stand outside the shops in question to carry out a "pedestrian count." Top Shop Estates v. Danino, [1985] E.G.L.R. 9 (Q.B. 1984)(arbitrator had been "acting under a misapprehension of his function," which is not "to play the part of a Perry Mason where he feels that the submissions or evidence of the parties might usefully be supplemented").

7. The conduct of an international arbitration is naturally likely to be influenced by the legal background and nationality of the arbitrators, and particularly of the chairman. Any given arbitral tribunal is likely to "develop its own microculture," see Jan Paulsson, "Differing Approaches to International Arbitration Procedures: A Harmonization of Basic Notions," ADR Currents, Fall 1996, pp. 17, 19. Arbitrators from civil-law jurisdictions may share the preference of judges in those systems for the submission and exchange of documentary evidence and written witness statements, de-emphasizing oral testimony. Written statements "may entirely replace oral testimony," as "the entire testimony of some witnesses and much of the testimony of others often goes unchallenged." See W. Laurence Craig et al., International Chamber of Commerce Arbitration § 24.05 (3rd ed. 2000); id. at § 26.02 (practice of taking depositions outside the presence of the arbitrators to be submitted to panel as part of documentary evidence). Arbitrators with a civil-law background are also likely to share the propensity of civil-law judges to take a more active role in the development of the facts. They may themselves routinely call—and examine—witnesses, obtain the assistance of experts, or order inspections or site visits, all on their own initiative.

The International Bar Association has issued suggested "Rules on the Taking of Evidence in International Commercial Arbitration," containing detailed ground rules for the production of documents and witness statements, expert reports, and evidentiary hearings. Under these rules, each party is required to provide in advance a statement from "each witness on whose testimony it relies," containing "a full and detailed description of the facts, and the source of the witness's information as to those facts, sufficient to serve as that witness's evidence in the matter in dispute." A witness who has submitted such a statement is expected to "appear for testimony at an Evidentiary Hearing"—although if the parties agree that he "does not need to appear," such an agreement "shall not be considered to reflect" any agreement "as to the correctness of the content" of the statement. See http://www.ibanet.org.

The "Forward" to the IBA Rules announces that they are intended to "reflect procedures in use in many different legal systems," and therefore should "be particularly useful when the parties come from different legal cultures." (Some critics have pointed out nevertheless that the rules seem to have "adopted a largely common law approach," see Gary B. Born, International Commercial Arbitration: Commentary and Materials 485 (2nd ed. (2001)). This set of rules is but one bit of evidence that some sort of harmonization of different national practices in international arbitration is gradually being achieved; it is in fact often suggested that a "convergence"—"embracing elements of both systems"—may be "gaining acceptance * * * as a middle ground acceptable to parties from both sides of the divide." Siegfried H. Elsing & John M. Townsend, Bridging the Common Law–Civil Law Divide in Arbitration, 18 Arb. Int'l 59 (2002); see also Yves Derains, La pratique de l'administration de la preuve dans l'arbitrage commercial international, [2004] Rev. de l'Arb. 781, 789 (noting the increasing practice of using "procedures that borrow the characteristic features of the taking of evidence in both civil-law and common-law countries—although sometimes watering them down—the overall result amounting to a sort of synthesis of these different traditions").

8. Is a non-attorney who represents a party in an arbitration engaged in the "unauthorized practice of law"? See In re Advisory Opinion on Nonlawyer Representation in Securities Arbitration, 696 So.2d 1178 (Fla.

1997)("we think that compensated nonlawyer representatives in securities arbitration are engaged in the unauthorized practice of law and the protection of the public requires us to step in where there is no [federal] legislation or regulation"); Florida Bar v. Rapoport, 845 So.2d 874 (Fla. 2003)(attorney licensed to practice law in District of Columbia but not in Florida is "enjoined from * * * the representation of parties in securities arbitration in this state").

But cf. Superadio Ltd. Partnership v. Winstar Radio Productions, LLC., 446 Mass. 330, 844 N.E.2d 246 (2006)("even assuming that the representation might constitute the unauthorized practice of law, the conduct would not provide a basis to vacate the award on the ground that it was procured by 'undue means' "). See also Model Rules of Professional Conduct, R. 5.5(c)(3), Appendix D infra; AAA Commercial Arbitration Rules, R. 24 ("Any party may be represented by counsel or other authorized representative").

d. DISCOVERY

Another illustration of the relative informality of arbitration is the sharply limited availability of discovery, both "pre-trial" and at the hearing itself.

A starting point is a common statutory provision such as § 7 of the Uniform Arbitration Act:

(a) The arbitrators may issue subpoenas for the attendance of witnesses and for the production of books, records, documents and other evidence, and shall have the power to administer oaths. * * *

(b) On application of a party and for use as evidence, the arbitrators may permit a deposition to be taken, in the manner and upon the terms designated by the arbitrators, of a witness who cannot be subpoenaed or is unable to attend the hearing.

Compare § 7 of the FAA.

Issuance or enforcement of a subpoena is, however, rarely necessary; an informal request for information by the arbitrator at a hearing usually suffices. At least where it is a *party* who has been requested to produce evidence, he will be reluctant to antagonize the arbitrator by refusing. Most importantly, the party will be aware that should he decline to produce relevant evidence within his control, the arbitrator is likely to draw the inference that it would have been unfavorable to him.[13] And so in most cases "an informal indication that such an inference will or may be drawn is sufficient to extract the document." [14]

---

13. See In re U.S. Dept. of Labor and American Federation of Govt. Employees, 98 Lab.Arb. 1129 (1992) (sexual harassment case; "I draw an adverse inference against Management from its failure to produce [the supervisor alleged to have harassed the grievant] to testify at the hearing to deny that he conducted himself as grievant testified or to otherwise explain his behavior").

14. Andreas Lowenfeld, The *Mitsubishi* Case: Another View, 2 Arb.Int'l 178, 184 (1986).

The provisions of § 7 leave it to the discretion of the arbitrator to decide what materials he feels he needs to resolve the dispute; a party has no "right" to the issuance of a subpoena.[15] Exercise of this discretion is likely to be limited to demands for the production of documents that can be "described with specificity (for example, if they are internally referenced in documents put into evidence by one side)."[16] It is conceivable that an arbitrator's refusal to order the production of evidence might lead to a successful challenge to the award: In one maritime case, for example, the arbitrators had refused to order the shipowner to produce the ship's logs during the proceeding; a court indicated that this could constitute a violation of § 10(a)(3) of the FAA at least if the charterer of the ship could "show prejudice as a result." The court noted that the ship's logs are "perhaps the most important items of documentary evidence in any maritime controversy," and failure to supply them before the hearing's end could prejudice the ability of a party "not only in cross examination of witnesses, but in the preparation of its own case."[17] Such judicial action is, however, extremely rare.

True "discovery" in the litigation sense—for example, interrogatories and depositions taken before "trial" for the purposes of "trial" preparation—is even more limited. Provisions such as § 7 of the Uniform Arbitration Act assume, of course, that the arbitrators have already been named. Even where the arbitration panel is in place, the power of arbitrators to order pre-hearing discovery—at least in the absence of an agreement between the parties—is uncertain. Note that § 7 of the FAA is written so as to allow the arbitrators to "summon in writing" any person *to attend before them or any of them as a witness and in a proper case to bring with him* any documents which may be deemed material as evidence. Despite this language, an arbitrator's authority to order the production of documents *in advance of a hearing* is usually upheld: "Implicit in an arbitration panel's power to subpoena relevant documents for production at a hearing is the power to order the production of relevant documents for review by a party prior to the hearing."[18] Occasionally, however, even this authority

15. See National Broadcasting Co., Inc. v. Bear Stearns & Co., Inc., 165 F.3d 184, 187 (2d Cir. 1999)("§ 7 explicitly confers authority only upon *arbitrators*; by necessary implication, the *parties* to an arbitration may not employ this provision to subpoena documents or witnesses").

16. Tupman, "Discovery and Evidence in U.S. Arbitration: The Prevailing Views," 44 Arb.J. (March 1989) at pp. 27, 32. Cf. Hunt v. Mobil Oil Corp., 654 F.Supp. 1487, 1512 (S.D.N.Y.1987) (arbitrators refused to issue a "broadcast subpoena" demanding "all documents" of various kinds; such a request "is not uncommon in litigation [but] is precisely the type of production demand that is

the exception rather than the rule in arbitration").

17. In the Matter of the Arbitration between Chevron Transport Corp. and Astro Vencedor Compania Naviera, S.A., 300 F.Supp. 179 (S.D.N.Y.1969).

18. Security Life Ins. Co. of Amer. v. Duncanson & Holt, Inc., 228 F.3d 865. 870–71 (8th Cir.2000)(our interest in "the efficient resolution of disputes through arbitration" is "furthered by permitting a party to review and digest relevant documentary evidence prior to the arbitration hearing"); see also Meadows Indemnity Co., Ltd. v. Nutmeg Ins. Co., 157 F.R.D. 42 (M.D.Tenn.1994) (considering "the sheer number of documents addressed by the subpoena," it would be

has been denied.[19] In any event the full range of discovery provided by the Federal Rules of Civil Procedure will not be available: While the Federal Rules apply to motions made under the FAA (for example, motions to compel arbitration or to confirm an award), it is clear that they do not apply *to the conduct of the actual proceedings* before the arbitrators.

The reluctance to make pre-hearing discovery more widely available in arbitration may reflect the concern that this would be inconsistent with the goal of rapid and inexpensive dispute resolution. Looming over the debate is likely to be the specter of the "abuse" of the discovery process— "unfocused, unthoughtful, often massive, and always expensive"—which many observers blame for the delay and excessive cost characterizing complex federal litigation.[20] The fear is often expressed that the use of pre-hearing discovery would add one further layer of complexity and "legalism" to a process which in the eyes of some observers has already come too much to resemble formal adjudication. In addition, there is a concern that judicial supervision and administration of the discovery process might interfere with the functions of the arbitrators chosen by the parties, and "preshape" the issues presented to them for decision. The point is also frequently made that by choosing arbitration, the parties have voluntarily accepted the risk that pre-hearing discovery and the other "procedural niceties which are normally associated with a formal trial" would not be available to them.[21] But at the same time, of course, limited discovery is likely to increase the risk that a party may come to the hearing with only an incomplete understanding of the issues, the nature of the opponent's case, and the evidence to be presented.

There are, however, some state statutes that do envisage more extensive arbitral discovery. For example, the Texas version of the Uniform Arbitration Act adds to § 7 that the arbitrators may authorize a deposition *"for discovery or evidentiary purposes* to be taken of an adverse witness," such a deposition to be taken "in the manner provided by law for a deposition in a civil action pending in a district court." Tex.Civ.Prac. & Rem.Code § 171.050. The recent Revised Uniform Arbitration Act adds that an arbitrator may "permit such discovery as the arbitrator decides is appropriate in the circumstances, taking into account the needs of the parties to the arbitration proceeding and other affected persons and the

---

"quite fantastic and practically unreasonable" for the arbitrators to require a witness to appear before the panel and to bring them all to the hearing; while the subpoena was directed not to a party in the arbitration, but to defendants in a related pending lawsuit, they were "intricately related to the parties involved in the arbitration" and were not "mere third-parties who have been pulled into this matter arbitrarily").

19. See North American Foreign Trading Corp. v. Rosen, 58 A.D.2d 527, 395 N.Y.S.2d 194 (1977) (arbitration panel "ex-

ceed[ed] its authority by directing pre-arbitration disclosure").

20. See Lundquist, In Search of Discovery Reform, 66 A.B.A.J. 1071 (1980). Cf. Mullenix, Discovery in Disarray: The Pervasive Myth of Pervasive Discovery Abuse and the Consequences for Unfounded Rulemaking, 46 Stan.L.Rev. 1393 (1994) (the notion of discovery abuse "is based on questionable social science, 'cosmic anecdote,' and pervasive, media-perpetuated myths").

21. Burton v. Bush, 614 F.2d 389, 390 (4th Cir.1980).

desirability of making the proceeding fair, expeditious, and cost effective." § 17(c). See also Cal.Code Civ.Pro. §§ 1283.05, 1283.1 ("right to take depositions and to obtain discovery" in arbitration of personal injury claims). And at the same time, it seems increasingly common to find explicit provisions in the arbitration agreement itself, or in institutional rules, that permit limited discovery in the form of document production or even depositions.[22]

The general unavailability of pre-hearing discovery in arbitration often leads parties to an arbitrable dispute to seek discovery ordered and supervised by a *court*. A fairly liberal attitude towards allowing discovery is exemplified by Bigge Crane & Rigging Co. v. Docutel Corp., 371 F.Supp. 240 (E.D.N.Y.1973). In *Bigge,* a subcontractor brought suit against a general contractor for payments due under a construction contract. The plaintiff, asserting that it had been given "no explanation" of the reasons it had not been paid for the work performed, then sought to take depositions of the defendant's employees and to obtain inspection of job records, contracts, and other documents. The defendant moved for a stay of the action under § 3 of the FAA and for an order compelling arbitration. The court granted the motion and stayed the trial pending completion of arbitration—"without prejudice," however, "to the rights of [the parties] to utilize the pretrial discovery procedures of the Federal Rules of Civil Procedure in a manner which does not delay the course of the arbitration":

> In this case there will have been considerable delay by the time the elaborate proceedings of the American Arbitration Association for the selection of arbitrators have been completed; and the arbitrators, selected for this particular case, may be under some pressure to complete their task promptly. On the other hand, discovery proceedings in the court action can go forward while the selection of arbitrators and scheduling of a hearing is under way.

* * *

> Arbitration is not a separate proceeding independent of the courts, as was sometimes thought. The courts are brigaded with the arbitral tribunal in proceedings to compel arbitration or stay judicial trials, proceedings to enforce or quash subpoenas issued by arbitrators and proceedings to enforce or set aside arbitral awards. * * * [T]he court believes that it should exercise discretion to permit discovery in this case because (1) discovery is particularly necessary in a case where the claim is for payment for work done and virtually completed, and the nature of any defense is unknown; (2) the amounts involved are so

---

22. E.g., Fernandez v. Clear Channel Broadcasting, Inc., 268 F.Supp.2d 1365 (S.D. Fla. 2003)(agreement provided that each party "shall have the right to take up to three depositions unless the arbitrator, on a showing of good cause, approves additional depositions," and that each party "also shall have the right to require the production of rele- vant documents from the other party"; plaintiff argued that the agreement was un- enforceable because it "fails to provide for reasonable discovery, thereby depriving plaintiff of an adequate forum for vindication of his rights," but the court compelled arbi- tration).

substantial that any expense in taking depositions is relatively small; [and] (3) the action has proceeded to such a point that the taking of depositions can probably be accomplished without delaying the arbitration.

Most cases, however, are considerably more restrictive than *Bigge* . There is a tendency to require that pre-arbitration discovery be "necessary" to a party to allow him to "present a proper case to the arbitrators," or even that "extraordinary circumstances" be present, before a court may order it.[23] For one such example, see Deiulemar Compagnia Di Navigazione S.p.A. v. M/V Allegra, 198 F.3d 473 (4th Cir.1999). Here an agreement for a time charter specified that the vessel would maintain a guaranteed speed of 12–13 knots; the agreement also provided for arbitration in London. When the vessel reached its final destination at Baltimore, the charterer claimed that the promised performance specifications had not been met, and tried to inspect the vessel in order to gather and preserve evidence to support its claim. The owner refused, and argued that all of the information sought "could be requested through the arbitration process" in London. The trial court granted the charterer's request for discovery under Rule 27 of the Federal Rules Civil Procedure, and the Fourth Circuit affirmed: A marine expert was permitted to inspect the vessel, observe repairs, take photographs, and copy documents. Since the ship's engine was scheduled for repair, "the circumstances and conditions extant today can never be recreated"; since the vessel was scheduled to leave the territorial waters of the United States immediately following repairs, the charterer "was in danger of losing access to any evidence of the ship's condition." "Given the time sensitive nature of [the charterer's] request and the evanescent nature of the evidence sought, we do not believe that the district court abused its discretion" in accepting the charterer's representation that it could not obtain "emergency discovery" from the London arbitrator "in time to preserve the rapidly changing condition of the ship." The sealed evidence gathered from the vessel was to be held *in camera* and transferred to the pending arbitration in London: "The arbitrator does not have to admit the evidence; nor does he have to suppress it; that choice is left entirely to the arbitrator."

As *Deiulemar* suggests, where a court order can be characterized—not as an order of "discovery" to produce evidence for later use in arbitration—but merely as an order to "preserve" or "perpetuate" existing evidence against destruction—judicial relief will be considerably easier to obtain.[24] See Section "e." below.

23.   See In re the Application of Moock, 99 A.D.2d 1003, 473 N.Y.S.2d 793 (App. Div. 1984); International Components Corp. v. Klaiber, 54 A.D.2d 550, 387 N.Y.S.2d 253 (1976) ("absolutely necessary"). Cf. Harry F. Ortlip Co. v. George Hyman Construction Co., 126 F.R.D. 494 (E.D.Pa. 1989) (staying discovery in lawsuit until after conclusion of arbitration between two of the parties on a related matter; depositions were being sought in order to "obtain testimony to be used in the forthcoming arbitration," and "[t]his [plaintiff] may not do"; " 'extraordinary circumstances' do not include an inability or a failure to obtain discovery for an arbitration proceeding").

24.   See also Sagot Jennings & Sigmond v. Sagot, 2003 WL 1873298 (Pa. Com. Pl.)(de-

NOTES AND QUESTIONS

1. "[I]n the large, complex case, discovery is almost inevitable." Robert H. Gorske, An Arbitrator Looks at Expediting the Large, Complex Case, 5 Ohio St.J.Disp.Res. 381, 394 (1990). In an increasing number of such disputes, procedures are being introduced aimed at insuring that both parties in arbitration will have available to them all the information they need for the full presentation of their cases. Experiments in this area usually arise out of some combination of arbitrator initiative and party cooperation.

In one large construction case—involving claims of almost $800 million and requiring more than 2 ½ years to complete—the arbitrators "proposed, and the parties agreed upon, a format similar to that used by numerous regulatory agencies whereby direct testimony and exhibits would be pre-filed in written form two weeks before each hearing session in order to reduce hearing time and to facilitate preparation for cross-examination." Discovery depositions of each sides' witnesses "were conducted by agreement of the parties or at the suggestion of the [panel] in order to reduce the likelihood that hearing time would be used for discovery" and as "the most efficient way for each side to prepare for cross-examination." This discovery was "closely supervised" by the arbitrators, who would often pass on any objections raised by one of the parties "within hours of their submission." Gorske, supra at 383–85; see also Reuben L Hedlund & Deborah C Paskin, Another View of Expediting the Large, Complex Case, 6 Ohio St.J.Disp.Res. 61 (1990); Gorske, A Reply, 6 id. 77 (1990).

As such devices have become more familiar, they have also become the subject of institutional rules that attempt to create a formal framework for information exchange prior to the actual hearings. For example, the AAA has recently published its "Optional Procedures for Large, Complex Commercial Disputes." These procedures—obviously influenced by the "case-management" practice of federal judges—call for a preliminary hearing shortly after the selection of the arbitrators. The preliminary hearing provides an opportunity to draw up a detailed statement of claims, damages, and defenses and "a statement of the issues asserted by each party," to stipulate to uncontested facts, to "exchange * * * those documents which each party believes may be offered at the hearing," and to identify witnesses and their expected testimony. The "Procedures" also provide:

> 4 (b) Parties shall cooperate in the exchange of documents, exhibits and information within such party's control if the arbitrator(s) consider such production to be consistent with the goal of achieving a just, speedy and cost-effective resolution of a Large, Complex Commercial Case.

parting partner of law firm removed files containing client records from the firm premises; court ordered the defendant to "maintain all files" as well as a "comprehensive and accurate list of those files'"; "if not enjoined, defendant may act in such a way that the [information contained in the files], which is essential to an arbitrator's decision, ... could be disposed [of] in part or in whole when the case comes before arbitration").

(c) The parties may conduct such discovery as may be agreed to by all the parties provided, however, that the arbitrator(s) may place such limitations on the conduct of such discovery as the arbitrator(s) shall deem appropriate. If the parties cannot agree on production of documents and other information, the arbitrator(s), consistent with the expedited nature of arbitration, may establish the extent of the discovery.

(d) At the discretion of the arbitrator(s), upon good cause shown and consistent with the expedited nature of arbitration, the arbitrator(s) may order depositions of, or the propounding of interrogatories to, such persons who may possess information determined by the arbitrator(s) to be necessary to determination of the matter.

2. If depositions of adverse witnesses have not been taken prior to the hearing, attorneys may feel compelled at the hearing itself to engage in protracted cross-examination that can become "a 'fishing expedition'—in effect, a deposition with the arbitrators looking on." Thomas J. Stipanowich, Rethinking American Arbitration, 63 Indiana L.J. 425, 451 (1988). See also John Wilkinson, "Streamlining Arbitration of the Complex Case," Disp. Res. J., Aug.–Oct. 2000 at pp. 8, 11 ("I have witnessed many cross-examinations at arbitration hearings that plod down one dead-end street after another, while the questioner endlessly gropes for any testimony that might be of help"). Alternatively, an arbitration proceeding may readily be adjourned or continued at the arbitrator's discretion, to allow a party to study and respond to information revealed as a result of testimony or document production—it is in this respect unlike a trial which once begun is likely to proceed more or less continuously. "If [the arbitrators] wish to allow the questioner further opportunity to investigate after receiving the answers they will do so. What more is there to an examination before trial?" Motor Vehicle Accident Indemnification Corp. v. McCabe, 19 A.D.2d 349, 243 N.Y.S.2d 495 (1963). See also Dean B. Thomson, Arbitration Theory and Practice: A Survey of AAA Construction Arbitrators, 23 Hofstra L.Rev. 137, 147–48 (1994) (survey indicates that 51% of construction arbitrators would grant a request for a continuance during the hearing on the ground that evidence is being "seen for the first time").

3. One study suggests that there is a "striking difference" between the settlement rate of cases that are litigated and those that are arbitrated: While only an insignificant fraction of court cases are fully adjudicated, perhaps half of AAA arbitrations proceed to a final award. See Herbert M. Kritzer and Jill K. Anderson, The Arbitration Alternative, 8 Justice System J. 6, 11 (1983); cf. Dispute Resolution Times, April–July 2005 at p. 14 (59% of AAA construction cases filed with the AAA through 2004 were resolved prior to a final award). Might the lower settlement rate of cases in arbitration be attributable to the relative unavailability of discovery? Is settlement less likely in part because the parties have not been led to clarify or narrow the issues in dispute, or to focus on the relative strengths and weaknesses of their cases and that of their opponents? Cf. Henry H. Perritt, "And the Whole Earth Was of One Language": A Broad View of

Dispute Resolution, 29 Villanova L. Rev. 1221, 1269 n.161 (1984)("The greater likelihood of an arbitration award that both parties can live with also reduces the incentives for negotiated settlement"). Or might there be other explanations as well? See, e.g., pp. 340–46 infra.

4. State and federal statutes give arbitrators the power to issue subpoenas not only to the parties themselves, but to *unrelated third parties*: This is in some tension with the usual notion that arbitration is in every respect a "creature of contract," isn't it? Understandably, courts are likely to police the exercise of this power somewhat more carefully than in the case of the contracting parties themselves. May arbitrators, for example, order non-parties to *produce documents prior to the hearing*, for inspection by a party? See Brazell v. American Color Graphics, Inc., 2000 WL 364997 (S.D.N.Y.)(yes); see also Integrity Ins. Co. v. American Centennial Ins. Co., 885 F.Supp. 69 (S.D.N.Y.1995) ("Documents are only produced once, whether it is at the arbitration or prior to it. Common sense encourages the production of documents prior to the hearing so that the parties can familiarize themselves with the contents of the documents"). To the contrary, though, see Hay Group, Inc. v. E.B.S. Acquisition Corp., 360 F.3d 404 (3d Cir. 2004)("the power to require a non-party 'to bring' items 'with him' clearly applies only to situations in which the non-party accompanies the items to the arbitration proceeding, not to situations in which the items are simply sent or brought by a courier"; the requirement that document production be made at an actual hearing "may, in the long run, discourage the issuance of large-scale subpoenas upon non-parties"). But see Note (2), above: Could arbitrators in the future simply order a third-party witness "to appear with documents before a single arbitrator"—note that FAA § 7 requires the attendance of the witness before the arbitrators *"or any of them"*—who could then promptly adjourn the proceedings? "In many instances, of course, the inconvenience of making such a personal appearance may well prompt the witness to deliver the documents and waive presence." 360 F.3d at 413 (Chertoff, J., concurring).

What about an order to a non-party directing him to appear for *a pre-hearing deposition?* See Atmel Corp. v. LM Ericsson Telefon, AB, 371 F.Supp.2d 402 (S.D.N.Y. 2005)(no; this "in effect would increase the burden on non-parties by creating the potential to require them to appear twice, both for discovery depositions and then for testimony at the hearing itself"); Hawaiian Elec. Industries, Inc. v. National Union Fire Ins. Co. of Pittsburgh, 2004 WL 1542254 (S.D.N.Y.)(claim under insurance policy; held, FAA § 7 does not authorize the issuance of subpoenas for pre-hearing testimony, even though the subpoenaed company and its employees "were involved as compensated agents * * * in negotiating the terms of the insurance at issue, and the experienced arbitrators have severely limited pre-hearing discovery to what is appropriate in this complex matter").

5. At an arbitration hearing the arbitrator orders the plaintiff to produce certain documents; the plaintiff refuses to comply, asserting that this material consists of the confidential communication of information to his attorney and is thus exempt from subpoena on the basis of the attorney-client privilege. The arbitrator then announces that following his usual practice, he will conclude that the evidence if produced would have been unfavorable to the plaintiff; his award is in favor of the defendant. On the plaintiff's motion to vacate the award, what result?

The California Evidence Code makes the testimonial privileges applicable in all "proceedings," a term defined to include arbitration and any other hearing "in which, pursuant to law, testimony can be compelled to be given." Cal.Evidence Code §§ 901, 910. Section 913 further provides that if a privilege is exercised not to testify or disclose information, "the trier of fact may not draw any inference therefrom as to the credibility of the witness or as to any matter at issue in the proceeding."

Odfjell ASA v. Celanese AG, 380 F.Supp.2d 297 (S.D.N.Y. 2005) provides a nice illustration of the elaborate procedural tangles that claims of privilege in arbitration may create. In an arbitration involving allegations of bid rigging in the parcel tanker shipping industry, the arbitrators issued a subpoena to O'Brien, the former general counsel and senior vice-president of Stolt–Nielsen, to testify and produce documents. (Neither Stolt–Nielsen nor O'Brien were parties to the proceedings). The court granted the claimant's motion to enforce the subpoena; Stolt's claim of attorney-client privilege was deemed "unripe" because objections on the ground of privilege "should first be heard and determined by the arbitrator." At an evidentiary hearing, the arbitral panel overruled most of the objections to O'Brien's testimony, but nevertheless—because of the threat of disciplinary action raised by Stolt's counsel—O'Brien refused to answer certain questions and to produce certain documents. The claimants asked the court to compel compliance with the arbitral subpoenas, and at the same time to "defer a substantive review of the arbitration panel's privilege rulings until the confirmation process." But the court decided nevertheless to consider the issue immediately—because the alleged privilege was a "separate issue" from the merits of the arbitration, and because as a non-party Stolt would be effectively unable to appeal the issue after the arbitration was completed. The court ultimately held that the arbitration panel had "abused its discretion" in not allowing Stolt to submit "supporting factual material" in support of its claim of privilege—concerning, for example, whether the subpoenaed testimony implicated only O'Brien's "non-legal responsibilities" at the company. Since such a refusal amounted to a "denial of elementary fairness," the question was remanded to the panel for further proceedings.

6. Consider the following provision in an arbitration clause:

> In no case shall the arbitrators order or permit any party to obtain from any other party documents, testimony, or any other evidence relating in any way to a transaction or occurrence other than the specific transaction or occurrence which is the subject of the arbitration proceeding.

Such a clause, it has been suggested, can ensure that "pattern and practice discovery"—which "permits plaintiffs' lawyers to rifle through company files looking for potential new clients and discovering potentially inflammatory fact situations which are analogous to their own cases"—"can be eliminated almost entirely in arbitration." Russel Myles & Kelly Reese, Arbitration: Avoiding the Runaway Jury, 22 Am. J. Trial Advoc. 129, 140 (1999). (This article was originally presented at a seminar for insurance executives and corporate counsel).

7. What sanctions can an arbitrator impose for the failure to comply with his discovery orders? In Interchem Asia 2000 Pte. Ltd. v. Oceana Petrochemicals AG, 373 F.Supp.2d 340 (S.D.N.Y. 2005), the arbitrator—a former federal district judge—ordered the respondent to produce certain documents, but found compliance "peculiarly sparse and unrevealing" and "patently dilatory and evasive." In his final award he ordered the respondent and its counsel to pay the claimant $70,000 in legal fees. The court found that both parties in their submissions to the arbitrator had requested attorneys' fees, and so—"regardless of whether the fees were categorized as sanctions"—the arbitrator's award *as to the respondent* was "pursuant to the parties' consent" and thus "within the scope of [his] authority." However, the award *against the attorney personally* was vacated: "While a *court* clearly can award attorneys' fees against an attorney as a sanction in certain circumstances," no authority supports the power of an arbitrator to do so. Cf. Polin v. Kellwood, 103 F.Supp.2d 238, 267–68 (S.D.N.Y. 2000)(panel awarded sanctions against the employee's attorney in the amount of half the employer's fees and expenses, totaling over $150,000, for having misled the panel, unduly prolonged the hearings, and for having committed "contempt of the panel" by making "highly defamatory" statements about the chairman to the AAA; held, award confirmed; under the AAA Rules for the Resolution of Employment Disputes, arbitrators were expressly authorized to grant any relief "that would have been available to the parties had the matter been heard in court").

8. Where an arbitration is to take place abroad, it was for a while thought that parties might be able to take advantage of 28 U.S.C. § 1782: This statute authorizes a federal district court to order an individual "to give his testimony or statement or to produce a document or other thing *for use in a proceeding in a foreign or international tribunal.*" A number of federal cases have, however, held that this statute simply "does not apply to private international arbitrations": "It is not likely that Congress would have chosen to authorize federal courts to assure broader discovery in aid of foreign private arbitration than is afforded its domestic dispute-resolution counterpart." Republic of Kazakhstan v. Biedermann Int'l, 168 F.3d 880 (5th Cir. 1999); see also National Broadcasting Co., Inc. v. Bear Stearns & Co., Inc., 165 F.3d 184 (2d Cir. 1999)(if "the broader evidence-gathering mechanisms provided for in § 1782" were applicable to private arbitral panels, it would be necessary to decide whether FAA § 7 "is exclusive, in which case the two statutes would conflict"; however, "we need not reach this issue" because we conclude that § 1782 refers only to "governmental or intergovernmental arbitral tribunals and conventional courts and other state-sponsored adjudicatory bodies"). The "dominant drafter" of § 1782 has termed these decisions "clearly incorrect," and asserts that "any unprejudiced reading of the term 'foreign or international tribunal' encompasses private arbitral tribunals created under either municipal law or international agreement." Hans Smit, The Supreme Court Rules on the Proper Interpretation of Section 1782: Its Potential Significance for International Arbitration, 14 Amer. Rev. of Int'l Arb. 295 (2003).

Even if § 1782 should be available in aid of a foreign arbitration, courts would presumably still retain the discretion to ensure that broad discovery would not interfere with the arbitral process. See, e.g., In re Application of Technostroyexport, 853 F.Supp. 695 (S.D.N.Y. 1994)(Russian company sought to obtain documents and deposition testimony from a New York company with whom it was involved in arbitrations both in Moscow and in Stockholm; held, even if the court had authority to grant the order, "it would be improper to order the discovery requested" since the Russian company had "made no effort to obtain any ruling from the arbitrators"; under both Russian and Swedish law—"consistent with United States law"—"it is the arbitrators, and not the courts, who are to decide the question of what discovery is to be obtained in arbitration proceedings," and parties "cannot bypass the arbitrators and go directly to court").

e. INTERIM MEASURES

Teradyne, Inc. v. Mostek Corp.

United States Court of Appeals, First Circuit, 1986.
797 F.2d 43.

[Mostek manufactured and marketed semiconductor components for use in computers and telecommunications equipment. Virtually all of Mostek's supply of laser systems and memory testers, which were essential to its manufacturing operations, were provided by Teradyne. Mostek always bought from Teradyne pursuant to the terms of a Quantity Purchase Agreement (QPA), which provided that Mostek would get price discounts on Teradyne equipment if it ordered certain minimum quantities, and that Mostek would be liable for cancellation and rescheduling charges if it cancelled an order.

[In early 1985 a dispute arose between the parties over cancellation charges claimed by Teradyne. At that time the 1984 QPA had expired; Mostek had held off entering into a QPA for 1985 because it was experiencing financial difficulties. As consideration for waiving the claimed charges, Teradyne demanded that Mostek place an order for twenty memory testers; Teradyne also supposedly "insisted" that before it would fill earlier orders placed by Mostek at the quoted prices, Mostek had to enter into a new QPA for 1985. In March 1985, Mostek did agree to enter into a QPA for 1985 and to place an order for twenty memory testers.

[Later that year, Mostek cancelled its orders; it refused to pay the cancellation charges demanded by Teradyne, assessed at 70% of the original purchase price. In September Teradyne requested arbitration, claiming approximately $3,500,000 for cancellation charges, goods and services invoiced, and incidental and consequential damages. In October Mostek's parent company announced that Mostek would cease operations; in November, substantially all of Mostek's assets were sold for approximately $71 million in cash. The proceeds of the sale were deposited in a separate bank account in Mostek's name and dedicated to the payment of the claims of its creditors. Teradyne then brought an action seeking an injunction ordering Mostek to set aside sufficient funds to satisfy a judgment pending the outcome of arbitration. The district court enjoined Mostek from disposing of or encumbering $4,000,000 of its assets and directed it to set that amount aside in an interest-bearing account to satisfy any arbitration award obtained by Teradyne.

[The First Circuit first held that the district court's "interlocutory order which has the attributes of both an attachment and an injunction" should be treated as a preliminary injunction, and was therefore appealable.

[The court then addressed Mostek's contention "that the policy of the Arbitration Act precludes the grant of preliminary injunctive relief in an arbitrable dispute."]

The Arbitration Act does not address this issue specifically and it has not previously been ruled upon by this circuit. Other circuits, however, have examined the issue in some detail. The Second, Fourth and Seventh Circuits all take the view that a court can, and should, grant a preliminary injunction in an arbitrable dispute whenever an injunction is necessary to preserve the status quo pending arbitration.

* * *

The Fourth Circuit's examination of this issue, in Merrill Lynch, Pierce, Fenner & Smith, Inc. v. Bradley, 756 F.2d 1048 (4th Cir.1985), focused on the effect of § 3 of the Arbitration Act on the court's power to issue preliminary injunctive relief. * * * Merrill Lynch sued Bradley, a former account executive, for damages for alleged breach of contract, and sought injunctive relief to prevent Bradley from using its records and soliciting its clients. The district court granted Merrill Lynch a preliminary injunction * * * and ordered expedited arbitration, both parties having agreed that the dispute was arbitrable. Bradley appealed, claiming that the injunction was an abuse of discretion because § 3 of the Arbitration Act precluded a court from considering the merits of an arbitrable dispute. The Fourth Circuit rejected this argument, holding that nothing in § 3 abrogated the equitable power of district courts to enter preliminary injunctions to preserve the status quo pending arbitration. The court also stated that it thought its decision would further rather than frustrate the policies underlying the Arbitration Act by ensuring that the dispute resolution would be a meaningful process.

* * *

Running counter to the approach taken by the Second, Fourth and Seventh Circuits is that taken by the Eighth Circuit in Merrill Lynch,

Pierce, Fenner & Smith, Inc. v. Hovey, 726 F.2d 1286 (8th Cir.1984) * * *. Hovey involved a petition by Merrill Lynch for an injunction against five former employees to prevent them from using Merrill Lynch's records and from soliciting Merrill Lynch clients. The employees counterclaimed, seeking to compel arbitration pursuant to New York Stock Exchange rules regulating dispute resolution procedures. The district court granted Merrill Lynch a preliminary injunction and refused to submit the dispute to arbitration. The employees appealed, claiming that the dispute was arbitrable. The Eighth Circuit held that the dispute was arbitrable and that issuing a preliminary injunction was, therefore, precluded by § 3 of the Arbitration Act. The court took the view that granting preliminary injunctive relief in an arbitrable dispute ran counter to the "unmistakably clear congressional purpose that the arbitration procedure, when selected by the parties to a contract, be speedy and not subject to delay and obstruction in the courts." (quoting *Prima Paint Corp.*).

* * *

[W]e are persuaded that the approach taken by the Second, Fourth and Seventh Circuits should be followed. We hold, therefore, that a district court can grant injunctive relief in an arbitrable dispute pending arbitration, provided the prerequisites for injunctive relief are satisfied. * * * We believe that the congressional desire to enforce arbitration agreements would frequently be frustrated if the courts were precluded from issuing preliminary injunctive relief to preserve the status quo pending arbitration and, ipso facto, the meaningfulness of the arbitration process. Accordingly, we hold that it was not error for the district court to issue the preliminary injunction before ruling on the arbitrability of this dispute. We next consider whether Teradyne established the prerequisites for such relief.

[The court then turned to the question whether the criteria for preliminary injunctive relief were satisfied. In the First Circuit, a court must find: "that plaintiff will suffer irreparable injury if the injunction is not granted"; "that such injury outweighs any harm which granting injunctive relief would inflict on the defendant"; and "that plaintiff has exhibited a likelihood of success on the merits."]

The district court here clearly articulated its reasons for finding that Teradyne had satisfied the prerequisites for injunctive relief. It held that Mostek's freedom to dispose of its assets created a substantial risk of irreparable harm to Teradyne, given that Mostek was in the process of winding down after selling the bulk of its assets, that it had failed to provide adequate assurances to alleviate Teradyne's concerns, and that it could at any time make itself judgment proof. Further, the court found that the affidavits submitted to it showed a likelihood that Teradyne would succeed on its contractual claims, and that the balance of hardships was in Teradyne's favor. The court dismissed Mostek's claims that the injunction would create a ripple effect whereby the creditors would rush to court seeking similar relief, noting that the injunction would have no precedential effect on other disputed claims, and that Mostek could pay undisputed claims and thereby avoid any possible ripple effect on them.

* * *

Although Mostek realized assets far exceeding Teradyne's claims when the sale of its assets occurred, the record shows that those assets were being used to pay off creditors' claims and wind down expenses in what Mostek itself described as an "orderly liquidation process." Further, the amount Mostek received for its assets was stated to be subject to a number of unspecified offsets and debits and no assurances were given that Mostek would be able to pay a Teradyne judgment.

* * * Under these circumstances, we affirm the district court's conclusion that the possible hardship to Teradyne of having a $3–4 million judgment prove worthless, outweighed the inchoate hardship to Mostek of having $4 million of its assets tied up in an interest bearing account pending judgment.

[The court then turned to the trial court's conclusion that Teradyne had a "reasonable likelihood of success on the merits." Mostek had argued that the 1985 QPA and the order for the twenty memory testers were "void for duress"; it asserted "that Teradyne took advantage of Mostek's weak financial condition and used its position, as Mostek's only source of supply, to force Mostek to sign the QPA and to place the new order."]

Mostek's allegations of undue pressure exerted on it by Teradyne are rebutted to some extent by Teradyne's account of the facts which indicates that Mostek entered the 1985 QPA voluntarily in order to obtain discounts on its 1984 orders and that it ordered the twenty memory testers of its own accord. But, even if the facts were as Mostek alleges, it is not clear that it has made out a prima facie case of economic duress.

It is well established that not all economic pressure constitutes duress. * * * [Under Massachusetts law,] "[m]erely taking advantage of another's financial difficulty is not duress," * * * the person alleging financial difficulty must allege that it was "contributed to or caused by the one accused of coercion," and the assertion of duress "must be proved by evidence that the duress resulted from defendant's wrongful and oppressive conduct and not by plaintiff's necessities." There is no indication here that Teradyne caused or contributed to Mostek's financial difficulties. Indeed, Mostek itself concedes that its difficulties came about as a result of a downturn in the semiconductor industry. Accordingly, we see no abuse of discretion in the trial court's conclusion that Teradyne had shown a likelihood of success on the merits.

Affirmed.

NOTES AND QUESTIONS

1. The AAA's Commercial Arbitration Rules provide (at Rule 34(a)) that

> The arbitrator may take whatever interim measures he or she deems necessary, including injunctive relief and measures for the protection or conservation of property and disposition of perishable goods.

In addition, the AAA has promulgated a separate set of "Optional Rules for Emergency Measures of Protection" which provides for the possibility of interim relief "prior to the constitution of the panel": If the parties have adopted these rules, the AAA will appoint within one business day "a single emergency arbitrator from a special AAA panel of emergency arbitrators designated to rule on emergency applications." Within two business days after his appointment, the emergency arbitrator must "establish a schedule for consideration of the application for emergency relief"; after giving each party a "reasonable opportunity * * * to be heard," he may then grant relief in the form of an "interim award" if he is satisfied "that immediate and irreparable loss or damage will result in the absence of emergency relief." This emergency procedure, however, must be separately and expressly agreed to by the parties—it may not be put into play merely by the usual generic arbitration clause incorporating AAA rules.

2. Provisional relief granted by an arbitrator will not, of course, always be an adequate substitute for the sort of judicial order approved in *Teradyne*. (Why not?) Nevertheless such relief, if backed by the courts, can often be an effective way of preserving the status quo pending a final decision. See, e.g., Sperry Int'l Trade, Inc. v. Government of Israel, 532 F.Supp. 901 (S.D.N.Y.1982), in which arbitrators required the parties to place the proceeds of a letter of credit in a joint escrow account, pending a later decision on the merits of the underlying claim. The district court temporarily enjoined one of the parties from taking any action to collect the proceeds and confirmed the arbitrators' order within two weeks: "An arbitration panel may grant equitable relief that a court could not"; "the Solomonic resolution of the award to take the money from both parties of course does not decide the merits [but] makes rational sense at this stage of the Arbitration."

The court in *Sperry* rejected the argument that the arbitral order was not "final" within the meaning of § 10(a)(4) of the FAA. For other cases also holding that arbitral orders of interim relief may constitute reviewable and enforceable final awards, see Banco de Seguros del Estado v. Mutual Marine Office, Inc., 344 F.3d 255 (2d Cir. 2003)(panel's interim order that reinsurer post, as prejudgment security, irrevocable letter of credit); Island Creek Coal Sales Co. v. City of Gainesville, 729 F.2d 1046 (6th Cir. 1984)(interim award required claimant to continue performance of a coal purchase contract until panel rendered a final award; held, award disposed of one "separate, discrete, independent, severable issue," namely, "whether the [claimant] is required to perform the contract during the pendency of the arbitration proceedings"). Cf. Hart Surgical, Inc. v. Ultracision, Inc., 244 F.3d 231 (1st Cir. 2001)(the parties agreed to bifurcate the arbitration into liability and damages phases; after the arbitrators found that the respondent had wrongfully terminated the distribution agreement, the respondent moved to vacate the award; held, this was a final partial award reviewable by the district court).

3. Will the arbitrator in *Teradyne* be bound by the views of the First Circuit as to "merits" of the controversy? Is he likely to be influenced by them? Might this "threaten the independence" of the arbitrator's ultimate determination? See also Tampimex Oil Ltd. v. Latina Trading Corp., 558 F.Supp. 1201 (S.D.N.Y. 1983)(plaintiff has demonstrated "probability of success on the merits"; "I think it unlikely ... that a court or arbitrator would construe this contract in accordance with defendant's contention," but even if it were so construed, "defendant appears to be in breach").

With this danger in mind, some courts have formulated *alternative tests for preliminary injunctive relief*: For example, some federal courts will issue injunctions after a finding merely of "irreparable harm" and a "balance of equities" favoring the plaintiff—at least if the case involves, in addition, questions "so serious, substantial, difficult and doubtful as to make the issues * * * deserving of more deliberate investigation." Dominion Video Satellite, Inc. v. Echostar Satellite Corp., 270 F.Supp. 2d 1205 (D. Colo.), *rev'd on other grounds,* 355 F.3d 1256, 1266 (10th Cir. 2004)(held, district court erred in finding "irreparable harm" because, "should [claimant] win in arbitration on the merits, any damage caused by [respondent's] breach of the exclusivity agreement can be quantified in damages"). Cf. Saferstein v. Wendy, 137 Misc.2d 1032, 523 N.Y.S.2d 725 (Sup. Ct. 1987) (in order to implement the policy of "keep[ing] 'hands off' the arbitrator's function," the court restricted its inquiry to the very narrow question *whether the claim was "so utterly without merit* or refuted by incontrovertible evidence as to deprive [it] of a rational basis").

And finally, consider the tour de force of reasoning accomplished in Guinness–Harp Corp. v. Jos. Schlitz Brewing Co., 613 F.2d 468, 471 (2d Cir.1980): Here a distributor requested an injunction to preserve the status quo of a beer distributorship pending arbitration of the brewer's right to terminate the agreement; the court issued the injunction, but asserted that the "merits" of the request did not really concern "the ultimate issue of contract termination" at all—that would be entirely a matter for the arbitrators—but "only *whether there can be termination in the interval prior to completion of arbitration."* As a consequence, the injunction was "preliminary" only "in a technical sense"—it was actually "in substance a final injunction, albeit one of limited duration."

4. Should the interim relief granted by a court in a case like *Teradyne* remain in effect until the award is handed down? Or should a party only be entitled to judicial preservation of the status quo until the arbitrators *themselves* can decide whether interim relief should be granted, and how it should be structured—so that the court order would "expire when the issue of preserving the status quo is presented to and considered by the arbitration panel"? The latter solution was adopted in Merrill Lynch, Pierce, Fenner & Smith, Inc. v. Dutton, 844 F.2d 726 (10th Cir.1988) (preliminary injunction preventing former employee from removing customer lists and soliciting former clients). See also Performance Unlimited, Inc. v. Questar

Publishers, Inc., 52 F.3d 1373 (6th Cir.1995) (license agreement; court should issue preliminary injunction requiring licensee "to pay only that amount of royalties necessary to ensure that [licensor] is not driven out of business prior to the time the arbitration proceeds"; "once the arbitration begins, it is for the arbitrators to decide how to maintain the status quo during the pendency of the arbitration process"); Merrill Lynch, Pierce, Fenner & Smith, Inc. v. Patinkin, 1991 WL 83163 (N.D. Ill.)(order "to maintain the status quo without prejudice to the merits" would stay in effect "until the case was presented to the arbitration panel, which could use its expertise and knowledge in this field to resolve the dispute present-ed").

Cf. Prudential Securities Inc. v. Schrimsher, 179 F.Supp.2d 1306 (N.D. Ala. 2001)(court refused to grant a preliminary injunction enjoining a former employee from soliciting the claimant's clients; the court "should defer" to the arbitral tribunal since the claimant "has conceded that it can obtain the same relief from the arbitrators that it can obtain from this court").

5. The California International Commercial Arbitration and Conciliation Act makes it clear that:

> It is not incompatible with an arbitration agreement for a party to request from a superior court, before or during arbitral proceedings, an interim measure of protection, or for the court to grant such a measure.

> Measures which the court may grant in connection with a pending arbitration include, but are not limited to:

> (a) An order of attachment issued to assure that the award to which applicant may be entitled is not rendered ineffectual by the dissipation of party assets.

> (b) A preliminary injunction granted in order to protect trade secrets or to conserve goods which are the subject matter of the arbitral dispute.

> See Cal.Code Civ.Pro. §§ 1297.91, 1297.92, 1297.93, 1297.171.

6. A seller allegedly refused to deliver certain goods that he had manufac-tured, and for which the buyer had paid in full. A court granted "injunctive relief in the form of replevin pending arbitration"—ordering the seller (upon the buyer's posting a bond) to "forthwith deliver" to the buyer possession of the goods. Danieli & C. Officine Meccaniche S.p.A. v. Morgan Construction Co., 190 F.Supp.2d 148 (D. Mass. 2002).

This kind of relief fits very uneasily into the notion that the purpose of provisional remedies is merely to *"preserve the status quo"* pending arbitra-tion. The "status quo," after all, consists of the seller's *withholding* the goods—and so couldn't the respondent plausibly argue that the relief sought would disturb, rather than preserve, that situation? Yet, the court noted, requiring delivery of the goods in exchange for a bond "would accomplish something unattainable by the strict maintenance of the status quo'': The buyer "would avoid any alleged irreparable harm that may befall it if the injunction is not imposed and it succeeds at arbitration"—for if it is unable to acquire the goods in the near future its contracts with third parties would be "irrefutably jeopardized" and it would be subject to substantial contractual penalties. 190 F.Supp.2d at 155. Similarly, the court in Ortho Pharmaceutical Corp. v. Amgen, Inc., 882 F.2d 806, 814 (3d Cir.1989) emphasized that the phrase "preservation of the status quo" is nothing more than a shorthand for the "need to protect the integrity of the applicable dispute resolution process": "If the existing status quo is currently causing one of the parties irreparable injury and thereby threatens to nullify the arbitration process, then it is necessary to alter the situation to prevent the injury." To the same effect, see Hughley v. Rocky Mountain Health Maintenance Org., Inc., 927 P.2d 1325 (Colo. 1996)(order requiring health insurer to pay or make a commitment for payment for high dose chemotherapy for the claimant's breast cancer; the claimant's "life expectancy and probability of ultimate survival diminished with each passing day," and "in the absence of injunctive relief, the evidence before the Court suggests that she may not be alive when this case reaches some determination on the merits").

7. The Eighth Circuit continues to adhere to the restrictive view that "injunctive relief is inappropriate in a case involving arbitrable issues unless the contract terms contemplate such relief and it can be granted without addressing the merits." In Manion v. Nagin, 255 F.3d 535 (8th Cir.2001), the district court had denied the request by a dismissed employee for interim relief in aid of arbitration; the arbitration clause stipulated that the agreement to arbitrate was "without prejudice to the right of a party under applicable law to request interim relief from any court * * *." The court of appeals affirmed: After all, the "provision allowing a party to *request* interim relief has been fulfilled since [the employee] filed a motion for a preliminary injunction and it was ruled on by the district court."

8. Under the New York Convention, each contracting state is required to "recognize" written agreements to arbitrate controversies; the courts of each nation, when seized of an arbitrable matter, "shall, at the request of one of the parties, refer the parties to arbitration * * *." (Art. II(3)). For many years—curiously enough—courts in New York would hold that this language barred them "from acting in any capacity except to order arbitration"; on this view they would have no power to take any interim measures in aid of international arbitrations to which the Convention applies. Cooper v. Ateliers de la Motobecane, S.A., 57 N.Y.2d 408, 456 N.Y.S.2d 728, 442 N.E.2d 1239 (1982). In this case the New York Court of Appeals, in denying an order of attachment, wrote:

> It is open to dispute whether attachment is even necessary in the arbitration context. Arbitration, as part of the contracting process, is subject to the same implicit assumptions of good faith and honesty that permeate the entire relationship. Voluntary compliance with arbitral awards may be as high as 85%. Moreover, parties are free to include

security clauses (e.g., performance bonds or creating escrow accounts) in their agreements to arbitrate. * * *

The essence of arbitration is resolving disputes without the interference of the judicial process and its strictures. When international trade is involved, this essence is enhanced by the desire to avoid unfamiliar foreign law.

Is this convincing? Does the language of the New York Convention require this result? Might it not be argued—given the complexity, delays, and risks inherent in international commercial disputes—that judicial intervention is *particularly* appropriate to insure that an arbitration award will ultimately be meaningful?

There was, happily, abundant authority to the contrary in other jurisdictions. See, e.g., China Nat'l Metal Prods. Import/Export Co. v. Apex Digital, Inc., 155 F.Supp.2d 1174 (C.D. Cal. 2001)(agreement between the parties provided for arbitration in China; held, "Article II(3) of the Convention does not deprive the court of subject matter jurisdiction over this action and particularly to order provisional relief, e.g., a pre-arbitral award writ of attachment pending reference to arbitration and pending the conclusion of the arbitration proceedings"). See generally Alan Scott Rau, Provisional Relief in Arbitration: How Things Stand in the United States, 22(1) J. of Int'l Arb. 1 (2005). The New York legislature has recently attempted to correct the anomaly: As a result of a 2005 amendment, the state statute now permits a court to make "an order of attachment [or] a preliminary injunction in connection with an arbitration that is pending or that is to be commenced inside or outside this state, *whether or not it is subject to the United Nations convention on the recognition and enforcement of foreign arbitral awards*, but only upon the ground that the award to which the applicant may be entitled may be rendered ineffectual without such provisional relief." N.Y. C.P.L.R. § 7502 (c).

9. Assume that the parties have agreed to arbitrate in New York, but the claimant instead files suit in Mexico. Having decided that the claims before the Mexican court "are properly the subject of arbitration, not litigation," an American court with personal jurisdiction may enjoin the claimants from proceeding with the Mexican suit: Indeed this exercise of the court's discretion to issue an "antisuit injunction" is "virtually mandated." Newbridge Acquisition I, L.L.C. v. Grupo Corvi, S.A., 2003 WL 42007 (S.D.N.Y.)(even forcing the respondent "to litigate arbitrability in Mexico when it is entitled to relief here would defeat the parties' clear choice of forum as embodied in the arbitration clause"). See also Paramedics Electromedicina Comercial, Ltda. v. GE Medical Systems Information Technologies, Inc., 369 F.3d 645 (2d Cir. 2004)(district court had issued an order compelling arbitration and enjoining Brazilian litigation; "to the extent that the claim is arbitrable, the district court's ruling is dispositive even if the claim is unique to [Brazilian law]"; anti-suit injunction "may be needed to protect the court's jurisdiction once a judgment has been rendered," especially since the foreign court might not give res judicata effect to a United States judgment).

However, in other circumstances—where the integrity of the arbitral process is not threatened so directly—considerations of international "comity" may counsel against enjoining foreign suits. For example, in Karaha Bodas Co., L.L.C. v. Perusahaan Pertambangan Minyak Dan Gas Bumi Negara, 335 F.3d 357 (5th Cir. 2003), a successful claimant in a Swiss arbitration sought to have its award enforced in the United States. The respondents in turn sought to have the award vacated in Indonesia. The claim of Indonesian jurisdiction was extremely dubious—but a trial court which enjoined the respondents from seeking annulment in Indonesia was nevertheless reversed for having abused its discretion: An injunction would "clash with the general principle that a sovereign country has the competence to determine its own jurisdiction and grant the kinds of relief it deems appropriate," and would "have the practical effect of showing a lack of mutual respect for the judicial proceedings of other sovereign nations." And—perhaps most important—an Indonesian order vacating the award would in no way prevent later confirmation in the United States. See generally Daniel Tan, Anti–Suit Injunctions and the Vexing Problem of Comity, 45 Va. J. of Int'l L. 283, 327–31 (2005); see also Section F. infra.

Should an "antisuit injunction" by which a court enjoins the initiation or continuation *of an arbitration proceeding* be treated in the same way? See "Determining the Jurisdiction of the Arbitrator," Section C.3.d. above. Cf. Julian D.M. Lew, Anti–Suit Injunctions Issued by National Courts to Prevent Arbitration Proceedings, in Emmanuel Gaillard (ed.), Anti–Suit Injunctions in International Arbitration 25, 39 (2005)("I find it difficult to imagine circumstances in which there would be a justification for a court to intervene in an arbitration, to stop the arbitration").

10. At the 2002 Winter Olympics in Salt Lake City, the judges—to the astonishment of many observers—awarded Russia the gold medal in the Figure Skating Pairs Competition; the Canadian pair—the clear favorite of the crowds—were given the silver. The next day, reports surfaced that the French judge had been directed by the President of the French Skating Federation to vote for the Russians, on the understanding that the Russians would then in exchange vote for the French team in another competition. Three days after the event, the National Olympic Committee for Canada asked a panel of the Court of Arbitration for Sport to award the Gold Medal to the Canadian skating pair. At the same time it filed an application for preliminary relief, in an effort to preserve any necessary testimony from the competition judges.

The arbitral panel issued an order that same day: It noted that although it was sitting in Salt Lake City, it was governed by Swiss arbitration law, under which the arbitral tribunal may enter provisional or conservatory orders at the request of one party—and that in cases of "particular urgency" the order can be made *ex parte*. So the arbitrators ordered the International Skating Union "to use its best endeavors to ensure" that the referees and judges from the competition "remain in Salt Lake City" until the ISU Council could render a decision on the matter. "The Panel does not think it necessary to make any request to the United

States Court at this time"; it also deferred any ruling on substantive relief until all remedies under ISU rules had been exhausted. An adversarial hearing between the claimant and the ISU was set for the following day. (The next morning, however, the International Olympic Committee announced that it would award a second gold medal to the Canadian team, and that the French judge would be suspended effective immediately. The arbitration proceeding was then terminated.). See COA v. ISU, III Digest of CAS Awards 2001–2003 at p. 592 (CAS ad hoc Division Feb. 14, 2002); cf. Gabrielle Kaufmann–Kohler & Blaise Stucki (eds.), International Arbitration in Switzerland 78 (2004)("Given that an arbitral tribunal and a court are in an analogous position, there is no reason in principle why arbitrators should not be vested with powers similar to those of a judge in this regard," but "in order to comply with the requirements of due process, an arbitral tribunal should only grant *ex parte* interim measures in situations of utmost urgency").

3. The Problem of Multi-Party Disputes

a. INTRODUCTION

Multi-party arbitration is arbitration's equivalent of squaring the circle. The conundrum arises because steps that may be perceived as necessary for the "efficient administration of justice"—consolidating related cases, joining all parties in a single arbitration, avoiding an ungainly number of arbitrators sitting on a tribunal—can run counter to the consensual nature of arbitration, which is generally considered its inviolable foundation.[1]

Many disputes that may be amenable to settlement by arbitration are considerably more complex than the simple two-party disputes we have been considering throughout this chapter. In a number of common fact patterns, several related players have an interest in resolving a controversy that has arisen out of a single transaction. For example:

(i) The Owner of a new building will have entered into separate contracts with the General Contractor (who is responsible for construction) and with an Architect (who acts as the Owner's representative in designing and overseeing the project). Owner may make a claim against Contractor for alleged defects in construction; Contractor may answer that any defects are attributable to Architect's failings in specifying materials or in inspecting the work. Should Contractor's defense be upheld, Owner may wish to assert a claim against Architect for negligence. Another common scenario is a claim by Contractor against Owner: Contractor may claim that he was unable to comply with the plans and specifications for the project because they called for the use of materials that were unobtainable; this, he asserts, caused him delay and economic loss. Should Contractor's claim be upheld,

---

1. Stephen R. Bond, " 'Equality' Is Required When Naming Arbitrators, Cour de Cassation Rules," 3(3) World Arb. & Med. Rep. at p. 70 (March 1992).

Owner's position will be that he is entitled to indemnification from Architect for anything he owes to Contractor.[2]

(ii) An owner of a ship suitable for transporting cargo will typically concern himself only with building, financing, and maintaining the vessel, and will enter into a long-term lease of the ship to a Charterer. The Charterer may himself be only a middleman speculating on increases in shipping rates; he may then "subcharter" the vessel to someone actually interested in carrying cargo for particular voyages. During the course of one such voyage, the ship may suffer structural damage. Shipowner will seek compensation from Charterer; Charterer in turn will claim that the Sub-charterer is responsible for the damage and will seek indemnity from him. [3]

(iii) The Egyptian Government purchased wheat from four American suppliers; it then chartered a vessel from a Shipper to carry the cargo from Texas to Egypt. During loading, it was discovered that the wheat contained insects; Shipper had to delay loading to fumigate the cargo, and claimed damages for the delay from the Government. The Government naturally took the position that it could not be held liable: "The flour must have been contaminated either before loading, in which case the Suppliers would be liable, or after loading, in which case [the Shipper] would be liable."[4]

In these cases, the party "in the middle"—for example, the Owner in case (i)—has an obvious interest in a single proceeding to resolve the interrelated disputes. If the Owner must first assert a claim against Contractor, and only later seek to hold Architect responsible, he is faced with more than just the duplication of time and expense inherent in separate proceedings. There is in addition the real possibility of inconsistent results in the two forums. In a first proceeding, the Owner may be unable to overcome the Contractor's defense based on deficiencies in the project specifications. In a *later* proceeding, however, it may be found that the defect was caused by poor workmanship rather than by the Architect's negligence in preparing the plans—leaving the Owner "holding the bag" alone. In such a case the Owner would much prefer to be able to sit back and let the Contractor and Architect fight out between themselves the cause of the construction defects.

Suppose, now, that the agreement between Owner and Contractor contains a clause providing for the arbitration of all disputes—but the agreement between Owner and Architect contains no arbitration clause at all. In such a case, is there any way to insure that all the claims are heard at the same time in a single proceeding? We are certainly familiar by now

2. See, e.g., Consolidated Pacific Engineering, Inc. v. Greater Anchorage Area Borough, 563 P.2d 252 (Alaska 1977); Litton Bionetics, Inc. v. Glen Construction Co., Inc., 292 Md. 34, 437 A.2d 208 (1981).

3. See Miller, Consolidated Arbitrations in New York Maritime Disputes, 14 Int'l Bus.Lawyer 58 (1986).

4. In the Matter of the Arbitration Between the Egyptian Co. for Maritime Transport and Hamlet Shipping Co., Inc., 1982 A.M.C. 874 (S.D.N.Y.1981).

with the truism that a party who has never agreed to arbitrate a dispute cannot be coerced into the process. By contrast, one powerful advantage of litigation is that a court with jurisdiction over all the interested parties can bring them all into the action: In a lawsuit against Contractor, Owner would be able to join a claim "in the alternative" against Architect (see Fed.R.Civ.P. 20(a)); if he is a defendant, Owner can "implead" Architect as a "third-party defendant." (See Fed.R.Civ.P. 14(a)). And if there are pending separate "actions involving a common question of law or fact," a court "may order a joint hearing or trial of any or all of the matters in issue in the actions" or may "order all the actions consolidated." (Fed. R.Civ.P. 42(a)).

b.   CONSOLIDATION

What if *both* contracts (between Owner and Contractor, and between Owner and Architect) contain provisions for the arbitration of future disputes? In such a case the Owner might wish to have the various arbitration proceedings "consolidated"—that is, heard jointly before a common arbitration panel. (The Contractor or the Architect, on the other hand, is very likely to object: Why?)

The long-standing policy of the AAA is that it will not consolidate separate arbitration proceedings unless all the parties consent or unless all the agreements explicitly provide for consolidation. The AAA has little incentive to force consolidation upon unwilling parties—and may, in fact, fear that doing so will impair the enforceability of the resulting award. So parties in the Owner's position will often attempt to seek a court order for the consolidation of the separate arbitrations. Once a court order has been issued, the AAA considers itself off the hook—and is then willing to administer the consolidated arbitrations.

The willingness of courts to order consolidated arbitration varies greatly. Some courts will do so even over the objections of one of the parties—at least when the arbitration agreement does not expressly forbid this. Such a power is asserted "as an incident of the jurisdiction statutorily conferred on a court generally to enforce arbitration agreements";[5] it will be stressed that "the same considerations of adjudicative economy that argue in favor of consolidating closely related court cases argue for consolidating closely related arbitrations."[6]

However, the general tendency of courts has been to refuse to order consolidation of related arbitrations in the absence of express consent of the parties to all the agreements. Many courts find the absence of "privity" between the Architect and the Contractor a barrier to ordering consolidated

---

5. Litton Bionetics, Inc., 437 A.2d at 217.

6. Connecticut General Life Ins. Co. v. Sun Life Assurance Co. of Canada, 210 F.3d 771 (7th Cir.2000)("we cannot see any reason why" the court should "place its thumb on the scale, insisting that it be 'clear,' rather than merely more likely than not, that the parties intended consolidation"; "practical considerations [are] relevant to disambiguating a contract, because parties to a contract generally aim at obtaining sensible results in a sensible way") (Posner, J.).

arbitration: To do so, it is suggested, would be to "rewrite" the contracts which these parties entered into. "A court is not permitted to interfere with private arbitration agreements in order to impose its own view of speed and economy."[7] And even if a court would generally be willing to order that the Owner–Contractor and the Owner–Architect arbitrations be heard together, further questions are still likely to arise. If it seems impossible to dovetail the provisions of two arbitration agreements that differ in important respects—for example, if one agreement calls for arbitration in Texas and the other in California, or if the agreements call for administration by different institutions—it may be expected that a court will be reluctant to consolidate the arbitrations.[8]

NOTES AND QUESTIONS

1. Under Rule 81(a)(3) of the Federal Rules of Civil Procedure, the federal rules apply "in proceedings under" the FAA "to the extent that matters of procedure are not provided for" in that statute. When a federal court is asked to compel arbitration, does this Rule give it the same power to order consolidation of related arbitrations involving a "common question of law or fact" as it would have to consolidate "actions" under Rule 42(a)? Or does the Rule simply mean that a court can consolidate two *judicial* proceedings to compel *two separate* arbitrations, or to enforce two separate awards, where there are common issues going to arbitrability or enforcement? See Robinson v. Warner, 370 F.Supp. 828 (D.R.I.1974) (relying on Rule 81 to order consolidation of arbitration proceedings); cf. Government of the United Kingdom v. Boeing Co., 998 F.2d 68 (2d Cir.1993) (§ 4 of the FAA precludes use of the Federal Rules to consolidate arbitrations "absent the parties' consent").

2. "If the parties haven't expressly provided for consolidation in their agreements, then for a court to order consolidation would violate the principle that arbitration is consensual." True or false? See Dominique Hascher, Consolidation of Arbitration by American Courts: Fostering or

---

7. American Centennial Ins. Co. v. National Casualty Co., 951 F.2d 107 (6th Cir. 1991); see also PaineWebber, Inc. v. Fowler, 791 F.Supp. 821 (D. Kans. 1992)("reading consolidation clauses into these contracts" defeats the purpose of protecting "the contractual integrity of arbitration agreements"); Rolls–Royce Industrial Power, Inc. v. Zurn EPC Services, Inc., 2001 WL 1397881 (N.D. Ill.)("there is no textual evidence to suggest that [the respondent] would have wanted to participate in consolidated proceedings with third parties who were non-signatories to the agreement"); Government of the United Kingdom v. Boeing Co., 998 F.2d 68 (2d Cir.1993); Glencore, Ltd. v. Schnitzer Steel Prods. Co., 189 F.3d 264 (2d Cir. 1999)("*Boeing*'s conclusion that there is no source of authority in either the FAA or the Federal Rules of Civil Procedure for the district court to order consolidation absent authority granted by the contracts ... applies with equal force to a court's order of joint hearing").

8. See Hyundai America, Inc. v. Meissner & Wurst GmbH & Co., 26 F.Supp.2d 1217 (N.D.Cal.1998)(consolidation of related arbitrations—one to take place in San Francisco under California law, and the other to take place in Eugene, Oregon under Oregon law—"would run contrary to the principal goal of the FAA which is to enforce agreements into which the parties have entered.").

Hampering International Commercial Arbitration, 1 J. Int'l Arb. 127, 134 (1984)(true; "if it had been the parties' intention to submit their disputes to a multiparty arbitration setting, they would have so provided in their contracts"); to the same effect is "A Critique of the Uniform Arbitration Act (2000)," World Arb. & Med. Rep., April 2001 at pp. 94, 100–101. But cf. Alan Rau & Edward Sherman, Tradition and Innovation in International Arbitration Procedure, 30 Tex. Int'l L.J. 89, 113–115 (1995)(not true; "as in most cases of contractual silence we are left with the need for some sort of default rule"; the problem of multiparty disputes is best approached "as one more inquiry into the choice of an appropriate presumption").

3. A number of statutes have reversed the usual American default rule, creating a new background rule in favor of consolidation. A California statute, for example, expressly provides that:

> A party to an arbitration agreement may petition the court to consolidate separate arbitration proceedings, and the court may order consolidation of separate arbitration proceedings when:
>
> (1) Separate arbitration agreements or proceedings exist between the same parties; or one party is a party to a separate arbitration agreement or proceeding with a third party; and
>
> (2) The disputes arise from the same transactions or series of related transactions; and
>
> (3) There is common issue or issues of law or fact creating the possibility of conflicting rulings by more than one arbitrator or panel of arbitrators.

West's Ann.Cal.Code Civ.Proc. § 1281.3. "In the event that the arbitration agreements in consolidated proceedings contain inconsistent provisions, the court shall resolve such conflicts and determine the rights and duties of the various parties to achieve substantial justice under all the circumstances." But see Parker v. McCaw, 125 Cal.App.4th 1494, 24 Cal.Rptr.3d 55 (2005)(to order consolidation before a single arbitrator would not "achieve substantial justice" where one agreement provides for a single arbitrator but the other calls for a three-person panel; "the contractual right to three arbitrators is substantial and may not be altered by the court").

The new Revised Uniform Arbitration Act has followed California's lead; § 10 (c) of the Act adds that a court may nevertheless not order consolidation "of the claims of a party to an agreement to arbitrate which prohibits consolidation." (Is this an unnecessary excess of caution?)

4. A group of investors wanted a racing yacht that could circumnavigate the globe in less than 80 days—in competition for the "Jules Verne Trophy"—and signed a contract with an Italian shipyard to build a yacht to be named the "Tag Heuer." The ship was to be "classified" by the American Bureau of Shipping, which would review the design and survey the ship to verify compliance with its quality standards and with the relevant international safety conventions. The builder accordingly entered into an agreement for "classification" with ABS; this builder-ABS agreement contained an arbitration clause. The ABS ultimately issued a certificate of classification, and the ship was delivered to the owners, but during a cruise to Venice it suffered serious hull damage as a result of defective design and poor construction. The builder sued ABS in Italy, while the owners filed claims against ABS in France; ABS sought to compel all the parties to arbitrate their claims. The court held that (1) the *builder* could be compelled to arbitrate, since it had been "acting on its own behalf" in signing the agreement with ABS. And it held (2) that *the owners too* were "bound to arbitrate with ABS, even though they never signed the arbitration agreement"; they were "estopped from denying" their obligation to arbitrate since they had received a "direct benefit" from the contract. Such benefits included lower insurance rates, and the ability to sail under the French flag—both of which would have been impossible without the certificate of classification. American Bureau of Shipping v. Tencara Shipyard S.p.A., 170 F.3d 349 (2d Cir. 1999).

In the course of its opinion, the *Tencara* court naturally had no occasion to discuss whether there should be any "consolidation" of the related arbitration proceedings involving the three parties. For another, somewhat simpler case in which a signatory to an agreement was also able to invoke an arbitration clause *to bind a non-signatory,* see Peltz v. Sears, Roebuck & Co., 367 F.Supp.2d 711 (E.D. Pa. 2005): During an extremely hot summer in Philadelphia, a couple died of heat exposure in their home when their air-conditioner malfunctioned and Sears failed to repair it promptly. The plaintiff filed a survival action for negligence and breach of warranty; as Administrator of the decedent's estate, the plaintiff was naturally thought to "stand in [the decedent's] shoes" and so was obligated to arbitrate pursuant to the arbitration clause in the maintenance agreement between the decedent and Sears. In addition—and more importantly—the plaintiffs had brought a *wrongful death action* on behalf of the decedent's *beneficiaries;* here the court held that even if the wrongful death claim "cannot be said to derive from [the decedent's] claims," the plaintiff was nonetheless "estopped from avoiding arbitration" because the wrongful death claims "rely upon" the maintenance agreement.

5. Finally, what about the case where a non-signatory to an agreement attempts *to compel a signatory* to arbitrate? This should be considerably easier than the cases in the preceding note, shouldn't it? For illustrations of this fact pattern see Choctaw Generation Ltd. Partnership v. American Home Assurance Co., 271 F.3d 403 (2d Cir. 2001)(contract between the builder of a power-generation facility, and the owner, contained an arbitration clause; after a dispute arose over delay in construction, the owner demanded that the insurer, as the builder's surety, replenish its letter of credit to fund the "rapidly accruing liquidated damages"; held, although the surety contract contained no arbitration clause, the owner, "as signatory, is estopped from avoiding arbitration with a non-signatory when the issues the nonsignatory is seeking to resolve in arbitration are intertwined with the agreement that the estopped party has signed"); see also Grigson v. Creative Artists Agency L.L.C., 210 F.3d 524 (5th Cir. 2000)(signatory of contract containing a "rent-a-judge" clause brought suit against a non-signatory for tortious interference with the contract; held, motion to compel arbitration granted); cf. Bridas S.A.P.I.C. v. Government of Turkmenistan, 345 F.3d 347, 361 (5th Cir. 2003)(in *Grigson*, "the parties resisting arbitration had expressly agreed to arbitrate claims of the very type that they asserted against the nonsignatory"; it "is more foreseeable, and thus more reasonable, that a party who has actually agreed in writing to arbitrate claims with someone might be compelled to broaden the scope of his agreement to include others").

Compare Bowater Inc. v. Zager, 901 So.2d 658 (Ala. 2004). Here a lessor under a timber lease filed a lawsuit against its lessee and also against 10 other defendants (logging companies and foresters), alleging that the defendants had conducted timber harvesting and road building "in a negligent and/or wanton manner or have otherwise committed waste on the property." The defendants moved to compel arbitration pursuant to an arbitration clause in the lease—the non-signatories on the theory that the claims asserted against them were "intertwined" with the claims against the lessee itself. The court held that arbitration should be compelled "consistent with the provisions of the arbitration agreement"—but it noted that under the agreement, the lessor was to choose one arbitrator, and the lessee another: Therefore the lessor was "contractually accorded the sole 'vote' on its 'side of the table,' and if the nonsignatory defendants wish to participate in the arbitration, they are obliged to accept the arbitrator chosen by [the lessee], the arbitrator chosen by the lessors, and the arbitrator chosen by those two arbitrators."

c. ESCAPING ARBITRATION IN MULTI–PARTY DISPUTES

It is likely, then, that the Owner—who may expect to be "in the middle" in most controversies—will not have the assurance that he will be able to settle all related disputes at the same time through consolidated arbitration. In such circumstances, then, he might often simply prefer to avoid arbitration completely. Some Owner–Contractor agreements in fact contain an "escape clause," freeing the Owner from any obligation to submit disputes with the Contractor to arbitration if the Owner, "in order to fully protect its interests, desires in good faith to bring in or make a party to any [dispute] * * * the Architect, or any other third party who has not agreed to participate in and be bound by the same arbitration proceeding." [9]

But suppose that the Owner has not been able through negotiation to obtain such an "escape clause," and suppose that the Owner is a party to an arbitration agreement with the Contractor, but not with the Architect. When the Contractor demands arbitration, the Owner may argue that for the sake of "efficiency," a court should simply refuse to compel arbitration so that the entire dispute can be resolved in one judicial proceeding.

9. See Garden Grove Community Church v. Pittsburgh–Des Moines Steel Co., 140 Cal.App.3d 251, 191 Cal.Rptr. 15 (1983).

Some states have in fact been receptive to such arguments by the Owner. See, e.g., Prestressed Concrete, Inc. v. Adolfson & Peterson, Inc., 308 Minn. 20, 240 N.W.2d 551 (1976) ("Where arbitration would increase rather than decrease delay, complexity, and costs, it should not receive favored treatment"); County of Jefferson v. Barton–Douglas Contractors, Inc., 282 N.W.2d 155 (Iowa 1979) ("prospect of multiple proceedings carrying a potential for inconsistent findings provides a basis for overriding the freedom to contract for arbitration"). The United States Supreme Court confronted this fact pattern in Moses H. Cone Memorial Hospital v. Mercury Construction Corp., 460 U.S. 1 (1983). Here Owner had filed a state court action against Contractor—seeking a declaratory judgment that their dispute was not arbitrable—and also against Architect, claiming indemnity for any liability to Contractor. Contractor then brought an action in *federal* court against Owner, under § 4 of the FAA, to compel arbitration. Since the Owner had taken the care in his own action to join a defendant who was not subject to an arbitration agreement, he was then in a position to argue that Contractor's action should be stayed—in order that the entire dispute could be disposed of in the parallel *state* action. Otherwise, he asserted, there would have to be "piecemeal litigation." The Supreme Court held that it was an abuse of discretion for the district court to grant a stay of the federal action, which at the time was "running well ahead of the state suit." To the Court, Owner's argument was misconceived: If the dispute between Owner and Contractor were in fact arbitrable, then "piecemeal litigation" was inevitable no matter *which* court, state or federal, decided the question of arbitrability. For "the relevant federal law *requires* piecemeal resolution when necessary to give effect to an arbitration agreement."

As we have seen in Note (3) above, California's arbitration statute permits a court to consolidate related arbitrations. But the statute also permits a court to *stay arbitration,* or *refuse enforcement* of an arbitration agreement, if one of the parties is also a party to pending *litigation* with a third party "arising out of the same transaction or series of related transactions," and if there is a "possibility of conflicting rulings on a common issue of law or fact." West's Ann.Cal.Code Civ.Proc. § 1281.2. In light of *Southland v. Keating,* would such a refusal or stay of arbitration pursuant to the California statute violate federal law?

The Supreme Court was faced with precisely this question in Volt Information Sciences, Inc. v. Board of Trustees of the Leland Stanford Junior University, 489 U.S. 468 (1989). Volt had entered into a construction contract with Stanford under which it was to install a system of electrical conduits on the Stanford campus. The contract contained an agreement to arbitrate all disputes between the parties "arising out of or relating to this contract or the breach thereof," and it also contained a choice-of-law clause providing that "[t]he Contract shall be governed by the law of the place where the Project is located." During the course of the project, a dispute developed regarding compensation for extra work: Stanford filed an action against Volt in the state courts of California alleging fraud and breach of contract, and in the same action Stanford also sought indemnity from two other companies involved in the construction project, with whom it did not have arbitration agreements. Volt moved to compel arbitration, and Stanford in turn moved to stay arbitration pursuant to § 1281.2. Relying on this legislation, the California courts denied Volt's motion to compel arbitration and stayed the arbitration proceedings pending the outcome of the litigation. The reasoning was that "by specifying that their contract would be governed by 'the law of the place where the project is located,' the parties had incorporated the California rules of arbitration, including § 1281.2, into their arbitration agreement."

The Supreme Court agreed with the state courts:

§ 4   of the FAA does not confer a right to compel arbitration of any dispute at any time; it confers only the right to obtain an order directing that "arbitration proceed *in the manner provided for in [the parties'] agreement.*" Here the Court of Appeal found that, by incorporating the California rules of arbitration into their agreement, the parties had agreed that arbitration would not proceed in situations which fell within the scope of [§ 1281.2.] This was not a finding that [Volt] had "waived" an FAA-guaranteed right to compel arbitration of this dispute, but a finding that it had no such right in the first place, because the parties' agreement did not require arbitration to proceed in this situation.

Such a finding, the Court went on, did not at all offend the principles underlying cases like *Moses H. Cone*—principles mandating that "questions of arbitrability ... be addressed with a healthy regard for the federal policy favoring arbitration," and that "any doubts concerning the scope of arbitrable issues ... be resolved in favor of arbitration." For "[t]here is no federal policy favoring arbitration under a certain set of procedural rules; the federal policy is simply to ensure the enforceability, according to their terms, of private agreements to arbitrate. Interpreting a choice-of-law clause to make applicable state rules governing the conduct of arbitration—rules which are manifestly designed to encourage resort to the arbitral process—simply does not offend the rule of liberal construction set forth in *Moses H. Cone,* nor does it offend any other policy embodied in the FAA. * * * [T]he FAA does not require parties to arbitrate when they have not agreed to do so, nor does it prevent parties who do agree to arbitrate from excluding certain claims from the scope of their arbitration agreement. It simply requires courts to enforce privately negotiated agreements to arbitrate, like other contracts, in accordance with their terms."

Arbitration under the Act is a matter of consent, not coercion, and parties are generally free to structure their arbitration agreements as they see fit. Just as they may limit by contract the issues which they will arbitrate, so too may they specify by contract the rules under which that arbitration will be conducted. Where, as here, the parties have agreed to abide by state rules of arbitration, enforcing those rules according to the terms of the agreement is fully consistent with the goals of the FAA, even if the result is that arbitration is stayed where the Act would otherwise permit it to go forward.

In dissent, Justice Brennan, joined by Justice Marshall, wrote that he could "accept neither the state court's unusual interpretation of the parties' contract, nor this Court's unwillingness to review it. * * * [I]nterpreting the parties' agreement to say that the California procedural rules apply rather than the FAA, where the parties arguably had no such intent, implicates the *Moses H. Cone* principle no less than would an interpretation of the parties' contract that erroneously denied the existence of an agreement to arbitrate. * * * The FAA requires that a court determining a question of arbitrability not stop with the application of state-law rules for construing the parties' intentions, but that it also take account of the command of federal law that those intentions [be] generously construed as to issues of arbitrability. * * * Construed with deference to the opinion of the California Court of Appeal, yet with a healthy regard for the federal policy favoring arbitration, it is clear that the choice-of-law clause cannot bear the interpretation the California court assigned to it."

For the dissent, the state court's construction of the parties' intent—especially given the total absence of any extrinsic evidence on the subject—was "at variance with the purposes for which choice-of-law clauses are commonly written and the manner in which they are generally interpreted." The "normal purpose of such choice-of-law clauses is to determine that the law of one State rather than that of another State will be applicable; they simply do not speak to any interaction between state and federal law." After all, "the law of any place in the United States"—even California—presumably embraces federal law. "Were every state court to construe such clauses as an expression of the parties' intent to exclude the application of federal law, as has the California Court of Appeal in this case, the result would be to render the Federal Arbitration Act a virtual nullity as to presently existing contracts. I cannot believe that the parties to contracts intend such consequences to flow from their insertion of a standard choice-of-law clause. Even less can I agree that we are powerless to review decisions of state courts that effectively nullify a vital piece of federal legislation."

NOTES AND QUESTIONS

1. Can there be any vitality or legitimacy at all left in the *Volt* decision in light of the Court's later opinion in *Mastrobuono*? See supra pp. 238–40. *Mastrobuono,* it will be remembered, involved the relevance of a New York choice-of-law clause to the question of arbitral authority to award punitive damages; the Court suggested that the "best way" to read the choice-of-law clause was simply as a reference to the "substantive rights and obligations that New York courts would apply"—but not to "any special rules limiting the authority of arbitrators."

Do you find persuasive the argument that *Volt* may still continue to have some purchase at least with respect to state law "favorable" to arbitration? See Note, An Unnecessary Choice of Law: *Volt, Mastrobuono,* and Federal Arbitration Act Preemption, 115 Harv. L. Rev. 2250, 2259

(2002)(in *Volt* "the state policy *furthered* the federal goal of encouraging arbitration," while in *Mastrobuono* "the policy at issue would have directly *impeded* the FAA's goals")(emphasis in original). In what sense is it accurate to say—as the Court does in *Volt*—that the California "rules" involved in that case "are manifestly designed to encourage resort to the arbitral process"? *Cf.* Alan Scott Rau, The UNCITRAL Model Law in State and Federal Courts: The Case of "Waiver," 6 Amer. Rev. Int'l Arb. 223, 250–54 (1995)(it "remains paradoxical that the effect of applying a state statute in *Volt* was to deny a motion to compel arbitration in precisely those circumstances that earlier cases applying the FAA had found to *require* such an order").

Or, perhaps, are you persuaded by the argument that *Volt* still survives because the California law involved in that case "determined only the efficient order of proceedings [but] did not affect the enforceability of the arbitration agreement itself"? See Doctor's Associates, Inc. v. Casarotto, 517 U.S. 681, 688 (1996).

2. The customary move in recent years has been to suggest that the *Volt* decision must now be "limited to its own facts." See, e.g., Ferro Corp. v. Garrison Industries, Inc., 142 F.3d 926, 936 (6th Cir. 1998)(the Supreme Court's "characterization of the California law at issue in *Volt* as merely determining the efficient order of proceedings appears to be another attempt by the Court to limit *Volt* to its facts"); Dean Witter Reynolds, Inc. v. Sanchez Espada, 959 F.Supp. 73, 83 (D.P.R. 1997)(*Volt*'s "holding is limited to its facts"); NOS Communications, Inc. v. Robertson, 936 F.Supp. 761, 765 fn. 1 ("later cases have held that the decision in *Volt* is restricted to its facts"). Now can you imagine a case that is thought to be properly decided—but which nevertheless, at the same time, is thought to have no resonance at all beyond its "own facts"? Can any such animal exist in a common-law system? And it is not a particularly striking phenomenon, is it, to find obsolete decisions "distinguished" away in order to mask changes of heart?

3. At least for the moment, though, California courts still feel able to refuse or to stay arbitration in multiparty disputes under § 1281.2 by continuing to rely on *Volt*. See Cronus Investments, Inc. v. Concierge Services, 35 Cal.4th 376, 107 P.3d 217, 25 Cal.Rptr.3d 540 (2005)(California choice-of-law clause; the arbitration clause specifically provided that "the designation of a situs or specifically a governing law for this agreement or the arbitration shall not be deemed an election to preclude application of the [FAA], if it would be applicable"); cf. Security Ins. Co. of Hartford v. TIG Ins. Co., 360 F.3d 322, 327 (2d Cir. 2004)(California choice-of-law clause; unlike the New York law at stake in *Mastrobuono,* § 1281.2 "does not limit the rights of the parties to arbitrate particular issues or the arbitrator's power to resolve the dispute").

4. Even if an overall dispute must be settled in "piecemeal" fashion, in separate proceedings, it should at least be possible for any lawsuit (say, between the Owner and the Architect) to be stayed until the conclusion of the arbitration between the Owner and the Contractor. See Hikers Industries, Inc. v. William Stuart Industries (Far East) Ltd., 640 F.Supp. 175 (S.D.N.Y.1986). In *Hikers* the exclusive licensee of a trademark brought suit against both his licensor and a retailer to whom the licensor had sold goods allegedly in violation of the license. The licensee had an arbitration agreement only with the licensor; however, the court held that "sound judicial administration" dictated that the suit be stayed as to the *retailer* also. The court noted that since the licensee's claims against the retailer were "derivative" of his claims against the licensor, the arbitrator's decision would be "helpful" and would "provide the court with insight into the issues of law and fact." (Note that a stay would also prevent the licensee from taking advantage of federal discovery in order to aid it in arbitration with the licensor.) The stay was to be lifted, however, if the licensor-licensee arbitration was not completed within six months.

Does this procedure tend to avoid duplication of effort and inconsistent results? In the suit against the retailer, what would be the effect of an arbitrator's decision that the licensor's sales were not in violation of the license agreement?

Where two *arbitration* proceedings are pending which cannot for some reason be consolidated, may a court order that one proceeding be stayed until the other is concluded?

d.   CLASS ACTIONS IN ARBITRATION

Green Tree Financial Corp. v. Bazzle

Supreme Court of the United States, 2003
539 U.S. 444, 123 S.Ct. 2402

■ JUSTICE BREYER announced the judgment of the Court and delivered an opinion, in which JUSTICE SCALIA, JUSTICE SOUTER, and JUSTICE GINSBURG join.

This case concerns contracts between a commercial lender and its customers, each of which contains a clause providing for arbitration of all contract-related disputes. The Supreme Court of South Carolina held (1) that the arbitration clauses are silent as to whether arbitration might take the form of class arbitration, and (2) that, in that circumstance, South Carolina law interprets the contracts as permitting class arbitration. We granted certiorari to determine whether this holding is consistent with the [FAA].

We are faced at the outset with a problem concerning the contracts' silence. Are the contracts in fact silent, or do they forbid class arbitration as petitioner Green Tree Financial Corp. contends? Given the South Carolina Supreme Court's holding, it is important to resolve that question. But we cannot do so, not simply because it is a matter of state law, but also because it is a matter for the arbitrator to decide. Because the record suggests that the parties have not yet received an arbitrator's decision on that question of contract interpretation, we vacate the judgment of the

South Carolina Supreme Court and remand the case so that this question may be resolved in arbitration.

I

In 1995, respondents Lynn and Burt Bazzle secured a home improvement loan from petitioner Green Tree. The Bazzles and Green Tree entered into a contract, governed by South Carolina law, which included the following arbitration clause:

"ARBITRATION—All disputes, claims, or controversies arising from or relating to this contract or the relationships which result from this contract ... *shall be resolved by binding arbitration by one arbitrator selected by us with consent of you.* This arbitration contract is made pursuant to a transaction in interstate commerce, and shall be governed by the Federal Arbitration Act at 9 U.S.C. section 1.... THE PARTIES VOLUNTARILY AND KNOWINGLY WAIVE ANY RIGHT THEY HAVE TO A JURY TRIAL, EITHER PURSUANT TO ARBITRATION UNDER THIS CLAUSE OR PURSUANT TO A COURT ACTION BY U.S. (AS PROVIDED HEREIN).... The parties agree and understand that the arbitrator shall have all powers provided by the law and the contract. These powers shall include all legal and equitable remedies, including, but not limited to, money damages, declaratory relief, and injunctive relief." (emphasis added, capitalization in original).

Respondents Daniel Lackey and George and Florine Buggs entered into loan contracts and security agreements for the purchase of mobile homes with Green Tree. These agreements contained arbitration clauses that were, in all relevant respects, identical to the Bazzles' arbitration clause. (Their contracts substitute the word "you" with the word "Buyer[s]" in the italicized phrase.)

At the time of the loan transactions, Green Tree apparently failed to provide these customers with a legally required form that would have told them that they had a right to name their own lawyers and insurance agents and would have provided space for them to write in those names. See S.C.Code Ann. § 37–10–102 (West 2002). The two sets of customers before us now as respondents each filed separate actions in South Carolina state courts, complaining that this failure violated South Carolina law and seeking damages.

In April 1997, the Bazzles asked the court to certify their claims as a class action. Green Tree sought to stay the court proceedings and compel arbitration. On January 5, 1998, the court both (1) certified a class action and (2) entered an order compelling arbitration. Green Tree then selected an arbitrator with the Bazzles' consent. And the arbitrator, administering the proceeding as a class arbitration, eventually awarded the class $10,935,000 in statutory damages, along with attorney's fees. The trial court confirmed the award, and Green Tree appealed to the South Carolina Court of Appeals claiming, among other things, that class arbitration was legally impermissible.

Lackey and the Buggses had earlier begun a similar court proceeding in which they, too, sought class certification. Green Tree moved to compel arbitration. The trial court initially denied the motion, finding the arbitration agreement unenforceable, but Green Tree pursued an interlocutory appeal and the State Court of Appeals reversed. The parties then chose an arbitrator, indeed the same arbitrator who was subsequently selected to arbitrate the Bazzles' dispute.

In December 1998, the arbitrator certified a class in arbitration. The arbitrator proceeded to hear the matter, ultimately ruled in favor of the class, and awarded the class $9,200,000 in statutory damages in addition to attorney's fees. The trial court confirmed the award. Green Tree appealed to the South Carolina Court of Appeals claiming, among other things, that class arbitration was legally impermissible.

The South Carolina Supreme Court withdrew both cases from the Court of Appeals, assumed jurisdiction, and consolidated the proceedings. That court then held that the contracts were silent in respect to class arbitration, that they consequently authorized class arbitration, and that arbitration had properly taken that form. We granted certiorari to consider whether that holding is consistent with the Federal Arbitration Act.

II

The South Carolina Supreme Court's determination that the contracts are silent in respect to class arbitration raises a preliminary question. Green Tree argued there, as it argues here, that the contracts are not silent—that they forbid class arbitration. And we must deal with that argument at the outset, for if it is right, then the South Carolina court's holding is flawed on its own terms; that court neither said nor implied that it would have authorized class arbitration had the parties' arbitration agreement forbidden it.

Whether Green Tree is right about the contracts themselves presents a disputed issue of contract interpretation. THE CHIEF JUSTICE believes that Green Tree is right; indeed, that Green Tree is so clearly right that we should ignore the fact that state law, not federal law, normally governs such matters, and reverse the South Carolina Supreme Court outright. THE CHIEF JUSTICE points out that the contracts say that disputes "shall be resolved ... by one arbitrator selected by us [Green Tree] with consent of you [Green Tree's customer]." And it finds that class arbitration is clearly inconsistent with this requirement. After all, class arbitration involves an arbitration, not simply between Green Tree and a *named customer,* but also between Green Tree and *other* (represented) customers, all taking place before the arbitrator chosen to arbitrate the initial, *named customer's* dispute.

We do not believe, however, that the contracts' language is as clear as THE CHIEF JUSTICE believes. The class arbitrator *was* "selected by" Green Tree "with consent of" Green Tree's customers, the named plaintiffs. And insofar as the other class members agreed to proceed in class arbitration, they consented as well.

Of course, Green Tree did *not* independently select *this* arbitrator to arbitrate its disputes with the *other* class members. But whether the contracts contain this additional requirement is a question that the literal terms of the contracts do not decide. The contracts simply say (I) "selected by us [Green Tree]." And that is literally what occurred. The contracts do not say (II) "selected by us [Green Tree] to arbitrate this dispute and no other (even identical) dispute with another customer." The question whether (I) in fact implicitly means (II) is the question at issue: Do the contracts forbid class arbitration? Given the broad authority the contracts elsewhere bestow upon the arbitrator, the answer to this question is not completely obvious.

At the same time, we cannot automatically accept the South Carolina Supreme Court's resolution of this contract-interpretation question. Under the terms of the parties' contracts, the question—whether the agreement forbids class arbitration—is for the arbitrator to decide. The parties agreed to submit to the arbitrator *"[a]ll* disputes, claims, or controversies arising from or relating to this contract or the relationships which result from this contract." *Ibid.* (emphasis added). And the dispute about what the arbitration contract in each case means (*i.e.,* whether it forbids the use of class arbitration procedures) is a dispute "relating to this contract" and the resulting "relationships." Hence the parties seem to have agreed that an arbitrator, not a judge, would answer the relevant question. And if there is doubt about that matter—about the " 'scope of arbitrable issues' "—we should resolve that doubt " 'in favor of arbitration.' " *Mitsubishi Motors Corp. v. Soler Chrysler–Plymouth, Inc.,* 473 U.S. 614, 626, 105 S.Ct. 3346, 87 L.Ed.2d 444 (1985).

In certain limited circumstances, courts assume that the parties intended courts, not arbitrators, to decide a particular arbitration-related matter (in the absence of "clea[r] and unmistakabl[e]" evidence to the contrary). *AT & T Technologies, Inc. v. Communications Workers,* 475 U.S. 643, 649, 106 S.Ct. 1415, 89 L.Ed.2d 648 (1986). These limited instances typically involve matters of a kind that "contracting parties would likely have expected a court" to decide. They include certain gateway matters, such as whether the parties have a valid arbitration agreement at all or whether a concededly binding arbitration clause applies to a certain type of controversy.

The question here—whether the contracts forbid class arbitration— does not fall into this narrow exception. It concerns neither the validity of the arbitration clause nor its applicability to the underlying dispute between the parties. [The] question is not whether the parties wanted a judge or an arbitrator to decide *whether they agreed to arbitrate a matter.* Rather the relevant question here is what *kind of arbitration proceeding* the parties agreed to. That question does not concern a state statute or judicial procedures, cf. *Volt Information Sciences, Inc. v. Board of Trustees of Leland Stanford Junior Univ.,* 489 U.S. 468, 474–476, 109 S.Ct. 1248, 103 L.Ed.2d 488 (1989). It concerns contract interpretation and arbitration procedures. Arbitrators are well situated to answer that question. Given these considerations, along with the arbitration contracts' sweeping language concerning the scope of the questions committed to arbitration, this matter of contract interpretation should be for the arbitrator, not the courts, to decide. Cf. *Howsam v. Dean Witter Reynolds, Inc.*, 537 U.S. 79, 83, 123 S.Ct. 588, 154 L.Ed.2d 491 (2002) [see supra pp. 130–31] (finding for roughly similar reasons that the arbitrator should determine a certain procedural "gateway matter").

III

With respect to this underlying question—whether the arbitration contracts forbid class arbitration—the parties have not yet obtained the arbitration decision that their contracts foresee. As far as concerns the *Bazzle* plaintiffs, the South Carolina Supreme Court wrote that the "trial court" issued "an order granting class certification" and the arbitrator subsequently "administered" class arbitration proceedings "without further involvement of the trial court." Green Tree adds that "the class arbitration was imposed on the parties and the arbitrator by the South Carolina trial court." Brief for Petitioner 30. Respondents now deny that this was so, Brief for Respondents 13, but we can find no convincing record support for that denial.

As far as concerns the *Lackey* plaintiffs, what happened in arbitration is less clear. On the one hand, the *Lackey* arbitrator (the same individual who later arbitrated the *Bazzle* dispute) wrote: "*I* determined that a class action should proceed in arbitration based upon *my* careful review of the broadly drafted arbitration clause prepared by Green Tree." And respondents suggested at oral argument that the arbitrator's decision was independently made.

On the other hand, the *Lackey* arbitrator decided this question after the South Carolina trial court had determined that the identical contract in the *Bazzle* case authorized class arbitration procedures. And there is no question that the arbitrator was aware of the *Bazzle* decision, since the *Lackey* plaintiffs had argued to the arbitrator that it should impose class arbitration procedures in part because the state trial court in *Bazzle* had done so. Record on Appeal 516–518. In the court proceedings below (where Green Tree took the opposite position), the *Lackey* plaintiffs maintained that "to the extent" the arbitrator decided that the contracts permitted class procedures (in the *Lackey* case or the *Bazzle* case), "it was a reaffirmation and/or adoption of [the *Bazzle* c]ourt's prior determination."

On balance, there is at least a strong likelihood in *Lackey* as well as in *Bazzle* that the arbitrator's decision reflected a court's interpretation of the contracts rather than an arbitrator's interpretation. That being so, we remand the case so that the arbitrator may decide the question of contract interpretation—thereby enforcing the parties' arbitration agreements according to their terms.

The judgment of the South Carolina Supreme Court is vacated, and the case is remanded for further proceedings.

So ordered.

■ JUSTICE STEVENS, concurring in the judgment and dissenting in part.

The parties agreed that South Carolina law would govern their arbitration agreement. The Supreme Court of South Carolina has held as a matter of state law that class-action arbitrations are permissible if not prohibited by the applicable arbitration agreement, and that the agreement between these parties is silent on the issue. There is nothing in the Federal Arbitration Act that precludes either of these determinations by the Supreme Court of South Carolina. See *Volt Information Sciences, Inc. v. Board of Trustees of Leland Stanford Junior Univ.*

Arguably the interpretation of the parties' agreement should have been made in the first instance by the arbitrator, rather than the court. See *Howsam v. Dean Witter Reynolds, Inc.*, 537 U.S. 79, 123 S.Ct. 588, 154 L.Ed.2d 491 (2002). Because the decision to conduct a class-action arbitration was correct as a matter of law, and because petitioner has merely challenged the merits of that decision without claiming that it was made by the wrong decisionmaker, there is no need to remand the case to correct that possible error.

Accordingly, I would simply affirm the judgment of the Supreme Court of South Carolina. Were I to adhere to my preferred disposition of the case, however, there would be no controlling judgment of the Court. In order to avoid that outcome, and because Justice BREYER's opinion expresses a view of the case close to my own, I concur in the judgment . .

■ CHIEF JUSTICE REHNQUIST, with whom JUSTICE O'CONNOR and JUSTICE KENNEDY join, dissenting.

* * * I would reverse because this determination is one for the courts, not for the arbitrator, and the holding of the Supreme Court of South Carolina contravenes the terms of the contracts and is therefore preempted by the FAA.

* * *

The decision of the arbitrator on matters agreed to be submitted to him is given considerable deference by the courts. The Supreme Court of South Carolina relied on this principle in deciding that the arbitrator in this case did not abuse his discretion in allowing a class action. But the decision of *what* to submit to the arbitrator is a matter of contractual agreement by the parties, and the interpretation of that contract is for the court, not for the arbitrator. * * *

Just as fundamental to the agreement of the parties as *what* is submitted to the arbitrator is to *whom* it is submitted [and] it is difficult to say that one is more important than the other. I have no hesitation in saying that the choice of arbitrator is as important a component of the agreement to arbitrate as is the choice of what is to be submitted to him.

* * *

I think that the parties' agreement as to how the arbitrator should be selected is much more akin to the agreement as to what shall be arbitrated, a question for the courts * * * , than it is to "allegations of waiver, delay, or like defenses to arbitrability," which are questions for the arbitrator under *Howsam*.

* * *

Under the FAA, "parties are generally free to structure their arbitration agreements as they see fit." *Volt, supra,* at 479, 109 S.Ct. 1248. Here, the parties saw fit to agree that any disputes arising out of the contracts "shall be resolved by binding arbitration by one arbitrator selected by us with consent of you." Each contract expressly defines "us" as petitioner, and "you" as the respondent or respondents named in that specific contract. (" 'We' and 'us' means the Seller *above,* its successors and assigns"; " 'You' and 'your' means each Buyer *above* and guarantor, jointly and severally" (emphasis added)). Each contract also specifies that it governs all "disputes ... arising from ... *this* contract or the relationships which result from *this* contract." (emphasis added). These provisions, which the plurality simply ignores, make quite clear that petitioner must select, and each buyer must agree to, a particular arbitrator for disputes between petitioner and that specific buyer.

While the observation of the Supreme Court of South Carolina that the agreement of the parties was silent as to the availability of class-wide arbitration is literally true, the imposition of class-wide arbitration contravenes the just-quoted provision about the selection of an arbitrator. To be sure, the arbitrator that administered the proceedings was "selected by [petitioner] with consent of" the Bazzles, Lackey, and the Buggses. But petitioner had the contractual right to choose an arbitrator for each dispute with the other 3,734 individual class members, and this right was denied when the same arbitrator was foisted upon petitioner to resolve those claims as well. Petitioner may well have chosen different arbitrators for some or all of these other disputes; indeed, it would have been reasonable for petitioner to do so, in order to avoid concentrating all of the risk of substantial damages awards in the hands of a single arbitrator. As petitioner correctly concedes, the FAA does not prohibit parties from choosing to proceed on a classwide basis. Here, however, the parties simply did not so choose.

"Arbitration under the Act is a matter of consent, not coercion." *Volt, supra,* at 479, 109 S.Ct. 1248. Here, the Supreme Court of South Carolina imposed a regime that was contrary to the express agreement of the parties as to how the arbitrator would be chosen. It did not enforce the "agreement to arbitrate ... according to [its] terms." I would therefore reverse the judgment of the Supreme Court of South Carolina.

[The dissenting opinion of Justice THOMAS is omitted].

NOTES AND QUESTIONS

1. In *Bazzle,* Justice Breyer thus fashioned a rule by which:

- under the federal common law of arbitration, this question—which went not to whether the parties had ever agreed to arbitrate, but "what kind of arbitration proceeding they had agreed to"—is presumptively a question for the arbitrators themselves, and

- under this common law, the presumption of arbitral competence is binding on state courts.

Taking these two points together, the question of classwide arbitration became one of construction with which the state courts had no business interfering. At least this was true once the contract was found by the Supreme Court to be sufficiently "unclear" as to warrant the exercise of arbitral interpretation. It is striking that Justice Breyer reached out for this formula—as far as I can tell—with no particular urging from either party. *See* Brief for Respondents in *Green Tree Financial Corp. v. Bazzle,* 2003 WL1701523 at *44–*45 ("if the error were that the court made a decision that should have been for the arbitrator, the remedy for resulting prejudice (had there been any) would have been to vacate and remand to the arbitrator, a remedy that [Green Tree] never sought here, could not now seek, and in any event does not want").

See Alan Scott Rau, Everything You Really Need to Know About "Separability" in Seventeen Simple Propositions, 14 Amer. Rev. of Int'l Arb. 1, 105–06 (2003).

The Court has of course been embroidering the same theme throughout other recent opinions: See, for example, the *Howsam* case, supra pp. 130–31 (Note, Loss of the Right to Arbitrate Through Delay or "Waiver")("procedural" questions growing out of the dispute do not limit the decisionmaking power of the arbitrators; "parties to an arbitration contract would normally expect a forum-based decisionmaker to decide forum-specific procedural gateway matters"); see also the *PacifiCare Health Systems* case, supra pp. 125–26 (Note, Determining the "Jurisdiction" of the Arbitrators)(whether the contract indicated an intention to waive the right to treble damages was a matter of contract interpretation that arbitrators are particularly well-placed to address; it was therefore a discrete controversy just like any other dispute between the parties going more conventionally to the "merits.").

2. What are the implications of *Bazzle* with respect to the problem of consolidating related arbitrations? A California court has held that in cases governed by the FAA "the arbitrator should likewise decide whether the parties' arbitration agreement permits consolidation of two arbitration proceedings"; where a "broad" arbitration agreement calls for the arbitration of "all disputes relating to the contract," "*Green Tree* mandates that consolidation is such an issue." It was therefore error for a court to order consolidation in its own discretion pursuant to Cal.Code Civ.Proc. § 1281.3. (See section "b" supra, "Consolidation," at note 3). Yuen v. Superior Court, 121 Cal.App.4th 1133, 18 Cal.Rptr.3d 127 (2004). *But see* Connecticut Gen. Life Ins. Co. v. Sun Life Assurance Co. of Canada, 210 F.3d 771, 773 (7th Cir. 2000)(Posner, J.)("there are compelling practical objections to remitting the question to the arbitrators"; "[a]rbitral panels are ad hoc, making it difficult to coordinate their decisions on such a question"); Irene M. Ten Cate, Multi–Party and Multi–Contract Arbitrations: Procedural Mechanisms and Interpretation of Arbitration Agreements Under U.S. Law, 15 Amer. Rev. of Int'l Arb. 133, 148 (2004)("the consequences of *Bazzle* are somewhat troubling where the unwillingness of parties to arrive at a joint nomination is at the heart of their opposition to consolidated proceedings"; "parties will often have to jointly appoint an arbitrator for the purpose of contesting the legitimacy of being forced to make such joint appointment").

American Arbitration Association, Supplementary Rules for Class Arbitrations

Effective Date October 8, 2003
www.adr.org

[Shortly after the *Bazzle* case was decided, the AAA announced that it would begin to administer demands for class arbitration "if (1) the underlying agreement specifies that disputes arising out of the parties' agreement shall be resolved by arbitration in accordance with any of the Association's rules, and (2) the agreement is silent with respect to class claims, consolidation or joinder of claims." At the same time the AAA warned that it would not accept demands for class arbitration "where the underlying agreement prohibits class claims, consolidation or joinder, unless an order of a court directs the parties to the underlying dispute to submit any aspect of their dispute involving class claims, consolidation, joinder or the enforceability of such provisions, to an arbitrator or to the Association." The Association would thus refrain from making decisions [as to whether an agreement that prohibits class actions is enforceable] "that the courts appear to have reserved for themselves."

[Note how closely the AAA's "Supplementary Rules" track Rule 23 of the Federal Rules of Civil Procedure, and how they depart in a number of substantial ways from the usual practice and procedure in arbitration]:

1. Applicability

(a) These Supplementary Rules for Class Arbitrations shall apply to any dispute arising out of an agreement that provides for arbitration pursuant to any of the rules of [the AAA] where a party submits a dispute to arbitration on behalf of or against a class or purported class, and shall supplement any other applicable AAA rules. These Supplementary Rules shall also apply whenever a court refers a matter pleaded as a class action to the AAA for administration, or when a party to a pending AAA arbitration asserts new claims on behalf of or against a class or purported class.

(b) Where inconsistencies exist between these Supplementary Rules and other AAA rules that apply to the dispute, these Supplementary Rules will govern. The arbitrator shall have the authority to resolve any inconsistency between any agreement of the parties and these Supplementary Rules, and in doing so shall endeavor to avoid any prejudice to the interests of absent members of a class or purported class.

(c) Whenever a court has, by order, addressed and resolved any matter that would otherwise be decided by an arbitrator under these Supplementary Rules, the arbitrator shall follow the order of the court.

2. Class Arbitration Roster and Number of Arbitrators

(a) In any arbitration conducted pursuant to these Supplementary Rules, at least one of the arbitrators shall be appointed from the AAA's national roster of class arbitration arbitrators.

(b) If the parties cannot agree upon the number of arbitrators to be appointed, the dispute shall be heard by a sole arbitrator unless the AAA, in its discretion, directs that three arbitrators be appointed. * * *

3. Construction of the Arbitration Clause

Upon appointment, the arbitrator shall determine as a threshold matter, in a reasoned, partial final award on the construction of the arbitration clause, whether the applicable arbitration clause permits the arbitration to proceed on behalf of or against a class (the "Clause Construction Award"). The arbitrator shall stay all proceedings following the issuance of the Clause Construction Award for a period of at least 30 days to permit any party to move a court of competent jurisdiction to confirm or to vacate the Clause Construction Award. * * * If any party informs the arbitrator within the period provided that it has sought judicial review, the arbitrator may stay further proceedings, or some part of them, until the arbitrator is informed of the ruling of the court.

4. Class Certification

(a) Prerequisites to a Class Arbitration

If the arbitrator is satisfied that the arbitration clause permits the arbitration to proceed as a class arbitration, as provided in Rule 3, or where a court has ordered that an arbitrator determine whether a class arbitration may be maintained, the arbitrator shall determine whether the arbitration should proceed as a class arbitration. For that purpose, the arbitrator shall consider the criteria enumerated in this Rule 4 and any law or agreement of the parties the arbitrator determines applies to the arbitration. In doing so, the arbitrator shall determine whether one or more members of a class may act in the arbitration as representative parties on behalf of all members of the class described. The arbitrator shall permit a representative to do so only if each of the following conditions is met:

(1) the class is so numerous that joinder of separate arbitrations on behalf of all members is impracticable;

(2) there are questions of law or fact common to the class;

(3) the claims or defenses of the representative parties are typical of the claims or defenses of the class;

(4) the representative parties will fairly and adequately protect the interests of the class;

(5) counsel selected to represent the class will fairly and adequately protect the interests of the class; and

(6) each class member has entered into an agreement containing an arbitration clause which is substantially similar to that signed by the class representative(s) and each of the other class members.

(b) Class Arbitrations Maintainable

An arbitration may be maintained as a class arbitration if the prerequisites of subdivision (a) are satisfied, and in addition, the arbitrator finds that the questions of law or fact common to the members of the class predominate over any questions affecting only individual members, and that a class arbitration is superior to other available methods for the fair and efficient adjudication of the controversy. The matters pertinent to the findings include:

(1) the interest of members of the class in individually controlling the prosecution or defense of separate arbitrations;

(2) the extent and nature of any other proceedings concerning the controversy already commenced by or against members of the class;

(3) the desirability or undesirability of concentrating the determination of the claims in a single arbitral forum; and

(4) the difficulties likely to be encountered in the management of a class arbitration.

5. Class Determination Award

(a) The arbitrator's determination concerning whether an arbitration should proceed as a class arbitration shall be set forth in a reasoned, partial final award (the "Class Determination Award"), which shall address each of the matters set forth in Rule 4.

(b) A Class Determination Award certifying a class arbitration shall define the class, identify the class representative(s) and counsel, and shall set forth the class claims, issues, or defenses. * * *

(c) The Class Determination Award shall state when and how members of the class may be excluded from the class arbitration. If an arbitrator concludes that some exceptional circumstance, such as the need to resolve claims seeking injunctive relief or claims to a limited fund, makes it inappropriate to allow class members to request exclusion, the Class Determination Award shall explain the reasons for that conclusion.

(d) The arbitrator shall stay all proceedings following the issuance of the Class Determination Award for a period of at least 30 days to permit any party to move a court of competent jurisdiction to confirm or to vacate the Class Determination Award. * * * If any party informs the arbitrator within the period provided that it has sought judicial review, the arbitrator may stay further proceedings, or some part of them, until the arbitrator is informed of the ruling of the court. * * *

6. Notice of Class Determination

(a) In any arbitration administered under these Supplementary Rules, the arbitrator shall, after expiration of the stay following the Class Determination Award, direct that class members be provided the best notice practicable under the circumstances (the "Notice of Class Determination"). The Notice of Class Determination shall be given to all members who can be identified through reasonable effort.

(b) The Notice of Class Determination must concisely and clearly state in plain, easily understood language:

(1) the nature of the action;

(2) the definition of the class certified;

(3) the class claims, issues, or defenses;

(4) that a class member may enter an appearance through counsel if the member so desires, and that any class member may attend the hearings;

(5) that the arbitrator will exclude from the class any member who requests exclusion, stating when and how members may elect to be excluded;

(6) the binding effect of a class judgment on class members;

(7) the identity and biographical information about the arbitrator, the class representative(s) and class counsel that have been approved by the arbitrator to represent the class; and

(8) how and to whom a class member may communicate about the class arbitration, including information about the AAA Class Arbitration Docket (see Rule 9).

7. Final Award

The final award on the merits in a class arbitration, whether or not favorable to the class, shall be reasoned and shall define the class with specificity. The final award shall also specify or describe those to whom the notice provided in Rule 6 was directed, those the arbitrator finds to be members of the class, and those who have elected to opt out of the class.

8. Settlement, Voluntary Dismissal, or Compromise

(a) (1) Any settlement, voluntary dismissal, or compromise of the claims, issues, or defenses of an arbitration filed as a class arbitration shall not be effective unless approved by the arbitrator.

(2) The arbitrator must direct that notice be provided in a reasonable manner to all class members who would be bound by a proposed settlement, voluntary dismissal, or compromise.

(3) The arbitrator may approve a settlement, voluntary dismissal, or compromise that would bind class members only after a hearing and on

finding that the settlement, voluntary dismissal, or compromise is fair, reasonable, and adequate.

(b) The parties seeking approval of a settlement, voluntary dismissal, or compromise under this Rule must submit to the arbitrator any agreement made in connection with the proposed settlement, voluntary dismissal, or compromise.

(c) The arbitrator may refuse to approve a settlement unless it affords a new opportunity to request exclusion to individual class members who had an earlier opportunity to request exclusion but did not do so.

(d) Any class member may object to a proposed settlement, voluntary dismissal, or compromise that requires approval under this Rule. Such an objection may be withdrawn only with the approval of the arbitrator.

9. Confidentiality; Class Arbitration Docket

(a) The presumption of privacy and confidentiality in arbitration proceedings shall not apply in class arbitrations. All class arbitration hearings and filings may be made public, subject to the authority of the arbitrator to provide otherwise in special circumstances. However, in no event shall class members, or their individual counsel, if any, be excluded from the arbitration hearings.

(b) The AAA shall maintain on its Web site a Class Arbitration Docket of arbitrations filed as class arbitrations. The Class Arbitration Docket will provide certain information about the arbitration to the extent known to the AAA, including:

(1) a copy of the demand for arbitration;

(2) the identities of the parties;

(3) the names and contact information of counsel for each party;

(4) a list of awards made in the arbitration by the arbitrator; and

(5) the date, time and place of any scheduled hearings.

NOTES AND QUESTIONS

1. Prior to the Court's decision in *Bazzle,* it had usually been assumed that the very existence of an arbitration clause would constitute a barrier to class adjudication of any kind: At the very least, a defendant's motion to compel arbitration could not be denied simply on the ground that a class action would be a more suitable means of resolving the problem. See Edward Dunham, The Arbitration Clause as Class Action Shield, 16 Franchise L.J. 141 (1997)("strict enforcement of an arbitration clause should enable the franchisor to dramatically reduce its aggregate exposure"); Johnson v. West Suburban Bank, 225 F.3d 366 (3d Cir. 2000)(consumer borrowers can be forced to arbitrate their claims under the Truth in Lending Act even if doing so prevents them from bringing class actions; while the statute "clearly contemplates" class actions, it does not "create a right to bring them," and the statute's "administrative enforcement provisions * * * offer meaningful deterrents to violators of the TILA if private enforcement actions should fail to fulfill that role"); cf. Caudle v. AAA, 230 F.3d 920 (7th Cir.2000)(Easterbrook, J.)("A procedural device aggregating multiple persons' claims in litigation does not entitle anyone to *be* in litigation; a contract promising to arbitrate the dispute removes the person from those eligible to represent a class of litigants").

2.   During oral argument in *Bazzle,* Justice Stevens asked, "Does this case have any future significance, because isn't it fairly clear that all the arbitration agreements in the future will prohibit class actions?" See 2003 WL 1989562 at *55. Cf. Myriam Gilles, Opting Out of Liability: The Forthcoming Near–Total Demise of the Modern Class Action, 104 Mich. L. Rev 373 (2005)("class actions will soon be virtually extinct"; "corporate caretakers have concocted an antigen, in the form of the class action waiver provision, that travels through contractual relationships and dooms the class action device. Where class actions are based on some sort of contractual relationship, this toxin is completely lethal").

3.   Suppose, then, that a drafter does indeed include a clause like the one envisaged by Justice Stevens—purporting to waive the right to proceed in classwide arbitration—and that the validity of this bar on classwide proceedings is challenged: In light of *Bazzle,* who—court or arbitrator—will decide whether it is enforceable?

See Jenkins v. First American Cash Advance of Georgia, LLC, 400 F.3d 868, 877 (11th Cir. 2005)("this claim alleges the Arbitration Agreements specifically are unconscionable because they preclude class action relief," and so the court may adjudicate the claim because "it places the making of the Arbitration Agreements in issue"). But see Hawkins v. Aid Ass'n for Lutherans, 338 F.3d 801, 807 (7th Cir. 2003)("Because the adequacy of arbitration remedies has nothing to do with whether the parties agreed to arbitrate or if the claims are within the scope of that agreement, these challenges must first be considered by the arbitrator"; "the same reasoning applies to [plaintiff's] complaint that they are prohibited from proceeding in arbitration as a class"). Cf. Jack Wilson, "No–Class–Action Arbitration Clauses," State–Law Unconscionability, and the Federal Arbitration Act: A Case for Federal Judicial Restraint and Congressional Action, 23 Quinnipiac L. Rev. 737, 781–83 (2004)(although the Seventh Circuit's approach "seems plainly inconsistent with *Prima Paint,*" it does avoid some "practical difficulty," and "arguably makes sense in certain cases," because it "permits the arbitrator to interpret the contract [to determine whether it permits class arbitration], determine the enforceability of any [clause prohibiting class actions], and decide the merits of the case, all without interruption").

In response to *Bazzle,* a number of lenders have begun modifying their consumer arbitration clauses to include "a statement to the effect that the validity, effect, and enforceability of the class-action waiver is to be determined solely by a court of competent jurisdiction and not by the arbitrator." See Hilary Miller, "Outside Counsel: Arbitration and Class Actions After JAMs' Flip–Flop," N.Y.L.J., May 4, 2005.

4. Following *Bazzle,* a number of courts have taken it upon themselves to determine the enforceability of a class-action waiver. As you might expect, no consensus has as yet emerged. A leading case is the California supreme court's decision in Discover Bank v. Superior Court, 36 Cal.4th 148, 113 P.3d 1100, 30 Cal.Rptr.3d 76 (2005). Here the plaintiff had filed a putative class action alleging that the Bank had breached his credit card agreement, and had violated the Delaware Consumer Fraud Act, by imposing an unauthorized late fee of $29. The agreement contained a Delaware choice-of-law clause, and also barred either party from arbitrating "any claim as a representative or member of a class." The court noted that not all class action waivers were "necessarily unconscionable," but laid down the rule that

> when the waiver is found in a consumer contract of adhesion in a setting in which disputes between the contracting parties predictably involve small amounts of damages, and when it is alleged that the party with the superior bargaining power has carried out a scheme to deliberately cheat large numbers of consumers out of individually small sums of money, then, at least to the extent the obligation at issue is governed by California law, the waiver becomes in practice the exemption of a party "from responsibility for [its] own fraud,"

and thus contrary to the state's public policy. This principle that class action waivers may be "unconscionable as unlawfully exculpatory" did not, the court went on, "specifically apply to arbitration agreements, but to contracts generally"—and therefore was not preempted by the FAA—which was, after all, never intended to "federalize the law of unconscionability." (Nevertheless the case was remanded to the lower court for a determination as to "whether and to what extent Delaware law should apply." On remand, the court determined that in fact Delaware had "a materially greater interest" than California in the issue of the waiver's enforceability: Although the named plaintiff was a California resident, he was asserting claims only under Delaware law, on behalf of a nationwide class, against a bank domiciled in Delaware—so "we fail to see how California has a greater interest [in the suit] than any other state." And a review of Delaware law indicated that under the law of that state, the class-action waiver would be "enforceable and not unconscionable." Discover Bank v. Superior Court, 134 Cal.App.4th 886, 36 Cal.Rptr.3d 456 (2005)).

See also Kinkel v. Cingular Wireless, LLC, 357 Ill.App.3d 556, 293 Ill.Dec. 502, 828 N.E.2d 812 (2005), *leave to appeal granted,* 298 Ill.Dec. 378, 216 Ill.2d 690, 839 N.E.2d 1025 (class action challenged Cingular's early-termination fee as both a breach of the service agreement and statutory fraud under the state Consumer Fraud and Deceptive Business Practices Act; since "the most" the plaintiff could hope to recover in an action of this nature is $150, "consumers in the plaintiff's position are left without an effective remedy in the absence of a mechanism for class arbitration or litigation"; however, since the remainder of the arbitration clause can be severed from the unconscionable prohibition on class arbitrations, "the claim can still be arbitrated if the arbitrator is free to determine that class arbitration is appropriate.").

But compare Walther v. Sovereign Bank, 386 Md. 412, 872 A.2d 735, 750 (2005)("numerous courts, both federal and state, have rigorously enforced no-class-action provisions in arbitration agreements and found them to be valid provisions of such agreements and not unconscionable")(collecting cases); Strand v. U.S. Bank Nat'l Association ND, 693 N.W.2d 918 (N.D. 2005)("the right to bring an action as a class action is purely a procedural right," and "all substantive remedies available to [the plaintiff] in a judicial action" would be available in arbitration; since the plaintiff would be entitled to an award of attorney fees if he prevails, and since he has provided "no empirical evidence that all attorneys would be unwilling to litigate these claims," there is at least "a chance that [the plaintiff] can be made whole through individual arbitration"). Cf. Schultz v. AT & T Wireless Services, Inc., 376 F.Supp.2d 685 (N.D. W.Va. 2005)(since the plaintiff seeks damages for "aggravation, annoyance and inconvenience, emotional distress, humiliation, anger, monetary losses, attorney's fees and expenses, and punitive damages," totaling in' excess of $75,000, his claim "cannot be considered 'small dollar' " and thus he can "effectively and cost-efficiently vindicate his rights through arbitration").

5.   The American Express cardholder agreement requires, in the middle of two columns of densely-printed text, that any claims shall be arbitrated "on an individual basis" and that "there shall be no right or authority for any Claims to be arbitrated on a class action basis or on bases involving Claims brought in a purported representative capacity on behalf of the general public, other Cardmembers or other persons similarly situated." However, it then goes on to provide that should such a restriction "be deemed invalid or unenforceable, then the entire Arbitration Provision (other than this sentence) shall not apply." The parenthetical phrase is an endearing bit of lawyerly caution, isn't it? More seriously, what do you suppose was the thinking behind this last sentence?

6.   What about the enforceability of an arbitration clause that purports to supersede class actions *that have already been filed*, where the consumer is a member of the putative class? Such a clause was held ineffective in In re Currency Conversion Fee Antitrust Litigation, 361 F.Supp.2d 237 (S.D.N.Y. 2005)("in the absence of candid disclosure" by the defendants, there was "no reasonable manner for cardholders to know that by failing to reject the arbitration clause they were forfeiting their rights as potential plaintiffs"; "the putative class members' rights in this litigation were protected as of the filing date of the complaint," and "indeed, when a defendant contacts putative class members for the purpose of altering the status of a pending litigation, such communication is improper without judicial authorization").

7.   JAMS, another of the leading arbitration providers, announced in November 2004 that it would no longer honor arbitration clauses prohibiting consumer and employment class actions: Taking the position that it was "inappropriate for a Company to restrict the right of a consumer to be a member of a class action arbitration," JAMS would henceforth accept any class-action arbitration filed with it—and would therefore "not enforce" a class-action preclusion clause. (Although the organization conceded that it had no "authority to dictate a result to the arbitrator," it would neverthe-less in such cases "proceed to manage the appointment of an arbitrator"). This new policy was immediately greeted with "loud complaints from general counsel and defense attorneys"; a number of large clients, such as Citibank, proceeded to write JAMS out of its contracts. And so in less than four months, JAMS reversed itself: Its position is now simply that "JAMS and its arbitrators will always apply the law on a case-by-case basis in each jurisdiction." See Hilary Miller, "Outside Counsel: Arbitration and Class Actions After JAMs' Flip–Flop," N.Y.L.J., May 4, 2005; "JAMS Reverses Class Action Policy," The Recorder, March 11, 2005.

On occasions where the AAA has accepted a case for class arbitration under its Supplementary Rules, counsel for the corporate defendants may take the opportunity to remind the AAA that as a result of the JAMS class-arbitration policies, "ADR users [have been] changing their clauses to delete JAMS as the chosen forum." And they may hint broadly that while as yet "the AAA has not seen an exodus of ADR users similar to that experienced by JAMS," the AAA should clarify its position on class-action waivers "so that ADR users can make an informed decision whether to include the AAA in their clauses." See In re Universal Service Fund Telephone Billing Practices Litigation, 370 F.Supp.2d 1135 (D. Kans. 2005)(suit against AT & T and Sprint; held, the plaintiff's argument that such a "threat destroyed the impartiality of the AAA" and will result in an award "procured by undue means," "must wait until the court reviews the arbitral award"; plaintiff's motion for relief from the court order compel-ling arbitration denied).

8. Houston plaintiffs' attorney John O'Quinn "has such a mesmerizing courtroom presence that a judge once accused him of hypnotizing jurors. He's so good other trial lawyers hire him to take their cases before a jury. He's won more than 250 verdicts of more than $1 million." Brenda Jeffreys, "Lawyers Wary of Arbitration Clauses in Fee Contracts," Texas Lawyer, Oct. 2, 2000, p. 1. O'Quinn represented 3000 women in litigation arising out of injuries allegedly caused by the use of silicone breast implants, and settled 2000 of those claims for close to $2 billion. But each of these clients had signed separate but identical contingent fee contacts containing a broad arbitration clause, and when a class action was brought against him on behalf of 2000 clients—claiming that he had taken too much in expenses out of their settlements—O'Quinn promptly moved to compel arbitration. The trial court did refer the claims to arbitration, but at the same time specifically authorized the arbitrator himself to decide the class certification issue. O'Quinn objected to this—and asked the court of appeals to order the trial court to refer each of the claims to a *separate* arbitration. The court of appeals instead directed the trial court to "determine whether the parties' agreement permitted class arbitration and, if so, whether to certify the class." On appeal to the state supreme court, this was held to be an abuse of discretion: "Contract interpretation [is] a task committed to the arbitrator," and "under the FAA, arbitrators make class arbitration decisions." In re Wood, 140 S.W.3d 367 (Tex. 2004).

Is this Note anything more than an exercise in cheap irony?

9. Securities arbitration rules provide that "a claim submitted as a class action shall not be eligible for arbitration"; they also provide that no NYSE or NASD member "shall seek to enforce any agreement to arbitrate against a customer" who has initiated a putative class action, or is a member of a putative class (unless class certification is denied, or unless the customer is excluded from, or has withdrawn from, the class). NASD Code of Arbitration Procedure § 10301(d), http://www.nasd.com; NYSE Rules of Arbitration, Rule 600(d), http://www.nyse.com. See also SEC, Order Approving Proposed Rule Change Relating to the Exclusion of Class Actions From Arbitration Proceedings, 57 FR 52659–02, 1992 WL 316267 (F.R.)("The Commission agrees with the NASD's position that, in all cases, class actions are better handled by the courts and that investors should have access to the courts to resolve class actions efficiently").

E.   Variations on a Theme

1.   Compulsory Arbitration

John Allison, The Context, Properties, and Constitutionality of Nonconsensual Arbitration

1990 Journal of Dispute Resolution 1, 6, 15.

Most ADR mechanisms have been and continue to be completely voluntary. Alongside the evolution of volitional alternatives, however, we recently have witnessed the accelerating use of nonconsensual ADR mechanisms in both the private claims and administrative contexts. [The author refers to arbitration as "nonconsensual" "when its selection as a dispute resolution mechanism is driven primarily by governmental power rather than by the volition of contracting parties."] Although several forms of nonconsensual ADR have been attempted for the resolution of private disputes,[25] the most ambitious and well-known is the "court-annexed arbitration" now found in a substantial number of states and federal districts.

Several important instances of nonconsensual ADR have been adopted within the administrative-regulatory realm, as well. When a nontraditional form of conflict resolution is imposed without the full consent of the parties in the administrative arena, arbitration appears so far to be the procedure of choice. Examples include * * * commodity futures customer-broker disputes, and data compensation disputes under the federal pesticide law.

---

25. Medical malpractice prescreening and early neutral evaluation are two examples. [See pp. 54–55 supra.—Eds.].

Use of nonconsensual ADR will probably become much more common in this setting than in the resolution of purely private claims, because in the former case (a) a substantial degree of government coercion is already established and expected and (b) the constitutional barriers to nonconsensual ADR will be easier to surmount. Perhaps the most unusual form of nonconsensual administrative ADR to date is the data compensation arbitration program of the Federal Insecticide, Fungicide, and Rodenticide Act (FIFRA).

———

Note: Data Compensation Disputes Under "FIFRA"

Pesticide manufacturers are required to register their products with the Environmental Protection Agency (EPA), and must submit research and test data to the EPA concerning the product's health, safety, and environmental effects. The development of a potential commercial pesticide may require the expenditure of millions of dollars annually over a period of several years. Frequently, after one product has been registered, *another* applicant may wish to register the same or a similar product. Can the EPA consider, in support of this second application, data already in its files that had been submitted by the previous registrant? By avoiding some duplication of test data, this would presumably result in lower costs and increased competition. (Such later registrations are colloquially known as "me too" or "follow on" registrations.)

The Federal Insecticide, Fungicide, and Rodenticide Act (FIFRA) allows the EPA to consider such data (after a 10–year period of exclusive use), but "only if the applicant has made an offer to compensate the original data submitter." 7 U.S.C.A. § 136a(c)(1)(F)(ii). "In effect, the provision instituted a mandatory data-licensing scheme." See Ruckelshaus v. Monsanto Co., 467 U.S. 986, 992 (1984). If the original data submitter and the second applicant fail to agree on the terms of compensation, then either may ask for binding arbitration.

The statute entrusts the arbitration program to the Federal Mediation and Conciliation Service (FMCS)—a federal agency whose primary function is to provide mediators and arbitrators to aid in the resolution of labor disputes. Since the FMCS "rarely arranges or conducts arbitration of commercial disputes," the Service has delegated its administrative functions to the AAA: The FMCS decided to use the commercial arbitration roster of the AAA, and to adopt the AAA's Commercial Arbitration Rules as its rules of procedure for FIFRA disputes. 45 Fed.Reg. 55,395 (1980). Under the statute, the award of the arbitrators is "final and conclusive," with no judicial review "except for fraud, misrepresentation, or other misconduct by one of the parties to the arbitration or the arbitrator." If the original data submitter fails to participate in an arbitration proceeding, he forfeits any right to compensation for the use of his data; if a "follow-on" applicant fails to participate, or fails to comply with an award, his application is denied or his registration is cancelled.

A number of large firms engaged in the development and marketing of pesticides challenged this arbitration scheme, claiming that Article III of the Constitution bars Congress from requiring arbitration of disputes concerning compensation "without also affording substantial review by tenured judges of the arbitrator's decision." A unanimous Supreme Court upheld the FIFRA arbitration scheme in Thomas v. Union Carbide Agricultural Prods. Co., 473 U.S. 568 (1985).

In an earlier case, the Supreme Court had suggested that Congress could not establish Article I "legislative courts" to adjudicate "private rights" disputes. Such disputes, involving "the liability of one individual to another under the law as defined," "lie at the core of the historically recognized judicial power." Northern Pipeline Construction Co. v. Marathon Pipe Line Co., 458 U.S. 50 (1982). Justice O'Connor, writing for the Court in *Thomas,* found that the situation presented by FIFRA was different:

> [T]he right created by FIFRA is not a purely "private" right, but bears many of the characteristics of a "public" right. Use of a registrant's data to support a follow-on registration serves a public purpose as an integral part of a program safeguarding the public health. Congress has the power, under Article I, to authorize an agency administering a complex regulatory scheme to allocate costs and benefits among voluntary participants in the program without providing an Article III adjudication. It also has the power to condition issuance of registrations or licenses on compliance with agency procedures. Article III is not so inflexible that it bars Congress from shifting the task of data valuation from the agency to the interested parties.
>
> * * * Congress, without implicating Article III, could have authorized EPA to charge follow-on registrants fees to cover the cost of data and could have directly subsidized FIFRA data submitters for their contributions of needed data. Instead, it selected a framework that collapses these two steps into one, and permits the parties to fix the amount of compensation, with binding arbitration to resolve intractable disputes. Removing the task of valuation from agency personnel to civilian arbitrators, selected by agreement of the parties or appointed on a case-by-case basis by an independent federal agency, surely does not diminish the likelihood of impartial decisionmaking, free from political influence.

* * *

The danger of Congress or the Executive encroaching on the Article III judicial powers is at a minimum when no unwilling defendant is subjected to judicial enforcement power as a result of the agency "adjudication." See, e.g., L. Jaffe, Judicial Control of Administrative Action 385 (1965) (historically judicial review of agency decisionmaking has been required only when it results in the use of judicial process to enforce an obligation upon an unwilling defendant).

We need not decide in this case whether a private party could initiate an action in court to enforce a FIFRA arbitration. But cf. 29 CFR pt. 1440, App. § 37(c) (1984) (under rules of American Arbitration Association, parties to arbitration are deemed to consent to entry of judgment). FIFRA contains no provision explicitly authorizing a party to invoke judicial process to compel arbitration or enforce an award. In any event, under FIFRA, the only potential object of judicial enforcement power is the follow-on registrant who explicitly consents to have his rights determined by arbitration. Finally, we note that FIFRA limits but does not preclude review of the arbitration proceeding by an Article III court. We conclude that, in the circumstances, the review afforded preserves the "appropriate exercise of the judicial function." FIFRA at a minimum allows private parties to secure Article III review of the arbitrator's "findings and determination" for fraud, misconduct, or misrepresentation. This provision protects against arbitrators who abuse or exceed their powers or willfully misconstrue their mandate under the governing law. * * * For purposes of our analysis, it is sufficient to note that FIFRA does provide for limited Article III review, including whatever review is independently required by due process considerations.

* * *

Our holding is limited to the proposition that Congress, acting for a valid legislative purpose pursuant to its constitutional powers under Article I, may create a seemingly "private" right that is so closely integrated into a public regulatory scheme as to be a matter appropriate for agency resolution with limited involvement by the Article III judiciary. To hold otherwise would be to erect a rigid and formalistic restraint on the ability of Congress to adopt innovative measures such as negotiation and arbitration with respect to rights created by a regulatory scheme.

Justice Brennan, joined by Justices Marshall and Blackmun, wrote in concurrence:

Congress has decided that effectuation of the public policies of FIFRA demands not only a requirement of compensation from follow-on registrants in return for mandatory access to data but also an administrative process—mandatory negotiation followed by binding arbitration—to ensure that unresolved compensation disputes do not delay public distribution of needed products. * * * Although a compensation dispute under FIFRA ultimately involves a determination of the duty owed one private party by another, at its heart the dispute involves the exercise of authority by a federal government arbitrator in the course of administration of FIFRA's comprehensive regulatory scheme. As such it partakes of the character of a standard agency adjudication.

NOTES AND QUESTIONS

1. In one FIFRA case arbitrators awarded Stauffer (the original registrant) one-half of its direct testing cost for a chemical, plus a royalty on all sales of the product by PPG (the second applicant) between 1983 and 1992. PPG asked the court to vacate this award; it argued that the arbitrators were limited to compensating Stauffer for the actual cost of producing the test data and could not make an award based on the value to PPG of earlier market entry. The court granted Stauffer's motion to dismiss, concluding that "Congress intentionally left to the arbitrators the choice of what formula to use in determining compensation." PPG Industries, Inc. v. Stauffer Chemical Co., 637 F.Supp. 85 (D.D.C.1986).

FIFRA had originally provided that in the absence of an agreement between the parties as to compensation, the figure was to be determined by the EPA. However, the court noted that "[t]he EPA found this task to be beyond its means":

> Congress concluded that the EPA lacked the requisite expertise in determining compensation, and Congress and the EPA agreed that a determination of compensation did not require "active government involvement." Consequently, Congress removed all suggestion of a standard from the statute and replaced EPA with binding arbitration as the mechanism for determining what compensation was proper. It seems quite reasonable to this Court that Congress intentionally obliterated all suggestion of a standard in view of the fact that not even the EPA could identify a formula which would adequately compensate a data submitter in every case. Congress determined to leave the matter to arbitrators who had more expertise and could evaluate each case individually.

The court also rejected the argument that such "standardless delegation" to private arbitrators was an unconstitutional delegation of legislative authority:

> [T]he concern with delegation to private parties has to do with the private party's interest in the industry being regulated. See, e.g., [A.L.A. Schechter Poultry Corp. v. United States, 295 U.S. 495 (1935)] (holding unconstitutional a statute delegating power to institute penal provisions to a body comprised of members of the industry involved). The private parties involved here are not members of the pesticide industry, but rather disinterested arbitrators appointed by the FMCS, which adopted the roster of the American Arbitration Association.

Is it important in FIFRA cases to develop a body of "common law" concerning the measure of compensation, in order to provide guidance for the future conduct of registrants and later applicants? Will a series of arbitration awards be likely to provide such standards and criteria of decision? See "Data Compensation Decision Seen as Victory by Both Sides in a Lengthy FIFRA Dispute," Pesticide & Toxic Chemical News, October 8, 1998 (in later case, arbitrators added a 25% "enhancement" to respondent's share of compensable costs "to reflect [its] early entry into the market by means of citations of claimants' data"; this was "the first time since the award in [PPG Industries] that an arbitration award has been based on the value of early entry"). How is the "expertise" of the individual arbitrators likely to aid in resolving the disagreement in *PPG* as to the choice of the appropriate standard of compensation?

2. The Supreme Court coyly left open in *Thomas* the question "whether a private party could initiate an action in court to enforce a FIFRA arbitration": Unsurprisingly, however, it now seems settled that the answer is "yes." "[I]f the phrase 'binding arbitration' is not given its usual meaning, i.e., that the award is enforceable in court, FIFRA's data-compensation scheme could be rendered meaningless." Cheminova A/S v. Griffin L.L.C., 182 F.Supp.2d 68 (D.D.C. 2002).

3. The Commodity Futures Trading Commission (CFTC) is an independent agency established by Congress. The CFTC requires members of commodity exchanges like the Chicago Board of Trade (CBOT) to submit disputes with customers to arbitration if their customers request it; at CFTC insistence, this requirement is incorporated into the rules of the exchanges. Geldermann, a member of the CBOT, refused to arbitrate a customer-initiated claim, and brought suit challenging the arbitration requirement. The court held that "by virtue of its continued membership in the CBOT," Geldermann had "consented to arbitration, and thus waived any right he may have possessed to a full trial before an Article III court." The court also rejected Geldermann's claim that the mandatory arbitration scheme violated its right to a jury trial: Since "Geldermann is not entitled to an Article III forum, the Seventh Amendment is not implicated." That Geldermann "had no choice but to accept the CBOT's rules" if it were to continue in business was irrelevant. Geldermann, Inc. v. CFTC, 836 F.2d 310 (7th Cir.1987).

The statute creating the CFTC also provides an alternative "reparations procedure" by which the agency itself may hear complaints brought by aggrieved customers of commodity brokers. In one such CFTC proceeding, the broker asserted a counterclaim for the balance owed by the investor on his account—a "traditional" state-law action for debt. The investor invoked Article III to challenge the CFTC's authority to hear the counterclaim, but the Supreme Court rejected this challenge: "[I]t seems self-evident that just as Congress may encourage parties to settle a dispute out of court or resort to arbitration without impermissible incursions on the separation of powers, Congress may make available a quasi-judicial mechanism through which willing parties may, at their option, elect to resolve their differences." CFTC v. Schor, 478 U.S. 833 (1986).

Is arbitration under FIFRA similarly limited to "willing parties"? Consider the Court's characterization in *Thomas* of the pesticide registration scheme as "voluntary," and its reliance on the fact that the follow-on registrant "explicitly consents to have his rights determined by arbitration." See also *Cheminova A/S,* note (2) above, 182 F.Supp.2d at 77 ("That the arbitration proceedings are required by federal statute does not vitiate [the second applicant's] consent").

4. The state's traditional supervisory authority over the legal profession has provided strong constitutional support for any requirement that attorneys submit to binding arbitration of fee disputes at the request of a client.

See Section B.4., supra. Cf. Shimko v. Lobe, 103 Ohio St.3d 59, 813 N.E.2d 669 (2004)(state disciplinary rule required that disputes over the division of fees between lawyers who are not in the same firm be resolved by arbitration through local bar association; "the critical support for the constitutionality of the compulsory arbitration schemes [lies] not in the fiduciary character of the attorney-client relationship or the attorney's position of dominance over the client, but in the relations existing between the bench and the bar, that is, in the recognition that lawyers are officers of the court and essential to the primary judicial function of administering justice"). Some courts have in addition found more fanciful justifications: Does an attorney somehow "waive" her right to a jury trial merely by engaging in the profession? See Kelley Drye & Warren v. Murray Indust., Inc., 623 F.Supp. 522 (D.N.J.1985) (New Jersey's mandatory fee arbitration program; "by taking advantage of the opportunity to practice law in New Jersey" the firm had "voluntarily given up its right to a trial of any kind" and had agreed to arbitration).

5. We have already come across a number of cases in which the state has chosen to require arbitration as a dispute resolution mechanism. Recall, for example, the statutory schemes making "lemon law" arbitration under AAA auspices mandatory on automobile manufacturers at the initiative of the consumer. See pp. 61–62 supra. There are many other instances. See, e.g., Nev. Rev. Stat. § 689A.0403 ("Each policy of health insurance must include a procedure for binding arbitration to resolve disputes concerning independent medical evaluations pursuant to the rules of the [AAA]"). The Amateur Sports Act of 1978 requires every amateur sports organization that wishes to be recognized as the national governing body for a particular sport to submit disputes over the rights of athletes to participate in competition—for example, disputes over alleged drug use—to arbitration; the arbitration is to be "conducted in accordance with the commercial rules of the [AAA]." See 36 U.S.C.A. §§ 371, 391(b)(3).

"Mandatory arbitration may indeed not benefit from the dynamic of self-government that often makes labor and commercial arbitration an extension of the parties' own negotiations. It may indeed lack the legitimacy of processes founded on consent, in which an arbitrator chosen and paid by the parties is charged with interpreting substantive standards laid down by them in their agreement, in accordance with procedures to which they have also consented. Mandatory arbitration is, instead, simply a form of economic or professional regulation." Alan Rau, Resolving Disputes Over Attorneys' Fees: The Role of ADR, 46 S.M.U.L.Rev. 2005, 2032–33 (1993).

6. Are there plausible claims that constitutional rights have been violated when a binding arbitration process is imposed on private parties? In GTFM, LLC v. TKN Sales, Inc., 2000 WL 364871 (S.D.N.Y.), a Minnesota distributor alleged that it had been wrongfully terminated in violation of the Minnesota Sales Representative Act, and brought suit against the manufacturer not only for violations of the Act, but also for failure to pay commissions and for breach of contract. There was no arbitration agreement between the parties—but the Act provided that a sales representative had the right to submit any such claims to "final and binding" arbitration. The court held that the MSRA's "mandatory and binding arbitration system operates to deny [the manufacturer] its right to a jury trial" guaranteed by the Seventh Amendment: Claims under the Act for wrongful termination were "analogous to actions at common law," for the Act "provides a specialized remedy for a breach of contract claim involving sales representatives and supplies additional terms to sales representative agreements regarding notice and grounds for termination." The Second Circuit, however, reversed, 257 F.3d 235 (2d Cir. 2001). The Seventh Amendment's guarantee of trial by jury clearly does not apply to the states. And when a case is in federal court only through diversity of citizenship, state arbitration law is "potentially outcome-affecting" under *Erie*—and must therefore be applied by federal courts as well. "[T]he mere fact that the parties are of diverse citizenship does not give the federal court the power to force [the distributor] to proceed in court on a State-created cause of action as to which the State has given [the distributor] the right to insist on arbitration." See *Bernhardt v. Polygraphic Co. of America*, supra p. 65.

Compare Motor Vehicle Manufacturers Ass'n of the U.S. v. New York, 75 N.Y.2d 175, 551 N.Y.S.2d 470, 550 N.E.2d 919 (1990), in which New York's "lemon law" arbitration statute was upheld against a claim that it deprived manufacturers of their right to a trial by jury. The statutory remedies—replacement of the vehicle or refund of the purchase price—were found analogous to claims for specific performance and restitution; since such remedies were "equitable in nature" they would not in any event "have been triable by jury under the common law." Nor did the law deprive them of their right to "have a court or public officer adjudicate their disputes" with consumers by "delegating sovereign judicial power to private arbitrators": The court reasoned that the legislature had "merely created a new limited class of disputes and provided a procedure for resolving them, much in the same way it removed automobile claims from judicial cognizance by the No–Fault Insurance Law." In addition, since "arbitrators are selected pursuant to detailed standards, the procedures they must follow are specified, the grounds for relief defined and their determinations are subject to judicial review," it followed that "the arbitration proceeding remains within the judicial domain." See also Lyeth v. Chrysler Corp., 929 F.2d 891 (2d Cir.1991) ("the compulsory alternative arbitration mechanism affords the basic procedural safeguards required by due process").

7. The Florida "lemon law" provides that an aggrieved consumer may apply for arbitration before the "New Motor Vehicle Arbitration Board"—whose members are appointed by the Attorney General—and that the consumer *must* submit to arbitration before filing a civil suit under the law. By contrast with the New York statute, either the consumer or the manufacturer in Florida is entitled to a trial de novo after completion of this "mandatory alternative dispute resolution procedure"; at such a trial the decision of the arbitration board is admissible in evidence.

In Chrysler Corp. v. Pitsirelos, 721 So.2d 710 (Fla.1998), the consumer prevailed before the arbitration board, and at the subsequent trial the judge instructed the jury that the board's decision was "presumed to be correct." The state supreme court held, however, that these instructions were erroneous: Indeed, to interpret the statute in this way would raise serious constitutional issues, since it "would diminish the right to have the ultimate decision in a case made by a court." The board's decision should be treated "only as evidence with its weight to be determined by the fact-finder." Nevertheless the court held that the manufacturer now had the burden of persuasion in establishing why the board's decision was erroneous: "The party appealing the Arbitration Board's decision carries the burden of proof"; to require the prevailing consumer to bear this burden "as if no previous proceeding had been held" would "relegate the mandatory arbitration to simply being a procedural impediment to the consumer." Does *Pitsirelos* appear to you to be a coherent decision?

Note: Mandatory Arbitration in Public Employment

A number of statutes require the arbitration of "interest" disputes concerning the terms of a new collective bargaining agreement between a state or local government, and a union representing its employees. Fairly typical examples of the growing number of such statutes are Rhode Island's Fire Fighter's Arbitration Act and Policemen's Arbitration Act.[1] In recognition of "the necessity to provide some alternative method of settling disputes where employees must, as a matter of public policy, be denied the usual right to strike," the legislation requires that where a city and a union cannot reach agreement, "any and all unresolved issues" shall be submitted to arbitration. One arbitrator is to be named by each of the parties and the third, in the absence of agreement, is selected under the rules of the AAA. The legislation attempts to enumerate the "factors" which the panel must take into account—including the "interest and welfare of the public," the "community's ability to pay," and a comparison of wage rates and employment conditions with prevailing local conditions "of skilled employees of the building trades and industry" and with police or fire departments in cities of comparable size.

It is obvious that "interest" disputes in public sector employment are intimately connected to the political process. Many public services, such as police protection and education, raise questions that are "politically, socially, or ideologically sensitive."[2] A number of such sensitive issues have in fact been held to be "non-bargainable"—despite their obvious impact on the working conditions of public employees—and thus outside the permissible scope of "interest" arbitration. Such "non-negotiable matters of governmental policy" might in public education include questions of curriculum or of class size; in police services, questions of the manpower level of the force or a civilian review board for police discipline. See, e.g., San Jose Peace Officer's Ass'n v. City of San Jose, 78 Cal.App.3d 935, 144 Cal.Rptr. 638 (1978) (police policy governing when officer is allowed to fire weapon;

---

1. R.I.Stat. § 28–9.1–1; R.I.Stat. § 28–9.2–1.

2. Harry Wellington & Ralph K. Winter, Jr., The Unions and the Cities 23 (1971).

"The forum of the bargaining table with its postures, strategies, trade-offs, modifications and compromises is no place for the 'delicate balancing of different interests: the protection of society from criminals, the protection of police officers' safety, and the preservation of all human life, if possible.' ").

In a more general sense, however, the resolution of *all* disputes over the terms of public employment—even disputes over nuts and bolts issues like wages—is inescapably "political." To resolve a wage dispute by applying the "factors" set out in the Rhode Island legislation requires an accommodation of the competing interests of employees, taxpayers, and the users of public services. The arbitrator will inevitably be led to determine priorities among various public programs, the level of public services, or the need and feasibility of increased public revenue. Such exercises of judgment are necessarily political compromises. Should such issues be resolved "in an arbitrator's conference room as an alternative to facing up to vexing problems in the halls of state and local legislatures"?[3] It has been suggested in fact that "interest" arbitration of public-sector disputes may be inconsistent with the democratic premise that governmental priorities are to be fixed by elected representatives, responsible to all the competing interest groups and responsive to the play of political forces. Resolving public sector "interest" disputes, it is asserted, is not an exercise in neutral, "objective" adjudication but rather one in "legislative" policymaking:

> The size of the budget, the taxes to be levied, the purposes for which tax money is to be used, the kinds and levels of governmental services to be enjoyed, and the level of indebtedness are issues that should be decided by officials who are politically responsible to those who pay the taxes and seek the services. The notion that we can or should insulate public employee bargaining from the political process either by arbitration or with some magic formula is a delusion of reality and a denigration of democratic government.[4]

It should not be surprising, then, that the constitutionality of compulsory interest arbitration in the public sector has repeatedly been challenged. Successful challenges have been rare.[5] Nevertheless, it is clear that there are real tensions here with the values traditionally underlying the arbitration process. It seems hard to justify compulsory "interest" arbitration on the usual rationale that the process is merely an extension of the parties' own bargaining, an application of "self-government" in the workplace. In the final analysis, how does compulsory "interest" arbitration in public-sector employment differ from decisions made directly by a govern-

---

3. Dearborn Fire Fighters Union v. City of Dearborn, 394 Mich. 229, 231 N.W.2d 226 (1975).

4. Summers, Public Sector Bargaining: Problems of Governmental Decisionmaking, 44 U.Cinn.L.Rev. 669, 672 (1975). See also Grodin, Political Aspects of Public Sector Interest Arbitration, 64 Cal.L.Rev. 678 (1976).

5. See, e.g., Salt Lake City v. International Ass'n of Firefighters, 563 P.2d 786 (Utah 1977) (the "legislature may not surrender its legislative authority to a body wherein the public interest is subjected to the interest of a group which may be antagonistic to the public interest").

mental agency? How different really is Rhode Island's compulsory arbitration statute from the Nebraska scheme—which entrusts the settlement of public-sector "interest" disputes to a state "Commission of Industrial Relations" consisting of five "judges" named for six-year terms by the Governor with the advice and consent of the legislature?[6]

Some years ago the Rhode Island Supreme Court rebuffed a constitutional attack on that state's compulsory arbitration statutes by the simple device of characterizing the arbitrators as "public officers" rather than as mere "private persons": The arbitration panel *must* be considered "an administrative or governmental agency," reasoned the court; after all, the arbitrators had been granted "a portion of the sovereign and legislative power of the government"![7] But such a semantic tour de force obviously does not resolve the problem. If the arbitrators are appointed on an ad hoc basis, with no continuing legislative or administrative oversight, there may be no real accountability to the electorate; these are "hit and run" decision-makers.[8] If, in contrast, the arbitrators are *not* to be private decision-makers and are instead made politically responsible, may not the neutrality of the entire process be called into question? Does the arbitrator not then become merely "an agent of government involved primarily in implementing public policy"?[9] Isn't it implicit in the very notion of an "impartial" or "neutral" arbitrator that the decision-maker is *not* to be responsive to political intervention, or to be held accountable for his decision by any constituency? Or might the personal "accountability" of private arbitrators be affected in any event by the well-known need of those in the profession to maintain their acceptability for future employment?

NOTES AND QUESTIONS

1.   Is the same judicial deference traditionally accorded arbitral awards appropriate in the case of compulsory "interest" arbitration in the public sector? In many states with such statutes, the arbitration panel is in fact treated for purposes of review much like an administrative agency: That is, a record of the proceedings and a written decision are commonly required, and courts may examine the result to see whether it is "supported by substantial credible evidence present in the record." See Hillsdale PBA Local 207 v. Borough of Hillsdale, 137 N.J. 71, 644 A.2d 564 (1994)(award must "identify and weigh" all the factors enumerated in the statute, "analyze the evidence pertaining to those factors, and explain why other factors are irrelevant").

---

6.   Neb.Rev.Stat. § 48–801; see also id. § 48–805 (the "judges" of the Commission "shall not be appointed because they are representatives of either capital or labor, but * * * because of their experience and knowledge in legal, financial, labor and industrial matters").

7.   City of Warwick v. Warwick Regular Firemen's Ass'n, 106 R.I. 109, 256 A.2d 206 (1969).

8.   Dearborn Fire Fighters Union v. City of Dearborn, 394 Mich. 229, 231 N.W.2d 226, 243 (1975) (Kavanagh, C.J., concurring).

9.   Grodin, supra n. 4, 64 Cal.L.Rev. at 693–94.

What is it that justifies a more extensive standard of judicial review here?

- Is it primarily the fact that "interest" rather than grievance arbitration is involved? See Charles Craver, The Judicial Enforcement of Public Sector Interest Arbitration, 21 B.C.L.Rev. 557, 572 (1980) (deference to arbitral determinations would give rise to the "possibility of catastrophic consequences resulting from an entirely intemperate award").

- Is it the fact that public-sector arbitration is more likely to involve "governmental" decisions—so that any delegation to arbitrators necessarily calls for a closer scrutiny of their evaluation of the "interest and welfare of the public"; *Hillsdale PBA*, supra, 644 A.2d at 570 ('the public is a silent party to the process,' and 'public funds are at stake' ").

- Or might it simply be the fact that the arbitration process is not grounded in the consent of the parties—so that there is lacking the legitimacy conferred by an exercise of private autonomy? See Mount St. Mary's Hosp. of Niagara Falls v. Catherwood, 260 N.E.2d 508 (N.Y. 1970). Here state law provided for the compulsory "interest" arbitration of the terms of collective bargaining agreements entered into by private voluntary or nonprofit hospitals. The court was concerned that if these arbitrations were to be governed by no more than the rules applicable to consensual arbitration, then "the relevancy of due process limitations" might be completely "eliminated." So it held that the general arbitration statute could be "adapted" "to the special uses and needs of compulsory arbitration": In such cases, then, awards could be reviewed, not only under the usual statutory criteria, but also to determine whether they are "supported by evidence or other basis in reason."

2. A "Model Termination of Employment Act" was approved by the National Conference of Commissioners on Uniform State Laws in 1991. Under this Act, an employee who has worked for the same employer for at least one year may not be fired without "good cause"—a term defined to include both the employee's misconduct and job performance, and the employer's good faith "exercise of business judgment" concerning the goals and organization of his operations and the size and composition of his work force. An employee who has been wrongfully terminated under the Act may be entitled to reinstatement or, alternatively, up to three years of severance pay, along with attorneys' fees. "[D]ecisionmaking by professional arbitrators is the preferred method of enforcing the Act"—although states that are concerned about "the possible extra expense of outside arbitrators" may instead choose hearing officers who are full-time civil service personnel, while states concerned "about possible constitutional problems" may leave enforcement in the hands of the courts. In addition to all the usual procedural grounds for overturning awards that are found in modern arbitration statutes, the arbitrator's decision may be vacated for "a prejudicial error of law." This standard of review was apparently thought necessary because "individual statutory rights are the issue, and arbitration as the enforcement method has been imposed upon, not agreed to by, the parties." Model Employment Termination Act, prefatory note, § 8 & cmt.

This Act has not as yet been adopted by any state.

Note: Mandatory Arbitration and Public Regulation

Nursing homes, and care facilities for the mentally retarded, must in Texas be licensed by the Texas Department of Human Services. As the state agency responsible for their regulation, the Department is required to inspect these facilities periodically to see if they are meeting state health and safety standards; if a facility is not in compliance with the state's standards, the Department may initiate enforcement action and may seek remedies such as the suspension or revocation of a license, or "administrative penalties." (In determining the amount of such a penalty, the Department is to consider "the seriousness of the violation, including the * * * hazard or potential hazard * * * to the health or safety of the public," and "deterrence of future violations." Tex. Health & Safety Code § 242.066.)

However, a 1995 statute now permits either the Department, or the nursing home or care facility itself, to "elect binding arbitration" of any such dispute; such arbitration "is an alternative to a contested case hearing" brought by the Department seeking suspension or revocation of a license or the imposition of a penalty. The arbitrator "must be on an approved list of a nationally recognized association that performs arbitrations" (or be otherwise qualified under rules promulgated by the state), and may not receive more than $500 per day in fees and expenses. The arbitrator's award may be vacated by a court if it was "arbitrary or capricious and against the weight of the evidence." (However, it is only the party who *has not elected arbitration*—but who "gets pulled into arbitration through the opposing party's election"—who may move to vacate an award; the party who has chosen arbitration apparently has no right to demand vacatur). Tex. Health & Safety Code §§ 242.252, 242.253, 242.254, 242.267; MicWal, Inc. v. State, 2004 WL 2569386 (Tex. App.).

The sponsor of this legislation claimed that it gives the state "a new tool to enforce the rules regulating nursing homes. If this tool is properly used, nursing homes who do not comply with basic standards of health and safety will face the quick collection of the appropriate fines and penalties." Austin American–Statesman, Dec. 20, 1995, at A14. Is this claim completely disingenuous? Is this statutory use of ADR appropriate? Is it consistent with the historical goals of alternative processes?

2. Final–Offer Arbitration

For almost 100 years professional baseball players were bound to their teams for life by the sport's infamous "reserve clause." In consequence, most players had little choice but to accept the salary their team was willing to pay them. In recent years, however, collective bargaining between the clubs and the players' union has replaced the old "reserve clause" with a system that considerably enhances player mobility between teams. At the same time, it has introduced a novel form of "interest" arbitration to fix salaries where player and team cannot agree.

Under the collective bargaining agreement between the teams and the players' union, players who have been in the major leagues for at least six years can choose to become "free agents"; they can thus have their salaries determined through negotiation in the free market with other teams that might be interested in them. Players with fewer than six years in the majors are still not free to look elsewhere, but are tied to their original team unless they are traded or released. However, those with at least *three* years service do have the right to submit the question of their salary to binding arbitration.

Salary arbitration hearings are held throughout the month of February. The collective bargaining agreement specifies a number of criteria which the "interest" arbitrators must consider in determining salaries for the coming season—for example, the player's contribution to the team during the past season (including his "overall performance, special qualities of leadership, and public appeal"), "the length and consistency of his career contribution," "comparative baseball salaries," and the "recent performance record of the Club," including its "League standing and attendance as an indication of public acceptance." They are instructed *not* to consider salary offers made by either party prior to arbitration, salaries in other sports or occupations, or the financial situation of the player or the team. The hearing is to be private and informal. Unless extended by the arbitrators, each party is limited to one hour for an initial presentation and one-half hour for rebuttal; awards are to be handed down by the arbitrators, without explanation, within 24 hours following the hearing.

The most distinctive feature of this arbitration scheme is the limits it places on the discretion of the arbitrators. The arbitrators are not free to choose whatever salary figure they think is appropriate. Instead, the player and the club each submits a "final offer" on salary for the coming season (these "final offers" need not be the figures offered during prior negotiations). The arbitrators may then award "only one or the other of the two figures submitted."

What is the rationale behind this "final-offer arbitration"? As we have seen, in conventional arbitration it is often assumed that arbitrators will have a tendency to compromise and "split the difference" between the parties in an effort to maintain their future acceptability. Conventional arbitrators may "use the parties' final offers to provide information on the range of settlements that bargainers are likely to view as acceptable."[10] Being aware of this, the parties at the bargaining stage are likely to hold back concessions that they would otherwise be willing to make, in order to avoid giving the game away. "If the parties view conventional arbitration as a procedure for securing compromise, bargaining tactics dictate that each party preserve a position *from* which the arbitrator can move to a

---

10. David E. Bloom, Empirical Models of Arbitrator Behavior Under Conventional Arbitration 17 (Nat'l Bureau of Econ. Res., Working Paper No. 1841, 1986).

compromise."[11] Indeed, the party which stakes out the *most extreme* initial position may hope to gain the most from an eventual arbitral compromise, and this is often said to have a "chilling effect" on good-faith bargaining.[12]

On the other hand, the constraints imposed by final-offer arbitration should have the opposite effect on the parties' negotiating behavior. Where the arbitrators may not compromise, each party may fear that if its offer is perceived as extreme or "unreasonable," the arbitrators will choose the offer of the *other* party. This may impel each party to adjust his bargaining position to make it more "reasonable"—and thus more likely to be chosen—than his opponent's. There is thus set up a movement of each party in the direction of the other, narrowing the differences between them——and at best, making any arbitration award at all completely unnecessary. Ideally, "final-offer arbitration" operates as a "doomsday weapon that invariably induces negotiated settlement."[13]

To some extent this dynamic can be observed in major league baseball. Typically, almost 90% of cases will settle after players have filed for arbitration and hearings have been scheduled. So only a handful of cases actually go through the arbitration process—in the years between 2000 and 2005, an average of around 9 cases per year.[14] "For most players, filing for arbitration and submitting salary proposals are stages of an ultimately successful bargaining process."[15] There are, of course, many other reasons for a high settlement rate in "baseball" arbitration. An arbitration hearing at which a player sits and listens to management's presentation of his many faults and shortcomings must inevitably strain the relationship between him and the club. And only if the parties settle can they be creative in designing a compensation package that may include bonuses, a no-trade clause, or a multi-year deal; the product of salary arbitration, on the other hand, is merely a standard player contract (contained in the "Uniform Player's Contract" that is made part of the collective bargaining agreement) for a single year at a defined salary.

Final-offer arbitration is also frequently used to resolve "interest" disputes in public-sector employment. In contrast to arbitration in major-league baseball, however, public-sector "interest" arbitrators are frequently charged with determining a wide range of bargainable issues in addition

11.   Chelius & Dworkin, An Economic Analysis of Final–Offer Arbitration as a Conflict Resolution Device, 24 J.Conflict Res. 293, 294 (1980).

12.   See Feuille, Final Offer Arbitration and the Chilling Effect, 14 Ind.Rel. 302 (1975).

13.   Id. at 307. See also Angelo S. DeNisi & James B. Dworkin, Final–Offer Arbitration and the Naïve Negotiator, 35 Ind. & Lab. Rel. Rev. 78 (1981)(study "clearly indicates that when negotiators fully understand and appreciate the final-offer procedure, they try harder to reach their own settlements and tend to feel more positively about their opponent in the negotiations").

14.   In those years 46 arbitration cases were actually heard, although 421 cases had been filed. See www.mlb.com; see generally Roger Abrams, The Money Pitch: Baseball Free Agency and Salary Arbitration 147, 152 (2000).

15.   Faurot & McAllister, Salary Arbitration and Pre–Arbitration Negotiation in Major League Baseball, 45 Ind. & Lab. Rel. Rev. 697, 701 (1992).

to salary—all going to make up the terms of employment in the new agreement. In some states, the statutory scheme calls for each party to present to the arbitrators a "package" that includes a position on *all* the bargainable issues not yet agreed on. The arbitrators must then choose what they consider to be the more reasonable of the two "packages." In other states, in contrast, the arbitrators are allowed to consider each issue separately—and to choose between the positions of the parties on an issue-by-issue basis. This variation enables the arbitrators to develop their own compromise "package" by balancing the parties' positions on the various issues. In New Jersey's complex scheme for collective bargaining for police and firefighters, cities and unions are given a choice of "terminal procedures" for resolving the issues in dispute: They may choose either

- conventional arbitration of all unsettled items;
- "final-offer" arbitration between the "single packages" proposed by the parties;
- "final-offer" arbitration on an "issue-by-issue basis," or
- arbitration in which as to any *"economic issues"*—essentially wages, vacations, insurance and other economic benefits—the arbitrator is to choose between the parties' contending *"packages,"* while as to any *noneconomic issues*, the arbitrator is to choose between the last offers submitted by each party for *"each issue in dispute."*[16]

NOTES AND QUESTIONS

1. How might the strategy and bargaining behavior of the parties differ depending on whether the final-offer arbitration is to be on an "issue-by-issue" or "package" basis?

2. It should be obvious that all forms of final-offer arbitration have the greatest impact on the party who is the more risk-averse. In determining its final offer, each party is faced with a trade-off. It must weigh the loss involved in making a particular concession (say, a reduction in salary demands) against the greater probability of having its offer chosen by the arbitrator should an award become necessary. The more risk-averse party will be likely to move further in adjusting his demand downwards, in the direction of "reasonableness," in order to reduce the chances of an unfavorable result. This is particularly likely where arbitration is on a "package" basis. There is some evidence that unions nominally "win" public-sector "interest" arbitrations more frequently than public employers, and this would seem to support the proposition that the unions are more likely than the employer to be risk-averse. See Henry S. Farber, An Analysis of Final–Offer Arbitration, 24 J.Conflict Res. 683 (1980); Susan Schwochau & Peter Feuille, Interest Arbitrators and Their Decision Behavior, 27 Ind.Rel. 37, 53–54 (1988) (union demands are much larger under conventional arbitration than under final offer arbitration, while offers by employers "show no significant differences").

16. N.J.S.A. § 34: 13A–16 (c).

See also Howard Raiffa, The Art and Science of Negotiation 118 (1982):

[I]t seems that the proportion of cases going to final-offer arbitration is smaller than the proportion going to conventional arbitration. This is often cited as an advantage of final-offer arbitration. Of course, the logic is marred a bit because conventional arbitration preceded by a round of Russian roulette would still do better.

3. The concern is often expressed that final-offer arbitration on a "package" basis may lead to results that are unworkable or inequitable. Consider, for example, the dilemma of the arbitrator in an "interest" dispute between a city and a firefighter's union. The union submits a proposal on salary and benefits which the arbitrators find preferable to the city's. However, the union has also included a "zinger," in the form of a demand for mandatory manning levels at certain fire stations—an unusual proposal that the arbitrators find objectionable. (Perhaps union negotiators slipped in this demand hoping that it would be carried along by the force of their "irresistible" economic package; perhaps they were forced to include it for reasons of internal union politics.) In such circumstances, arbitrators often express frustration at being limited to choosing one package or the other. Cf. In re Monroe County, 113 Lab. Arb. 933 (1999)("If I had the authority to decide this on an issue by issue basis, I would adopt the [union's] wage proposal and the [employer's] vacation proposal. Unfortunately, I do not possess that authority. It is all or nothing").

Is it a sufficient answer to such concerns to say that the *whole point* of final-offer arbitration is to discourage actual arbitration, and that "if the case reaches the arbitrator, the parties both deserve whatever they get"? Arnold Zack, Final Offer Selection—Panacea or Pandora's Box, 19 N.Y.L.F. 567, 585 (1974). Consider the following proposal for an alternative system of final-offer arbitration by "package": Each side is to submit *three* different final offers. The arbitrator chooses one of the six packages presented to him but does not reveal his choice to the parties; instead, he merely announces *which side* has made the better offer. The *losing party* is then allowed to choose one of the three packages submitted by the winning party, and this becomes the final award. See Cliiff Donn, Games Final–Offer Arbitrators Might Play, 16 Ind.Rel. 306, 312 (1977). What might be the advantages of such a system?

4. Consider this variation of final-offer arbitration: The arbitrator first draws up a proposed award without having seen the respective final offers of the parties. The final offer that was "closest" to this proposed settlement by the arbitrator then becomes the actual award binding on the parties. This is sometimes referred to as "night baseball." What are the possible advantages of this variant?

5. Final-offer arbitration has as yet been little used to resolve commercial disputes. In one highly-publicized case, however, the IRS and Apple Computer chose to resort to this mechanism in order to settle a "transfer pricing" dispute. The IRS had asserted a $114 million deficiency against Apple, claiming that the company had unlawfully reduced its U.S. income by overpaying for parts manufactured by its Singapore subsidiary—that is, by setting the prices higher than if the work had been done "at arm's length" for an unrelated company. Apple and the IRS spent nine months negotiating a 40–page agreement setting out the procedure for the arbitration. There would be a panel of three arbitrators—a retired federal judge, an economist, and an industry expert. For each taxable year in dispute, the parties would each present the panel with one amount, and the arbitrators must "select one of the amounts * * * and no other"; the arbitrators would not be bound by legal precedents if those cases "conflicted with industry practices." "IRS and Apple Submit Transfer Pricing Case to 'Baseball' Arbitration by Industry Experts," 10 Alternatives to High Cost Litig. 47 (1992); see also Jay A. Soled, Transfer Tax Valuation Issues, the Game Theory, and Final Offer Arbitration: A Modest Proposal for Reform, 39 Ariz. L. Rev. 283, 306 (1997); cf. id. at 289 (studies suggest that by contrast, "courts tend to compromise valuation estimates").

In another dispute, arising out of a real estate transaction in the Czech Republic, the arbitrator was instructed to choose the offer of one of the parties, but was permitted to "depart from that figure by up to $500,000 in either direction." See Al–Harbi v. Citibank, N.A., 85 F.3d 680 (D.C. Cir.1996).

6.   Under some statutes governing public-sector employment, "interest" disputes may be submitted to a neutral "fact-finder," who after hearing evidence from the parties makes a "recommendation." The term "fact-finder" may be chosen to lend an air of precision and inevitability to the process—but the fact-finder, in issuing his recommendations, is still likely to make the same sorts of value judgments and show the same concern for the acceptability of his conclusions to the parties as is typical of the "interest" arbitrator. The fact-finder's recommendations are usually made public, in the hope that the resulting public scrutiny and pressure of "public opinion" may make it more difficult for the parties to reject them. See, e.g., Ore.Rev.Stat. § 243.722(3), (4) (fact-finder's recommendations shall be "publicized" unless parties agree to accept them or agree to submit the dispute to final and binding arbitration). As you might expect, however, in all but the most exceptional cases there is room for considerable skepticism as to the extent of any public awareness of or concern for the reports of public-sector fact-finders.

In some states, fact-finding is the final prescribed stage in the resolution of public-sector "interest" disputes. In others, both mediation and then fact-finding are imposed as preliminary steps before mandatory arbitration. Such arbitration is often of the "final-offer" variety. Iowa's version adds further flexibility to the process: The arbitrators are allowed to choose not only one of the parties' last offers, but also—as a third option—the recommendation of the fact-finder on "each impasse item." Iowa Code §§ 20.21, 20.22. This recommendation, unsurprisingly, usually turns out to be a compromise, an intermediate position between the positions taken by the parties. And in those cases where an award proves necessary, the arbitrators tend overwhelmingly to choose the recommendation of the fact-finder. Even in jurisdictions where this option is not given to the arbitrator, the fact-finder's recommendation will often simply be incorporated into the final offer of one of the parties; the arbitration may then become a "show cause" hearing as to why this offer should not be accepted. "For those disputes that are not going to get resolved at the bargaining table, fact-finding is where the concrete for the foundation of an arbitration award is first poured." Steinar Holden, Final Offer Arbitration in Massachusetts, 31 Arb.J. 26, 28–29 (1976).

What might be the advantages and disadvantages of combining fact-finding and arbitration in this way? Might this two-step process tend to dilute the supposed benefits of final-offer arbitration? See generally Bierman, Factfinding: Finding the Public Interest, 9 Rutgers–Camden L.J. 667 (1978).

3. "Med–Arb"

There are many different styles of arbitration. One arbitrator may see himself chiefly as a passive adjudicator, presiding over the confrontation of adversaries. At the other extreme may be found the arbitrator who intervenes actively, in an effort to help the parties reach their own mutually agreeable settlement without the need for an imposed award.

Combining the roles of mediator and adjudicator poses a unique challenge to an arbitrator's skill: "When you sit there with the parties, separately or together—listening, persuading, cajoling, looking dour or relieved—your responsibility is a heavy one. Every lift of your eyebrow can be interpreted as a signal to the parties as to how you might eventually decide an issue if agreement is not reached."[17] This style of arbitration is seen most frequently in public-sector "interest" disputes. In fact, one survey estimates that arbitrators with experience in such disputes first attempt to mediate in at least 30 to 40 percent of their cases.[18]

Frequently, the statutory procedure for the settlement of public-sector disputes encourages and even institutionalizes "med-arb." The New Jersey statute, for example, expressly mandates that in the "interest" disputes of police and firefighters, the arbitrators "may mediate or assist the parties in reaching a mutually agreeable settlement" "throughout formal arbitration proceedings."[19] The arbitrators may accept revisions of the parties' "last offers" until the hearings are closed—and "arbitrators have successfully used mediation in many instances to obtain revised offers that significantly narrowed the differences between the parties."[20] It is not uncommon for the arbitrators, after hearing evidence, to remand the dispute to the parties for further negotiations before the ultimate "final" offers must be submit-

---

17. Bairstow, The Canadian Experience, Proceedings, 34th Annual Meeting, Nat'l Academy of Arbitrators 93 (1982).

18. James L. Stern et al., Final–Offer Arbitration: The Effects on Public Safety Employee Bargaining 140 (1975).

19. N.J.S.A. § 34: 13A–16f(3).

20. See Newark Firemen's Mutual Benevolent Ass'n, Local No. 4 v. City of Newark, 90 N.J. 44, 447 A.2d 130, 134, 136 (1982)("Nothing is gained by a rigid application of final offer arbitration that requires the selection of an unreasonable offer after the parties have narrowed their differences").

ted. In the course of the hearing, the arbitrator may indicate that on a particular issue he is "leaning towards" the position of one party. It does not require much imagination to see how this may influence the settlement process, and may force an adjustment in the position taken by the *other* party.

Arbitrators under this statute are often quite outspoken in inducing settlement by advising parties of the unacceptability of their positions. This is what has often been termed "mediation with a club." One arbitrator explained that "I beat up on the parties. I believe that scaring them helps them to settle their own dispute."[21]

Lon Fuller, Collective Bargaining and the Arbitrator

Proceedings, Fifteenth Annual Meeting, National Academy of Arbitrators 8, 29–33, 37–48 (1962).

There remains the difficult problem of mediation by the arbitrator, where instead of issuing an award, he undertakes to persuade the parties to reach a settlement, perhaps reinforcing his persuasiveness with "the gentle threat" of a decision. Again, there is waiting a too-easy answer: "Judges do it." Of course, judges sometimes mediate or at least bring pressure on the parties for a voluntary settlement. Sometimes this is done usefully and sometimes in ways that involve an abuse of office. In any event the judiciary has evolved no uniform code with respect to this problem that the arbitrator can take over ready-made. Judicial practice varies over a wide range. If the arbitrator were to pattern his conduct after the worst practices of the bench, arbitration would be in a sad way.

Analysis of the problem as it confronts the arbitrator should begin with a recognition that mediation or conciliation—the terms being largely interchangeable—has an important role to play in the settlement of labor disputes. There is much to justify a system whereby it is a prerequisite to arbitration that an attempt first be made by a skilled mediator to bring about a voluntary settlement. This requirement has at times been imposed in a variety of contexts. Under such systems the mediator is, I believe, invariably someone other than the arbitrator. This is as it should be.

Mediation and arbitration have distinct purposes and hence distinct moralities. The morality of mediation lies in optimum settlement, a settlement in which each party gives up what he values less, in return for what he values more. The morality of arbitration lies in a decision according to the law of the contract. The procedures appropriate for mediation are those most likely to uncover that pattern of adjustment which will most nearly meet the interests of both parties. The procedures appropriate for arbitration are those which most securely guarantee each of the parties a meaningful chance to present arguments and proofs for a decision in his favor.

21. Weitzman & Stochaj, Attitudes of   New Jersey, 35 Arb.J. 25, 30 (1980).
Arbitrators toward Final–Offer Arbitration in

Thus, private consultations with the parties, generally wholly improper on the part of an arbitrator, are an indispensable tool of mediation.

Not only are the appropriate procedures different in the two cases, but the facts sought by those procedures are different. There is no way to define "the essential facts" of a situation except by reference to some objective. Since the objective of reaching an optimum settlement is different from that of rendering an award according to the contract, the facts relevant in the two cases are different, or, when they seem the same, are viewed in different aspects. If a person who has mediated unsuccessfully attempts to assume the role of arbitrator, he must endeavor to view the facts of the case in a completely new light, as if he had previously known nothing about them. This is a difficult thing to do. It will be hard for him to listen to proofs and arguments with an open mind. If he fails in this attempt, the integrity of adjudication is impaired.

These are the considerations that seem to me to apply where the arbitrator attempts to mediate before hearing the case at all. This practice is quite uncommon, and would largely be confined to situations where a huge backlog of grievances seemed to demand drastic measures toward an Augean clean-up. I want now to pass to consideration of the case where the arbitrator postpones his mediative efforts until after the proofs are in and the arguments have been heard. * * *

One might ask of mediation first undertaken after the hearing is over, what is the point of it? If the parties do not like the award, they are at liberty to change it. If there is some settlement that will effect a more apt adjustment of their interests, their power to contract for that settlement is the same after, as it is before, the award is rendered. One answer would be to say that if the arbitrator undertakes mediation after the hearing but before the award, he can use "the gentle threat" of a decision to induce settlement, keeping it uncertain as to just what the decision will be. Indeed, if he has a sufficiently Machiavellian instinct, he may darkly hint that the decision will contain unpleasant surprises for both parties. Conduct of this sort would, however, be most unusual. Unless the role thus assumed were played with consummate skill, the procedure would be likely to explode in the arbitrator's face.

There is, however, a more convincing argument for mediative efforts after the hearing and before the award. This lies in the peculiar fact—itself a striking tribute to the moral force of the whole institution of adjudication—that an award tends to resist change by agreement. Once rendered it seems to have a kind of moral inertia that puts a heavy onus on the party who proposes any modification by mutual consent. Hence if there exists the possibility of a voluntary settlement that will suit both parties better than the award, the last chance to obtain it may occur after the hearing and before the award is rendered. This may in fact be an especially propitious moment for a settlement. Before the hearing it is quite usual for each of the parties to underestimate grossly the strength of his adversary's case. The hearing not uncommonly "softens up" both parties for settlement.

What, then, are the objections to an arbitrator's undertaking mediative efforts after the hearing and before rendering the award, this being often so advantageous a time for settlement? Again, the objection lies essentially in the confusion of role that results. In seeking a settlement the arbitrator turned mediator quite properly learns things that should have no bearing on his decision as an arbitrator. For example, suppose a discharge case in which the arbitrator is virtually certain that he will decide for reinstatement, though he is striving to keep his mind open until he has a chance to reflect on the case in the quiet of his study. In the course of exploring the possibilities of a settlement he learns that, contrary to the position taken by the union at the hearing, respectable elements in the union would like to see the discharge upheld. Though they concede that the employee was probably innocent of the charges made by the company, they regard him as an ambitious troublemaker the union would be well rid of. If the arbitrator fails to mediate a settlement, can he block this information out when he comes to render his award?

It is important that an arbitrator not only respect the limits of his office in fact, but that he also appear to respect them. The parties to an arbitration expect of the arbitrator that he will decide the dispute, not according to what pleases the parties, but by what accords with the contract. Yet as a mediator he must explore the parties' interests and seek to find out what would please them. He cannot be a good mediator unless he does. But if he has then to surrender his role as mediator to resume that of adjudicator, can his award ever be fully free from the suspicion that it was influenced by a desire to please one or both of the parties?

* * *

These, then, are the arguments against the arbitrator's undertaking the task of mediation. They can all be summed up in the phrase, "confusion of role." Why, then, should any arbitrator be tempted to depart from his proper role as adjudicator? In what follows I shall try to analyze the considerations that sometimes press him toward a departure from a purely judicial role.

* * *

[Fuller then discusses "polycentric" (that is, "many-centered") problems— the type of problem exemplified by the testator who in her will left a varied collection of paintings to two museums "in equal shares." See p. 24 supra.]

[P]robably the nearest counterpart to Mrs. Timken's will is the following case: Union and management agree that the internal wage structure of the plant is out of balance—some jobs are paid too little in comparison with others, some too much. A kind of wage fund (say, equal to a general increase of five cents an hour) is set up. Out of this fund are to be allotted, in varying amounts, increases for the various jobs that will bring them into better balance. In case the parties cannot agree, the matter shall go to arbitration. Precisely because the task is polycentric, it is extremely unlikely that the parties will be able to agree on most of the jobs, leaving for arbitration only a few on which agreement proved impossible. Since in the allotment every job is pitted against every other, any tentative agreements reached as to particular jobs will have to lapse if the parties fail in the end to reach an agreement on the reorganization of the wage structure as a whole. In short, the arbitrator will usually have to start from scratch and do the whole job himself.

Confronted with such a task the arbitrator intent on preserving judicial proprieties faces a quandary much like that of a judge forced to carry out Mrs. Timken's "equal" division through adjudicative procedures. * * *

What modifications of his role will enable the arbitrator to discharge this task satisfactorily? The obvious expedient is a resort to mediation. After securing a general education in the problems involved in reordering the wage scale, the arbitrator might propose to each side in turn a tentative solution, inviting comments and criticisms. Through successive modifications a reasonably acceptable reordering of rates might be achieved, which would then be incorporated in an award. Here the dangers involved in the mediative role are probably at a minimum, precisely because the need for that role seems so obvious. Those dangers are not, however, absent. There is always the possibility that mediative efforts may meet shipwreck. Prolonged involvement in an attempt to work out a settlement agreeable to both parties obscures the arbitrator's function as a judge and makes it difficult to reassume that role. Furthermore, a considerable taint of the "rigged" award will in any event almost always attach to the final solution. The very fact that this solution must involve a compromise of interests within the union itself makes this virtually certain.

* * *

There is one general consideration that may incline the arbitrator to resolve any doubts presented by particular cases in favor of assuming a mediative role. This lies in a conviction—to be sure, not expressed in the terms I am about to employ—that all labor arbitrations involve to some extent polycentric elements. The relations within a plant form a seamless web; pluck it here, and a complex pattern of adjustments may run through the whole structure. A case involving a single individual, say a reclassification case, may set a precedent with implications unknown to the arbitrator, who cannot see how his decision may cut into a whole body of practice that is unknown to him. The arbitrator can never be sure what aspects of the case post-hearing consultations may bring to his attention that he would otherwise have missed.

That there is much truth in this observation would be foolish to deny. The integrity of the adjudicative process can never be maintained without some loss, without running some calculated risk. Any adjudicator—whether he be called judge, hearing officer, arbitrator, or umpire—who depends upon proofs and arguments adduced before him in open court, with each party confronting the other, is certain to make occasional mistakes he would not make if he could abandon the restraints of his role. The question is, how vital is that role for the maintenance of the government—in this case a system of industrial self-government—of which he is a part?

In facing that question as it arises in his practice, the arbitrator ought to divest himself, insofar as human nature permits, of any motive that might be called personal. It has been said that surgeons who have perfected some highly specialized operation tend strongly to favor a diagnosis of the patient's condition that will enable them to display their special skills. Can the arbitrator be sure he is immune from a similar desire to demonstrate virtuosity in his calling? It is well known in arbitrational circles that combining the roles of arbitrator and mediator is a tricky business. The amateur who tries it is almost certain to get in trouble. The veteran, on the other hand, takes an understandable pride in his ability to play this difficult dual role. He would be less than human if he did not seek out occasions for a display of his special talents, even to the point of discerning a need for them in situations demanding nothing more than a patient, conscientious judge, about to put a sensible meaning on the words of the contract.

* * *

Sometimes judgment on the issues here under discussion is influenced by a kind of slogan to the effect that an agreed settlement is always better than an imposed one. As applied to disputes before they have gone to arbitration, this slogan has some merit. When the case is in the hands of the arbitrator, however, I can see little merit in it, except in the special cases I have tried previously to analyze. After all, successful industrial self-government requires not only the capacity to reach and abide by agreements, but also the willingness to accept and conform to disliked awards. It is well that neither propensity be lost through disuse. Furthermore, there is something slightly morbid about the thought that an agreement coerced by the threat of decision is somehow more wholesome than an outright decision. It suggests a little the father who wants his children to obey him, but who, in order to still doubts that he may be too domineering, not only demands that they obey but insists that they do so with a smile. After having had his day in court, a man may with dignity bend his will to a judgment of which he disapproves. That dignity is lost if he is compelled to pretend that he agreed to it.

NOTES AND QUESTIONS

1. One arbitrator has noted that,

    [y]ou have to recognize the danger is there even by the mere overture to the arbitrator to step outside and "Let's have a look at this." It could be nothing more than one side broadly indicating, "Yes, we are ready to compromise this," and the other side saying, "Under no circumstances. We think we have a solid case." Back we go into the room, and you have to decide. It is conceivable that that conversation

is going to influence the arbitrator. * * * I just don't think you can say even in the most cautious way that there won't be some prejudice.

Panel Discussion (Valtin), Proceedings, 33rd Annual Meeting, National Academy of Arbitrators 232 (1981).

Is it fair to suggest, then, that the "med-arb" process may often serve as an invitation to the parties to be candid—an invitation which only the more inexperienced or ingenuous of the two is likely to accept?

2.   A recent survey asked members of the National Academy of Arbitrators whether they would ever "meet separately with the parties to mediate an arbitration dispute." On a scale in which "1" signified "always," and "5" signified "never," the average response was "3.95." Michel Picher et al., The Arbitration Profession in Transition: A Survey of the National Academy of Arbitrators 30–32 (Cornell/PERC Institute on Conflict Resolution 2000).

3.   Where in other legal cultures arbitrators routinely engage in efforts to induce a negotiated settlement, they do not seem overly troubled by Fuller's concern with respect to a possible "confusion of role." See pp. 39–40 supra. "As the Chinese put it: who better to be the arbitrator than the failed conciliator"? Neil Kaplan, Hong Kong and the UNCITRAL Model Law, 4 Arb.Int'l 173, 176 (1988). See also Arthur Marriott, The Role of ADR in the Settlement of Commercial Disputes, 3 Asia Pacific L.Rev. 1, 15 (1994) ("the Chinese concept of * * * a rolling arbitration, whereby the arbitrator could become a conciliator and then revert to an adjudicatory role if the search for compromise and consensus proved in vain"). Attempts by arbitrators to facilitate compromise, suggest formulas for settlement, and induce agreement are not only seen in the Far East; such activity is also apparently quite common in Northern European arbitration. See, e.g., Johannes Trappe, Conciliation in the Far East, 5 Arb.Int'l 173 (1989) (approach of "concilio-arbitration," combining arbitration and mediation, "makes German practice, at least to a certain extent, similar to the Chinese"); cf. James T. Peter, Med–Arb in International Arbitration, 8 Amer. Rev. Int'l Arb. 83 (1997)(referring to a "low-intensity form of mediation" used in Swiss and German arbitrations; "there is minimal, if any, intervention in the negotiation process," and "confidential private caucusing is not commonly used.").

4.   The Hong Kong Arbitration Ordinance provides expressly that the arbitrator "may act as a conciliator," and in so doing may meet with the parties "collectively or separately." Where the parties fail to reach an agreement, the arbitrators may then "resume" the arbitration process. But in such a case, how should the arbitrators treat the confidential information that they were bound to receive in the course of their earlier efforts? The Ordinance requires the arbitrator to "disclose to all other parties * * * as much of [the confidential] information as he considers is material to the arbitration proceedings." § 2B. What do you think of this solution?

5.   Consider a process by which the arbitrator *first* hears evidence and reaches a decision in the traditional manner; an award is written and placed in a sealed envelope without having been revealed to the parties. Only *then* does she attempt to bring the parties to a consensual agreement through mediation; if she is successful in doing so, the award is simply destroyed. (This in effect is "arb-med.") What might be the advantages of such a process?

6.   A survey of litigators indicated that the overwhelming majority of them preferred judges in settlement conferences to "actively offer suggestions and observations" for the settlement of the case: "They want the judge's opinions. They want the judge's suggestions. They want the perspective of the experienced neutral." See Wayne Brazil, Settling Civil Disputes 44–46 (1985). Does this affect in any way your view of Fuller's criticisms respecting arbitrators who depart from the proper "judicial role"?

7.   A trial judge offered to mediate a lawsuit that (the) Ted Williams had brought against one Vincent Antonucci. The parties agreed to the mediation attempt, but no settlement was reached. The defendant then moved to disqualify the judge. (Matters escalated so that the defendant's attorney was later adjudged guilty of criminal contempt). The defendant complained that after he had made a settlement offer, the judge had told him to "get real," and that he had made comments "regarding the costs of protracted litigation and [his] likelihood of prevailing." The trial judge apparently also told Antonucci that "there'll always be people like [you] around, but let's face it, there's only one Ted Williams." The court of appeals noted:

> Regardless of the good faith of all concerned, this case more than points out the basic fallacy in such an agreement—that a judge can act as both mediator and judge. [W]e suggest that mediation should be left to the mediators and judging to the judges. If a judge decides to mediate a case with the consent of all concerned parties, the judge should act only as a settlement judge for another judge who will hear and try the matter in the event mediation fails * * *.

Evans v. State, 603 So.2d 15 (Fla. App. 1992). Cf. Township of Aberdeen v. Patrolmen's Benevolent Ass'n, 286 N.J.Super. 372, 669 A.2d 291 (1996)(in his award in a compulsory interest arbitration, the arbitrator rather naively "described in great detail the Township's shifting positions during the mediation process" that preceded the arbitration, and was "clearly exasperated" by its breach of confidentiality in having "leaked" information to the press about bargaining sessions; his award was largely in favor of the union; held, award vacated; the arbitrator had "violated his obligations to act fairly and impartially and to decide the issues solely on the evidence adduced before him at the arbitration hearings"; "mediation would be a hollow practice if the parties' negotiating tactics could be used against them by the arbitrator in rendering the final decision").

8.   Some schemes of "med-arb" provide for the different functions of mediation and arbitration to be performed by different individuals. If mediation fails, the dispute is then entrusted to a separate arbitrator who has the power to make a binding award. See Iowa Code §§ 20.20–20.22; Stephen Goldberg, The Mediation of Grievances Under a Collective Bargaining Contract: An Alternative to Arbitration, 77 Nw.U.L.Rev. 270 (1982).

In some cases, however, the mediator is charged also with making a *recommendation* to the ultimate decision-maker as to how the dispute should be resolved. This is true, for example, under California's mandatory mediation scheme, where the mediator may make a recommendation to the court as to child custody and visitation matters. See Cal.Fam.Code, §§ 3170, 3183. How might the possibility of such a recommendation by the mediator affect the mediation process? See Jay Folberg & Alison Taylor, Mediation 277–78 (1984):

> The consensus among mediators appears to confirm that the trust and candor required in mediation are unlikely to exist if the participants know the mediator may be formulating an opinion or recommendation that will be communicated to a judge or tribunal. The recommendation of the mediator, particularly in a child custody and visitation case, would generally be given such great weight that the mediator, in effect, would be switching roles from decision facilitator to decision maker. The confusion and suspicion created by this crossover role taint the validity, effectiveness, and integrity of the mediation process.

> The participants may, in some circumstances, agree or contract for the mediator to decide the matter if they are unable to do so or to testify as to a recommendation. Using the informal, consensual process of mediation with no evidentiary or procedural rules as the basis for an imposed decision does, however, create a considerable risk that the more clever or sophisticated participant may distort or manipulate the mediation in order to influence the mediator's opinion.

9. In addition to the effect on the neutrality of the ultimate decisionmaker, what other sorts of problems may be posed by the "med-arb" process? Are mediation and arbitration likely to call on different skills, and are these often to be found united in a single individual? Consider the following excerpt:

> [S]ome critics fear that having the power to arbitrate makes mediators too forceful, resulting in a decision that unduly reflects the views of the mediator. This may be a more pressing concern when the third party is primarily an arbitrator, [since] an arbitrator naturally, over time, develops personal concepts of what makes a good solution ... Arbitrators who lack mediation experience may even become offended when the parties reject their suggestions during mediation, and they may then pressure the parties into what they feel is an acceptable solution.
> * * *

> In a study comparing mediation, med-arb with the same mediator and arbitrator, and med-arb with a different mediator and arbitrator, it was observed that during the mediation stage the use of heavy pressure tactics—threats and strong advocacy of a particular solution—was greater in med-arb with the same mediator and arbitrator. Furthermore, it was observed that some med-arbiters pushed for a particular

solution after only a few minutes of mediation and that disputants appeared particularly anxious to follow the suggestions of and to please the mediator, perhaps because mediator prestige was greatest in this condition.

Megan Elizabeth Telford, Med–Arb: A Viable Dispute Resolution Alternative 3 (Industrial Relations Centre 2000).

10. The AAA has devised a program it refers to as "MEDALOA"— mediation combined with last-offer arbitration. Under this mechanism, parties mediate their dispute under the AAA's Commercial Mediation Rules; if they are unable to reach a settlement, they agree that a neutral appointed by the AAA—or the mediator himself if the parties prefer—will select between their final negotiated positions, that selection being binding on them. "During the mediation phase each party has made concessions and has developed some sort of feel for the other party's concessions and views. * * * Often the offers come so close together that the arbitrator's choice is of no real importance—you get what in effect is a mediated compromise." It has even been claimed that this "little-known-little used process * * * is the process of choice in the vast majority of commercial cases." Tom Arnold, A Vocabulary of ADR Procedures, in PLI, 1 Patent Litigation 1994 at pp. 287, 330–31; Robert Coulson, MEDALOA: A Practical Technique for Resolving International Business Disputes, 11 (2) J. of Int'l Arb. 111 (1994).

11. Christian Bühring–Uhle has suggested that a "mediation window" might usefully be inserted *in the course of an ongoing arbitration*, for the purpose of conducting a more or less structured settlement attempt: "Setting aside a few days" for such a mediation attempt need not "disrupt the arbitration since there are long periods during any arbitration where no hearings are conducted and the participants simply prepare for the next step in the proceedings." Even where a separate mediator is used, it would still be possible to efficiently integrate the two processes: For example, a mediator may be involved from the very beginning as a "stand-by" who could "shadow the arbitration proceedings"—"reading the most important briefs and participating as a tacit observer," becoming informed about the dispute so he could "step in as soon as the parties thought mediation attempts might make sense." This would give the parties "a mediation option available in case an opportunity for settlement talks arose during the course of the arbitration." Christian Bühring–Uhle, Arbitration and Mediation in International Business 370–381 (1996).

12. In conventional arbitration, the decisionmaker is expected to find the facts, decide whether they give rise to liability, and then determine the appropriate remedy. What if instead the contracting parties choose to structure their arbitration differently—so that "the neutral decisionmaker is to award *her estimate of the expected value of the outcome at trial*—that is, the average of the possible outcomes with each weighted by its likelihood of occurring"? By relying on expected value, this form of arbitration "essentially offers the imposition by a neutral party of an objectively reasonable settlement"—"a compromise that incorporates uncertainty";

the outcome for the parties "should be the same as if they tried their case repeatedly in court and took the average result." "There should be no shortage of arbitrators who are experienced in both practicing in a given area of the law and assigning an expected value to a case." See Joshua Davis, Expected Value Arbitration, 57 Okla. L. Rev. 47 (2004); see generally Rau, Sherman & Peppet, Processes of Dispute Resolution (4th ed. 2006), Chapter II at Section A.3.b.

Is it likely that an arbitrator will be able in such a process "to separate her view of the facts and the law from the views others might hold"—or, despite the contract, is it likely that she will have an unfortunate "tendency to decide issues on the merits"? Under what circumstances would you counsel a client to agree to this form of arbitration? See Davis, supra, 57 Okla L. Rev. at 121 ("This option should attract two, overlapping groups: (1) disputants who wish to compromise but cannot agree on the terms of a settlement, and (2) parties who are averse to [the risks of trial] but want the benefit of a neutral assessment of their legal rights").

4. "Rent a Judge"

A California statute provides that "upon the agreement of the parties," a court may "refer" a pending action to any person or persons whom the parties themselves may choose. The court may also "refer" an action where the parties had previously entered into a written contract calling for a referee to hear controversies that might arise in the future. Referees may be asked:

> to try any or all of the issues in an action or proceeding, whether of fact or of law, and to report a statement of decision thereon; [or] to ascertain a fact necessary to enable the court to determine an action or proceeding.

Cal.Code Civ.Pro. §§ 638, 640.

After hearing the case, the referees are to report their decision to the court within twenty days after the close of testimony; judgment must then be entered on the referees' decision "in the same manner as if the action had been tried by the court." Cal.Code Civ.Pro. §§ 643, 644.

Barlow F. Christensen, Private Justice: California's General Reference Procedure

1982 American Bar Foundation Research J. 79, 81–82, 103.

The statute says nothing at all about the qualifications of referees. Presumably, the parties might agree to have a case referred to almost anyone—to another lawyer, perhaps, or even to a layman. But parties using this statutory procedure are seeking judicial determination of their causes, and so references are made to retired judges selected by the parties. The reasons are obvious. A retired judge who would be acceptable to both parties would almost surely possess acknowledged judicial skills and, in many instances, expertise in the particular kind of case at issue, thus ensuring a trial that is both expeditious and fair.

The statute is also silent about the time and place of trials by referees. As a consequence, the parties and the referee are free to select the times and places that will be most convenient. This has obvious advantages with respect to such things as securing the presence of witnesses, and it means that trials can be scheduled at times that will be most advantageous to counsel. Moreover, because the procedure is most often used by parties who want to get to trial promptly, both sides know that when they do go to trial both parties will be ready, thus avoiding the continuances and postponements that are often so frustrating in the course of regular trials in courts.

Trials by referees are conducted as proper judicial trials, following the traditional rules of procedure and evidence. Transcripts are made of the proceedings, and the judgment of the referee becomes the judgment of the court. It is thus enforceable and appealable, as any other judgment would be. One lawyer who uses the reference procedure suggests that parties might agree to submit disputes to retired judges for decision independently, without any court order, but that they use the statutory procedure to preserve their rights of enforcement and appeal. * * *

In theory, almost any kind of case might be referred to a referee for trial. The consensual portion of the statute imposes no restrictions. In practice, however, the procedure has been used primarily in technical and complex business litigation involving substantial amounts of money. The case in which the procedure was first used, for instance, was a complicated dispute between a medical billing company and two attorneys who had acquired interests in the company. Other examples have been a suit by major oil companies against a California governmental agency over air pollution control standards, a contract dispute between a nationally known television entertainer and his broadcasting company employer, and an action between a giant motor vehicle manufacturer and one of its suppliers over the quality of parts supplied.

The compensation of a retired judge appointed to try a case as a referee is also the subject of agreement between the parties, and the cost is borne equally by the parties.

NOTES AND QUESTIONS

1. A survey of private ADR firms and independent neutrals offering dispute resolution services in Los Angeles is reported in Elizabeth Rolph et al., Escaping the Courthouse: Private Alternative Dispute Resolution in Los Angeles, 1996 J. Disp. Resol. 277. According to this study, the total "private ADR caseload" in Los Angeles grew at an average rate of 15% per year between 1988 and 1993—while during that period, the *public* court caseload declined an average of about 0.5%; private ADR, however, still represented only 5% of the total dispute "caseload" filed both in private fora and in the public courts (small claims, municipal, and superior courts) combined. Claims involving amounts in controversy greater than $25,000 accounted for between 60–70% of the private caseload, as compared to only 14% of the public court caseload.

This private ADR market was dominated by arbitration (58% of disputes) and by mediation (22%): Only 5% of private forum disputes were handled in "private judging" proceedings under the California statute (including discovery matters that courts often refer to private judges even without the consent of the parties, see Cal. Code Civ. Pro. Sec. 639 (e)). About 91 former judges are now offering their services in Los Angeles as neutrals in private ADR; most of these retired from the bench following 20 years of service, and "therefore cannot be characterized as leaving the bench 'prematurely.' " Of those neutrals who were characterized as "heavy hitters"—each handling 100 or more disputes in a year—almost half came from the bench. Unsurprisingly, while attorneys tended to dominate the provision of arbitration services, "former judges provide voluntary settlement conferences and private judging much more often than do attorneys."

2. The California statute appears to be the most often-used, and is certainly the most highly-publicized, in the country. However, comparable procedures exist in some other states. In some cases, the "referee" is *required* to be a retired judge. Under the Texas statute, for example, a "special judge" must be a retired or former district, county, or appellate judge with at least four years service, who has "developed substantial experience in his area of specialty" and who each year completes five days of continuing legal education courses. Here too, however, the parties are free to select their own "special judge" and to agree with him on the fee that he is to be paid. See Texas Trial by Special Judge Act, Tex.Civ.Prac. & Rem.Code § 151.001 et seq.

3. How does the California or Texas reference procedure differ from arbitration? Are there reasons why parties might prefer to utilize the reference procedure rather than to submit an existing dispute to arbitration?

Consider the following provisions of the Texas statute:

Sec. 151.005. Rules and statutes relating to procedure and evidence in the referring judge's court apply to a trial under this chapter.

Sec. 151.006. (a) A special judge shall conduct the trial in the same manner as a court trying an issue without a jury.

(b) While serving as a special judge, the special judge has the powers of the referring judge except that the special judge may not hold a person in contempt of court unless the person is a witness before the special judge.

Sec. 151.011. The special judge's verdict must comply with the requirements for a verdict by the court. The verdict stands as a verdict of the referring judge's court. * * *

Sec. 151.013. The right to appeal is preserved. * * *

4. In response to a number of criticisms of the "rent-a-judge" system, the Judicial Council of California approved new rules in February 1993 to govern trials by privately compensated judges. What objections were these rules intended to address—and how adequately do they deal with the perceived problems?

California Rules of Court, R.244.1. Reference by Agreement:

(b) A court must not use the reference procedure * * * to appoint a person to conduct a mediation. Nothing in this subdivision is intended to prevent a court from appointing a referee to conduct a mandatory settlement conference or, following the termination of a reference, from appointing a person who previously served as a referee to conduct a mediation.

(c) In addition to any other disclosure required by law, * * * a referee must disclose to the parties: * * *

> (2) Any significant personal or professional relationship the referee has or has had with a party, attorney, or law firm in the instant case, including the number and nature of any other proceedings in the past 24 months in which the referee has been privately compensated by a party, attorney, law firm, or insurance company in the instant case for any services, including, but not limited to, service as an attorney, expert witness, or consultant or as a judge, referee, arbitrator, mediator, settlement facilitator, or other alternative dispute resolution neutral.

(e) A party who has elected to use the services of a privately compensated referee * * * is deemed to have elected to proceed outside the courthouse; therefore, court facilities and court personnel must not be used, except upon a finding by the presiding judge that the use would further the interests of justice. * * *

(f) The presiding judge or supervising judge, on request of any person or on the judge's own motion, may order that a case before a privately compensated referee must be heard at a site easily accessible to the public and appropriate for seating those who have made known their plan to attend hearings. * * * The order may require that notice of trial or of other proceedings be given to the requesting party directly. * * *

(g) * * * A motion to seal records in a cause before a privately compensated referee must be served and filed and must be heard by the presiding judge or a judge designated by the presiding judge. The moving party must mail or deliver a copy of the motion to the referee and to any person or organization who has requested that the case take place at an appropriate hearing site.

A motion for leave to file a complaint for intervention in a cause before a privately compensated referee must be served and filed, and must be assigned for hearing as a law and motion matter. The party seeking intervention must mail or deliver a copy of the motion to the referee. If intervention is allowed, the case must be returned to the trial court docket unless all parties stipulate * * * to proceed before the referee.

See also Tex.Civ.Prac. & Rem.Code § 151.009(c) ("The state or a unit of local government may not pay any costs related to a trial under this chapter"); § 151.010 ("A trial under this chapter may not be held in a public courtroom, and a public employee may not be involved in the trial during regular working hours").

5. The following excerpts from a student-written note raise a number of objections to the California reference procedure. In light of everything that you have read in this chapter on arbitration, how do you assess these criticisms?

> While the comparatively affluent can realize the cost and time savings of hiring a referee, other litigants may not. Those appearing pro se, for example, or who are represented by Legal Aid or by attorneys appearing pro bono or on a contingency fee basis, may be able to afford little or no out-of-pocket expenditure prior to entry of a judgment and hence will be unable to hire a referee. The use of referees paid by the parties, then, in effect creates two classes of litigants: wealthy litigants, who can afford the price of a referee, and poorer litigants, who cannot. The former group obtains all of the advantages of reference, while the latter must endure all the systemic disadvantages that led wealthy litigants to seek reference in the first place.

> Such a system of reference is clearly unfair to the poorer litigant and may even run against the best interests of society. It would allow, in the extreme case, an utterly frivolous suit to obtain a speedy trial solely because the litigants were wealthy, while forcing a suit involving issues important to society and vital to the parties to languish for a considerable time awaiting trial. Even if the suits are similar, the bias against the poor is still striking. If, for example, the poor litigant is in court because he needs to protect a valuable property interest affected by the dispute, his interest is kept in jeopardy for a longer period of time than that of a similarly situated litigant using the referee system. The state's action in according the wealthy the privilege of using a faster form of procedure gives them an additional property right, the right to be more secure in their ownership.

* * *

> A due process problem may arise when referees are privately paid, particularly if overloading in the regular court system has driven some parties to a reference procedure they otherwise might not have chosen. As early as 1215, Magna Charta declared that it was wrong for the government to sell justice or to delay or deny it to anyone. In a private reference system, the state does not sell justice, but it does sanction the payment of private adjudicators to act in its place. The ultimate product purchased by these payments is a judgment that is entered on the court rolls and enforced by state authority. To whom the payments ultimately go is not nearly so important as the fact that they are made, with the sanction of the state, in order to obtain a state-monopolized enforceable order.

Note, The California Rent–A–Judge Experiment: Constitutional and Policy Considerations of Pay–As–You–Go Courts, 94 Harv.L.Rev. 1592, 1601–02, 1607–08 (1981). Similar arguments are advanced in Note, Rent–A–Judges and the Cost of Selling Justice, 44 Duke L.J. 166 (1994) ("The rent-a-judge system is an unconstitutional, elitist institution that unfairly grants privileges to the wealthy").

6. Other states have devised different sorts of hybrids between litigation and arbitration, some of which envisage a greater role for the public court system: For example, as an alternative to nonbinding "court-annexed arbitration," parties to a civil action in Nevada may agree to proceed under the "Short Trial Rules" promulgated by the state supreme court; such an agreement must be "entered into at the time of the dispute and not be a part of any previous agreement between the parties," and must be entered into "knowingly and voluntarily." Nev. Stat. § 38.250. Short trials are conducted by judges whom parties may select from a state-maintained panel; they may select either sitting judges, or "pro tempore judges" from the panel. "Pro tempore judges" are either practicing attorneys with 10 years civil trial experience or retired judges; they are paid $150 per hour—with a maximum of $1500 for the entire case—for which the parties are equally responsible, and while serving they have "all the powers and authority of a district court judge." If a jury is used, jurors are chosen from the county jury pool; the default size is four persons, three of whom have to concur for a valid verdict. The local court is to provide courtroom space.

Under the court's short-trial rules, the trial is to be calendared no later than 240 days after the parties' written stipulation agreeing to enter the program. Each party is allowed only three hours to present its case, and—as is common in many forms of arbitration—the parties are to create a "joint evidentiary booklet" including all evidence to be presented; any evidentiary objections are to be raised at a pre-trial conference or else deemed waived. A judgment under the short-trial program may not exceed $40,000 per plaintiff exclusive of attorneys' fees and costs unless the parties agree otherwise; either party may appeal an adverse judgment directly to the state supreme court, unless they have agreed "that the results of the short trial are binding." Nev. Short Trial R.32.

Is this "Short Trial" program open to the same objections as the California and Texas "rent-a-judge" schemes?

F. TRANSNATIONAL ARBITRATION: SOME FURTHER PROBLEMS

Throughout earlier sections of this chapter, we have already had a number of occasions to look at particular problems posed by the law and practice of transnational arbitration: Refresh your memory by looking again at the general introduction to the subject in Section B.2 ["Some Frequent Uses of Arbitration"]. In addition, there are further discussions of specific legal and procedural questions at pp. 128–29 ["Note, Determining the 'Jurisdiction' of the Arbitrator," note (4)]; p. 174 ["Note, Judicial Review of Awards and 'Public Policy,'" note (6)]; pp. 265–66 ["Arbitral Impartiality"]; pp. 278–79 ["Evidence," note (7)]; pp. 289–90 ["Discovery," note (8)]; pp. 297–300 ["Interim Measures," notes (8), (9) and (10)]; p. 352 ["Med–Arb," note (3)].

Given the likelihood that they will be considerably more complex than purely domestic transactions, transnational ventures—involving parties of different nationalities, or performance in different states—require considerable care and attention at the drafting stage. The potential involvement of more than one legal system should also force the parties to devote some thought to the question of which courts will hold themselves out as ready to supervise the arbitral process—or to interfere with it, and which courts will undertake to police the resulting award. (Indeed, the parties must face the possibility that they may be subject to overlapping assertions of jurisdiction.). In the following excerpt, the former Secretary General of the ICC Court of Arbitration discusses several key provisions that parties should consider when drafting an international arbitration clause.

Stephen R. Bond, How to Draft an Arbitration Clause

6(2) J. of Int'l Arb. 65, 66, 72, 74–75, 76, 78 (June, 1989).

[T]oo often, as has been said, the dispute resolution clause is done as an afterthought, and without very much thought. Preparation and study of the matter is essential. [In addition,] the other party may have very different ideas as to what constitutes an ideal clause. The relative bargaining strength of the parties comes into play and the negotiator must know what is essential to his interests and what can safely be given up. [And finally,] the all-purpose clause may not, in fact, be suitable for all situations. For example, it is all very well to provide clearly in the ideal arbitration clause for payment of interest, but if you ever have to execute upon an award based on such a clause in Saudi Arabia or certain other Muslim countries, the mention of interest may render the entire arbitration clause and award invalid. So too, it is generally preferable to indicate in the arbitration clause the place of arbitration. However, if that place is in a particularly unstable country so that there is a chance that when a dispute arises it might not be possible, for political or security reasons, to hold the arbitration in the place designated, the result may be to render the clause unworkable and to forfeit the right to arbitrate.

Still, the fact remains that because of the consensual nature of arbitration and the various requirements for the validity of the arbitral clause, if you desire that arbitration be the method of dispute resolution between yourself and a business partner, you will have to have an arbitral clause. It is also true that many of the difficulties that most often complicate and delay an arbitral proceeding and the possible enforcement of an arbitral award can be removed or diminished by a well-drafted arbitration clause.

Also, the more effective the arbitration clause you negotiate, the less likely it is that it will ever be used. This is because an ineffective dispute resolution clause will be less of a deterrent to a party that is considering a breach of contract. So, even businessmen who wish to deal with lawyers as little as possible have a major interest in involving an attorney in the negotiation of the dispute settlement provision, unless those businessmen wish to prove, once again, the old adage that arbitration is a procedure that has too few lawyers in the beginning (when the clause is drafted) and too many in the end (when an arbitration is actually under way).

I would like to present some thoughts as to elements which should be considered in drafting and negotiating an arbitration clause.

* * *

c. THE PLACE OF ARBITRATION

The importance of the place of arbitration cannot be overestimated. Its legislation determines the likelihood and extent of involvement of national courts in the conduct of the arbitration (either for judicial "assistance" or "interference"), the likelihood of enforceability of the arbitral award (depending on what international conventions the *situs* State is a party to), and the extent and nature of any mandatory procedural rules that you will have to adhere to in the conduct of the arbitration. (For example, in Saudi Arabia, the arbitrators must be Muslim and male.) Such factors are of far greater importance than the touristic attractions of any particular place that sometimes appear to be the decisive factor in making this decision. * * * This mention of *situs* is, after the choice of applicable law, the element most often added to the basic ICC arbitration clause. The choice of the place of arbitration may literally determine the outcome of the case. In one ICC arbitration between a Finnish corporation and an Australian corporation. London was selected as the place of arbitration in the arbitration clause. The case involved royalty payments allegedly not made and the purported cancellation of the relevant agreement in 1976. In 1982 the licensor initiated arbitration. The arbitrator found that because the arbitration was taking place in England, the statute of limitations contained in the U.K. Limitation Act had to be applied. So, even assuming that Finnish law was applicable and Finnish law had no comparable statute of limitations, the arbitrator applied the relevant U.K. 6–year statute of limitations and barred all claims arising prior to 1976, which effectively meant all claims.

* * *

d. APPLICABLE LAW

While the choice of the law to be applied by the arbitrators to determine the substantive issues before them is not an element necessary for the validity of an arbitration clause, it is certainly desirable for the parties to agree upon the applicable law in the arbitration clause if at all possible. Failure to do so is a significant factor in increasing the time and cost of an arbitration. Moreover, the decision of the arbitral tribunal on the matter (for it is an issue to be decided by the arbitrators, even if institutional arbitration is used) may bring an unpleasant surprise to one of the parties. Finally, where an institution is to select the chairman or sole arbitrator it is, as a practical matter, far easier to appoint the best possible person when it is known in what country's law the arbitrator should be most expert.

For these reasons, the element most often added to the contract, often directly in the arbitration clause itself, is that of the law applicable to the contract.

* * *

A few points should be borne in mind in deciding upon an applicable law and I will very briefly mention them.

Firstly, it is preferable that the legal system you agree upon in fact is developed in regard to the specific issues likely to arise.

Secondly, you may wish to exclude the conflict of laws principles of the chosen law, either explicitly or by specifying the "substantive law" of the particular country concerned.

Thirdly, be sure that the law you choose considers the subject matter of the contract to be arbitrable. Copyright or patent law questions, antitrust matters, etc. are often not permitted to be resolved by arbitration, but only in the national courts.

e. Composition of the Arbitral Tribunal

The next element which should be given the most serious attention is that of the composition of the arbitral tribunal. How many arbitrators do you want? How should they be selected? Should they have any particular qualifications? No broad generalities can cover all the situations likely to arise. * ** * [In many cases] where the arbitration clause did not determine the number of arbitrators, the parties were able to reach agreement between themselves on the point prior to the ICC Court having to make a decision. This would indicate that, as a practical matter, it will often be possible to reach agreement on this element even after a dispute has developed. Consequently, it is less urgent to reach agreement on this point in negotiating the arbitration clause than on certain others. * * *

Arbitration clauses tend to include no mention of other elements relating to the arbitral panel [such as nationality or professional qualifications. However,] it may well be that ICC clauses are not typical in this regard because parties know that the quality of ICC arbitrators is excellent and the ICC Rules require an arbitrator from a country other than those of the parties. Thus, with regard to the selection of arbitrators, confidence in the arbitral institution may well have reduced the amount of detail parties would otherwise have put in an *ad hoc* arbitration clause, for example.

* * *

f. Language of the Arbitration

Many parties may mistakenly believe that the language in which the contract is written will automatically be the language of any arbitration arising out of that contract. It is true that the ICC Rules, for example, state in Article 15(3) that the arbitrator shall give "due regard ... in particular to the language of the contract" in determining the language of the arbitration. It will, however, be for the arbitral tribunal to decide the question should the parties not have agreed on it.

As can well be imagined, simultaneous interpretation at hearings and translation of all documents into two or more languages are enormously expensive and time-consuming. If it is not possible to agree on a language in the arbitration clause then it would be desirable to try to agree either that costs for interpretation and translation are shared or else borne by the party requiring the interpretation or translation.

* * *

CONCLUSIONS

I will not end this presentation by revealing to you the all-purpose, miraculous arbitration clause, because there is probably no single clause that is appropriate in every case. You cannot escape the need, each time you negotiate an arbitration clause, to engage in a rigorous analysis of the circumstances related to the particular transaction in order to produce an arbitration clause tailored to the situation at hand. In the long run, this work will result in immeasurable savings of time and money.

Note: The New York Convention and "The Place of Arbitration"

The United Nations Convention on the Recognition and Enforcement of Foreign Arbitral Awards (the "New York Convention") was adopted in 1958. The United States ratified it in 1970,[15] and by the end of 2005, 137 states had become parties to the Convention—a number that obviously includes most major commercial states.[16] This widespread adoption of the Convention has made it "the single most important pillar on which the edifice of international arbitration rests"[17]—the Convention might even "lay claim to be the most effective instance of international legislation in the entire history of commercial law."[18] The full text of the Convention appears in Appendix B.

The principal impetus behind the adoption of the Convention was the need to provide a mechanism for the enforcement of "foreign" arbitral awards—that is, arbitral awards rendered abroad, "in the territory of a State other than the State where the recognition and enforcement of such

---

15. In that same year, §§ 201–208 were added to the FAA in order to provide a mechanism for enforcing agreements and awards falling within the Convention.

16. For the current status, see http://www.uncitral.org/uncitral/en/uncitral_texts/arbi-tration/NYConvention_status.html. Taiwan, which is not a signatory to the Convention, constitutes perhaps the only exception to this statement.

17. J. Gillis Wetter, The Present Status of the International Court of Arbitration of the ICC: An Appraisal, 1 Am. Rev. Int'l Arb. 91, 93 (1990).

18. Lord Mustill, Arbitration: History and Background, 6(2) J. of Int'l Arb. 43, 49 (1989).

awards are sought." See Art.I(1), first sentence. The site of an international arbitration is, after all, often chosen precisely because it represents a "neutral" location—and this usually means a place where the defendant may not have his principal place of business and where he may not have substantial assets. It is therefore often necessary for a successful claimant to take the award to some more appropriate jurisdiction, where there is a greater possibility of enforcing the award by execution. It is true that most arbitration awards are paid without enforcement action, but experienced practitioners report that awards tend to be paid more promptly when enforcement seems a live and imminent alternative. Under the Convention, enforcement in other jurisdictions of a foreign arbitral award has become considerably more simple and certain than would be the enforcement of the judgment of a foreign court.

The key provision of the Convention is therefore Article III, which establishes a state's general obligation to recognize and enforce foreign arbitral awards: Such awards are to be enforced "in accordance with the rules of procedure" used in the enforcing state with respect to domestic awards. Article I (3) gives each state the option of limiting this obligation to awards made only in the territory of *another contracting state*—the so-called "reciprocity" reservation—or to disputes "arising *out of legal relationships, whether contractual or not, which are* considered as commercial under [its] national law."[19] The United States has adopted both of these reservations (although the former, given the near-universal adoption of the Convention, is becoming increasingly irrelevant).

Courts of contracting states *must* enforce an arbitral award falling within the Convention, unless one of a small number of specified exceptions applies. In such a case a court "may" then refuse to enforce the award. (The exceptions are therefore permissive, within the discretion of the enforcing court.)[20] The grounds that can be asserted by a party against whom enforcement is sought, in order to contest enforcement of a foreign award, are set out in Art. V(1): Some of these are already quite familiar from our discussion of the "domestic" FAA—they naturally include due process violations such as the denial of a fair hearing or "the opportunity to present [a party's] claim in a meaningful manner";[21] irregular composi-

---

19. While this reservation apparently excludes arbitration awards arising out of family disputes, or disputes concerning succession to property, the fact that a government is a party to a transaction "does not destroy its commercial character; indeed, the fact that an agreement to arbitrate is in the contract between a government and a private person may confirm its commercial character and may constitute a waiver of sovereign immunity." Restatement, Third, Foreign Relations Law of the United States § 487 at cmt. f.

20. Cf. Jan Paulsson, *May* or *Must* Under the New York Convention: An Exercise in

Syntax and Linguistics, 14 Arb. Int'l 227, 229 (1998)("four of the five official languages of the Convention clearly leave room for judicial discretion. Only the French text contains a hint of a contrary intention, but it is not explicit").

21. E.g., Iran Aircraft Industries v. Avco Corp., 980 F.2d 141 (2d Cir.1992). At a pre-hearing conference the claimant had requested guidance as to the appropriate method for proving certain of its claims, which were based on voluminous invoices. The "neutral" arbitrator expressed reluctance about "getting kilos and kilos of invoices" and approved the claimant's proposal that its

tion of the arbitral tribunal; and an award that exceeds the contractual authority of the arbitrator or one that deals with an "inarbitrable" subject matter. In fact it is usually assumed that on such matters the standards of the Convention are essentially the same as those of the FAA generally:[22]

> Of course the verbal formulations differ—but then, they differ across various jurisdictions within this country in "domestic" FAA cases, without altering our recognition that "[h]owever nattily wrapped, the packages are fungible." I freely admit that waving the banner of "international comity" in cases with strong foreign overtones can often be a useful way of intimidating a judge into being more than usually circumspect in review. But as a general matter I think it is reasonably safe to assume that in operation the standards of the Convention and the FAA will be identical: In both cases the stated grounds for challenging awards are mere signposts—aimed at alerting a court on review that something has gone seriously wrong in the conduct of the arbitration, whether in the form of arbitral overreaching or the denial of a fair hearing. They are (to change the metaphor) expandable categories, which—in the rare case that seems to demand it—can be filled with a court's reaction that an award simply ought not to be honored.[23]

Now, does the New York Convention add any other possible grounds of review? See particularly Art. V(1)(a) and V(1)(e). What role does the Convention envisage for the courts and the law in the country where the award was made? (And what could be possibly meant by the words, "in which or under the law of which"?)

It is usually assumed that the law of the place where the arbitration is to be held—what is usually referred to as the arbitral "seat," or "situs"—will be the law that governs the arbitration process. (This applicable body of law, in the rather esoteric terminology of international arbitration, is inevitably referred to as the *"lex arbitri"*). The *lex arbitri* will regulate such matters as the selection of the arbitral tribunal, the extent of judicial assistance to—or interference in—the arbitral process, the conduct of the proceedings, the power of the arbitrators, and the making of the award.[24]

---

claims be documented by audited accounts receivable ledgers. However, by the time of the actual hearing, two of the three arbitrators had resigned and been replaced, and the panel ultimately disallowed certain claims that were asserted "solely on the basis of an affidavit and a list of invoices, even if the existence of the invoices was certified by an independent audit." The court held that the panel had "misled" the claimant, "however unwittingly," and enforcement of the award was denied under art. V(1)(b) of the Convention.

22. See, e.g., Management & Technical Consultants S.A. v. Parsons–Jurden Int'l Corp., 820 F.2d 1531 (9th Cir.1987) ("In interpreting the grounds specified [for overturning awards], it is generally recognized that the Convention tracks the Federal Arbitration Act").

23. Alan Scott Rau, The New York Convention in American Courts, 7 Amer. Rev. of Int'l Arb. 213, 236–37 (1996).

24. For a list of 14 "issues potentially governed by [this] procedural law," see Gary B. Born, International Commercial Arbitration: Commentary & Materials 412 (2nd ed. 2001).

"In very few cases is there any serious doubt but that the law of the seat applies."[25] At this point, then, we can fully appreciate Stephen Bond's admonition that "the importance of the place of arbitration cannot be overestimated." "The folklore of international arbitration is replete with accounts of how places of arbitration were fixed in City X at the insistence of one of the negotiators, whose sole reason turned out to be the convenience of airline connections. It is a safe bet that anyone who has participated even once in an international arbitration will never again base the selection of the place of arbitration on such a criterion."[26]

Why did the drafters of the Convention envisage (a) that an award may be scrutinized and set aside in local courts, if it is in conflict with mandatory local rules governing the arbitration process? And (b) that such a successful local challenge to the award may also make it impossible to enforce the award abroad in other jurisdictions where the respondent has assets?

In addition to the critical obligation to enforce foreign *awards*, the Convention, in Art. II, obligates each contracting state to "recognize *an agreement in writing*" under which the parties have agreed to arbitrate a dispute "concerning a subject matter capable of settlement by arbitration." Where a court is "seized of an action in respect of which the parties have made" an arbitration agreement, then the court must "refer the parties to arbitration, unless it finds that the said agreement is null and void, inoperative or incapable of being performed."

It has been said that the phrase "refer to arbitration" "[lacks] a precise legal meaning" and rarely appears in national arbitration laws: The Convention thus merely "mandates a result but leaves Contracting States free as to the means by which they are to achieve it."[27] In non common-law countries, the usual method for a court to give effect to an arbitration agreement is to dismiss an action or to "declare that it has no jurisdiction"; in common law countries, by contrast, statutes more commonly provide that a court shall leave the parties to their agreed remedy by staying

25. Adam Samuel, The Effect of the Place of Arbitration on the Enforcement of the Agreement to Arbitrate, 8 Arb. Int'l 257, 263, 268 (1992); see also Alain Hirsch, The Place of Arbitration and the *Lex Arbitri*, 34 Arb. J. 43 (1979) ("If, as is more often the case, the arbitration clause provides only for the place of arbitration, it is normally assumed that the *lex arbitri* of the same country will apply. Indeed, this is normally the aim of such a clause, rather than only providing for a geographical place for the proceedings"); XL Ins. Ltd. v. Owens Corning, [2000] 2 Lloyd's L. Rep. 500 (Q.B.)(by stipulating for arbitration in London, "the parties chose English law to govern" matters such as "the formal validity of the arbitration clause and the jurisdiction of the arbitral tribunal; and

by implication chose English law as the proper law of the arbitration clause"); cf. Gary B. Born, International Commercial Arbitration: Commentary and Materials 110–111 (2nd ed. 2001) (application of the law of the arbitral situs to arbitration agreements "can be explained as an implied choice of law by the parties (through their selection of the arbitral situs")).

26. W. Laurence Craig et al., International Chamber of Commerce Arbitration 93–94 (3rd ed. 2000).

27. Aron Broches, The 1985 UNCITRAL Model Law on International Commercial Arbitration: An Exercise in International Legislation, 18 Netherlands Yrbk. of Int'l Law 3, 16–17 (1987).

judicial proceedings pending the completion of the arbitration proceedings. In addition, a stay could help preserve a court's authority to order preliminary relief "[s]hould.... the court deem preliminary injunctive relief necessary to ensure that the arbitration process remains a meaningful one."[28] A number of American courts have found that a stay pending arbitration is an appropriate method in Convention cases of "referring" the parties to arbitration;[29] in other cases—where there is perhaps "no question" as to the arbitrability of the claims and "it appears that the grant of a stay serves no function other than that of postponing the inevitable dismissal of such actions until the completion of arbitration"—dismissal for "lack of subject matter jurisdiction" may be the appropriate means of complying with the Convention.[30]

NOTES AND QUESTIONS

1. In DaPuzzo v. Globalvest Management Co., L.P., 263 F.Supp.2d 714 (S.D.N.Y. 2003), a partnership agreement mandated arbitration in the Bahamas under ICC rules. After an investor brought suit alleging that his investment had been fraudulently induced, the defendant moved to stay the litigation and compel arbitration. The court held that it lacked any authority to compel arbitration in the Bahamas, which had not ratified the New York Convention. Nevertheless it stayed the litigation, both pursuant to FAA § 3 and as "an incident to its inherent power to control its own docket"; it was reluctant to declare itself "powerless to devise an adjudication that gives legal effect to what the parties agreed, and that also pays due homage to the spirit and salutary goals of the FAA." The court acknowledged that any award the investor might receive through arbitration in the Bahamas could not ultimately be enforced in the United States—but that "does not mean that [he] would not have recourse to enforce the award in the Bahamas." See also National Iranian Oil Co. v. Ashland Oil, Inc., 817 F.2d 326 (5th Cir. 1987). Here the agreement provided for arbitration in Teheran; however, since Iran had not at the time ratified the Convention, the district court lacked the power to compel arbitration there under FAA § 206—nor did it have the power to order arbitration anywhere else under FAA § 4 ("the court shall make an order directing the parties to proceed to arbitration in accordance with the terms of the agreement"). It was "Iran or nowhere." It should be noted, though, that Iran has since—effective 2002—become a party to the Convention.

2. Note the definition in Art. II(2) of an "agreement in writing." Surely such a creaky text could use some adjustment to take account of more

---

28. Tennessee Imports, Inc. v. Filippi, 745 F.Supp. 1314, 1325 (M.D.Tenn.1990).

29. E.g., Rhone Mediterranee Compagnia Francese di Assicurazioni e Riassicurazoni v. Lauro, 555 F.Supp. 481, 486 (D.V.I. 1982), aff'd, 712 F.2d 50 (3d Cir.1983).

30. See Filanto, S.p.A. v. Chilewich Int'l Corp., 789 F.Supp. 1229, 1241–42

(S.D.N.Y.1992) (court issued final judgment containing a mandatory injunction to arbitrate and held that staying action and retaining jurisdiction "would serve no purpose" since the entire dispute "will be resolved by arbitration").

modern forms of communication? In November 2005, the United Nations General Assembly adopted a "Convention on the Use of Electronic Communications in International Contracts": Under the new Convention, a requirement that a contract be "signed by a party" is satisfied by an electronic communication, as long as some method is used "to identify the party and to indicate that party's intention," and the method is "as reliable as appropriate for the purpose for which the electronic communication was generated or communicated, in the light of all the circumstances." These provisions are specifically made applicable to communications looking to the formation of an arbitration agreement under the New York Convention. See http://www.uncitral.org/uncitral/en/uncitral_texts/electronic_com merce/2005Convention.html, and in particular Arts. 9 and 20.

What, though, of the case where one of the parties has not given any written assent to arbitration *in any form*? Suppose, for example, that a written proposal to arbitrate is sent by one party and then accepted orally—or even tacitly—by the other party. In such circumstances, of course, under ordinary principles of American contract law—as well as under the domestic law of many other jurisdictions—it would not be difficult for a court to find that an enforceable arbitration agreement has been created. See Section C.3.a., supra; see also Zambia Steel & Bldg. Supplies Ltd. v. James Clark & Eaton Ltd., [1986] 2 Lloyd's Law Rep. 225 (C.A. 1986) ("assent to the written terms may be proved by other evidence," and so "any evidence which proves that the party has agreed to be bound by an agreement to [arbitrate] contained in a document or documents is sufficient to make the document or documents an agreement in writing").

But do these facts allow us to find an "agreement in writing" within the meaning of the Convention? The drafters apparently intended for the answer in such a case to be "no." See Albert Jan van den Berg, The New York Convention of 1958: Towards a Uniform Judicial Interpretation 196 (1981)("The text of Article II(2) does not leave any doubt on this point"; the legislative history also "confirms that the drafters of the Convention wished to exclude the oral or tacit acceptance of a written proposal to arbitrate"). Is it really necessary, though, to read the Convention in such a restrictive manner? One ingenious way out of the dilemma is suggested by Sphere Drake Ins. PLC v. Marine Towing, Inc., 16 F.3d 666, 669 (5th Cir.1994): On the court's reading of the structure of Art.II(2), an "agreement in writing" includes *either*

    (1) an arbitral clause in a contract, *or*

    (2) an arbitration agreement that is

        (a) signed by the parties or

        (b) contained in an exchange of letters or telegrams."

And so, "because what is at issue here is an arbitral clause in a contract, the qualifications applicable to arbitration agreements do not apply," and a signature is "therefore not required." The Second Circuit, on the other hand, refused to go down that seductive path in Kahn Lucas Lancaster, Inc. v. Lark Int'l Ltd., 186 F.3d 210 (2d Cir. 1999)(the comma immediately following the words "an arbitration agreement" "suggests that the modifying phrase is meant to apply to both elements in the series" and any other interpretation "would render the comma mere surplusage"; in addition, in both the equally authoritative French-and Spanish-language versions of the Convention, the word for "signed" appears in the plural, thereby "unambiguously apply[ing] to both" antecedents).

Assume, then, that—despite all our efforts—we are unable to bring this fact pattern within the syntax of Art. II: Are we necessarily forced to conclude that the agreement loses all the protection of the Convention? (Is there any particular significance in Article II(2)'s use of the word "include"?) See Sen Mar, Inc. v. Tiger Petroleum Corp., 774 F.Supp. 879 (S.D.N.Y.1991). Here an arbitration clause was contained in a telex sent by one party only, and the court refused to compel arbitration—because the arbitration clause was "not found in a signed writing nor is it found in an exchange of letters" as required by the Convention. Cases in which courts had, under the FAA, enforced arbitration clauses "contained in [an] unsigned writing" were deemed simply irrelevant—because the court was authorized to "enforce the arbitration clause only if it satisfies *the Convention's more stringent requirement.*" See also Paul D. Friedland, "U.S. Courts' Misapplication of the 'Agreement in Writing' Requirement for Enforcement of an Arbitration Agreement under the New York Convention," 13 (5) Mealey's Int'l Arb. Rep. at pp. 21, 15 (May 1998)(the "implicit assumption [made by non-U.S. courts] that Art. II(2) leaves no room for application under Art. II of more permissive local law standards is a reasonable one"). Can the *Sen Mar* result possibly be defended? Is there any reason why the Convention should be viewed as laying down—not *the minimum that states must do to* enforce arbitral agreements—but rather the maximum that they are *allowed* to do? Under the result in *Sen Mar,* does it necessarily follow that the agreement has become completely unenforceable? What is the significance here of Art. VII of the Convention?

3. The Convention, as we have seen, allows a court to refuse to enforce an arbitration agreement that it finds to be "null and void, inoperative or incapable of being performed." What does this mean? If, as is likely, differing national laws have varying requirements concerning the validity of arbitration clauses, what body of law will then determine whether the agreement is enforceable?

For example, suppose that an arbitration agreement provides for arbitration to take place in Italy. A lawsuit is brought in the United States; the defendant moves to compel arbitration, and the plaintiff argues that the arbitration agreement is not enforceable under Italian law. The agreement fails to comply with Italian law, he asserts, because under Italian law arbitration clauses are unenforceable (a) where the agreement does not appear above the signatures of both parties, (b) if all of the defendants to a lawsuit are not parties to the agreement, or (c) if they call for an even number of arbitrators. In such circumstances, some American courts have nevertheless stayed the litigation once they were convinced that an "agreement in writing" exists under *American* law. See Marchetto v. DeKalb Genetics Corp., 711 F.Supp. 936 (N.D.Ill.1989) ("The possibility that Italian law might divest a panel of Italian arbitrators of jurisdiction is not determinative of this court's duty to enforce an otherwise valid arbitration agreement"; "underlying the Supreme Court's willingness to enforce arbitration agreements is the assumption that signatory nations to the Convention will honor arbitration agreements and reject challenges to arbitration based on legal principles unique to the signatory nation"). See also Rhone Mediterranee Compagnia Francese Di Assicurazioni E Riassicurazoni v. Lauro, 712 F.2d 50 (3d Cir.1983) (an arbitration agreement is "null and void" under Art.II(3) of the Convention only "when it is subject to an internationally recognized defense such as duress, mistake, fraud, or waiver, or when it contravenes fundamental policies of the forum state").

Can these cases be right? A quick glance at the Convention shows that while the undertaking to honor arbitral awards is the subject of detailed regulation in Articles I, III, and V, the scope of the obligation to honor *agreement*s—by contrast—is completely undeveloped. (It appears in fact that Art. II was the product of last-minute drafting and discussion at the conference that produced the text of the Convention, and little or no thought was paid to the question of how far the obligation to enforce agreements should extend). So what conclusions should we draw? It has been argued that the silence of the text imposes a duty to enforce arbitration agreements that is unqualified and unconditional: See, e.g., Martin Domke, Domke on Commercial Arbitration § 50:3 (3d ed. 2005)("since the limitations on the scope of [the enforcement of awards] are not set forth in Art. II, the enforcement of agreements is mandated even with respect to transactions that would not be considered international under Art. I"). But doesn't it seem more sensible to conclude instead that the obligations of the Convention are "congruent for both agreements and awards"? Alan Scott Rau, The New York Convention in American Courts, 7 Amer. Rev. of Int'l Arb. 213, 233 & fn. 81 (1996). In this respect, isn't Art. V(1)(a) helpful here by analogy? Isn't the obvious inference that Art. II "can be deemed to incorporate Art. V(1)(a)," and that, failing a contrary designation by the parties, "the law applicable to the arbitration agreement" is "the law of the country where the award *will be made*"? Albert Jan van den Berg, The New York Convention of 1958: Towards a Uniform Judicial Interpretation 127 (1981). Can you imagine reasons why a state should be obligated to give effect to an arbitration agreement when it would have no obligation under the Convention to enforce the resulting award?

Gary Born suggests that cases like *Marchetto* may best be explained as "forum non conveniens decisions"; an unwillingness to hold the agreement invalid under Italian law may simply reflect a recognition that "Italian courts are much better placed than U.S. courts to apply Italian arbitration statutes, and ought to be given the opportunity to do so." Gary Born, International Commercial Arbitration in the United States 315 (1994). Some support for this assertion be found in Pepsico Inc. v. Oficina Central De Asesoria y Ayuda Tecnica, C.A., 945 F.Supp. 69 (S.D.N.Y.1996): In

Pepsico the parties' agreement provided that it would be governed by the law of Venezuela; disputes were to be settled by arbitration in New York under ICC Rules, and "the arbitrators shall apply the substantive law of the State of New York." The court considered that it made "obvious good sense, as well as offering a considerable savings of judicial time and resources, for this Court to have the benefit of a Venezuelan court's speedy determination of a threshold question of Venezuelan law that must be resolved before" arbitration could be compelled. So it retained jurisdiction but stayed proceedings for 60 days "to afford the Venezuelan court the opportunity to determine, if it chooses," the question of arbitrability.

4. The discussion above hardly exhausts the complexity of the Convention. What about the problem that is, in a sense, the converse of the one in note (3) above: Is the enforcement of an *award* under Art. V dependent on satisfying the requirements of a "written agreement" under Art. II? That is, does Art. V "incorporate" Art. II—so that a state only has the obligation to enforce an award where an adequate written agreement can be presented? Cf. China Minmetals Materials Import & Export Co., Ltd. v. Chi Mei Corp., 334 F.3d 274, 286 & fn. 13 (3d Cir. 2003)(court should not enforce an award "where the parties did not reach a valid agreement to arbitrate, at least in the absence of a waiver of the objection to arbitration by the party opposing enforcement"; however, there remains "some distinction" between Art. II and Art. V, since the former "explicitly requires 'an agreement in writing' while [the latter, by contrast], requires only that the parties have reached an agreement as to arbitrability under ordinary contract principles"). Compare id. at 292–3 (Alito, J., concurring and writing "separately to elaborate on the importance of Art. IV(1)(b)" of the Convention; to "comport with fundamental principles of arbitration," a party seeking enforcement must produce an "agreement in writing within the meaning of Art.II").

5. There has traditionally been considerable unwillingness to submit to foreign arbitration in Latin America, where historical memory of one-sided international arbitrations dominated by European or North American partners is still vivid. See Section B.2. supra. In response to the view that Latin Americans may "trust global organizations less than they trust themselves," a regional convention was drafted in order to encourage the use of international commercial arbitration in Latin American countries. This is the Inter–American Convention on International Commercial Arbitration (the "Panama Convention"), adopted in 1975, and to which the United States became a party in 1990. (At the same time, §§ 301–307 were added to the FAA in order to provide a mechanism for enforcing agreements and awards falling within the Convention.). At the present time 18 nations have ratified the Convention (all of whom, by the way, are also parties to the New York Convention). See http://www.oas.org/juridico/english/Sigs/b–35.html. The full text of the Convention appears in Appendix C.

The text of the Panama Convention was obviously modeled after that of the New York Convention and is quite similar to the earlier treaty. It might even be said that the Panama Convention is "redundant in view of the New York Convention." See generally Albert Jan van den Berg, The New York Convention 1958 and the Panama Convention 1975: Redundancy or Compatibility, 5 Arb. Int'l 214, 229 (1989). Some textual differences may be attributable to the fact that the Panama Convention is drafted in a style that reflects legal concepts familiar to the region, but these differences are unlikely to entail any substantive significance. See, e.g., Progressive Casualty Ins. Co. v. C.A. Reaseguradora Nacional de Venezuela, 802 F.Supp. 1069, 1074–75 (S.D.N.Y.1992), rev'd on other grounds, 991 F.2d 42 (2d Cir.1993) (New York Convention provides that arbitration clause must be in "a contract or an arbitration agreement" while Panama Convention refers to "an instrument," but "I am not inclined to build a brick of substantive difference from such frail straws"). Courts have held that the scope of the two conventions should be interpreted similarly since "Congress intended the Inter–American Convention to reach the same results as those reached under the New York Convention," Productos Mercantiles E Industriales, S.A. v. Faberge USA, Inc., 23 F.3d 41, 45 (2d Cir.1994).

There is, however, one striking and unusual feature of the Panama Convention: Under article 3, unless the parties expressly provide otherwise, arbitrations under the Convention are to be conducted in accordance with the rules of procedure of the Inter–American Commercial Arbitration Association; see also FAA § 306. Few if any other examples can be found in which an international convention has incorporated, as positive law, the rules of a private institution. ICAC rules call for administered arbitration, and in the United States the AAA, as the "national section" of the ICAC, administers these arbitrations. See generally John P. Bowman, The Panama Convention and Its Implementation Under the Federal Arbitration Act 23–33 (2002).

William Laurence Craig, Uses and Abuses of Appeal from Awards

4 Arbitration International 174, 174–179, 182–185, 190–192 (1988).

International arbitration has become the ordinary way of resolving international commercial disputes. One of the reasons for this success has been the relative ease with which awards rendered in a foreign jurisdiction can be enforced at the debtor's domicile or in any jurisdiction where the debtor has assets. That ease has been due, in large part, to the New York Convention of 1958, a treaty which provides that the courts of each signatory country will enforce arbitration awards from other countries. The Convention provides relatively few grounds for courts to deny recognition and enforcement of foreign awards. The same spirit which gave rise to the Convention has also led many jurisdictions to look favourably upon enforcing foreign awards even where the Convention does not apply. The internal laws of some countries have provided for even more liberal enforcement of foreign awards than envisioned in the New York Convention.

The rising number of international commercial arbitration awards–and wide dissemination of information about these awards in a number of excellent publications—has produced an increasingly cohesive practice among nations in the recognition and enforcement of awards. In other words, recognition and enforcement of foreign awards is a success story; and the present system can be expected to continue its process toward a uniform international system for recognition and enforcement of awards.

On the other hand, however, no international agreements control how national courts supervise arbitrations taking place on their own territory. Each State is free to apply whatever measures of judicial control it wishes to international arbitration taking place within its own jurisdiction. The most dramatic judicial intervention in the arbitral process is appeal or judicial review at the seat of arbitration. A successful appeal cuts the awards off "at its roots" and leaves it unenforceable anywhere because the New York Convention provides that "recognition and enforcement of the award may be refused" on proof that "the award. . . . has been set aside or suspended by a competent authority in which, or under the laws of which, that award was made."

Unlike the unifying trend in recognition and enforcement of foreign awards, judicial review is heteroclite, changing rapidly by reforms of arbitration laws in various jurisdictions. Appeal of arbitration awards is a field of frequently unpredictable results. With more and more awards involving important parties and substantial amounts of money, one may expect ever more testing of judicial review at the seat of arbitration. A party disappointed with an arbitration award will try to have the award set aside at the seat of arbitration because success means that the New York Convention, with its limited grounds for refusing the enforcement of an award, will never come into play.

* * *

We should start with a definitional problem: Is it correct to speak about "appeal" from an arbitral award? I chose that word because when a party is disappointed with an arbitral award, the first question he asks is, How can I appeal?

Technically the term is either too narrow or too broad to describe the process by which a court at the seat of arbitration may take steps affecting the validity of the award itself. It might be useful to set out the lexicon of the awkward relationship between judicial courts and international arbitration awards.

There are two basic ways by which a party disgruntled with an arbitration award can test it judicially. First, he can oppose recognition and enforcement of the award in any jurisdiction where the winner seeks judicial enforcement of the award. If he succeeds in opposing enforcement, he defeats the award only in that jurisdiction. The winner may still try to enforce the award in any other jurisdiction where the loser has assets.

The alternative is to take the offensive and seek "judicial review" of the award in the jurisdiction where it was rendered. I will refer to the jurisdiction where the award was rendered as the arbitration's home jurisdiction or as the seat of arbitration. When judicial review in the home jurisdiction nullifies, vacates, overturns or reverses the arbitral award, it cannot be enforced anywhere.

It is difficult to find a single word appropriate for all jurisdictions to describe the process of judicial review of an award at the seat of arbitration. In referring to review in the home jurisdiction, the broadest and most encompassing term is "challenge" of an award. Challenge captures the idea of an offensive effort to overturn an award, as distinct from mere resistance to enforcement. It covers recourse to a court for the setting aside or the revision of an award; it also covers an appeal on a point of law which might lead to the setting aside or revision of an award.

* * *

[It] should be recognised that parties can in a certain measure influence the extent and scope of judicial review. The choice of the seat of arbitration is effectively a choice of law with respect to judicial review of the award. The parties may agree to hold their arbitration in a jurisdiction which guarantees rights of full appeal or what is commonly called ordinary appeal. Ordinary appeal allows a court to conduct a complete review of the arbitrator's decision on the merits, regarding both factual and legal determinations. In some cases ordinary appeal permits the judge to substitute his own decision if he finds that the arbitral tribunal erred. More frequently, parties will seek to hold their arbitration at a place providing only for judicial review or "extraordinary" appeal—appeal only for fundamental irregularities which tainted the arbitral decision.

* * *

The relationship between courts and arbitrations is neither purely adversarial nor purely complementary. As Berthold Goldman points out, the interaction between the courts and arbitral tribunals can be summarized as both "arbitration, the rival of the judge" and "arbitration, dependent on the judge." When one of the parties is seeking the court's powers of compulsion to advance arbitral proceedings which have been stalled because of the other party, the court has a role of assistant to the arbitral process. At the stage of annulment, however, the court exercises its right of control over the arbitral process so as to prevent the award from being received into the legal order of the State. At such moments, one can perhaps see, at least from time to time the role of the courts as rival to arbitration.

At the stage of confirmation proceedings for recognition and enforcement of an award—or its counterpart, judicial challenge—the State faces a choice. It must make the decision whether it will accept the results of an essentially contractual procedure as an award within its legal order. In keeping with this function, a court will not exercise the powers of the State to compel enforcement of the award unless it can be convinced that the award presents certain minimum characteristics which justify the State's use of its sovereign powers. With respect to foreign awards, most States have agreed by treaty greatly to restrict the grounds upon which they may refuse enforcement of an award. This is because the proponents of world trade and commerce have been able to convince the major nations of the world that business efficacy requires that an award, if valid where rendered, should be given an "international currency" and should be enforced in other jurisdictions.

A State court's action in recognition and enforcement of a foreign award has much less impact than the same court's action in reviewing an arbitration award that was rendered in its own territory. The decision within the recognition State will have an effect only on the award in that jurisdiction. Refusal to recognise the award has no effect on the award itself, which the winner can carry from State to State looking for other forums where the loser has assets and where the courts are amenable to enforcement. However, successful appeal at the *seat of arbitration* may prevent the award from being recognised anywhere else in the world.

Not only is the impact greater, but the court's discretion is wider. The reviewing court will not be limited to determining whether the award fulfills the "international currency" criterion but will be free to decide whether the award meets any other requirements necessary for welcoming arbitral awards into the domestic legal order. These requirements may be much more stringent than treaty grounds for recognition. Moreover, the reviewing court will be exercising powers which the State enjoys over any activity taking place within its territory. Thus, review by a court of an award taking place within the territory of its State determines whether contractual proceedings have ripened into an award fulfilling the requirements of a jurisdictional act of that State.

There is a very simple way to contrast judicial review at the seat of arbitration with recognition proceedings and other measures of judicial assistance. Recognition proceedings and other measures are triggered by the request of a person who wishes either to advance the arbitral process or to secure the enforcement of an arbitral award already obtained. He is a party crying to keep the contractual commitment to arbitration alive. In judicial review, the moving party seeks the annulment of an arbitral award. His goal is to render the arbitral process meaningless both at the seat of arbitration and elsewhere. Since the effect of judicial review is so drastic, we should examine the interests of the State in the exercise of such powers.

It is almost universally accepted that there should be only limited rights of appeal from an arbitration award. Indeed, limited rights to judicial review are just one aspect of the doctrine that parties who choose arbitration are intentionally choosing not to have the advantages and disadvantages of the courts. Courts will deny applications for discovery when the dispute is subject to arbitration because if the parties had wanted the paraphernalia of discovery, they should have agreed to judicial resolution and not to arbitration. In the same vein, if the parties had wanted full rights of appeal, they should not have agreed to arbitrate.

* * *

[Perhaps the most acceptable rationale for the necessity of judicial review has been given by Sir Michael Kerr, a Lord Justice of Appeal]:

> With the exception of the Sovereign and the Judicial Committees of the House of Lords and Privy Council, there is virtually no body, tribunal, authority or individual in England whose acts or decisions give rise to binding legal consequences for others, but who are altogether immune from judicial review in the event of improper conduct, breaches of the principle of natural justice, or decisions which clearly transcend any standard objective reasonableness. Such islands of immunity as remain are constantly shrinking. These limited powers of judicial review are exercised by judges whose decisions are themselves controllable ... ultimately by the House of Lords ... with each member of the higher courts exercising considerable influence over the view of the others. No one having the power to make legally binding decisions in the country should be altogether outside and immune from this system. This system is our bulwark against corruption, arbitrariness, bias, improper conduct and—where necessary—sheer incompetence in relation to acts and decisions with binding legal effect for others. No one below the highest tribunals should have unreviewable legal powers over others. Speaking from experience, I believe this to be as necessary in relation to arbitrations in England and abroad as in all other contexts.[25]

This seems to me to offer the true rationale of limited review at the seat of arbitration. In countries devoted to the constitutional principle of "no man above the law", it is difficult to give anyone the power to bring about final legal consequences without the possibility of any judicial body of the land questioning those consequences.

In common-law countries it is very easy to compare judicial review over arbitration proceedings to the powers that courts exercise over quasi-judicial bodies of all kinds (magistrates, land tribunals, housing councils, etc.). One could also make some comparisons with court review of administrative agency action in the United States. The essential problem with this analysis is that the reviewing court begins to perceive the arbitral tribunal as a part of its own legal system and as an inferior tribunal at that. This is an acceptable position for domestic arbitrations or even for arbitrations having international character but having a strong link with the local law and procedure, but it does not suit arbitrations in the purely international context.

* * *

It is no surprise that the relationship between arbitrations and judicial review at the seat of the arbitration has not been regulated in a New York Convention fashion. Setting any international standards for how courts should handle arbitrations rendered in their jurisdiction would be a far greater invasion of a State's sovereignty than are international standards

---

25. Michael Kerr, Arbitration and the Courts: The UNCITRAL Model Law, 34 Int'l & Comp. L.Q. 1 (1985).

for honoring an arbitration award from abroad. Arbitrations in the "home jurisdiction" are much more likely to involve domestic concerns. In large, relatively self-contained economies, the majority of arbitrations will be purely domestic affairs. The relationship between an arbitration and the courts of its home jurisdiction is built on a far different model than the relationship between an arbitration and a foreign court.

Yet a large number of the arbitrations conducted in the world today do not have any meaningful link to their home jurisdiction. Often, the jurisdiction is home to the arbitration without being home to either side in the dispute. In fact, this is a natural result of the nature of international arbitration. Arbitration is often chosen because neither side wants to end up in the courts of the other. Similarly, each side may be suspicious of holding an arbitration in the other side's country. A third country with a proper image of neutrality becomes the chosen site of arbitration. Hence, cities such as Geneva, Stockholm, and Vienna become favored sites for international arbitrations.

Arbitration in a third country is also a natural consequence of the fact that international arbitration is centered on a few arbitration institutions, such as the London Court of International Arbitration (LCIA), the International Chamber of Commerce in Paris, the International Centre for Settlement of Investment Disputes (ICSID) in Washington, or the Stockholm Chamber of Commerce. While all these institutions permit arbitrations under their auspices to be held all over the world, there is an understandable tendency to hold the arbitration in the city where the institution is headquartered. A Brazilian and a Danish company which have agreed to arbitrate their contract by ICC Rules may pick Paris as the seat of arbitration simply because they have no reason to pick any other place and they know the ICC is headquartered there.

The most extreme example of the lack of connection between the dispute and the seat of arbitration arises when the parties have failed to elect a venue in their contract and the seat of arbitration is chosen by the arbitral institution. In the case of the ICC, when the parties have not chosen a seat of arbitration, the ICC will select a neutral site, often based on the domicile of the president of the arbitral tribunal or simply on a location convenient for the parties and arbitrators. It is sometimes said that the result of this exercise is a site equally inconvenient to everyone. More important, the result of this exercise may be selection of a site of arbitration which neither of the parties contemplated in contracting.

The result is a large number of international arbitrations which have nothing to do with the home jurisdiction, except that they use conference rooms in the home jurisdiction's Hilton hotel. The arbitration involves no national of the home jurisdiction, involves no direct financial impact on the home jurisdiction, and applies a substantive law foreign to the home jurisdiction. In the case where the arbitration institution chooses the venue, the seat of arbitration is not even a conscious choice of the parties. Even the procedural rules of the arbitration tend to be those of an arbitration institution, with the procedural law of the home jurisdiction relegated to the second string.

Few of the traditional interests of the courts in overseeing domestic arbitration remain. There is no national to protect; there is no national interest to protect; there may be little domestic law that the arbitral panel can be accused of having misunderstood or misapplied. All that is left is the most abstract of sovereign interests—a pure concern of the government for what happens on its sovereign territory.

The principal interest the national courts have in these kinds of arbitration might arguably be termed interests of national prestige. Arbitral awards from a particular jurisdiction could come to have a certain reputation and that reputation indirectly but inevitably would reflect on the judiciary of that nation. Such subjective feelings hardly seem to be a sufficient foundation upon which to construct a theory of judicial review, however. Nor is it a sufficiently principled response to say that judicial review of international awards should follow the model of domestic review simply because the controlling legislation makes no distinction and judges have been trained to think that way.

This is not to say that a nation hosting international arbitrations has absolutely no legitimate interests in policing those arbitrations. While the principal criterion of determining the applicability of the New York Convention is simply whether the award is "foreign", the "nationality" of the award will have some relevance in determining whether the award was final and, for countries using the reciprocity section, whether the award comes from another signatory State. Courts may have the reaction that an award rendered on their territory should not enter the international stream of enforcement and attain the status of international currency without facing at least the prospects of judicial review. That is, the national judiciary could feel that it is performing its judicial duty or its government's international duty. Judicial review could stem from a sense of national responsibility in the international arena. Finally, courts may demand to exercise some judicial review on the theory that a government has some responsibility to see that justice is done—or, at least, that injustice is not done—within its frontiers. As Alan Redfern and Martin Hunter have written:

> It is generally accepted, however, that a state should insist upon the observance of a minimum standard of objectivity and justice in quasi-judicial proceedings held within its territory, whether they are the proceedings of a jockey club or of an arbitral tribunal.[43]

There can be little doubt that this is a desirable standard for civilised nations, but national courts should occasionally be reminded that often their citizens have more interests at stake in the meeting of the local jockey club than in the proceedings of an international arbitral tribunal.

---

43. Alan Redfern & Martin Hunter, International Commercial Arbitration 320 (1986).

NOTES AND QUESTIONS

1. An important case illustrating the distinction between attempts to "set aside" or "vacate" an award (at the "seat" of arbitration), and resistance to enforcement proceedings elsewhere, is International Standard Elec. Corp. v. Bridas Sociedad Anonima Petrolera, Industrial Y Comercial, 745 F.Supp. 172 (S.D.N.Y. 1990). Here a joint venture agreement provided that it would be "governed by and construed under and in accordance with the laws of the State of New York"; the ICC, which was to administer the arbitration, named a Mexican attorney as the chairman of the panel—and "since the parties here are an American Company and an Argentine Company, it is not difficult to understand why" the ICC selected Mexico City as the place of arbitration. The arbitrators ultimately awarded the claimant damages of almost $7 million, plus $1 million in legal fees, and costs of $400,000. The respondent moved in a U.S. district court to vacate the award, while the claimant "cross petitioned to enforce" it under Art. III of the Convention. The court held that it lacked any jurisdiction to set aside the award: The reference in Art. V to the country "under the laws of which [the] award was made" should be understood, it held, as a reference

> exclusively to procedural and not substantive law, and more precisely, to the regimen or scheme of arbitral procedural law under which the arbitration was conducted, and not the substantive law of contract which was applied in the case. * * * The "competent authority" as mentioned in Article V(1)(e) for entertaining the action of setting aside the award is virtually always the court of the country in which the award was made. * * * It is clear, we believe, that any suggestion that a Court has jurisdiction to set aside a foreign award based upon the use of its domestic, substantive law in the foreign arbitration defies the logic both of the Convention debates and of the final text, and ignores the nature of the international arbitral system. * * * The whole point of arbitration is that the merits of the dispute will *not* be reviewed in the courts, wherever they be located.

The court then turned to the claimant's cross-petition, and proceeded to enforce the award.

It is an obvious corollary of *Bridas* that the Convention has nothing whatsoever to say about—it imposes no restraint whatever on—the ability of *the courts of Mexico* to vacate the award according to that state's own domestic standards:

> Thus in the country of origin a losing party may obtain a setting aside on a ground not mentioned in Article V of the Convention. He can subsequently resist enforcement on ground *e* of Article V(1) that the award has been set aside in the country of origin. This has the effect that the grounds for refusal of enforcement of the Convention may indirectly be extended by the grounds for setting aside contained in the arbitration law of the country of origin.

Albert Jan van den Berg, The New York Convention of 1958: Towards a Uniform Judicial Interpretation 22 (1981).

2. As *Bridas* itself illustrates, it is a commonplace proposition that an arbitration clause may be governed by a different body of law than the overall contract in which it is embedded. See, e.g., Deutsche Schachtbau–Und Tiefbohrgesellschaft v. Ras Al Khaimah National Oil Co., [1987] 2 Lloyd's L. Rep. 246 (C.A.), rev'd on other grounds, [1988] 2 Lloyd's Law Rep. 293 (H.L. 1988) (ICC arbitration held in Geneva; even if "the proper law of the substantive contract" was the law of Ras Al Khaimah, where the contract was to be performed, "the proper law of the arbitration" was Swiss; "an arbitration agreement constitutes a self-contained contract collateral or ancillary to the substantive agreement and * * * not be governed by the same law as that agreement"); XL Ins. Ltd. v. Owens Corning, [2000] 2 Lloyd's L. Rep. 500 (Q.B.)("parties' freedom of choice includes freedom to choose different systems of law to govern different aspects of their relationship").

This is just a corollary of the doctrine of "separability," isn't it? See Section C.3.b. supra; see also Alan Scott Rau, Everything You Really Need to Know About "Separability" in Seven Simple Propositions, 14 Amer. Rev. of Int'l Arb. 1, 43 (2003):

> The law governing the arbitration agreement may be that of the arbitral forum—often, after all, chosen precisely because it is perceived as having little or no connection with the parties or with the underlying transaction—or it might be some "international" standard spun out directly from the New York Convention. In any case, it should seem perfectly natural that the validity of an arbitration agreement (under its proper law) need not at all be affected by the supposed invalidity or "non-existence" of a container contract that is subject to a quite different legal regime. So it is barely worth a second thought—it is not even a paradox—to find that arbitrators might well have the final word to the effect that the overall contract—in which the arbitration clause is embedded—is and has been from the beginning, under its own proper law, a nullity.

3. In Productos Mercantiles e Industriales, S.A. v. Faberge USA, Inc., 23 F.3d 41 (2d Cir.1994), the Second Circuit held that a district court had the authority under the Panama Convention to "modify" a Convention award. (The dispute, between corporations of Guatemala, El Salvador, and the United States, arose out of an agreement to license trademarks in Central America). Is that result in tension with the decision in *Bridas?* The court found support for its holding in FAA § 307, which permits the "domestic FAA"—and hence § 11—to apply on a "residual" basis when not in actual conflict with the Convention. See also § 208 (New York Convention). Is this a strategic move that might possibly work also for § 10 motions to vacate? The *Productos* court was careful to note that modification in that case "did not concern the merits of the award" since the district court had merely adjusted amounts to account for the arbitrators' own earlier correction of "a typographical error." In addition—although the *Productos* opinion betrays absolutely no understanding of why this might possibly be relevant—it seems noteworthy that the award in question was actually rendered in New York. See "Note: Coverage of the New York Convention," infra.

4. KBC (a Cayman Islands company which builds electric generating stations using geothermal sources) and Pertamina (an oil, gas, and geothermal energy company owned by the Republic of Indonesia), entered into a contract for the construction and operation of an electrical power plant in Indonesia. The contract contained an arbitration clause under which "the site of the arbitration shall be Geneva, Switzerland"; it also recited that "in accordance with Section 641 of the Indonesian Code of Civil Procedure," neither party "shall appeal to any court from the decision of the arbitral panel," and that the parties "waive the applicability" of certain provisions in the Indonesian Code (among them provisions imposing time limits on the arbitral process and requiring that the arbitrators be "bound by strict rules of law").

The project was later suspended by the government of Indonesia; KBC instituted arbitration proceedings, and an *ad hoc* arbitral tribunal ultimately rendered an award—reciting that it was "made in Geneva"—in the claimant's favor. KBC sought to enforce its award in the United States, as well as in Hong Kong and Canada; while these enforcement proceedings were pending, Pertamina sought to have the award vacated in Switzerland. The Swiss courts dismissed the annulment proceedings on the ground that court costs had not been paid; having failed in this attempt, Pertamina then sought to have the award set aside in Indonesia—and this time, unsurprisingly, it was successful. What effect should an American court give to the Indonesian decree of annulment? Should it decline to enforce the award?

The Fifth Circuit concluded that the parties' agreement designating Switzerland as the site for the arbitration "presumptively designated Swiss procedural law as the *lex arbitri,* in the absence of any express statement making another country's procedural law applicable." And there can be *"only one national court system that has jurisdiction to consider an application for annulment of an award."* "Such 'exclusive' primary jurisdiction in the courts of a single country is consistent with the New York Convention's purpose; facilitates the 'orderliness and predictability' necessary to international commercial agreements; and implements the parties' choice of a neutral forum." It followed, then, that the action of the Indonesian courts in setting aside the award could not be a defense to enforcement under the Convention; the court affirmed a summary judgment of enforcement in favor of KBC.

Such a holding could have been predicted rather easily. But the same court—a year earlier—had nevertheless held it to be an "abuse of discretion" to issue an antisuit injunction, with the effect of *prohibiting* Pertamina from pursuing annulment proceedings in Indonesia:

> By allowing concurrent enforcement and annulment actions, as well as simultaneous enforcement actions in third countries, the Convention necessarily envisions multiple proceedings that address the same substantive challenges to an arbitral award. * * * Inasmuch as the Con-

vention provides for multiple proceedings and a more limited role for enforcement jurisdictions, Pertamina's actions in Indonesia, even if spurious, are less vexatious and oppressive than they would be outside of this treaty structure. * * * Not only did KBC contract to arbitrate its dispute in a foreign country (Switzerland), but it also instituted enforcement proceedings in several countries, including the United States. Indeed, but for Pertamina's initiation of a law suit in Indonesia, or perceived bias there, KBC conceivably might have attempted enforcement there as well.

In these circumstances—and "given the absence of a practical, positive effect that any injunction could have"—the court concluded that "more weighty considerations of comity" militated against the injunction; the antisuit injunction could only "have the practical effect of showing a lack of mutual respect for the judicial proceedings of other sovereign nations" and would amount to "an assertion of authority not contemplated by the New York Convention." Although there was indeed "strong evidence" suggesting that Switzerland was "the paramount country of primary jurisdiction under the Convention,"—and indeed that Pertamina "appears to be" "acting in bad faith by pursuing annulment in Indonesia"—that "is an issue that is not directly before us today." "A sovereign country has the competence to determine its own jurisdiction and grant the kinds of relief it deems appropriate."

Among the many opinions in this litigation—which metastasized at an alarming rate—see Karaha Bodas Co., L.L.C v. Perusahaan Pertambangan Minyak Dan Gas Bumi Negara, at 335 F.3d 357 (5th Cir. 2003), and at 364 F.3d 274 (5th Cir. 2004). See also Section D.2.e. supra, at note (9).

5. A Mexican subsidiary of a U.S. company (Metalclad) owned a development site for a waste disposal facility in Mexico. Although Mexican federal officials had approved the facility—and had assured Metalclad that no further permissions were necessary—municipal officials later refused to issue a municipal construction permit; after construction began at the site, a state "Ecological Decree" declared the entire area an "ecological preserve [to protect] species of cacti"—which of course had the effect of proscribing the project entirely. Metalclad brought a claim against Mexico under the North American Free Trade Agreement (NAFTA). See generally Section B.2, supra ("Note, Investment Disputes"). Chapter 11 of NAFTA, as we have seen, extends to aggrieved investors of one contracting state the right to institute binding arbitration against another contracting state. An investor may choose to arbitrate:

- under the ICSID Convention—but only where *both* involved states are parties to the treaty [This has been irrelevant since neither Mexico nor Canada has as yet signed the ICSID Convention]; or

- under the ICSID's "Additional Facility Rules" [These arbitrations are administered by ICSID, but are not governed by the ICSID Convention framework that makes ICSID a public-law body whose awards are unchallengeable], or

- as an hoc arbitration, under rules promulgated for non-administered arbitrations by the United Nations Commission on International Trade Law [UNCITRAL].

Metalclad instituted an "Additional Facility" arbitration; the three arbitrators were all extremely distinguished attorneys and academics—Sir Elihu Lauterpacht [see http://www.20essexst.com/bar/q_lauter-pacht_e/lauterpacht.htm], Benjamin Civiletti [see http://www.vena-ble.com/attorneys.cfm?action=view & attorney_id=14], and Professor José Luis Siqueiros. Hearings took place in Washington, where ICSID is located, but "it was proposed by the Tribunal, and agreed by the parties, that the place of the arbitration would be Vancouver." The arbitral panel ultimately awarded Metalclad $16,685,000 in damages, having made two critical findings:

- The various conflicting state and federal decrees were inconsistent with NAFTA's requirement of "transparency": There appeared to be "no clear rule" as to whether a municipal permit was required, and in any event no established practice or procedure governing permit applications. So Mexico had "failed to ensure a transparent and predictable framework for Metalclad's business planning and invest-ment"; "transparency" was understood "to include the idea that all relevant legal requirements for the purpose of initiating, completing and successfully operating investments should be capable of being readily known to all affected investors," and "that there should be no room for doubt or uncertainty."

- In addition, the state environmental decree was tantamount to an "expropriation" without compensation.

The award was challenged in the British Columbia Supreme Court, which proceeded to review it under the province's International Commer-cial Arbitration Act. Like most modern legislation, the Act made no provision for judicial review of awards for legal error, but the court vacated the tribunal's first holding on the familiar ground of excess of power—that the arbitrators "had made decisions on matters beyond the scope of the submission to arbitration." For the arbitral tribunal had grounded its decision "on the basis of transparency," and there are simply "no transpar-ency obligations contained in Chapter 11 of NAFTA." It is true that Art. 1105 of NAFTA does require states to accord investments "fair and equitable treatment" "in accordance with international law"—and the situation might have been very different if the arbitrators had "simply *interpret[ed]*" this language "to include a minimum standard of transparen-cy." But the tribunal had not purported to "interpret the wording of Article 1105," but rather, it "*misstated* the applicable law to include transparency obligations." So although the tribunal's second holding was upheld, the award was "partially set aside"—with the result that interest could only be awarded Metalclad for the period following the date of the Ecological Degree. See United Mexican States v. Metalclad Corp., [2001] BCSC 664, 89 B.C.L.R. (3d) 359 (2001).

Does this use of the rhetoric of "jurisdiction" represent a heightened standard of judicial review, at odds with the usual deference given to private tribunals? Did the court honor the usual presumption that an arbitral tribunal acted within the scope of its powers? Would such heightened review be justified by the fact that—as the Government of Mexico argued—NAFTA decisions "have significant public policy ramifications" on issues of general concern, including public health and the environment? See Gus van Harten, Judicial Supervision of NAFTA Chapter 11 Arbitration: Public or Private Law?, 21 Arb. Int'l 493 (2005)("the principle of party autonomy—so central to commercial arbitration"—may be less relevant to NAFTA since the treaty standards "could be viewed as analogous to rules of domestic public law that protect individuals by limiting state authority"); Charles H. Brower, Investor–State Disputes Under NAFTA: The Empire Strikes Back, 40 Colum. J. Transnat'l L. 43 (2001)("The prospect of lengthy annulment proceedings by itself threatens to diminish investor confidence"; "[i]f municipal courts take the annulment process one step further by permitting the easy reopening of awards, they will cripple a system of neutral adjudication designed to promote the flow of capital across the borders of NAFTA Parties").

Metalclad also reminds us that under the NAFTA framework, the elaboration over time of the meaning of this international treaty is confided to different national courts operating within the New York Convention. Is this a sensible structure? Is it likely to lead to a uniform understanding of what the treaty means? See Jack J. Coe, Jr., Domestic Court Control of Investment Awards: Necessary Evil or Achilles Heel Within NAFTA and the Proposed FTAA?, 19 (3) J. of Int'l Arb. 185 (2002)(even uniform modern legislation relies "on local law for substantive content" and different courts "may interpret the common text differently"; the present Chapter 11 mechanism "encourages participants to forum shop, promotes inefficiency through its lack of centralization and provides an unsuitable vehicle for elaborating, unifying and legitimizing NAFTA law").

Note: Centers of Control: The Place of Arbitration and the Place of Enforcement

As we have seen, it has become commonplace to distinguish between the "primary" jurisdiction—the state "in which the arbitration was sited and the award was rendered," "or in other words the state where the arbitration took place"—and the "secondary" or "enforcement" jurisdiction. (The terminology can be traced to W. Michael Reisman, Systems of Control in International Adjudication and Arbitration: Breakdown and Repair 113–14 (1992)). For many authors, nullification in a primary jurisdiction must necessarily "have a universal effect," which "uproots" or indeed "kills" the award entirely:

> If an award is rendered [in] Switzerland and is nullified under Swiss law, nothing should be enforceable in any other jurisdiction. However, if the award is rendered in Switzerland but enforcement is refused in France where the award debtor has property, the French judgment should have no effect outside of France, even if it explicitly bases itself

on a ground of nullity which would have nullified the award *erga omnes* had it been rendered in a primary jurisdiction.[1]

This view has been carried forward into certain national laws: Legislation in both Italy and the Netherlands, for example, makes it *mandatory* for local courts to refuse enforcement of an arbitral award that has been set aside in the state where it was rendered.[2] But why should this be true?

Chromalloy Aeroservices v. Arab Republic of Egypt

United States District Court, District of Columbia, 1996.
939 F.Supp. 907.

■ JUNE L. GREEN, DISTRICT JUDGE.

I.   Introduction

This matter is before the Court on the Petition of Chromalloy Aeroservices, Inc., ("CAS") to Confirm an Arbitral Award, and a Motion to Dismiss that Petition filed by the Arab Republic of Egypt ("Egypt"), the defendant in the arbitration. This is a case of first impression. The Court GRANTS Chromalloy Aeroservices' Petition to Recognize and Enforce the Arbitral Award, and DENIES Egypt's Motion to Dismiss, because the arbitral award in question is valid, and because Egypt's arguments against enforcement are insufficient to allow this Court to disturb the award.

II.   Background

This case involves a military procurement contract between a U.S. corporation, Chromalloy Aeroservices, Inc., and the Air Force of the Arab Republic of Egypt.

On June 16, 1988, Egypt and CAS entered into a contract under which CAS agreed to provide parts, maintenance, and repair for helicopters belonging to the Egyptian Air Force. On December 2, 1991, Egypt terminated the contract by notifying CAS representatives in Egypt. On December 4, 1991, Egypt notified CAS headquarters in Texas of the termination. On December 15, 1991, CAS notified Egypt that it rejected the cancellation of the contract "and commenced arbitration proceedings on the basis of the arbitration clause contained in Article XII and Appendix E of the Contract." Egypt then drew down CAS' letters of guarantee in an amount totaling some $11,475,968.

On February 23, 1992, the parties began appointing arbitrators, and shortly thereafter, commenced a lengthy arbitration. On August 24, 1994, the arbitral panel [rendered an award substantially in favor of CAS]. On October 28, 1994, CAS applied to this Court for enforcement of the award. On November 13, 1994, Egypt filed an appeal with the Egyptian Court of

---

1. Reisman, supra at 114; see also W. Michael Reisman et al., International Commercial Arbitration 1081 (1997).

2. See Roy Goode, The Role of the *Lex Loci Arbitri* in International Commercial Arbitration, 17 Arb. Int'l 19, 24 (2001).

Appeal, seeking nullification of the award. * * * On December 5, 1995, Egypt's Court of Appeal at Cairo issued an order nullifying the award. * * *

Egypt argues that this Court should deny CAS' Petition to Recognize and Enforce the Arbitral Award out of deference to its court. CAS argues that this Court should confirm the award because Egypt "does not present any serious argument that its court's nullification decision is consistent with the New York Convention or United States arbitration law."

III. Discussion
* * *

B. Chromalloy's Petition for Enforcement
* * *

1. The Standard under the Convention

* * * In the present case, the award was made in Egypt, under the laws of Egypt, and has been nullified by the court designated by Egypt to review arbitral awards. Thus, the Court *may,* at its discretion, decline to enforce the award.

While Article V provides a discretionary standard, Article VII of the Convention *requires* that, "The provisions of the present Convention *shall not* ... deprive any interested party of any right he may have to avail himself of an arbitral award in the manner and to the extent allowed by the law ... of the count[r]y where such award is sought to be relied upon." In other words, under the Convention, CAS maintains all rights to the enforcement of this Arbitral Award that it would have in the absence of the Convention. Accordingly, the Court finds that, if the Convention did not exist, the [FAA] would provide CAS with a legitimate claim to enforcement of this arbitral award. Jurisdiction over Egypt in such a suit would be available under 28 U.S.C. §§ 1330 (granting jurisdiction over foreign states "as to any claim for relief in personam with respect to which the foreign state is not entitled to immunity ... under sections 1605–1607 of this title") and 1605(a)(2) (withholding immunity of foreign states for "an act outside ... the United States in connection with a commercial activity of the foreign state elsewhere and that act causes a direct effect in the United States").

2. Examination of the Award under 9 U.S.C. § 10
* * *

In the present case, the language of the arbitral award that Egypt complains of reads:

> The Arbitral tribunal considers that it does not need to decide the legal nature of the contract. It appears that the Parties rely principally for their claims and defences, on the interpretation of the contract itself and on the facts presented. Furthermore, the Arbitral tribunal holds

that the legal issues in dispute are not affected by the characterization of the contract.

[The] arbitrators in the present case made a procedural decision that allegedly led to a misapplication of substantive law. After considering Egypt's arguments that Egyptian administrative law should govern the contract, the majority of the arbitral panel held that it did not matter which substantive law they applied-civil or administrative. At worst, this decision constitutes a mistake of law, and thus is not subject to review by this Court.

In the United States, "[W]e are well past the time when judicial suspicion of the desirability of arbitration and of the competence of arbitral tribunals inhibited the development of arbitration as an alternative means of dispute resolution." *Mitsubishi Motors Corp. v. Soler Chrysler–Plymouth, Inc.*, 473 U.S. 614, 626–27, 105 S.Ct. 3346, 3354, 87 L.Ed.2d 444 (1985). In Egypt, however, "[I]t is established that arbitration is an exceptional means for resolving disputes, requiring departure from the normal means of litigation before the courts, and the guarantees they afford." (Nullification Decision at 8.) Egypt's complaint that, "[T]he Arbitral Award is null under Arbitration Law, . . . because it is not properly 'grounded' under Egyptian law," reflects this suspicious view of arbitration, and is precisely the type of technical argument that U.S. courts are not to entertain when reviewing an arbitral award.

The Court's analysis thus far has addressed the arbitral award, and, as a matter of U.S. law, the award is proper. *See Sanders v. Washington Metro. Area Transit Auth.*, 819 F.2d 1151, 1157 (D.C.Cir.1987) (holding that, "When the parties have had a full and fair opportunity to present their evidence, the decisions of the arbitrator should be viewed as conclusive as to subsequent proceedings, absent some abuse of discretion by the arbitrator"). The Court now considers the question of whether the decision of the Egyptian court should be recognized as a valid foreign judgment.

As the Court stated earlier, this is a case of first impression. There are no reported cases in which a court of the United States has faced a situation, under the Convention, in which the court of a foreign nation has nullified an otherwise valid arbitral award. This does not mean, however, that the Court is without guidance in this case. To the contrary, more than twenty years ago, in a case involving the enforcement of an arbitration clause under the FAA, the Supreme Court held that:

> An agreement to arbitrate before a specified tribunal is, in effect, a specialized kind of forum-selection clause. . . . The invalidation of such an agreement . . . would not only allow the respondent to repudiate its solemn promise but would, as well, reflect a parochial concept that all disputes must be resolved under our laws and in our courts.

Scherk v. Alberto–Culver Co., 417 U.S. 506, 519, 94 S.Ct. 2449, 2457, 41 L.Ed.2d 270 (1974) In *Scherk*, the Court forced a U.S. corporation to arbitrate a dispute arising under an international contract containing an arbitration clause. In so doing, the Court relied upon the FAA, but took the opportunity to comment upon the purposes of the newly acceded-to Convention:

> The delegates to the Convention voiced frequent concern that courts of signatory countries in which an agreement to arbitrate is sought to be enforced should not be permitted to decline enforcement of such agreements on the basis of parochial views of their desirability or in a manner that would diminish the mutually binding nature of the agreements.... [W]e think that this country's adoption and ratification of the Convention and the passage of Chapter 2 of the United States Arbitration Act provide strongly persuasive evidence of congressional policy consistent with the decision we reach today.

Id. at n. 15.

The Court finds this argument equally persuasive in the present case, where Egypt seeks to repudiate its solemn promise to abide by the results of the arbitration.[4]

C.   The Decision of Egypt's Court of Appeal

1.   The Contract

"The arbitration agreement is a contract and the court will not rewrite it for the parties." The Court "begin[s] with the 'cardinal principle of contract construction': that a document should be read to give effect to all its provisions and to render them consistent with each other." Article XII of the contract requires that the parties arbitrate all disputes that arise between them under the contract. Appendix E, which defines the terms of any arbitration, forms an integral part of the contract. The contract is unitary. Appendix E to the contract defines the "Applicable Law Court of Arbitration." The clause reads, in relevant part:

> "It is * * * understood that both parties have irrevocably agreed to apply Egypt (sic) Laws and to choose Cairo as seat of the court of arbitration. * * * * * * The decision of the said court shall be final and binding and cannot be made subject to any appeal or other recourse." (Appendix E ("Appendix") to the Contract.)

This Court may not assume that the parties intended these two sentences to contradict one another, and must preserve the meaning of both if possible. Egypt argues that the first quoted sentence supersedes the second, and allows an appeal to an Egyptian court. Such an interpretation, however, would vitiate the second sentence, and would ignore the plain language on the face of the contract. The Court concludes that the first sentence defines choice of law and choice of forum for the hearings of the arbitral panel. The Court further concludes that the second quoted sentence indicates the clear intent of the parties that any arbitration of a dispute arising under the contract is not to be appealed to any court. This

---

4. The fact that this case concerns the enforcement of an arbitral *award,* rather than the enforcement of an agreement to arbitrate, makes no difference, because without the knowledge that judgment will be entered upon an award, the term "binding arbitration" becomes meaningless.

interpretation, unlike that offered by Egypt, preserves the meaning of both sentences in a manner that is consistent with the plain language of the contract. The position of the latter sentence as the seventh and final paragraph, just before the signatures, lends credence to the view that this sentence is the final word on the arbitration question. In other words, the parties agreed to apply Egyptian Law to the arbitration, but, more important, they agreed that the arbitration ends with the decision of the arbitral panel.

2.   The Decision of the Egyptian Court of Appeal

The Court has already found that the arbitral award is proper as a matter of U.S. law, and that the arbitration agreement between Egypt and CAS precluded an appeal in Egyptian courts. The Egyptian court has acted, however, and Egypt asks this Court to grant *res judicata* effect to that action.

The "requirements for enforcement of a foreign judgment ... are that there be 'due citation' [*i.e.,* proper service of process] and that the original claim not violate U.S. public policy." *Tahan v. Hodgson,* 662 F.2d 862, 864 (D.C.Cir.1981) (*citing Hilton v. Guyot,* 159 U.S. 113, 202, 16 S.Ct. 139, 158, 40 L.Ed. 95 (1895)). The Court uses the term "public policy" advisedly, with a full understanding that, "[J]udges have no license to impose their own brand of justice in determining applicable public policy." Correctly understood, "[P]ublic policy emanates [only] from clear statutory or case law, 'not from general considerations of supposed public interest.'" *Id.*

The U.S. public policy in favor of final and binding arbitration of commercial disputes is unmistakable, and supported by treaty, by statute, and by case law. The Federal Arbitration Act "and the implementation of the Convention in the same year by amendment of the Federal Arbitration Act," demonstrate that there is an "emphatic federal policy in favor of arbitral dispute resolution," particularly "in the field of international commerce." *Mitsubishi v. Soler Chrysler–Plymouth,* 473 U.S. 614, 631, 105 S.Ct. 3346, 3356, 87 L.Ed.2d 444 (1985) (internal citation omitted); *cf. Revere Copper & Brass Inc., v. Overseas Private Investment Corporation,* 628 F.2d 81, 82 (D.C.Cir.1980) (holding that, "There is a strong public policy behind judicial enforcement of binding arbitration clauses"). A decision by this Court to recognize the decision of the Egyptian court would violate this clear U.S. public policy.

* * *

4.   Choice of Law

Egypt argues that by choosing Egyptian law, and by choosing Cairo as the sight of the arbitration, CAS has for all time signed away its rights under the Convention and U.S. law. This argument is specious. When CAS agreed to the choice of law and choice of forum provisions, it waived its right to sue Egypt for breach of contract in the courts of the United States in favor of final and binding arbitration of such a dispute under the Convention. Having prevailed in the chosen forum, under the chosen law,

CAS comes to this Court seeking recognition and enforcement of the award. The Convention was created for just this purpose. It is untenable to argue that by choosing arbitration under the Convention, CAS has waived rights specifically guaranteed by that same Convention.

5.   Conflict between the Convention & the FAA

As a final matter, Egypt argues that, "Chromalloy's use of [A]rticle VII [to invoke the Federal Arbitration Act] contradicts the clear language of the Convention and would create an impermissible conflict under 9 U.S.C. § 208," by eliminating all consideration of Article V of the Convention. *See Vimar Seguros y Reaseguros, S.A. v. M/V Sky Reefer*, 515 U.S. 528, 533, 115 S.Ct. 2322, 2325, 132 L.Ed.2d 462 (1995) (holding that, "[W]hen two statutes are capable of coexistence ... it is the duty of the courts, absent a clearly expressed congressional intention to the contrary, to regard each as effective"). As the Court has explained, however, Article V provides a permissive standard, under which this Court *may* refuse to enforce an award. Article VII, on the other hand, mandates that this Court *must* consider CAS' claims under applicable U.S. law. * * *

Article VII does not eliminate all consideration of Article V; it merely requires that this Court protect any rights that CAS has under the domestic laws of the United States. There is no conflict between CAS' use of Article VII to invoke the FAA and the language of the Convention.

IV.   Conclusion

The Court concludes that the award of the arbitral panel is valid as a matter of U.S. law. The Court further concludes that it need not grant *res judicata* effect to the decision of the Egyptian Court of Appeal at Cairo. Accordingly, the Court GRANTS Chromalloy Aeroservices' Petition to Recognize and Enforce the Arbitral Award, and DENIES Egypt's Motion to Dismiss that Petition.

NOTES AND QUESTIONS

1. Is it likely that the *Chromalloy* opinion was motivated, at least in part, by suspicions about the behavior of the Egyptian courts in overturning an arbitral award rendered against the Egyptian Government? (The Cairo court referred at one point to the "irreparable serious harm" that the award would supposedly inflict on Egypt.). The attorney for Chromalloy has written that while his client "could present no 'smoking gun' to demonstrate conclusively that the Egyptian court, or the country's entire judiciary, was biased or corrupt, it was able to show that Egyptian courts have had a disturbing propensity to nullify awards in favor of foreign parties against Egyptians or its government for seemingly arbitrary reasons." Gary H. Sampliner, Enforcement of Foreign Arbitral Awards After Annulment in Their Country of Origin, 11 (9) Mealey's Int'l Arb. Rep., Sept. 1996 at 22, 28. In these circumstances, was it preferable for the court to rest its decision on Art. VII of the New York Convention rather than relying on the discretionary standard of Art. V(1)(e)?

2. What did the contract in question here mean when it said that "the decision of the said court shall be final and binding and cannot be made subject to any appeal or other recourse"? If an agreement indeed envisages that "the arbitration ends with the decision of the arbitral panel," does this really mean that each party has waived its right to seek annulment of the award? Is it fair to say that by seeking to vacate the award, Egypt has "repudiate[d] its solemn promise to abide by the results of the arbitration"?

3. Was the court in *Chromalloy* correct in relying as it did on Art. VII of the New York Convention? For one thing, "the law * * * of the country where such award is sought to be relied upon" includes, among other things, § 207 of the FAA, doesn't it? And doesn't § 207 override § 10? See also FAA § 208. For another thing, could FAA § 10 apply in any event to awards rendered outside the United States? See Stephen T. Ostrowski & Yuval Shany, Note, *Chromalloy*: United States Law and International Arbitration at the Crossroads, 73 N.Y.U. L. Rev. 1650, 1675–77 (1998)(whether Chromalloy "would have been able to enforce an award rendered in Egypt in a United States court in the absence of the New York Convention is doubtful. Thus, it is difficult to see what more favorable rights of domestic law Article VII could have pointed to in this case").

4. Do cases like *Chromalloy* "encourage expensive and anarchical forum shopping"?:

> The prevailing party in the arbitration would begin to look for the most liberal and open-handed judge, as soon as any debts, bank deposits or any other assets belonging to the respondent, no matter how small, could be found within his jurisdiction. This race to enforcement could only lead to an uncertainty and a relativism that would be harmful to the image of international arbitration, and that would impair the stability and growth of this means of resolving disputes in international commerce.

See Philippe Fouchard, La portée internationale de l'annulation de la sentence arbitrale dans son pays d'origine, [1997] Rev. de l'Arbitrage 329, 343 (ultimately concluding, however, that "it is not legitimate to entrust to the judges of one single state the power to annihilate, throughout the entire world, an award that they didn't like"). See also W. Michael Reisman, Systems of Control in International Adjudication and Arbitration 117 (1992)("the winner of a defective award could fail in enforcement in any forum and still continue to go to others in an effort at enforcement, harassing the other party and forcing it either to settle for a nuisance value factored by the number of jurisdictions in which it could be pursued or to expend great amounts of time and effort to block and block again enforcement efforts without ever securing a terminal annulment").

5. Under French law, the same standards of judicial review apply to the recognition and enforcement of *foreign* awards as to awards rendered *in*

France in international arbitral proceedings: That is, French courts may refuse to recognize or enforce a foreign award *only* if: a) there was no arbitration agreement; b) the tribunal was "irregularly composed"; c) the arbitrator's decision was rendered "in a manner incompatible with the mission conferred upon him"; d) due process was not respected, or e) there was a violation of international public policy.

As a consequence, "France may recognize a foreign award which the New York Convention does not require to be recognized, since the French statute does not permit nonenforcement on the ground that the award has been set aside by the courts of the country where the arbitration took place." See W. Laurence Craig, Some Trends and Developments in the Laws and Practice of International Commercial Arbitration, 30 Tex. Int'l L.J. 1, 32 (1995).

Suppose that the parties to an American arbitration have contracted for "expanded review" by a court of any possible "error of law" on the part of the arbitrators—and that a district court, heeding these instructions, reviews and vacates the award on this ground. See Section C.4, supra. Is the party who prevailed in the arbitration able to shop around and take the award to a jurisdiction—like France—where the local courts may enforce it anyway despite the American annulment? Should he be able to do so?

6.   A number of leading international arbitrators and scholars have been attracted by the notion that international arbitration awards are "autonomous, being unconnected to any national legal system and deriving their force solely from the agreement of the parties." This is an idea that in particular has "captured the Gallic imagination." It is thought to follow that awards, as soon as they are rendered, become "the prospective beneficiary of the recognition laws of a putative foreign state of enforcement," but that they should be unaffected by any subsequent order setting the award aside in the country of origin:

> In other words, at the very moment of its birth, produced by the consensual coupling of the parties in the arbitration process, the award took off and disappeared into the firmament, landing only in those places where enforcement was sought.

Roy Goode, The Role of the *Lex Locus Arbitri* in International Commercial Arbitration, 17 Arb. Int'l 19, 21 (2001); see also note (5) supra.

The goal therefore is to "free the international arbitral process from domination by the law of the place of arbitration." In the words of a leading proponent, the traditional vision of "die-hard territorialists" simply

> does not correspond to contemporary commercial reality. Japanese and American businessmen may meet in an Indian airport hotel and sign a contract relating to a European venture and given legal effect in Europe without anyone pausing to consider whether the contract is "heretical" because it has not complied with Indian formalities. Similarly, an arbitrator is not an emanation of a sovereign, and when he resolves an international dispute his award may be given effect without

necessary reference to the acceptance or tolerance of the legal system of the place where he rendered his award.

Jan Paulsson, The Case for Disregarding LSAs (Local Standard Annulments) Under the New York Convention, 7 Amer. Rev. of Int'l Arb. 99, 109 (1996); see also Jan Paulsson, Enforcing Arbitral Awards Notwithstanding a Local Standard Annulment, 9 ICC Int'l Ct. Arb. Bull. 14 (May 1998).

For an energetically-expressed contrary view, see William W. Park, Duty and Discretion in International Arbitration, 93 Amer. J. of Int'l L. 805 (1999), who argues that deference to local annulments should follow "not from any explicit treaty mandate but from the parties' mutual commitments":

> "Merchants who contract for an arbitral situs should be held to the implicit consequences of the bargain, whether this means narrow or broad judicial scrutiny. If the chosen review standards appear problematic on postdispute reflection, market forces will direct future arbitrations elsewhere. * * * Just as an agreement to arbitrate in London means driving to hearings on the left side of the road, so it means that proceedings are subject to the English Arbitration Act."

Is Professor Park's argument at all weakened by the fact that in 17% of the cases administered by the ICC between 1989 and 1999, it was *the ICC itself* (rather than the parties) which chose the site of the arbitration? See W. Laurence Craig et al., International Chamber of Commerce Arbitration 185–6 (3d ed. 2000). Why not?

7. Cases like *Chromalloy*, then, may represent "a shift in the control function [of awards], away from the court of the country of arbitration to those of the country of execution of awards." See Jan Paulsson, Arbitration Unbound in Belgium, 2 Arb. Int'l 68, 69 (1986). Another very different form of such a displacement can be seen in legislation which restricts or even eliminates any review of "international" awards *at the very seat of the arbitration.*

For example, in 1985, Belgium amended its arbitration statute to provide that a Belgian award could be vacated *only* where one of the parties to the dispute was a resident of Belgium, or a Belgian national, or "a legal entity created in Belgium or having a branch in Belgium": In other words, where *neither party* had any connection to the country, there was no way at all to challenge an award rendered in Belgium. One of the principal proponents of the bill commented that it would exclude "judicial control of arbitral awards which in no manner concern our country, because this control is often used today for purely dilatory purposes, as the award is to be enforced abroad."

It might have been thought that the Belgian reform would serve to attract arbitration business—an important form of invisible export—to that country: "Belgium has now instantly emerged as a major contender in the arbitration venue sweepstakes, and has overtaken everyone in its efforts to please those who want arbitration without court interference. * * * For those who want to find a neutral venue for arbitration where they can be sure not to have to defend themselves before the local courts after the award is rendered, Belgium is the promised land." Paulsson, supra, at 68–69. See also Reisman, supra at 131 ("Belgians" are "free riders," "engaging in an unfair trade practice by exploiting a noneconomic variable in order to make themselves more attractive to a class of potential consumers"). In practice, however, the effect of this reform was somewhat different: Apparently it served to *"divert more arbitrations away from Belgium* than it attracted arbitrations *to* Belgium." Bernard Hanotiau & Guy Block, *La loi du 19 mai 1998 modifiant la législation belge relative à l'arbitrage*, 16 Bulletin of the Swiss Arb. Ass'n 528, 532 (1998). (Query: Why might contracting parties have been reluctant to entrust *all* the control function to the court where the winning party seeks enforcement—that is, where the losing party has assets?) So in 1998, the Belgian legislation was amended once again—this time, to substitute a milder default rule of "opting out": Where neither of the parties has the requisite connection to Belgium, henceforth, they may waive in advance any right to vacate an award only by an "express declaration" to that effect; for this purpose a mere reference in the contract to the rules of some arbitral institution will probably not suffice.

8.   Compare Baker Marine (Nig.) Ltd. v. Chevron (Nig.) Ltd., 191 F.3d 194 (2d Cir. 1999). Baker Marine and Danos jointly entered a contract with Chevron to provide barge services. The contract specified that the the arbitration "procedure * * * shall be governed by the substantive laws of the Federal Republic of Nigeria" and that the contracts "shall be interpreted in accordance with the laws of the Federal Republic of Nigeria." After Baker Marine charged Chevron and Danos with violating the contracts, the parties submitted to arbitration before arbitration panels in Lagos; one panel awarded Baker Marine $2.23 million in damages against Danos and a second panel awarded Baker Marine $750,000 in damages against Chevron. The Nigerian courts later set aside the two awards—concluding, in the Chevron action, that the arbitrators had improperly awarded punitive damages, gone beyond the scope of the submissions, incorrectly admitted parole evidence, and made inconsistent awards; and in the Danos action, that the award was unsupported by the evidence.

Baker Marine moved for confirmation in New York, but the district court relied on Article V(1)(e) in declining to enforce the awards, holding that under the Convention and principles of comity, "it would not be proper to enforce a foreign arbitral award under the Convention when such an award has been set aside by the Nigerian courts." The Second Circuit affirmed:

> It is sufficient answer [to Baker Marine's argument] that the parties contracted in Nigeria that their disputes would be arbitrated under the laws of Nigeria. The governing agreements make no reference whatever to United States law. Nothing suggests that the parties intended United States domestic arbitral law to govern their disputes. Furthermore Baker Marine has made no contention that the Nigerian courts acted contrary to Nigerian law.

Can *Baker Marine* be squared with the earlier decision in *Chromalloy*? The Second Circuit purported to "distinguish" *Chromalloy* on the ground that unlike the petitioner in that case, "Baker Marine is not a United States citizen, and it did not initially seek confirmation of the award in the United States. Furthermore, Chevron and Danos did not violate any promise in appealing the arbitration award within Nigeria." Furthermore, the court noted, "as a practical matter, mechanical application of domestic arbitral law to foreign awards under the Convention would seriously undermine finality and regularly produce conflicting judgments." If a party whose arbitration award has been vacated at the site of the award can automatically obtain enforcement of the awards under the domestic laws of other nations, a losing party will have every reason to pursue its adversary "with enforcement actions from country to country until a court is found, if any, which grants the enforcement."

9.   An investment agreement was entered into between an Italian company and the Government of Ethiopia. The contract contained ambiguous dispute resolution provisions: It was apparently common ground that the "place" of the arbitration was to be in Ethiopia. The Government, however, took the position that the contract called for *ad hoc* arbitration; the Italian investor—taking the position that the parties had agreed to ICC arbitration—filed a claim with the ICC in Paris. The ICC decided to "set this arbitration in motion" and confirmed the appointment of an arbitral tribunal (made up of professors from Italy, France, and Ireland).

For the Government, the contractual choice of Ethiopia as the "place of arbitration" at the very least "created a presumption" that the hearings would physically take place in Addis Ababa—which would also allow the tribunal to make a visit to the site of the project. In a preliminary ruling, however, the arbitrators decided "that it would be more convenient to hold at least the first meeting in Paris." The Government strongly objected to this decision, which it claimed "was evidence of a lack of impartiality"— supposedly the tribunal "had improperly and abusively had regard to its own convenience and the convenience of the Claimant and its witnesses"— and made a formal challenge to the continued service of the arbitrators. The ICC rejected this challenge, and the Government appealed to the Ethiopian courts; it also obtained from the courts of Ethiopia an injunction "suspending the arbitration," and temporarily enjoining the claimant from proceeding, until the courts could resolve the challenge and finally determine the jurisdiction of the ICC. But with the Government boycotting the proceedings—considering "that any such hearing would be a contempt of court and illegal"—the tribunal went ahead anyway: "The Arbitral Tribunal will continue to prosecute these arbitral proceedings in accordance with its duty to the parties":

> An international arbitral tribunal is not an organ of the state in which it has its seat in the same way that a court of the seat would be. The primary source of the Tribunal's powers is the parties' agreement to arbitrate. An important consequence of this is that the Tribunal has a duty *vis à vis* the parties to ensure that their arbitration agreement is

not frustrated. In certain circumstances, it may be necessary to decline to comply with an order issued by a court of the seat, in the fulfillment of the Tribunal's larger duty to the parties.

* * *

The Tribunal would be slow to render an award that is likely to be set aside at the seat, taking into account the principle according to which the Tribunal must make every effort to render an enforceable award. This does not mean, however, that the arbitral tribunal should simply abdicate to the courts of the seat the tribunal's own judgment about what is fair and right in the arbitral proceedings. In the event that the arbitral tribunal considers that to follow a decision of a court would conflict fundamentally with the tribunal's understanding of its duty to the parties, derived from the parties' arbitration agreement, the tribunal must follow its own judgment, even if that requires non-compliance with a court order.

Under the ICC rules, the tribunal stressed, decisions by the ICC with respect to challenges to arbitral impartiality are to be "final"; equally under the ICC rules, decisions with respect to the jurisdiction of the arbitrators are to be made in the first instance "by the Arbitral Tribunal itself":

> The appropriate occasion for the Ethiopian courts to consider the issue of jurisdiction is in the context of an action to set aside the Tribunal's award, after the Tribunal has determined its own jurisdiction. The courts cannot, in the meantime, pre-empt the Tribunal's decision on its own jurisdiction. More generally, if respondents were able to stay the proceedings in this way, through applications made to the courts of the seat during the course of the proceedings, it would have disastrous consequences for international arbitration in general.

Salini Costruttori S.p.a. v. Federal Democratic Republic of Ethiopia, 20 (3) Mealey's Int'l Arb. Rep. at A–1 (March 2005). See also Section C.3.d., supra (Note, "Determining the Jurisdiction of the Arbitrator").

Gabrielle Kaufmann–Kohler, Identifying and Applying the Law Governing the Arbitration Procedure: The Role of the Law of the Place of Arbitration*

International Council for Commercial Arbitration, Congress series no. 9 (Paris/1999), 336, 342–365.

What Is the Place of Arbitration?

So arbitrations are generally governed by the law of the place where they are held. But is the place a legal connection or a physical, geographical

---

* [A revised version of this article appeared as Gabrielle Kaufmann–Kohler, *Le lieu de l'arbitrage à l'aune de la mondialisa-* *tion: réflexions à propos de deux formes récentes d'arbitrage*, [1998] Rev. de l'arb. 517.—Eds.]

location? How is it selected? Can part or even all procedural steps be carried out elsewhere?

Pursuant to Art. 20(1) of the [UNCITRAL] Model Law**, the parties are free to select the place of arbitration. They may do so directly or by delegation to an institution. In the absence of an agreement by the parties, the arbitrators have the power to choose the place, which they must do taking into account "the circumstances of the case, including the convenience of the parties". This latter phrase refers to the *legal* convenience as well, especially to the suitability of the applicable procedural law. Indeed, in addition to its factual significance (the arbitration is in principle expected to be held there), the choice of the place has legal consequences under the Model Law: it determines the applicability of the Model Law and the place of origin of the award for enforcement purposes.

According to the second paragraph of Art. 20, subject to the parties' contrary agreement, the arbitral tribunal may meet at any place it considers appropriate "for consultation among its members, for hearing witnesses, experts or the parties, or for inspection of goods, other property or documents". * * * [A]ll stages of the arbitration are covered in [this] version. Therefore, an arbitration may take place in its entirety outside the place of arbitration, which is reduced to "nothing but a fiction."

Recognizing that the Model Law attached legal consequences to the "constructive" place of arbitration determined pursuant to Art. 20(1) and that no "genuine link" was required between that place and the actual location of the proceedings, Norway made a proposal during drafting, pursuant to which the "constructive" place of the arbitration would lack at least part of its legal consequences, if "there is no genuine link between that place and the actual arbitral proceedings". The proposal was not followed up and the provision was adopted without a requirement for any kind of link between the "constructive" and the actual place of arbitration. This makes sense: the constructive place is often chosen for its neutrality, i.e., for its absence of connection to either party, while the actual place may be chosen precisely for the opposite reason, because it shows a link to a party due, for instance, to the presence of witnesses.

There was general agreement about the contents of Art. 20 when it was drafted. Hence, the countries adopting the Model Law enacted it without significant changes. Germany, as a newcomer to the Model Law club, deserves a special mention. Its Sect. 1043 ZPO is almost identical to Art. 20. Schlosser views the second paragraph (allowing that procedural steps be taken abroad) as a hidden way out of the rigidity of the territorial

---

** [The UNCITRAL Model Law on International Commercial Arbitration was adopted by UNCITRAL [the United Nations Commission on International Trade Law] in 1985. By the end of 2005, legislation based on the Model Law had been enacted in 44 countries, including Australia, Canada, Germany, Hong Kong, India, Ireland, Japan, Mexico, Norway, Russia, Singapore, Spain, and Scotland—and also, bizarrely, in a number of states in the United States, including California and Texas.—Eds.]

connection newly adopted by German arbitration law, since the entire proceedings can be conducted abroad.[53]

Recent non-Model Law legislations provide the same rules. Among these, English law calls for a particular comment. Sect. 3 of the English Arbitration Act 1996 expressly states that the seat in the meaning of the Act is a legal, juridical connection. In *Naviera Amazonica Peruana SA v. Compañia Internacional de Seguros del Peru*, Lord Justice Kerr for the English Court of Appeal had emphasized the "distinction between the legal localisation of an arbitration on the one hand and the appropriate or convenient geographical locality for hearings of arbitration on the other hand".[55] This distinction is confirmed by Sects. 43 and 2(3)(a) of the Act, which permit a court to secure attendance of witnesses present in the United Kingdom, provided the hearing takes place there, even though the seat of the arbitration is located abroad.

Similarly, the Swiss Supreme Court has recently stressed the same distinction, as well as the legal nature of the place or seat:

> By choosing a Swiss legal domicile [*ein schweizerisches Rechtsdomizil*] for the arbitral tribunal, the parties manifestly intended to submit their dispute to Swiss arbitration law, not to provide for an exclusive location for meetings among arbitrators at the place of arbitration.... [T]he determination of a given place of arbitration is of significance to the extent that the award is deemed to be rendered at such place. It is irrelevant that a hearing was effectively held or that the award was effectively issued there.

Indeed, although there is no statutory provision to this effect, it is generally accepted that hearings and meetings in a Swiss arbitration may take place outside of Switzerland.

Most major arbitration rules confirm the parties' freedom to choose the place of arbitration and the possibility to hold meetings and hearings elsewhere. * * * Interestingly, the 1998 ICC Rules contain new provisions on this very subject. Pursuant to Art. 14(2) and (3), the arbitral tribunal may "after consultation with the parties, conduct hearings and meetings at any location it considers appropriate, unless otherwise agreed by the parties" and "deliberate at any location it considers appropriate". This codifies existing practice and confirms the broad consensus found in recent legislations.

---

53. This is how I understand the statement that it is not necessary for parties and arbitrators *ever* to meet in Germany for the arbitration to be German. See also F.A. Mann, "Where is an Award Made?", Arbitration International (1985) p. 107 et seq. (the award is made at the arbitral seat, which is "by no means necessarily identical with the place or places where hearings are being held" or, further, which is "independent of the place of meetings of the arbitrators, hearings with the parties").

55. Decision of 10 November 1987, *Yearbook* XIII (1988) p. 157. The same decision confirms that * * * there is a presumption that the law of the place where the arbitration is held has the strongest connection and should thus govern and vice versa (i.e., a choice of a given procedural law implies a choice of a place). * * *

Sports Arbitration

Before our traveller brings his sightseeing memories home, he will make two additional stops: one at the Olympic Games and one in cyber-space. Let us start with the Olympics.

The Court of Arbitration for Sport (CAS) is an arbitration institution dealing with the resolution of international disputes related to sports.*** * * *

CAS has its main office in Lausanne and local offices in the USA and in Australia, which provide the logistics for proceedings held locally and managed in consultation with the main office. In addition, CAS sets up a special arbitration body for the duration of the Olympic Games, which resolves all disputes arising during the Games on site, as a rule within 24 hours. * * *

Wherever a CAS arbitration takes place physically, [CAS rules provide that] it always has its legal place or seat in Lausanne. This applies to all CAS arbitrations, wherever the hearings take place, whether they are managed by the Lausanne office exclusively or in conjunction with a decentralized office, and it includes arbitrations handled on the site of the Olympic Games.

There are three main reasons for the choice of a sole seat, regardless of the actual place of arbitration. First, that choice provides a uniform procedural regime for all CAS arbitrations, not only in terms of applicable rules under the Code, but also with respect to the arbitration law governing the proceedings. The Games move around, but the legal framework is stable.

Second, conducting the arbitration at the site of the Games is intended to make arbitration as convenient as possible for the parties and to resolve disputes as expeditiously as possible. It is not meant to have any legal significance.

Third, the equal treatment so achieved is consistent with the equal standards that govern the activities giving rise to disputes, i.e., sports competition. A time on a stopwatch is the same wherever the race takes place. It is further consistent—which may be of even greater significance here—with the choice of substantive law governing sports disputes. According to Art. 17 of the CAS ad hoc Rules, the arbitral tribunal must resolve the dispute "pursuant to the Olympic Charter, the applicable regulations, general principles of law and the rules of law, the application of which it deems appropriate".

All these sets of rules (except possibly for the last one, which in practice never comes to bear) are transnational, universal, global. Their application is not dependent on a territorial nexus, nor is it restricted

*** [See pp. 37–38 supra.—Eds.]

territorially. This global substantive law is matched by a uniform procedural law thanks to the choice of a sole seat for all CAS arbitrations.

* * *

[T]he example of sports arbitration is striking because it demonstrates that the legal place of an arbitration can become pure fiction for perfectly legitimate reasons.

Online Arbitration

Leaving the Olympics, the traveller now takes the leap into cyberspace to observe that online arbitration is just another illustration of a purely fictional (or fictitious?) place of arbitration.

Imagine an arbitration where the request and later written pleadings are filed, procedural orders issued, and all other communications sent by electronic mail, where procedural hearings take the form of so-called "chats" (even if the term is not really flattering . . .), and witnesses are heard by videoconference.

An unreal, imaginary world? No. Although still very limited in scope, several dispute resolution mechanisms of this kind already exist.**** * * * Another example of online dispute resolution are the proposed WIPO-administered Internet domain name procedures.*****

Where do online arbitrations physically take place? "In cyberspace" is an easy, but wrong answer: cyberspace is misnamed, "there is no 'there' there", no space, simply a telecommunication network. So where then? Nowhere? Or at the places where the participants access the network? Maybe, but for purposes of connection to a given arbitration law, such a plurilocalization is highly impracticable. The real problem is that on the Internet our traditional concept of place, which implies space, distances, territories, borders, is meaningless. There is no such thing as a physical place of online arbitrations.[98] If the territorial connection is to stand, then we are left to rely on a legal place, which by essence will be nothing but a fiction.

* * *

Virtual arbitration is not limited to full online arbitrations administered by specialized institutions. Tribunals in conventional "real-space" arbitrations, are starting to use electronic communication tools too, for

---

**** [See, e.g., the websites of Dispute Resolution Services, www.drs-adr.com ("the ElectronicCourthouse®'s Web-enabled international dispute resolution service"), and of "Virtual Magistrate," www.vmag.org. "Virtual Magistrate" bills itself as "a service for resolution of disputes among online computer users, computer operations and persons harmed by the posting of wrongful online messages," including such matters as "spam-

ming, defamation or inappropriate messages," "requesting the removal of a message or posted web page," or "contract or property or tort disputes regarding on-line issues."—Eds.]

***** [See pp. 169–70, supra.—Eds.]

98. At best, if one really insists on determining a place, there are multiple places, which is of little help to identify the applicable law.

instance to hear a far away witness unable to travel or to save travel expenses.

Because it saves time and costs, which are major concerns to present-day users of arbitration, it is likely that electronic communication will increasingly be used in arbitrations. WIPO intends to make its online mechanism available for intellectual property arbitrations other than domain name disputes. * * * And "traditional" arbitrators, even if they are no computer freaks, will increasingly resort to new telecommunication facilities.

* * *

A Paradox which Fosters Uniformity

Having returned from his trip, the traveller tells of two main evolutions. First, the territorial connection nowadays prevails, primarily because it is easy to handle and provides certainty. In other words, to identify the law applicable to the arbitration procedure, one must define the place of arbitration. Second, that place is increasingly viewed as a fiction which has no necessary connection to the physical location of the proceedings. This trend is evident, even if in the great majority of cases the legal place still coincides with the physical location. With the continuing globalization of the world and the changes brought about by the technological revolution, this evolution cannot but gain in importance. * * * The choice of a place ends up being nothing but a choice of the law governing the arbitration. It delocalizes the arbitration proceedings, removing the authority of the local lex arbitri and the powers of the local courts to supervise the proceedings and set aside the award.

Delocalization, denationalization, deterritorialization gave rise to passionate arguments a number of years ago. Will the once-heated debate be revived by phenomena such as online, Olympic or similar delocalized arbitrations?

If it is accepted that the (legal) place may be a fiction, then the issue of delocalization becomes moot, because delocalization is in fact achieved, though indirectly. One of the main purposes of delocalization as it was once discussed was to eliminate the unintended effects of peculiarities of the law of the place where the arbitration happened to be held. By the choice of an arbitration-friendly fictional place of arbitration, that goal is fully met. It is not threatened by uncertainties or conflicts about competent courts, if courts consistently apply the concept of a legal place or seat and accept jurisdiction in aid and control of arbitration only at that place. * * * [If] by way of the choice of a place, one can avoid inhospitable features of the law where the dispute is physically heard, then denationalization loses much of its practical interest. Not to speak of the fact that the increasing uniformity of arbitration laws makes the search for hospitable fora less of a necessity.

* * *

Conclusion and Outlook

At the close of his journey, the traveller cannot but conclude that the role of the law of the place of arbitration keeps decreasing. Based on his observations, one can see four reasons for this decline. First, in a "global village", geographical places tend to be immaterial. The activities giving rise to disputes are increasingly globalized; technological communication means abolish distances; the place is becoming a non-issue.

Second, legal places follow suit, with a growing acceptance of the place as a pure fiction and a powerful wave of uniformization of arbitration laws, which tend to become interchangeable.

Third, this uniformization process goes together with a general consensus over two hard-core principles of arbitration law, procedural autonomy and its due process limitation.

Fourth and last is * * * the emergence of a worldwide arbitration culture, which runs parallel to the normalization of arbitral proceedings and—if this writer can be forgiven the term—the "standardization" of the international arbitrator.

What about the future? Will the decline of the law of the place of arbitration continue? Will its role shrink to the point where its sole significance will be to offer a link to a court? Are we moving towards a procedural lex mercatoria? These are the issues; to find the answers, we will have to take another trip sometime in the twenty-first century.

NOTES AND QUESTIONS

1. The notion that CAS arbitrations necessarily have their "site" in Lausanne was first tested in the New South Wales Court of Appeal, in Australia, in 2000. The Judo Federation of Australia had nominated Angela Raguz as a member of the 2000 Australian Olympic Team in the women's under/52 kg category. The nomination was challenged by Rebecca Sullivan, another member of the "JFA Shadow Team," who alleged that she was entitled to the nomination on the grounds of selection criteria contained in an agreement between the JFA and the Australian Olympic Committee. After an internal JFA Appeal Tribunal rejected the challenge, Sullivan initiated an arbitration proceeding with the CAS office in Sydney. A hearing took place in Sydney 24 days later, and at the end of the hearing, the panel announced its decision in favor of Sullivan: After finding that the selection of Raguz had been in error—that the "points" awarded Sullivan throughout her competitions had been added incorrectly—the panel ordered the JFA to nominate Sullivan to the team instead of Raguz.

Raguz challenged the award in the Australian courts. In order to be eligible for selection to the Olympic Team, each athlete had been required to sign a Team Membership Agreement; the court had no difficulty in finding that by doing so, each had become a party to an "integrated scheme"—including a consent to CAS arbitration—which bound the JFA, the AOC, "and all the relevant athletes." The Team Membership Agreement provided that any decision of the CAS "will be final and binding on the parties and * * * neither party will institute or maintain proceedings in any court or tribunal other than [the CAS]."

The critical problem was the jurisdiction of the courts of Australia: Under Australian legislation, a court could entertain an appeal on a question of law arising out of an arbitral award, unless (1) there was an "exclusion agreement" which "excludes the right of appeal," and (2) if and only if the arbitration agreement was a "domestic arbitration agreement"—that is, one that "does not provide, expressly or by implication, for arbitration *in a country other than Australia*." It was apparent that the CAS arbitration clause did in fact constitute an "exclusion agreement"—but was the agreement a "domestic" one? The court concluded that it was not: The legislation, it held, was concerned "with the legal place of the arbitration"—a "juridical concept"—rather than the "physical place of the arbitration." The statutory scheme of judicial review should not change every time there was a "temporary change of hearing venue"; the legislature obviously wished to permit parties "to select a single legal place of arbitration and to leave the choice of the physical location of hearings to the felt necessities of a specific dispute." Since under the CAS rules the "seat" of every CAS panel was deemed be Lausanne, the "exclusion agreement" was valid, and so the appeal was dismissed. Raguz v. Sullivan, [2000] NSWCA 240; 15(10) Mealey's Int'l Arb. Rep. (Oct. 2000), at p. D–1.

2. The internet domain-name system administered by ICANN, the Internet Corporation for Assigned Names and Numbers, requires registrants of domain names to agree to the Uniform Domain Name Dispute Resolution Policy (the UDRP). See pp. 169–70, supra. Cf. Elizabeth G. Thornburg, Fast, Cheap, and Out of Control: Lessons From the ICANN Dispute Resolution Process, 6 J. Small & Emerging Bus. L. 191 (2002):

> The UDRP [uses] a "hearing" process that is a poor model for any dispute that involves contested facts, especially contested facts not embodied in pre-existing documents. * * * Under [this] dispute resolution procedure, any kind of hearing would be highly unusual. The Rules virtually prohibit even video conferences, telephone conferences, and web conferences. Instead of hearing witnesses, the arbitrator makes her decision based on written submissions and accompanying documents. This is fast, but not helpful. * * * The procedure would prove completely inadequate should the arbitrator need to decide whether a product was defective, a statement libelous, or a market monopolized if an ICANN-like procedure were used to resolve other types of Internet disputes. Also, when disputes involve decisions about the amount of damages, not the case in the ICANN process, an additional layer of factual disputes may require resolution. * * * Even in the limited context of domain name disputes, arbitrators have noted the impact of the UDRP when credibility issues are involved. Responding to a complainant's request to cross-examine respondent's evidence in order to establish bad faith, the panel responded that a matter requiring this kind of credibility check would be better resolved in "a

forum, like a United States court, that permits for a more probing, searing search for the truth. This proceeding is not conducive to such credibility determinations given the lack of discovery and, in the normal course, the lack of live testimony."

See also Daniel Girsberger & Dorothee Schramm, Cyber–Arbitration, 2 European Bus. Org. L. Rev. 605 (2002).

3. Look again at art. V(1)(e) of the New York Convention: What does the Convention mean when it refers to the country "in which" an award is "made"? Does the Convention envisage the possibility of an award rendered *"in"* one country, but yet at the same time *"under the [arbitration] law"* of another—so that the law governing the arbitration may be different from the law of the state where the award was made? Given Professor Kaufmann–Kohler's demonstration that the "legal place of an arbitration can become pure fiction"—amounting in essence to little more than "a choice of the law governing the arbitration"—is such a question even meaningful?

Most academic commentary admits—at least as a matter of theory— the possibility that an agreement may provide "that one country will be the site of the arbitration but the proceedings will be held under the arbitration law of another country"—but treats such clauses as

"exceptional"; "almost unknown"; a "purely academic invention"; "almost never used in practice"; a possibility "more theoretical than real"; and a "once-in-a-blue-moon set of circumstances."

Karaha Bodas Co., L.L.C v. Perusahaan Pertambangan Minyak Dan Gas Bumi Negara, 364 F.3d 274, 291 (5th Cir. 2004). Or more simply, "international commercial arbitration is complicated enough, without such flights of fancy." See Alan Redfern & Martin Hunter, Law and Practice of International Commercial Arbitration 91–92, 299–0300, 431–32 (2nd ed. 1991). Obviously, such a silly clause would double the number of jurisdictions with a plausible interest in entertaining actions to supervise proceedings or vacate awards.

See, e.g., Hiscox v. Outhwaite, [1991] 3 All E.R. 641 (H.L.). Here a contract of reinsurance called for arbitration in London; the hearings took place in London, but the arbitrator, an English barrister, signed the final award when he was in Paris. In his opinion for the House of Lords, Lord Oliver of Aylmerton found it "anomalous and regrettable that the fortuitous circumstance of signature in Paris should stamp what was clearly intended to be an award subject to all the procedural regulations of English arbitration with the character of a Convention award"—but found such a conclusion "irresistible": "A document is made when and where it is perfected. An award is perfected when it is signed." In fact the House of Lords held *both*

- that the award had been "made in France"—so that it fell within the New York Convention;
- and, at the same time, that it could be vacated by English courts because it had been made subject to English curial law.

So in this case, "the country of the award" and "the country having jurisdiction over the conduct of the arbitration" turned out to be different jurisdictions. This curious result was much criticized—for where an award was signed could obviously "vary subject to the whims or the clumsiness of the arbitrators"—and it has been reversed by the English Arbitration Act of 1996: The Act now provides straightforwardly that "the seat of the arbitration" is "the juridical seat" designed by the parties (or, if authorized by them, by an arbitral institution or the arbitrators themselves), and that "an award shall be treated as made at the seat of arbitration, regardless of where it was signed, dispatched or delivered to any of the parties." Okezie Chukwumerije, Reform and Consolidation of English Arbitration Law, 8 Amer. Rev. Int'l Arb. 21, 29–33 (1997); Emmanuel Gaillard, Note, [1996] Rev. de l'Arbitrage 106, 108; Arbitration Act 1996 §§ 3, 100(2).

Note: Coverage of the New York Convention

As we have seen, the Convention was intended to apply primarily to "foreign" awards—that is, to arbitral awards rendered abroad, "in the territory of a State other than the State where the recognition and enforcement of such awards are sought." But note also the second sentence of art. I(1), telling us that in addition, the Convention may also apply to awards rendered within *the territory of the state where enforcement is sought*, if in that state the award is "not considered as [a] domestic award." Apparently, then, in some cases the Convention may create binding obligations on American courts *even in the case of an arbitration award rendered within the United States*. See FAA, § 202; see also Alan Scott Rau, The New York Convention in American Courts, 7 Amer. Rev. of Int'l Arb. 213, 230–31 (1996):

> The first sentence of § 202 announces the overarching principle—apparently absolute—that all agreements or awards "arising out of" a "commercial" "relationship" come within the Convention. The second sentence * * * is then presumably necessary to introduce the inevitable limitations. The intention here was obviously to carve out, from the Convention, agreements or awards that are to remain strictly within the "domestic" FAA of Chapter I—insuring at a minimum that an American award, between two American parties and without some relation to a foreign state, must not fall within the treaty. Once such awards are eliminated, it seems logical to conclude that American awards would come within the Convention where some reasonable relation with a foreign state does exist. For awards entirely between American citizens, this seems to follow both from the overall structure of § 202 and by negative implication from its language; where one or more foreign nationals are involved, this must be an a fortiori case. * * * The logic of the classic argument *a contrario* would dictate that some "reasonable relation" with a foreign state is required by § 202 *only* when the award is "entirely between citizens of the United States"—and not otherwise. It seems surprising but inevitable, then, that a Texas award, arising out of a transaction in which an American citizen conveys property in Texas jointly to another American citizen

and her resident-alien spouse—all three resident in Texas—will be a Convention award.

See Lander Co., Inc. v. MMP Investments, Inc., 107 F.3d 476 (7th Cir.1997) (agreement between two American companies by which one was to become the exclusive distributor of the other's products in Poland; arbitration to take place in New York); Fuller Co. v. Compagnie des Bauxites De Guinee, 421 F.Supp. 938 (W.D.Pa.1976) (contract between two American companies for the design and installation of a plant in Guinea; arbitration to take place in Pittsburgh).

But why should it even matter whether, in some abstract sense, the Convention "applies" to awards rendered within the United States? After all, where an arbitration is to take place within this country, doesn't the FAA already provide a ready framework within which courts must give effect to arbitration agreements and awards? What is the significance, then, for such arbitrations, of the scheme of the Convention? The answer is that there are a number of ways in which the enforcement scheme of the Convention may differ from that of the "domestic" FAA. And while some of these disparities are of marginal or disappearing significance, others may have real "bite."

(a) Perhaps the greatest significance of the Convention for American arbitrations is with respect to the jurisdiction of federal courts. Since the FAA itself confers no subject matter jurisdiction, a plaintiff in federal court seeking to compel arbitration or to confirm an award must point to an independent source of federal jurisdiction, such as diversity of citizenship. By contrast, a case falling within the New York Convention is automatically "deemed to arise under the laws and treaties of the United States"—so that federal courts have jurisdiction to entertain such motions even in the absence of diversity and regardless of the amount in controversy. See FAA § 203. So bringing a case within the Convention can have real importance, for example, where two aliens have agreed to arbitrate in the United States;[1] in the absence of the Convention the only available forum may be a state court.[2] In addition, the rights given by § 205 to state court defen-

---

1. In fact, diversity jurisdiction is lacking not only where a suit is in the form "Alien A v. Alien B," but also where an American citizen has been joined in a suit with aliens on each side, i.e., in the form "Alien A v. Minnesota citizen and Alien B." See 13B Charles Alan Wright et al., Federal Practice & Procedure § 3604 (2d ed. 1984); Productos Mercantiles E Industriales, S.A. v. Faberge USA, Inc., 1993 WL 362391, at *3 (S.D.N.Y. Sept. 14, 1993), aff'd, 23 F.3d 41 (2d Cir. 1994)(Guatemala plaintiff v. El Salvador and Minnesota defendants; no diversity jurisdiction).

2. A related jurisdictional problem may arise from the fact that the FAA is limited in

scope to "maritime transaction[s]" and to contracts "evidencing a transaction involving commerce"—that is, "commerce among the several States or with foreign nations." Some older cases have held that this statutory language does not extend to contracts, between two foreign parties, which do not appear to directly involve any American trade, see, e.g., Petroleum Cargo Carriers, Ltd. v. Unitas, Inc., 31 Misc.2d 222, 220 N.Y.S.2d 724, 727 (Sup. Ct. 1961), aff'd, 15 A.D.2d 735, 224 N.Y.S.2d 654 (App. Div. 1962)(contract between a Panamanian company and a Liberian company to pay for condenser tubes manufactured in Germany and shipped to Japan; this "obviously is not commerce ... as defined in the Act"). Where the FAA does not

dants, allowing them to remove to federal court cases falling within the Convention, are considerably broader than rights under the general federal removal statute (28 U.S.C. § 1441).[3]

(b) Section 9 of the FAA provides that a party may apply for an order confirming the award "at any time within one year after the award is made." On the face of it, this looks very much like a statute of limitations—suggesting that summary confirmation under the statute would be barred after a year has passed. In this case a prevailing party might need to bring himself within the Convention—since in Convention cases, a motion to confirm may be made within three years after the award. [4]

(c) When a court grants an order compelling arbitration under § 4 of the FAA, it must direct the parties to arbitrate "in accordance with the terms of agreement." However, § 4 also provides that the arbitration proceedings ordered by the court "shall be within the district in which the

apply at all, it obviously cannot be enforced in either state or federal court. By contrast, the Convention does not rest on the commerce power of the federal government at all. And our reservation by which the treaty's scope is limited to relationships deemed to be "commercial" in nature could not have been intended to restrict the Convention to American commerce. See Sumitomo Corp. v. Parakopi Compania Maritima, S.A., 477 F.Supp. 737, 740 (S.D.N.Y. 1979), aff'd, 620 F.2d 286 (2d Cir. 1980)(" 'commercial' disputes involving only foreign entities" may come within the Convention even if they do not involve commerce "with foreign nations" within the meaning of FAA § 1).

3. Here are two examples: In most removal cases *all* properly joined defendants must timely file for, at least consent to, a notice of removal, by contrast, it is not necessary in Convention cases under § 205 that *all* defendants consent to removal: "Foreign businesses who understand that their access to federal courts can be denied by one local party defendant are likely to think carefully before contracting with an American business." Acosta v. Master Maintenance & Construction, Inc., 52 F.Supp.2d 699 (M.D. La. 1999). In addition, in most removal cases a proceeding can be removed to federal court only within 30 days of receiving the initial pleading; by contrast, § 205 permits removal "at any time before the trial"—although even before "trial" some notions of timeliness may still come into play, and removal may be disallowed if a defendant is held to have "waived" his right to removal by engaging in substantial state court litigation; see

Certain Underwriters at Lloyd's v. Bristol–Myers Squibb Co., 51 F.Supp.2d 756 (E.D. Tex. 1999)("although § 205 may have been enacted to facilitate removal of cases coming under the Convention, it certainly was not designed to enable parties to invoke the jurisdiction of state court and willingly proceed with discovery and trial only to remove when the first bite of what appears to be a ripe apple turns out in fact to be extremely sour").

4. Photopaint Technologies, LLC v. Smartlens Corp., 335 F.3d 152 (2d Cir. 2003)("Our construction of the text is not inevitable, but it is intuitive: for example, tax returns may be filed anytime up to April 15, but one senses at once that the phrase is permissive only up to a point"; moreover, "this result advances important values of finality"). Some courts have nevertheless held that the one-year period of § 9 is nothing more than "permissive rather than mandatory," so that judicial confirmation would still be possible after a year has passed. Note that an award that has been neither confirmed or vacated has the same effect as a contract between the parties: It can therefore still be the subject of an ordinary action on the contract, even after the time for making a statutory motion to confirm has expired. Courts that find the one-year period in § 9 to be merely "permissive" rely on the fact that "an action at law remains a viable alternative to confirmation proceedings"; as a consequence, they hold, "reading § 9 as a strict statute of limitations would be an exercise in futility," Sverdrup Corp. v. WHC Constructors Inc., 989 F.2d 148, 151 (4th Cir. 1993).

petition for an order directing such arbitration is filed." These two provisions must be taken together: So where an arbitration agreement calls for arbitration to take place in New York, a federal district court in Texas may under § 4 lack any power to compel arbitration at all: Arbitration in New York would not be "within the district in which the petition" was filed, and arbitration in Texas would not be "in accordance with the terms of the agreement." By contrast, in cases falling within the Convention, any court with jurisdiction over the parties is empowered to order that arbitration be held "in accordance with the agreement at any place therein provided for, whether that place is within or without the United States." See FAA § 206. Cf Oil Basins Ltd. v. Broken Hill Proprietary Co. Ltd., 613 F.Supp. 483, 487 (S.D.N.Y.1985) (§ 4 is superseded by § 206 only "to the extent that the parties specify an arbitration site in the contract"; where "no place was specified explicitly or implicitly," court could order the parties to arbitrate only in its own district).

Of course, even though the agreement may not explicitly identify the site of the arbitration, the parties may have given authority to an administering institution or to the arbitrators themselves to choose the location— and that should suffice under the Convention. See United States Lines, Inc. v. Liverpool & London Steamship Protection & Indemnity Ass'n, Ltd., 833 F.Supp. 350 (S.D.N.Y.1993) (arbitration clause did not specify venue but provided that if the parties could not agree on an arbitrator, the arbitrator was to be appointed by the President of the Law Society of England; "the Law Society has made it clear that its practice would be to appoint an English arbitrator, and that arbitrator would decide whether England or the United States is the more appropriate venue"; held, parties are "directed to arbitrate at the time and place set by the arbitrator" named by the Law Society).

(d) Finally, what about the scope of judicial review of awards? It is not likely in any event—as we saw at the beginning of this Section—that the grounds for challenge specified in the Convention will differ substantively in any significant respect from the grounds for vacatur provided in the "domestic" FAA. Perhaps a more important point, though, is this: Where an award has been rendered in the United States, § 10 of the FAA should continue to be available to the losing party who wishes to move to vacate the award: This is because the Convention assumes that an award can always be set aside "in the country in which it was made," and—since the Convention itself provides no grounds for setting aside an award—any court wishing to do so must presumably look to the grounds for vacatur specified in the arbitration law of the situs. That is the thrust of the Second Circuit's opinion in Yusuf Ahmed Alghanim & Sons, W.L.L. v. Toys "R" Us (HK) Ltd., 126 F.3d 15 (2d Cir. 1997).

This case involved a dispute over the termination of a franchise that Toys "R" Us had extended to a Kuwaiti business, to operate stores in the Middle East. The arbitrators had awarded the franchisee $46 million for lost profits under the agreement. The franchisee moved to confirm the award; Toys "R" Us cross-moved to vacate on the ground that it "was clearly irrational, in manifest disregard of the law [because the award of damages was 'speculative'], and in manifest disregard of the terms of the agreement." Although the arbitration had taken place in the United States, the court quite naturally found that "the Convention's applicability in this case is clear." It is true, the court said, that the grounds set forth in article V of the Convention are the "only grounds," the "exclusive" grounds for refusing to recognize a Convention award: Nevertheless, "under Article V(1)(e), the courts of the United States are authorized to apply United States procedural arbitral law, i.e., the FAA, to nondomestic awards rendered in the United States":

> The defense in Article V(1)(e) incorporates the entire body of review rights in the issuing jurisdiction. . . . If the scope of judicial review in the rendering state extends beyond the other six defenses allowed under the New York Convention, the losing party's opportunity to avoid enforcement is automatically enhanced.

The court therefore examined the award under the standards of the FAA—including the non-statutory ground that the arbitrators may have "manifestly disregarded" the law. But "our application of the FAA's implied grounds for vacatur is swift." Since, as we have seen, challenges on the basis of "manifest disregard" are uniformly rejected anyway—"mere error in the law or failure on the part of the arbitrators to understand or apply the law is not sufficient"—the court had little difficulty in confirming the award.

NOTES AND QUESTIONS

1. Cf. Alan Scott Rau, The New York Convention in American Courts, 7 Amer. Rev. of Int'l Arb. 213, 240 (1996), which characterizes cases like *Toys "R" Us* in this way:

> One can—if this helps—conceive of an American court that (under § 10 of the FAA) vacates an award, and then (under the Convention) refuses to enforce the award it has just vacated, as being "two separate courts with the judges wearing two different hats." But all this of course is unnecessary conceptualism: Combining the two functions retains the supervisory functions of the forum state, while still giving the broadest possible currency to international arbitration agreements and awards.

2. Cf. Industrial Risk Insurers v. M.A.N. Gutehoffnungshutte GmbH, 141 F.3d 1434 (11th Cir. 1998). A suit against a German turbine manufacturer—alleging that a "tail gas expander" it had supplied had been defectively designed and manufactured—was, pursuant to the agreement, referred to AAA arbitration in Tampa, Florida. The arbitrators ruled in favor of the respondent, and the claimant moved to vacate the award, alleging that the panel had improperly and prejudicially admitted certain evidence, and that the award was "arbitrary and capricious"—a non-statutory ground for vacatur accepted in theory by certain federal courts. (This ground apparently permits vacatur where an award "exhibits a wholesale departure from the law or where the reasoning is so palpably faulty that no judge could ever conceivably have made such a ruling"). The district court confirmed the award, finding that the procedures followed by the arbitrators were in accordance with AAA rules and the agreement of the parties, and that the award was not "arbitrary and capricious," and the Eleventh Circuit affirmed.

Arbitration proceedings, it held, "need not follow all the niceties of the federal courts, [but] need provide only a fundamentally fair hearing"; the rules to which the parties agreed "left wide discretion" to the arbitrators to admit or exclude evidence "how and when they see fit." At the same time, the court added that the non-statutory ground of vacatur for "arbitrary and capricious" awards was not in any event available with respect to arbitrations falling within the Convention—its "omission [from the Convention] is decisive." The *Toys "R" Us* case was quoted simply for the proposition that the "Convention's enumeration of defenses is exclusive"—and for nothing else. So the court completely failed to grasp the point of the *Toys "R" Us* analysis, didn't it?

3. In both *Toys "R" Us* and *Industrial Risk Insurers,* it was assumed that the "non-domestic" elements of the dispute were enough to bring even an "American" arbitration—that is, one held in the United States—within the scope of the Convention. What about the converse case? Consider this surprisingly common fact pattern: A yacht owned by an American couple—and whose home port is in Freeport, New York—is struck by a wave and beached on Long Island while on a short journey from Connecticut; a professional salvor—also from Freeport—is called, and tows the vessel approximately six miles to a marina. Before it will perform any towing or salvage services, however, the salvage company insists that the owners sign a Lloyd's Standard Form of Salvage Agreement. This agreement ("Lloyd's Open Form," or "LOF") provides that the salvor's compensation shall be fixed by a Lloyd's Arbitration Panel in London. Later the salvor does in fact initiate an arbitration proceeding in London, but the owners resist by filing an action in federal court in New York. Obviously there is no foreign connection here other than that the contemplated place of arbitration is abroad.

In such cases courts have regularly held that arbitration cannot be ordered in London, because the Convention did not apply. See Jones v. Sea Tow Services Freeport NY Inc., 30 F.3d 360 (2d Cir.1994)(lower court was held to have "exceeded its jurisdiction" in ordering arbitration in England, since "the relation with a foreign state that is required to invoke the Convention is lacking"). So "the saving grace in this case is that the [owners] will be able to defend in the United States, rather than in a foreign forum, the salvage claim asserted against them." See also Reinholtz v. Retriever Marine Towing & Salvage, 1993 WL 414719 (S.D.Fla.1993). In *Reinholtz* the parties had actually proceeded to arbitration in London; the court held that the resulting award in favor of the salvors could not be enforced, because there was missing the "requisite link to another nation" needed to bring it under the Convention. To the same effect is Brier v.

Northstar Marine, Inc., 1993 A.M.C. 1194, 1992 WL 350292 (D.N.J.) (salvor's motion for an order compelling arbitration in London was denied; excluding "purely domestic matters between citizens of the United States * * * would not appear to do any harm to the purposes of the Convention * * * and has the salutary effect of minimizing the expansion of federal jurisdiction into areas traditionally the province of the state judiciary").

These cases seem to rest on two distinct propositions:

- In order for the Lloyd's agreement to be "cognizable under the Convention," the "reasonable relation" test of FAA § 202 must be satisfied—that is, it is necessary, *even where the arbitration is to be held abroad, to identify some "reasonable relation" that the transaction has with a foreign state;*

- And on this fact pattern, no such "reasonable relation" can be found—"there is no connection with England independent of the LOF" itself. As the court put it in *Reinholtz*, the argument that the arbitration clause providing for arbitration in London provides the requisite link to another nation is "circular," since "the arbitration agreement itself must possess, not supply, the requisite nexus to a foreign forum to allow a federal court to assert jurisdiction under the Convention."

But both of these propositions are highly dubious, aren't they? Doesn't the first proposition directly violate the language and structure of the Convention? Recall that the first sentence of Art. I(1) establishes the basic principle that the Convention applies to all "foreign" awards, that is, "awards made in the territory of [another] State": The Convention was thus extended to foreign awards independent of the citizenship of the parties, or the presence of any other factors linking the dispute with the state where enforcement is sought. The second sentence of Art. I(1) was added to create a separate, additional category of awards that a state may choose to treat as "non-domestic"—and which *by definition* can apply only in those cases where enforcement is sought in the country *where the award was rendered.* When the Convention was being drafted, an amendment was proposed by one delegation that was intended to exclude from the scope of the Convention some awards rendered abroad but nevertheless considered by the enforcing state as "domestic"; this amendment was rejected by over two-thirds of the votes cast. Thus, the applicability of the Convention to awards handed down in another state "does not depend on the existence of any factor connecting the [dispute] with a foreign state. This is not unreasonable as domestic disputes are not seldom referred to foreign arbitration which appears to be particularly well-suited to accommodate the needs of a specific trade." 1 Giorgio Gaja, International Commercial Arbitration: New York Convention at I.A.3 & n.17 (1984).

So, isn't the better interpretation of § 202 simply that it defines the scope of "non-domestic" awards *rendered within the United States*—and that it does not limit the obligation to recognize and enforce *foreign awards* or agreements calling for *foreign arbitration*?

As for the second proposition, see simply Ian R. Macneil et al., Federal Arbitration Law § 44.9.4 (1999): "If an agreement to arbitrate in a foreign jurisdiction and under its laws does not 'envisage . . . enforcement abroad' [within the language of 202], what does?"

In *Brier*, a magistrate judge—after first rejecting the assertion that the contract was a product of fraud or coercion—found that since the arbitration clause "failed to satisfy the foreign relation requirement" of § 202, it was therefore "unenforceable and invalid." It apparently followed that it was "impossible" for the court even to stay the litigation under § 3 of the FAA; the owner was allowed to proceed to discovery. In *Reinholtz*, the court granted summary judgment to the salvors as to liability and "deferred resolution of the issue of damages * * * until trial." The sweeping implication of both cases, then, is that agreements and awards that do not fall within the Convention are simply dead letters—and that the court may therefore itself proceed to determine salvage. Can this result be defended at all? Is the implementing legislation for the Convention intended to affect the validity of an agreement—operating to strike down agreements that the court has already found, on the usual contract-law grounds, to be enforceable? Is it not just a tad ironic that an agreement which fails to be sufficiently "international" to satisfy the Convention has even less currency than it would have had the Convention never existed?

FEDERAL ARBITRATION ACT 9 U.S.C. § 1 (1925)

CHAPTER 1. GENERAL PROVISIONS

§ 1. "Maritime Transactions," and "Commerce" Defined; Exceptions to Operation of Title

"Maritime transactions," as herein defined, means charter parties, bills of lading of water carriers, agreements relating to wharfage, supplies furnished vessels or repairs of vessels, collisions, or any other matters in foreign commerce which, if the subject of controversy, would be embraced within admiralty jurisdiction; "commerce," as herein defined, means commerce among the several States or with foreign nations, or in any Territory of the United States or in the District of Columbia, or between any such Territory and another, or between any such Territory and any State or foreign nation, or between the District of Columbia and any State or Territory or foreign nation, but nothing herein contained shall apply to contracts of employment of seamen, railroad employees, or any other class of workers engaged in foreign or interstate commerce.

§ 2. Validity, Irrevocability, and Enforcement of Agreements to Arbitrate

A written provision in any maritime transaction or a contract evidencing a transaction involving commerce to settle by arbitration a controversy thereafter arising out of such contract or transaction, or the refusal to perform the whole or any part thereof, or an agreement in writing to submit to arbitration an existing controversy arising out of such a contract, transaction, or refusal, shall be valid, irrevocable, and enforceable, save upon such grounds as exist at law or in equity for the revocation of any contract.

§ 3. Stay of Proceedings Where Issue Therein Referable to Arbitration

If any suit or proceeding be brought in any of the courts of the United States upon any issue referable to arbitration under an agreement in writing for such arbitration, the court in which such suit is pending, upon being satisfied that the issue involved in such suit or proceeding is referable to arbitration under such an agreement, shall on application of one of the parties stay the trial of the action until such arbitration has been had in accordance with the terms of the agreement, providing the applicant for the stay is not in default in proceeding with such arbitration.

§ 4.   Failure to Arbitrate Under Agreement; Petition to United States Court Having Jurisdiction for Order to Compel Arbitration; Notice and Service Thereof; Hearing and Determination

A party aggrieved by the alleged failure, neglect, or refusal of another to arbitrate under a written agreement for arbitration may petition any United States district court which, save for such agreement, would have jurisdiction under Title 28, in a civil action or in admiralty of the subject matter of a suit arising out of the controversy between the parties, for an order directing that such arbitration proceed in the manner provided for in such agreement. Five days' notice in writing of such application shall be served upon the party in default. Service thereof shall be made in the manner provided by the Federal Rules of Civil Procedure. The court shall hear the parties, and upon being satisfied that the making of the agreement for arbitration or the failure to comply therewith is not in issue, the court shall make an order directing the parties to proceed to arbitration in accordance with the terms of the agreement. The hearing and proceedings, under such agreement, shall be within the district in which the petition for an order directing such arbitration is filed. If the making of the arbitration agreement or the failure, neglect, or refusal to perform the same be in issue, the court shall proceed summarily to the trial thereof. If no jury trial be demanded by the party alleged to be in default, or in the matter in dispute is within admiralty jurisdiction, the court shall hear and determine such issue. Where such an issue is raised, the party alleged to be in default may, except in cases of admiralty, on or before the return day of the notice of application, demand a jury trial of such issue, and upon such demand the court shall make an order referring the issue or issues to a jury in the manner provided by the Federal Rules of Civil Procedure, or may specially call a jury for that purpose. If the jury find that no agreement in writing for arbitration was made or that there is no default in proceeding thereunder, the proceeding shall be dismissed. If the jury find that an agreement for arbitration was made in writing and that there is a default in proceeding thereunder, the court shall make an order summarily directing the parties to proceed with the arbitration in accordance with the terms thereof.

§ 5.   Appointment of Arbitrators or Umpire

If in the agreement provision be made for a method of naming or appointing an arbitrator or arbitrators or an umpire, such method shall be followed; but if no method be provided therein, or if a method be provided and any party thereto shall fail to avail himself of such method, or if for any other reason there shall be a lapse in the naming of an arbitrator or arbitrators or umpire, or in filling a vacancy, then upon the application of either party to the controversy the court shall designate and appoint an arbitrator or arbitrators or umpire, as the case may require, who shall act under the said agreement with the same force and effect as if he or they had been specifically named therein; and unless otherwise provided in the agreement the arbitration shall be by a single arbitrator.

§ 6. Application Heard as Motion

Any application to the court hereunder shall be made and heard in the manner provided by law for making and hearing of motions, except as otherwise herein expressly provided.

§ 7. Witnesses Before Arbitrators; Fees; Compelling Attendance

The arbitrators selected either as prescribed in this title or otherwise, or a majority of them, may summon in writing any person to attend before them or any of them as a witness and in a proper case to bring with him or them any book, record, document, or paper which may be deemed material as evidence in the case. The fees for such attendance shall be the same as the fees of witnesses before masters of the United States Courts. Said summons shall issue in the name of the arbitrator or arbitrators, or a majority of them, and shall be signed by the arbitrators, or a majority of them, and shall be directed to the said person and shall be served in all the same manner as subpoenas to appear and testify before the court; if any person or persons so summoned to testify shall refuse or neglect to obey said summons, upon petition the United States court in and for the district in which such arbitrators or a majority of them, are sitting may compel the attendance of such person or persons before said arbitrator or arbitrators, or punish said person or persons for contempt in the same manner provided on February 12, 1925, for securing the attendance of witnesses or their punishment for neglect or refusal to attend in the courts of the United States.

§ 8. Proceedings Begun by Libel in Admiralty and Seizure of Vessel or Property

If the basis of jurisdiction be a cause of action otherwise justiciable in admiralty, then, notwithstanding anything herein to the contrary, the party claiming to be aggrieved may begin his proceeding hereunder by libel and seizure of the vessel or other property of the other party according to the usual course of admiralty proceedings, and the court shall then have jurisdiction to direct the parties to proceed with the arbitration and shall retain jurisdiction to enter its decree upon the award.

§ 9. Award of Arbitrators; Confirmation; Jurisdiction; Procedure

If the parties in their agreement have agreed that a judgment of the court shall be entered upon the award made pursuant to the arbitration, and shall specify the court, then at any time within one year after the award is made any party to the arbitration may apply to the court so specified for an order confirming the award, and thereupon the court must grant such an order unless the award is vacated, modified, or corrected as prescribed in sections 10 and 11 of this title. If no court is specified in the agreement of the parties, then such application may be made to the United

States court in and for the district within which such award was made. Notice of the application shall be served upon the adverse party, and thereupon the court shall have jurisdiction of such party as though he had appeared generally in the proceeding. If the adverse party is a resident of the district within which the award was made, such service shall be made upon the adverse party or his attorney as prescribed by law for service of notice of motion in an action in the same court.

§ 10. Same; Vacation; Grounds; Rehearing

(a) In any of the following cases the United States court in and for the district wherein the award was made may make an order vacating the award upon the application of any party to the arbitration—

(1) where the award was procured by corruption, fraud, or undue means;

(2) Where there was evident partiality or corruption in the arbitrators, or either of them;

(3) Where the arbitrators were guilty of misconduct in refusing to postpone the hearing, upon sufficient cause shown, or in refusing to hear evidence pertinent and material to the controversy; or of any other misbehavior by which the rights of any party have been prejudiced; or

(4) Where the arbitrators exceeded their powers, or so imperfectly executed them that a mutual, final, and definite award upon the subject matter submitted was not made.

(b) If an award is vacated and the time within which the agreement required the award to be made has not expired the court may, in its discretion, direct a rehearing by the arbitrators.

(c) The United States district court for the district wherein an award was made that was issued pursuant to section 580 of title 5 may make an order vacating the award upon the application of a person, other than a party to the arbitration, who is adversely affected or aggrieved by the award, if the use of arbitration or the award is clearly inconsistent with the factors set forth in section 572 of title 5.

§ 11. Same; Modification or Correction; Grounds; Order

In either of the following cases the United States court in and for the district wherein the award was made may make an order modifying or correcting the award upon the application of any party to the arbitration—

(a) Where there was an evident material miscalculation of figures or an evident material mistake in the description of any person, thing, or property referred to in the award.

(b) Where the arbitrators have awarded upon a matter not submitted to them, unless it is a matter not affecting the merits of the decision upon the matter submitted.

(c) Where the award is imperfect in matter of form not affecting the merits of the controversy.

The order may modify and correct the award, so as to effect the intent thereof and promote justice between the parties.

§ 12. Notice of Motions to Vacate or Modify; Service; Stay of Proceedings

Notice of a motion to vacate, modify, or correct an award must be served upon the adverse party or his attorney within three months after the award is filed or delivered. If the adverse party is a resident of the district within which the award was made, such service shall be made upon the adverse party or his attorney as prescribed by law for service of notice of motion in an action in the same court. If the adverse party shall be a nonresident then the notice of the application shall be served by the marshal of any district within which the adverse party may be found in like manner as other process of the court. For the purposes of the motion any judge who might make an order to stay the proceedings in an action brought in the same court may make an order, to be served with the notice of motion, staying the proceedings of the adverse party to enforce the award.

§ 13. Papers Filed with Order on Motions; Judgment; Docketing; Force and Effect; Enforcement

The party moving for an order confirming, modifying, or correcting an award shall, at the time such order is filed with the clerk for the entry of judgment thereon, also file the following papers with the clerk:

(a) The agreement: the selection or appointment, if any, of an additional arbitrator or umpire; and each written extension of the time, if any, within which to make the award.

(b) The award.

(c) Each notice, affidavit, or other paper used upon an application to confirm, modify, or correct the award, and a copy of each order of the court upon such an application.

The judgment shall be docketed as if it was rendered in an action.

The judgment so entered shall have the same force and effect, in all respects, as, and be subject to all the provisions of law relating to, a judgment in an action; and it may be enforced as if it had been rendered in an action in the court in which it is entered.

§ 14. Contracts Not Affected

This title shall not apply to contracts made prior to January 1, 1926.

§ 15. Inapplicability of the Act of State Doctrine

Enforcement of arbitral agreements, confirmation of arbitral awards, and execution upon judgments based on orders confirming such awards shall not be refused on the basis of the Act of State doctrine.

§ 16. Appeals

(a) An appeal may be taken from—

(1) an order—

(A) refusing a stay of any action under section 3 of this title,

(B) denying a petition under section 4 of this title to order arbitration to proceed,

(C) denying an application under section 206 of this title to compel arbitration,

(D) confirming or denying confirmation of an award or partial award, or

(E) modifying, correcting, or vacating an award;

(2) an interlocutory order granting, continuing, or modifying an injunction against an arbitration that is subject to this title; or

(3) a final decision with respect to an arbitration that is subject to this title.

(b) Except as otherwise provided in section 1292(b) of title 28, an appeal may not be taken from an interlocutory order—

(1) granting a stay of any action under section 3 of this title;

(2) directing arbitration to proceed under section 4 of this title;

(3) compelling arbitration under section 206 of this title; or

(4) refusing to enjoin an arbitration that is subject to this title.

CHAPTER 2. CONVENTION ON THE RECOGNITION AND ENFORCEMENT OF FOREIGN ARBITRAL AWARDS

§ 201. Enforcement of Convention

The Convention on the Recognition and Enforcement of Foreign Arbitral Awards of June 10, 1958, shall be enforced in United States courts in accordance with this chapter.

§ 202. Agreement or Award Falling Under the Convention

An arbitration agreement or arbitral award arising out of a legal relationship, whether contractual or not, which is considered as commercial, including a transaction, contract, or agreement described in section 2 of this title, falls under the Convention. An agreement or award arising out of such relationship which is entirely between citizens of the United States shall be deemed not to fall under the Convention unless that relationship involves property located abroad, envisages performance or enforcement abroad, or has some other reasonable relation with one or more foreign states. For the purpose of this section a corporation is a citizen of the United States if it is incorporated or has its principal place of business in the United States.

§ 203. Jurisdiction; Amount in Controversy

An action or proceeding falling under the Convention shall be deemed to arise under the laws and treaties of the United States. The district courts of the United States (including the courts enumerated in section 460 of title 28) shall have original jurisdiction over such an action or proceeding, regardless of the amount in controversy.

§ 204. Venue

An action or proceeding over which the district courts have jurisdiction pursuant to section 203 of this title may be brought in any such court in which save for the arbitration agreement an action or proceeding with respect to the controversy between the parties could be brought, or in such court for the district and division which embraces the place designated in the agreement as the place of arbitration if such place is within the United States.

§ 205. Removal of Cases From State Courts

Where the subject matter of an action or proceeding pending in a State court relates to an arbitration agreement or award falling under the Convention, the defendant or the defendants may, at any time before the trial thereof, remove such action or proceeding to the district court of the United States for the district and division embracing the place where the action or proceeding is pending. The procedure for removal of causes otherwise provided by law shall apply, except that the ground for removal provided in this section need not appear on the face of the complaint but may be shown in the petition for removal. For the purposes of Chapter 1 of this title any action or proceeding removed under this section shall be deemed to have been brought in the district court to which it is removed.

§ 206. Order to Compel Arbitration; Appointment of Arbitrators

A court having jurisdiction under this chapter may direct that arbitration be held in accordance with the agreement at any place therein provided for, whether that place is within or without the United States. Such court may also appoint arbitrators in accordance with the provisions of the agreement.

§ 207. Award of Arbitrators; Confirmation; Jurisdiction; Proceeding

Within three years after an arbitral award falling under the Convention is made, any party to the arbitration may apply to any court having jurisdiction under this chapter for an order confirming the award as against any other party to the arbitration. The court shall confirm the award unless it finds one of the grounds for refusal or deferral of recognition or enforcement of the award specified in the said Convention.

§ 208. Chapter 1; Residual Applications

Chapter 1 applies to actions and proceedings brought under this chapter to the extent that chapter is not in conflict with this chapter or the Convention as ratified by the United States.

CHAPTER 3. INTER–AMERICAN CONVENTION ON INTERNATIONAL COMMERCIAL ARBITRATION

§ 301. Enforcement of Convention

The Inter–American Convention on International Commercial Arbitration of January 30, 1975, shall be enforced in United States courts in accordance with this chapter.

§ 302. Incorporation by Reference

Sections 202, 203, 204, 205, and 207 of this title shall apply to this chapter as if specifically set forth herein, except that for the purposes of this chapter "the Convention" shall mean the Inter–American Convention.

§ 303. Order to Compel Arbitration; Appointment of Arbitrators; Locale

(a) A court having jurisdiction under this chapter may direct that arbitration be held in accordance with the agreement at any place therein provided for, whether that place is within or without the United States. The court may also appoint arbitrators in accordance with the provisions of the agreement.

(b) In the event the agreement does not make provision for the place of arbitration or the appointment of arbitrators, the court shall direct that the arbitration shall be held and the arbitrators be appointed in accordance with Article 3 of the Inter–American Convention.

§ 304. Recognition and Enforcement of Foreign Arbitral Decisions and Awards; Reciprocity

Arbitral decision or awards made in the territory of a foreign State shall, on the basis of reciprocity, be recognized and enforced under this chapter only if that State has ratified or acceded to the Inter–American Convention.

§ 305. Relationship Between the Inter–American Convention and the Convention on the Recognition and Enforcement of Foreign Arbitral Awards of June 10, 1958

When the requirements for application of both the Inter–American Convention and the Convention on the Recognition and Enforcement of Foreign Arbitral Awards of June 10, 1958, are met, determination as to which Convention applies shall, unless otherwise expressly agreed, be made as follows:

(1) If a majority of the parties to the arbitration agreement are citizens of a State or States that have ratified or acceded to the Inter–American Convention and are member States of the Organization of American States, the Inter–American Convention shall apply.

(2) In all other cases the Convention on the Recognition and Enforcement of Foreign Arbitral Awards of June 10, 1958, shall apply.

§ 306. Applicable Rules of Inter–American Commercial Arbitration Commission

(a) For the purposes of this chapter the rules of procedure of the Inter–American Commercial Arbitration Commission referred to in Article 3 of the Inter–American Convention shall, subject to subsection (b) of this section, be those rules as promulgated by the Commission on July 1, 1988.

(b) In the event the rules of procedure of the Inter–American Commercial Arbitration Commission are modified or amended in accordance with the procedures for amendment of the rules of that Commission, the Secretary of State, by regulation in accordance with section 553 of title 5, consistent with the aims and purposes of this Convention, may prescribe that such modifications or amendments shall be effective for purposes of this chapter.

§ 307. Chapter 1; Residual Application

Chapter 1 applies to actions and proceedings brought under this chapter to the extent chapter 1 is not in conflict with this chapter or the Inter–American Convention as ratified by the United States.

UNITED NATIONS CONVENTION ON THE RECOGNITION AND ENFORCEMENT OF FOREIGN ARBITRAL AWARDS

[The New York Convention]

June 10, 1958

Article I

1. This Convention shall apply to the recognition and enforcement of arbitral awards made in the territory of a State other than the State where the recognition and enforcement of such awards are sought, and arising out of differences between persons, whether physical or legal. It shall also apply to arbitral awards not considered as domestic awards in the State where their recognition and enforcement are sought.

2. The term "arbitral awards" shall include not only awards made by arbitrators appointed for each case but also those made by permanent arbitral bodies to which the parties have submitted.

3. When signing, ratifying or acceding to this Convention, or notifying extension under article X hereof, any State may on the basis of reciprocity declare that it will apply the Convention to the recognition and enforcement of awards made only in the territory of another Contracting State. It may also declare that it will apply the Convention only to differences arising out of legal relationships whether contractual or not, which are considered as commercial under the national law of the State making such declaration.

Article II

1. Each Contracting State shall recognize an agreement in writing under which the parties undertake to submit to arbitration all or any differences which have arisen or which may arise between them in respect of a defined legal relationship, whether contractual or not, concerning a subject matter capable of settlement by arbitration.

2. The term "agreement in writing" shall include an arbitral clause in a contract or an arbitration agreement, signed by the parties or contained in an exchange of letters or telegrams.

3. The court of a Contracting State, when seized of an action in a matter in respect of which the parties have made an agreement within the meaning of this article, shall, at the request of one of the parties, refer the parties to arbitration, unless it finds that the said agreement is null and void, inoperative or incapable of being performed.

Article III

Each Contracting State shall recognize arbitral awards as binding and enforce them in accordance with the rules of procedure of the territory where the award is relied upon, under the conditions laid down in the following articles. There shall not be imposed substantially more onerous conditions or higher fees or charges on the recognition or enforcement of arbitral awards to which this Convention applies than are imposed on the recognition or enforcement of domestic arbitral awards.

Article IV

1. To obtain the recognition and enforcement mentioned in the preceding article, the party applying for recognition and enforcement shall, at the time of the application, supply:

(a) The duly authenticated original award or a duly certified copy thereof;

(b) The original agreement referred to in article II or a duly certified copy thereof.

2. If the said award or agreement is not made in an official language of the country in which the award is relied upon, the party applying for recognition and enforcement of the award shall produce a translation of these documents into such language. The translation shall be certified by an official or sworn translator or by a diplomatic or consular agent.

Article V

1. Recognition and enforcement of the award may be refused, at the request of the party against whom it is invoked, only if that party furnishes to the competent authority where the recognition and enforcement is sought, proof that:

(a) The parties to the agreement referred to in article II were, under the law applicable to them, under some incapacity, or the said agreement is not valid under the law to which the parties have subjected it or, failing any indication thereon, under the law of the country where the award was made; or

(b) The party against whom the award is invoked was not given proper notice of the appointment of the arbitrator or of the arbitration proceedings or was otherwise unable to present his case; or

(c) The award deals with a difference not contemplated by or not falling within the terms of the submission to arbitration, or it contains decisions on matters beyond the scope of the submission to arbitration, provided that, if the decisions on matters submitted to arbitration can be separated from those not so submitted, that part of the award which contains decisions on matters submitted to arbitration may be recognized and enforced; or

(d) The composition of the arbitral authority or the arbitral procedure was not in accordance with the agreement of the parties, or, failing such agreement, was not in accordance with the law of the country where the arbitration took place; or

(e) The award has not yet become binding on the parties, or has been set aside or suspended by a competent authority of the country in which, or under the law of which, that award was made.

2. Recognition and enforcement of an arbitral award may also be refused if the competent authority in the country where recognition and enforcement is sought finds that:

(a) The subject matter of the difference is not capable of settlement by arbitration under the law of that country; or

(b) The recognition or enforcement of the award would be contrary to the public policy of that country.

Article VI

If an application for the setting aside or suspension of the award has been made to a competent authority referred to in article V (1)(e), the authority before which the award is sought to be relied upon may, if it considers it proper, adjourn the decision on the enforcement of the award and may also, on the application of the party claiming enforcement of the award, order the other party to give suitable security.

Article VII

1. The provisions of the present Convention shall not affect the validity of multilateral or bilateral agreements concerning the recognition and enforcement of arbitral awards entered into by the Contracting States nor deprive any interested party of any right he may have to avail himself of an arbitral award in the manner and to the extent allowed by the law or the treaties of the country where such award is sought to be relied upon.

2. The Geneva Protocol on Arbitration Clauses of 1923 and the Geneva Convention on the Execution of Foreign Arbitral Awards of 1927 shall cease to have effect between Contracting States on their becoming bound and to the extent that they become bound, by this Convention.

Article VIII

1. This Convention shall be open until 31 December 1958 for signature on behalf of any Member of the United Nations and also on behalf of any other State which is or hereafter becomes a member of any specialized agency of the United Nations, or which is or hereafter becomes a party to the Statute of the International Court of Justice, or any other State to which an invitation has been addressed by the General Assembly of the United Nations.

2. This Convention shall be ratified and the instrument of ratification shall be deposited with the Secretary–General of the United Nations.

Article IX

1. This Convention shall be open for accession to all States referred to in article VIII.

2. Accession shall be effected by the deposit of an instrument of accession with the Secretary–General of the United Nations.

Article X

1. Any State may, at the time of signature, ratification or accession, declare that this Convention shall extend to all or any of the territories for the international relations of which it is responsible. Such a declaration shall take effect when the Convention enters into force for the State concerned.

2. At any time thereafter any such extension shall be made by notification addressed to the Secretary–General of the United Nations and shall take effect as from the ninetieth day after the day of receipt by the Secretary–General of the United Nations of this notification, or as from the date of entry into force of the Convention for the State concerned, whichever is the later.

3. With respect to those territories to which this Convention is not extended at the time of signature, ratification or accession, each State concerned shall consider the possibility of taking the necessary steps in order to extend the application of this Convention to such territories, subject, where necessary for constitutional reasons, to the consent of the Governments of such territories.

Article XI

1. In the case of a federal or non-unitary State, the following provisions shall apply:

(a) With respect to those articles of this Convention that come within the legislative jurisdiction of the federal authority, the obligations of the federal Government shall to this extent be the same as those of Contracting States which are not federal States;

(b) With respect to those articles of this Convention that come within the legislative jurisdiction of constituent states or provinces which are not, under the constitutional system of the federation, bound to take legislative action, the federal Government shall bring such articles with a favourable recommendation to the notice of the appropriate authorities of constituent states or provinces at the earliest possible moment;

(c) A federal State Party to this Convention shall, at the request of any other Contracting State transmitted through the Secretary–General of the United Nations, supply a statement of the law and practice of the federation and its constituent units in regard to any particular provision of this Convention, showing the extent to which effect has been given to that provision by legislative or other action.

Article XII

1. This Convention shall come into force on the ninetieth day following the date of deposit of the third instrument of ratification or accession.

2. For each State ratifying or acceding to this Convention after the deposit of the third instrument of ratification or accession, this Convention shall enter into force on the ninetieth day after deposit by such State of its instrument of ratification or accession.

Article XIII

1. Any Contracting State may denounce this Convention by a written notification to the Secretary–General of the United Nations. Denunciation shall take effect one year after the date of receipt of the notification by the Secretary–General.

2. Any State which has made a declaration or notification under article X may, at any time thereafter, by notification to the Secretary–General of the United Nations, declare that this Convention shall cease to extend to the territory concerned one year after the date of the receipt of the notification by the Secretary–General.

3. This Convention shall continue to be applicable to arbitral awards in respect of which recognition or enforcement proceedings have been instituted before the denunciation takes effect.

Article XIV

A Contracting State shall not be entitled to avail itself of the present Convention against other Contracting States except to the extent that it is itself bound to apply the Convention.

Article XV

The Secretary–General of the United Nations shall notify the States contemplated in article VIII of the following:

(a) Signatures and ratifications in accordance with article VIII;

(b) Accessions in accordance with article IX;

(c) Declarations and notifications under articles I, X and XI;

(d) The date upon which this Convention enters into force in accordance with article XII;

(e) Denunciations and notifications in accordance with article XIII.

Article XVI

1. This Convention, of which the Chinese, English, French, Russian and Spanish texts shall be equally authentic, shall be deposited in the archives of the United Nations.

2. The Secretary–General of the United Nations shall transmit a certified copy of this Convention to the States contemplated in article VIII.

Inter-American Convention on International Commercial Arbitration

[The Panama Convention]

January 30, 1975

PREAMBLE

The Governments of the Member States of the Organization of American States, desirous of concluding a convention on international commercial arbitration, have agreed as follows:

Article 1

An agreement in which the parties undertake to submit to arbitral decision any differences that may arise or have arisen between them with respect to a commercial transaction is valid. The agreement shall be set forth in an instrument signed by the parties, or in the form of an exchange of letters, telegrams, or telex communications.

Article 2

Arbitrators shall be appointed in the manner agreed upon by the parties. Their appointment may be delegated to a third party, whether a natural or juridical person. Arbitrators may be nationals or foreigners.

Article 3

In the absence of an express agreement between the parties, the arbitration shall be conducted in accordance with the rules of procedure of the Inter-American Commercial Arbitration Commission.

Article 4

An arbitral decision or award that is not appealable under the applicable law or procedural rules shall have the force of a final judicial judgment. Its execution or recognition may be ordered in the same manner as that of decisions handed down by national or foreign ordinary courts, in accordance with the procedural laws of the country where it is to be executed and the provisions of international treaties.

Article 5

1. The recognition and execution of the decision may be refused, at the request of the party against which it is made, only if such party is able to prove to the competent authority of the State in which recognition and execution are requested:

a. That the parties to the agreement were subject to some incapacity under the applicable law or that the agreement is not valid under the law to which the parties have submitted it, or, if such law is not specified, under the law of the State in which the decision was made; or

b. That the party against which the arbitral decision has been made was not duly notified of the appointment of the arbitrator or of the arbitration procedure to be followed, or was unable, for any other reason, to present his defense; or

c. That the decision concerns a dispute not envisaged in the agreement between the parties to submit to arbitration; nevertheless, if the provisions of the decision that refer to issues submitted to arbitration can be separated from those not submitted to arbitration, the former may be recognized and executed; or

d. That the constitution of the arbitral tribunal or the arbitration procedure has not been carried out in accordance with the terms of the agreement signed by the parties or, in the absence of such agreement, that the constitution of the arbitral tribunal or the arbitration procedure has not been carried out in accordance with the law of the State where the arbitration took place; or

e. That the decision is not yet binding on the parties or has been annulled or suspended by competent authority of the State in which, or according to the law of which, the decision has been made.

2. The recognition and execution of an arbitral decision may also be refused if the competent authority of the State in which the recognition and execution is requested finds:

a. That the subject of the dispute cannot be settled by arbitration under the law of the State; or

b. That the recognition or execution of the decision would be contrary to the public policy ("ordre public") of that State.

Article 6

If the competent authority mentioned in Article 5.1.e has been requested to annul or suspend the arbitral decision, the authority before which such decision is invoked may, if it deems it appropriate, postpone a decision on the execution of the arbitral decision and, at the request of the party requesting execution, may also instruct the other party to provide appropriate guaranties.

Article 7

This Convention shall be open for signature by the Member States of the Organization of American States.

Article 8

This Convention is subject to ratification. The instruments of ratification shall be deposited with the General Secretariat of the Organization of American States.

Article 9

This Convention shall remain open for accession by any other State. The instruments of accession shall be deposited with the General Secretariat of the Organization of American States.

Article 10

This Convention shall enter into force on the thirtieth day following the date of deposit of the second instrument of ratification.

For each State ratifying or acceding to the Convention after the deposit of the second instrument of ratification, the Convention shall enter into force on the thirtieth day after deposit by such State of its instrument of ratification or accession.

Article 11

If a State Party has two or more territorial units in which different systems of law apply in relation to the matters dealt with in this Convention, it may, at the time of signature, ratification or accession, declare that this Convention shall extend to all its territorial units or only to one or more of them.

Such declaration may be modified by subsequent declarations, which shall expressly indicate the territorial unit or units to which the Convention applies. Such subsequent declarations shall be transmitted to the General Secretariat of the Organization of American States, and shall become effective thirty days after the date of their receipt.

Article 12

This Convention shall remain in force indefinitely, but any of the States Parties may denounce it. The instrument of denunciation shall be deposited with the General Secretariat of the Organization of American States. After one year from the date of deposit of the instrument of denunciation, the Convention shall no longer be in effect for the denouncing State, but shall remain in effect for the other States Parties.

Article 13

The original instrument of this Convention, the English, French, Portuguese and Spanish texts of which are equally authentic, shall be deposited with the General Secretariat of the Organization of American States. The Secretariat shall notify the Member States of the Organization of American States and the States that have acceded to the Convention of the signatures, deposits of instruments or ratification, accession, and denunciation as well as of reservations, if any. It shall also transmit the declarations referred to in Article 11 of this Convention.

APPENDIX D

AMERICAN BAR ASSOCIATION MODEL RULES OF PROFESSIONAL CONDUCT (2004) EDITION

RULE 1.1   Competence

A lawyer shall provide competent representation to a client. Competent representation requires the legal knowledge, skill, thoroughness and preparation reasonably necessary for the representation.

RULE 1.2   Scope of Representation and Allocation of Authority Between Client and Lawyer

(a) Subject to paragraphs (c) and (d), a lawyer shall abide by a client's decisions concerning the objectives of representation and, as required by Rule 1.4, shall consult with the client as to the means by which they are to be pursued. A lawyer may take such action on behalf of the client as is impliedly authorized to carry out the representation. A lawyer shall abide by a client's decision whether to settle a matter. In a criminal case, the lawyer shall abide by the client's decision, after consultation with the lawyer, as to a plea to be entered, whether to waive jury trial and whether the client will testify.

(b) A lawyer's representation of a client, including representation by appointment, does not constitute an endorsement of the client's political, economic, social or moral views or activities.

(c) A lawyer may limit the scope of the representation if the limitation is reasonable under the circumstances and the client gives informed consent.

(d) A lawyer shall not counsel a client to engage, or assist a client, in conduct that the lawyer knows is criminal or fraudulent, but a lawyer may discuss the legal consequences of any proposed course of conduct with a client and may counsel or assist a client to make a good faith effort to determine the validity, scope, meaning or application of the law.

RULE 1.6   Confidentiality of Information

(a) A lawyer shall not reveal information relating to representation of a client unless the client gives informed consent, the disclosure is impliedly authorized in order to carry out the representation or the disclosure is permitted by paragraph (b).

(b) A lawyer may reveal information relating to the representation of a client to the extent the lawyer reasonably believes necessary:

(1) to prevent reasonably certain death or substantial bodily harm;

(2) to prevent the client from committing a crime or fraud that is reasonably certain to result in substantial injury to the financial interests or property of another and in furtherance of which the client has used or is using the lawyer's services;

(3) to prevent, mitigate or rectify substantial injury to the financial interests or property of another that is reasonably certain to result or has resulted from the client's commission of a crime or fraud in furtherance of which the client has used the lawyer's services;

(4) to secure legal advice about the lawyer's compliance with these Rules;

(5) to establish a claim or defense on behalf of the lawyer in a controversy between the lawyer and the client, to establish a defense to a criminal charge or civil claim against the lawyer based upon conduct in which the client was involved, or to respond to allegations in any proceeding concerning the lawyer's representation of the client; or

(6) to comply with other law or a court order.

RULE 1.7 Conflict of Interest: Current Clients

(a) Except as provided in paragraph (b), a lawyer shall not represent a client if the representation involves a concurrent conflict of interest. A concurrent conflict of interest exists if:

(1) the representation of one client will be directly adverse to another client; or

(2) there is a significant risk that the representation of one or more clients will be materially limited by the lawyer's responsibilities to another client, a former client or a third person or by a personal interest of the lawyer.

(b) Notwithstanding the existence of a concurrent conflict of interest under paragraph (a), a lawyer may represent a client if:

(1) the lawyer reasonably believes that the lawyer will be able to provide competent and diligent representation to each affected client;

(2) the representation is not prohibited by law;

(3) the representation does not involve the assertion of a claim by one client against another client represented by the lawyer in the same litigation or other proceeding before a tribunal; and

(4) each affected client gives informed consent, confirmed in writing.

RULE 1.8 Conflict of Interest: Current Clients: Specific Rules

(a) A lawyer shall not enter into a business transaction with a client or knowingly acquire an ownership, possessory, security or other pecuniary interest adverse to a client unless:

(1) the transaction and terms on which the lawyer acquires the interest are fair and reasonable to the client and are fully disclosed and transmitted in writing in a manner that can be reasonably understood by the client;

(2) the client is advised in writing of the desirability of seeking and is given a reasonable opportunity to seek the advice of independent legal counsel on the transaction; and

(3) the client gives informed consent, in a writing signed by the client, to the essential terms of the transaction and the lawyer's role in the transaction, including whether the lawyer is representing the client in the transaction.

(b) A lawyer shall not use information relating to representation of a client to the disadvantage of the client unless the client gives informed consent, except as permitted or required by these Rules.

(c) A lawyer shall not solicit any substantial gift from a client, including a testamentary gift, or prepare on behalf of a client an instrument giving the lawyer or a person related to the lawyer any substantial gift unless the lawyer or other recipient of the gift is related to the client. For purposes of this paragraph, related persons include a spouse, child, grandchild, parent, grandparent or other relative or individual with whom the lawyer or the client maintains a close, familial relationship.

(d) Prior to the conclusion of representation of a client, a lawyer shall not make or negotiate an agreement giving the lawyer literary or media rights to a portrayal or account based in substantial part on information relating to the representation.

(e) A lawyer shall not provide financial assistance to a client in connection with pending or contemplated litigation, except that:

(1) a lawyer may advance court costs and expenses of litigation, the repayment of which may be contingent on the outcome of the matter; and

(2) a lawyer representing an indigent client may pay court costs and expenses of litigation on behalf of the client.

(f) A lawyer shall not accept compensation for representing a client from one other than the client unless:

(1) the client gives informed consent;

(2) there is no interference with the lawyer's independence of professional judgment or with the client-lawyer relationship; and

(3) information relating to representation of a client is protected as required by Rule 1.6.

(g) A lawyer who represents two or more clients shall not participate in making an aggregate settlement of the claims of or against the clients, or in a criminal case an aggregated agreement as to guilty or nolo contendere pleas, unless each client gives informed consent, in a writing signed by the client. The lawyer's disclosure shall include the existence and nature of all the claims or pleas involved and of the participation of each person in the settlement.

(h) A lawyer shall not:

(1) make an agreement prospectively limiting the lawyer's liability to a client for malpractice unless the client is independently represented in making the agreement; or

(2) settle a claim or potential claim for such liability with an unrepresented client or former client unless that person is advised in writing of the desirability of seeking and is given a reasonable opportunity to seek the advice of independent legal counsel in connection therewith.

(i) A lawyer shall not acquire a proprietary interest in the cause of action or subject matter of litigation the lawyer is conducting for a client, except that the lawyer may:

(1) acquire a lien authorized by law to secure the lawyer's fee or expenses; and

(2) contract with a client for a reasonable contingent fee in a civil case.

(j) A lawyer shall not have sexual relations with a client unless a consensual sexual relationship existed between them when the client-lawyer relationship commenced.

(k) While lawyers are associated in a firm, a prohibition in the foregoing paragraphs (a) through (i) that applies to any one of them shall apply to all of them.

RULE 2.1 Advisor

In representing a client, a lawyer shall exercise independent professional judgment and render candid advice. In rendering advice, a lawyer may refer not only to law but to other considerations such as moral, economic, social and political factors, that may be relevant to the client's situation.

RULE 3.1 Meritorious Claims and Contentions

A lawyer shall not bring or defend a proceeding, or assert or controvert an issue therein, unless there is a basis in law and fact for doing so that is not frivolous, which includes a good faith argument for an extension, modification or reversal of existing law. A lawyer for the defendant in a criminal proceeding, or the respondent in a proceeding that could result in incarceration, may nevertheless so defend the proceeding as to require that every element of the case be established.

RULE 3.2 Expediting Litigation

A lawyer shall make reasonable efforts to expedite litigation consistent with the interests of the client.

RULE 3.3   Candor Toward the Tribunal

(a) A lawyer shall not knowingly:

(1) make a false statement of material fact or law to a tribunal or fail to correct a false statement of material fact or law previously made to the tribunal by the lawyer;

(2) fail to disclose to the tribunal legal authority in the controlling jurisdiction known to the lawyer to be directly adverse to the position of the client and not disclosed by opposing counsel; or

(3) offer evidence that the lawyer knows to be false. If a lawyer, the lawyer's client, or a witness called by the lawyer, has offered material evidence and the lawyer comes to know of its falsity, the lawyer shall take reasonable remedial measures, including, if necessary, disclosure to the tribunal. A lawyer may refuse to offer evidence, other than the testimony of a defendant in a criminal matter, that the lawyer reasonably believes is false.

(b) A lawyer who represents a client in an adjudicative proceeding and who knows that a person intends to engage, is engaging or has engaged in criminal or fraudulent conduct related to the proceeding shall take reasonable remedial measures, including, if necessary, disclosure to the tribunal.

(c) The duties stated in paragraphs (a) and (b) continue to the conclusion of the proceeding, and apply even if compliance requires disclosure of information otherwise protected by Rule 1.6.

(d) In an ex parte proceeding, a lawyer shall inform the tribunal of all material facts known to the lawyer that will enable the tribunal to make an informed decision, whether or not the facts are adverse.

RULE 3.8   Special Responsibilities of a Prosecutor

The prosecutor in a criminal case shall:

(a) refrain from prosecuting a charge that the prosecutor knows is not supported by probable cause;

* * *

(d) make timely disclosure to the defense of all evidence or information known to the prosecutor that tends to negate the guilt of the accused or mitigates the offense, and, in connection with sentencing, disclose to the defense and to the tribunal all unprivileged mitigating information known to the prosecutor, except when the prosecutor is relieved of this responsibility by a protective order of the tribunal;

(e) not subpoena a lawyer in a grand jury or other criminal proceeding to present evidence about a past or present client unless the prosecutor reasonably believes:

(1) the information sought is not protected from disclosure by any applicable privilege;

(2) the evidence sought is essential to the successful completion of an ongoing investigation or prosecution; and

(3) there is no other feasible alternative to obtain the information;

(f) except for statements that are necessary to inform the public of the nature and extent of the prosecutor's action and that serve a legitimate law enforcement purpose, refrain from making extrajudicial comments that have a substantial likelihood of heightening public condemnation of the accused and exercise reasonable care to prevent investigators, law enforcement personnel, employees or other persons assisting or associated with the prosecutor in a criminal case from making an extrajudicial statement that the prosecutor would be prohibited from making under Rule 3.6 or this Rule.

RULE 3.9   Advocate in Nonadjudicative Proceedings

A lawyer representing a client before a legislative body or administrative agency in a nonadjudicative proceeding shall disclose that the appearance is in a representative capacity and shall confirm to the provisions of Rules 3.3(a) through (c) * * *.

TRANSACTIONS WITH PERSONS OTHER THAN CLIENTS

RULE 4.1   Truthfulness in Statements to Others

In the course of representing a client a lawyer shall not knowingly:

(a) make a false statement of material fact or law to a third person; or

(b) fail to disclose a material fact to a third person when disclosure is necessary to avoid assisting a criminal or fraudulent act by a client, unless disclosure is prohibited by Rule 1.6.

RULE 4.4   Respect for Rights of Third Persons

(a) In representing a client, a lawyer shall not use means that have no substantial purpose other than to embarrass, delay, or burden a third person, or use methods of obtaining evidence that violate the legal rights of such a person.

(b) A lawyer who receives a document relating to the representation of the lawyer's client and knows or reasonably should know that the document was inadvertently sent shall promptly notify the sender.

RULE 5.5   Unauthorized Practice of Law; Multijurisdictional Practice of Law

(a) A lawyer shall not practice law in a jurisdiction in violation of the regulation of the legal profession in that jurisdiction, or assist another in doing so.

(b) A lawyer who is not admitted to practice in this jurisdiction shall not:

(1) except as authorized by these Rules or other law, establish an office or other systematic and continuous presence in this jurisdiction for the practice of law; or

(2) hold out to the public or otherwise represent that the lawyer is admitted to practice law in this jurisdiction.

(c) A lawyer admitted in another United States jurisdiction, and not disbarred or suspended from practice in any jurisdiction, may provide legal services on a temporary basis in this jurisdiction that:

(1) are undertaken in association with a lawyer who is admitted to practice in this jurisdiction and who actively participates in the matter;

(2) are in or reasonably related to a pending or potential proceeding before a tribunal in this or another jurisdiction, if the lawyer, or a person the lawyer is assisting, is authorized by law or order to appear in such proceeding or reasonably expects to be so authorized;

(3) are in or reasonably related to a pending or potential arbitration, mediation, or other alternative dispute resolution proceeding in this or another jurisdiction, if the services arise out of or are reasonably related to the lawyer's practice in a jurisdiction in which the lawyer is admitted to practice and are not services for which the forum requires pro hac vice admission; or

(4) are not within paragraphs (c)(2) or (c)(3) and arise out of or are reasonably related to the lawyer's practice in a jurisdiction in which the lawyer is admitted to practice.

(d) A lawyer admitted in another United States jurisdiction, and not disbarred or suspended from practice in any jurisdiction, may provide legal services in this jurisdiction that:

(1) are provided to the lawyer's employer or its organizational affiliates and are not services for which the forum requires pro hac vice admission; or

(2) are services that the lawyer is authorized to provide by federal law or other law of this jurisdiction.

RULE 5.6 Restrictions on Right to Practice

A lawyer shall not participate in offering or making:

(a) a partnership, shareholders, operating, employment, or other similar type of agreement that restricts the right of a lawyer to practice after termination of the relationship, except an agreement concerning benefits upon retirement; or

(b) an agreement in which a restriction on the lawyer's right to practice is part of the settlement of a client controversy.

RULE 8.4 Misconduct

It is professional misconduct for a lawyer to:

(a) violate or attempt to violate the Rules of Professional Conduct, knowingly assist or induce another to do so, or do so through the acts of another;

(b) commit a criminal act that reflects adversely on the lawyer's honesty, trustworthiness or fitness as a lawyer in other respects;

(c) engage in conduct involving dishonesty, fraud, deceit or misrepresentation;

(d) engage in conduct that is prejudicial to the administration of justice;

(e) state or imply an ability to influence improperly a government agency or official or to achieve results by means that violate the Rules of Professional Conduct or other law; or

(f) knowingly assist a judge or judicial officer in conduct that is a violation of applicable rules of judicial conduct or other law.

FURTHER REFERENCES

Here are some selected additional sources that may be particularly useful to the reader for reference.

Websites:

www.adr.org (American Arbitration Association)

www.naarb.org (National Academy of Arbitrators)

www.arbitrators.org (Chartered Institute of Arbitrators)

www.lcia-arbitration.com (LCIA)

www.jamsadr.com (JAMS)

www.iccwbo.org (ICC)

www.cpradr.org (CPR Institute of Dispute Resolution)

www.worldbank.org/icsid (ICSID)

www.tas-cas.org (Court of Arbitration for Sport).

www.nasd.com (Securities Arbitration)

www.arb-forum.com (NAF)

www.naftaclaims.com

Books:

Bishop, R. Doak (ed.), The Art of Advocacy in International Arbitration (2004).

Brunet, Edward, Richard Speidel, Jean R. Sternlight, and Stephen Ware, Arbitration Law in America: A Critical Assessment (2006).

Born, Gary, International Commercial Arbitration: Commentary and Materials (2nd ed. 2001).

———, International Arbitration and Forum Selection Agreements: Planning, Drafting, and Enforcing (1999).

Bowman, John P., The Panama Convention and Its Implementation Under the Federal Arbitration Act (2002).

Bühring-Uhle, Christian, Arbitration and Mediation in International Business: Designing Procedures for Effective Conflict Management (1996).

Carbonneau, Thomas E., AAA Handbook on Commercial Arbitration (2006).

———, Cases and Materials on Commercial Arbitration (1997).

———, The Law and Practice of Arbitration (2004).

Cooper, Laura J., Dennis R. Nolan, & Richard A. Bales, ADR in the Workplace (2nd ed. 2005).

Craig, W. Laurence, William W. Park & Jan Paulsson, International Chamber of Commerce Arbitration (3d ed. 2000).

___, Craig, Park, & Paulsson's Annotated Guide to the 1998 ICC Arbitration Rules: with Commentary (1998).

Dezalay, Yves & Bryant G. Garth, Dealing in Virtue: International Commercial Arbitration and the Construction of a Transnational Legal Order (1996).

Derains, Yves & Eric A. Schwartz, A Guide to the New ICC Rules of Arbitration (1998).

Drahozal, Christopher R. & Richard W. Naimark (eds.), Towards a Science of International Arbitration: Collected Empirical Research (2005).

Fairweather, Owen & Ray J. Schoonhoven (eds.), Fairweather's Practice and Procedure in Labor Arbitration (4th ed. 1999).

Frommel, Stefan N. & Barry A. K. Rider (eds.), Conflicting Legal Cultures in Commercial Arbitration: Old Issues and New Trends (1999).

Gaillard, Emmanuel & John Savage (eds.), Fouchard Gaillard Goldman on International Commercial Arbitration (1999).

___ (ed.), Anti–Suit Injunctions in International Arbitration (2005).

Haagen, Paul (ed.), Arbitration Now: Opportunities for Fairness, Process Renewal and Invigoration (1999).

Bernard Hanotiau, Complex Arbitrations: Multiparty, Multicontract, Multi–Issue and Class Actions (2005).

Kaufmann–Kohler, Gabrielle, Arbitration at the Olympics: Issues of Fast–Track Dispute Resolution and Sports Law (2001).

___ & Thomas Schultz, Online Dispute Resolution: Challenges for Contemporary Justice (2004).

Lookofsky, Joseph & Ketilbjórn Hertz, Transnational Litigation and Commercial Arbitration: An Analysis of American, European and International Law (2d ed. 2004).

Macneil, Ian R., American Arbitration Law: Reformation, Nationalization, Internationalization (1992).

___, Richard E. Speidel, & Thomas J. Stipanowich, Federal Arbitration Law: Agreements, Awards, and Remedies Under the Federal Arbitration Act (1994).

Redfern, Alan, & Martin Hunter, Law and Practice of International Commercial Arbitration (4th ed. 2004).

Reisman, W. Michael, W. Laurence Craig, William Park & Jan Paulsson, International Commercial Arbitration: Cases, Materials and Notes on the Resolution of International Business Disputes (1997).

Ruben, Alan Miles (ed.), Elkouri and Elkouri: How Arbitration Works (6th ed. 2003) (labor arbitration).

Smit, Hans & Vratislav Pechota, International Commercial Arbitration and the Courts (4th ed. 2004).

Várady, Tibor, John J. Barceló III, & Arthur T. von Mehren, International Commercial Arbitration: A Transnational Perspective (2d ed. 2003).

Zack, Arnold M. (ed.), Arbitration in Practice (1984) (labor arbitration).

——, Grievance Arbitration: Issues on the Merits in Discipline, Discharge, and Contract Interpretation (1989).

Zimny, Max, William F. Dolson, & Christopher A. Barreca, Labor Arbitration: A Practical Guide for Advocates (1990).

Articles:

Allison, John R., The Context, Properties and Constitutionality of Non–Consensual Arbitration, 1990 J. Disp. Resol. 1 (1990).

Alvarez, Guillermo Aguilar & William W. Park, The New Face of Investment Arbitration: NAFTA Chapter 11, 28 Yale J. Int'l L. 365 (2003).

Bruff, Harold H., Public Programs, Private Deciders: The Constitutionality of Arbitration in Federal Programs, 67 Tex. L. Rev. 441 (1989).

Brunet, Edward, Arbitration and Constitutional Rights, 71 N.C.L.Rev. 81 (1992).

——, Replacing Folklore Arbitration with a Contract Model of Arbitration, 74 Tul. L.Rev. 39 (1999).

Carbonneau, Thomas E., The Exercise of Contract Freedom in the Making of Arbitration Agreements, 36 Vand. J. Transnat'l L. 1189 (2003).

——, The Ballad of Transborder Arbitration, 56 U. Miami L. Rev. 773 (2002).

Carrington, Paul D. & Paul H. Haagen, Contract and Jurisdiction, 1996 Sup. Ct. Rev. 331 (1997).

Choi, Stephen J., The Problem With Arbitration Agreements, 36 Vand. J. Transnat'l L. 1233 (2003).

Dezalay, Yves, & Bryant Garth, Merchants of Law as Moral Entrepreneurs: Constructing International Justice from the Competition for Transnational Business Disputes, 29 Law & Society Rev. 27 (1995).

Drahozal, Christopher R., In Defense of Southland: Reexamining the Legislative History of the Federal Arbitration Act, 78 Notre Dame L. Rev. 101 (2002).

——, Privatizing Civil Justice: Commercial Arbitration and the Civil Justice System, 9 Kan. J.L. & Pub. Pol'y 578 (2000).

——, Commercial Norms, Commercial Codes, and International Commercial Arbitration, 33 Vand. J. Transnat'l L. 79 (2000).

——, "Unfair" Arbitration Clauses, 2001 U. of Illinois L. Rev. 695.

Getman, Julius G., Labor Arbitration and Dispute Resolution, 88 Yale L.J. 916 (1979).

Ginsburg, Tom, The Culture of Arbitration, 36 Vand. J. Transnat'l L. 1335 (2003).

Hill, Elizabeth, Due Process at Low Cost: An Empirical Study of Employment Arbitration Under the Auspices of the American Arbitration Association, 18 Ohio St. J. on Disp. Resol. 777 (2003).

Kerr, Sir Michael, International Arbitration vs. Litigation, J. Bus. L. 164 (May, 1980).

Mentschikoff, Soia, Commercial Arbitration, 61 Colum. L. Rev. 846 (1961).

——, The Significance of Arbitration–A Preliminary Inquiry, 17 Law & Contemp.Probs. 698 (1952).

Park, William W., Duty and Discretion in International Arbitration, 93 Am. J. Int'l L. 805 (1999).

——, Arbitration in Banking and Finance, 17 Ann. Rev. Banking L. 213 (1998).

——, Arbitration's Discontents: Of Elephants and Pornography, 17 Arb. Int'l 263 (2001).

——, Amending the Federal Arbitration Act, 13 Am. Rev. Int'l Arb. 75 (2002).

——, The Specificity of International Arbitration: The Case for FAA Reform, 36 Vand. J. Transnat'l L. 1241 (2003).

Peter, James T., Med–Arb in International Arbitration, 8 Amer. Rev. Int'l Arb. 83 (1997).

Rau, Alan Scott, Resolving Disputes Over Attorneys' Fees: The Role of ADR, 46 S.M.U. L. Rev. 2005 (1993).

——, The UNCITRAL Model Law in State and Federal Courts: The Case of "Waiver," 6 Am. Rev. Int'l Arb. 223 (1995).

——, The New York Convention in American Courts, 7 Am. Rev. Int'l Arb. 213 (1996).

——. Contracting Out of the Arbitration Act, 8 Am. Rev. of Int'l Arb. 225 (1997).

——, Integrity in Private Judging, 14 Arbitration International 115 (1998).

——, "The Arbitrability Question Itself," 10 Am. Rev. of Int'l Arb. 287 (1999).

——, Does State Arbitration Law Matter at All?, in ADR & the Law 199 (AAA 2000).

——, All You Need to Know About Separability in Seventeen Simple Propositions, 14 Am. Rev. of Int'l Arb. 1 (2003).

——, The Culture of American Arbitration and the Lessons of ADR, 40 Tex. Int'l L.J. 449 (2005).

Rogers, Catherine A., The Vocation of the International Arbitrator, 20 Amer. U. Int'l L. Rev. 957 (2005).

Sternlight, Jean R., Rethinking the Constitutionality of the Supreme Court's Preference for Binding Arbitration: A Fresh Assessment of

Jury Trial, Separation of Powers, and Due Process Concerns, 72 Tul. L. Rev. 1 (1997).

——, Mandatory Binding Arbitration and the Demise of the Seventh Amendment Right to a Jury Trial, 16 Ohio St. J. on Disp. Res. 669 (2001).

Stipanowich, Thomas J., Rethinking American Arbitration, 63 Ind.L.J. 425 (1988).

——, Contract and Conflict Management, 2001 Wis. L. Rev. 831.

Symposium on International Commercial Arbitration, 30 Tex. Int'l L.J. No. 1 (Winter 1995).

Symposium, Mandatory Arbitration, 67 Law & Contemp. Probs. Nos. 1 & 2 (Winter/Spring 2004).

Ware, Stephen J., Default Rules from Mandatory Rules: Privatizing Law Through Arbitration, 83 Minn. L. Rev. 703 (1999).

——, The Effects of Gilmer: Empirical and Other Approaches to the Study of Employment Arbitration, 16 Ohio St. J. on Disp. Resol. 735 (2001).

—— & Sarah Rudolph Cole, Introduction: ADR in Cyberspace, 15 Ohio St. J. on Disp. Res. 589 (2000).

In addition, the following journals regularly publish a large number of important and interesting articles concerning arbitration:

American Review of International Arbitration (available on Westlaw *www.westlaw.com*).

Arbitration International (available on KluwerArbitration *www.kluwerarbitration.com*).

Journal of American Arbitration (available on Westlaw *www.westlaw.com*).

Journal of International Arbitration (available on KluwerArbitration *www.kluwerarbitration.com*).

†